ETIQUETTE

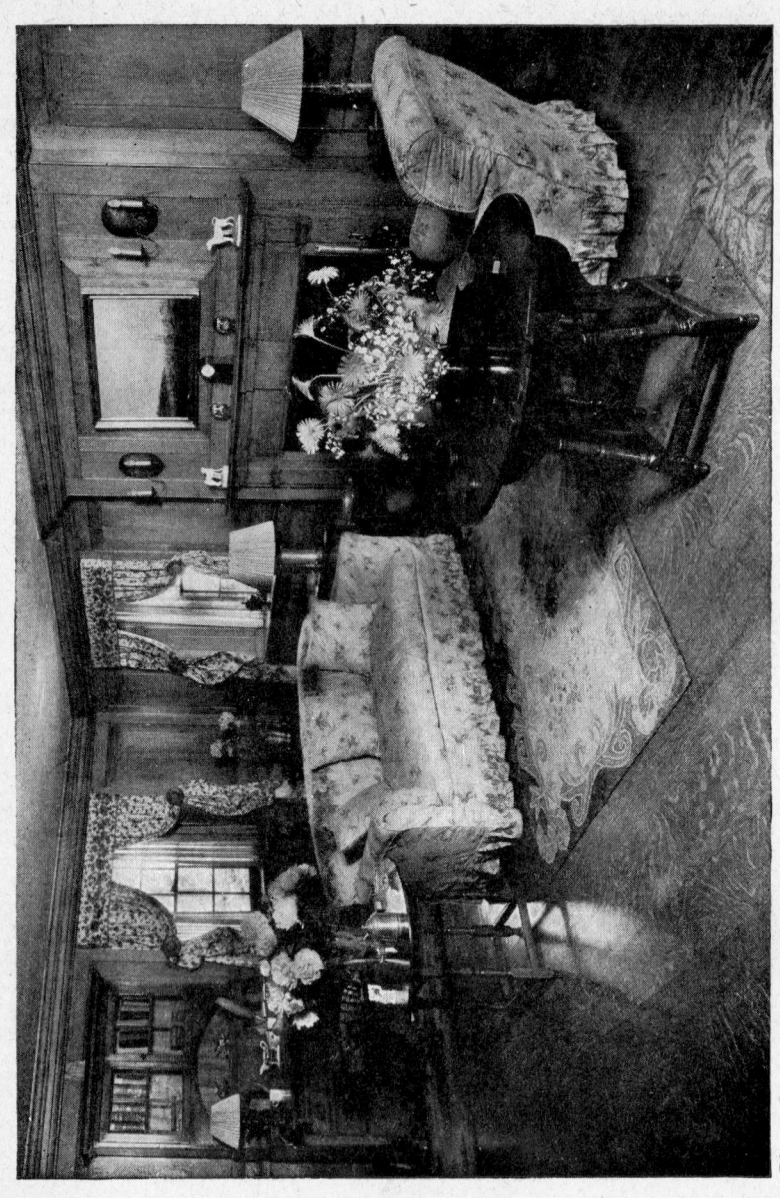

Photograph by Mattie Edwards Hewitt

THE PERSONALITY OF A HOUSE IS INDEFINABLE

But there never lived a hostess of cultivation and charm whose home, whether a palace or a bungalow, did not reflect the quality of inviting comfort.

ETIQUETTE

"The Blue Book of Social Usage"

BY EMILY POST
(MRS. PRICE POST)

Director, Emily Post Institute, Inc.

Author of "Children Are People" and "The Personality of a House"

ILLUSTRATED WITH PHOTOGRAPHS
AND FACSIMILES OF SOCIAL FORMS

NEW EDITION

*Completely Rewritten and Reset
Including Military and Post-War Etiquette*

FUNK & WAGNALLS COMPANY, PUBLISHERS
NEW YORK

COPYRIGHT, 1945, BY
FUNK & WAGNALLS COMPANY
ORIGINAL EDITION COPYRIGHT, 1922
REVISED EDITIONS, COPYRIGHT, 1927, 1931, 1934, 1937, 1940 AND 1942, BY
FUNK AND WAGNALLS COMPANY

Copyright Under the Articles of the Copyright Convention
of the Pan-American Republics and the United States

[PRINTED IN THE UNITED STATES OF AMERICA]

1945 Copyright Edition, Completely Rewritten

[Seventieth Printing, 1947]

To ANNE KENT
MY INVALUABLE ASSISTANT
IN AFFECTIONATE RECOGNITION OF HER
LIBERALIZING INFLUENCE
THROUGHOUT OUR LONG ASSOCIATION

Contents

CHAPTER		PAGE
	In Answer to a Letter	xi
1.	The True Meaning of Etiquette	1
2.	Introductions	3
3.	Greetings	15
4.	Good Taste in the Use of Names	23
5.	Words, Phrases, and Pronunciation	27
6.	Conversation	40
7.	On the Street and in Public	49
8.	Restaurant Etiquette	55
9.	At the Opera, the Theater, and Other Public Gatherings	61
10.	Visiting Cards and Their Uses	71
11.	Invitations, Acceptances and Regrets and All Engraved Forms	91
12.	Teas and Other Afternoon Parties	125
13.	Balls and Dances	135
14.	The Débutante	144
15.	Popularity and Hospitality at College	149
16.	The Vanished Chaperon and Other Lost Conventions	160
17.	Modern Man and Girl	171
18.	Engagements	180
19.	First Preparations for a Wedding	187
20.	The Day of the Wedding	222
21.	Simplified Wedding Details for a Bride in Everyday Clothes	257
22.	The Stranger at a Wedding	260
23.	Making One's Position in the Community	263
24.	Christenings	266
25.	Funerals	271
26.	The Well-Appointed House	286
27.	Flat Silver—Its Choice and Usage—Condensed Table Setting	316
28.	Formal Dinners	323
29.	Modern Dinner Giving	363
30.	Luncheons, Breakfasts and Suppers	372
31.	Mrs. Three-in-One Gives a Dinner Party	379
32.	Simple Party Giving	385
33.	American Neighborhood Customs	401

34.	Hospitable Hosts	407
35.	The Country House and Its Hospitality	413
36.	Whether You Are Hostess or Guest	426
37.	Telephoning, Smoking, and Out-In-Company Manners	438
38.	The Clothes of a Lady	454
39.	The Clothes of a Gentleman	468
40.	Table Manners	482
41.	Formal Correspondence	495
42.	How to Address Important Personages	527
43.	Longer Letters	536
44.	Etiquette in Business	544
45.	Clubs and Club Etiquette	560
46.	Games and Sports	573
47.	Manners for Motorists	581
48.	The Code of a Gentleman	587
49.	What We Contribute to the Beauty of Living	591
50.	Traveling Etiquette	599
51.	In Official Washington	613
52.	Concerning Military and Post-War Etiquette	624
	Index	641

Illustrations

	FACING PAGE
The Personality of a House is Indefinable	*Frontispiece*
The Formal Afternoon Tea Table	128
The Every-Day Afternoon Tea Table	129
Looking up the Bride's Aisle in a Double-Aisled Church	192
A Bride's Bouquet	193
The Bride's Table	224
A Gem of a House	*Between* 288 *and* 289
The Modern Ideal of Hospitality	*Between* 288 *and* 289
Maids' Dining Alcove in an Apartment	*Between* 288 *and* 289
Flat Silver	320
The Perfectly Appointed Formal Dinner Table in a Great House	*Between* 328 *and* 329
Detail of a Formal Dinner Table	*Between* 328 *and* 329
Correct Setting of Each Course at a Formal Dinner	*Between* 328 *and* 329
Dessert and After-Dinner Coffee Service	*Between* 328 *and* 329
A Lovely Dinner Service Without Silver Decoration	368
The Correctly Set Every-Day Lunch Table	*Between* 376 *and* 377
Correct Setting of Each Course at Luncheon	*Between* 376 *and* 377
A Seated Buffet Supper Table of Unusual Beauty	*Between* 376 *and* 377
The Buffet Supper Appeals to Almost Everyone	392
At Tea Time in a City Yard	393
Sitting-Room Convertible into Bedroom	416
The Tray for a Guest Who Breakfasts in Bed	417
Correct Choice and Use of Table Implements	*Between* 488 *and* 489

In Answer to a Letter

AGAIN, by way of preface to this newly revised edition of "Etiquette," I am reprinting this letter that was sent me at a time when the term "Café Society" was coined to apply to an unclassifiably mixed group of restaurant and night-club habitués. This letter is today as applicable to the subject of this book as it was before the war.

Dear Mrs. Post:

While waiting my turn in a doctor's office, I happened to read in one of America's greatest magazines an amazingly frank article about the publicity-craving of what the author calls café society and evidently believes to be New York's smartest society.

As I finished this story about people whose social position was seemingly proclaimed by being placed by the headwaiter at a ringside table, I said to myself, "And so what? Who cares whether the So-and-So's are given a front-row table in a high-priced restaurant, or whether they eat at an automat?"

But to my own surprise I find myself suddenly caring very much, because it is assumed that the rest of us are satisfied to have these same society headliners represent the American social ideal.

This article and hundreds like it depict a world that is pretentious and vulgar. And no one, so far as I know, is saying a word in Society's defense. Or has it no defense? I'd like to know the truth, Mrs. Post; that's why I'm writing to you.

Is it true that these people I have been reading about are the same ones as those whose opinions you so often refer to as authoritative? Or was there (is there) another Best Society, which must have been shamed into seeking greater and greater privacy? And yet this doesn't follow through, because the names figuring conspicuously in several front-page scandals have been those of families whose prestige has always been looked up to as representative of America's Best.

I have been trying to think why I should care. I think it is this: Reformers of sorts may write all they please about the bad taste of Hollywood, but we, the countless "middle-class" people of the nation, look there for entertainment and not for the patterns of highest social and ethical traditions. On the other hand, we not only look to, but are as a nation represented by those who are assumed to comprise our highest social class.

As you see from the stamping on my letter paper, I live far from New York; and if I, who am so far removed from the super-rich and super-smart of a far-off city, can feel so strongly about this disloyalty to all sense of *noblesse oblige* on the part of those who are thought to be the top, because holding the foremost social citadel of the nation, what must you feel, who all your life have been of the social world of New York?

Perhaps you won't answer me—perhaps you can't. Perhaps the society depicted by these others is what that of all great cities has come to. But if you can, I do wish you would give us who are your readers a reassuring glossary for such terms as "Best Society," "People of Quality," "People of Taste," "The Smart or the Modern or the Fashionable World." Or if you can't, won't you be frank with us who believe you, and who are bringing our children up according to your precepts, and tell us the truth?

Is this society of names advertised and rated by where they walk in the parade and where a headwaiter seats them in a restaurant—or by a published list of "ten best-dressed ladies"—also your society? Is the admirable world of Society that I have thought I could read between the lines of what you write real, or do you make it up?

No, I do not "make up" the people of whom I write nor the society that I define as "best." But I admit that the reassuring glossary you ask for is almost as difficult to make clear as it would be to separate each color that has gone into the painting of a picture.

In the general picture of this modern day, the smart and the near-smart, the distinguished and the merely conspicuous, the real and the sham, and the unknown general public are all mixed up together. The walls that used to enclose the world that was fashionable are all down. Even the car tracks that divided cities into smart and not-smart sections are torn up.

On the other hand, there are countless private houses whose walls are standing intact and whose shades are pulled down when the indoor lights are lighted. And within the walls of the houses there are enclosures where the owners spend their days and into which intimate friends go at their pleasure. But out in the big concourse, where the reporters gather with their cameras, the crowd is the same public one that goes to the races or to the restaurants, or to the night clubs.

There is nowhere to go to see Best Society on parade, because parading is one thing that Best Society does not intentionally do. And yet it is true (and this is one of the things hardest to make clear) that in the forefront of the public parade are to be found a certain few who are really best. But they are best in spite of, and not because of, the publicity they attract.

When I say that "people of taste do this or think that," I naturally have in mind definite people whose taste is the most nearly perfect among all those whom I know. Or on occasion, perhaps, I go back in memory to the precepts of those whose excellence has remained an ideal.

In other words, when I write of people of quality or fashion or taste, I always select the individual people who ideally serve as models, exactly as I select flowers in my garden which are to be put in a certain room. Or more particularly, if I am choosing the best varieties to be exhibited at the flower show, I certainly don't go into the garden and pick half a dozen blooms of the first plant that happens to be labeled a good variety—even though they are all grown from seeds that came in the same packet and have been given the same cultivation. But I carefully choose the most perfect individual blooms I can find. This figure of speech perhaps explains how it can happen that a certain Elaine Eminent can have not a single characteristic that one labeled with that name should have.

In other words, to return to our glossary, Best Society, Best People, or People of Quality can all be defined as people of cultivation, courtesy, taste and kindness—people, moreover, who are very rarely dissociated from their backgrounds. In thinking of them, you think of their home surroundings, their families, their intimates, their work, their interests. But when you ask for the meaning of smart, fashionable and modern, the qualities implied may include fastidious taste, alert perceptions, appreciative knowledge of every forward-looking movement of the day; or, on the other hand, it may mean no more than a flair for the trend of the moment—or no less than a love of the limelight.

So you can see how hard it is to try to explain who's who—let alone the much harder what's what. A fact I should like to bring out is that the rating by superficial appearance or the accident of publicity has little to do with an accurate appraisal of intrinsic worth—or worthlessness. Real value is something back of and apart from publicity value. There is all the difference between climbing on the band wagon in order to be noticed by the public standing on the side lines, and impulsively jumping on board because one can see better what *is* at the moment going on.

Emily Post

New York

ETIQUETTE

1

The True Meaning of Etiquette

ONE is apt to think of Etiquette as being of importance to none but brides or diplomats or persons lately elected to political office. As a matter of fact, there is not a single thing that we do, or say, or choose, or use, or even think, that does not follow (or break) one of the exactions of taste, or tact, or ethics, or good manners, or etiquette —call it what you will.

Considering manners even in their superficial aspect, no one—unless he be a recluse who comes in contact with no other human being— can fail to reap the advantage of a proper, courteous and likable approach, or fail to be handicapped by an improper, offensive and resented one. And certainly the greatest asset that a man or woman or even a child can have is charm. And charm cannot exist without good manners—meaning by this, not so much manners that precisely follow particular rules, as manners that have been made smooth and polished by the continuous practice of kind impulses.

It is hard to say why the word "etiquette" is so inevitably considered merely a synonym of the word "correct," as though it were no more than the fixed answer to a sum in arithmetic. In fact, it might be well to pull the word "correct" out by the roots and substitute "common sense." In short, I wish that those whose minds are focused on precise obedience to every precept would ask themselves, "What is the purpose of this rule? Does it help to make life pleasanter? Does it make the social machinery run more smoothly? Does it add to beauty? Is it essential to the code of good taste or to ethics?" If it serves any of these purposes, it is a rule to be cherished; but if it serves no helpful purpose, it is certainly not worth taking very seriously.

On the subject of the thousands of detailed rules essential to all ceremonial procedures, the importance of knowing the unending details, such as when to sit and when to stand, what to say and what to do upon this or that occasion, is most practically illustrated by a church service. It would be shocking to have people trotting in and out of pews, talking out loud or otherwise upsetting devotional tranquillity. For this reason we have set rules for all ceremonial functions, so that marriages, christenings, funerals, as well as Sunday services, shall be conducted with ease and smoothness. It is also essential to ease of living that certain mechanical conventions be observed.

The real point to be made is that rules of etiquette have not been contrived in order to make those who know them seem important and to make those who happen not to know them miserably chagrined. Actually the so-called rules are nothing but the findings of long experience handed down for reasons of practical use. This does not mean that the principles of good taste, or of beauty, or of consideration for the rights or feelings of others can be discarded—ever! As a matter of fact, good taste is necessarily helpful! It must be the suitable thing, the comfortable thing, the useful thing for the occasion, the place, and the time, or it is not in good taste.

In the same way the code of ethics—for generations known as the code of a gentleman—is an immutable law of etiquette. Too many of us are likely to assume a rich man a gentleman. No qualification could be further from the truth, since the quality of a gentleman is necessarily measured by what he is and never by what he has. We've all heard the term "nature's nobleman," meaning a man of innately beautiful character who, never having even heard of the code, follows it by instinct. In other words, the code of a thoroughbred, whether it be applied to a man or a woman, or to a half-grown child, is the code of instinctive decency, ethical integrity, self-respect and loyalty. Decency means not merely propriety of speech and conduct, but honesty and trustworthiness in every obligation. Integrity includes not only honesty but a delicacy of motive and of fairness in judging the motives of others. Self-respect, among many other things, means refusal to accept obligations that one is unwilling to return. This word "unwilling" is of importance, since there is no more contemptible person than one who takes all he can get and gives as little as he can. Loyalty means faithfulness not only to friends, but to principles.

Etiquette, if it is to be of more than trifling use, must go far beyond the mere mechanical rules of procedure or the equally automatic precepts of conventional behavior. Actually etiquette is most deeply concerned with every phase of ethical impulse or judgment and with every choice or expression of taste, since what one is, is of far greater importance than what one appears to be. A knowledge of etiquette is of course essential to one's decent behavior, just as clothing is essential to one's decent appearance; and precisely as one wears the latter without being self-conscious of having on shoes and perhaps gloves, one who has good manners is equally unself-conscious in the observance of etiquette, the precepts of which must be so thoroughly ingrained that their observance is a matter of instinct rather than of conscious obedience.

2

Introductions

THE most ceremonious introduction possible is

"Mrs. Distinguished, may I present Mr. Traveler?" or
"Mrs. Young, may I present Professor Gray?"

The word "present" is more formal than the word "introduce," but the word "introduce" is equally proper.

The younger person is always introduced to the older or more distinguished, but a gentleman is always presented to a lady, even though he is an old gentleman of great distinction and the lady a mere slip of a girl.

No woman is ever presented to a man, except to the President of the United States, a royal personage, or a dignitary of the church.

The correct introduction of either a man or woman is:

To the President

"Mr. President, I have the honor to present Mrs. Jones." Or, if officially, "Mrs. Jones of Chicago."

(Mrs. Jones bows deeply. If the President offers his hand, Mrs. Jones gives him hers.)

To a Reigning Sovereign

Much formality of presenting names on lists is gone through beforehand; at the actual presentation an "accepted" name is repeated from one functionary to another and nothing is said to the king or queen except "Mrs. Jones."

Mrs. Jones bows and, if the king offers to shake hands, Mrs. Jones bows again deeply as she gives him her hand.

To a Cardinal

"Your Eminence, may I present Mrs. Jones?"

A non-Catholic behaves exactly as to a king, but a Roman Catholic drops on the right knee, places the right hand, palm down, under the cardinal's extended hand and kisses the cardinal's ring.

A woman is always presented to archbishops and monsignori, and it is not incorrect to present her to a priest.

A woman is also presented to any member of a reigning family.

"Your Royal Highness (or whatever the title), may I present Mrs. Jones?"

But a foreign ambassador is presented. "Your Excellency, may I present you to Mrs. Jones?" Or "Mrs. Jones, may I present His Excellency, the British Ambassador?" An introduction to an archbishop is, "Your Grace, may I present Mrs. Jones?" But to those who know him socially, a duke is never "His Grace" nor a lord "His Lordship." A hostess says, "Mrs. Jones, may I present the Duke of Overthere?" or "Lord Blank?" "The Honorable" is merely Mr. Lordson or Mr. Holdoffice. A doctor, a judge, a bishop are addressed and introduced by their titles. The Protestant clergy are usually "Mister" unless they hold the title of Doctor, or Dean, or Canon, in which case the surname is added: "Dean Wood," "Doctor Starr," "Canon Cope." A Catholic priest is "Father Kelly." To call him "Mister" is a breach of courtesy.

A senator is always introduced as "Senator Davis," whether he is still in office or not. But the President of the United States, once he is out of office, is merely "Mister" and not "Ex-President."

An ex-governor and an ex-ambassador are both actually "The Honorable." But usually one would in courtesy introduce the latter as "Ex-Ambassador" and the former as "Ex-Governor." On an important occasion one would present "The Honorable Alfred E. Smith, ex-governor of the State of New York."

Unless the occasion is really formal; unless, let us say, you are a chairman introducing a speaker or a hostess presenting people to a guest of honor, the formal introduction is not often used. The typical introduction, suitable not only on informal occasions but whenever two individuals are introduced, is the mere pronouncing of two names.

"Mrs. Worldly. Mrs. Norman."

If the two names are said in the same tone of voice, it is not apparent who is introduced to whom; but by accentuating the more important person's name, it can be made as clear as though the words "May I present" had been used.

The more important name is said with a slightly rising inflection; the secondary as a mere statement of fact. For instance, suppose you say, "Are you there?" and then, "It is raining!" Use the same inflection exactly and say, "Mrs. Worldly! — Mrs. Younger!"

A man is also introduced. "Mrs. Worldly!—Mr. Norman!" A mother introducing a man to her daughter would say, "Mr. Eminent —my daughter Mary!" or if she is married "—my daughter Mary Smartlington."

The reason why it is discourteous as well as in very bad taste to speak of one's husband as "Mr. Smith" or one's daughter as "Miss

Smith" is that it seems to put the person spoken to into the position of one's social inferior (the same type of rudeness as signing a letter "Mrs. Smith" without any parenthesis). But if one's daughter has a different name, the name can be said with a pause between that makes a parenthesis. "My daughter (pause, and then) Mrs. Smartlington." "My sister—Mrs. Lake."

Although the name of a stranger or of the older or more notable person is properly said first, this is no longer considered of importance —except that a woman's name should be said before that of a man, unless the preposition "to" is prefixed to the lady's name. For instance, if you find yourself saying Mr. Norman's name first, it is very simple to make this polite by adding, "May I introduce you to Mrs. Smith?" Or with greater friendliness, "Mr. Norman, I should like to introduce you to Mrs. Smith."

Formally, a man introduces another man to his wife. "Mr. Brown, may I present you to my wife?" Or if this seems to you to imply that you are asking Mr. Brown's permission to present him to your wife, you can say, "Mr. Brown, I should like to introduce you to my wife."

A lady introduces her husband to friends as "John" and to acquaintances as "my husband." The two names of safety are "my husband" and "my wife," since they are proper no matter whether you are talking to an archbishop or a climber whom you particularly dislike. The tabu of Mr. and Mrs. is purely social. In business "Mr. Brown" and "Mrs. Brown" are quite correct.

To an old friend a husband would say, "Jim, I want you to meet my wife" (on no account "the wife"!). Then he adds as though in parenthesis, "Jim Buyer" or "Mr. Buyer." Or if they are all very young, he probably says, "Mary, this is Bob Ace," since he is really introducing his friend, not to Mrs. Jones, but to Mary.

It might be emphasized that an introduction prefaced by the phrase "This is," when said with an enthusiastic inflection, can express a warmth and charm that other introductions lack. This was once illustrated in London *Punch*, in the drawing of a small boy approaching his mother and holding an abashed small girl by the hand, radiantly exclaiming, "Mummy! THIS is HER." In the same way a child would introduce a beloved teacher enthusiastically, "Mother, *this* is Miss Brown." Or, on the other hand, to exclaim, "Miss Brown, *this* is my mother!"—in the sense of "Behold! this is she—my mother"—has an affectionate emphasis (when affectionately said) that other introductions lack.

OTHER FORMS OF INTRODUCTION

There are many other forms of introduction which might be called conversational introductions: such as,

"Mrs. Jones, do you know Mrs. Norman?" or
"Mrs. Jones, you know Mrs. Robinson, don't you?"

(On no account say "Do you not?" Best taste always prefers "Don't you?") Or one may say, "Mrs. Robinson, have you met Mrs. Jones?" or, to attract her attention, "Mary! you have met Mrs. Jones, haven't you?—Mrs. Towne" (Mary's name).

These are all good forms, whether gentlemen are introduced to ladies, ladies to ladies, or gentlemen to gentlemen. In introducing a gentleman to a lady, you may ask Mr. Smith if he has met Mrs. Jones, but you must *not* ask Mrs. Jones if she has met Mr. Smith!

It makes not the least difference whether those introduced happen to be married or single. A married man is introduced to a single girl; a young married woman is introduced to an older spinster.

INTRODUCING RELATIVES-IN-LAW

A lady introduces her son's wife, formally to acquaintances, as "My daughter-in-law," or to friends as "Dick's wife." Or, with greater display of affection, "This is my Mary—Dick's wife." But this would be said only to an old friend. To an acquaintance "My daughter-in-law" would depend for its warmth on the tone in which it is said. And this, as already noted in a foregoing paragraph, is of course a very important point in all introductions. By tone alone the same words can convey every shade of feeling from cool indifference to adoration. If you are the daughter-in-law, you in turn introduce your mother-in-law as "My husband's mother" or "My mother-in-law"; or in less formal communities you perhaps say, "Mother Green, this is Aunt Susie"—or the other way about. When introducing other relatives-in-law, "My husband's sister" and "My brother John's wife" (or "Jim's sister" and "John's wife" to one who knows who they are). These names are more clearly understood than "My sister-in-law"; but this does not matter unless the person to whom they are introduced cares about your husband's family or your brother John.

Although they are not really your relatives in law, it is quite proper to speak of the husband of your sister-in-law as "my brother-in-law" and the wife of your brother-in-law as "my sister-in-law."

FORMS OF INTRODUCTION TO AVOID

Do *not* say, "Mr. Jones, shake hands with Mr. Smith" or "Mrs. Jones, I want to make you acquainted with Mrs. Smith." Never say "make you acquainted with," and do not, in introducing one person to another, call one of them "my friend." You can say "my aunt," or "my sister," or "my cousin"—but to pick out a particular person as "my friend" is bad manners, for it implies that the other person is not.

If you are introducing someone to another who is a very special friend, you may say, "Mrs. Smith, I want you to meet Mrs. Jones." But you should never say, "Mrs. Smith, meet Mrs. Jones."

Do not repeat "Mrs. Jones! Mrs. Smith! Mrs. Smith! Mrs. Jones!" To say each name once is quite enough, unless it is a foreign one that is difficult to pronounce. Saying this a second time, and slowly, is not only helpful but gives one who could not remember a chance to ask later on, "Won't you tell me again how to pronounce your name?"

Most people very much dislike being asked their names. To say, "What is your name?" is always abrupt and unflattering. If you want to know with whom you have been talking, you can generally find a third person later and ask, "Who was the lady with the gray feather in her hat?" The next time you see her you can say, "How do you do, Mrs. ——?" (calling her by name).

TITLELESS YOUTH

In no way to be compared with the bad taste of total strangers' using first names in introductions on certain radio quiz programs is the younger generation's practice of introducing all friends by first names. Muriel Manners, for example, taking a friend to the Country Club, greets a group of friends with "Hello, everybody. This is Sally." In the modern fashionable world the titles Mister, Missis and Miss are literally never said except to outsiders. If Sarah Stranger is accepted as a member of a certain group, she is at once called Sarah or Sally, or quite likely Sal. To be called Miss Stranger (or Mrs. Stranger if she is in the early twenties) announces that she is not a member of the group. Maybe she does not care to join it—maybe they don't want her—but, whatever the reason, she does not "belong." Obviously, then, introductions among our younger groups are titleless. "Sally Stranger, Lucy and Bob Gilding!" Or, "Lucy, this is Sally Stranger," and then to Sally, "That is Bob Gilding, and that is Tom Brown." But even so, a man is always introduced to a girl.

Also, if Muriel were not really a friend of Sarah Stranger, she would introduce her—and her own friends as well—by their titles of Missis, Miss or Mister, as formally as her mother would. The stranger, by the way, must wait to be called by her first name before calling others by theirs. If you are a younger person, you should never call an older person by her (or his) first name unless you are asked to. Whether older people choose to have those who are a generation younger call them by their first names is a question for them to decide. But it is safe to keep in mind that age attempting to masquerade as youth is, to youth itself, inevitably an object of scorn.

YOUNG WOMAN TO MAN AT DINNER

When a young woman finds herself next to an unknown man at a dinner party, she more likely than not merely talks to him without telling him her name. But if he introduces himself to her, she perhaps says in turn, "I'm one of the Smiths that live on X Street." She can't very well say, "I'm Miss Smith," unless she is at least approaching the mid-thirties and she might not want him to call her "Mary," which he would be quite likely to do were she to say, "I'm Mary Smith." It is of course an unbreakable rule that all people who find themselves seated together at table must talk. To sit side by side without speaking is one of the greatest discourtesies a guest can show a hostess.

Under all informal circumstances the roof of a friend serves as an introduction, but at a very large party—such as a dance or a formal tea or wedding reception—it is not customary to speak with those whom you don't know, unless you and another guest find yourselves apart from the others. In such a case you do not introduce yourself, but you perhaps make a casual remark about the beauty of the bride, or a comment upon the weather. Whether to talk or not usually depends upon mutual willingness, except, as already noted, with those sitting on either side of you at lunch or dinner, to whom you must talk, first to one and then to the other, throughout the meal.

WHAT TO SAY WHEN INTRODUCED

Under all possible circumstances the reply to an introduction is "How do you do?" It may be said gladly, casually, coolly or unthinkingly, as the case may be, and it may be varied in pronunciation or emphasis. "How do you *do?*" "*How* d'you do?" "How d'oo?" "How d'you *do-oo?*"

It does sound limited, but so is holding one's knife and fork and so is drinking coffee after meals. And one can often say nothing at all—just smile! True, the same smile can become equally monotonous. At all events, when Mr. Bachelor says, "Mrs. Worldly, may I present Mr. Struthers?" Mrs. Worldly says, "How do you do?" Struthers bows, and says nothing. To sweetly echo "Mr. Struthers?" with a rising inflection on "—thers?" is *not* good form. Saccharine chirpings should be classed with crooked little fingers, high handshaking and other affectations. All affectations are bad form.

Persons of distinction do not say, "Charmed" or "Pleased to meet you." When it is actually true, you can say, "I am VERY glad to meet you." But you may *never* say, "I am pleased to make your acquaintance." "Make your acquaintance" is a bad phrase. The tabu of tabus was, "Pleased to meet you." In the last few years it has almost died out. On an occasion when you meet someone whom you have heard much about and long wanted to meet, you may of course say, "Oh, I am so *glad* to meet you."

When a young girl is introduced to another who is the friend of an intimate friend of her own, she naturally explains, "Mary has so often talked about you." A girl should say less than this to a boy. She should not tell him how much Mary has talked about him. A boy, on the other hand, may properly tell a girl that his roommate is always talking about how wonderful she is. Often the first remark is the beginning of a conversation. Sidney Struthers is introduced to Muriel Manners. She smiles and perhaps says, "Tommy tells me you are going to be in New York all winter." Struthers answers, "Yes, I am an interne at Medical Center."

The one occasion when something more than "How do you do?" is necessary is when a friend brings a stranger to your house and tells you, "I have brought Mrs. Blank, who is visiting us." You reply, "I'm so glad you did!" Then to the stranger, "I'm delighted to see you, Mrs. Blank."

WHEN TO SHAKE HANDS

When gentlemen are introduced to each other, they always shake hands.

When a gentleman is introduced to a lady, she generally smiles, bows slightly, and says, "How do you do!" Strictly speaking, it is her place to offer her hand or not, as she chooses; but if he puts out his hand, she of course gives him hers. Nothing could be more ill-bred than to treat any spontaneous friendliness curtly.

Those who have been drawn into a conversation do not usually shake hands on parting. But there is no fixed rule. One is more likely to shake hands with someone whom one finds sympathetic than with one who is the contrary.

Nearly all rules of etiquette are elastic, and none more so than those governing the acceptance or rejection of the strangers you meet.

There is a wide distance between rudeness and reserve. You can be courteously polite and at the same time reserved to someone who does not appeal to you, or you can be welcomingly friendly to another whom you like on sight. Individual temperament should also be taken into consideration; one person is naturally austere, another genial. The latter shakes hands far more often than the former.

At times a few words of explanation make the introduction of a stranger smoothly pleasant. "Mrs. Worldly! Miss Jenkins—her penname is Grace Gotham." Or "Mr. Neighbor, I should like you to meet Mr. Dusting—he has just returned from Egypt, where he's been searching for buried Pharaohs."

But this can be very much overdone, and the hostess who habitually exploits her friends as though she were the barker at a side-show is a bore no less than a pest.

WHEN TO RISE

On formal occasions a hostess always stands at the door and the host near-by. Both shake hands with every arrival. On informal occasions they both rise and go forward to greet each guest—a man as well as a woman, but not necessarily a child. The children in the family should rise to receive another child, as well as rise for every grown person who enters the room, and stand until the older person is seated. Grown as well as half-grown members of the family rise to greet guests but do not necessarily shake hands. A woman guest does not stand when introduced to someone at a distance, nor when shaking hands with a friend of her own or with anyone unless very much older. Should an old lady enter the room in which many other ladies are seated, the others—unless members of the family who live in the house—do not rise, since seven or eight all getting up at once would produce an effect not so much of politeness as of confusion. But every gentleman stands as long as his hostess or any other lady does.

HOW VISITOR TAKES LEAVE

When a visitor is ready to leave, she (or he) merely stands. To one with whom she has been talking, the visitor says, "Good-by. I hope I shall see you again soon"—or "sometime"—or "I've enjoyed our talk so much." Naturally a woman is less effusive in what she says to a man than in what she says to another woman. And yet she may very well exclaim, "I've been completely thrilled!" if he has told her anything that can be truthfully described as thrilling, but not otherwise. Furthermore, any comment in praise of his opinion, or of his achievement, or of any especial work he has done is proper. But any remark flattering to his personal appearance or charm would be in worst possible taste. Whatever pleasant remark one person makes, the other person answers, "Thank you." The one who told of his adventures perhaps answers, "I think you've been very good to listen to me." Or a woman replies to another who hopes to see her again, "I hope so, too." Usually "Thank you" is all that is necessary.

In taking leave of a group of strangers—it makes no difference whether you have been introduced or merely included in their conversation—you bow "good-by" to any who happen to be looking at you, but you do not attempt to attract the attention of those who are unaware that you are turning away.

ONE PERSON TO A GROUP

On formal occasions, when a great many people are present, one person is not introduced to each and every member of the group. An arrival may be introduced to one or two people, or he may be left to talk with those near-by without exchanging names.

But at a small lunch, for instance, let us suppose you are the hostess. Your position is not necessarily near, but it is toward the door. Mrs. King is sitting quite close to you, and also Mrs. Lawrence. Miss Robinson and Miss Brown are much farther away. Mrs. Jones enters. You go a few steps forward and shake hands with her, then stand aside, as it were, to see whether Mrs. Jones goes to speak to anyone. If she apparently knows no one, you say, "Mrs. King, Mrs. Jones." Mrs. King, if she is young, rises, shakes hands with Mrs. Jones and sits down. If Mrs. King is of about the same age as Mrs. Jones, Mrs. King merely extends her hand and does not rise. Having said "Mrs. Jones" once, you do not repeat it immediately, but turning to the other lady sitting near you, you say, "Mrs. Lawrence." You can, if you choose, look across the room and continue, "Miss Robinson, Miss Brown; Mrs. Jones!" The two bow but do not rise.

It is much more practical to repeat the names of those present before that of the new arrival, because the attention of each is attracted by hearing her own name, whereas the one entering is naturally paying attention.

At a very big lunch you would introduce Mrs. Jones to Mrs. King and possibly to Mrs. Lawrence, so that Mrs. Jones might have some one to talk to. But if other guests come in at this moment, Mrs. Jones finds a place for herself, and after a pause, falls naturally into conversation with those she is next to, without giving her name or asking theirs.

Typical of many American communities is the practice of the hostess who takes each arriving guest—especially a stranger—up to every other guest at a large party. This is a kind procedure but one likely to fail of its friendly intent because, after hostess and guest have made a grand circuit of the room, new arrivals claim the hostess, and the guest is left with no one. It is really better for a hostess to seat a stranger and introduce her to those near-by. At a small party of five or six, a stranger is usually introduced to everyone in turn. But if not, people *always* talk with those seated near them in the house of a friend. It would be a breach of etiquette not to!

WHEN TO INTRODUCE

The question as to when introductions should be made, or not made, is one of the most elusive points of social knowledge. One occasion that requires introductions is the presentation of everyone to a guest of honor. If one arrives after the receiving line has ended, he must look for this guest and present himself, since it is the height of rudeness to go to an entertainment given in honor of someone and fail to "meet" him. (Even though one's memory is too feeble to remember him afterward!)

At a dance, when an invitation has been asked for a stranger, the friend who vouched for him should personally present him to the hostess. "Mrs. Worldly, this is Mr. Robinson (or if he is young, 'John'), whom you said I might bring." The hostess shakes hands and smiles and says, "I am very glad to see you, Mr. Robinson."

A guest in a box at the opera or horse show or county fair introduces to her hostess any gentleman who comes to speak to her, unless other people block the distance between so that an introduction would be forced and awkward.

At a formal dinner (a dinner of ceremony) the host should see that every gentleman either knows or is presented to the lady he is to "take in" to dinner, and also, if possible, to the one who is to sit at the other side of him. If the latter introduction is overlooked, people sitting next each other at table introduce themselves. A gentleman says, "I am Arthur Robinson." Or showing her his place card, "This is my name." Or the lady says first, "I am Mrs. Hunter Jones." And the man answers, "My name is Titherington Smith." In any case, those seated together are obliged to talk.

(For beginning a conversation see Index.)

Should you take a friend visiting you to the house of another friend, it is always safer to introduce your visitor to those whom you encounter than to expect a hostess to remember a stranger's name.

WHEN NOT TO INTRODUCE

A newly arriving visitor in a lady's drawing room is not introduced to another who is taking leave. Nor is an animated conversation between two persons interrupted to introduce a third.

You must never introduce people to each other in public places if you have reason to doubt that the introduction will be agreeable to both. You cannot commit a greater blunder than to introduce to a notable person someone she does not care to know, especially on shipboard, in hotels, or in other very small, rather public communities where people are so closely thrown together that it is correspondingly difficult to avoid presuming acquaintances who have been given the wedge of an introduction.

When two people—either friends or acquaintances—are walking together and they meet a third who stops to speak to one of them,

INTRODUCTIONS

the other walks slowly on and does not stand awkwardly by and wait for an introduction. If the third is asked by the one she knows to join them, the sauntering friend is overtaken and an introduction made. The third, however, must not join the others unless invited to do so.

At a very large dinner, people are not collectively introduced. After dinner, men in the smoking room or left at table always talk to their neighbors whether they have been introduced or not, and ladies in the drawing room do the same.

Quaint writers on etiquette speak of "correct introductions" that carry "obligations of future acquaintance" and "incorrect introductions" that seemingly obligate one to nothing.

Degrees of introduction are utterly unknown to best society. One person is welcomed by those he comes in contact with because he happens to be clever or sympathetic or attractive. Another is rejected by those who find him antipathetic or boring. Introductions can no more detract from the charm of the one than they can add to the unacceptability of the other.

CONVERSATION WITHOUT INTRODUCTION

On occasions it happens that in talking to one person you want to include another in your conversation without making an introduction. For instance, suppose you are talking to a seedsman and a friend joins you in your garden. You greet your friend, and then include her by saying, "Mr. Smith is suggesting that I dig up these cannas and put in delphiniums." Whether your friend gives an opinion about the change in color of your flower bed or not, she has been made part of your conversation.

HALFWAY INTRODUCTION OF DOMESTIC EMPLOYEE

Ordinarily the introduction of a maid or butler or a chauffeur or any domestic employee to a guest would be as out of place as introducing the driver of a bus to the passengers. But there are many occasions when, for one reason or another, a halfway introduction is made. For example, Mrs. Kindhart, having offered the use of her car to Celia Lovejoy, says as the chauffeur opens the door at her own house, "Carlson, take Mrs. Lovejoy wherever she wants to go this afternoon, and that will be all for today." Or, for example, to a house guest as the maid who is to unpack the visitor's clothes approaches, "Will you give Selma the keys to your bags?" Or to a man, "If you ring four times, Dawson will look after you."

A real introduction is made only when the servant has been long in the family and is held in affectionate esteem. In the South certainly, and very likely elsewhere, a young man would tell his fiancée,

"Muriel, this is my Louisa who brought me up!" and to Louisa, "And you don't have to be told that this is Miss June Night, do you?"

And it is not at all unusual—especially in a small household—for the mistress of the house to introduce—or call friendly attention to—one who has been long in her employ. "This is our Hilda" or "Aunt Jane, I'm sure you remember Hilda!"

INTRODUCING ONESELF

If there is a good reason for knowing someone, it is quite proper to introduce yourself. For instance, you would say, "Mrs. Worldly, aren't you a friend of my mother's? I am Mrs. Titherington Smith's daughter." Mrs. Worldly says, "Yes, indeed, I am. I am so glad you spoke to me."

But if a strange man says, "Aren't you Muriel Manners?" Muriel says "Yes" and waits for his explanation; and then if the stranger continues, "I think my sister Millicent—Millicent Brown—is a friend of yours," Muriel at once offers her hand and, smiling, asks, "Are you George or Alec?"

"I'm Alec." Whereupon Muriel probably says, "Hello, Alec!"

But unless he is the brother of a friend, or a particular friend of a friend, a man should say, "Are you Miss Manners? I am Arthur Jones, I met you at a dinner at Mrs. Worldly's last winter." Whereupon Muriel would greet him with the inevitable "How d'you do, Mr. Jones?"—or if she is willing to be called Muriel, she says, "Hello, Arthur."

In spite of this titleless custom of the younger generation, certain conventions prevail. It would be in very bad taste to introduce yourself to Mrs. Worldly if your mother knew her only slightly, or for any man without credentials to introduce himself to Muriel, and more especially to think of calling her Muriel.

THE RETORT COURTEOUS TO ONE FORGOTTEN

Suppose someone you have forgotten says, "You don't remember me, do you?" Since it is rather hurting to one's pride to be forgotten, the only kind thing to do is to say, "Of course I do." And then find out later who it was, if you can.

INTRODUCTION BY LETTER

An introduction by letter is far more binding than any spoken introduction, which commits you to nothing.

(For fuller explanation and example letters, see pages 517-520.)

3

Greetings

ACKNOWLEDGING INTRODUCTIONS

As explained in the foregoing chapter, the correct formal greeting is "How do you do?" abbreviated to "How d'you do" or "'D' you do." Whether Mrs. Younger is presented to Mrs. Worldly or the French ambassador is presented to her, all say the same, or merely bow.

One gentleman* says to another, "I'm very glad to meet you" or "—Delighted to meet you." Or, if in his own office, "Very glad to see you!" Friends greet each other with "Good morning" or "Good evening" or "How are you?" But "Good afternoon" is rarely if ever heard in fashionable society as a greeting to a friend. It is sometimes used as a greeting by public speakers, but its more typical use is as a phrase of dismissal. A lady terminates an interview with a stranger who has come to see her on business by bidding him "Good afternoon." On similar occasions she would say, "Good morning" or "Good evening," but not "Good-by" or "Good night"—both of which are said to friends.

"Hello!" This seemingly too-free salutation has become as widely accepted among friends as on the telephone. It is approved or disapproved according to the tone in which it is said. To shout "Hullow!" is vulgar because the mispronunciation is a vulgar one. But "Hello, Mary" or "How 'do, John" are practically interchangeable. It may even be that "Howdy" will move across the car tracks. It doesn't suit Mrs. Worldly very well, but it has a pleasant and friendly sound that fits in with the trend toward simplified living.

Sometimes, to one who is a chronic invalid or is in great sorrow or anxiety, the greeting "Hello. How are you?" is very disconcerting, since to answer truthfully would make the situation serious and even emotional. In such a case the only thing to reply is, "All right, thank you." One may be worse and everything all wrong, but to confess to either is to open the floodgates—which one fears. "All right, thank you" is an impersonal and therefore strong bulwark against further comment or explanation.

* In this chapter it is impossible to substitute the general terms *man* and *woman* for the specific meaning of the words *gentleman* and *lady*. In conversation, *man* and *woman* are to be preferred.

TAKING LEAVE

Whether you are a man or a woman bidding good-by to a new acquaintance, either man or woman, you shake hands and say, "Good-by. I am very glad (or so glad) to have met you." To one who has been especially interesting, or who is somewhat of a personage, you say, "It's been a great pleasure to meet you." The other answers, "Thank you" or "Thank you very much" or "I've enjoyed meeting *you*" or "I'm so glad to have met *you*."

There are only two forms of farewell: "Good-by" and "Good night." Never say "Au revoir" unless you have been talking French. Never interlard your conversation with foreign words or phrases when you can possibly translate them into English; and the occasions when our mother tongue will not serve are extremely rare.

Very often in place of the over-worn "How d'you do?" or "Hello Jane!" perhaps more often than not, people skip the words of greeting and say "I'm so glad to see you!" or "I haven't seen you for ages" or "What have you been doing lately?" The weather, too, fills in with equal faithfulness. "Isn't it a heavenly day!" or "Horrid weather, isn't is?"

GREETINGS IN CHURCH

People do not greet each other in church, except at a wedding. At weddings people do speak to friends sitting near them, in a low tone. It would be shocking to enter a church and hear a babel of voices.

Ordinarily in church, if a friend happens to catch your eye, you may perhaps smile, but never actually bow. If you go to a church not your own and a stranger offers you a seat in her pew, you should, on leaving, turn to her and say, "Thank you." But you do not greet any one until you are out on the church steps, when you naturally speak to your friends as you encounter them.

SHAKING HANDS

Intimate friends rarely shake hands when they meet in public or even when they come in or go out of each other's houses. But the rule that a hostess must shake hands with every guest whom she has invited to a party is so ingrained that a well-bred hostess invariably goes forward and shakes hands with a guest even though she may have seen her but a few minutes before. Guests also shake hands with each other particularly if they know each other formally. Young people shake hands only when guests or hostesses or hosts, and—when introduced.

Gentlemen always shake hands when they are introduced to each other—even crossing a room to do so. Ladies rarely shake hands when introduced, except with someone standing near. Boys and girls follow the example of their elders.

EXCUSE MY GLOVE

A gentleman *wearing an outdoor glove* never shakes hands with a lady without first removing his right glove. But at a ball, or if he is usher at a wedding, he does *not* remove a glove intended to be worn indoors. If in the street he cannot free his left hand to pull his right glove off, he says, "Excuse my glove." But he does not ask that an indoor glove be excused.

A lady *never* takes off her gloves to shake hands—correctly she puts them *on!* and never asks that her glove be excused unless she is wearing muddy gardening gloves when she is encountered in her garden. If she can't get these off, she says she is sorry she can't shake hands.

PERSONALITY OF A HANDSHAKE

A handshake often creates a feeling of liking or of irritation between two strangers. Who does not dislike a "boneless" hand extended as though it were a spray of sea-weed or a miniature boiled pudding? It is equally annoying to have one's hand clutched aloft in grotesque affectation and shaken violently sideways, as though it were being used to clean a spot out of the atmosphere. What woman does not wince at the viselike grasp that cuts her rings into her flesh and temporarily paralyzes every finger?

The proper handshake is made briefly; but there should be a feeling of strength and warmth in the clasp, and, as in bowing, one should at the same time look into the countenance of the person whose hand one takes. In giving her hand to a foreigner, a married woman always relaxes her arm and fingers, as it is customary for him to lift her hand to his lips (except in the "movies" the hand of an unmarried girl is *not* kissed). But by a relaxed hand is not meant a wet rag; a hand should have life even though it be passive. A woman should always allow a man who is only an acquaintance to shake her hand; she should never shake his. To a very old friend she gives a much firmer clasp, but he shakes her hand more than she shakes his. Younger women usually shake the hand of the older; otherwise women merely clasp hands, give them a dropping movement rather than a shake, and let go.

GREETINGS FROM YOUNGER TO OLDER

It is the height of rudeness for young people not to go and shake hands with an older lady of their acquaintance when they meet her away from home, if she is a hostess to whose house they have often gone. It is not at all necessary for either young women or young men to linger and enter into a conversation, unless the older lady detains them, which she should not do beyond the briefest minute.

Older ladies who detain young people with long stories or questions, or who, worse yet, are always dragging young men up to unprepossessing partners, are studiously avoided and with reason; but otherwise it is inexcusable for any youth to fail in this small exaction of polite behavior. If a young man is talking with someone when an older lady enters the room, he bows formally from where he is, as it would be rude to leave a young girl standing alone while he went up to speak to Mrs. Worldly or Mrs. Toplofty. But a young girl passing near an older lady can easily stop for a moment, say, "How do you do, Mrs. Jones!" and pass on—and nothing will win Mrs. Jones' friendship so completely as this momentary courtesy, *if* done with genuine friendliness.

People do not cross a room to speak to anyone unless it be to show politeness to an acquaintance who is a stranger there, to speak to an intimate friend, or to talk to someone about something in particular.

A GENTLEMAN REMOVES HIS HAT

A gentleman takes off his hat and holds it in his hand when a lady enters the elevator in which he is a passenger, but he puts it on again in the corridor. A public corridor is like the street, but an elevator in an hotel or apartment house or club or opera house is suggestive of a room, and a gentleman does not keep his hat on in the presence of ladies in a house—ever!

But in public buildings, such as offices or stores or buildings which contain neither apartments nor assembly rooms, the elevator is considered as public a place as an omnibus or a trolley car. What is more, the elevators in such business structures are usually so crowded that the only room for a man's hat is on his head!

When a gentleman stops in the street to speak to a lady of his acquaintance, taking his hat and his glove off, and getting his stick and his cigarette out of the way, constitute a maneuver that must need considerable practice to be done without effort, though the process is easy enough to describe. First of all, he transfers cigarette and stick (if encumbered with either) to his left hand, takes off hat and transfers it to left hand, and at the same time grips fingers of right glove, pulling it off! He then gives her his gloveless right hand. All of which perhaps explains why the smart world never carries anything but a crooked-handled malacca stick which can be hung on the left arm. If the gentleman and lady walk ahead together, he puts his hat on; but while he is standing in the street talking to her, he should remain hatless, no matter how cold the wind nor how torrid the sun, for so long as she may be pleased to stand and talk to him. Nor may he smoke. In the country he may very well be bareheaded and also be smoking a pipe, but in a city street there is no vulgarity greater than for a man to stand talking to a lady with his hat on and a cigar in his mouth.

It is not necessary to add that every American citizen stands with his hat off at the passing of the flag* and when the national anthem is played. If he didn't, some other more loyal citizen would take it off for him. Also every man should stand with his hat off in the presence of a funeral.

A GENTLEMAN LIFTS HIS HAT

Lifting the hat is a conventional gesture of politeness shown to strangers only, not to be confused with bowing, which is a gesture used to acquaintances and friends. In lifting his hat, a gentleman merely lifts it slightly off his forehead—by the brim of a stiff hat or by the crown of a soft one—and replaces it; he does not smile or bow, nor does he even look at the object of his courtesy. No gentleman ever subjects a lady to his scrutiny or his apparent observation if she is a stranger.

If a lady drops her glove, a gentleman should pick it up, hurry ahead of her—on no account nudge her—offer the glove to her and say, "I think you dropped this!" The lady replies, "Thank you." The gentleman should then lift his hat and turn away.

If he passes a lady in a narrow space, so that he blocks her way or in any manner obtrudes upon her, he lifts his hat as he passes.

If he gets on a street car and the car gives a lurch just as he is about to be seated and throws him against another passenger, he exclaims, "I beg your pardon" and lifts his hat as soon as he regains his balance. If he would be thought a person of social position, he must *not* say, "Pardon *me!*" nor—unless spoken in French with an unmistakable accent, "Parr *dohn.*" The English word "pardon" is a social pariah except in the complete sentence, "I *beg* your pardon." If a man has to ask someone to let him pass by to enter or leave the car, he says, "Excuse me!" He must not take a seat if there are ladies standing. But if he is sitting and ladies enter, should they be young, he may with perfect propriety keep his seat. If a very old woman, or a young one carrying a baby, enters the car, a gentleman rises at once, lifts his hat slightly as he indicates the proffered seat, and lifts his hat again when she thanks him (unless he is clinging to the strap with one hand and has a package in the other!).

If the car is very crowded when he wishes to leave it and a lady is

---

* For Flag-etiquette—also respect to National Anthem see page 639.

directly in his way, he asks, "May I get through, please?" As she makes room for him to pass, he lifts his hat (if he has a free hand!) and says, "Thank you!"

If he is in the company of a lady anywhere in public, he lifts his hat to a man who offers her a seat or who picks up something she has dropped or shows her any other civility.

He lifts his hat if he asks a woman or an old gentleman a question, and always, if, when walking on the street with either a lady or another man, his companion bows to another person.

In other words, a gentleman lifts his hat whenever he says "Excuse me," "Thank you," or speaks to or is spoken to by either a lady or a gentleman. Needless to say, he always takes his pipe, cigar, or cigarette out of his mouth when he lifts his hat, takes it off or bows. And a gentleman always lifts his hat to his wife when he encounters her, or joins her, or takes leave of her in public.

A BOY TAKES OFF HIS HAT

A young boy must, of course, take off his hat to a lady or a gentleman. He should also take it off to a girl—or at least lift it. To another boy he either makes a gesture of salute, or waves his hand, or very likely calls out, "Hi, Jimmy!"—unless the boy is with his mother or other lady, in which case he takes off his hat if he knows her, or tips it if he does not.

When a boy is wearing no hat, he bows to a lady or a gentleman exactly as he would indoors, but he would probably raise his hand to his forehead in a salute to a girl, and either salute or wave to a boy.

A GENTLEMAN RISES

A gentleman always rises when a lady comes into a room. In public places men do not jump up for every strange woman who happens to approach. But if any woman addresses a remark to him, a gentleman stands as he answers her. In a restaurant,* when a lady bows to him, a gentleman merely makes the gesture of rising by getting up halfway from his chair and at the same time bowing. Then he sits down again.

When a lady goes to a gentleman's office on business† he should stand up to receive her, offer her a chair, and not sit down until after she is seated. When she rises to leave, he must get up instantly and stand for as long as she stands (no matter *how* long that is!) and then go with her as far as the door, which he holds open for her.

* For restaurant etiquette in detail, see Index.
† See chapter 44, "Etiquette in Business."

THE BOW OF CEREMONY

The standing bow, made by a gentleman when he rises at a dinner to say a few words, in response to applause, or across a drawing room at a formal dinner when he bows to a lady or an elderly gentleman, is usually the outcome of the bow taught little boys at dancing school. The instinct of clicking heels together and making a quick bend over from the hips and neck, as though the human body had two hinges, a big one at the hip and a slight one at the neck, and was quite rigid in between, remains in a modified form through life. The man who as a child came habitually into his mother's drawing room when there was "company" generally makes a charming bow when grown, a bow wholly lacking in self-consciousness. There is no apparent "heel-clicking," but a camera would show that the motion is there.

THE INFORMAL BOW

The informal bow is merely a modification of the bow of ceremony; it is easy and unstudied, but it should suggest the ease of controlled muscles, not the floppiness of a rag doll.

In bowing on the street, a gentleman should never take his hat off with a flourish, nor should he sweep it down to his knee; nor is it graceful to bow by pulling the hat over the face as though examining the lining. The correct bow, when wearing a high hat or derby, is to lift it by holding the brim directly in front, take it off merely high enough to escape the head easily, bring it a few inches forward, the back somewhat up, the front down, and put it on again.

If a man is wearing a soft hat, he takes it by the crown instead of the brim, lifts it slightly off his head and puts it on again.

A gentleman does not look at a stranger to whom he lifts his hat, but he always looks at a person whom he knows.

The bow to a friend is made with a smile, to a very intimate friend often with a broad grin that fits exactly with the word "Hello"; whereas the formal bow is mentally accompanied by the formal salutation, "How do you do!"

THE BOW OF A WOMAN

Nothing is so easy for any woman to acquire as a charming bow. It is such a short and fleeting duty. Not a bit of trouble really; just to incline your head and spontaneously smile as though you thought, "Why, *there* you are! How glad I am to see you!"

Even to a stranger who does her a favor, a woman of charm always smiles as she says "*Thank* you!" As a possession for either woman or man, a ready smile is more valuable in life than a ready wit; the latter may sometimes bring enemies, but the former always brings friends.

WHEN TO BOW

In Europe a gentleman bows to a lady first; in the United States a lady is supposed to bow first; but few people of today observe this formality.

In meeting the same person many times within an hour or so, one does not continue to bow after the second, or at most third, meeting. After that one either looks away or merely smiles.

Unless one has a good memory for people, it is always better to bow to someone whose face is familiar than to run the greater risk of ignoring an acquaintance. It is often difficult to recognize people whom one has met when they are wearing a different type of dress—sports clothes or evening dress, for instance.

But the habit that causes most unintended rudeness is absent-mindedness. Absorbed in their own thoughts, the unmindful have no idea that they are "blocking a passage," spreading over the only available seat, blotting out another's view, not hearing the voice or seeing the motions made by someone trying to speak to them. They pass a friend unaware of his proximity. It may be annoying to be passed by an "unseeing" acquaintance, but one should be careful not to confuse absentminded unseeingness with intentional slight.

THE "CUT DIRECT"

For one person to look directly at another and not acknowledge the other's bow is a breach of civility that only gravest cause can warrant. Therefore one must be careful not to confuse poor sight or a forgetful memory with an intentional cut. Anyone whose eyes are not sharp or who is not quick of memory can all too easily fail to recognize good friends as well as newly made acquaintances by whom they were much attracted. This does not excuse the bad memory, but it explains the unintended rudeness.

A "cut" is very different. It is a direct stare of blank refusal, and is not only insulting to its victim but embarrassing to every witness. Happily it is practically unknown in polite society.

4

Good Taste in the Use of Names

NAME OF SAFETY

THE so-called "name of safety" used by every well-bred man or woman or child when speaking to a stranger about any member of the family is "my wife" or "my husband" or "my daughter" or "my mother"—or if necessary "my sister Alice" or "my son George." No matter to whom these merely descriptive names are said, they can't be wrong. On the other hand, should one whom you have met socially speak of her husband as "Mister," this would seem very rude.

When a lady is talking with someone who has presumed to call her husband by his first name and she wishes to register her disapproval of the address, she speaks of him as "Mister."

FORMALITY IN USE OF TITLES

They are fantastic—the extremes to which we go! When Charles Dickens came to the United States almost a century ago, it is said that we deeply resented his criticism of our manners in his *American Notes*. He especially ridiculed the preposterous custom of the American wife who not only spoke about her husband as "Mr. Jones" but who never called him anything but "Mr. Jones" herself. Today we find this just as absurd as he did. Absurd also was the custom of the gay 90's when every débutante, aged eighteen, was called "Miss" by all the young men who were introduced to her after her "coming out," even by her most devoted beaux—aged nineteen to twenty-odd! She in turn called them "Mister," not only until she knew them better, but for life, even though she might see them every day! Only when a man and a girl became engaged did they call each other by their first names!

First names were "bad form" to such a degree that even those girls and men who had been playmates in childhood and called each other by first names always when at home or among others of their own group, before strangers spoke to each other as Miss or Mister—always.

TODAY'S OUTSTANDING CHEAPNESS

And yet, absurd as this prim formality sounds to us, surely there is little to be said in favor of present-day familiarity in the use of first names by those supposedly at the upper end of the social scale who voluntarily choose to do the very thing that to others less fortunately placed carries unavoidable distress. It is ironical that a dignified elderly woman who is nurse or maid has to submit to being called Mary or Selma by butcher boy or baker boy or anyone else because of a custom that is beyond her powers to change.

First names should indicate that people know each other well, and the degree of friendship implied among those beyond college years should increase in proportion to age. Yet we all know that there are countless people of middle age, and older, who seem to think that being called Lily or Tommy by Dora Débutante and Freddy Freshman is to be presented with a cup of the elixir of youth.

It may be true that "Lily" or "Tommy" does suggest camaraderie; that "Mrs. Autumn" or "Mr. Sere" do not—and if they individually like the former, certainly no one else has the right to object—though one wonders how Mrs. Autumn would feel should she overhear those who, she has supposed, were accepting her as their own contemporary, say, "Here comes Old Lil!"

COURTESY TO ELDERLY DOMESTIC EMPLOYEES

In contrast to the lack of dignity shown by "Old Lil" in the foregoing paragraph is the unjust indignity shown to every woman, as well as man, who is in domestic service. From the point of view of good taste, as well as courtesy, a dignified, elderly, unmarried domestic employee should be addressed by strangers as "Miss Margaret" or "Miss Selma," exactly as she would be were she in her own home. The fact that certain foolish old women of the fashionable world choose to discard their dignity makes it doubly unfair that others wholly worthy of respect are, because of their classification by the word "servant" instead of their personal qualifications, unable to avoid the opprobrium of a titleless name.

DEFINITE RULES

As already noted at the head of this chapter, a lady says "my husband" when speaking to an acquaintance, but to a friend or the friend of a friend she speaks of him as "John." But this does not give anyone the privilege of calling him John unless otherwise told to do so. In the same way, Mr. Worldly speaks of "Edith" to friends of course, and also to every woman whom they both know socially, whether they themselves call her Edith or Mrs. Worldly. But to a man not an intimate friend and to a woman who is a stranger he talks about "my wife." To all business friends and acquaintances, as well as to servants or strangers, he calls her "Mrs. Worldly." She says "Mr.

Worldly" to her own employees and to workmen who come to repair the house, as well as to tradesmen or salesmen—to all, in fact, whom she meets on other than social occasions.

WHEN FIRST NAMES ARE IN WORST TASTE

In speaking about other people, one says "Mrs.," "Miss" or "Mr." as the case may be. It is very bad form to go about saying "Edith Worldly" to those who do not call her Edith, and to speak thus familiarly of one whom one perhaps does not even know, is done only by the climbers and snobs who speak with familiarity of persons of prominence in order to impress their hearers with their own importance. (With the quite opposite effect upon all but the ignorant.)

A CHILD'S USE OF NAMES

On the subject of the widespread laxity which has in many instances encouraged children to call their parents' friends by their first names, the rule is that every child must at least be taught that he may never call a grown person by his or her first name—unless told to do so by that person. Even so, according to good taste this is not quite fair to the child in that it prejudices those who take it for granted that his apparent lack of respect is a shortcoming of his own.

In many cases, really intimate friends who are devoted to the children—those who do not like the formality of "Mr." and "Mrs." and yet do not want to be called by their first names—suggest nicknames for themselves. Otherwise everyone is of course called "Mr." and "Mrs." There is a strong (and reasonable) prejudice of modern taste against a general practice of teaching children to call their parents' friends Aunt, Uncle or Cousin when intimacy and devotion are not sufficient to endorse a genuinely wished-for relationship.

NAMES FOR PARENTS-IN-LAW AND STEP-PARENTS

The question of what a bride is to call her parents-in-law is one that has no definite answer, except the old-fashioned one of "Mother Jones" and "Father Jones." Among the moderns, choice of names is purely personal. In unusually formal families, for example, one hears "Mr." and "Mrs.," which does to most of us sound very uncaring. Usually—and more naturally—parents-in-law are called by names which mean mother and father but are not the names which the bride uses for her own parents. Or perhaps they are called "Mr." and "Mrs." by the bride (or groom) until a grandchild's nicknames gradually become theirs. Curiously enough, the less intimate relationships of aunts, uncles and even grandparents never come into question since the bride calls all of her husband's relations exactly what he does, and he in turn does the same in speaking to hers.

Nearly all step-parents of half-, or quite-, grown sons and daughters —depending, of course, upon their ages—choose to be called by their first names. When they are not young or when they do not want to be called by first names, they are either called Aunt and Uncle or else they choose one of the names described in the foregoing paragraph for parents-in-law.

OVER THE TELEPHONE

On the telephone, a woman says to another whom she knows socially, "Hello, Mrs. Smith. This is May Jones." Mrs. Smith answers, "How do you do, Mrs. Jones" (or Miss Jones). A man calling a woman whom he knows socially would never under any circumstances announce himself as Mr. Smartling. He would say, "This is George Smartling." But a man calling a woman on business says, "This is Mr. Smartling of Dash & Sons." If he were calling a business man, he would be likely to say, "This is Smartling of Dash & Sons."

NAMES LEGALLY CHANGED

Whatever may have been the reason for changing the name by which one has been known, social and business associates should be notified of the change if embarrassing situations are to be avoided. The quickest and simplest way of telling them is to send out formal announcements.

MR. AND MR. JOHN ORIGINAL NAME
ANNOUNCE THAT BY PERMISSION OF THE COURT
THEY AND THEIR CHILDREN
HAVE TAKEN THE FAMILY NAME OF
BROWN

5

Words, Phrases, and Pronunciation

SPEECH, THE X-RAY OF QUALITY

IT is rather curious that we Americans, who care so very much about the idea of "Culture" in the abstract, are often unaware that the measure of our own cultivation is made evident the moment we speak. Nothing so instantly, and so irrefutably, reveals the social quality of our background—our advantages or our disadvantages—as the words we choose and the way we pronounce them. To use English of distinction may seem simple enough; the dictionary is meticulous in its definitions, and grammar determines every word's use, and yet (and this is where the subject becomes almost as dangerous to handle as TNT) the groups of cultivated persons who for generations comprised what was recognized as best society gradually throughout these generations established a special list of "approved" and "disapproved" words and pronunciations. Moreover, since these innate approvals or prejudices were universal among all persons of social tradition, our speech of today proclaims that we too have inherited the same traditions or that we have not.

This is most difficult to explain, particularly because it may seem too trifling to be included in a seriously and honestly intended book. And yet, the truth is that had this chapter been untrue, neither this book, nor its author, would ever have been accepted as authoritative by anyone qualified to judge.

THE SOCIAL IMPORTANCE OF SPEECH

To compare the world of cultivated society to a fraternity, with the avoidance of certain seemingly unimportant words as the sign of recognition, is not a fantastic simile. People of the fashionable world invariably use certain expressions and instinctively avoid others; therefore when a stranger uses an "avoided" one, he proclaims that he "does not belong," exactly as a pretended Freemason proclaims himself an "outsider" by giving the wrong "grip"—or whatever it is by which Masons recognize one another.

Today the social groups are so much larger; moreover, yesterday's defining car-tracks are all pulled up. And to what degree the postwar world will keep to the traditions of the past, no one can say. In the meantime so much attention is being paid to purity of speech that the test of today is of importance only so far as this: To speak as the cultivated element in one's own home town speaks is sufficient for all social and domestic purposes.

For those who are going to make public speeches to the Nation at large—one who, for example, is seeking Federal office—any local accent or vocabulary is a handicap. The reason is that any local accent connotes (in the listener's mind) a locality-limited mind.

Appearance, on the other hand, often passes muster. For example, Miss Nobackground and Miss Oldlineage, standing side by side, are equally attractive to look at, equally graceful, and wear equally good clothes. But the moment they speak the difference in their social backgrounds is made plain. Let Miss Nobackground, for example, say "Hully Gee," or call out to her friend, "Say, Murree, the new drapes in my home are dandy," and what is her background then? On the other hand, Miss Oldlineage, in the vernacular of today, may very well say "It looks swell," answer "Fine" when asked how she is, and speak of a "boy-friend or girl-friend" and yet leave the impression of her background intact. The reason why "say," "drapes" and "dandy" are still outcast, whereas "swell," "boy-friend" and "fine" have been welcomed everywhere, is something which must merely be reported as a fact but which cannot be explained. Not all the dressmakers, milliners and beauty experts in the world, however, can camouflage the complete history of family origin made clear by speech.

IN SPITE OF ILLITERACY

Another angle of this difficult subject of admitted or excluded words is that, at the illiterate extreme, certain exceptional people can seemingly overcome all handicaps. People who say "I come," and "I seen it," and "I done it" prove by their lack of grammar that they have had little education. But they may at the same time be exceptional characters, respected by everyone who knows them, because they are what they seem and nothing else. But the caricature "lady" with the comic-picture "society manner" who says "Pardon me" and talks of "retiring," and "residing," and "desiring," and "being acquainted with," and "attending" this or that with "her escort," and who curls her little finger over the handle of her teacup and prates of "cult-your" is not sensitive to the exactions of taste and never will be. The offense of pretentiousness is committed oftener perhaps by women than by men, who are usually more natural and direct. A genuine, sincere, kindly American man—or woman—can go anywhere and be welcomed by everyone, provided, of course, that he be a man of some natural talent, ability, wit, or grace. One finds him all over the world, neither aping the manners of others nor treading on the sensibilities of those less fortunate than himself.

Often too we encounter men and women in whose conversation is perceptible the influence of much reading of the Bible. Such are seldom if ever stilted or pompous or long-worded, but are invariably distinguished for the simplicity and dignity of their English.

There is no better way to cultivate taste in words than by constantly reading books of proved literary standing. But it must not be forgotten that there can be a vast difference between literary standing and popularity, and that many of the "best sellers" have no literary merit whatsoever.

To be able to separate best English from merely good English needs a long process of special education, but in order to recognize simple, direct and beautiful speech from that which is redundant and pretentious, one need merely see whether the same thing might be said in shorter, simpler Anglo-Saxon form. For example:

NEVER SAY	SAY INSTEAD
I desire to purchase	I should like to buy
I trust I am not trespassing	I hope I am not in the way (unless trespassing on private property is actually meant)
Request (suitable for third-person invitations and their answers or for official communications)	Ask (the proper word under usual circumstances)
Will you accord me permission?	Will you let me? or May I?
He expressed a desire to make your acquaintance	He said he would like to meet you
Permit me to assist you	Let me help you
I presume	I suppose
Tendered him a banquet	Gave him a dinner
Converse	Talk
Partook of liquid refreshment	Had something to drink
Perform ablutions	Wash
A song entitled (unless used in legal sense)	A song called
I will ascertain	I will find out
Residence (except in printing or engraving)	House
Mansion	Big house
I recall	I remember
Realtor	Real-estate agent
Mortician	Funeral director

"Attended" instead of "went to"—in the everyday sense of attended the theater, attended such a school, attended a dinner—is in bad taste. But "attended the peace conference" is quite proper.

The objection to such words as purchase, partake, ablutions is that they have a pseudo-elegance about them that is on a par with curled up third and little fingers holding a teacup.

In best—meaning most distinguished—society no one arises, or retires or resides in a residence. One gets up, goes to bed, and lives in a house. In other words, everything that is simple and direct is better form than the cumbersome and pretentious.

In contrast to words which are pretentious, below are several never used by persons of best taste.

NEVER SAY	SAY INSTEAD
Brainy	Brilliant or clever
Make you acquainted with	(See Introductions)
Pardon *me!*	I beg your pardon. Or, Excuse me! Or, I'm sorry!
Lovely food	Good food
Elegant home	Beautiful house—or place
A stylish dresser	She dresses well, or she wears lovely clothes
Charmed! Or pleased to meet you!	How do you do! Or, I'm very glad to meet you!
Formals	Formal clothes
Fellow or chap	Man (or, boy, if under twenty-one years of age)
Boy (when over twenty-one years of age)	Man
Young lady	Girl is proper according to good usage for any unmarried young woman not in business, and not older than early twenties
"Keeping company with" or "walking out with"	(There is no proper equivalent for the phrase because according to etiquette no such situation exists. No man is given the exclusive right to be devoted to any girl unless he is engaged to her.)
Gentleman friend	Man friend or "a man who is a friend of mine"
Lady friend	Woman friend or my best girl
Close friend	A best friend or intimate friend; on occasion, good friend

WORDS, PHRASES, AND PRONUNCIATION

NEVER SAY	SAY INSTEAD
Social affair	A party (an "affair" is something more than friendship between a man and a woman. One speaks of affairs—with an s—of business or state. Otherwise affair suggests a badly-put-together contraption. In best society one dines or lunches or goes to a party, but no one ever heard a person of taste speak of "attending a social affair")
In the home	In someone's house or at home
Drapes	Curtains, or, if necessary, draperies. ("Drapes" is seen in the advertising pages every day, but it is still a flagrant example of bad taste.)
Photo, auto, mints. (All abbreviated words should be avoided, but business has gradually lessened the tabu against phone—except for those who have no "business custom" excuse.)	Telephone, photograph, automobile (or motor), peppermints

A few such words as "wealthy," meaning "well-to-do" or "rich," or such phrases as "they entertained us," meaning "invited us to dinner" or "gave a tea for us," are approved of in certain localities. But they should be avoided by those who would not be thought provincial.

"Dearie," said to strangers, is very bad form. "My dear," said to friends, is entirely proper.

"Gent," "girlie," "hubby," "little woman" are unspeakable.

"Tintinnabulary summons," meaning "bell," and "bovine continuation," meaning "cow's tail," are more amusing than offensive, but they illustrate the theory of bad style that is pretentious.

As examples of the very worst offenses that can be committed, the following are offered:

"Pray accept my thanks for the flattering ovation you have tendered me."

"Yes," says the preposterous bride, "I am the recipient of many admired and highly prized gifts."

"Will you permit me to recall myself to you?"

Speaking of bridesmaids as "pretty servitors," "dispensing hospitality," asking anyone to "step this way."

Many other expressions are provincial and one who seeks purity of speech should, if possible, avoid them, but as "offenses" they are minor. They include

Reckon, guess, calculate, or figure, meaning think.
Allow, meaning agree.
Folks, meaning family.
Visiting with, meaning talking with.

There are certain words which have been singled out and misused by the indiscriminating until their value is destroyed.

"HOME" AND "HOUSE"

In its true meaning, "home" is the sentiment, the atmosphere, the spirit, the personality, the hospitality that the room or the apartment of the house in which you dwell expresses. "Home" is not a synonym for "house." To people of taste a house is built of wood or brick or stone. It is shocking to be offered an icebox as though it were an attribute of family loyalty. You can love your home, work for your home, and be at home, or have or do whatever you please at home. You can also eat home cooking, do home designing and home sewing, meaning food cooked in your kitchen, designing or sewing done by yourself or done under your roof; but if you are sensitive to the traditions of taste, you never put a piece of furniture "in *the* home" unless you mean a charitable institution. You would say, "Our home was an old Georgian house," but not "We had a Georgian home."

OTHER WORDS TO AVOID

Long ago "elegant" was turned from a word denoting the essence of refinement and beauty into gaudy trumpery. "Refined" and "dainty" are both affected. But the pariah of the language is "culture," a word rarely used by those who truly possess it, but so constantly misused by those who understand nothing of its meaning that it is becoming a synonym for vulgarity and imitation. To speak of the proper use of a finger bowl or the ability to introduce two people without a blunder as being "evidence of culture of the highest degree" is precisely as though evidence of highest education were claimed for whoever can do sums in addition and read words of one syllable. Culture in its true meaning is widest possible education, *plus* sensitive and discriminating appreciation of excellence.

Whether you should say "girl" or "young woman" when you mean a young person between the age of eighteen and twenty-five depends upon whether you are speaking according to the dictionary or according to social traditions. In business one speaks of men and young women always. Socially one speaks of men and girls. The reason for this is arbitrary custom. If, in society, one were to speak of men and young women, one would immediately transfer the scene from ballroom or terrace to office.

WORDS, PHRASES, AND PRONUNCIATION

Girls, meaning maidservants (used even by the highest class when speaking of themselves) has always been and in great measure is still very bad form, but the feeling of opprobrium that is attached to the word "servant" has made it not unusual to hear elderly ladies speak of several as "my girls." A single one is called by name always. In big and formally appointed houses, the word "servants" remains in use.

The term "lady," which once denoted elegance and cultivation, long ago became a mere synonym for respectability which deteriorated into having no meaning at all. Every female in America expects to be spoken of as "this lady." Consequently a real lady under most circumstances speaks of herself and her friends as women.

"FORMAL" AND "INFORMAL"

But the most misused words in the dictionary are "informal" when formality is intended, and "formal" for other occasions which have not an attribute of formality about them! Formal is a synonym for ceremonial. A formal party is always conducted according to rules of ritualistic or established forms of ceremony.

In certain houses—such as the Worldlys' for instance—formality is inevitable no matter how informal may be her "will you dine informally" intention!

On the other hand, the Kindharts can invite a hundred guests, half of them strangers, and at the same time achieve a party that has nothing formal about it. In short, the ordinary pleasant social intercourse between friends and neighbors should, it is to be hoped, never be characterized as formal.

SLANG

The fact that slang is apt and forceful makes its use irresistibly tempting. Coarse or profane slang is beside the mark, but the "movies," "deadly" (meaning dull), "swell" (meaning first-rate), "divine" (meaning pleasant), "hunch," and "O.K." and even such phrases as "and how!" "so what?" and "you betcha" are words and phrases in such common use—at least by our husbands and sons—that their exclusion would leave our American vernacular rather stilted.

It must be remembered that all slang is so greatly modified by the tone of voice in which it is said that the vocabulary as printed may give an inaccurate impression. Slang, to be acceptable, must be fresh and applicable, or it is as unappetizing as a left-over buckwheat cake. Moreover, it is like underscoring written words, and to be effective must be sparingly used.

All colloquial expressions are little foxes that spoil the grapes of perfect diction, but they are very little foxes; the false elegance of stupid pretentiousness, however, is an annihilating blight that destroys root and vine.

PRONUNCIATION

Traits of pronunciation which are typical of whole sections of the country, or accents inherited from European parents, must not be confused with crude pronunciations that have their origin in illiteracy. A gentleman of Irish blood may have a brogue as rich as plum cake, or another's accent be soft Southern, or flat New England, or rolling Western; and to each of these the utterance of the others may sound too flat, too soft, too harsh, too refined, or drawled, or clipped short, but not uncultivated.

To a New York ear, which ought to be fairly unbiased since the New York accent is a composite of all accents, English women chirrup and twitter. But the beautifully modulated, clear-clipped enunciation of a cultivated Englishman, one who can move his jaws and not swallow his words whole, comes as near to perfection in English as the diction of the Comédie Française comes to perfection in French.

The Boston accent is very crisp and in places suggestive of the best English, but the vowels are so curiously flattened that the speech has a saltless effect. There is no rhyming word as flat as the way they say "heart"—"haht." And "bone" and "coat"—"bawn," "cawt," to rhyme with awe!

Then, South, there is too much salt—rather too much sugar. Everyone's mouth seems full of it, with "I" turned to "ah" and every staccato a drawl. But the voices are full of sweetness and music unknown north of the Potomac.

Charm is perhaps in the ear of the listener. But there are few listeners who are not fascinated by Charleston's way of saying "The Kyart is in the Gyarden." In Maryland, a child's mother calls, "Come hyeur Ehm-leh!" And of course every Southerner says "*Idea*," "You all," "Ah reckon!" and calls architectural columns "pillahs."

The Pennsylvania burr is perhaps the mother of the Western one. It is strong enough to have mothered all the r's in the wor-r-rld!

The smartest of smart in Philadelphia say, "Owrchie had a mawervellous howrrt" and the "uiyly buiyd chuiyped and chuiyped." Chicago calls itself Chicawgo and eats chawklut. Many Omurricuns go on fourn tours and eat awerunges, and what their accent does to European languages is exactly like taking stones out of a gurgling brook and throwing them into a stone crusher. All of which merely indicates the part of the country we are from. "Water," pronounced as though it were the watt of electric measure—watter—came, so it is said, from German settlers who pronounced it like Wasser. "Bot" and "thot" sound ugly to us who say "bought" and "thought." But it is very possible that "bought" and "thought" sound ugly to the others, just as "lowng" and "strowng" sound ugly to the English, who always say "lahng" and "strahng."

Philadelphia's "haow" and "caow" for "how" and "cow," and "mee" for "my," are quite as bad as the "water-r" and "thot" of the West.

N'Yawk is supposed to say "yeh" and "Omurica" and "Toosdeh," and "puddin'." "Whazza us'n tell'n' yuh?" And "Thuh spoim erl wuz berled" (the sperm oil was boiled). Probably five per cent of it does, but as a whole it has no accent, because it is a composite of all in one.

In best New York society there is perhaps a generally accepted pronunciation which seems chiefly an elimination of the accents of other sections. Probably that is what all people think of their own pronunciation. Or do they not know whether their inflection is right or wrong? Nothing should be simpler to determine. If they pronounce according to a standard dictionary, they are correct; if they don't, they have an "accent" or are ignorant; it is for them to determine which. Such differences as those between saying "wash" or "wawsh," "cahn't" or "can't," "ad*ver*tisement" or "adver*tise*ment" are of small importance. But one who considers himself able to qualify as a person of education should know better than to commit errors such as the following.

These illiterate pronunciations are of course *never* heard in good society:

Tark to rhyme with bark	for	Talk (Tawk)
Gempmun	for	Gentleman
Forn	for	Foreign (far-ren)
Otta*mo*bile	for	Automo*bile*
Reely	for	Real-ly
Cherce	for	Choice
Fambly	for	Family
Pitcher	for	Picture
Merrige (Het and Ket)	for	Marriage (Hat and Cat)
Atha-let-ic	for	Ath-let-ic
Pur runt	for	Parent
Av viator	for	Ay viator
Ar tchi tek	for	Ark ki tect
Ben	for	Been or bin
Jest or jast	for	Just
Fillum	for	Film
Et	for	Ate
Goil	for	Girl

Erl	for	Oil
Eggsit	for	Exit
Muh*ree*	for	*Ma*rie (a as in fat)
Luk a mo tuv	for	Lo co mo tive
Strenth	for	Strength
Sing ging	for	Sing ing
Kep	for	Kept
*R*ee fined	for	Re*fined*
Col-yum	for	Column

These pretentious pronunciations are only pseudo-elegant:

IN BAD TASTE	IN GOOD TASTE
Cult your	Cultcha
Par ris (with trilled "r" and hissing "s")	Paris
At-all	A-tall
Iss-you	Issue (ishue)
Press-i-yus	Precious (preshus)

Incorrect pronunciations most frequently encountered:

Feb u ary	for	Feb ru ary
Toos day	for	T(you)s day
Youman	for	Human
Abzorb	for	Absorb (sibilant s)
Gov er ment	for	Gov ern ment
Leezure	for	Lez zure
Wite	for	White

Pronunciations in the "A" list are correct with unanglicised American pronunciation of "can't" to rhyme with "pants," and terminal *r* sounded.

The "B" list is correct with pronunciation of *a* as in "art" and terminal *r* as *h*.

A	B
To may to	To ma(h) to
May onnaise	Mai onnaise (my-onnaise)
Recipe	Receipt. (Receipt has a more distinguished ancestry, but since recipe is used by all modern writers on cookery, only the immutables insist on receipt.)

This does not mean that the "A" pronunciation would be approved by lovers of diction, but that speech of a pattern is better than one that is of the unmatching patch-work that has resulted from our borrowed accents.

THE ACCENTS WE BORROWED FROM LONDON

In not very happy contrast to the ugliness of our native American twang and burr, it became the fashion a few years ago to copy London and to say "figger," "cahfee," "shedule," "squeer-ril," "*la-bore*-atory," "secretree" and "lahng"—for "figure," "coffee," "schedule," "squirrel," "*lab*ratory," "secretary" and "long." But those who adopt these pronunciations should remember to adapt the rest of their speech to match. Otherwise, the imported words will suggest velvet patches on native overalls.

But those of us who are inclined to think America's speech is alone bad and England's alone perfect can perhaps find amusement as well as consolation in the comment made by H. W. Seaman, an Englishman writing from London, who describes an evening at a cinema where an American film is to be shown, as follows:

"A tramp crawls into a box car. A young man behind me says to his girl, " 'E's a 'aowbaow." An actress on the screen says, "I jest kean't go through wuth ut; I jest kean't." The voice behind says, "I daown't mawnd the blinkin' sleng; it's the neyesal tweng I cawn't stick."

FRENCH WORDS IN ENGLISH SPEECH

Although the point must be made that sprinkling French words throughout English speech does not give elegance to conversation, but on the contrary suggests a limited vocabulary in English, it is true that certain words which have become part of our language are unavoidable and should therefore be said properly. Especially important is it to learn those which have no English equivalents. Many of these are as easy to say as any words in our language, and their mispronunciation has no excuse. For instance:

Bouquet is pronounced boo-kay, not bo- to rhyme with go.

Vaudeville—vaude is pronounced voad- to rhyme with road; ville as veal, a meat; voad-veal.

Chauffeur is not *show*fer, but show*fur*, accent apparently even, but actually on the last syllable, which is pronounced *fur*.

Garage is not gurrodge, but gar-*razhe*—gar as in garret, and zhe like the ge in rouge.

The bill of fare in every restaurant is not a may-*noo*. The actual French pronunciation has no English equivalent, but an acceptable prounuciation is *men* (plural of man) -*you:* menyou.

The underwaist now advertised as a "bra" was never a brazeer but a brassière. Brass like the metal, and -ière like the slang "yeah" for yes!—brassière.

Débutante is day-bu (like the first syllable of beauty) -tant (said like aunt with a moderately broad *a*).

Amateur is not amachure. Say quickly I *am at her* house, and you can't help pronouncing amateur perfectly.

One who is engaged is a fiancé (masculine) or fiancée (feminine); both words are pronounced alike. The first syllable is fee (same as the fee a doctor charges); the second has no English equivalent, but the nearest is the "an" in want. The last syllable is *say*—fee-ahn-*say* as though the final y were broken off in mid-air. But these syllables are only approximate.

Première—not prum *eer*, but *prerm* to rhyme with term and ière like *oh yeah*—with sound of r at end of h.

Words which ought to be banned because they cannot be written with our alphabet include "bouillon," "bon-bon," "lingerie," and "ensemble." Much better to say "clear soup," "candy," "underthings," and "dress with coat to match"—in plain English, instead of murdering our own tongue as well as that of the French with "bull yon," "bonn bonn," "long ger ay" and "enn sem-bel." The nearest to "in" in lingerie is like the *an* in sang, long drawn out without pronouncing the g, ger like the g as in rouge and rie is a *trilled* ree. The nearest to "ensemble" is "ahn sahm-m-bl"—"en" very much like a groan of pain.

HOW TO CULTIVATE AN AGREEABLE SPEECH

The often-heard expression, "You know she is a lady as soon as she opens her mouth," is not an exaggeration. The first requirement for charm of speech is a pleasing voice. A few singing lessons—even though you have no gift for music and will never sing a note—are of inestimable value in teaching you to place your speaking voice and in teaching you to breathe. A low voice—low in pitch, not in range—is always more pleasing than one forced up against the ceiling and apparently let out through a steam-vent in the roof! On the other hand, a voice uttered with so little strength that it threatens to be extinguished or so low as to be heard with effort is even more trying. Making yourself heard is chiefly a matter of enunciation; if you breathe properly and pronounce distinctly, a low voice carries well and delights a sensitive ear. Few people with loud voices have any idea that their steam-whistle screaming is not only ear-splitting but, in public, extremely bad form, as it attracts the attention of everyone within shouting radius.

As a nation we do not talk so much too fast, as too loud. Tens of thousands twang and slur and shout and burr! Many of us drawl and many others of us race tongues and breath at full speed, but, as already said, the speed of our speech does not matter so much. Pitch of voice matters very much, and so do pronunciation and enunciation, both of which are absolutely essential to the comfort of the listener.

THE ATTRIBUTES OF CHARM OF SPEECH

No speaker who searches for words is interesting. Beautiful speech is like a brook that ripples on and on. Irritating speech is like the puffing of a locomotive, each puff broken with er-er—and-er, the listeners sharing in the search and also sharing in the effort with which each word is pronounced.

There is no better way to cultivate a perfect pronunciation, apart from association with cultivated people, than by getting a small pronouncing dictionary of words in ordinary use, and reading it word by word, marking and studying any that you use frequently and mispronounce. When you know them, read any book at random slowly aloud to yourself, very carefully pronouncing each word.

You should, moreover, look up in a dictionary every word you meet that you do not thoroughly know. Another convenient way to enlarge your vocabulary as well as to correct your faults of pronunciation is that of a notable lawyer, whose early advantages had not taught him good English, but who won a high reputation for the purity of his speech. The secret of his achievement was that for years he wrote words or phrases, a few at a time, on his bathroom mirror with soap! Then he practiced these words by saying them over and over to himself, day after day, while he shaved and dressed. Later on, when these words were thoroughly fixed in his mind, other words were written in their place. The consciousness of these exercises may make you stilted in conversation at first, but by and by the "sense" or "impulse" to speak correctly will come.

This is a method that has been followed by many men handicapped in youth through lack of education, who have become prominent in public life, and by many women who, likewise handicapped by circumstances, have not only made possible a creditable position for themselves, but have then given their children the inestimable advantage of learning their mother tongue correctly at their mother's knee.

6

Conversation

IDEAL conversation must be an exchange of thought, and not, as many of those who worry most about their shortcomings believe, an eloquent exhibition of wit or oratory. Happily for most of us, it is not necessary to have any very special gift of cleverness to be a person with whom others are delighted to talk.

BE TRANQUIL! DON'T BE AFRAID!

But if you are one of those who dread meeting strangers because you are afraid you won't be able to think of anything to say, you might do well to remember that most of the faults of conversation are committed not by those who talk little, but by those who talk too much. A bore is almost always one whose voice is never still. A tactless person invariably rushes in with what ought never to be said. On the other hand, those who have great difficulty in carrying on a conversation are usually those who for reasons known only to themselves are terrified of silence. This terror is very like the terror of sinking felt by those who are learning to swim. It is not just the first stroke that overwhelms them, but the thought of all the strokes that must follow. In the same way it is not making a first remark that is dismaying, but the endless effort to keep on thinking of further remarks, with the result that the frightened talker hears not a word said to him because he is so desperately trying to think what he is going to have to say next. So the practical rule for continuing a conversation is the same as that for swimming: "Don't get frightened. Don't splash violently. Just take it calmly." Or, to change the simile, the old sign at the railroad crossing, "STOP, LOOK, LISTEN," is excellent advice under many circumstances other than when waiting to cross the tracks. In conversation, for example, "Stop" would mean not to rush recklessly forward; "Look" would mean pay attention to the expression of the person with whom you are talking; and "Listen"—meaning exactly that—is the best advice possible, since the person whom most people love to sit next to is a sympathetic listener who makes others want to talk. It must, of course, be remembered that a sympathetic listener really listens. To hold a fixed expression of sympathy and let your mind wander elsewhere won't do at all.

Obviously, conversation should be a matter of equal give and take,

CONVERSATION

but too often it is all "take." The voluble talker—or chatterer—rides his own hobby straight through the hours without giving anyone else, who might also like to say something, a chance to do other than exhaustedly await the turn that never comes. Once in a while—a very long while—one meets a brilliant person whose talk is a delight; or still more rarely a wit who manipulates every ordinary topic with the agility of a sleight-of-hand performer, to the ever-increasing rapture of his listeners.

But as a rule the man who has been led to believe that he is a brilliant talker has been led to make himself a pest. No conversation is possible between others whose ears are within reach of his insistent voice. There is a simple rule by which, if one is voluble, one can at least refrain from being a pest or a bore. And the rule is merely to stop and think.

"THINK BEFORE YOU SPEAK"

Nearly all the faults or mistakes in conversation are caused by not thinking. For instance, a first rule for behavior in company is "Try to do and say only that which will be agreeable to others." Yet how many people who really know better, people who would be perfectly capable of intelligent understanding if they didn't let their brains remain asleep or locked tight, go night after night to dinner parties, day after day to other social gatherings, and absent-mindedly chatter about this or that without ever taking the trouble to *think* what they are saying and to whom they are saying it! Would a young mother describe twenty or thirty cunning tricks and sayings of the baby to a bachelor who has been helplessly put beside her at dinner if she *thought?* She would know very well, alas! that not even a very dear friend would really care for more than an *hors d'oeuvre* of the subject at the board of general conversation.

IF YOU ARE A DOTING MOTHER—DON'T

The older woman is even worse, unless something occurs (often when it is too late) to make her wake up and realize that she not only bores her hearers but prejudices everyone against her children by the unrestraint of her own praise. The daughter who is continually lauded as the most captivating and beautiful girl in the world seems to the wearied perceptions of enforced listeners annoying and plain. In the same way the "magnificent" son is handicapped by his mother's —or his father's—pride and love in exact proportion to its displayed intensity. On the other hand, the neglected wife, the unappreciated husband, the misunderstood child, take on a glamor in the eyes of others equally out of proportion. That great love has seldom perfect wisdom is one of the great tragedies in the drama of life. In the case of the overloving wife or mother, someone should love *her* enough to make her *stop and think* that her loving praise is not merely boring her hearers but handicapping unfairly those for whom she would gladly lay down her life—and yet few would have the courage to point out to her that she would far better lay down her tongue.

THOSE WHO TALK TOO EASILY

People who talk too easily are likely to talk too much, and at times imprudently, and those with vivid imagination are often unreliable in their statements. On the other hand, the "man of silence," who never speaks except when he has something "worth while" to say, tends to wear well among his intimates, but is not likely to add much to the gaiety of a party.

ONCE IS EFFECTIVE; TWICE IS BORING

Try not to repeat yourself, either by telling the same story again and again or by going back over details of your narrative that seemed especially to interest or amuse your hearer. Many things are of interest when briefly told and for the first time; *nothing* interests when too long dwelt upon or told a second time. The possible exception is something very pleasant that you have heard about A, or more especially A's child, which having already told A you can then tell B, and later C in A's presence. Avoid this as a habit, however, because an over-dosage of praise is very like ten lumps of sugar in coffee: only an insatiable sugar lover can swallow it.

Certain subjects, even though you are very sure of the ground upon which you are standing, had best be shunned; such, for example, as the criticism of a religious creed or disagreement with another's political conviction. Also, since few can parry an opponent's thrusts with good temper as well as skill, be careful not to let amiable discussion turn into contradiction and argument. The tactful person keeps his prejudices to himself and even when involved in a discussion says, "It seems to me thus and so." One who is well bred never says, "Nothing of the kind!" If he finds another's opinion utterly unreasonable, he turns to another subject for a pleasanter channel of conversation.

When someone is talking to you, it is inconsiderate to be repeating, "What did you say?" Those who are deaf are often obliged to ask that a sentence be repeated. Otherwise their irrelevant answers would make them appear half-witted. But countless persons, with perfectly good hearing, say, "What?" from force of habit and inattention.

THE GIFT OF HUMOR

The joy of joys is the person of light but unmalicious humor. If you know anyone who is gay, beguiling and amusing, you will, if you are wise, do everything you can to make him prefer your house and your table to any other, for where he is, the successful party is also. What he says is of no moment. It is the twist he gives to it, the intonation, the personality he puts into his quip or retort or observation that delights his hearers, and to his case the ordinary rules do not apply.

Our greatly beloved Will Rogers could tell a group of people that it had rained today and would probably rain tomorrow, and make everyone burst into laughter—or tears if he chose—according to the way it was said. But the ordinary rest of us must, if we would be thought sympathetic, intelligent or agreeable, "go fishing."

GOING FISHING FOR TOPICS

In talking to a stranger who has just been introduced to you and about whom you are in complete ignorance, there is really nothing to do but try one topic after another just as a fisherman searches for the right fly. "You "try for nibbles" by asking a few questions, such as "Are you fond of the theater?" If the answer is, "Yes, very," you can talk theater. When the subject runs down, you try another, or perhaps you talk of something you have been doing or thinking about—planting a garden, planning a journey, contemplating a job or similar safe topics. Do not snatch at a period of silence. Let it go for a little while. Conversation is not a race that must be continued at breakneck pace.

BEGIN, "I AM JANE JONES"

To a total stranger it is sometimes easiest to begin with a description of yourself. Say frankly, for instance, "My name is Mrs. John Jones. That's my husband sitting opposite you. We live in the country and raise prize poultry and dahlias, but we come to town very often in the winter to hear music." The one spoken to is very likely to reply that he lives in the city, knows nothing about music or prize flowers and poultry, but his favorite occupations are golf and fishing. Probably after this you talk fishing and this leads to other things. If these topics fade out, he perhaps asks about poultry and what one must know to take prizes. It's really very simple. Or, another helpful thing, if you are a woman talking to a man, is to ask advice. "We want to motor through the South. Do you know about the roads?" Or. "I'm thinking of buying a radio. Which make do you think is best?" In fact, it is safe to ask his opinion on almost anything. Politics, sports, the stock market, the trend of behavior—anything. Or, if you are a man talking to a young woman, ask her what she thinks about life, love, work, amusement, romance, almost any question about the relative values of the things people do or think or try for. If she is an older woman, she will probably talk to you.

CRAMMING FOR CONVERSATION

Making an outline of what to say before you go out is sensible only in this, that it does in most cases inspire confidence. This does not mean that you should study some subject and then lecture on it. Heaven forbid! But if you glance through your newspaper, in which every imaginable topic is proffered, you can't very well go out feeling completely unprepared. Whatever you do, don't deliberately read up on a topic that you think will give an impression of your cleverness. That is the way bores are made! Be sure to choose topics that truly appeal to you. It doesn't matter so much what the subjects are; your enthusiasm about what you have to say is almost sure to kindle a responsive enthusiasm in your listener. And yet, a paradox: If you care too intensely about a subject, it is dangerous to allow yourself to say anything. That is, if you can only lecture about your fixed point of view, then you should never mention it except as a platform speaker. But if, on the other hand, you are able to listen with an open mind, the chances are that you need put no barriers whatever on any subject. At the present moment Mrs. Oldname and Mrs. Kindhart—really the most devoted of neighbors—are so violently opposed to each other on a certain political question of today that their neighbors have made a rule to which both have amiably agreed: the first person who mentions the tabu topic must pay a fine.

After all, a conversation between one person and you is very simple. You find one topic on which you agree—a topic that is pleasant to both. Then you stumble on another about which you don't agree. Careful here! Much better withdraw unless you can argue without bitterness or bigotry. Argument between cool-headed skilful opponents is delightful, but very, very dangerous for those who may become hot-headed or unreasoning.

THE CRUELTY OF TACTLESS BLUNDERING

None but the insane could feel impelled to clutch at a neighbor's dress and tear it off. Yet the tactless do the comparably unfit thing time and time again.

Thoughts and feelings of seclusion and sacredness are ruthlessly laid bare by such remarks as, "Oh, but your son's lameness is getting much worse!" "I suppose you feel lonely since the death of your daughter?" "Is it true that you are going to be divorced?"

These examples sound unbelievable, yet each of these crude remarks has actually been made on occasion by persons of supposed education who had not a semblance of excuse for their cruelty.

Commonplace examples of tactlessness include the mean-to-be-agreeable elderly man who says to an old acquaintance, "Twenty years ago you were the prettiest woman in town." Or, in the pleasantest tone of voice to one whose only son has married, "Why is it, do you suppose, that young wives always dislike their mothers-in-law?"

If you have any ambition to be sought after, you must not talk about the unattractiveness of old age to the elderly, about the joys of dancing and skating to the lame, or about the advantages of ancestry to the self-made. It is also dangerous, as well as needlessly unkind, to ridicule or criticize others, especially for what they can't help. To say, "She looks as though her mother had been scared by a white mouse" may make your listeners laugh at a girl who is very blonde and shy and pale, but it is a cheap trick and not worth taking.

A young girl who admired her own facile adjectives said to a casual acquaintance, "How *can* you go about with that moth-eaten, squint-eyed bag of a girl!" "Because," answered the youth, whom she had intended to dazzle, "the lady of your flattering epithets happens to be my sister."

It is scarcely necessary to say that one whose tactless remarks ride roughshod over the feelings of others is not welcomed by many.

THE TIMETAKERS

People of this character would undoubtedly be shocked if told that they ever took anything from anyone without payment, and yet they take great sections out of the busy lives of others, thus forced to sit in an empty room politely looking at a blank wall—which is exactly what unfinished conversation is like. There is always time to listen to something that is interesting or amusing, but a long encounter with words that have absolutely no "furnishing thoughts" behind them—that are uttered without a glimmer of other intention than filling time with pleasantly modulated sound—is in this intensive age scarcely pleasanter than an encounter with an actual thief who steals one's actual watch!

THE BORE

A bore is said to be "one who talks about himself when you want to talk about yourself!" This is superficially true, but a bore might more accurately be described as one who insists on telling you at length something that you don't want to hear about at all. He insists that you hear him out to the bitter end in spite of your plainly shown disinclination. He will tell the same story for the thousandth time; every tiresome detail is held up and turned about as a morsel of delectability; to him each pea in a pod differs from another with the entrancing variety that artists find in tropical sunsets.

On the other hand, to be bored is a bad habit, and one only too easy to fall into. As a matter of fact, it is impossible, almost, to meet anyone who has not *something* of interest to tell you if you are but clever enough yourself to find out what it is. Also you might remember that in every conversation with a "dull" person, half of the dulness is your own. There are certain always delightful people who refuse to be bored. Their attitude is that no subject need ever be utterly uninteresting, so long as it is discussed for the first time. Repetition alone is deadly dull. Besides, what is the matter with trying to be agreeable yourself? Not *too* agreeable. Alas! it is true: "Be polite to bores and so shall you have bores always round about you." Furthermore, there is no reason why you should be bored when you can be otherwise. But if you find yourself sitting in the hedgerow with nothing but weeds, there is no reason for shutting your eyes and seeing nothing, instead of finding what beauty you may in the weeds. To put it cynically, life is too short to waste it in drawing blanks. Therefore, it is up to you to find as many pictures to put on your blank pages as possible.

TABUS OF CONVERSATION

The safest rule to remember is that conversation must never be taken out of the drawing room. Vivid details of operations, ills or personal blemishes, descriptions concerning bed or bathroom, as well as appurtenances of the dressing room, are not suitable topics, nor are personal jokes in good taste. It is very bad form to talk freely to acquaintances, or worse yet to strangers, about your private concerns.

DANGERS TO BE AVOIDED

In conversation the dangers are very much the same as those to be avoided in writing letters. Talk about things which you think will be agreeable to your hearer. Don't dilate on ills, misfortunes, or other unpleasantnesses. The one in greatest danger of making enemies is the man or woman of brilliant wit. If sharp, wit tends to produce a feeling of mistrust even while it stimulates. Furthermore, the applause which follows every witty sally becomes in time breath to the nostrils, and perfectly well-intentioned people, who mean to say nothing unkind, in the flash of a second "see a point," and in the next second score it with no more power to resist than a drug addict has to refuse a dose put into his hand!

The mimic is a joy to his present company, but eccentric mannerisms are much easier to imitate than charm of personality, and the subjects of the habitual mimic are all too likely to become enemies.

You need not, however, be dull because you refrain from the rank habit of a critical attitude, which like a weed will grow all over the place if you let it have half a chance. A very good resolve to make and keep, if you would also keep any friends you make, is never to speak of anyone without, in imagination, having him or her overhear what you say. One often hears the exclamation "I would say it to her face!" At least be very sure that this is true, and not a braggart's phrase, and then—nine times out of ten—think better of it and refrain. Preaching is all very well in a textbook, schoolroom or pulpit, but it has no place in society. Society is supposed to be a pleasant place; telling people disagreeable things to their faces or behind their backs is *not* a pleasant occupation.

PERSONAL REMARKS

Although personal remarks are always in bad form, it is proper and always pleasant to say something appreciative about something one has done. "That was a splendid speech," "You gave us such a delicious dinner," "I've never seen such beautiful flowers," "You always know how to make a room inviting," etc. But it is bad taste to say, "What a lovely nose you have and what an enchanting mouth."

THE "OMNISCIENCE" OF THE VERY RICH

Why a man, because he has millions, should assume that they confer omniscience in all branches of knowledge is something which may be left to the psychologist to answer, but most people thrown much in contact with millionaires will agree that an attitude of infallibility is typical of a fair majority.

A professor who has devoted his life to a subject modestly makes a statement. "You are all wrong," says the man of millions. "It is this way——" As a connoisseur he seems to think that because he can pay for anything he fancies, he is an accredited expert as well as a potential owner. Topics he has a smattering of he simply appropriates; his prejudices are, in his opinion, expert criticism; his taste impeccable; his judgment infallible; and to him the world is a pleasure built for his sole pleasuring. But to the rest of us, who also have to live in it with as much harmony as we can, such persons are certainly elephants at large in the garden. We can sometimes induce them to pass through gently, but they are just as likely at any moment to pull up our fences and push the house itself over on our defenseless heads.

There are countless others, of course, very often the richest of all, who are authoritative in all they profess, who are human and helpful and respecters of the garden enclosure of others.

MAXIMS FOR THOSE WHO TALK TOO EASILY!

The faults of commission are far more serious than those of omission; regrets are seldom for what you left unsaid.

The chatterer reveals every corner of his shallow mind; one who keeps silent cannot have his depth plumbed.

Don't pretend to know more than you do. To say you have read a book and then seemingly to understand nothing of what you have read, proves you a half-wit. No real person hesitates to say, "I don't know."

Above all, stop and *think* what you are saying! This is really the first, last and only rule. If you "stop," you can't chatter or expound or flounder ceaselessly; and if you *think*, you will find a topic and a manner of presenting your topic so that your neighbor will be interested rather than long-suffering.

Remember also that the sympathetic—not apathetic—listener is the delight of delights. The person who looks glad to see you, who is seemingly eager for your news or enthralled with your conversation, who looks at you with a kindling of the face and gives you spontaneous and undivided attention, is the one to whom the palm for the art of conversation would undoubtedly be awarded.

(Please always consult the Index for additional details, which may quite possibly be included in other chapters. For example, "Conversation" is touched upon in seven different chapters.)

7

*On the Street and in Public**

THE rule of convention says that a gentleman, whether walking with two ladies or one, takes the curb side of the pavement, and that he should never sandwich himself between them. The second part of this rule is always observed when they are walking, but it is not considered improper that he sit between them in church or in a motor—or even at a concert or in a theater—unless they have aisle seats, in which case the gentleman sits on the aisle. But there is a strong modern tendency toward paying no attention to the "curb," since the danger from runaway horses, which the gentleman was once supposed to avert, no longer exists, and therefore it does seem senseless that he keep circling back of her every time they cross the street, instead of giving her the position of courtesy on his right. In short, modern rules of behavior approve of his walking on the curb side of the pavement or on the lady's left as he chooses, but not on her right and away from the curb at the same time.

DON'T ATTRACT ATTENTION

The most important rules of behavior in the street are those against doing things that are conspicuous.

All people in the streets, or anywhere in public, should be careful not to talk too loudly. They should especially avoid pronouncing people's names, or making personal remarks that may attract passing attention or give a clue to their identity.

There is nothing that stamps the vulgarian more than advertising his possessions or achievements by loud word of mouth—anywhere!

Not to attract attention to oneself in public is one of the fundamental rules of good breeding. Shun a loud voice, staring at people, knocking into them, talking across anyone; in a word, do not attract attention to yourself. Do not expose your private affairs, feelings or innermost thoughts in public. You are knocking down the walls of your house when you do.

One should never call out a name in public, unless it is absolutely

* Although the words *gentleman* and *lady* have through misuse become tabu, it is impossible to avoid their use in a book such as this, since rules of best taste do not necessarily govern all men and women, but they do govern all people who can be qualified as "gentle."

unavoidable. A young girl who was separated from her friends in a baseball crowd had the presence of mind to take off her hat and hold it above the people surrounding her so that her friends might find her.

GENTLEMEN AND BUNDLES

Victorian books on etiquette which said that a gentleman must offer to carry a lady's bundles have been thought amusingly quaint for many, many years. Bundles never suggested either ladies or gentlemen in the first place. But since the Second World War's shortage of delivery trucks, package carrying has become necessary even for officers, who had hitherto been forbidden to carry so much as a box of candy or a single book! Suddenly they found themselves obliged, when on leave at home, either to carry the groceries or go supperless. The rules, therefore, have undergone a change. It is still true, however, that a gentleman will gladly stagger under golf bags and suitcases—but carry a "bundle"? Not twice! War or no war, an unthinking young woman who asks an admirer to carry something suggestive of a pillow, done up in crinkled paper and odd lengths of joined string, will wonder, as her grandmother did, why John Nubeau never calls upon her any more!

Of course, every man is willing to carry an umbrella that looks at all masculine in style. He will also very willingly carry a woman's field glasses or her camera or her polo coat or even her coonskin coat, or anything that might be his own.

It is true that the belle of the days when that word was in use handed most of her belongings (and all of them conspicuously feminine) to her beaux to carry. But the girl of today wears or uses what she takes with her, and the present-day man does not consider it a privilege to be an animated clothes rack even for HER.

A GENTLEMAN OFFERS HIS ARM

To an old lady or to an invalid or to any lady on any occasion when she may need his support, a gentleman of course offers his arm. Otherwise a lady does not take a gentleman's arm in the daytime.

But in accompanying a lady anywhere at night, whether down the steps of a house or when walking a distance, a gentleman always offers his arm, not only because it is a courtesy, but because stilt-heeled sandals are fairly perilous to walk in when it is too dark for a woman to see her foothold clearly.

When he offers his arm, he says, "Will you take my arm?" or perhaps, "You'd better take my arm!" or "Wouldn't it be easier if you took my arm along here?" Otherwise the only occasions on which a gentleman offers his arm to a lady are in taking her in at a formal dinner, or in to supper at a ball, or when he is an usher at a wedding. Even in walking across a ballroom, except at a public ball in the grand march, it is the present fashion for the younger generation to walk side by side rather than hand on arm. This, however, is merely an instance where etiquette and the custom of the moment differ. An old-fashioned gentleman still offers his arm, and it is, and long will be, in accordance with etiquette to do so. But etiquette does *not* permit a gentleman to grab a lady by the arm or the elbow and shove her along. Only when he is assisting her to get into a motor or taxi or bus is it good form for him to put his hand under her elbow. When he helps her out, he should alight first and offer her his hand. Over dangerous footing or up a few rickety steps he also goes first and then leans over and offers her his hand.

Under all ordinary circumstances, indoors or out, the gentleman precedes her only if the way is dangerous or uncertain. The reason for his alighting first from a carriage dates from the era of the horse-drawn vehicle, when the horses might start suddenly, and he stood ready to catch or assist her should she trip. He alights first from a motor today because of the habit of getting out of a carriage first. He also precedes her down a very steep or slippery stairway. "Let me go first; the stairs are bad." The idea of protecting her should she slip is quite out of key with the fleet-footed young women who as easily qualify for the women's services as Diana herself might have done! Even so, etiquette requires that he make the gesture of stepping into a boat first and being ready to help her. Moreover it may be well to remember that charm in a woman still presupposes feminine grace rather than masculine hardihood, which does not deny the fact that a young woman's helplessness is a thing of the past, but is intended merely to suggest that many of the precepts of propriety are to manners what beauty preparations are to appearance. Overdone, they are very bad; but applied with taste, they can be very enhancing. In other words, without any of the traditional observances behavior becomes crudely unpleasant, like rough hands, broken nails and unwashed hair.

ON COUNTRY BY-PATHS

It is still impossible to imagine a lady as walking on a city street and either chewing gum or smoking. Nor does a gentleman walk with a lady on a city street and at the same time smoke. On the other hand, many things which are "not done" in the city are permissible in the country, where a man's pipe, like his dog, is his inseparable companion. That a young woman's cigarette may properly go along with the man and his pipe and his dog is now taken for granted in almost every community. But, for walking on the street in a city, the answer is still definitely No.

A LADY NOT ON THE LEFT

In former days there was a rule of utmost importance, that a lady was never seated on a gentleman's left, because according to etiquette a lady "on the left" was *not* a "lady." But today in America all that remains of this rule is that, when equally practical, it is always more polite that a gentleman seat a lady on his right. A few definite rules about sitting on the right include the seating of a guest of honor on the right of the host or hostess or chairman and the military rule by which the senior officer walks as well as sits on his junior's right. There is also a fixed rule that in her own car a lady always sits on the right-hand side of the rear seat of a motor that is driven by a chauffeur. This is "the owner's" seat, and therefore a woman friend—who of course enters the car first—must remember to take the left-hand seat so that the owner may take her own place always, unless she relinquishes it to a guest, such as the wife of the President or the Governor, whose rank is above her own, or anyone whom she wishes especially to honor.

THE QUESTION OF PAYING

It is becoming much less customary than it used to be for a gentleman to offer to pay a lady's way, especially if they happen to meet by chance. For example, if a young woman and a man happen to find themselves taking the same train and she stops at the news-stand to buy magazines, the man instinctively starts to pay for them. If she knows him very well and the total is very small, she perhaps lets him pay. But if he is someone she knows slightly or if she has bought a stack of the higher-priced ones, she answers, "Don't bother; I have it!" and puts the money on the counter. It would be awkward for him to protest, and bad taste to press the point. In this case, too, she buys her ticket and tips the porter for carrying her bag. On the other hand, if she has gone on his invitation to spend the day in the country or to lunch or to dinner or to a theater, he of course pays for everything that can be included in the ordinary obligations of every host—or hostess.

(For further details on this subject, see Index.)

A gentleman who finds himself sitting next to a lady whom he knows very slightly, on a train or boat, should not offer to pay for her seat or for anything she may buy from the vendor. At least he should on no account force her to accept his gratuities. One of the hall-marks of the socially ignorant is his insistence upon making everyone whom he meets his debtor.

THE ENJOYMENT OF PUBLIC PLACES

Apart from the courtesies which all of us are expected to show to friends and neighbors, there are endless other exactions of ordinary human kindness which well-bred people unfailingly show to the public at large, and which they have the right to expect will be shown in turn to them. Therefore, the following items cannot be taken too much to heart by those of us who, no matter how good our intentions, are inclined to be forgetful of the rights or unaware of the feelings of others.

PICNIC IN PUBLIC

When you picnic anywhere in public, don't forget to choose a place well out of the way of traffic. And do, moreover, make sure not only to tidy up before you leave, so that no trace will be left, but be careful, while you are eating and opening papers, that you don't carelessly throw them aside where they will blow out on the road. On the property of a private owner the least payment you can make is to be sure that nothing which belongs to him has been despoiled.

In the woods, for example, vandal picnickers not only pick flowers, but break off large branches and sometimes even pull out whole bushes and drive blithely away leaving cardboard boxes and tin cans scattered behind in their places. Needless to say, if you picnic in the woods and have lighted a fire, the ashes must be safely covered over with earth before you leave. Although most picnickers are careful about this, there are many who seem utterly unaware that leaving an untidy mess behind them is not the way to repay the owners for the temporary use of their property.

AT A PUBLIC BEACH

At a public beach the first rule is to avoid crowding—at least as much as you possibly can. Those of you who have children should choose places as near as you can to where the children are going to wade in and out of the water and dig canals and build sand castles. It is dangerous to have little children paddling in the water far away. And it is also natural for a child to fill his pails and run back and forth from his family to the water, kicking sand and spilling water all over those who may be sitting in his path. Or even though they run very steadily, people are likely to be nervous for fear of having water poured over them.

It is also important not to let a child thrust its attentions upon strangers. While spontaneous friendliness is one of the most appealing traits a child can have, and most people are inclined to like children, it must nevertheless be remembered that certain individuals do not. Therefore it is necessary to notice whether it is the strangers who are showing particular interest in Johnny or whether it is Johnny who is alone showing interest in the strangers!

PARKS AND PLAYGROUNDS

Behavior at one of the public parks is practically the same as that at the beach. Again, don't crowd against other groups if you can help it. Don't spread your picnic baskets and personal belongings over two or three tables when your share is one. Although picnicking table manners are less exacting than those at a set table at home, this does not grant to the children the privilege of eating like little savages—ever.

On the other hand, the public parks and picnic grounds are excellent training schools in that they teach children to take their turn and be satisfied with their own share of time on the slides and swings and see-saws, and in any other pleasures offered to all children.

LIFE IN CROWDED CITIES

Even more important than the need for consideration of others on beaches and in parks is that of the dwellers in city flats so closely packed that every sound made by one family is likely to be heard by several others. In fact, sound can appear to be intensified by distance. In the room with the children, their play does not seem overloud; a radio program—even a jazz band—sounds scarcely loud enough to bother anyone not close to it. But to the family living on the floor below, the patter of little feet sounds like a stable full of percherons. The toys they drop seem all of iron! The jazz band crashes through each separate convolution of a neighbor's brain. As for young musicians' "practicing"—there is no manager of an apartment house who is not at his wits' end to solve this chief cause of complaint—approached only by slamming doors or a banging shutter.

There are certain annoyances to others that can't be helped; babies must sometimes cry, children scream, dogs bark, or someone gets a hacking cough. The best one can do is to try to soften such sounds as much as possible by shutting a window temporarily, muffling one's mouth and little by little training children and dogs.

An angle that is evidently difficult to understand is that in nearly all communal buildings in close neighborhoods, there are always those few who seemingly show no feelings for others because their own insensitiveness is, as it were, on another wave length. It is very hard to remember—or even to understand—that things which greatly annoy us—such as the unceasing sound of music—may not disturb others at all, whereas things to which we don't object quite easily torture our neighbors.

8

Restaurant Etiquette

In a fashionable restaurant a man leaves his hat and coat in the coat room or checks them at the entrance of the restaurant. A woman leaves her wrap in the dressing room—or, if she prefers, she goes into the dining room and sits down at the table as she is. She then merely throws the shoulders of her wrap back of her, over her chair.

In the daytime she wears a hat and keeps it on, of course. In spite of the vagaries of transient fashion, a hat is correct with a street dress, just as boots are correct with a riding habit. At night she wears a hat if in daytime clothes, an evening hat if she chooses with semi-evening clothes, and no hat ever if in formal evening dress. The fee to the maid in the dressing room—given when she returns the coat check and is helped on with her wrap—is twenty-five cents—in every restaurant or hotel that can be called luxurious. In a very simple hotel, one whose clothes are equally simple usually gives ten cents. The fee to the check-rack boy or girl who takes care of a man's hat and coat is ten cents—or in a super-smart restaurant a little more.

When entering a restaurant or hotel dining room, always stand near the door. The headwaiter or waitress will show you where to sit. If you are staying at an American-plan hotel, you usually sit at the same table in the dining room, and after your first entrance you go to your place at table without waiting to be shown—although the headwaiter will hurry, if he can, to pull your chair out for you. In a restaurant, even though you have the same special table reserved for you, you are always shown to your place by the headwaiter or one of his assistants—very often both.

The waiter always pulls out the choice seat first (the seat which he considers choice because it is facing the room or the view or whatever is supposed to be of interest). A woman dining with a man naturally takes it, unless for some reason she definitely prefers another, in which case she stands beside the other chair, saying, "I'd rather sit here." A woman who has invited another woman to lunch or dine with her naturally lets her guest go first and take the choice seat.

When a woman is lunching or dining with two men, they will of course seat her between them. A man lunching or dining with two women will sit between two who are not related to him, but he will sit opposite his wife. In a restaurant that has sofa seats the women always sit against the wall (or partition), and the man or men sit on the chairs facing them.

If a woman and two men are lunching or dining in an alcove (a table with benches) the woman takes her place first against the wall; the man who is not related sits beside her, and her husband or brother sits opposite. If this number is reversed, the two women sit next the wall and the man sits beside her who is not related to him.

AT A DINNER GIVEN IN A RESTAURANT

The women always follow the headwaiter and the men follow them. If a man is giving a party of six or more, the women stand at the table until told by their host where to sit. If they are only four and neither woman is married, the women seat themselves facing each other without direction.

Also, if Mary Lone and John Batchler dine with the Joneses, it is better that Mary and Mrs. Jones sit opposite—in spite of the tabu of seating a wife next her husband—in order to let Mary sit next to Batchler instead of between the Joneses. When the Joneses and the Gaylings dine together, husbands and wives sit opposite each other.

It is said that in certain localities husbands and wives are purposely seated together when out in company. This, if true, is certainly contrary to all precepts of etiquette!

In all first-class restaurants each dish is presented to the host or hostess as soon as it arrives from the kitchen. The host is not expected to help himself, but merely to approve of its preparation. He nods "all right" and the waiter then serves it, or passes it to the guests.

ORDERING THE MEAL

When invitations are given beforehand to a lunch party or to a dinner in a restaurant, the host or hostess should order the meal in advance, and the guests eat what is put before them exactly as at a dinner in someone's house. But when the dinner has been made up at the spur of the moment, or when one woman lunches with another or dines with a man and the meal has not been ordered, and the host or hostess asks what the guests would like, it is better frankly to name a dish or two than to answer, "Oh, anything," which means nothing whatever and leaves the host helplessly staring at that utterly impersonal dictionary of dishes, and *à la carte* menu.

But don't ask the waiter for explanations of every dish and change your order so that he has to rub it out as fast as he writes it down. And unless you know that your host is fabulously rich, you should show some consideration and not choose caviar, terrapin, breast of guinea-hen, and so on!

A GIRL DINES IN A RESTAURANT WITH A MAN

When a girl lunches or dines in a restaurant with a man, she takes the seat the headwaiter holds for her. This is usually the seat facing the door—if near the door—or possibly the view. She is supposed to sit opposite—at a small table—or on his right on a sofa seat against the wall. But this "on the right" rule is not important in the United States and they sit where they choose.

On occasion a man who may want to order a special dish—or dishes—gives this order beforehand. Usually, however, the man, the girl and the waiter hold a three-sided conversation, something like this:

Man: "What would you like? Fruit cocktail? Oysters?"
Waiter: "Our shrimps are particularly fine."
Man to Girl: "Would you like shrimps?"
Girl: "Yes, very much," or else, "I'd rather have oysters."
Man to waiter: "Bring one order of shrimps, one of oysters."
Man to girl: "Soup?"
Girl: "No, I'd like just one dish, chicken—or something like that, and a dessert."

Or when asked what she would like, she says in the beginning what she wants. Or she says nothing except "very nice" to whatever he suggests. One point: Unless she knows the man is very well off, or the restaurant is a *table d'hote* one, the girl ought to show some consideration for her companion's purse. A young woman who says sweetly "yes" to his necessary suggestions of *"Hors d'oeuvres?" "Soup?" "Fish?" "Entrée?" "Roast?" "Salad?" "Dessert?" "Coffee?"* is not very likely to be asked to dine with him soon again—if ever!

At a *table d'hôte*, each person usually gives her or his individual order to the waiter—or waitress.

TABLE D'HÔTE OR À LA CARTE

Table d'hôte (the table of the host) means a set price for each meal, irrespective of how many courses you order. "Club" breakfasts and lunches, "blue plate" dinners or any meals at fixed prices, whether fifty cents or five dollars a cover, are *table d'hôte*. *À la carte* means that you order "according to the card," and you pay for each dish ordered.

"American plan" means so much a day for room, including *table d'hôte* meals.

In the "European plan" hotel the prices of rooms include no food. And the restaurant charge is so much for each dish ordered.

Usually it is very easy to know which is which, because the price follows each item on an *à la carte* menu, whereas no prices are listed on a *table d'hôte* bill of fare. Very often a separate card or a box inset on the *à la carte* menu reads "Special dinner $1.25" (or whatever the price may be), which means that you can order whatever you choose on this special list for a dollar and twenty-five cents, but that any item taken from the big menu will be charged for as an extra.

There is one word of warning against mistaking an *à la carte* menu without prices printed on it for a *table d'hôte* bill of fare. But this need concern you only if you patronize those few among the highest-priced restaurants which, copying those for which Paris is famous, present you with a menu without prices printed on it. Should you encounter this, you can remember that it is entirely correct to hand it back—as does every European—and say, "Bring me the menu with prices."

In an *à la carte* restaurant, the check—meaning a list of what you have ordered with the price of each item and the total of the bill—is brought to you by the waiter who serves you. In first-class restaurants it is always turned face down on a plate or a small silver tray. You turn it over and pay the waiter. He then brings your change, and you give him a tip.

DE LUXE RESTAURANT TIPS

It is impossible to give definite schedules for tipping, because it all depends upon where you go, and upon what you order, and upon the service given you—or that you exact.

The conventional ten per cent of a restaurant bill was correct in the days when people ordered an excessive amount of food. But today, when most people go to the other extreme and "rations vie with diets" in limiting your order, ten per cent of your bill must be qualified as "ten per cent if *above the minimum* tip for the class of restaurant you are in" and for the class of person you *appear* to be. That is, if you patronize restaurants of greatest luxury and wear obviously expensive clothes with valuable accessories or if you are critical and difficult to please, greater "compensation" is expected than if your appearance were simpler and your manners more kind.

In New York at an ultra-smart restaurant of greatest luxury, the smallest tip you can give is thirty-five cents if you lunch alone, twenty per cent of a bill of three dollars or less, seventy-five cents on a total of five dollars and ten per cent above this. For two persons, add about fifteen cents to each of these sums. The tipping system may be a bad plan and the trend is up! But in restaurants of this type the waiters depend upon tips for their wages. A lunch or dinner-party tip would be a minimum of twenty-five cents a person and ten per cent in addition to this base.

TIPS IN AN AVERAGE FIRST-CLASS RESTAURANT

In an average first-class restaurant a reasonably accurate rule is a minimum tip of twenty-five cents, whether for one person or two, for a bill that totals less than two dollars; thirty-five cents for one up to three dollars; forty cents for one from three dollars to four dollars. And a minimum of twenty cents a person for a lunch or dinner party.

If you are having a party of ten or twelve or more, ten per cent would be quite enough divided between the waiters who serve you, if the bill comes to two dollars a person or more. Otherwise you would give two dollars, or two dollars and a half, and perhaps as much again to the headwaiter if he has taken particular pains to have the service efficient or if he made you a special per-person price. On the other hand, if he does nothing for you, you give him nothing. Some people are very unfair in that the tips they give to waitresses are less than those given to waiters.

In a bare-tabled café or tea room, a tip of fifteen or even ten cents is possible for a dollar meal. In a restaurant with tablecloths, you would add five cents (laundry?) tip.

(For other varieties of tips, see Index.)

American-plan-hotel meal cards are often bought at the hotel desk. Country hotels sometimes ask you to register and pay for the meal later, but sometimes the check is paid to the waiter or waitress as in a restaurant. It is always easy enough to ask whoever serves you, "Where do I pay?" In any event you tip the one who served you, unless the management is one that forbids tipping. In this case a ten per cent fee is added to the bill. You pay the check at the cashier's desk and leave nothing on the table.

PREPAYING THE RESTAURANT CHECK

Not so very long ago a host—as well as a hostess—found the moment when the waiter presented the check embarrassing. In fact, the hostess who had no charge account either ordered the meal ahead of time and paid for it (which was impractical because no one could count on how many would, or would not, take cocktails or cigarettes or cigars). Many hostesses made it a practice to have the bill brought to them at the door of the ladies' dressing room.

Today, however, all questions of payment are taken as a matter of course—even when a man alone is dining with a woman. In this case, if possible, she takes him to her club, where she necessarily signs the voucher, and there can be no question about the propriety of her paying. But if they dine in a restaurant where she has no charge account, there is no reason why a man should feel embarrassed to have a woman friend who, let us say, has dined with him time and again take the check and pay it. In other words, Mrs. Grundy has lost nearly all of her influence during the war. If a woman who wants to return a man's many invitations to her would like to ask him to dine with her, he can decline (ungenerously) if he chooses. But if he accepts her invitation, he must *not* make her and himself conspicuous by refusing to accept the situation in a matter-of-fact way.

When a woman gives a dinner of any size, she usually makes the man she knows best her banker by giving him the money beforehand. He pays the bills and makes an accounting to her afterwards.

RESTAURANT MANNERS

When one lady, passing another seated at a table in a restaurant, stops and shakes hands, the one who is seated does not rise unless she is very young and the one passing is quite old. All the gentlemen at the table of course rise and stand until the visiting lady has departed, whether she is known to them or not.

This detail of behavior is one that every lady should take seriously, since every gentleman MUST stand as long as she stands. It doesn't change the situation a bit for her to say, "Please sit down," because a man who is seen sitting and eating while a "lady" stands is automatically proclaimed "no gentleman" by each person who catches a glimpse of this behavior.

Very expert waiters save the situation by instantly placing a chair behind the knees of any woman inclined to linger. As soon as she sits, the men may sit—and continue eating. If the visitor sits down, she is introduced to the two or three others at a very small table, or to those next her at a large one; but should she merely stand, the friend with whom she stops to speak does not make any introduction, unless she *knows* that one of those at the table and the visitor are for some reason anxious to meet each other.

If the ladies are introduced, the ones at the table do not rise—unless very young and the visitor very elderly.

Gentlemen at table do not rise when another gentleman stops at the table unless there is a great difference in age. All younger men rise for a really old gentleman.

CONSIDERATION FOR THOSE WHO SERVE US

Lack of consideration for those who in any capacity serve us—whether in restaurants or hotels or stores, or in public places anywhere—is always an evidence of ill-breeding as well as inexcusable selfishness. (For further details on the subject of store etiquette, see Index.) It is only those who are afraid that someone may encroach upon their exceedingly insecure dignity who show neither courtesy nor consideration except to those whom they think it would be to their advantage to please.

9

At the Opera, the Theater, and Other Public Gatherings

There is perhaps some question about the usefulness of prerving this and one or two other chapters in this revision which illustrate an extreme formality of deportment that may never return. But since the opera will lose much of its prestige if its manners grow lax, this chapter is being left untouched.

EXCEPT on occasions of religious ceremonial, nowhere is greater dignity of manner required than in a box at the opera. For a gentleman, especially, etiquette at the opera is more than exacting.

In walking about in the foyer, a gentleman leaves his coat in the box—or in his orchestra chair—but he always wears his top hat. The "opera" hat—collapsible high hat—was designed for use in the seats rather than in the boxes, but because of its serviceability it has almost completely replaced the silk one. (If a man has only one high hat, it should obviously be a silk one, which is proper both day and evening.) A gentleman must always be in full dress—tail coat, white waistcoat, and white tie—when he is going to sit in a box. But it is no longer necessary that he wear gloves. In fact, white gloves are at present worn nowhere indoors, except when serving as usher at an evening wedding. A gentleman properly wears "tails" even when seated in the orchestra.

As people usually dine with their hostess before the opera, they arrive together. The gentlemen assist the ladies to lay aside their wraps; one of the gentlemen (whichever is nearest) draws back the curtain dividing the ante-room from the box, and the ladies enter, followed by the gentlemen, the last of whom closes the curtain again. If there are two ladies besides the hostess, the latter places her more distinguished or older guest in the corner nearest the stage. The seat furthest from the stage is always her own. The older guest takes her seat first, then the hostess takes her place, whereupon the third lady goes forward in the center to the front of the box, and stands until one of the gentlemen places a chair for her between the other two. This maneuver is necessary because three chairs placed side by side take up the width of the box. The chairs are always arranged by the caretaker in three rows of two, with an aisle between, so that the third lady's chair, brought from the second row, closes the aisle.

One of the duties of the gentlemen is to see that the curtains at the back of the box remain tightly closed, as the light from the ante-room shining into the faces of others in the audience across the house is very disagreeable to them.

A gentleman never sits in the front row of a box, even though he is for a time alone.

VISITING THE BOXES

It is the custom for a gentleman who is a guest in one box to pay visits to friends in other boxes during the entr'actes. He must visit none but ladies of his acquaintance and must never enter a box in which he knows only the gentlemen, and expect to be introduced to the ladies. A lady's box at the opera is actually her house, and only those who are welcome visitors in her house should take it upon themselves to go into her box.

But it is quite correct for a gentleman to go into a stranger's box to speak to a lady who is a friend of his, just as he would go to see her if she were staying in a stranger's house. But he should not go into the box of one he does not know, to speak to a lady with whom he has only a slight acquaintance, since visits are not paid quite so casually to ladies who are themselves visitors. Upon a gentleman's entering a box, it is obligatory for whoever is sitting behind the lady whom the arriving gentleman has come to see to relinquish his chair. Another point of etiquette is that a gentleman must never leave the ladies of his own box alone. Occasionally it happens that the gentlemen in Mrs. Gilding's box, for instance, have all relinquished their places to visitors and have themselves gone to Mrs. Worldly's or Mrs. Jones's or Mrs. Town's boxes. Mrs. Gilding's guests must, from the vantage point of the Worldly, Jones or Town boxes, keep a watchful eye on their hostess and instantly return to her support when they see her visitors about to leave, even though the ladies whom they are visiting be momentarily left to themselves. It is of course the duty of the other gentlemen who came to the opera with Mrs. Worldly, Mrs. Jones or Mrs. Town to hurry to them.

A gentleman must never stay in any box that he does not belong in after the lowering of the lights for the curtain. Nor, in spite of cartoons to the contrary, does courtesy either to the musicians or to the audience permit conversation during the performance or during the overture. Box holders arriving late or leaving before the final curtain do so as quietly as possible and always without talking.

A "BRILLIANT OPERA NIGHT"

Whether a "brilliant opera night," which one so often heard spoken of before this war, will ever come into usage again is something that none can at present answer. This was, in its day, generally a night when a leader of fashion, such as Mrs. Gilding or Mrs. Toplofty, was giving a ball, and most of the holders of the parterre boxes were in ball dresses, with an unusual display of jewels. Or a house was particularly "brilliant" if a very great singer were appearing in a new role or a personage of eminence were to be present as especial guest of honor.

DRESSING FOR THE OPERA

The exactions of dress at the opera have always been very strict. Gentlemen in the orchestra seats, as well as in the boxes (parterre as well as first tier), *must* wear formal evening dress. Those in the first balcony wear dinner coats (tuxedos). Above that, clothes are not necessarily formal. Dark business suits are almost as numerous as dinner coats. On the other hand, occasional tail coats are also seen.

The women's clothes follow the same ruling: very best evening dresses in the parterre boxes; simple evening dresses in the orchestra and first tier boxes; afternoon dresses in the first balcony; all varieties of day dresses above that.

WILL YOU DINE AND GO TO THE PLAY?

There is no more popular or agreeable way of entertaining people than to ask them to "dine and go to the play." The majority do not even prefer to have "opera" substituted for "play," because those who care for serious music are a minority compared with those who like the theater.

Unfortunately, theater tickets (in New York, for example) have become so expensive that a "party" of four is more typical than six—which is the outside number. The old-fashioned one of twenty or over is practically unheard of—except when that of a club.

So let us consider the little party of six—or four.

When a man invites three friends to go to the theater, he usually takes them to dine at an "amusing" restaurant, but married people living in their own house are likely to dine at home.

When the invitation is telephoned by butler or maid, the wording is: Will Mr. and Mrs. Lovejoy dine with Mr. and Mrs. Norman at half past seven on Tuesday and go to see "Love Distilled." (One should always name the play, because nothing is duller for both hosts and guests than to find that the latter are sitting through the same play for the nth time!) In New York, where plays run for months—sometimes for years—Mr. Clubwin Doe telephones: "Will you dine on Saturday at the Colonial? And what play would you like to see?"

Mrs. Norman's guests go to her house. Mr. Doe's guests meet him in the foyer of the Colonial. But the guests at both dinners are taken to the theater by their host. If the hostess has no car, a guest will sometimes ask, "Don't you want me to have the car come back for us?" The hostess can say either, "Why, yes, thank you very much," or "No, thank you just the same—I have ordered a taxi." There is no rule beyond her own feelings in the matter.

TICKETS BOUGHT IN ADVANCE

Not only must a host get seats in advance, but he must get good ones. It is little compliment and less pleasure to be invited to spend an evening in theater seats from which you can neither see nor hear more than half of the performance. It is scarcely necessary to say that one must *never* ask people to go to a place of public amusement and then stand in line to get seats at the time of the performance.

It is also practical as well as polite to ask, "How near do you like to sit?" and then get seats near to the stage—or to the platform at a concert or a lecture—or farther back accordingly.

GOING DOWN THE AISLE OF A THEATER

The host, or whichever gentleman has the tickets (if there is no host, the hostess usually hands them to one of the gentlemen before leaving her house), goes down the aisle first and gives the checks to the usher, and the others follow in the order in which they are to sit and which the hostess must direct. It is necessary that each shall know who follows whom, particularly if the party arrives after the curtain has gone up. Going down the aisle is not a question of precedence, but a question of seating. The one who is to sit sixth from the aisle, whether a lady or a gentleman, goes first, then the fifth, and if the gentleman with the checks is fourth, he goes in his turn and the third follows him.

If a gentleman and lady go to the theater alone, the question as to who goes down the aisle first depends on where the usher is. If the usher takes the checks at the head of the aisle, she follows the usher. If the usher is not at the head of the aisle, the gentleman with the tickets goes first, until having given the tickets to the usher, he lets the lady precede him the rest of the way. In any event, he stands at the end of their seats and lets her take her place first and then takes the seat on—or nearest to—the aisle.

Do not however judge hastily if this rule is not followed. Arthur Norman, for example, is stone deaf in his left ear and his wife always sits on his right no matter where that position happens to place **her**. Others for any similar reasons do the same.

GOOD MANNERS AT THE THEATER

In passing strangers, gentlemen as well as ladies face the stage and always press as close to the backs of the seats they are facing as they can. They should remember however not to drag anything across the heads of those sitting in the row in front. At motion-picture theaters, especially when it is dark and difficult to see, any loose hanging coat or dress front, let alone a coat on an arm passing behind a chair, can literally devastate the "hair-do" of a lady occupying it.

If you are obliged to cross in front of someone who gets up to let you pass, say, "Thank you" or "Thank you very much" or "I am very sorry." Do *not* say, "Pardon *me!*" or "Beg pardon!" Yet you may say, "I beg your pardon." That, however, would be more properly the expression to use if you brushed your coat over their heads, or spilled water over them, or did something to them for which you should actually *beg* their pardon.

When you are seated and others pass you, you must give them a clear right of way. Usually the rows of seats are far enough apart for you to make plenty of room by merely turning your knees sideways. When the curtain is up or a picture is on the screen, this is much better than standing and further blotting out the view of those behind. But if you can't make sufficient room, then stand—and sit down again—quickly! Remember that during every second you stand, you are cutting off the view of all who are seated behind you.

TO AVOID BEING CLIMBED OVER

Young people have much to say about the ill manners of certain middle-aged men as well as women, who practically refuse to allow anyone to pass. It is quite true that having to gather up opera glasses, program, bag, and stand while each person on a long aisle goes out and comes back separately after every act can be far from pleasurable. But if one hasn't sufficient self-control not only to seem but to *be* amiable about whatever annoyances one encounters, one should at least take enough trouble to avoid the obvious annoyances or else stay at home. As an example of the obvious, why not take pains to get seats away from an aisle instead of *on* it? In a theater that has no center aisle, get seats in the mid-center and sit undisturbed. It is true that, where there is a center aisle and seats become less desirable as distance from the aisle increases, it comes to a question of choosing between sitting at the side or being climbed over twice (once out and once in) by everyone in the row, after each act.

HATS OFF!

All women whose hats rise high above the skull line or have any sticking-up bows or feathers should take them off without having to be asked to do so. Many of those who are made perfectly miserable by an upturned brim, or whose eyes are tortured by a wabbling feather, are often made almost equally miserable by being obliged to ask the owner of the offending hat to take it off. True, at the movies those who can not see can usually change to other seats; but even so, if every one tried to find other seats, the entire audience would soon be playing "Going to Jerusalem"!

THEATER PESTS

Talking, coughing, rattling programs, jingling bangles—not to speak of those who rattle cellophane when opening candy boxes!—and coming back for each act after the curtain has gone up not only annoy the audience but frequently disturb the actors. Most people are seemingly unaware that sound travels as well one way across the footlights as another. And the comments of those in the first few rows of the audience, and the constant coughing throughout a bronchial disturbance, have actually made it impossible for the company to give a good performance. Very young people love to go to the theater in droves called theater parties and absolutely ruin the evening for others who happen to sit in front of them. If Mary and Johnny and Susy and Tommy want to talk and giggle, why not arrange chairs in rows for them in a drawing room, turn on a phonograph as an accompaniment, and let them sit there and chatter!

If those behind you insist on talking, it is never good policy to turn around and glare. If you are young they pay no attention, and if you are older—most young people think an angry older person the funniest sight on earth! The small boy throws a snowball at an elderly gentleman for no other reason! The only thing you can do is to say amiably, "I'm sorry, but I can't hear anything while you talk." If they still persist, you can ask an usher to call the manager.

The sentimental may as well realize that every word said above a whisper is easily heard by those sitting directly in front, and those who tell family or other private affairs might do well to remember this also.

As a matter of fact, comparatively few people are ever anything but well behaved. Most people take their seats as quietly and quickly as they possibly can, and are quite as much interested in the play and therefore as attentive and quiet as you are.

LEAVING THE THEATER

The gentleman on the aisle, or nearest the aisle, naturally stands in the aisle a moment so that the lady who necessarily follows him can walk with or, if the crowd makes two abreast impossible, precede him. Under nearly all circumstances a lady goes first. An exception to this is where the crowd is really dense; in this case he goes first to make a wedge for her. She follows as closely behind him as possible in order to take advantage of the space he makes for her. In a theater party of six the first gentleman should let the lady who sat next to him go ahead of him, but usually he does not wait to follow the remaining two.

PROPER DRESS AT THE THEATER

During the opening weeks and at the evening performance in New York of a play or musical comedy presenting stars of highest rank, a lady sitting "down front" in the orchestra wears a semi-evening dress, a gentleman a "tuxedo." White ties and tails and low-cut evening dress are never worn at the theater except by those who are going on to a party later. Whether or not people are going on elsewhere later naturally affects their choice of dress. The present trend of fashion leans, however, very decidedly toward ordinary day clothes for both men and women, especially when the play has been running for several months.

PRINKING IN PUBLIC

Prinking and making up in public are all part of an age which cannot see fun in a farce without bedroom scenes and actors in pajamas and actresses running about in panties! An audience which night after night watches people dressing and undressing can hardly help thinking "making up" in public the most natural thing in the world. In other days it was always thought that so much as to adjust a hair-pin or glance in the glass of a vanity case was evidence of a lack of breeding. For example, when Mrs. Cleveland, in her early twenties, made her first appearance at a state dinner, the British Ambassador, afterwards commenting on the charm of the President's lovely bride, especially noted that "not once during the entire evening did she raise her hands to her dress, her face or her hair!"

This merely illustrates yesterday's training of every young girl who was expected to become a woman of beauty and charm. She was taught that she must dress as carefully as possible, but when she turned away from the mirrors in her dressing room, she must never look in a glass or "take note of her appearance" until she dressed in front of hers again. But today young women in theaters, restaurants, and other public places are continually studying their reflection in little mirrors and patting their hair and powdering their noses; and perhaps we should be grateful that they do not take off shoes and stockings, sit in public places in their "undies," or file their nails or use a tooth-brush in public—as yet!

A BIG THEATER PARTY

A big theater party has always been a favorite entertainment given for a débutante by very well-to-do parents or an equally well-to-do aunt or grandmother.

The invitations may be written formally or informally. If the party is given by her parents, the débutante very likely writes the invitations herself—or even telephones them. But if the party is a formal one and given by a prominent hostess, her "general utility" invitation usually is filled in, as follows:

To meet Miss Millicent Gilding

Mrs. Toplofty

requests the pleasure of

Miss Rosalie Gray's

company at *the Thespis Theater*

on *Tuesday the sixth of January*

at *8.15*

R. s. v. p.

All those who accept the invitation have tickets sent them. Each ticket sent to a débutante is accompanied by a visiting card on which is written:

"Please be in the lobby of the Thespis Theater at 8:15."

On the evening of the theater party, Mrs. Toplofty stands in the lobby to receive the guests. As soon as those who are to sit next one another have arrived, they are sent into the theater. Each gives her (or his) ticket to an usher and sits in the place allotted to her (or him). When the last young girl has arrived, Mrs. Toplofty goes to her own seat in the theater.

After the play, buses drive them to the house of the hostess. Occasionally if the house is large enough, musicians are provided and the young people dance. Usually, however, they have a very simple supper and then go home.

(For a dance see Index.)

DON'T BE LATE

When you are dining before going to the opera or theater, or lunching before going to a game or any sort of performance, you *must not be late!* Nothing is so unfair to others who are keen about whatever it is you are going to see than to make them miss the beginning of a performance through your selfishness.

AT GAMES, THE CIRCUS OR ELSEWHERE

Considerate and polite behavior by each member of an audience is the same everywhere. At outdoor games, or at the circus, it is not necessary to stop talking. In fact, a good deal of noise is not out of the way in "rooting" at a match, and a circus band does not demand silence in order to appreciate its cheerful blare. Of great annoyance to many are the careless smokers. (For etiquette for smokers see Index.)

Another serious annoyance met with at ball games or parades or wherever people occupy seats on the grandstand is that produced by a few in front who get excited and insist on standing up. If those in front stand—those behind naturally have to! Generally people call out "Down in front!" If they won't stay "down," then all those behind have to stay "up." Also, umbrellas entirely blot out the view of those behind.

ANSWERS TO READERS' QUESTIONS

FIRST DOWN THE AISLE

When there are no ushers and no reserved seats, should I or the gentleman I am with go down the aisle first?

At the movies, or wherever there are no reserved seats, you go first; and unless the man you are with is your husband or your fiancé or someone with whom you go often and know where you both like to sit, you generally turn to him before taking a seat and ask, "Is this all right?" which gives him a chance—should he be near- or far-sighted—to say, "Let's go nearer" or "Not so near."

"EXCUSE ME, PLEASE"

When do you say, "I beg your pardon" and when "Excuse me!" and when are you "Sorry"?

You say "I beg your pardon" after any real awkwardness, such as tripping over anyone in a moving-picture theater where you have to grope for a seat in the dark. But when merely passing in front of someone you say "Excuse me." For a slight awkwardness, such as delay in finding tickets, or going back for something forgotten, you say "I'm sorry." Or, in the second case, you say, "I'm sorry to disturb you," and "Thank you," as they let you pass.

SEATING TWO WIVES AND HUSBANDS

I have always been under the impression that two couples, going to the theater together, sit in this order: first a man, then the two women, and last a man on the aisle. Some one now tells me that this is correct in church, but not at the theater. What is right, and why is any difference made?

There is no fixed rule about seating four people in a theater except that a man should sit on the aisle—if they have aisle seats. If two married couples go to a theater, they do usually sit as you suggest, so that a man shall not be seated next to his wife. But if Mr. and Mrs. A took Miss B and Mr. C to the theater, Mr. A would sit on the aisle and then Miss B, then Mr. C, and then Mrs. A. But if Mr. C and Miss B are engaged, the A's would sit together, since the pair who are in love might as well be counted as absent. In other words, sit in whichever order you think most pleasant.

A WOMAN LEFT ALONE BETWEEN ACTS

May a man leave a woman alone while he goes out between the acts?

The modern woman usually goes out with him. But if he is with an old-fashioned type of woman who does not smoke, it is quite proper to leave her briefly during one entr'acte; or should the play have more than three acts, he might go out for two. Of course, it depends somewhat upon whom he is with. He could leave his wife oftener than anyone else, which does not mean he should leave her at each curtain-fall to sit alone until the house is darkened for the curtain's rise.

10

Visiting Cards and Their Uses

WHO was it that said—in the Victorian era probably, and a man of course—"The only mechanical tool ever needed by a woman is a hairpin?" He might have added that with a hairpin and a visiting card she is ready to meet most emergencies.

Although the principal use of a visiting card, at least the one for which it was originally invented—to be left as an evidence of one person's presence at the house of another—has gone gradually out of ardent favor in fashionable circles, its usefulness seems to keep a nicely adjusted balance. In New York, for instance, the visiting card has entirely taken the place of the written note of invitation to informal parties of every description. Messages of condolence or congratulation are written on it; it is used as an endorsement in the giving of an order; it is even tacked on the outside of express boxes. The only employment of it which is not as flourishing as formerly is that of being left in quantities and with frequency at the doors of acquaintances. This will be explained further on.

SIZE AND ENGRAVING

The sizes of visiting cards vary, necessarily, according to length of name (a short name on a squarer card than that chosen for a long name), but a married woman's card is usually about $2\frac{7}{8}$ to $2\frac{3}{4}$ inches long by 2 to $2\frac{1}{4}$ inches high, although the smaller of these two dimensions has been for many years in fashion. Very young girls customarily use a card smaller still. A man's card is narrower in shape—from $2\frac{7}{8}$ to $3\frac{1}{4}$ inches long, and from $1\frac{1}{4}$ to $1\frac{5}{8}$ inches high if plate-marked; otherwise, subtract $\frac{1}{4}$ inch from both width and height. Plate-marking is very suitable for wedding invitations and announcements and their enclosures, but it is chosen for visiting cards by comparatively few of the smart. There is no valid objection to plate-marking—especially on the card of a young girl—but it is a little effeminate for a man. The cards are made of white or cream-white glazed or unglazed cardboard of medium thickness, but those made of thin parchment paper are convenient because a greater quantity may be carried easily.

The engraving much in use is shaded Roman. Script is always good form, and various other letterings, brought out by engravers from time to time, have a temporary vogue, but all overlarge or ornate lettering should be avoided.

All people who live in cities should have the address in the lower right corner, engraved in very small letters. In the country, addresses are less important, as everyone knows where everyone else lives. People who have town and country houses usually have separate cards for these addresses.

In America it is not customary for a married man to have a club address on his card. Unmarried men use no other address than that of a club, especially if they live in transient quarters; but young men who live at home use their home address.

CORRECT NAMES AND TITLES

To be impeccably correct, initials should not be engraved on a visiting card. A gentleman's card should read "Mr. John Hunter Titherington Smith"; but since names are sometimes awkwardly long, and it is the American custom to cling to each and every one given in baptism, he engraves his cards "Mr. John H. T. Smith" or "Mr. J. H. Titherington Smith," as suits his fancy. So, although, according to high authorities, he should drop a name or two and be Mr. Hunter Smith or Mr. Titherington Smith, it is very likely that to the end of time the American man, and necessarily his wife, who must use the name as he does, will go on cherishing initials. Her card must of course be the duplicate of his, and not read "Mrs. J. Hunter Smith" when his reads "Mr. John H. Smith."

A curious custom in certain localities is the discarding by a widow of her husband's Christian name and sometimes her wedding ring as well. Of course if he made her so bitterly unhappy that the thought of him is hateful—and she doesn't care who knows it!—one can understand her getting rid of everything suggestive of him. But it is impossible to imagine a sorrowing wife's repudiation of a beloved husband's name and ring, the most sacred emblems of her life with him.

A WIDOW SHOULD KEEP HER HUSBAND'S NAME

A man gives his name to his wife for life—or until she herself through re-marriage relinquishes it. A widow, therefore, should always continue to use her husband's Christian names. She is Mrs. John Hunter Titherington Smith (or, Mrs. J. H. Titherington Smith), but *never* Mrs. Sarah Smith, if she cares at all about good taste.

SOCIAL TABU, "MRS. MARY," UNAVOIDABLE IN BUSINESS

In business and in legal matters it is often impossible to avoid addressing a woman by her own Christian name, because she uses it in her signature. But one should never address a personal or social letter "Mrs. Sarah Smith." In best taste a woman who has earned a professional title uses her title or professional name in public, and in private life uses the name of her husband. A spinster who is a practising physician uses the title of Doctor socially as well as professionally. But if she is, for instance, a Doctor of Philosophy, a woman of sensitive taste would never call herself "Doctor" except in a classroom or when introduced as a speaker.

WHEN WIDOW AND SON HAVE SAME NAME

When a widow's son, who has the name of his father, marries, the widow may have Sr. added to her name; or if she is the head of the family, she very often omits all Christian names, and has her card engraved "Mrs. Smith." (Smith is not a very good name as an example, since no one could very well claim the distinction of being *the* Mrs. Smith. It, however, illustrates the point.)

This is necessary if they live at the same address—or in a village where no street address is used. If they live in different cities, they can both be Mrs. John Hunter Smith.

For the daughter-in-law to continue to use a card with Jr. on it when her husband no longer uses Jr. on his is a mistake made by many people. A wife always bears the name of her husband. To have a man and his mother use cards engraved respectively "Mr. J. H. Smith" and "Mrs. J. H. Smith" and the son's wife a card engraved "Mrs. J. H. Smith, Jr.," would announce to anyone upon whom the three cards were left, that Mr. and Mrs. Smith and *their* daughter-in-law had called.

YOUNG GIRL'S CARD

The cards of a young girl after she is fourteen, always, and often earlier, have "Miss" before her name, which should be her real and never a nickname: "Miss Sarah Smith," not "Miss Sally Smith."

MEANING OF "JR." AND "2ND"

The fact that a man's name has "Jr." added at the end in no way takes the place of "Mr." His card should be engraved "Mr. John Hunter Smith, Jr.," and his wife's "Mrs. John Hunter Smith, Jr." It is rather the fashion to have the "junior" engraved in full. It is not spelled with a capital J if spelled out.

It is improper for a man to continue adding Jr. to his name after the death of his senior. In the same way it is improper to continue calling a boy John Smith 3rd if either John Smith or John Smith Jr. has died. "Junior" always means the son—or possibly the grandson—

of a man of the same name; "2nd" means the nephew or cousin of a man of the same name. The following diagram will perhaps make this much-misunderstood order clear:

```
                    Silas Acres
            ┌───────────┴───────────┐
        Silas Acres Jr.          Jotham
            │                       │
        (A) Silas 3rd           Silas 2nd
                                    │
                                (B) Silas 3rd
```

Since there is no way to distinguish between (A) and (B), the latter is usually given a different middle name, and is christened Silas John Acres. Since this changes the name, he has no suffix, and his son is called Silas John Acres, Jr.

Upon the death of the senior Silas Acres, the names of his family are changed to:

```
            ┌───────────┴───────────┐
        Silas Acres              Jotham
            │                       │
        Silas Jr.               Silas 2nd (no change)
            │                       │
        Silas 3rd               Silas 3rd (or Silas John Acres)
```

And yet once in a great while and for definite reasons, a son continues to call himself "Jr." after his father has died. For example, when a father has been so celebrated that the son cannot possibly take his father's place, or when the mother is a celebrity who cannot very well be expected to add "Sr." to her name, and sometimes for other reasons when it is practical or very important that the son keep his own identity as junior, he continues to use the suffix. But this is not the usual procedure.

When a mother or daughter are both known professionally, the daughter is "Mary Notable, younger" or "second" (junior is a masculine suffix).

"MR." ON BOY'S CARD

A boy never puts "Mr." on his cards until he leaves school, and many use cards without "Mr." while in college.

TITLES ON CARDS

A doctor, a clergyman or a military officer in active service, and holders of title-bestowing offices all have their cards engraved with

VISITING CARDS AND THEIR USES

their titles: Doctor Henry Gordon; The Reverend William Goode; Colonel Thomas Doyle; Judge Horace Rush; Senator Widelands. But a man holding high degrees does not add their letters to his name, and his cards are not engraved "Professor" unless he is a public teacher of highest rank who holds an established chair in a university.

The double card reads "Dr. and Mrs. Henry Gordon," "Judge and Mrs. Horace Rush," "Professor and Mrs. Scholar," etc. It is best form to engrave titles in full.

A woman who is divorced takes her maiden name in place of her husband's Christian name. "Mrs. Henry Green" who was "Mabel Smith" calls herself "Mrs. Smith Green," according to good taste, *never* "Mrs. Mabel Green." If her husband's surname is distasteful, she sometimes takes back her own maiden name to which she prefixes that of her mother. If her mother was a Miss Brown, her daughter calls herself "Mrs. Brown Smith." In business or on the stage she may be known as "Miss Mabel Smith" but NOT in private life. There are occasions when a married woman, intensely disliking to be called Miss, and obliged to choose between Mrs. Mabel and plain Mabel, prefers the former. Otherwise Mrs. Mabel is tabu.

*DIVORCEE TAKES NAME OF HUSBAND BEFORE LAST

A seemingly accepted custom is that of a widow who remarries, then divorces her second husband and takes back her first husband's name. The propriety of this maneuver depends upon her motive, which is usually that of wanting to have the same name as her children.

CARDS OF PERSONAGES

The correct card for a governor is

The Governor of Nevada

on a card that is slightly larger (or squarer) than an ordinary man's card. Less correct, but not inadmissible, is his ordinary card with "Governor of Nevada" added in small letters under his name. Occasionally an over-modest incumbent objects to the correct form because he thinks it looks too self-important. But he must remember that the card is representative of the highest office of his State and not that of a private citizen.

* The laws of the United States permit anyone to change his (or her) name without applying to the courts, if able to give proof that this was done with no intent to defraud.

The card of a mayor may read either

The Mayor of Chicago

or

Mr. John Lake
Mayor of Chicago

as he personally chooses.

It is unnecessary to continue this list, as each official certainly "knows his own name"! But it may be as well to add that titles of "courtesy" have no place either in a signature or on a visiting card.

The American title of courtesy, "The Honorable," (unlike this title given to sons of Earls, Vicounts and Barons) is never correct on a card.

The professional card of a doctor or surgeon is "James Smith, M.D." His social card is "Dr." or "Doctor James Smith," as he prefers. (*Dr.* is perfectly correct. But *Doctor* is somewhat better form.)

The visiting card for a doctor and his wife is engraved "Dr. (or preferably Doctor) and Mrs. James Smith." If his wife is also a physician who prefers using her own title, it is best not to use a double card ever. But if they insist upon this, it must read "Dr. James and Dr. Julia Smith." "Doctor" written in full twice would make many names too long.

A woman physician who is practicing her profession is "Doctor Julia Smith" or "Julia Smith, M.D."—as she may prefer.

CHILDREN'S CARDS

That very little children should have visiting cards is not so "silly" as might at first thought be supposed. To acquire perfect manners, and those graces of deportment that Lord Chesterfield so ardently tried to instil into his son, training cannot begin early enough, since it is through lifelong familiarity with the niceties of behavior that much of the distinction of those to the manner born is acquired. Many mothers think it good training in social personality for children to have their own cards, even though they are used only to send with gifts and upon very rare occasions.

At the rehearsal of a wedding, the tiny twin flower girls came carrying their wedding present for the bride between them, to which they had themselves attached their own small visiting cards. One card was bordered and engraved in pink, and the other bordered and engraved in blue, and the address on each read "*Chez Maman.*"

And in going to see a new baby cousin each brought a small 1830 bouquet, and both sent to their aunt their cards, on which, after seeing the baby, one had printed, "He is very little," and the other, "It has a red face." This shows that if modern society believes in beginning social training in the nursery, it does not believe in hampering a child's natural expression.

SPECIAL CARDS AND WHEN TO USE THEM

The double card, reading "Mr. and Mrs.," is sent with a wedding present, or with flowers to a funeral, or with flowers to a débutante, and is also used in paying formal visits.

The card on which a débutante's name is engraved under that of her mother is used most frequently when no coming-out entertainment has been given for the daughter. Her name on her mother's card announces, wherever it is left, that the daughter is "grown" and "eligible" for invitations. Although general card leaving is going each year more and more out of fashion, it is still correct when paying visits to leave the cards of all sons and daughters who are grown.

FOLD-OVER CARDS

Fold-over cards—known as "informals"—are convenient when one wants to write a very brief note but one that requires more space than is afforded by a visiting card. Fold-over cards are substitutes for note paper and not to be left in place of visiting cards.

THE P. P. C. CARD

This is merely a visiting card, whether of a lady or a gentleman, on which the intials P. P. C. (*pour prendre congé*—to take leave) are written in ink in the lower left corner. This is usually sent by mail to acquaintances when one is leaving, and means nothing except "I've gone away—Good-by." It is in no sense a message of thanks for especial kindness, for which a visit should be paid or a note of farewell and thanks written.

Since there is a tendency at present to translate French words into English for their more practical use, many are now writing T. s. g. b.! (To say good-bye), which is certainly sensible in this particular instance.

CARDS OF NEW OR TEMPORARY ADDRESS

In a case where change of address is not readily found, a visiting card with new address on it is the proper way to notify one's acquaintances as well as friends.

Cards are also sent, with a temporary address written in ink, when one is in a strange city and wishes to notify friends—either men or women—where one is stopping.

THE VANISHING VISIT OF EMPTY FORM

Somewhat more than a generation ago, Mrs. Social Leader, after her annual ball, put all the cards left upon her into a certain box, and a few weeks later these cards, carefully noted, made up the list of those to be invited next year, and the absent were left out. But about twenty years ago the era of informality set in and has been gaining ground to such extent that, if lists were kept according to "party call" cards, the once-smart hostess would find herself reduced to the middle-aged and the climbers, while the younger world of fashion flocked to the Cigret Colcreme's and the Sunrise Breakfasts of the Uppal Knights and cared very little whether Mrs. Toplofty and Mrs. Social Leader asked them to their balls or not. And as Society can have distinction and dignity without youth, but not gaiety, hostesses have capitulated and "party calls" by the younger set are no longer exacted.

But though punctilious card-leaving, visiting, and "days at home" have gone out of fashion in New York, this is no reason why these really important observances should not be in the height of fashion elsewhere. Nor, on the other hand, must anyone suppose, because the younger New Yorkers pay few visits and never have days at home, that they are a bit less careful about the things which they happen to consider essential to proper behavior.

But there are circumstances in which even the most indifferent to social obligations *must* leave cards.

WHEN CARDS MUST BE LEFT

It is still considered necessary that one leave a card within a few days after taking a first meal in a lady's house; or if one has for the first time been invited to lunch or dine with strangers, it is inexcusably rude not to leave a card upon them, whether one accepted the invitation or not—unless one return their hospitality with an invitation. In this day an invitation cancels a mere party call everywhere except perhaps in Washington diplomatic or official circles. If you want to be utterly correct, you leave your cards within three days and send your invitation within a week after your visit. But few people leading private lives are as punctilious as this.

One must also return a first visit. It is supposed that only a real "cause" can excuse the affront to an innocent stranger that the refusal to return a first call would imply. Today one *should* return such a visit certainly! But card leaving has become such a neglected practice that a neighbor should be given the benefit of the doubt before she is believed intentionally rude.

Strictly speaking, a card should be left with a first invitation—if a

VISITING CARDS AND THEIR USES

visit has not previously been paid. For example, let us suppose Miss Philadelphia takes a letter of introduction to Mrs. Newport. Mrs. Newport, inviting Miss Philadelphia to her house, should leave her invitation and her card at Miss Philadelphia's hotel. Good form demands that an old resident pay a visit on a newcomer before issuing a first invitation. Sometimes a note of explanation is sent asking that the formality be waived, but it is never disregarded, especially in the case of Mrs. Worldly, who has her own car and chauffeur, so that leaving a card with her invitation requires no effort. On the other hand, Mrs. Author, who has neither chauffeur nor time nor perhaps even a car, should not be expected to show the same measure of time-taking courtesy that is expected of a woman of leisure.

It seems scarcely necessary to add that anyone not entirely heartless must leave a card on, or send flowers to, a friend who has suffered a recent bereavement. One should also leave cards of inquiry or send flowers to sick friends, or, on occasion, to acquaintances.

INVITATION IN PLACE OF RETURNED VISIT

People who are old friends pay no attention to how often or how seldom one goes to see the other, unless there is an illness, a death, a birth, or a marriage. People invite each other to their houses and don't leave cards at all. Nor do they ever consider whose "turn" it is to invite whom. But first visits are paid and returned with considerable formality—especially the visit that must be paid after a *first* invitation to lunch or dine or take supper—either in someone's house or in a club or elsewhere.

If hospitality has been shown you by two (or more) hostesses together, you are indebted to both or all equally, if you know them equally. But if you have been asked by one, it is not necessary that you return the hospitality of the other (or others) to the full degree —nor ever—unless opportunity offers. In any event, when returning the hospitality of these several hostesses, it is never necessary that you invite them together.

"NOT AT HOME"

When a maid or butler at a door says "Not at home," this phrase means that the lady of the house is "Not at home to visitors." This answer neither signifies nor implies—*nor is it intended to imply*—that Mrs. Jones is out of the house. Some people say "Not receiving," which means actually the same thing, but the "Not at home" is infinitely more polite; in the former you know she is in the house but won't see you, whereas in the latter case you have the pleasant uncertainty that it is quite possible she is out.

To be told, "Mrs. Jones is at home but doesn't want to see you" would certainly be unpleasant. And to "beg to be excused"—except in a case of illness or bereavement—is very chilling. But "not at home" means that she is not sitting in her living room ready to receive you; that and nothing else. She may be out or she may be lying down or otherwise occupied. Nor should anyone find the slightest objection if a hostess, happening to recognize the visitor as a particular friend, calls out, "Come in, Mary! I *am* at home to *you!*"

Anyone who talks about this phrase as being a "white lie" either doesn't understand the meaning of the words, or is going very far afield to look for untruth. To be consistent, these over-literals should also exact that when a guest inadvertently knocks over a teacup and stains a sofa, the hostess, instead of saying, "It is nothing at all! Please don't worry about it," ought for the sake of truth to say, "See what your clumsiness has done! You have ruined my sofa!" And when someone says, "How are you?" instead of answering with conventional politeness, "Very well, thank you," the same truthful one should perhaps take an hour by the clock and mention every symptom of indisposition that she can accurately subscribe to.

While "not at home" is merely a phrase of politeness, to say "I am *out*" after a card has been brought to you is both an untruth and an inexcusable rudeness. Or to have an inquiry answered, "I don't know, but I'll see," and then to have the servant, after taking a card, come back with the message "Mrs. Jones is out" cannot fail to make the visitor feel rebuffed. Once a card has been admitted, the visitor *must* be admitted also, no matter how inconvenient receiving her may be. You may send a message that you are dressing but will be very glad to see her if she can wait ten minutes. The visitor can either wait or say she is pressed for time. But if she does not wait, then *she* is rather discourteous.

It may be a nuisance to be obliged to remember either to turn an "in" and "out" card in the hall, or to ring a bell and say, "I am going out," and again, "I have come in." But whatever plan or arrangement you choose, no one at your front door should be left in doubt and then repulsed. It is something that does at times occur in the houses of all of us; we run next door or up the street, or we go somewhere just for a moment, never thinking it important to tell whoever answers our door that we have gone. But even though it may on occasion happen to most of us, to give a visitor the chance to think we have been at home is bad manners.

A member of the family may also give the message "Mother is not at home"—meaning "not to visitors." But to leave whoever answers our door unaware of whether we are in or out is very bad housekeeping.

VISITING CARDS AND THEIR USES

PAYING A VISIT TO A LADY WHO HAS NO MAID

Let us say you go to see a stranger who has come to live in your neighborhood, and that when you ring the bell the lady herself opens the door—or let us say you find her sitting on her veranda. In either case you say, "How do you do—I'm Mrs. Jones. I live in the brick house across the way." The new neighbor says, "How do you do. I'm very glad to see you," or "How kind of you to come to see me!" She then invites you into her living room or asks whether you think it pleasanter on the veranda. In any case you sit and talk. From fifteen to twenty minutes is the time allotted for a formal visit. This is not a strict rule, but it is well to keep within this time unless you have much to talk about, and unless your hostess says, "Oh, do stay a little longer" or "Oh, don't go so soon," in which case you stay for a few minutes longer, or say "I'm sorry! I'd love to but I can't today. Do come and see me soon!" The new neighbor says, "I'll be glad to." You both say, "Good-bye," and that's all.

MODERN CARD-LEAVING

Yesterday's fashion of card-leaving, which required endless time going from house to house, sending the footman or chauffeur up the steps with cards without ever asking whether anyone was at home or not, is almost obsolete except in Washington. Even so, there are occasions when the visitor must ask to see the hostess (see Chapter 30); but under the following circumstances cards are left without asking whether a lady is at home.

Having been asked to lunch or dine with a lady whom you know but slightly, you should leave your card whether you accepted the invitation or not, within three days if possible, or at least within a week after the date for which you were invited. It is not considered necessary (in New York at least) to ask whether she is at home; promptness in leaving your card is, in this instance, better manners than delaying your "party call" and asking whether she is at home. This matter of asking at the door is one that depends upon the customs of each state and city; but as it is always wiser to err on the side of politeness, it is the better policy, if in doubt, to ask, "Is Mrs. Blank at home?" than to run the risk of offending a lady who may like to see her visitors.

VISITS WHICH EVERYONE MUST PAY

Paying visits differs from leaving cards in that you must ask to be received. A visit of condolence should be paid at once to a friend when a death occurs in her immediate family. A lady does not call on a man. but writes him a note of sympathy.

In going to inquire for convalescing friends, you should ask to be received, and it is always thoughtful to take them a gift of a book or fruit or flowers, or perhaps something from your kitchen.

If a relative announces his engagement, you must at once go to see his fiancée. Should she be out, you do not ask to see her mother. You do, however, leave a card upon both ladies, and you invite both to your house or wherever else you can.

A visit of congratulation is also paid to a new mother and a present taken to the baby.

MESSAGES WRITTEN ON CARDS

"With sympathy" or "With deepest sympathy" is written on your visiting card with flowers sent to a funeral. This same message is written on a card and left at the door of a house of mourning, if you do not know the family well enough to ask to be received.

"To inquire" is often written on a card left at the house of a sick person, but not if you are received.

In going to see a friend who is visiting a lady whom you do not know, whether you should leave a card on the hostess as well as on your friend depends upon the circumstances. If the hostess is one who is socially prominent and you are unknown, it would be better taste not to leave a card on her, since your card afterward found without explanation might be interpreted as an uncalled-for visit made in an attempt for a place on her list. If, on the other hand, she is the unknown person and you are the prominent one, your card is polite but unwise unless you mean to include her name on your list. But if she is one toward whom you have friendly inclinations, you naturally leave a card for her.

In leaving a card on a lady stopping at a hotel or living in an apartment house, you should write her name in pencil across the top of your card, to insure its being given to her, and not to someone else.

At the house of a lady whom you know well and whom you are sorry not to find at home, it is "friendly" to write "Sorry not to see you!" or "So sorry to miss you!"

Bending a card means merely that the card was left at the door by the visitor and not sent by mail. This has very little sense today when cards are left seldom and mailed, without a message, scarcely ever.

HOW A FIRST VISIT IS MADE

In very large cities (New York, for example) neighbors seldom call on each other. But when strangers move into a neighborhood in a small town or more especially in the country, it is very unfriendly of their neighbors not to call on them. The new residents always must wait for the old residents to call on them—or at least invite those much younger to come to see them—or more likely to come in for a cup of tea.

Or, if two ladies are both newcomers, either one may say, "I wish you would come to see me." To which the other replies, "I'd love to."

Everyone invited to a wedding should call upon the bride on her return from the honeymoon. And when a man marries a girl from a distant place, courtesy absolutely demands that his friends and neighbors go to see her as soon as she is at home.

ON OPENING THE DOOR TO A VISITOR

On the hall table in every house, there should be a small silver or other card tray, a pad and a pencil. The nicest kind of pad is one that, when folded, makes its own envelope, so that a message, when written, need not be left open. There are all varieties and sizes at all stationers.

When the doorbell rings, the servant on duty, who can easily see the chauffeur or lady approaching, should have the card tray ready to present on the palm of the left hand. Whoever is on duty at the door should never take the cards in his (or her) fingers.

CORRECT NUMBER OF CARDS TO LEAVE

When the visitor herself rings the doorbell and the message is "not at home," the butler or maid proffers the card tray on which the visitor lays a card of her own and her daughter's for each lady in the house and a card of her husband's and son's for each lady and gentleman. The number of cards to leave is very simple. You leave your own cards for women only, because you do not call upon a man. But your husband's card is left upon every man as well as every woman. That is all there is to it. But three is the greatest number ever left of any one card. In calling on Mrs. Town, who has three grown daughters and her mother living in the house, and a Mrs. Stranger staying with her whom the visitor was invited to a luncheon to meet, a card on each would mean a packet of six. Instead, the visitor should leave three—one for Mrs. Town, one for all the other ladies of the house, and one for Mrs. Stranger. In asking to be received, her query at the door should be, "Are any of the ladies at home?" Or in merely leaving her cards she should say, "For all of the ladies."

WHEN THE VISITOR LEAVES

The butler or maid must stand with the front door open until a visitor reenters her motor, or if she is walking, until she has reached the sidewalk. It is bad manners ever to close the door in a visitor's face.

When a chauffeur leaves cards, the door may be closed as soon as he turns away.

WHEN THE LADY OF THE HOUSE IS AT HOME

When the door is opened by a waitress or a parlor maid and the mistress of the house is in the drawing room, the maid says, "This way, please" and leads the way. She goes as quickly as possible to present the card tray. The guest, especially if a stranger, lags in order to give the hostess time to read the name on the card.

The maid meanwhile moves aside to make room for the approaching visitor, who goes forward to shake hands with the hostess. If a butler is at the door, he reads the card himself; picking it up from the tray and, opening the door of the drawing room, he announces: "Mrs. So.-and-so," after which he puts the card on the hall table.

The duration of a formal visit should be in the neighborhood of twenty minutes. But if other visitors are announced, the first one—on a very formal occasion—may cut her visit shorter. Or if conversation becomes especially interesting, the visit may be prolonged five minutes or so. On no account must a visitor stay an hour!

A hostess always rises when a visitor enters, unless the visitor is a very young woman or man and she is seated behind the tea table so that rising is difficult. She should always receive a visitor graciously. She says, "How nice of you to come to see me!" Or "I'm very glad to see you. Won't you sit here?"

If the lady of the house is "at home" but upstairs, the servant at the door leads the visitor into the reception room, saying, "Will you take a seat, please?" and then carries the card to the mistress of the house.

On an exceptional occasion, such as paying a visit of condolence or inquiring for a convalescent, when the question as to whether he will be received is necessarily doubtful, a gentleman does not take off his coat or gloves, but waits in the reception room with his hat in his hand. When the servant returning says either "Will you come this way, please?" or "Mrs. Town is not well enough to see anyone, but Miss Alice will be down in a moment," the visitor divests himself of his coat and gloves, which the servant carries, as well as his hat, out to the front hall.

A gentleman visitor always leaves his hat and coat in the hall and also removes and leaves his gloves—and rubbers should he be wearing them. A gentleman entering a room in which there are several people who are strangers, shakes hands with his hostess and slightly bows to all the others, whether he knows them personally or not. He, of course, shakes hands with any who are friends, and with all men to whom he is introduced, but with a lady only if she offers him her hand.

HOW TO ENTER A DRAWING ROOM

To know how to enter a drawing room is supposed to be one of the supreme tests of social skill. But there should be no more difficulty in entering the drawing room of Mrs. Worldly than in entering the sitting room at home. Perhaps the best instruction would be: "Take plenty of time; don't struggle and don't splash about!" Good manners are not unlike swimming after all!

Before entering a room full of people, it is best to pause on the threshold and see where the hostess is and the most unencumbered approach to her. The way *not* to enter a drawing room is to dart forward and then stand awkwardly bewildered and looking about in every direction. After greeting the hostess, talk with her for a few minutes and then either join friends of your own, or those to whom the hostess introduces you.

HOW TO SIT GRACEFULLY

To sit gracefully one should not perch stiffly on the edge of a straight chair, nor sprawl at length in an easy one. The perfect position is one that is easy, but dignified. In other days, no lady of dignity ever crossed her knees, held her hands on her hips, or twisted herself sideways, or even *leaned back in her chair!* Today all these things are done; and the only etiquette left is on the subject of how not to exaggerate them. No young girl—let alone older lady—should cross her knees when wearing knee-length skirts that are also lacking in fullness; neither should her foot be thrust out so that her toes are at knee level. An arm akimbo is *not* a graceful attitude, nor is a twisted spine! Everyone, of course, leans against a chairback (except in a box at the opera and in a ballroom). A gentleman who is a guest in a lady's house should not sit on the middle of his backbone with one ankle supported on the other knee, and both as high as his head. If too weak to sit up, he should stay at home.

The proper way for a lady to sit is in the center of her chair, or slightly sideways in the corner of a sofa. She may lean back, of course, and easily, her hands relaxed in her lap, her knees together, or if crossed, her foot must not be thrust forward like a pump-handle, or hooked around the chair leg in vine fashion. On informal occasions she can lean back in an easy chair as far as she chooses, with her hands on the arms. In a ball dress a lady of distinction never leans really backward. One cannot picture a beautiful and high-bred woman, wearing a tiara and other ball-room jewels, *leaning* against anything. This is, however, not so much a rule of etiquette as a question of beauty and fitness.

A gentleman, on very formal occasions, leans against the back of his chair, but he must give the appearance of sitting on a chair, not of lying at ease on a sofa.

POSTSCRIPTS ON VISITS

When you are paying a formal visit, the important rules are: Don't outstay other visitors who arrive after you, or one who may have come before you but who is plainly an intimate friend in whose news the hostess seems interested. In such a situation, the rule of safety is to stay ten minutes at most.

Do not, however, fidget and talk about leaving. Sit down as though your leaving immediately were not on your mind, but after a very few minutes stand up and say "Good-by" and go.

Never make remarks such as "I'm afraid I have overstayed my welcome" or "I must apologize for hurrying off" or "I am afraid I have bored you to death talking so much." All such expressions are self-conscious and stupid. If you really think you are staying too long or leaving too soon or talking too much—don't!

Above all, don't keep your hostess standing while you make parting remarks for half an hour! Having risen to go, *go!*

OTHER VISITING DETAILS

Visits of condolence are never returned.

A lady never pays a party call on a gentleman. But if the gentleman who has given a dinner has his mother (or sister) staying with him and if the mother (or sister) chaperoned the party, cards should, of course, be left upon her.

Few Americans are so punctilious as to pay their dinner calls within twenty-four hours; but it is the height of correctness and good manners to do so.

CHRISTMAS CARDS

The ever-increasing impulse to send out Christmas cards as messages of friendship and goodwill is plainly not a mere caprice of fashion, but evidence of a country-wide trend toward a broadened and more friendly social relationship.

The present tendency is toward sending personal cards to those whom not many years ago we would have considered rather formal acquaintances.

When ordering Christmas cards the inclusion of Mr. and Mrs. as part of the signature is proper when the names are engraved or printed like engraving and are put at the head of the message.

For example, "Mr. and Mrs. Christopher Holly send you their best wishes for a Merry Christmas and a Happy New Year." This is better form than "Best Wishes for a Merry Christmas and a Happy New Year, from Mr. and Mrs. Christopher Holly."

Sending cards as bought without any signature and then enclosing a visiting card is suitable for the extremely impersonal greeting sent to clients or customers or business acquaintances. When sent to friends, it rather suggests evidence of having been ordered too late to have them properly engraved—or perhaps it shows a frugal mind, since if the card is unmarked, it will be just as good as new for the receiver to send on to someone else next year.

An important point to be made is that engraving of names on Christmas cards naturally follows the rules for the engraving of names on visiting cards. For example, a woman's name should never be engraved without the prefix Mrs. or Miss. A man's card is of course on many occasions left without a prefix. It is sensible, therefore, if one can, to order two varieties of cards: one that is formal in subject and either engraved or formally printed in the style of engraving; the other an informal card with informal printing, and the signature printed to match and without title, these to be sent to intimate friends. And then one should select a few separate others for those of one's friends who are ill or in sorrow and upon which one's personal messages are added by hand.

It is always proper of course to buy cards as they come, for everyone, and to sign them or to have our names printed.

IS HUSBAND'S OR WIFE'S NAME WRITTEN FIRST?

When the cards are sent by husband and wife, the one who writes the names courteously writes his or her own name last. But when cards are printed, there is no rule about whether the husband's or the wife's name shall be first. "Mary and John" seems more polite to Mary, but "John and Mary" does of course follow the conventional Mr. and Mrs. form. Moreover, when children's names are included, the father's name comes first—always. For example: "John and Mary and the Baby" is better than "Mary and John and the Baby." Sometimes, by the way, a baby's arrival at any time during the year is announced by adding his name on the Christmas cards—"John and Mary and their new son Timothy." Cards sent to intimate friends, by a family having several children, might be from "The John Smiths —all Five" or from "The Smiths—John, Mary, Johnny, Marie and Tim." There is of course no rule about anything so informal as this.

On the formal cards sent by a widow and her grown son together, or widower and his grown daughter, the name of the parent would be engraved on one line and that of the son or daughter on the line below. Or if written by hand, the parent's name would come first: "Aunt Jane and Tim" or "Henry Green and Mary Green," or to those who call the parent by first name, "Henry and Mary."

Engaged people often send cards together to their intimate friends with their first names either written by hand or printed to match that on an informal card. But their two names are not very suitable when formally engraved.

There is practically no limit to the list of those to whom one may send Christmas cards, beginning with dearest friends and ending with the slightest acquaintances, but they *should* stop at acquaintances. Tradespeople should not commercialize the spirit of the most beautiful day in the year by sending cards intended to solicit customers. This does not mean that it is improper to send Christmas cards as a purely friendly greeting to customers whom they know personally.

CARD FOR WHOLE FAMILY

When a card is intended for the whole family and one dislikes the ambiguousness of Mr. and Mrs. Brightmeadow and Family, it is best to address the envelope Mr. and Mrs. and then on the card itself and below the wording of the message write in ink "Love to the children too" or "We all in our house send best Christmas wishes to all of you in your house," or whatever message is suitable.

CARDS TO BUSINESS ACQUAINTANCES

When sending cards to a business acquaintance whom one's husband (or wife) does not know, one properly signs one's name alone; but when the acquaintance is a social one or when sending a card to anyone who is really a friend and whom one would very much like one's husband or wife to meet, the name of the latter may be included. Both these answers apply to cases of uncertainty. In the usual case you would do what your own impulse tells you, and send an impersonal one alone and a friendly one together. And this applies to people working in business with you, for you, and above you.

A CHRISTMAS CARD TO SOMEONE IN MOURNING

A card to someone who is in deep mourning can be kind if its picture in some way illustrates the birth of Christ or the promise of peace, or if its message be of loving friendly thought. But please do **not** send a picture of a grave or gravestone—nor on the other hand a gay card shouting "Merry Christmas and Happy New Year." Whether or not those who are themselves in mourning send cards depends entirely upon their own feelings. Naturally they would not send cards to mere acquaintances, but certainly there is no impropriety in wishing their friends happiness, if they can forget their own unhappiness enough to do so. On the other hand, no one could possibly want them to do anything that could add to the strain of what must be to them the hardest of days to endure.

COLORED INKS FOR GAILY COLORED CARDS

Although red and orange and green ink are still tabu for social usage, there is no tabu against signing cards in red or other colored ink to match the wording on a gaily informal Christmas card. Also Christmas envelope linings can be as vividly colorful as you please. It is quite all right to paste return address stickers or to write your address on envelopes going to people whose address you are not certain about.

BIRTHDAY AND OTHER GREETING CARDS

Birthday and anniversary cards and all other messages of friendship are charming evidences of good wishes from family and friends. But the engraved or printed card intended as a substitute for a written note of thanks is abominably rude and utterly lacking in taste.

ANSWERS TO READERS' QUESTIONS

ANSWERING A VISITING-CARD INVITATION

I am much puzzled about the inconsistency of replying in the formal third person to an invitation sent out on a visiting card. If I, for example, wrote informally on a visiting card, "Buffet supper, Sunday at 7 o'ck," and then everyone answered in the third person, I would be anxious about the kind of party they might expect!

I agree with you that it is inconsistent to answer a visiting-card invitation, which is never quite formal, with a note of acceptance or regret written in the third person. Nevertheless, this is the accepted convention, probably because its first use was considered as a substitute for the formal engraved third-person invitation form which was merely "filled" in with a few words. At the present time only comparative strangers answer in the third person. Intimate friends invariably reply in kind, "Coming!" "Accept." "Sorry can't come!" And it is reasonable to suppose that the custom will spread further. In fact, even though the third-person reply is still conventionally correct, I see no objection whatever to replying to "Wed. Nov. 1, 7:30 o'ck, Buffet supper" on one's own card, "Accept with pleasure Nov. 1" or even "So sorry cannot accept for Wed."

"MISS ONLYDAUGHTER"

What about the form "Miss Onlydaughter"? Is it more popular elsewhere than in America, and just what does it mean? In cases where it can be properly used, would you advise it?

To create a term, it means "senior spinster of the clan"—the oldest daughter of the oldest son—though she might herself be younger than a cousin whose father was a younger son. Its use is solely a matter of personal choice. In this modern day it sounds very old-maidish—at least it does to me. If I saw a card reading "Miss Green" I would suppose her to be at least sixty, though she might very well be sixteen.

MESSAGES OF VISITING CARDS

I want to leave my card on one daughter in a large family. How can I leave it so that the right one receives it? Her sisters don't know me!

Write "For Miss Mary Smith" across the top of the card.

When a message is written on a visiting card, is it better to write on the face of the card or on the reverse side? Is there any other rule than that of space on the card?

Better on the face, because a message on the back might be overlooked, should the one who receives it read the name and not turn the card over.

11

Invitations, Acceptances and Regrets and All Engraved Forms

ALL formal invitations—and their acceptances and regrets—whether they are to be engraved or to be written by hand, are invariably in the third person, and good usage permits no deviation from this form. The words must be placed on specified lines and centered as evenly as possible. Names of hosts belong on the first line; "request the pleasure of" on the second; name of guest on the third; and so forth.

Among the many engraved forms adapted to our social life, a few are of unusual importance.

WEDDING INVITATIONS

The invitation to the wedding ceremony is customarily engraved on the first page of a sheet of white note paper either plain or with a raised margin formed by a "plate mark." If the family of the bride has one, their coat of arms—or the crest only—is embossed without color at top center of the sheet. Otherwise the invitation bears no device. The engraving may be in script, which is a standard style, or in any of the several other letterings which from time to time come into fashion.

The invitation to the church should always request "the honour" of your "presence," and never the "pleasure" of your "company." The invitation to the reception requests the "pleasure" of your "company." (Honour is spelled in the old-fashioned way with a "u" instead of "honor.")

ENCLOSED IN TWO ENVELOPES*

Two envelopes are rarely used except for wedding invitations or announcements; but they with their accompanying cards are conventionally enclosed, first in an inner envelope that has no mucilage on the flap and is superscribed "Mr. and Mrs. Jameson Greatlake," without address, and then in an outer envelope which is sealed and addressed.

* This is correct but not possible for the duration of war shortages.

> Mr. and Mrs. Jameson Greatlake
> 24 Michigan Avenue
> Chicago, Illinois

It is bad form to abbreviate the state, but it is quite proper to omit it when the invitations are posted in the same city, or when otherwise unnecessary. New York, for example, is never written twice.

To those who are only "asked to the church" no house invitation is enclosed.

ADDRESSING ENVELOPES

Envelopes should not be addressed

> Mr. and Mrs. James Greatlake
> and Family

"And Family" has never been completely approved because it is too indefinite as to how many of the family are invited. Correctly, Miss Mary Greatlake, or The Misses Greatlake, may be written under the names of their parents, but otherwise each grown member of the family should receive a separate invitation, or else all names be included.

When double envelopes are again available, the children's names are written on the inner envelopes this way:

> Priscilla, Penelope, Harold and Jim

enclosed in an outside envelope addressed to the Misses Greatlake and the Messrs. Greatlake.

On the inside envelopes of the invitations to relatives who are very dear to the bride or to the groom—especially if they are simple people who might not understand that the formality of writing "Mr. and Mrs." is prescribed and not intended—"Aunt Kate and Uncle Tom" or "Grandmother" may, of course, be written in the handwriting of the bride—or the groom. This, however, is a personal exception and quite apart from etiquette, which is more particularly concerned with the wording of the engraving or the addressing of the envelope that goes to the post.

ENVELOPE AND INVITATION IN ONE

Wedding invitations and announcements are sometimes engraved on a sheet with a gummed flap at the top; when folded, this paper makes its own envelope. This style cannot possibly replace the conventional fine-quality kid-finish paper enclosed in two envelopes—which is in best possible taste. But, if there are no enclosures, it might serve as well as those invitations sent in one envelope—as a paper-saving measure. When paper of the smoothness and texture of a gardenia petal becomes available again, two envelopes should, of course, be used.

In the examples of correct wording, spacing, and styles of engraving which follow, it is important to note the lack of punctuation, except after abbreviations and initials and when phrases requiring separation by punctuation occur on the same line.

THE CHURCH INVITATION

The proper form for an invitation to the church ceremony.

Mr. and Mrs. John Huntington Smith

request the honour of

Miss Pauline Town's

presence at the marriage of their daughter

Mary Katherine

to

Mr. James Smartlington

Tuesday, the first of November

at twelve o'clock

St. John's Church

The invitation may be about 5½ inches wide by 7⅜ inches deep or a little smaller and fold into its envelope, or about 4⅜ inches and 5¾ inches go into the envelope without folding; but the fashion in this varies from time to time and other sizes may be used, according to the mode of the moment.

The invitation to the breakfast reads

Mr. and Mrs. John Huntington Smith
request the pleasure of

Miss Pauline Town's

company at breakfast
Tuesday, the first of November
at half after twelve o'clock
43 Park Avenue

R.s.v.p.

Or the following on a small card is enclosed with the invitation to the church

Reception

immediately following the ceremony

895 Park Avenue

R.S.V.P.

When the bride's father has a coat of arms, it is always embossed without color on wedding invitations and announcements; but when invitations are sent out in the name of the bride's mother (or any woman alone), a coat of arms is improper. She can, however, have the device on the shield of her husband's coat of arms impaled with that of her own family on a lozenge.

* On an actual invitation this is embossed without color and does not have the heavy black effect caused by this printed example.

Plain script is in very best taste for invitations ornamented with a **coat** of arms or a lozenge.

Mr. and Mrs. Charles Robert Oldname
request the honour of your presence
at the marriage of their daughter
Carolyn Marie
to
Mr. John Frederick Hamilton
Saturday, the twenty-ninth of April
at four o'clock
Church of the Heavenly Rest
New York

* See note on page 94.

INVITATION TO A WEDDING AT THE HOUSE OF A FRIEND

Mr. and Mrs. Richard Littlehouse

request the honour of *

presence at the marriage of their daughter

Betty

to

Mr. Frederic Robinson

Saturday, the fifth of November

at four o'clock

at the residence of Mr. and Mrs. James Sterlington.

Tuxedo Park, New York

R.s.v.p.

In this form the invitations are issued by the parents of the bride. although the wedding takes place at a home other than their own.

THE BRIDE WITH ONE PARENT

When the bride's own father (or mother) is not living and she has a step-parent, the invitations are worded:

Mr. and Mrs. John Huntington Smith
request the honour of your presence
at the marriage of her daughter
Mary Alice Towne
etc.

---

* At one time it was customary to request the "pleasure of . . . company" instead of the "honour of . . . presence" at a house wedding because the invitation necessarily included the reception. But the bad taste of requesting the pleasure of your company at a solemn church rite is now universally recognized and invitations, even in the smallest houses, request the honour of your presence.

INVITATION TO A DOUBLE WEDDING

Mr. and Mrs. Henry Smartlington
request the honour of your presence
at the marriage of their daughters

Marian Helen

to

Mr. Judson Jones

and

Amy Caroline

to

Mr. Herbert Scott Adams

Saturday, the tenth of November
at four o'clock
Trinity Church

The wording of a double wedding invitation, when the brides are not sisters, must necessarily include the surnames of the brides.

Mr. and Mrs. Henry Smartlington
and
Mr. and Mrs. Arthur Lane
request the honour of your presence
at the marriage of their daughters
Marian Helen Smartlington
to
Mr. Judson Jones
and
Mary Alice Lane
to   etc.

If the surnames of the brides are omitted, there is, at the moment, danger that strangers may suppose the invitation one of those divorced-parents offenses occasionally perpetrated.

THE CARDS FOR RESERVED PEWS

To the family and very intimate friends who are to be seated in specially designated pews, the same admission card which is sent to others may be sent, but with the words "Pew No.   " engraved in the lower left-hand corner, the number of the pew being written in by hand.

But the more usual custom is for the mother of the bride and the mother of the bridegroom each to write on her personal visiting card the number of the pew destined for each member of the family and each very intimate friend to occupy.

```
┌─────────────────────────────────────────┐
│                                         │
│   Pew No. 7                             │
│                                         │
│                                         │
│     Mrs. John Huntington Smith          │
│                                         │
│                                         │
│                                         │
│              600 East Fifty-Seventh Street │
│                                         │
└─────────────────────────────────────────┘
```

A few years ago all numbers were written out, but according to best present fashion house numbers are given in figures and street numbers are written out. The street numbers may also be given in figures.

A card for a reserved enclosure consisting of a certain number of front pews, but for no special pew, and inscribed "Within the ribbon" may be enclosed with the invitations, or the words may be added in the lower left-hand corner of a requisite number of admission cards of the customary form. If admission cards are not necessary, "Within the ribbon" may be written on a visiting card.

THE INVITATION TO THE HOUSE

The invitation to the breakfast or reception following the church ceremony is engraved on a card to match the paper of the church invitation and is a little smaller than the size of the latter after it is folded for the envelope.

Wedding invitations frequently request "your" presence, but invitations to the house preferably have the name of the guest written in the space left for the purpose.

INVITATIONS AND REGRETS

THE CEREMONY AND RECEPTION INVITATION IN ONE

Occasionally, especially for a country wedding or when the reception is taking place in the assembly room of the church and everyone is invited to remain, the invitation to the breakfast or the reception is added to the invitation to the ceremony.

Mrs. Alexander Oldname

requests the honour of

Mr. and Mrs. Worldly's

presence at the marriage of her daughter

Hester

to

Mr. James Town, junior

Tuesday, the twenty-first of October

at three o'clock

Church of the Resurrection

Ridgemont, New York

and afterwards at the reception

Bright Meadows

R. s.v. p.

Or the invitation reads, "At twelve o'clock, Church of the Resurrection, Ridgemont, New York, and afterwards at breakfast at Bright Meadows."

THE BRIDE WHO HAS NO PARENTS

When the bride has no parents, generally the eldest brother sends her marriage announcements. Or, if another relative has taken the part of parent to her, this one's name is used. The bride whose several sisters, or brothers, are younger than she may prefer to announce her own marriage, in which case the form would be

>Miss Mary Jane Smith
>and
>Mr. John Henry Bridegroom
>have the honour of announcing
>their marriage
>etc.

Whoever gives her the wedding sends the invitations. Or she invites her own guests.

WHEN PARENTS OF BRIDE ARE DIVORCED

Threatening to spread like an epidemic across the whole country is the present wave of poor taste that reaches a climax in the invitation to a wedding sent out by divorced parents of the bride *together!*

>Mr. and Mrs. Oldhusband
>and
>Mr. and Mrs. Newhusband
>request the honour of your presence
>at the marriage of
>Mr. Oldhusband's and Mrs. Newhusband's daughter
>Mary
>etc.

Anything more starkly affronting the sacredness of marriage is hard to imagine.

If we suppose that the bride is a young woman who, like the majority of the children of the divorced, takes her own marriage with intense seriousness, such invitations to her wedding (quite apart from taste and propriety) are not very auspicious. We may know that her parents have been divorced and remarried, but to have our attention called to their shattered and rehashed pledges upon the same sheet of paper that calls upon us to witness the solemn taking of these same breakable pledges by their daughter would not seem to be giving the latter's marriage a fair chance at the start.

A number of other examples are less shocking only in degree. One of them reads "Mr. A. Aye and Mrs. Z. Zee announce the marriage

INVITATIONS AND REGRETS

of their daughter Margaret." Properly the announcement of Margaret Aye's marriage should be sent out by her mother. It is still more important that the invitations to Mary Oldhusband's wedding should read

Mrs. Newhusband
requests the honour of your presence
at the marriage of her daughter
Mary Oldhusband
etc.

The invitation to the reception held at the house of Mary's mother and step-father is worded

Mr. and Mrs. Newhusband
request the pleasure of your company
on Saturday, the third of November
at half after four o'clock

An important reason why the invitations should be sent out by the mother of the bride is that the father takes the same part no matter who gives the wedding. He goes with his daughter to church and walks up the aisle with her and gives her away. Whereas, if the invitations are sent out by the bride's father, her mother is made an outsider unless the father's present wife generously cedes the front pew, or unless the all-mixed-together relationship of the divorced and their new partners is taken with camaraderie by all concerned.

THE INVITATION TO A HOUSE WEDDING

This is the same except that "at Sunlawn" or "at 400 Park Avenue" is put in place of "Saint John's Church," and an invitation to stay on at a house, to which the guest is already invited, is not necessary.

The wording of an invitation to a house wedding includes a house address in place of the name of the church, and R.s.v.p. is added.

THE TRAIN CARD

If the wedding is to be in the country, the transportation of guests is one of the obligations of the bride's family. For a wedding of average size, a special car is added to a regular train; but for a very big wedding, a special train is engaged. In either case a train card about three inches wide and two inches deep is enclosed, as follows:*

---

* Although entirely unknown since the beginning of the war, weddings of similar importance will probably take place somewhere, sometime.

A special train will leave
Grand Central Terminal for Ridgemont
at 12.45 p.m.
and, returning, will arrive in New York
at 7.02 p.m.
Please present this card in place of a ticket

The most flattering wedding invitation possible to receive is a note of invitation personally written by the bride.

Sally Dear

Our wedding is to be on Thursday the tenth at half-past twelve, Christ Church Chantry. Of course we want you and Jack and the children! And we want all of you to come afterward to Aunt Mary's, for a bite to eat and to wish us luck.

Affectionately
Helen

Or

Dear Mrs. Kindhart

Dick and I are to be married at Christ Church Chantry at noon on Thursday the tenth. We both want you and Mr. Kindhart to come to the church and afterward for a very small breakfast at my Aunt's—Mrs. Slade—at Two Park Avenue.

With much love from us both,

Affectionately
Helen

The bride's mother may also write similar notes to a few of her intimate friends.

Dear Jane

Helen and Dick are to be married, etc.

INVITATION TO THE RECEPTION ONLY

On occasion the ceremony is private and a big reception follows. This plan is chosen where the nearest relative is an invalid who can perhaps go down to the drawing room with only the immediate families, but could not otherwise be present.

Under these circumstances the invitations to the ceremony are given verbally, or else "Ceremony at 4 o'ck" is written on the visiting card of the bride's mother.

The invitations to the reception are engraved on sheets of note paper like those used for church invitations, but the "pleasure of your company" is requested in this case instead of the "honour of your presence."

When the wedding reception—or any other entertainment—is given at a club through the courtesy of a friend of the hostess, the following announcement is always engraved in the lower right corner: "Through the courtesy of Mrs. John Smith Jones." This is put in the right corner because the left is reserved for the R.s.v.p.

WEDDING ANNOUNCEMENTS

If no general invitations have been issued to the church, an announcement engraved on note paper like that of the invitation to the ceremony is sent to the entire visiting list of both the bride's and the groom's family.

Mr. and Mrs. John Fairplay

have the honour of

announcing the marriage of their daughter

Madeleine Anne,

to

Mr. George Followes Highseas
Ensign United States Navy

Tuesday, the twenty-seventh of March

One thousand nine hundred and forty-five

Washington, D. C.

Three forms of announcement are equally correct: "have the honour to announce," or "have the honour of announcing" or merely the one word "announce." At present "have the honour of announcing" is in fashion. Also in fashion is "Tuesday, April 24th, 1945" in place of "Tuesday, the twenty-fourth" on one line and "One thousand nine hundred and forty-five" below. (See Military and Post-War Supplement for additional Army and Navy Forms.)

Announcements go out in the name of the nearest kin—whether actually present or absent. An invalid mother's name is included in the Mr. and Mrs. of the invitation. A father actually abroad is present on the engraved line.

Announcements are never sent to those who have been invited to the wedding.

An announcement means that, for some reason or other, you were not (or *could not be*) invited. An announcement requires no gift or acknowledgment except that of your own interest and impulse.

THE SECOND MARRIAGE

Invitations to the marriage of a widow—if she is very young—are sent in the name of her parents exactly as were the invitations to her first wedding, except that her name, instead of being merely Priscilla, is now written Priscilla Barnes Leaming, thus:

> Mr. and Mrs. Maynard Barnes
> request the honour of your presence
> at the marriage of their daughter
> Priscilla Barnes Leaming
> to
> etc.

Forms that are tabu include a title following a possessive pronoun denoting relationship. "Their daughter, Mrs." and "their niece, Miss" are equally wrong. One excuse given is that if Mr. and Mrs. Jones announce the marriage of their daughter, Mary Jones Smith, no one will know that this is her second marriage. It would be difficult to see how it could be plainer. On the other hand, without the Jones in her name she might of course be the daughter of Mrs. Jones, who might first have been a Mrs. Smith; or the bride may be marrying again. But, after all, invitations to second weddings are supposed to be sent to people who know the Joneses or the bride really well. If they do not recognize any of the names, it would scarcely have been necessary to send announcements, let alone invitations.

Announcements for a young widow's marriage are also the same as for a first wedding.

> Mr. and Mrs. Maynard Barnes
> announce the marriage of their daughter
> Priscilla Barnes Leaming
> etc.

But the announcement of the marriage of a widow of maturer years reads

INVITATIONS AND REGRETS

Mrs. Eben Hoyt Leaming*
and
Mr. Worthington Adams
have the honour to announce their marriage
on Monday, the second of November
at Saratoga Springs, New York

CONCERNING DIVORCÉE'S REMARRIAGE

Sending out engraved invitations to, or announcements of, the remarriage of a divorcée is permissible only when circumstances so strongly favor an innocent wife that public opinion gives its approval of her right to find happiness in a second marriage. But in the all-too-typical shifting of partners by means of whatever convenient cause complacent laws allow, announcements of a second or third marriage, particularly one that took place within a few hours of release by divorce, is in worst possible taste.

On the other hand, the fact that the groom has been divorced does not interfere with the announcement of his new bride's marriage.

CARDS OF ADDRESS

If the bride and groom wish to inform their friends of their future address, the following form without any name is enclosed in the invitation:

After the first of December
25 Alderney Place, Detroit, Michigan

THE INVITATION TO A WEDDING ANNIVERSARY

For a wedding anniversary celebration, the year of the wedding and the year in which the invitation is issued are usually stamped at the top of the invitation. Sometimes the couple's initials are added.

1895–1945
Mr. and Mrs. James Neighbor
at Home
Tuesday, the fifth of September
from four until six o'clock

The latter would indicate a much simpler form of entertainment. Invitations to a very simple anniversary tea or evening party are written by hand—or are telephoned.

---

* In this single instance the tabu of Mrs. followed by a woman's Christian name is proper because of the questionable propriety of including her first husband's name in such close proximity to that of her second.

When the invitations are sent out by half a dozen children, married and unmarried, a practical form is

In honour of the
Fiftieth Wedding Anniversary of
Mr. and Mrs. John Darby
their sons and daughters
request the pleasure of

(space for name of guest)

company on Tuesday, the twenty-third of June
at nine o'clock
in the small Ballroom of the Fitz-Cherry
R.S.V.P.
(to whoever is selected
to receive the replies)

ANSWERING A WEDDING INVITATION

An invitation to the church only requires no answer whatever (unless the wedding is so small that the invitation is a personally written note). An invitation to the reception or breakfast is answered on the first page of a sheet of note paper; and although it is written "by hand," the spacing of the words must be followed as though they were engraved. This is the form of acceptance:

Mr. and Mrs. Robert Gilding, Jr.
accept with pleasure
Mr. and Mrs. John Huntington Smith's
kind invitation for
Tuesday, the first of June

The regret reads:

Mr. and Mrs. Richard Brown
regret that they are unable to accept
Mr. and Mrs. John Huntington Smith's
kind invitation for
Tuesday, the first of June

OTHER FORMAL INVITATIONS

All other formal invitations are engraved—never printed from type —on white suède-finish cards, either plain or plate-marked like those for wedding-reception cards.

Monograms, addresses, personal devices are not used on engraved invitations. But a coat of arms (or the crest alone) embossed without color on wedding cards is correct for all who have a right to such a device. To use one without this right is to pretend to something that is not true.

The size of the card of invitation varies with personal preference. The most graceful proportion is three units in height to four in width —or four high by three wide.

The lettering is a matter of personal choice, but the plainer the design, the safer. Punctuation is used only where words requiring separation occur on the same line, and in certain abbreviations, such as R.s.v.p. It is absolutely correct in this abbreviation to use small letters for the s.v.p. Capitals, R.S.V.P., which went out of fashion a few years ago, are at the present moment coming back into favor.

THE INVITATION TO A BALL

The word "ball" is rarely used except in an invitation to a public one, or at least a semi-public one, such as may be given by a committee for a charity or a club or association of some sort. For example:

>The Entertainment Committee of the Greenwood Club
>requests the pleasure of your company
>at a Ball
>to be held at the club house
>on the evening of Thursday, the seventh of November
>at ten o'clock
>for the benefit of
>The Neighborhood Hospital
>Tickets five dollars

INVITATION TO BE A PATRON

If fifty or more names are to be included in the list of those invited to become patrons, the correct wording is as follows:

>The Committee of the Midwinter Ball
>has the honour to invite
>(name written by hand)
>to be a Patron of the Ball
>for the benefit of
>The Children's Hospital
>at the Hotel Grand
>Friday evening, the thirtieth of October
>at nine o'clock

Usually a card with return envelope is enclosed with the invitation for the convenience of the patron's answer. The most elaborate of these is worded:

I accept the Committee's invitation to be a Patron of the SCHOLARSHIP BALL, at the HOTEL GRAND, Friday Evening, October thirtieth. Please reserve for me:

............BOXES; First Tier (seating eight persons. Supper served in the box)..............$

............SINGLE TICKETS (including Table Reservations on the ballroom terrace, Supper and All Events of the Evening)..each $

............SINGLE TICKETS (including Buffet Supper and All Events of the Evening) each $

      Each patron is requested to be responsible for at least four tickets at $— or $— each.
      As tables will be allotted in the order in which acceptances are received, early reservations are advisable.

NAME ....
      (Please write name as you wish it to appear on Patron List)

ADDRESS ....

Checks, made payable to the SCHOLARSHIP COMMITTEE, should be mailed to Room 540, Blank Building, Blanktown.

INVITATIONS TO A PRIVATE BALL

Invitations to a private ball, no matter whether the ball is to be given in a private house or the hostess has engaged an entire floor of the largest hotel in the world, announce merely that Mr. and Mrs. Somebody will be "At Home,"—both words written with a capital letter—and the word "Dancing" is added, almost as though it were an afterthought, in the lower left or right corner. *This is the most punctilious and formal invitation that it is possible to send.* It is engraved in script usually, on a card of white bristol board about five and a half inches wide and three and three-quarters inches high. Like the wedding invitation, it has an embossed crest without color, or *nothing.*

The precise form is

Mr. and Mrs. Davis Jefferson

At Home

Monday, the third of January

at ten o'clock

Town and Country Club

Kindly send reply to   *Dancing*
Three Vernon Square

but may of course be engraved in whatever style of lettering the family prefers.

THE BALL FOR A DEBUTANTE DAUGHTER

Very occasionally an invitation is worded

Mr. and Mrs. Davis Jefferson

Miss Alice Jefferson

At Home

if the daughter is a débutante and the ball is for her; but it is not strictly correct to have any names except those of the host and his wife above the words "At Home."

The proper form of invitation when the ball is to be given for a débutante is as follows:

Mr. and Mrs. de Puyster

request the pleasure of

Miss Rosalie Grey's

company at a dance in honour of their daughter

Miss Alice de Puyster

Monday the tenth of January

at ten o'clock

One East Fiftieth Street

R.s.v.p.

The only explanation of why the wording "their daughter Miss" is permitted in the invitation to a ball and forbidden in an invitation to a wedding is that the wedding is a church sacrament. The marriage (sacrament) of "their daughter Miss" (or Mrs.) is shocking. But all the young men are invited to meet and to dance with Miss Alice de Puyster. Or if this explanation is not satisfactory, we must fall back on the fact that social convention has always said "yes" to one and "no" to the other.

INVITATIONS AND REGRETS

Or the invitation to the ball may read

Mr. and Mrs. James Town
Miss Pauline Town

request the pleasure of

Mr. and Mrs. Greatlake's

company on Monday, the third of January

at ten o'clock

One East Fiftieth Street

Dancing
R. s. v. p.

The form most often used by fashionable hostesses in New York and Newport is

Mr. and Mrs. Gilding

request the pleasure of

company at a small dance
Monday, the first of January

at ten o'clock

900 Fifth Avenue

R. s. v. p.

Even though the ball is given for a débutante daughter, her name does not necessarily appear, and it is called a "small dance" whether it is really small or big.

If the dance or dinner, or whatever the entertainment is to be, is given at one address and the hostess lives at another, both addresses are always given.

> Mr. and Mrs. Sidney Oldname
>
> request the pleasure of
>
> Miss Pauline Town's
>
> company at a dance
>
> Monday evening, January the third
>
> at ten o'clock
>
> The Fitz-Cherry
>
> Kindly send response to
> Brookmeadows,
> Long Island

If the dance is given for a young friend who is not a relative, Mr. and Mrs. Oldname's invitations read

> request the pleasure of
>
> company at a dance in honour of
>
> Miss Rosalie Grey

ASKING AN INVITATION FOR A STRANGER

One may never ask for an invitation for oneself anywhere! And one may not ask for an invitation to a luncheon or a dinner for a stranger. But an invitation for any general entertainment may be asked for a stranger—especially for a house guest—still more especially for a man.

Example

> Dear Mrs. Worldly,
>   My nephew, David Park, is staying with us. May I send him to your dance on Friday?
>   Very sincerely yours,
>   Caroline Robinson Town.

INVITATIONS AND REGRETS

If the nephew had been a niece instead, Mrs. Town would have added, "If it will be inconvenient for you to include her, please do not hesitate to say so." This would give Mrs. Worldly a chance to answer, if necessary, that her list of dancing men was rather short, and that she would be glad to have Mrs. Town send a man as well as Miss Stranger.

But most properly—and probably—Mrs. Worldly sends a telephoned answer. "Mrs. Worldly will be delighted to see Mr. Park (or Miss Stranger) on the tenth."

A very young girl may of course take a man to a dance; in fact several dancing men will be more than welcomed!

INVITATIONS TO SIMPLE DANCE SENT BY SEVERAL MEMBERS OF A FAMILY

This form intended for several members of one family should be printed and not in formal type.

> Mary, Sara, and Jack Brown
> hope you will come to their dance
> on Friday evening, February 23rd
> at 10 o'clock
> at the Blank Club
> Do say yes!

THE CARD OF GENERAL INVITATION

Invitation to important entertainments are nearly always specially engraved, so that nothing is written except the name of the person invited. But for the hospitable hostess, a card which is engraved in blank, so that it may serve for dinner, luncheon, dance, lecture, musicale, or whatever she may care to give, is indispensable.

> Mr. and Mrs. Stevens
>
> request the pleasure of
>
> company at
>
> on
>
> at   o'clock
>
> Two Knob Hill

THE HALF-ENGRAVED UTILITY INVITATION

The blank form which may be used for all parties is

Mr. and Mrs. Huntington Jones
request the pleasure of

company at

on

at   o'clock
645 Fifth Avenue

INVITATIONS TO RECEPTIONS AND TEAS

Invitations to receptions and teas differ from invitations to balls in that the cards on which they are engraved are usually somewhat smaller. Formerly the words "At Home" with capital letters were always changed to "will be at home" with small letters. At present the wording "At Home" is in fashion. The time is not set at a certain hour, but extends over a definite period indicated by a beginning and a terminating hour. Also, except on very unusual occasions, a man's name does not appear. The name of the débutante for whom the tea is given is put under that of her mother, and sometimes under that of her sister or the bride of her brother.

Mrs. James Town
Mrs. James Town, junior
Miss Pauline Town
will be at home
Tuesday, the eighth of December
from four until six o'clock
850 Fifth Avenue

Because afternoon teas are supposedly given by women, Mr. Town's name is omitted from this invitation, and Mrs. Town brings her daughter out at a tea alone. Mr. Town shares her responsibility if the party is given in the evening, and he, of course, assumes the responsibility of host in the afternoon as well. (Just why his name is omitted has no answer further than "It's always been that way.")

Mr. Town's name would probably appear with that of his wife if he were an artist and the reception were given in his studio to view his pictures; or if a reception were given to meet a distinguished guest, such as a bishop or a governor, in which case "In honour of

INVITATIONS AND REGRETS

the Right Reverend William Ritual" or "To meet His Excellency the Governor of California" would be engraved at the top of the invitation.

Suitable wording for an evening reception.

Mr. and Mrs. James Town
at Home
Tuesday, the eighth of December
from nine until eleven o'clock

This use of the little "a" and capital "H" and small-size "at Home" is a new form borrowed from England. It is pleasing, because it emphasizes the hospitable thought of Home and denotes neither the ceremoniousness of At Home nor the impersonal inclusion of one's whole visiting list at an afternoon tea which "will be at home" announces.

THE FORMAL INVITATION WHICH IS WRITTEN

When the formal invitation to dinner or luncheon is written instead of engraved, note paper stamped with house address or personal device is used. The wording and spacing must follow the engraved models exactly.

39 EAST 79TH STREET

Mr. and Mrs. John Kindhart

request the pleasure of

Mr. and Mrs. Robert Gilding jr.'s

company at dinner

on Tuesday, the sixth of December

at eight o'clock.

It must *not* be written

39 EAST 79TH STREET
PLAZA 4-7572

[handwritten:] Mr & Mrs J. Kindhosrt request the pleasure of Mr & Mrs James Town's Company at Dinner on Tuesday

etc.

This incorrect invitation has four faults:

(1) Letters in the third person must follow the prescribed form. This does not. (2) The writing is crowded against the margin. (3) The telephone number should be used only for business and informal notes and letters. (4) The full name "John" should be used instead of the initial "J."

RECALLING AN INVITATION

If for illness or other reason invitations have to be recalled, the following forms are correct. They are always printed instead of engraved, there being no time for engraving.

Owing to the sudden illness of their daughter
Mr. and Mrs. John Huntington Smith
are obliged to recall their invitations
for Tuesday, the tenth of June

When a wedding is broken off after the invitations have been issued

Mr. and Mrs. Benjamin Nottingham
announce that the marriage of their daughter
Mary Katharine
to
Mr. Jerrold Atherton
will not take place

THE FORMAL ACCEPTANCE OR REGRET

Answers to informal invitations are telephoned more often than not. The formal acceptance of an invitation, whether it is to a dance, a wedding breakfast or a ball, is identical in general form.

> Mr. and Mrs. Donald Lovejoy
> accept with pleasure
> Mr. and Mrs. Worldly's
> kind invitation for dinner
> on Monday, the tenth of December
> at eight o'clock

The formula for regret.

> Mr. Clubwin Doe
> regrets extremely that a previous engagement
> prevents his accepting
> Mr. and Mrs. Worldly's
> kind invitation for dinner
> on Monday, the tenth of December

Or

> Mr. and Mrs. Timothy Kerry
> regret that they are unable to accept
> Mr. and Mrs. Smith's
> kind invitation for the tenth of December

"Monday, December the tenth" is sometimes used, but the wording above is best form.

In accepting an invitation, the day and hour must be repeated so that, in case of mistake, it may be rectified and prevent one from arriving on a day when one is not expected. But in declining an invitation, it is not necessary to repeat the hour.

MORE THAN ONE HOSTESS

If the names of two or more hostesses appear on an invitation, the envelope is addressed to the one at whose house the party is to take place; or, if it is to be at a club or hotel, to all the names exactly as in the invitation. The acceptance usually reads:

> Mrs. Donald Lovejoy
> accepts with pleasure
> the kind invitation of
> Mrs. White and
> Mrs. Black and
> Mrs. Grey
> for Tuesday, the tenth of November
> at half after four o'clock

If, however, only one of the hostesses is known to you, it would be quite permissible to accept "your kind invitation for Tuesday the tenth—" and, leaving out all names, address the envelope to whichever hostess happens to be your friend.

Or you may write numerals: Tuesday, November 10th.

INVITATION SENT BY AN ORGANIZATION

To meet
Mrs. Leigh Notable

The X Y Chapter
of
X Y Z
requests the pleasure of your company
on Monday, the twenty-third of February
at four o'clock
at the X Y House
2 Campus Row

VISITING CARD INVITATIONS

With the exception of invitations to house parties, dinners and luncheons, the writing of notes is past. For an informal dance, musicale, picnic, for a tea to meet a guest, or for bridge, a lady uses her ordinary visiting card. The following examples are absolutely correct in every detail—including the abbreviations.

To meet
Miss Millicent Gilding
MRS. JOHN KINDHART
Tues. Jan. 7.
Dancing at 10. o'ck.
350 PARK AVENUE

INVITATIONS AND REGRETS

> *Wed. Jan. 8.*
> *Bridge at 4. o'ck.*
>
> MRS. JOHN KINDHART
>
> *R.s.v.p.*
>
> 350 PARK AVENUE

Strictly speaking, answers to invitations written on visiting cards should be worded in the third person as though the invitation were engraved. But to an intimate friend a return card saying

> *With pleasure!*
> *Wednesday at 4.*
>
> Mrs. Robert Gilding, junior
>
> 1000 Fifth Avenue

is sensible, and fundamentally quite as correct as the invitation.

TELEGRAPHED INVITATIONS

That telegrams are rapidly taking the place of telephoned as well as written invitations sent out by hosts and hostesses of highest fashion is not surprising. In the first place nothing is simpler than handing a list of names with a form note to a telegraph operator and letting the telegraph company do the rest. Or for that matter, telephoning a message and fifty names to the telegraph office takes at most five minutes, whereas calling each of the fifty numbers (including busy signals and messages left for those not at home, and enforced conversation with those who, answering themselves, talk for half an hour) would take anywhere from twice to ten times as long as writing notes.

But the greatest advantage of telegraphing is that, when giving a spur-of-the-moment party, everyone not only answers but answers at once.

THE BACHELOR'S INVITATIONS

The bachelor's invitations are the same as those sent out by a hostess. There is absolutely no difference. He telephones himself or else his butler or waitress telephones, "Will Mr. and Mrs. Norman dine with Mr. Bachelor on Wednesday?" Or he writes a note or uses the engraved dinner card. In giving a party of any size, it is correct for him to write on his visiting card, regardless of his address.

> *Saturday April 7.*
> *at 4. o'ck.*
>
> **Mr. Anthony Dauber**
>
> *To hear Tonini play.* **Park Studio**

INFORMAL INVITATIONS AND THEIR ANSWERS

Informal invitations are those which are written in the second person, and, though called "informal" because they have greater latitude than the utterly prescribed pattern of the third-person invitation and reply, they, too, follow a fairly definite formula. (The *colon* ":" is not used after the form of address in a social note. Either no punctuation or a comma, as you prefer.)

The informal dinner and luncheon invitation is not spaced according to set words on each line, but is written merely in two paragraphs.

Dear Mrs. Smith
    Will you and Mr. Smith dine with us on Thursday, the seventh of January, at eight o'clock?
      Hoping so much for the pleasure of seeing you,
                   Very sincerely
                             Caroline Robinson Town

A note written to one person, Miss Mary Bright—"Will you and your brother lunch with us," etc.—is entirely proper, but an envelope addressed to

              Miss Mary Bright
              Mr. Thomas Bright

is very bad, and "Miss Mary Bright and brother" is worse.

THE INFORMAL NOTE OF ACCEPTANCE OR REGRET

Dear Mrs. Town
It will give us much pleasure to dine with you on Thursday the seventh at eight o'clock.
Thanking you for your kind thought of us,
Sincerely yours
Constance Style

Wednesday.

Or

Dear Mrs. Town
We are so sorry that we cannot accept your kind invitation for Saturday because of another engagement.
With many thanks for thinking of us, and hope to see you soon.
Sincerely
Ethel Norman

To more intimate friends

Dear Caroline
Will you and John dine with us next Monday (the eighth) at seven o'clock promptly, and go afterwards to the new Russian opera?
Affectionately
Lucy

Acceptance

Dear Lucy
John says "yes"! and I am simply thrilled at the thought of hearing the new opera and—with you.
With love.
Caroline

Regret

Dear Lucy
John won't.
You were sweet to ask us, and I would love it—but John is working out a new organization, and it is literally keeping him at a desk sixteen hours out of the twenty-four.
Much love, and I know you will understand.
Affectionately
Caroline

Informal

> Dear Sally
>
> Will you and Jack (and the baby and nurse, of course) come out the 28th (Friday) and stay for ten days? Morning and evening trains take only forty minutes, and it won't hurt Jack to commute for the weekdays between the two Sundays! I am sure the country will do you and the baby good, or at least it will do me good to have you here.
>
> With much love.
>
> Affectionately
Ethel

To intimate friends

> Dearest Mary
>
> WHEN will you come? And of course I mean all of you! Don't write me such nonsense as that it is too much to descend upon us five strong! I should be delighted if you were ten! I mean it.
>
> As you know, the house is plain but perfectly comfortable, and you certainly know that seeing the children (and hearing them) about the place is just what Tom and I like best!
>
> So we are back at the beginning.
>
> When? and for how long? The very longest long you can make it! All of July and August, too! Please!
>
> Your devoted
Jane

> Dear George,
>
> How about spending the Fourth with us? From Friday the second to Thursday the eighth—surely you can stay away from the office till Monday the twelfth? Can't you?
>
> Sally

Or Mrs. Gilding, junior, writes

> Dearest Sally
>
> Am I never to see you again? Won't you come out for a week in June? Any one you will. Do! I'll come in and get you the day and hour you say.
>
> Devotedly
Lucy

Answers

> Dearest Lucy
>
> Yes, with joy! Will be waiting June 8 at three. It will be heavenly to see you!
>
> Devotedly
Sally

BRIEF NOTES AT PRESENT IN FASHION

One may write a note on the front page of a small sheet of note paper, quite as typically as on the inside of a folded card.

Dear Alice
    Will you lunch on Monday at 1:30, here?
Affect'ly
Grace

Answer

Dear Grace
    Delighted! 1:30 Monday!
With love
Alice

TYPICAL NOTES OF YOUNGER GENERATION

Cora darling
    Giving big lunch 1:30 Jan. 26. You've GOT to come.
Kit

Answer

    All right darling! I've written it down.
Cora

THE FORMAL INVITATION BY TELEPHONE

Custom, which has altered many ways and manners, has taken away all opprobrium from the formal invitation by telephone. Such messages, however, follow very closely a prescribed form.

"Is this Lenox 0000? Will you please ask Mr. and Mrs. Smith if they will dine with Mrs. Grantham Jones next Tuesday, the tenth, at eight o'clock?

"Mrs. Jones' telephone number is Regent 4-0011."

The answer

"Mr. and Mrs. Huntington Smith regret very much that they will be unable to dine with Mrs. Jones on Tuesday, the tenth, as they are engaged for that evening."

Or

"Please tell Mrs. Jones that Mr. and Mrs. Smith are very sorry they will be unable to dine with her next Tuesday, and thank her for asking them."

Or

"Please tell Mrs. Jones that Mr. and Mrs. Smith will dine with her on Tuesday, the tenth, with pleasure."

The formula is the same, whether the invitation is to dine or lunch, or play bridge or tennis or golf, or motor, or go on a picnic.

"Will Mrs. Smith play bridge with Mrs. Grantham Jones this afternoon at the Country Club, at four o'clock?"

"Hold the wire, please. * * * Mrs. Smith will play bridge with pleasure at four o'clock."

REMINDER CARDS, AND NOTES

When invitations have been telephoned, cards reminding guests of their acceptance are in good usage and very sensible. Those who entertain a great deal have cards engraved with blank spaces to fill in with the word "lunching," "dining," "playing bridge" or whatever.

> To remind you
> that you are..................
> with Mrs. John Smith
> on............ at ...... o'clock

Otherwise you write on your visiting card: "To remind you—Wednesday 10th, 7:30."

For a more important engagement, one perhaps writes a note.

Dear Helen

Just to remind you that you and Dick are coming here on the sixth. Will meet you on arrival of the 5.10!

Love,
Muriel

12

Teas and Other Afternoon Parties

Except at a wedding, the function strictly understood by the word "reception" went out of fashion, in New York at least, during the reign of Queen Victoria, and its survivor is a public or semi-public affair presided over by a committee, rather than a hostess or host.

The very word "reception" brings to mind an aggregation of personages, very formal, very learned, among whom the ordinary mortal cannot do other than wander helplessly in the labyrinth of the specialist's jargon at a varnishing-day reception, or be obliged to say something appreciative to an explorer and not know where or what he explored, or to a celebrated author and not have the least idea whether he wrote detective stories or expounded Taoism!

Yet the difference between a reception and a tea is one of atmosphere only, like the difference in furnishing twin houses. A reception always takes itself seriously. A tea, no matter how formal it pretends to be, is friendly and inviting. One does not go to be impressed or instructed, but merely to see one's friends and be seen by them.

THE AFTERNOON TEA WITH DANCING

The afternoon tea with dancing is today's substitute for yesterday's débutante ball. It may equally well be given to introduce a new daughter-in-law.

Before the war, the engraved invitations were usually

Mrs. Grantham Jones
Miss Muriel Jones
At Home
on Tuesday, the third of December
from four until seven o'clock
The Fitz-Cherry

Dancing

Today, such invitations, especially those to introduce the brides of sons, are usually written on a visiting card of the hostess with "To meet Mrs. So-and-So" across the top.

> To meet Mrs. Grantham Jones, Jr.
>
> Mrs. Grantham Jones
>
> Tuesday, Dec. 3.
> from 4 until 7 O'clock
> Tea and dancing

Formerly it was customary to invite the hostess' complete "general" visiting list, but today the list is usually limited to the special friends of the hostess and all the young people possible to think of. And since houses large enough for dancing are comparatively few, and growing fewer, a coming-out tea is usually given at the clubhouse or in the small ballroom of a hotel. Remember, however, it is a mistake to choose too big a room, because too much space for too few people gives an effect of emptiness which always is suggestive of failure; also one must not forget that an undecorated room needs more people to make it look "trimmed." Although a "crush" may be unpleasant, it always gives the effect of "success."

The arrangements for a tea with dancing are much the same as for a dance. A grouping of palms behind which the musicians sit (unless they sit in a gallery), perhaps a few festoons of green here and there, and the débutante's own bouquets banked on tables near where she stands to receive form the typical decoration.

Whether in a public ballroom or a private drawing room, the curtains over the windows are drawn and the lights lighted as though for a dance in the evening.

(For details see Chapters 13 and 14.)

AFTERNOON TEA MENU IS LIMITED

Only tea, chocolate, bread and cakes are served. There may be all sorts of sandwiches, made with rolls and made with bread. There may be layer cake, sliced cake and all imaginable kinds of little cakes, but nothing else, or it becomes a "reception." (Hot breads are reserved for the informal varieties of teas.) At the end of the table or on a separate table nearby, there are bowls or pitchers of orangeade or lemonade or punch for the dancers, exactly as at an evening dance.

Guests go to the table and ask whoever is "pouring" for chocolate or tea and help themselves to sandwiches or cakes, which they eat standing at the table—with cup and saucer held in the left hand.

AFTERNOON TEAS WITHOUT DANCING

Afternoon teas without dancing are given in honor of visiting celebrities or new neighbors or engaged couples, or to "warm" a new house, or for a house guest from another city; or, most often, for no reason other than that the hostess feels hospitably inclined.

The invitation is a visiting card of the hostess with "To meet Mrs. So-and-So" across the top of it and "Jan. 10, Tea at 4 o'clock" in the lower corner, opposite the address.

TABLE HOSTESSES POUR

At a tea of this description, tea and chocolate may be passed on trays or poured by two intimate friends of the hostess. The ladies who "pour" are always especially invited beforehand, and are always chosen because they can be counted on for gracious manners to everyone and under all circumstances.

It does not matter that a guest going into the dining room does not know the deputy hostesses who are "pouring." It is perfectly correct for a stranger to say, "May I have a cup of tea?"

The one pouring should smile and answer, "Certainly! How do you like it? Strong or weak?"

If the visitor says "Weak," she adds *boiling* water and, watching for the guest's indication, adds cream or lemon or sugar. Or, preferring chocolate, the guest asks the hostess at the other end of the table for a cup of that. If either hostess is surrounded with people, she smiles as she hands it out, and that is all. But if she is unoccupied and her momentary "guest by courtesy" is alone, she makes a few pleasant remarks. Very likely when asked for chocolate she says, "How nice of you! I have been feeling very neglected. Everyone seems to prefer tea." Whereupon the guest ventures that people are afraid of chocolate because it is so fattening or so hot. After an observation or two about the beauty of the table or how good the little cakes look, the guest finishes her chocolate.

If the table hostess is still unoccupied, the guest smiles and slightly nods "Good-by;" but if the hostess is talking with someone else, she who has finished her chocolate leaves unnoticed.

If another lady coming into the dining room is a friend of one of the table hostesses, the new visitor draws up a chair, if there is room, and drinks her tea or chocolate at the table. But as soon as she has finished, she should give her place to a later arrival. Except in a public tea room, a tea table is seldom set with places. But at a table where deputy hostesses are pouring, and especially at a tea that is informal, a number of chairs are usually ready to be drawn up for those who like to take their tea at the table.

Whether or not strangers standing in a queue or at the table in the dining room at very large and formal entertainments speak to each other, depends upon the friendliness or aloofness (possibly shyness) of individuals. But at a luncheon, a dinner, or any small party, the roof of a friend serves as an introduction, and strangers who find themselves *seated* together always talk.

THE EVERYDAY AFTERNOON TEA TABLE

The everyday afternoon tea table is familiar to everyone; there is not the slightest difference in its service, whether in the tiny band-box house of the newest bride, or in the drawing room of Mrs. Worldly of Great Estates. Always the tea tray stands on a low table in front of the hostess, who pours. Correctly, the tea table should be of the drop-leaf variety because it is more easily moved than a solid one.

Correctly, its height should be five or six inches above the knees of the hostess, which depends upon the height of the chair or sofa that she always sits upon. It is usually about 26 inches high, between 24 to 26 inches wide, and from 27 to 36 inches long, or it may be oval or oblong. A table that has a second deck above the main table is not good because the tea tray perched on the upper deck is neither graceful nor convenient. Nor is a tea wagon in best taste for *tea!* It is however excellent for cold drinks of all sorts which require a quantity of bottles, pitchers, and glasses (one of chromium and glass preferred).

CORRECT EQUIPMENT OF TEA TABLE

But to return to the table prepared for the proper serving of tea. Except on a table of chromium and glass or mirror, a cloth must always be first placed on the table before putting down the tray. It may barely cover the table, or it may hang half a yard over each edge. A yard and a quarter is the average size. A tea cloth can be colored, but the conventional one is of white linen, with little or much needlework or lace, or both.

On this is put a tray big enough to hold everything except the plates of food. The tray may be a massive silver one that requires

THE FORMAL AFTERNOON TEA TABLE

Chocolate, either hot or iced, often takes the place of the punch bowl. For a wedding collation the tea service is omitted and the wedding cake added.

THE EVERY-DAY AFTERNOON TEA TABLE

Correctly, the equipment and arrangement of the tea table are as strictly prescribed as in the case of the formal dinner table.

strong arms to be lifted, or it may equally well be of lacquered tin. Many of these lacquered trays are exquisite in design and color. Many of the old Chinese or English ones are also priceless. In any case, on it should be the most important item of the tea equipment—a *practical* kettle in which the water should have been boiling before being brought in, with a spirit lamp under it. If carried by a maid, it is lighted as soon as the tray is down but *never before*, as a terrible accident can too easily occur, through the catching on fire of her apron or dress.

Also on the tray is an empty teapot, a caddy of tea, a tea strainer and slop bowl, cream pitcher and sugar bowl, and, on a glass dish, lemon in slices.

(In a house without any servants the hostess would of course set the tray with everything except the boiling water before her guests arrive, leaving the water kettle on the range in the kitchen. When she is ready for tea, she fills the tea-tray kettle from the kitchen kettle and carries it in.)

As already said—especially in a small house—the tea tray is equally smart if made of modern and not expensive tin, the tea set of china and the water kettle of glass. In fact there is a charm in watching water come to boil through a glass kettle that is entirely lost through the opaqueness of silver.

A pile of cups and saucers and a stack of little tea plates, all to match, with a napkin (about 12 inches square, to match the tea cloth) folded on each of the plates, like the filling of a layer cake, complete the paraphernalia. Each plate is lifted off with its own napkin. Then on the tea table, back of the tray, or on the shelves of a separate "curate," (a stand made of three small shelves each big enough to hold a dish or plate or platter) are three varieties of tea foods.

THINGS PEOPLE EAT AT TEA

The typical variety would be one plate of cake, one of sandwiches, and one of hot bread, but the selection of these items is limited only by the imagination and the skill of the hostess. Many provide no more than crackers or wafers or cookies. Others pile an extra table as well as the curate with toasted crumpets or muffins—cinnamon toast as well as pastry, or cheese-cakes and sandwiches of several varieties. All of which is of less importance to the subject of etiquette than the reminder that certain implements must be provided for certain foods. Small tea forks for pastries or "gooey" cakes and small knives to spread jam and to cut crumpets or English muffins are obviously essential to comfort.

THE ETIQUETTE OF TEA

Correctly, the hostess herself "makes" the tea and pours it.

The most important item of the tea service is boiling water, and plenty of it. The least amount of water not actually bubbling as it is poured over tea leaves turns the flavor to hay! (A fact that not one hotel in a thousand takes note of!) Nothing is easier than tea-making; nothing is rarer than the hostess who knows *how!*

To make good tea. First, rinse the pot with a little boiling water and pour it into a slop bowl. Then put in a rounded teaspoonful of tea leaves or one tea bag for each person—or half this amount if the tea is super-quality. Then pour on enough *actually boiling* water to cover the tea leaves about half an inch. It should steep about five minutes before additional boiling water is poured in. Then pour half tea, half boiling water for those who like it "weak"; pour it straight for those who like it strong.

The requirement of a cup of *good* tea is that it should be too strong without the addition of a little lively boiling water to give it freshness. For half an hour the tea is still good if the cup is rinsed and boiling water poured over half—or a third—of a cupful of the tea. But if the water is not boiling *hard* the stale tea will be vile.

Since the beginning of the war quite a number of hostesses are having tea set on the dining-room table. Martha Kindhart, for instance, thinks it simpler and more comfortable for eight or ten—or even six. Most people, however, have little glass-topped individual tables to hold plates or ash trays or any other things that must otherwise be balanced on their knees placed next to the guests.

When offering a cup, the hostess asks, "How do you like your tea?" Guest answers, "Strong, with lemon and one lump" or "Weak, please, no sugar, quite a lot of cream." And it is poured accordingly, tea in cup first, then water, then sugar, then a slice of lemon, or else little or much cream.

If there are likely to be more than five or six people for tea, water must be kept boiling in the kitchen kettle so that it will quickly again come to a boil in the replenished kettle on the table.

Those sitting near the hostess put out their hands for their cup and saucer. If any ladies are sitting farther off and a gentleman is present, he, of course, rises and takes the tea from the hostess to the guest. He also then passes the "curate," afterward putting it back where it belongs and resuming his seat. If no gentleman is present, a lady gets up and takes her own tea—which the hostess hands her—carries it to her own little individual table, comes back, takes a plate and napkin, helps herself to what she likes and goes to her place. If there are no little tables, she either surreptitiously draws near to any self-offering piece of furniture, or manages as best she can to balance plate, cup and saucer on her lap.

COCKTAILS

When served late in the afternoon, with or instead of tea, cocktails are either made in the pantry and passed around on a tray, or else the makings of several varieties are put out on a big tray or a glass-topped table, or wherever convenient, and people mix their own.

WHAT TO SERVE WITH COCKTAILS

At a "cocktail party" you may serve literally every sort of in-fingers-eaten hors d'oeuvres or appetizers that *you* think taste good and look tempting. Olives (either raw or wrapped in bacon and broiled) or very little sausages, broiled, canapés or thin bread rolled around cheese or bacon, skewered and toasted, or crackers spread with sandwich paste, crabmeat, or lobster in mouthful pieces on little wooden picks with which to dip them in mayonnaise are favorites.

Before a meal, it is not customary to serve a great variety of canapés. One or two varieties of appetizers on one platter are ample.

Cocktails proffered before a meal are either made in the pantry and passed on a tray by a servant, or else mixed and handed around by the host.

SAYING "NO" AT A COCKTAIL PARTY

There should always be at least one kind of non-alcoholic drink, such as tomato juice, for those who do not like the stronger drinks. This is in fact an exaction of good taste which should be underscored, since lack of consideration for those who for one reason or another do not—or cannot—take alcohol is always a source of uneasiness to such abstainers. Moreover, many such people hesitate to accept invitations to parties which they would very much like to go to for the sake of sociability, because they are afraid of being looked upon as "wet blankets" if they are obliged to sit empty-handed. However, should none but alcoholic cocktails be served, it is *not* considered rude to refuse them, unless, of course, the manner of doing so is plainly unfriendly and disapproving.

As to this general subject of saying "No" when we want to, one wonders why so many people who feel embarrassed when refusing cocktails have no hesitation whatever in refusing foods—particularly those to which they are allergic! The reason is probably this: The censorious attitude of those who disapprove of alcohol, no matter how temperate its use, has brought about a connotation of disapproval in its refusal. One may refuse to eat bread or fish or strawberries, and this may cause regret on the part of the hostess who knows that her biscuits are superlatively good or the fish caught but a few hours before the meal, or the strawberries picked at just the right hour of the day in the garden, but no disapproval can possibly be implied on the part of the guest who says, "No, thank you."

Not so many years ago, when diet fads had not come into fashion, and the scientific study of balanced rations, vitamins, and allergics and so on was unknown outside of the laboratories, it was considered very discourteous to refuse whatever one's host or hostess proffered. A well-behaved guest took at least a little of everything passed and ate or drank that little. Today no one is ever expected to eat any items to which one is personally antipathetic. In fact, the increasing present-day use of the word allergic has been more helpful to the acceptance of the phrase "No, thank you," than anything that ever happened.

HOST'S DISCOURTESY, NOT YOURS

As a matter of fact, the real point of etiquette as it concerns the subject of politeness in refusing alcoholic beverages is that the obligation of courtesy is not that of the guest, but of the host and hostess. It is they who are at fault if they serve only alcoholic cocktails and offer a guest who refuses wines or spirits no alternate choice.

In a really well-appointed house, tomato juice or other plain fruit juice is always proffered in addition to whatever other drinkables may be the host's specialty. At table it is now absolutely proper to say, "No, thank you" before any wine is poured into your glass. In fact, the expert servant always asks, "Chablis, Madam?" "Claret, Sir?"

If the host himself urges you, naming a fine vintage, you answer with a wishful look of regret, "Sorry—wish I might!" or "*Very* sorry, no!" or just "No, nothing for me, thank you."

YOUNG PEOPLE AFRAID TO SAY "NO"

The most serious "No, thank you" problem is of course that of young people who are afraid of saying "No" to whatever others suggest, because they fear it may lessen their popularity. Wanting to be popular is natural. It is also natural to go along with the crowd, do what the others are doing, and think what they think. In matters which are not important this is quite the right thing to do. But when an inner small voice says, "Don't do that! It's cheap; it's wrong," then it is time to say "No," and hold on to it. As for permanent popularity —it does not really belong to the sheep, after all.

In school, in college, in society, in politics, or anywhere else, the person who follows a leader into doing things with which his own conscience does not agree is taking the first step, not toward success, but toward being held in contempt even by those whom he follows. A real leader is one who says "No" lightly, and yet this "No" has an immutable finality. Such a person says very little about what he will or won't do. In fact, he rarely forces his opinion upon anyone, but if asked, he gives his answer as truthfully, as uncritically and as briefly as possible—especially if he thinks his opinion may be in serious disagreement with that of the other persons. Such people never lose the confidence of their friends.

"NO" CAN BE MADE AS FRIENDLY AS "YES"

Of course, the obvious point to be made is that frankness must be adjusted to courtesy by means of the warmth of one's manner. It is quite amazing how frank we can be when our manner is sympathetic, eager, or appreciative. We can say "No" and make it sound almost as nice as "Yes." On the other hand, we can say "No" and make it sound cold, critical, and almost as affronting as a blow. We can say, "I'm sorry, no," and make it sound a poignant regret, or as casual and light-hearted as the flitting of a butterfly. Or it can come down upon the sensibilities of others with the weight of a sledge hammer.

The secret of how this is done is first of all an innate attitude by which, while we refuse, we hold no criticism of those who do not refuse. At the very moment we set ourselves up with an "I am better than thou" attitude, we become as intolerable to others as we ourselves are intolerant.

THE GARDEN PARTY

A really formal garden party is as out of key with the picture of today as the blue-flannel below-knee-length bathing suits! They were the two extremes of the gay nineties and not in the picture of modern today.

But since in a book such as this the formal garden party cannot be left out, let us describe the typical one as being like the most elaborate wedding reception imaginable, transplanted from midwinter in a city to midsummer and outdoors. Only the bride seems to be missing from the picture, since all the guests look as though they might be either bridesmaids or mothers of the principals, and, barring the white boutonnières, every man present might be taken for the bridegroom or an usher or the father of the bride. As a background for this replica of a wedding scene, there is, of course, a garden with terraced lawns and marble balustrades. There is always music (sometimes two alternating orchestras); there is a marquee covering an adequate dance floor and another marquee under which is set the most elaborate collation imaginable, and lacking nothing but the bridal cake. Here and there about the lawn are large gay-colored umbrella tents with chairs and tables beneath them.

If it should rain, the sides of the marquees are necessarily dropped at least on the windward side, and awning corridors connect the marquees with the veranda of the house, so that, although appreciation of the garden may be dampened, the afternoon party continues just the same. It is possible, of course, that garden parties of this elaboration may somewhere at some time come back. But it is not easy to imagine where or when. Meanwhile, however, garden parties have been replaced by less formal entertainment.

PARTIES IN THE GARDEN

The difference between a party in the garden and a real garden party is much the same as that between a simple buffet supper and a dinner of ceremony. If many people are expected, a large table is set as for an afternoon tea, outdoors—the weather permitting—or else on the veranda or in the dining room, and the accent is on cold beverages. Tea is iced and has plenty of mint and usually lemon, and perhaps other fruit juices are added. If there is chocolate, it is cold and poured into glasses with whipped cream. Food consists of nothing but breads and cakes. These can be of whatever variety, and as many or few as one may choose. Usually there are thin sandwiches cut either in diamond or heart shapes but not otherwise fancy.

A very pleasant hospitality that began to be popular before the war was that of being at home in the garden on several successive Saturdays or Sundays, or possibly on several days in the same week—the object being to show the garden when it is at its very best. There is a period in almost every garden when it is just a little more beautiful than it is likely to be at another time. These invitations, usually written on visiting cards, are "At home in the garden" (or other similar writing) and then the dates and hours:

> Mon. Wed. and Sat.
> July 20-22-25
> between 5 and 6 o'ck

13

Balls and Dances

ALTHOUGH great private balls have of course been unknown during the war, this book would be incomplete were descriptions of all balls of splendor omitted. Therefore, this is the way one is given.

A HOSTESS PREPARES TO GIVE A BALL

If she does not put all the arrangements into the hands of a social specialist, the hostess goes to see the manager of the hotel she prefers, or of other suitable assembly rooms, and finds out which evenings are available. She then telephones—or most likely the manager telephones for her—and engages the two best orchestras for the evening on which both the orchestras and the ballroom are at her disposal. Of the two, music is of more importance than choice of place. You cannot give a ball or a dance that is anything but a dull promenade if you have dull music.

At all balls there must be two orchestras, so that the moment one finishes playing the other begins. At dignified private balls, dancers do not stand in the middle of the floor and clap as they do elsewhere because the music does not stop until the ball is over.

Having secured the music and engaged the ballroom, dressing rooms and lounge or other rooms—where guests can talk and smoke and very probably play cards—as well as the main restaurant after it is closed to the public, the hostess next makes out her list and orders and sends out her invitations.

INVITATIONS

The fundamental difference between a ball and a dance is that, while only those of approximately one age are asked to a dance, ball invitations include all the personal friends of the hostess, no matter what their age.

If the ball is for a débutante, all the débutantes whose mothers are on the "general visiting list" are asked, as well as all young dancing men in these same families. All the débutante's own friends are of course asked, but older members of their families are not necessarily included.

WHEN A LIST IS BORROWED

A lady who has a débutante daughter, but who has not given any general parties for years—or ever—and whose daughter, having been away at boarding school or abroad, has therefore very few friends of her own, must necessarily, in sending out invitations to a ball, take the list of young girls and men from a friend or a member of her family.

In a small community it is especially cruel to leave out any of the young people whose friends are all invited, and a hostess can, of course, be as generous as she chooses in allowing extra invitations for friends of friends.

ASKING FOR AN INVITATION TO A BALL

It is always permissible to ask a hostess if you may "bring" a dancing man who is a stranger to her; men who dance are always an asset, and the more the better, but it is rather difficult to ask for an invitation for an extra girl unless she is to be "looked after" by the person asking for the invitation. In that case the hostess is delighted to write her. Invitations for older people are rarely asked for. Nor are invitations ever asked for persons whom the hostess already knows. This is a definitely established rule of etiquette which assumes that she would have sent them an invitation had she cared to. It is, however, not at all out of the way for an intimate friend to remind her of someone who, in receiving no invitation, has more than likely been overlooked.

DECORATIONS

Ball decorations have on occasions been literally astounding, but as a rule no elaboration is undertaken other than greens in corners and trailing vines wherever most effective.

THE BALL BEAUTIFUL

Certain sounds, perfumes, places always bring associated pictures to mind. Restaurants, Paris! Distinguished audiences, London! The essence of charm in society, Rome! Beguiling and informal joyousness, San Francisco! The delightful afternoon visit, Washington! Unlimited amusements, New York! Beautiful balls, Boston!

There are three reasons (probably more) why the balls in Boston have always had what can be described only by the word "quality."

First: Best Society* in Boston, having kept its social traditions intact, has preserved a quality of unmistakable cultivation.

Second: Boston hostesses of position have never failed to demand

---

* For definition of "Best Society," see letter at beginning of this book.

BALLS AND DANCES

of those who would remain on their party lists something of the "grand manner" characteristic of every lady and gentleman.

Third: Boston's older ladies and gentlemen always dance at balls, and the fact that older ladies of distinction dance with dignity has an inevitable effect upon younger ones, so that dancing at balls has not degenerated into the vulgarities of wriggling contortions.

The extreme reverse of a "smart" Boston ball is one—no matter where—which has a roomful of people who dance like Apaches or jiggling music-box figures, and who scarcely suggest an assemblage of even decent—let alone well-bred—people.

SUPPER

The sit-down supper is the most elaborate ball supper of today. But a buffet supper that begins at one and continues until three or later, and to which people go when they feel like it, is in highest fashion. A sit-down supper is always served in the restaurant, which is closed to the public at one o'clock; the entrance is then curtained or shut off from the rest of the hotel. The tables are decorated with flowers and the supper service opened for the ball guests. Guests sit where they please, either "making up a table," or a man and his partner finding a place wherever there are two vacant chairs. At a private ball guests do not pay for anything or tip the waiters because the restaurant is for the time being the private dining room of the host and hostess.

Suppers are no longer as elaborate. Years ago no balls were given without champagne at supper. In fact, champagne is still one of the heaviest items of expenditure, especially at small dances given by older or young married groups for themselves.

There is always an enormous glass bowl of punch or orangeade—sometimes two or three bowls, each containing a different iced drink—in a room adjoining the ballroom. And in very cold climates it is the thoughtful custom of some hostesses to have a cup of hot chocolate or bouillon offered each departing guest. This is an especially welcome attention at a holiday dance in the country to those who have a long drive home.

A DANCE

A dance is merely a ball on a smaller scale. Fewer people are asked to it and it usually has simpler decorations and provisions.

But the real difference is that invitations to balls always include older people—as many as if not more than younger ones—whereas invitations to a dance for a débutante, for instance, include none but very young girls and young men; or, if the dance is given by a hostess for herself, it includes only her personal group of intimate friends.

A dance, as well as a ball, may be given in the banquet room or smaller ballroom of a hotel, or in the assembly or ballroom of a club.

Simple dances as well as other informal parties will be found in Chapter 32 on Simple Party-Giving.

BALL OR FORMAL DANCE IN A PRIVATE HOUSE

For a ball there is always an awning and a red carpet down the front steps of the house. A chauffeur at the curb opens the car doors. If there is a great crush, there is a detective in the hall to investigate any one who does not have himself announced to the hostess. In fact, it has become customary in New York and other big cities to have admission cards engraved and sent to all those who have accepted.

All the necessary appurtenances, such as awning, red carpet, coat-hanging racks, ballroom chairs, as well as crockery, glass, napkins, waiters and food, are supplied by hotels or caterers. In houses like the Gildings', footmen's liveries to match those of their own footmen are always supplied to the caterer's men. In other words, fifteen of the twenty footmen in "Gildings' liveries" who wait at big parties are caterer's men and five, or fewer, their own.

Unless a house has a ballroom (which practically none has today), the room selected for dancing must have all the furniture moved out of it; and if there are adjoining rooms and the dancing room is not especially big, it adds considerably to the floor space to put no chairs around it. Those who dance seldom sit around a ballroom, anyway, and the more informal grouping of chairs in the hall or library is a better arrangement than the wainscot row or wallflower exposition grounds. The floor, it goes without saying, must be smooth and waxed.

THE HOSTESS RECEIVES

The hostess must be ready to receive on the stroke of the hour specified in her invitations. If the ballroom opens on a foyer at the head of a stairway, she usually receives at this place. Otherwise she ceives in the ballroom near the door of entrance.

THE HOSTESS AT A BALL

Guests arriving are announced, as at an afternoon tea, and after shaking hands with the hostess, they pass on. A man who has received an invitation through a friend is usually accompanied by the friend, who presents him. Otherwise, when the butler announces him to the hostess, he says, "Mrs. Norman asked you if I might come." And the hostess shakes hands and says, "How do you do. I am very glad to see you."

THE PERFECT HOST

The duty of seeing that guests are looked after, that shy youths are presented to partners, that shyer girls are not left on the far wallflower outposts, that the dowagers are taken in to supper, and that elderly gentlemen are provided with good cigars in the smoking-room, falls to the "perfect host."

BALLROOM ETIQUETTE

A ballroom is still the one background against which gentlemen and ladies behave with almost exaggerated decorum. Ladies do not and women must not sit with crossed knees lolling against their chairs. Properly a lady doesn't lean back at all. Neither a man nor a woman can smoke in a ballroom without destroying the distinction of the whole assemblage.

But even so, an onlooker at any modern ball is too often impressed with the utter gracelessness of the young people who walk across a ballroom floor. The athletic young woman of today strides across the ballroom floor as though she were on the golf course; the happy-go-lucky one ambles—shoulders stooped, arms swinging, hips and head in advance of chest; others trot, others shuffle, others make a rush for it. The young girl who can walk across a room with grace is rare.

Older gentlemen still give their arms to older ladies in all "promenading" at a ball, since the customs of a lifetime are not broken by one short and modern generation. Those of today walk side by side, except when going to supper. At public balls, when there is a grand march, the lady always takes her partner's right arm.

DISTINCTION VANISHED WITH COTILLION

The glittering display of tinsel satin favors that used to be the featured and gayest decoration of every ballroom is gone; the cotillion leader, his hands full of "seat checks," his manners a cross between those of Lord Chesterfield and a traffic policeman, is gone; and much of the distinction that used to be characteristic of the ballroom is gone with the cotillion. There is no question that a cotillion was prettier to look at than a mob scene of dancers crowding each other for every few inches of progress.

The reason why cotillions were conducive to good manners was that people were on exhibition, where now they are unnoticed components of a general crowd. When only a sixth, at most, of those in the room danced while others had nothing to do but watch them, it was only natural that those "on exhibition" should dance as well as they possibly could, and since their walking across the room and asking others to dance by "offering a favor" was also watched, grace of deportment and correct manners were not likely to deteriorate.

USHERS AT A BALL—OR DANCE

The hostess who would insure the success of a dance of any size chooses from among the young men whom she knows best a number who are tactful and self-possessed to act as ushers. They are distinguished by white boutonnières like those worn by ushers at a wedding as deputy hosts. They must see that wallflowers are not left decorating the seats in the ballroom, and it is also their duty to relieve a partner who has too long been planted beside the same "rosebud."

The ushers have little chance to follow their own inclinations, and unless the "honor" of being chosen by a prominent hostess has some measure of compensation, the appointment—since it may not be refused—is a doubtful pleasure. An usher has the right to introduce any man to any girl without knowing either one of them personally, and without asking permission. He may also ask a girl (if he has a moment to himself) to dance with him, whether he has ever met her or not, and he can also leave her promptly, because any "stag" called upon by an usher must dance. The usher in turn must release every "stag" he calls upon by substituting another, and the second by a third, and so on. In order to make a ball "go," meaning to keep everyone dancing, the ushers have on occasions to spend the entire evening in relief work.

At a ball where there are ushers, a girl standing or sitting alone would at once be rescued by one of them, and a rotation of partners presented to her. If she is "hopeless"—meaning a poor dancer—even the ushers are helpless! The answer is of course that she must either learn to dance or seek her popularity otherwise.

On the other hand, on an occasion when none of her friends happen to be present, the greatest belle of the year can spend an equally distressing evening.

THE DANCE PROGRAM

The program or dance-card has some undeniable advantages. A girl can give as many dances as she chooses to whomever she chooses; and a man can be sure of having not only many but uninterrupted dances with the one he mosts wants to be with—provided "she" is willing. Why the dance-card is unheard of at private balls is probably because the youth of today does not care to take his pleasure on schedule. He likes to dance when the impulse moves him; he also likes to be able to stay or leave when he pleases. In New York there are often two or three dances given on the same evening, and he likes to drift from one to the other just as he likes to drift from one partner to another, or not dance at all if he does not want to. A man who writes himself down for the tenth dance must be eagerly appearing on the stroke of the first bar. And if he does not engage his partners busily at the opening of the evening, he cannot dance at all—he may not want to, but he hates not being able to.

So again we come back to the problem of the average young girl, whose right it is, because of her youth to be light-heartedly happy—and not to be terrified, wretched and neglected. The one and only solution seems to be for her to belong to a group.

THE FLOCK SYSTEM OR ANY OTHER GROUP IDEA

If a number of young girls and young men come together—better yet, if they go everywhere together, always sit in a flock, always go to supper together, always dance with one another—they not only have a good time, but they are sure to be popular with drifting odd men also. If a man knows that, having asked a girl to dance, one of her group will inevitably "cut in," he is eager to dance with her. Or if he can take her "to the others" when they have danced long enough, he is not only delighted to be with her for a while but to sit with her "and the others" off and on throughout that and every other evening, because since there are always "some of them together" he can leave them again the moment he chooses.

A certain group sits in precisely the same place in a ballroom, to the right of the door, or the left, or in a corner. One might almost say they form a little club (a doe club to balance the stag line); they dance as much as they like, but come back "home" between whiles. They all go to supper together, and whether individuals have partners or not is scarcely noticeable, not even known by themselves.

"CUTTING IN"

When one of the "stags" standing in the doorway sees a girl whom he wants to dance with dance past, he darts forward, lays his hand on the shoulder of her partner, who relinquishes his place in favor of the newcomer, and a third in turn does the same to him.

When "cutting in," the following rules must be observed:

1. The partner who was first dancing with a girl must not cut back on the man who took her from him. He can cut in on a third man if he wants to, especially if he is "giving her a rush."

2. He must not continue to cut in on the same man when the latter dances with other partners.

For instance, Jim Norman is dancing with Pauline Towne. Basil Newling cuts in. Ollie Gilding cuts in on Newling. Newling must not go and cut in on Jim Norman, who is now dancing with Constance Style. Having cut in on Norman once, he if possible avoids cutting in on him again too soon.

THE REFUSAL TO DANCE

If a girl is sitting in another room, or on the stairs, with a man alone, a second one should not interrupt, or ask her to dance. If she is sitting in a group, he can go up and ask her, "Don't you want to dance some of this?" She then either smiles and says, "Not just now—I am very tired," or if she likes him, she may add, "Come and sit with us!"

To refuse to dance with one man and then immediately dance with another is an open affront to the first one—excusable only if he was intoxicated or otherwise actually offensive so that the affront was justifiable. But under ordinary circumstances, if she is "dancing," she must dance with everyone who asks her; if she is "not dancing," she must not make exceptions.

A girl who is dancing may not refuse to change partners when another "cuts in." This is the worst phase of the "cutting in" custom; those who particularly want to dance together are often unable to take a dozen steps before being interrupted. Once in a while a girl will shake her head "No" to a "stag" who darts toward her. But that is considered rude. In certain communities, a girl dancing with her eyes shut is recognized as signaling that she does not want to be "cut in on." This is an excellent practice, but not one to be followed either often or for too long a time. This is done sometimes to give those who dance well together a chance to enjoy at least one long dance.

At a public ball or cabaret—or wherever "cutting in" is not practiced—it is always the privilege of the girl to stop dancing; a man is supposed to dance on and on, until she—or the music—stops.

Another unhappy phase of cutting in is that the man with whom she dances best invariably makes her own dancing conspicuously graceful, and therefore every stag in the room wants to cut in. On the other hand, a man who dances like a jumping-jack, stamping on her toes, is not only a torture to her but makes her seem almost as awkward as he, and no one comes to her rescue. A wise girl therefore stops dancing at once, saying, "Let's sit out the rest of this dance."

ASKING FOR A DANCE

When a man is introduced to a girl, he says, "May I have some of this?" or "Would you care to dance?" She either replies, "Certainly" or "Yes, I'd like to very much" or usually she says nothing but gets up, or turns to him, and dances. At the end of the dance, whether it

BALLS AND DANCES

has lasted one minute or sixty, the man says, "Thank you!" Sometimes he adds, "That was wonderful!" If they have danced only a few steps, she says nothing when cut in on unless she says, "Sorry" so low that the one cutting in does not hear. At the end of quite a long dance, when he says, "Thank you" she also says, "Thank you" (generally accented, "thank *you*") or possibly, "Thank you too."

A girl never asks a man to dance, or to go to supper with her, though she may, if she is one of a "flock," say, "Come and sit at our table!" This however would not imply that in sitting at "their" table he is supposed to sit next to her.

In asking a girl to go to supper, a man says, "May I take you to supper?" He should never say, "Have you a partner?" as she is put in an awkward position in having to admit that she has none, and is "left rather flat" if he says nothing about having supper with him.

A BALL IS NOT A DANCING SCHOOL

Since a girl may not without rudeness refuse to dance with a man who "cuts in," a man who does not know how to dance is inexcusably inconsiderate if he "cuts in" on good dancers. If at home, or elsewhere, a girl volunteers to "teach" him, that is another matter, but the ballroom is no place to practice.

PUBLIC BALLS

When a ball is a ball given for a benefit or charity, tickets are sold to the public, either at hotels or at the house of the secretary of the committee. A properly brought-up young girl does not go to a public ball without a chaperon. This is one of the few occasions where this almost forgotten person makes a temporary return to office.

SUPPER CLUBS AND CABARETS

In London, supper clubs are "clubs" in reality; but, with very few exceptions, those in America are merely restaurants to which the public goes after the theater. People sit at small tables ranged around a small dancing floor space upon which a short vaudeville performance is given. Before and after the performance there is general dancing.

Those sitting at the same table dance only with each other; there is no interchange of cordialities between the groups at different tables.

These clubs come properly under the head of restaurants, for which details of behavior are to be found in Chapter 8.

14

The Débutante

"Presenting a débutante to society" has a quaintly archaic flavor, reminiscent of social customs long past. And yet it is not at all out of order for a present-day mother to give whichever of these various entertainments she may choose for her daughter's "coming out" (or being "presented to society").* The most elaborate of these, possible only to parents of wealth, is a ball. Less elaborate, and far more popular, is a small dance which "presents" the débutante to her own friends. Third, is a tea dance. Sending out a mother's visiting card, with her daughter's name below her own to announce to the world that the daughter is eligible for invitations is now extinct.

A BALL FOR A DÉBUTANTE

The ball for a débutante is the typical ball! The débutante "receives" standing beside her mother or whoever else may be hostess and furthest from the entrance, whether that happens to be on the latter's right or left. As they enter, the guests approach the hostess first, who, as she shakes hands with each, turns to the débutante and says, "My daughter" or "You remember Cynthia, don't you?" or merely, "Cynthia" or "My daughter."

Each arriving guest shakes hands with the débutante as well as with the hostess; if there is a queue of people coming at the same time, there is no need of saying anything beyond "How do you do?" and passing on as quickly as possible. If there are no others entering at the moment, each guest makes a few pleasant remarks—for instance, how beautiful the débutante's bouquets are. A friend of her mother probably says, "You look too lovely, Cynthia dear" or "Your dress is enchanting!"

Cynthia's particular friends are, of course, apt to tell her that her dress is wonderful or more likely, "simply divine."

It is customary in most cities to send a débutante a bouquet at her "coming-out" party. They may be "bouquets" really, or baskets or other decorative flowers, and are sent by relatives, friends of the family, her father's business associates, as well as by younger men who are her friends. These "bouquets" are always banked around the

---

* During the war the only large débutante parties are those given by a number of parents together for their débutante daughters.

THE DÉBUTANTE

place where she stands to receive. The débutante usually holds one of the bouquets while receiving, sometimes the same one, sometimes several in succession.

THE FRIENDS OF THE DÉBUTANTE RECEIVE

At a ball, where the guests begin coming about half past ten, the débutante must stand beside the hostess and "receive" until at least twelve o'clock—later if guests continue to arrive.

At all coming-out parties, the débutante invites a few of her best girl friends to receive with her. Being asked to "receive" is a form of expression merely, as they never stand in line, and other than wearing their prettiest clothes and thus adding to the picture, they have no "duties" beyond that of their own amusement.

AT SUPPER

The débutante goes to supper with a partner whom she herself chooses. Very likely he has spoken for the privilege. But whether he has or not, she always makes up her own table, which includes her most intimate friends. Her table is usually in the center of the dining room, and somewhat larger than the other tables surrounding it. Also, a card on it says "reserved." If the supper is a buffet one, the débutante's special group sit together wherever they find space.

The afternoon tea dance to introduce a débutante is described in the chapter on Teas, and the very small dance needs little comment, because, except for size and decoration, its pattern is precisely the same.

When the dance or tea is given in a private house, most of the furniture is, of course, moved out.

THE DÉBUTANTE'S DRESS

At a ball, the débutante wears her very prettiest evening dress. Old-fashioned sentiment prefers that it be white and that it ought to suggest something light and airy and gay and, above all, young. For one to whom white is unbecoming, a color is perfectly suitable as long as it is not scarlet or Yale blue, and on no account black, no matter how sophisticatedly *chic* she thinks she would look in it.

At an afternoon tea the débutante wears a semi-evening dress. Her mother wears an afternoon dress, not an evening one. Both mother and daughter wear gloves, and neither they, nor the young girls receiving, wear hats. (Hats are worn at a wedding reception because it follows a religious service.)

IN CONFIDENCE TO A DÉBUTANTE

Let us pretend a worldly godmother is speaking, and let us suppose that you are a young girl on the evening of your coming-out ball.

You are excited! Of course you are! It is your evening! There is music, and there are lights, and there are flowers everywhere, tables heaped with bouquets—all for you! You have on the dress that of all those you looked at seemed to you the prettiest. Even your mother and married sister have for the moment become, for all their smartness, merely background; and you alone are the center of the picture. Up the wide staircase to the ballroom come those persons of importance—who mean "the world." They are coming on purpose to see you! You can't help feeling that the glittering dresses of the beautiful women, the stiff white shirt-fronts of the men, as well as the best clothes of all the younger people, were all put on for you.

You shake hands and smile to a number of older ladies and gentlemen. Then suddenly, halfway up the stairs you see Betty and Anne and Fred and Ollie. Of course your attention is drawn to them. You are vaguely conscious that the butler is shouting some stupid name you never heard of—that you don't care in the least about. Your mother's voice is saying, "Mrs. Zzzzzz——"

Impatiently you give your hand to someone—you haven't the slightest idea who it is. So far as your interest is concerned, you might as well be brushing away annoying flies. Your smiles are directed to Betty and Anne. As they reach the top of the stairs, you dart forward and enter into an excited conversation, deliberately overlooking a lady and gentleman who, without trying further to attract your attention, pass on. Later in the winter you will perhaps wonder why you alone among your friends were not invited to the cabaret party of the Joneses. The answer is that the lady and gentleman of whom you were so rudely unaware happened to be Mr. and Mrs. Jones. And now you have entirely forgotten that you are a hostess, and furthermore that you have the whole evening, beginning at supper, when you can talk to these friends of yours! You can dance with Fred and Ollie and Jimmy all the rest of the evening; you can spend most of your time with them for the rest of your life if you and they choose. But at a party of which you are the hostess, commonest civility demands that you behave courteously to *your* guests.

It takes scarcely five seconds to listen to the name that is said to you, to look at the one to whom the name belongs, to put out your hand willingly and not as though doing something hateful to you, and with a smile say, "How do you do, Mrs. Jones?" who then passes on. It takes no longer to be cordial and attentive than to be distrait and casual and rude, yet the impression made in a few seconds of time may easily gain or lose a friend. When no other guests are arriving, you can chatter to your own friends as much as you like; but as you turn to greet another, you must show pleasure, not annoyance, in giving him your attention.

THE DÉBUTANTE

A happy attitude to cultivate is to think that strangers are like packages in a grab-bag, and that you can never tell what any of them may prove to be until you know what is inside the outer wrappings!

As friends who have sent you flowers approach, you must thank them; you must also write later an additional note of thanks to older people. But to your family or your own intimate friends, your verbal thanks—if appreciatively made—are sufficient.

A FEW DON'TS FOR DÉBUTANTES

Don't think that because you have a pretty face, you need neither brains nor manners. Don't think that you can be rude to anyone and escape being disliked for it.

Whispering and giggling are always rude. Everything that shows lack of courtesy toward others is rude.

If you would be thought likable, don't nudge or paw or finger people. Don't hold hands or walk arm-about-waist in public. Don't allow anyone to paw you. "Petting" is cheap—and pawing common. Don't hang on anyone for support, unless necessary! Don't walk across a ballroom floor swinging your arms. Don't talk or laugh loudly enough to attract attention, and on no account force yourself to laugh. Nothing is flatter than laughter that is lacking in mirth. If you laugh only because there is something irresistibly funny, the chances are that your laugh will be irresistible too. In the same way, a smile should be spontaneous, because you *feel* happy, and pleasant. Nothing has less allure than a mechanical grimace, as though you were trying to imitate a tooth paste advertisement.

WHERE ARE THE "BELLES" OF YESTERDAY?

In other days a young girl's social success was measured by the number of her partners in a ballroom. Today, although ballroom popularity is still important, it is by no means the beginning and end it used to be.

As repeated several times in this book, the day of the belle is past; beaux belong to the past too. Today is the day of woman's equality with man; and if in proving her equality she has come down from a pedestal, her pedestal was perhaps a theatrical "property" at best and not to be compared for satisfaction with the level ground of the entirely solid position she now occupies.

There was a time when "wallflowers" went night after night to balls where they either sat beside a chaperon or spent the evening in the dressing room in tears. Today a young girl who finds she is not a ballroom success avoids ballrooms and seeks her success otherwhere. She sizes up the situation exactly as a boy might size up his own chances to "make" the baseball or the football team.

TODAY'S SPECIALISTS IN SUCCESS

The girl of today soon discovers, if she does not know it already, that to be a ballroom belle it is necessary first of all to dance really well. A girl may be as beautiful as a young Diana or as fascinating as Circe, but if she is heavy or steps on her first partner's toes, never again will he ask her to dance. And the news spreads in an instant.

The girl of today therefore knows she must learn to dance well, which is difficult, since dancers are born, not made; or she must go to balls for supper only, or not go to balls at all *unless*—she plays a really good game of bridge! In which case, her chances for popularity at the bridge tables, which are at all balls today, are quite as good as though she were a young Pavlowa in the ballroom. Or perhaps she skates, or hunts, or plays a really good game of tennis or golf, each one of which opens a vista leading to popularity and the possibilities for a "good time," which was after all the mainspring of old-fashioned ballroom success.

And since the day of femininity that is purely ornamental is gone by, it is the girl who does things well who finds life full of interests and of friends and of happiness. The old idea that measures a girl's popular success by the number of trousered figures around her has also passed. It is quality, not quantity, that counts; and the girl who surrounds herself with indiscriminate and possibly "cheap" youths excites, not the envy, but the derision of beholders. To the highest type of young girl today it makes very little difference whether, in the inevitable "group" in which she is perpetually to be found, there are more men than girls or the opposite.

This does not mean that human nature has changed—scarcely! There always are and doubtless always will be any number of women who love to parade a beau just as they love to parade a new dress. But the tendencies of the time do not encourage the tasteless parading attitude. It is not considered a triumph to parade a new beau every day any more than to parade a new dress every day, but rather an evidence of lack of discriminating taste.

WOULD YOU KNOW THE SECRET OF POPULARITY?

The secret of popularity is unconsciousness of self, enthusiastic interest in almost anything that turns up, and inward generosity of thought and impulse outwardly expressed in good manners.

15

Popularity and Hospitality at College

To all young men and girls looking forward to their freshman year at college comes a dream of fellowship, and to most of these the dream includes their own popularity. Advice on acquiring this gift is alas confusingly contradictory. On the one hand there is a vivid, impelling gift for salesmanship, an innate sureness; on the other hand there is a complete unself-consciousness that results NOT in self-assertion but in knowledge, or talent, or beauty, or skill, *taken casually*. One who is puffed up with pride in what he has or what he knows or what he can do cannot possibly have a trace of personality that is likable. People who are very much beloved and who make lasting friends wherever they go are invariably the givers of the world, not the takers; invariably, too, they are simple in precisely the way that the truly great are simple.

It is easy and trite to say, "Be kindly disposed toward the whole world. *Care enough about people* to find that which is interesting in each person you meet, and you will at the same time find a world full of friends." No trait brings greater rewards. There is a difference, however, between interest and prying curiosity, between generosity and shiftless squandering. There is a saying that he who is a friend to all men is the friend of none. This is only a half-truth and a misleading one—except when applied to those who, making popularity their goal, shift their opinions to match those of each person they meet, exactly as a chameleon changes color to match each change of background. There is a very nice adjustment between the person of charm and courtesy who shows consideration for the opinions of persons with whom he does not agree by listening with an open mind, and the popularity-seeker who ends by becoming a chronic hand-clapper and what in the vernacular of today is known as a "yes man."

LASTING OR TRANSIENT POPULARITY

Lasting friendships are built on sympathetic qualities of character or on interests shared in common—which draw people together. General popularity is often the result of achievement such as that felt for persons of exceptional skill or talent or courage. But, all things being equal, we are naturally inclined to like those who *show their liking for us* by showing appreciation of our good points and kind tolerance of our shortcomings.

TO MAKE OURSELVES LIKED

To make ourselves liked—in the sense of being much-sought-after persons out in the world in general, in business or in society, or in our circle of friends, which means the same thing—there are two maxims again in confusing contradiction to each other. The first says: Cultivate sensitiveness of perception. The second says: Don't be over-sensitive. Which of course mean that if our sensitiveness have for its object the understanding of the point of view and feelings of others, so that we shall not in any thoughtless way ride roughshod over their sensibilities, *this* is a step in the right direction.

In the first place, most people are not thinking about us at all! In the second, most people are kindly intended toward us unless we have made ourselves dislikable. And there is no surer way of doing this than by being easily "offended" or "hurt."

DON'T WEAR MIRROR-LINED DIVERS' HELMETS

The trouble with permitting ourselves to develop a sense of inferiority is that our vision becomes focused inward. This is not meant to be cruel, but one thing that would vastly increase the popularity of introspective and over-sensitive young girls and women (and men too!) would be to stop getting into a chronic habit of thinking about themselves, as though they kept putting their heads into mirror-lined boxes fastened on like divers' helmets. If only they would look about them and see as much and as far as they possibly can, they would not only be happier themselves but would certainly add to the happiness of their families as well as to the pleasure of their friends.

FRATERNITY HOUSE-PARTY WEEK

With the continual spreading of the co-educational plan it may be that Fraternity House-Party Week will, at almost any moment, come to an untimely end! Meanwhile, however, even though Sally is herself a Co-ed at X-University, she is just as pleased as was her older sister to be invited by Jim to his Fraternity House-Party Week, and just as eager to have a score of questions answered!

The questions obviously are those of how to be a credit to Jim and to be thought attractive by his classmates.

WHAT SHALL SHE WEAR?

The cost of clothes for the occasion is likely to be a real problem. The first question that Sally probably asks her mother, even as she reads the invitation, is, "What can I wear?" And almost always this will be followed by, "Oh, Mother, I *must* have—" and her list may run on through half a dozen formidable items. It may be impossible for her mother to find the extra money for even one new dress, especially if Sally is herself away at college. On the other hand, it may be that Sally's mother could give her everything necessary. Even so Sally should cut her list to the fewest items practical.

It is always tempting to the "new" girl to take along every attractive item she owns or can buy, but she must not lose sight of the fact that she will have to share—with one or maybe two other girls—a very little closet room and drawer space cleared out for their use by the boys, who can't very well move out everything they own! Since the only sensible way to make a list of clothes is to decide what will be suitable for each of the events that will take place, the following schedule is offered as being typical of house-party week.

All the girls are expected to arrive at the house—on Thursday usually—in time to dress for the dinner and dance given at the house on Thursday evening. For this Sally wears the prettiest evening dress she owns. Her clothes, by the way, must have an effect of simplicity suitable to her age. College faculties do not look with approval at bare backs, dripping earrings and obvious make-up. Moreover, the boy who invited Sally to the house party likes her as he remembered her at home and does not want a blasé woman who looks thirty-five in her place.

On Friday morning a plain country type dress will be best to wear all day, either outdoors or in, until late in the afternoon, when it is likely that there will be tea and dancing at some of the houses in Fraternity Row. For this, an afternoon dress of crêpe or fine wool or quite possibly velvet is worn. On Friday evening the guests and their hosts and chaperons dine informally at the house and later go to the formal "Prom" in the gymnasium for everyone at college. At this dance she perhaps wears the same dress without the jacket which she wore with it on Thursday evening. If she happens to have two evening dresses, one old and one new, she would wear the old one to the big dance which is so crowded that clothes are not as conspicuous as at the house dance on Thursday.

Saturday morning is usually spent sleeping late, probably until lunch time. Saturday afternoon is a repetition of Friday. On Saturday evening each fraternity house has "open house" and in many colleges it is customary for the members and guests of one house to go to whichever of the houses they choose. The same dress which was worn for tea is probably worn again.

Since Sunday dinner is to be served at noon, the girls wear the same dresses or suits in which they arrived, and in which they will go back home on an afternoon train.

According to this, one sports dress (at most two), one afternoon dress and one evening dress (or at most two) is the maximum. The warm loose coat she arrives in serves as evening wrap as well as daytime coat.

WHEN WRONG CLOTHES SPELL FAILURE

If the college should happen to be in a warm climate, naturally foularde dresses or cotton prints would take the place of the warm woolens. But at a college that is, let's say, snowbound for many months, it is important that the clothes be warm and that heavy gloves, low-heeled shoes and galoshes be included. Nothing could be more unappealing to a boy than a girl in such unsuitable clothes that she can take no part in any outdoor sports. High-heeled evening slippers in which to walk on frozen snow, and thin fluffy clothes when the thermometer is zero, will not impress any boy as alluring, but will make him wish he hadn't handicapped himself with such a nuisance.

THE "THANK YOU" PRESENT

Except for whatever she may get in the way of clothes, a girl's expenses are limited to those of traveling. It is true that in a number of colleges it is the rather charming custom to contribute toward a "thank you" present donated to the house. Usually one who has been at the previous year's house party fixes a box with a money slit in it and each girl puts into it what she can. No one knows how much each puts in. Whatever amount has been collected is then entrusted to the House President to buy some item for the house—if possible this is marked with the date, and ever afterwards known to the brothers as the present from the girls of that year's party.

DON'TS FOR ALL HOUSE-PARTY VISITORS

To begin with packing: DON'T put off looking at your bag until the last moment, unless it is new or you know it is in perfect condition. DON'T arrive with a shabby, down-at-heel suitcase with handle half off or lock broken, or packed with straps carelessly hanging out, which to every fastidious man will discount the effect of your otherwise lovely appearance as completely as though you wore unshined oxford ties with laces made of knotted-together string. Neat, compact, good-looking luggage will please a man much more than the smartest hat ever bought.

DON'T forget to dress mentally as you pack. Stockings? Now, shoes? Slip? Dress? What goes with it? Belt, clips or flowers or other accessories, bag, etc. No one is less likely to be pleasing than the girl who begins to borrow from the other girls, or sends a boy on repeated trips to the drugstore for the comb or tooth paste or whatever else she forgot. And yet: DON'T make your luggage one inch bigger or one ounce heavier than necessary, unless you are driving your own car! Any girl who brings more than one moderate-sized bag will not add to her popularity either with the others who are going in the same motor or with her host who meets her at the station and perhaps has to carry it for several blocks up a steep hill to the house where she is to stay. DON'T forget that on holiday occasions in small college towns there may not be taxis or cars for more than about one out of ten. Therefore DON'T count on being that "one."

Upon your arrival at the House, DON'T greet the House Mother and other chaperons as though they were inanimate objects upon whom you need waste no attention. DON'T show an alive and interested manner toward the boys and indifference towards the girls. When you are shown to the room which you are to share with another girl, DON'T claim the bed you like best by throwing your bag on it. At least make the gesture of asking the other girl if she cares which she takes.

DON'T take up more than exactly your share of the closet space and drawer space. If you have brought too many things for the space that is yours, you must leave some of them packed in your bag and leave the bag neatly closed.

DON'T monopolize the bathroom. Remember that others are waiting. If you have a bathroom to yourself at home, all the more reason for remembering this. DON'T leave your personal belongings around on all the bedroom furniture. DON'T leave powder scattered over everything. Later, when you pack to leave, DON'T leave powder or smears of lipstick, or hairpins, or curlers in the bureau drawer. Also open a lower drawer wide to be sure you have not left step-ins or other very personal items behind. DON'T pretend to have forgotten an especially fetching scrap of chiffon and lace, in the belief that it will increase John's interest in you. This is a cheap trick and is plainly recognized for what it is. DON'T leave rubbish behind you, either. Remember that the men may have to move back into the house before there is time to have their rooms cleaned. DON'T forget, throughout your stay, to respect the wishes of the House Mother (and other chaperons) as if she were your own mother. Be sure to say good-bye to her and to the others, and to thank them for their many kindnesses.

But now, to turn back to the evening of your arrival—at the time, let us say, when you all congregate before dinner. Introductions will be made by the men rather than by you. At the dinner given in the fraternity house with no outsiders except each brother's "best girl," introductions would very likely be not only by first names but by nick-names: "Sally, this is Slim," and Babe, and so on. But if outsiders are included, then introductions will be "Miss Jones, Mr. —."

DON'T wait for introductions under the house roof. Friendliness should be your natural inclination. It would be too bad to be thought a snob when you are really only shy. If you are afraid you won't make friends, don't forget that nearly every other girl is feeling exactly the same!

If you don't know anything about the boy seated beside you at dinner, ask your personal host (who should be seated at your left) about him first so as to know what to talk to him about. This is cynical advice, but it is as true today as it was in the day of Aspasia that a man is rarely bored if you talk—but with some intelligence—about him. Don't, however, get his abilities confused with those of someone else, and don't in any case lay flattery on with a trowel!

At the dances, greet the chaperons as though you liked them. The moment of enthusiastic attention that courtesy demands is one of the easiest and most rewarding social investments you can make.

DON'T refuse to dance with whoever cuts in.

Throughout the days of your visit, DON'T think only of what you like to do; that is, DON'T insist on playing ping-pong if your host would like you to make a fourth at bridge—unless your bridge is very bad indeed. In this case tell him you would be delighted to play, only you know how sorry everyone else will be if you do. In the same way also don't attempt to go skating or skiing if you have never done either. But otherwise to do whatever the majority suggest is no more than what is expected of you everywhere—unless what is suggested is something which is contrary to your own code of ethics. It does not fit into the present picture, but there is no obligation to drink anywhere at any time—unless you choose to.*

DON'T be jealous of every attention your best boy friend pays to another girl. The more you show your dislike for this "interest," the more jealous he is likely to try to make you. DON'T show that you hate to be teased or you'll be a target for even those who never thought of teasing until you showed how badly you take it.

DON'T show chagrin or disappointment, ever. The fundamental secret of the popular house-guest is to show delight in everything pleasing, and to be blind, deaf and insensible to annoyance or disappointment. Above all, DON'T do anything that can seem unappreciative of the efforts made for your pleasure by the man who is your host. It is not playing the part of a fascinating woman of the world to try to impress him with your powers by attracting one of his classmates; on the contrary, it is the maneuver of an extremely stupid as well as vain young woman, whose lack of loyalty to a brother is resented by every member of his fraternity. The methods of a real siren are quite different. She makes all other men wish they were in

---

* For tact in refusing cocktails, see index.

her host's shoes. Never, therefore, should you risk letting one of them think your treatment of a friend of theirs unfair, even though your motive may be free from guile. DON'T forget that appreciation of your friend is the ace of trumps. Certainly you can like his friends, but chiefly because they *are* his friends.

Above all, DON'T forget that the friendship of other girls is the crown of your own success. Popularity with girls may not make you popular with men, but earning their dislike by treating them with contempt and by trying to take their boy friends will end in ostracism of yourself. The really popular girl is popular with girls as well as boys.

In short, DON'T try to be the house-party coquette in an attempt to see how many of the men you can add to your chain of admirers! It is natural that every man wants the girl he asks to this big social event at his fraternity to be liked by all his brothers. But you must not confuse the friendliness shown you under these circumstances with that which might otherwise be given to you for yourself alone. There is a close bond in the brotherhood that is much stronger than any interest in a strange girl—a fact which every girl should notice and respect.

GRADUATION

Any definite schedule for Commencement week cannot be given, since it necessarily differs in each of our thousands of colleges. But let us say that graduation exercises take place on a Monday. On the Friday preceding, there is probably a senior ball. This is as different in character from all the house-party dances that have preceded it throughout the year as a christening is from a children's party!

Instead of scenes of romance multiplied almost as many times as there are girls or men in college, the Commencement picture is of a festivity that includes the whole family. Parents, grandparents, aunts, uncles, and little brothers and sisters arrive in hordes.

Because visiting families stay either at the hotel or the inn or in the houses of those who take boarders during this period, a graduate's best girl usually comes with his family. Or perhaps she has already made arrangements to go with her own family (if her brother or a relative is also a member of the graduating class), or with an intimate girl friend whose family is taking her. She goes to her friend's fraternity house, of course, to dinner or to afternoon tea or to whatever each house can give for its visitors during this week.

Another typical event of Commencement week is a baseball game on Saturday afternoon. This is either a serious game between the home team and that of a neighboring college, or possibly a burlesque between the present team and picked stars of yesterday. And on Saturday night perhaps a show is put on by the graduates of five or ten or fifteen years back. Or possibly on Saturday evening there is a torchlight parade that ends in dancing around a bonfire made of barrels and boxes into which are thrown the books of whichever subject each student disliked most.

At a small but beautiful college for women, a pageant is always given outdoors at sunset on the verdant campus, from which the sun, sinking into the waters of a distant lake, makes a dazzling horizon against which the departing pageant fades into a processional silhouette. And there are dozens of similar customs, which are carried away year after year in the affectionate memories of the graduates.

The most important event on the week's calendar is the Sunday morning service in chapel, at which the baccalaureate sermon is preached. The sermon is addressed to the students, but the families and friends are expected to be present also. In the afternoon, perhaps, the president of the college and his wife are at home to students and their families, and the rest of this day is spent much as each fraternity, sorority or group has arranged.

Graduation also brings the necessity for observing many details of courtesy, which should be emphasized. A note of thanks written by hand and on note paper must go to everyone who has sent a present either to a young man or to a young woman. This note need not be long, but it should express appreciation and be written as promptly as possible.

"I can't thank you enough, dear Aunt Agatha, for the check you sent me, which will be a wonderful help toward—" whatever it is to be used for; or "Dear Aunt Martha, Thank you for the beautiful flowers you sent me. They could not take your place, but they were a reminder of your loving thought." Or "Dear Uncle John, Your letter was the finest thing possible to receive. And I shall certainly try to do my best in the job you are offering me."

Since invitations to graduation exercises are usually limited to a very small number for each student, the impropriety of sending announcements that say So-and-So will be graduated on such-and-such a day must be stressed. To send them out afterwards, as all other announcements are sent, would be entirely proper.

COLLEGE GIRLS ASK

MAY A GIRL GIVE HER PICTURE TO A BOY IN COLLEGE?

May I give a boy my picture to take to college? If yes, how shall I sign it?

If he is an old friend, there is no reason why you should not give him your picture, but don't sign it, because a name on a girl's picture in a college man's room is likely to challenge the sort of attention that every well-bred man hates. In other words, it makes Mary a conspicuous personality in his room, whereas the face of a girl is as impersonal as the face in any picture on his wall.

IMPROPRIETY OF REFERENCE WITHOUT PERMISSION

Recently I sent in an application blank to the college to which I am going this year. On the blank I gave two references. A friend of mine has since told me that this was a rude thing to do without first asking for permission to use their names.

Your friend is right—unless you know those whose names you used intimately. And even in this case, you ought to have written and told them you had done so. If you don't know them very well, you ought to write at once and apologize for not having written to ask them first.

GREETING CHAPERONS AT BIG DANCE

Is it necessary to greet the chaperons of a dance where there are approximately a thousand in attendance?

If they are not receiving, you don't. If they are receiving, you follow the custom of your university—probably shake hands and introduce your partner: "Mrs. Chaperon, Mr. Gray," "Mrs. Patron, Mr. Gray," etc. Or if you don't know the names of the ladies in the receiving line, you shake hands and say to the lady at the head of the line, "I'm Mildred Senior," and then, turning to him slightly, "This is Mr. Gray." Then shake hands with the others and merely say, "How do you do." Or if it is customary to curtsy, you make your one deep curtsy to the line of receiving ladies and then pass on. Mr. Gray bows. That is all.

LOST AT A PROM

What do you do at the formal Prom when you get "stuck" at the end of a dance and there is no hope of your next partner's finding you in the mob, and you know that your present partner must hurry to the girl he is dancing with next?

You say, "Will you take me over near the door so that my partner can find me?" Whatever you do, you should try to take the situation lightly and not get ballroom panic. After all, you would not be terrified if you were to be left for a few minutes alone on the veranda of a golf club!

BREAD-AND-BUTTER LETTER FOR "BLIND DATE"

May I write a bread-and-butter letter to a boy who had his roommate ask me (for him) to come with his best girl, who is my best girl friend, to a fraternity dance at their House? This boy was a stranger to me until we arrived at the station, but I like him and I'd like to thank him again for the good time he showed me. And of course I'd like to see him again!

Certainly, write to your host and tell him what a good time you had at the dance. Also ask him to let you know when he comes to town because you'd like to ask him to your house.

CUTTING IN ON STRANGERS

Is it correct at a college dance for a man to cut-in on a girl to whom he has not been introduced?

At a Fraternity dance, yes; at a Prom, no.

PICK-UPS ON THE CAMPUS

Is it permissible to speak to a man whom you meet repeatedly on the campus and who is a member of your class, although you have never been formally introduced?

Yes. After noticing each other day after day, you'd naturally say "Good morning." Then somewhere, sometime, perhaps talk. At certain colleges, everybody speaks after the big all-college party the first week end.

TITLES OF THE FACULTY

When meeting professors socially—entertaining them at tea, for instance—does one use the title "Professor" or "Mister"?

If he holds the title of Doctor, call him that; otherwise call him "Professor." If he is an instructor, call him "Mister."

FRATERNITY PIN ENGAGEMENT

Does a man's giving his fraternity pin mean that he considers himself engaged to the girl?

By most people it is supposed that, when a man gives a girl his pin, his intentions are of a future engagement. A man's fraternity usually means everything to him; if he gives a girl its official pin, he must think a great deal of her.

DINING ROOM ETIQUETTE IN SORORITY HOUSE

While visiting in a sorority house recently I was puzzled by happenings apparently contrary to usual rules of etiquette. The house mother, or chaperon, always led the way to the dining room with one of the girls who, after seating the chaperon at the end of the table, took the first seat to the right. Now I would like to know: (1) Isn't the usual place of honor in this seat? (2) Where should the girl escorting the chaperon be seated? (3) At such a table, what would be the correct seating of a man or a woman guest, or both at once? (4) Should the chaperon enter with a guest or leave the guest to another girl? (5) *All food was served from the kitchen by two men waiters, except water and milk poured by a girl at the other end of the table and passed down the table. Is this correct or should the waiter pass it?* (6) *The chaperon was always served first. Was this right?* (7) *If coffee is poured at the table, should it be done by the chaperon or by a girl at the other end of the table?* (8) *On one occasion the chaperon entered the dining room late for lunch. Every girl rose at once and stood until she was seated. Was this necessary?* (9) *At a buffet supper the chaperon entered the dining room first and served herself first. Is this correct?*

Replies: (1) Yes. (2) At her usual place at table. (3) If only one man is present, he would probably sit on the chaperon's left and the woman guest on her right. If two men, one sits on either side of her and a woman guest on the right of man at the right of the chaperon. (4) First guest with chaperon. Second, or many guests with girl, or many girls. Since the chaperon is much older, she would go first; but if there is a guest of honor, the chaperon would accompany her. Two girls (taking turns perhaps at this "escorting duty") would follow closely and hold chairs for the chaperon and the guest (one girl only, if the guest is a man). (5) It should be poured by a waiter. Otherwise several pitchers on the table would seem more practical. (6) Chaperon before any of the girls, or a man, yes. But on no account should she be served before a woman guest. (7) By the chaperon probably, but a girl might do this equally well. (8) Correctly, yes. (9) Not if other women—or even girl—guests were present.

INVITATION TO COMMENCEMENT

Will you please tell me how invitations to commencement are worded?

Invitations to the various commencement exercises are usually sent out in the following form:

> The President and Faculty
> of X College
> request the pleasure of your company
> at the Commencement Exercises
> on Wednesday morning, the twentieth of June
> at eleven o'clock
> in the Gymnasium

Each graduate encloses his own card.

WHEN A GIRL IS HOSTESS SHE PAYS

Does an invitation to a man who is not a student at college, oblige the girl who invites him to pay the expenses of the evening?

If the word "invitation" is meant, yes. Otherwise, she is a seller of tickets and not a hostess.

16

The Vanished Chaperon and Other Lost Conventions

In no detail of etiquette has the modern generation effected so marked a change as in its increasing freedom from the perpetual presence of a chaperon. Of course there have always been chaperons and chaperons! But it must be said that the very word has a repellent school-teacherish sound. One instinctively pictures a humorless tyrant whose "correct" manner plainly reveals her true purpose, which is to take the joy out of life. That she can be—and often is—a perfectly human and sympathetic person, whose unselfish desire is merely to smooth the path of one who is the darling of her heart, in nothing alters the feeling of gloom or rebellion that settles upon the spirit of youth at the mention of the very word "chaperon." Nevertheless it is true no young girl may live alone. Under ordinary circumstances one who has no parents lives with other relatives. But in the case of a young girl who has no immediate family but who has an ample estate, her guardians usually engage a resident chaperon to look after her and to protect her reputation from the still able-bodied Mrs. Grundy and her ilk, until she is married or old enough to persuade a doubting world that she is thoroughly able to protect herself. This, until a few years ago, was set at beyond the age of thirty—and still is for her whose interests in life are solely those of her own amusement. A girl who has a career is granted considerable freedom, usually proportionate to the seriousness of her calling.

A chapter on the chaperon is, however, more closely related to the social than to the business aspects of life. So let us consider the chaperon who comes nearest her prototype of yesterday.

THE RESIDENT CHAPERON

It goes without saying that a chaperon is always a lady, but she need not be an old lady! She can perfectly well be reasonably young, and a spinster. Usually the chaperon "keeps the house," but she is never called a "housekeeper." Nor is she a "secretary," though she probably draws the checks and audits the bills.

THE DUTIES OF A CHAPERON

Let us consider a few of the requirements of a resident chaperon. First of all, a perfect chaperon (which title, by the way, also applies to parents) should be neither inquisitive nor interfering unless for a seriously considered reason. If a really objectionable young man—meaning one who is lacking in the ordinary impulses of decency—begins to show particular interest in Marie, it is her chaperon's duty to discourage the friendship if she can. It is unnecessary to add that a chaperon—if she is to be of any real use—must be a person of wisdom as well as sympathy and tact, for it is of vital importance that confidence exist between the chaperon and her charge. No young girl is likely to be influenced by opinions that she has not learned to believe in. Making Marie aware of Heppy Heel's worthlessness is not so simple as it sounds, since the criticism of him must be accurate, and his failings serious according to the standards which Marie herself respects. To judge him without fairness or tolerance would be fatal—not to Marie's interest in him, but to her confidence in her chaperon.

To think of a chaperon solely as someone professionally employed to look after the morals, as well as the manners, of one—or several—young girl would be a misuse of this space, were it not that the problems confronting such a chaperon are those of almost every mother and father in the land.

TODAY'S REVERSAL OF YESTERDAY'S PRECEPTS

The most important change in the entire chaperon situation is that training is taking the place of protection.

The hen on the bank and the ducklings in the pond represent more truly than ever the situation of the new-fashioned girl and the old-fashioned mother.

MOTHER HEN OF YESTERDAY

A mother hen, willing to realize that her children are ducks who must learn to swim as strongly and as expertly as possible and not chickens to keep huddled close to her on the bank, has taken the one essential step forward. What she really should do (if she is not able to turn herself into a duck) is to stand as near the water as she can and help her ducklings swim. She should not only watch the currents and the whirlpools but note the failure and success of the other ducklings and then cluck encouragement to her own.

This is a very threadbare fable, but it still ideally illustrates a hard, cold, modern fact. Or, to change the metaphor, if a child is to be a high-wire performer in a circus, she is trained from babyhood to keep her balance on a wire which is gradually put up higher and higher until she is in no danger of being overcome with dizziness and falling without a net. Since there are to be no chaperons—of any kind—the youngest age is none too soon to begin training a child in self-control and level-headedness, that she may not be overcome with dizziness in a netless world.

THE BEST CHAPERON—HERSELF

From an ethical standpoint, the only chaperon worth having in this present day is a young girl's own efficiency in chaperoning herself. The girl who has been trained to appraise every person and situation she meets, much as an expert automobile driver has been trained to appraise speed and distance and to counter the probable impulses of other drivers, needs no one to sit beside her and tell her what to do. In short, the girl who, in addition to trained judgment, has the right attributes of proper pride and character needs no chaperon—ever. If she lacks these qualities, not even Argus could watch over her! But apart from the questions of ethics, which are concerned with what she herself thinks or feels, and the motive behind what she says or does, there still remain the appearances to be considered.

THE CHAPERON WAS FOR PROTECTION

Since the modern girl is to go without protection, she must develop expertness in meeting unprotected situations. She must be able to gauge the reactions of various types of persons—particularly men, of course—under varying circumstances. She must know which man has the instincts of a gentleman—meaning that he is one to whom she can unfailingly turn for help—and which others, if given provocation or opportunity, are likely to revert to something quite different.

One fact, however, should perhaps be emphasized: the tenets of decency are still immutable, no matter what reversed theories of morality may be devised. It would seem that unlimited freedom for women, which is occasionally talked about (perhaps practiced by a certain daring and self-destructive minority), is not debatable.

The laws of morality, whether we think of them as ethics or the proprieties, are, after all, rules of the Game of Life—rules essential to know so thoroughly that obedience to them is as instinctive as a thoroughbred's obedience to the rules of sportsmanship. It is as true now as always, that women, whether young or old, cannot flout Mrs. Grundy's antiquated yet none the less potent consideration for appearances. If you doubt this, you might note that old woman's efficiency in turning into total darkness the most brilliantly lighted names even in the convention-immune citadel of Hollywood. But this, while the depth of the subject, is not its most important phase, since those who have been smirched by scandal are happily so few as to be negligible.

WHEN YOUNG WOMEN ARE NOT PARTICULAR

But what happens when young women are not particular, when their manners are too free and the precepts of the formalities forgotten, is not the melodrama's story of wrecked reputation so much as one of lost romance through being no longer able to sense or to exact its fastidious requirements.

Continuous pursuit of thrill and consequent craving for greater and greater excitement gradually produce the same result as that which a drug produces in an addict; or, to change the metaphor, promiscuous crowding and shoving, petting and cuddling, have the same cheapening effect as that produced on merchandise which has, through constant handling, become faded and rumpled, smudged or frayed and thrown out on the bargain counter in a marked-down lot. One danger of a certain dominant iconoclasm that might be called the chaperonless attitude is that values may be appreciated too late. And when one of these reckless squanderers longs for something of real value to give, there may be nothing left worth giving.

PROPRIETIES THAT HAVE BEEN REPEALED

Until very lately it was not considered proper for a young girl in her early teens ever to be alone as hostess, but in recent years it has become customary to allow not only a débutante, but her little sister of thirteen or so, to invite her friends to a party without the necessity of a chaperon other than that of her parents' roof. No young girl under eighteen, however, should be allowed to give a party in a restaurant or a theater unless a proper chaperon be present—though not necessarily seated with the young people.

PARENTS WHO ARE LATCHKEYS

A strong wave of sentiment against the "lack of proper home background" illustrated by a latchkey with which a young girl is permitted to let herself in when she is escorted home by a man alone from a dance or other late evening party has started a widespread custom among mothers (and fathers) of serving as latchkeys themselves, not because they fear to trust their daughter, but because they do not want to give any man the impression that her family is not only ignorant of good form but indifferent to her well-being.

On returning home from a party, a girl must not invite or allow any man to "come in for a while." If he insists, she should answer casually but quite as a matter of fact, "Sorry! It's against the rules." And bid him "Good night."

Not long ago, certain members of the Junior League started a practice that has been followed by other groups in a score of our States—merely telephoning home just before leaving a dance. The telephone rings just in time for her mother to tidy her hair, put on a long coat or a negligée that is not too undressed in effect, and be ready to open the door when her daughter rings.

At first thought the plan may sound unreasonably Victorian and interfering with the freedom that is the keynote of today. So let us consider this from the daughter's point of view. Having to telephone her mother is not unreasonable. There is a telephone everywhere she goes. The real point to be made is that she can make her practice of telephoning an evidence of respect for her mother, or she can make it one of derision, *according to the attitude that she assumes*. If herself is cheap, shallow, snobbish and unsure of herself, she will make her mother seem ridiculous. On the other hand, if she has poise, loyalty and good temper, there will be no more question about her going to the telephone than about going to get her wrap! Moreover, if she has these attributes of character, the chances are that she will agree that the type of man who might resent her mother's presence is one who is inclined to drink too much or to be in other ways one whose attentions are eventually likely to prove more annoying than pleasant.

AN OVER-NIGHT JOURNEY

Convention still decrees that a young girl should not, even with her fiancé, go on a long-distance motor trip and stop over-night in a hotel without a chaperon; nor is it supposed to be proper to go on any other journey that can last longer than the day. And yet there are occasions when it would be caviling to say that he and she cannot properly take a long trip by train, especially in a pullman car where every other passenger in the car is necessarily a chaperon.

THE GIRL OF FIFTEEN

A girl in her middle teens may perfectly well have a boy she knows well take dinner with her in her parents' house on an evening when they are dining out. She may also, with their consent, go with him to the movies—especially to an early showing neighborhood movie—and stop at a drugstore for ice cream or soda. It is also proper for a boy and girl to go to a club or even hotel restaurant in the afternoon to dance and take tea; but in the evening they must be with a group of others or in care of someone who can be considered a chaperon. But she certainly may not go to the theater or anywhere else that would keep her out late in the evening with a boy alone.

"MRS. GRUNDY"

Of course everyone has his own portrait of Mrs. Grundy, and some idea of the personality she shows to him; but has anyone ever tried to ferret out that disagreeable old woman's own position, to find out where she lives and why she has nothing to do but meddle in affairs which do not concern her? Is she a lady? One would imagine she is not. One would also imagine that she lives in a solid, well-repaired, square brownstone house with a cupola used as a conning tower and equipped with periscope and telescope and wireless. Furthermore, her house is situated on a bleak hill so that nothing impedes her view and that of her two pets, a magpie and a jackal. And the business in life of all three of them is to track down and destroy the good name of every woman who comes within range, especially if she is young and pretty—and unchaperoned! The pretty young woman living alone is their particular quarry. The magpie never leaves her window sill; and the jackal sits on the door mat. And the news of her every going out and coming in, of everyone whom she receives, when they come, how long they stay and at what hour they go, is spread broadcast. And yet if a young woman behaves with natural propriety, she is not likely to bring censure upon herself, even though the gossip of Mrs. Grundy still influences a world which seldom takes the trouble to sift appearance from fact.

MAY A YOUNG WOMAN GO ALONE TO A MAN'S APARTMENT?

This question is more often asked and harder to answer than any other question of the present day. Considered solely from the point of view of etiquette, the answer is NO. Considered in regard to a girl in her teens or to a young woman who is not very worldly-wise, the answer is No. In fact, it is a question that had not even a proper place in the earlier editions of this book. But times have changed, and the point of view of the modern world has turned from the consideration of etiquette as applied to society, and exacted that young women with professional careers—young women of new independence—be considered too. Therefore, this greatest question that has followed the disappearance of the chaperon must be included in a chapter such as this. And yet—any attempt to apply the rules of propriety to a young woman's going alone to the apartment of a man would be the same as attempting to give directions for applying a flame to a high explosive. Plenty of explosives can be approached with a flame—so they say. Plenty of young women do dangerous or foolish or stupid things and suffer not the slightest effects—either ill or otherwise. And yet that doesn't alter the fact that being shut in behind the latch-locking door in a man's rooms alone is, from every angle, as flagrant a reversal of propriety as is possible to describe—that is, granting a certain element of attraction between the woman and the man. If there is not the slightest personal interest further than stone-cold liking, would she be going to see him? True, she might dine with him on an evening when she has nothing else to do. Or perhaps they are old friends from the same home town and both more or less lonely strangers in an unaware city. The situation in either case is in no way a deviation from convention.

But how can this question be brought down to a particular case, and how is it possible to say definitely "no" or "yes" with any degree of accuracy of judgment or fairness? Each girl and each man and each background presents a different problem, requiring almost as many different answers as there are young men and women.

However, let us take yourself for an example. How are you to know whether you very well might—or positively shouldn't—go alone to dine in the rooms of a certain man? Why not ask yourself a few plain questions? Would you be embarrassed should someone you know see you going in or coming out? Do you think your going is anything not to be talked about? Would you call your mother from his apartment and tell her where you are? In short, will it be an adventure, or will it be nothing at all except having dinner with Tommy at his rooms instead of having it, as usual, in yours? You really know the answers much better than anyone else can, because you know all of the elements that enter into your personal situation. For instance, you know that dining with Tommy is just about the same as having tea in his rooms in college with your brother Hubert. Very well, then, add another angle: Is it worth having old Mrs. Grundy whisper about you, all because of dining alone with Tommy, which couldn't be less thrilling? Or take that angle away and let us say that in the group you go with not a thought will be given you, and that to Mrs. Grundy you are utterly unknown. Then dining with Tommy has not a single "no" against it.

But now let us say you want to dine with the fascinating man you met the other night. You know perfectly well you shouldn't go. Why look for the answer here? In any case, why not make it a dinner of four? Objection to a dinner of four instead of two is just that much weight added to the "no" side of the scale.

It is not necessary to add that a silly or emotionally inclined young woman who in pursuit of thrills accepts about any invitation from almost any man is certainly more likely than not to become shopworn or tarnished or otherwise marked down in value.

How late may you stay? If you dine alone, you should leave before ten, which is the hour that the servants in most houses are supposed to go off duty for the night. If you are four, you need not closely watch the clock. But even so, you should remember that past midnight is too late for a well-bred young woman—even two together—to be leaving Bachelor Flats.

The difference between going to a man's apartment and seeing him alone in yours is much the same as that which certain small boys find between the flavor of cherries eaten in the highest branches of the tallest tree and those same cherries on the dinner table. Even though the unchaperoned situation be precisely the same—there is a flavor of adventure in going to a man's rooms in contrast to the commonplaceness of receiving him in yours, probably because you are hostess almost every day in the year and it is likely that he is host but seldom. Other effects that add to or detract from the emotional emphasis that a particular situation may hold are those of alluring background, or the contrary. It is true that certain people are much more responsive to beauty or ugliness of surroundings than are others. But to most women, delightfully furnished rooms and the perfect service of a delicious meal, whether prepared by an expert cook and served by a butler, or cooked and served by the host himself, add just so much more flavor!

THE BACHELOR HOST AND THE CHAPERON

Barring the one fact that a "chaperon" should be on hand before young or "single" women guests arrive, and that she may not leave until after those whom she has chaperoned have left, there is no difference whatsoever in an entertainment given at the house of a bachelor and one given by a hostess.

A BACHELOR'S HOUSE PARTIES

Bachelors who live in the country often have both men and women staying with them. Any married couple is, of course, a proper chaperon for a girl, unless the host's mother or sister may be staying—or living—in the house.

There is always something unusually alluring about a bachelor's entertaining. Especially his house parties. Where do so many men living alone get those nice and so very respectable elderly housekeepers? They can't all have been their nurses! It is true that quite a few are inherited from their families, at that.

It is hard to determine what the "something" is in a bachelor's house that is so very friendly and comfortable and yet so entirely different from a woman's house, though it would be difficult to define wherein the difference lies.

A possible reason why bachelors seem to make such good hosts is that only those who have a talent for it make the attempt. There is never any obligation on a man's part to invite ladies to stay with him; whereas it is part of every woman's duty, at least occasionally, to be a hostess, whether she has talent, or even inclination, for the position or not.

However, repeated courtesies of hostesses can be returned by occasionally sending flowers or candy (to friends it might be something to the children or for the house) and by showing them polite attention when he meets them out. Of course, if he lives in a house or an apartment of his own, people are always especially pleased to go to any sort of party that a bachelor can give. On the other hand, if he is regularly keeping house, his obligation to return the hospitality of his friends is the same as that of all householders.

ANSWERS TO READERS' QUESTIONS

A MAN WHO IS A NEWCOMER ASKS ABOUT RETURNING HOSPITALITY

What return is a man alone who has come to a new town expected to make to the invitations which he receives (and accepts) to the houses of his neighbors? Is it on an eye-for-an-eye basis when a man is not married?

To this the answer is that returning the hospitality of one's friends is *never* on an eye-for-an-eye basis. Naturally, one is expected to make whatever return for repeated hospitality he can. This might very well be nothing more than payment of "oneself"—meaning, by putting oneself out to be courteous and agreeable and a very real help to one's hostess—in short, to be the sort of guest every hostess is delighted to welcome.

YESTERDAY'S PARENTS OF TODAY'S DAUGHTERS

Shall my daughter Cynthia be allowed to do the things the other girls do—things which to her father and me are shocking—or shall she be deprived of the joy that is the portion and right of her youth? We live in a small town (not far away from New York). It is customary for many of the supposedly nicest girls in town to go to New York alone with a man; dine in a restaurant, go to a play, go somewhere and dance afterward, and come home on the "milk train" at six in the morning. And our refusal to let Cynthia do the same thing is causing Cynthia continuous heartache.

The gist of the true answer to every such question is necessarily this: Whether Cynthia may be allowed to go out alone with a man depends first of all on the sort of girl Cynthia is and what her training has been. If she has been brought up with the same lack of practice in the responsibility of looking after herself that her mother very probably had, the answer is, "Decidedly no!" But if she is a clear-headed young modern, incapable of being nonplussed by any situation in which she may find herself, the answer, so far as her personal danger is concerned, might quite probably be, "Yes." But there is still the question of Mrs. Grundy—in other words, public opinion—for which Cynthia cares not at all.

To Cynthia, therefore, the question to put is this (said not tearfully or tensely, but casually, good-humoredly): "Going alone with Tom? Safe enough, certainly, but why collect fresh fish for all the old cats who can see you? Why not get Jane and George to go too?"

This is not literal, but it is the idea. Never admit "danger," because "danger" is the synonym of "thrill." Don't present Mrs. Grundy as a personage of importance, but as a trap-setter. And who'd be such a fool as to walk into a trap?

As a matter of fact, there is a second situation that is far more menacing and vital than Cynthia's, and that is the situation of daughters who are separated from all interference of their parents by the impenetrable static of misunderstanding between the older generation and the younger moderns. The unreasonable type of parent who commands the static to clear, or who insists that the annoying condition is caused by the deliberate insubordination of Mary or Lilian or Lucile, will never clear the air by such edicts as "I forbid you—and that is sufficient." The ensuing estrangement, if not deceit, is the inevitable and unfortunate result of any act of coercion.

To talk about sympathy, love, and understanding between parents and their daughters sounds sobby. I hate sobbishness every bit as much as does the youngest modern; and yet, how else can it be said? How else can perfect communication be established?

Frankly, the only parents who have any chance (and it is they who must take the chance) are those who can sink their emotions completely in order to overcome the bias of their own prejudices. The real cause of static is the inability as well as unwillingness of most parents to understand that the parental autocracy of yesterday is a thing of the past, and that the change is one which must be met with selfless courage. In no other way can the modern mother or father win the friendship and confidence of the modern daughter. Never in the world, probably, has it been so heart-searingly difficult to be an ideal parent. It is no light achievement to succeed in being lovingly wise and coolly impersonal at the same time.

ANOTHER HELPLESS MOTHER

What can I do to keep my sixteen-year-old daughter from running wild? I know I never gave my parents as much trouble as she is giving us. She has no respect for our opinions—in fact she seems to think she knows better than we. She is capable and clever, and yet will not agree that we know best what is for her good.

I wouldn't for an instant pretend to be an infallible expert on how to behave though a parent, but I *do* know some things *not* to do. There is no excuse for the stupidity of a mother or father who illustrates all arguments with bygone pictures.

The younger generation are not impressed, but bored, by being told what was thought proper when you were young, or how much you relied on your parents' wisdom. Those who have been brought up to have good manners will assume an expression of looking pleasant before a camera, but they will *think*, "Why can't the family of Noah be left in the ark?"

And on the subject of their father's claim of superior wisdom, their reply is a mental challenge that he "prove it!"

But whether children are frankly combative, stubbornly silent, or resentfully obedient, the present lack of adjustment between them and their parents is fundamentally the inability to speak the same language.

The modern home is like nothing so much as the Tower of Babel. Parents say words that have no meaning whatever to their sons and daughters. Sons and daughters say words that utterly terrify their parents, who try to interpret the sounds according to archaic definitions and find their meaning unintelligible.

Exclaim, "How shocking!" and a modern girl laughs. Tell her she is outrageous, and she is delighted. Tell her that she is cheap, and she looks you straight in the eye—in anger—unless you can give her equally straight reasons for your opinion. If you can, she will take it exactly as a boy will take a blow that is deserved. But if you have no grounds for your accusations, she returns your injustice with everlasting contempt.

What to do about it? I have theories. I'm sure you have theories. In fact, nearly all of us have theories of one sort or another—but which of us can prove that any of his theories is halfway right? As a grandmother I ought to be far less in sympathy with the youngest generation than are their mothers, who are usually much younger than I am. Instead, I have an enormous sympathy and liking for what I should call the "typical moderns" of the young generation. I like their honesty of outlook, their complete frankness (if given a chance to be frank). I admire their courage, their self-confident pride in being able to cope with whatever may turn up. "Cope," by the way, ranks with "divine" as a favorite expression. Perhaps they have pulled the wool over my eyes, but at least it is my honest belief that appreciation of knowledge was never greater than today. But response to cant, to false sentiment, to pretended wisdom, is a cut wire.

The fact that a man happens to have cumbered the earth with his utterly mediocre abilities for half a century or so is no reason why he has any right whatever to instruct either a young man or a young woman whose intelligence, quite possibly, is greater than his. Coming from an "expert" on manners, this sounds curiously iconoclastic, perhaps; but remember that the chief object of manners is consideration of others, and consideration is not shown by forcing our opinions on those made helpless by the requirements of good manners to resent them. After all, one must, in fairness, grant two sides to the question.

The intelligent mother builds what foundations she may by personal example, by evincing an open mind, by keeping away from the personal and sentimental. The father who is loved, respected, and willingly obeyed is one whose sympathy springs from keenness of understanding, and whose opinions are founded on wisdom of judgment—even if he has to work like a student to acquire it. The truth is that passing a college-entrance examination is nothing as compared with passing an examination as an adorable and infallibly wise father or mother.

17

Modern Man and Girl

QUESTIONS OF PAYMENT

Perhaps no other situations of the modern day present so many unsolved problems as that of the girl, the man, and questions of payment. If a man be really well-to-do, then in all situations that can be termed social the conventional exaction that all payments be assumed by him is followed without question; but when his pay envelope is a thin one, it is merest common sense to give this fact reasonable consideration.

In this modern day, when women are competing with men in politics, in business and in every profession, it is really senseless to cling to that one obsolete convention—no matter what the circumstances—that the man must buy the tickets, pay the check, pay the taxi, or else be branded a gigolo or a parasite. The modern point of view has changed in every particular save this one! Certainly it does not seem logical that an otherwise modern man-and-girl situation should still be depicted as that of a Victorian lady dependent for her safety in public upon the protection of a chivalrous gentleman, instead of the modern one of girl friend and boy friend—or one business associate and another.

Ethically this subject comes down to a question of underlying motive. The man who is deliberately "out for what he can get" from a woman is a type of parasite that is not even mentionable. And it is natural that every man of decent impulse shun the faintest likeness to one of these pariahs. Therefore, it is very hard to say how the various angles of a man's self-respect are to be reckoned with, and at the same time solve the typical situation of Mary who is wondering what has changed Jim, who used to be the life of the party, but who never wants to go anywhere any more! In other words, what can the girl, who likes Jim better than any other man, do about it except to make believe that above everything she likes to cook and stay home and to listen to the radio?

The only real advice to be offered is, first of all, to take whatever the situation may be, frankly and unself-consciously.

THE YOUNG MAN OF MODERATE MEANS AND THE TOO EXPENSIVE INVITATIONS

Many young men are learning that they dare not risk accepting the invitations of careless hostesses who put them into the embarrassing position of having to spend money that they can't afford.

To illustrate: Let us say John Graduate goes to a dinner of twelve at the Junior Executives. After dinner three bridge tables are set up. Mrs. Executive asks John, "You play, of course?" Knowing that, without a fourth, three others won't be able to play, he answers, "Yes, but not very well!" Reassuringly she says, "Then I'll put you at this table with me." They take their places; nothing is said about what they are playing for. John, who is a stranger, feels he can't ask. *But* having told his hostess that he doesn't play well, he trusts to her understanding of his situation, and the protection which he, as her guest, should have a right to expect. He has bad luck in cards, and worse luck in cutting the same devastating partner, who persists in overbidding, until the end of the evening finds John six thousand points down, which he now learns was at half a cent a point. It is a loss that will take him weeks of saving to pay; and at this he is deeply humiliated in having to give an I. O. U.

In John's place a woman would have said frankly in the beginning, "I don't play for money" or "I never play for more than a hundredth of a cent." A man ought to be able to take the situation lightly and say the same. But the typical man, especially among strangers, is made to feel that equal frankness on his part is a confession of financial failure. Although his hostess should have noticed his hesitation and have asked him if half a cent was all right, actually the fault was John's. When he was asked whether he played, this was his cue to say, "Yes, but I only play for a tenth" (or "I don't play for money"). And the sooner he learns this the better!

The second situation of needless embarrassment is a dinner given by a woman in a restaurant. At the end of dinner the waiter bringing the check more than likely puts it down in front of the man he takes for the host. It may seem simple enough for the man to tell the waiter, "Give it to the lady in black." But the typical American is embarrassed and therefore, he pays the check—if he *can*.*

As a third example, let us say that a group of young people dining at the Richards decides to go to the movies. Let's say that Mary Richards and two other girls and two boys arrive at the theater. One boy pays for the taxi; the other is hurried by Mary toward the box office, where he of course buys five seats! Night after night a boy dining with one hostess and another who casually suggests going to

* For payment of check by hostess, see "Restaurant" in Index.

the movies buys five or any other number of tickets. Moreover, he gets no credit for this expenditure, which he has possibly saved toward giving a party himself. And presently he declines duplicate invitations; he *has* to. It would be quite simple for a hostess to buy and keep a strip of tickets for her favorite picture house for just such occasions. Arrived at the theater, she would then hand the right number to the first boy, saying, "Here are the tickets, Jim!"

Hostesses whose incomes are moderate invariably think of these considerate measures for the protection of their daughters' guests, where those who are well-to-do forget that a dollar or two can mean much to one whose salary is small.

HOW CAN A MAN WITH ALMOST NO MONEY TAKE A NICE GIRL OUT?

Let us imagine a young man who is lucky enough to have a regular job, but whose pay leaves very little for luxuries, in which he naturally includes amusements. The question that he asks himself is this: How can he take a *nice* girl out? How can he ask a girl, let us say, like Sally Hiborn, used to luxury as she is, to spend an evening that couldn't help being—well, not very impressive? Jim Clerking hasn't a car at all. He can't possibly buy her orchids; he dare not even risk the bill for luncheon, let alone dinner, at a high-class restaurant; and "down in front" orchestra seats at a successful play are entirely out of reach. So what can he do?

Of course, the point to make is that Sally is precisely the type of girl who wouldn't care whether he bought seats for the latest musical comedy or went to a second-showing picture theatre. Having all her life been used to the things that many people look upon as luxuries, she finds that they in themselves mean nothing to her.

It is the girl with an inferiority fear who wants to be driven in a high-powered car to the Fritz-Cherry, to be conspicuously decorated with orchids, because she has no standards except those of cost.

To Sally Hiborn, on the other hand, the one thing that really counts is the man she is going out with. Given her choice between dining at the Fritz-Cherry with Dullan Rich and going to a cafeteria with Bob Bright, she would choose the cafeteria every time.

So, to you who hesitate because you do not think that whatever you have in mind is good enough for the nicest girl in the world, the advice is: Ask her by all means, to whatever you can afford. In fact, if it is simple, the way she responds is rather a measure of the quality of girl she is—and of her liking for you. The important thing is to be unself-consciously frank yourself, and to take the fact of having or not having money casually.

"PAY PARTY" CHECK

When several men and girls go on a "pay party," there are two ways of having checks presented. The fairer arrangement is having separate checks whereby each man pays for exactly what he and his own guest have ordered. The other is dividing the total check in equal parts among the men. On occasion, the latter means that a man and girl who perhaps ordered no more than coffee and doughnuts must help pay for the extravagance of another who ordered caviar and champagne. Usually those who go on pay parties are intimate friends whose tastes are similar. However, if one chooses to give an especially extravagant order, he should insist on paying his own check separately.

On occasion, when agreed to beforehand, girls as well as men pay their own checks.

IF YOU WOULD BE THOUGHT GLAMOROUS DON'T!

It would be hard to think of anything more at variance with charm than a woman who is continually looking at herself in her vanity mirror, making moues, and fussing at her hair and dabbing at her face. It is not only bad form, but evidence of ignorance of the meaning of charm.

To begin with, the sense of her own value would not allow any woman of charm to risk giving evidence that her natural face is far from satisfactory. After all, it is obvious that one does not mend china unless it is broken, smear ink eradicator on a letter unless there is a blot, or put a patch on something except to hide a hole.

A man may not stop to reason whether Gloria Gorgeous would have gray lips, pallid cheeks and a shiny, red nose without her make-up; but to see her continually daubing and painting and patching cannot fail to impress his subconscious mind with the shortcomings that her natural face must have, to need such constant attention.

ALL THOROUGHBREDS HATE CHEAPNESS

If there is one thing that a really well-bred individual cannot overlook, it is cheapness of behavior. Cheapness of behavior has nothing whatever to do with lack of money. The great heiress can be cheaper than cheap—and the poorest girl in town a complete thoroughbred. But no one can be both cheap and a thoroughbred.

The typical meaning of the word "cheapness" is exemplified in the girl or woman who puts no value on herself; who shows no reserves mentally, morally, or physically; who confides most personal and intimate details of her life to strangers; who, exacting no courtesy, does not mind being nudged or pushed or shoved; and, having no sense of personal value, is willing to be kissed and petted—in other words, to put herself in a class with the food on a free-lunch counter.

THAT WHICH IS GOOD REMAINS GOOD

At the moment it is distressing not to be able to hold the gates closed against many things that are utterly shocking to taste—in fact, against everything that gives the impression that the scene is laid in a dressing room or at a public bath. But it must be realized that nothing much can be done while popular taste temporarily stampedes.

There is, however, one hope to which we can look forward with reasonable certainty. Excellence is alone imperishable. Bad taste, bad manners, vulgar fashions, crude behavior will assuredly go the way they have always gone—into the discard; and whatever of excellence this same present day has furthered will permanently remain.

THE MAN MUST TAKE THE INITIATIVE

At the country club, or perhaps at a mountain-resort hotel, at the dance on a Saturday night, John Towne is introduced to Mary Lovely. They dance several dances and they sit out several more. She likes him more than anyone she has met—so much so that she walks over to the hotel next day with the definite hope that he may be there and that he will single her out again as at the dance the night before.

There is no sign of him, but on the veranda there is one group of her friends and in the lounge another group. Knowing that if she joins either group she will be hopelessly anchored should he appear, she goes into the dressing room to waste time. Other women come in, and she can't continue to stand looking out the window. She may miss him entirely if she is out of sight too long. So she goes back and joins the group in the lounge. Presently four or five other people bring up chairs and shut her in securely. And then he arrives. From across the room he bows to her; but because she is with a dozen people who to him are strangers, he wanders out of the room and in again and at last picks up a magazine and sits down not far from the entrance.

Meanwhile, Mary is perfectly well aware that everyone who saw her dancing most of the evening before with that same man is alert and watching like a hawk to see which reason she is going to pretend to have for crossing the room, and that any sudden impulse to telephone or to go off into the writing room would be only too transparent. Moreover, her equally good sense objects to giving him the chance to think to himself, "Mm-hm, here she comes!" So quite helplessly she just sits.

Or, changing this situation, let us say that most of the people she is sitting with are friends of his and that he joins the group but there is no vacant chair near her. She, trying to listen to what Elmer Boresome is telling her, wishes that she had got up the moment she saw John and gone off by herself, no matter where, and not cared what he or anyone else might have thought. But at last, let us say, the group disperses, leaving Mary and John alone. Manlike, he probably asks,

"Why did you go and bury yourself in the middle of all those people?"

And she replies, "What would you have liked me to do?"

To which the chances are that he has no practical answer, because apart from such transparent excuses as going to the telephone, or to see whether the mail has come, there was nothing Mary could have done. But there were many ways whereby John himself could have handled the situation with ease!

In the two examples given—wandering around aimlessly or sitting down and reading in the first, and joining the group in the second—both were wrong moves. Properly, in the first instance, all he had to do was to follow the formal dinner precept: when a gentleman finds that the lady he selects is sitting in the midst of others, he stands before her, bows and says, "Will you come and talk to me?" In the instances described, John would not bow or say these words; but in the example where she was seated with strangers he could perfectly well have sent her a note by a bell-boy (or whatever messenger he could find) saying, "Will you take a walk with me?" or any other invitation that presented itself.

As a matter of fact, sending a messenger is very much simpler when she is with strangers than it would be were she sitting with people whom he also knows, and who may very well include other young women who resent his preferring Mary to themselves. About the best way to meet this last situation is to show no self-consciousness, but upon seeing her, walk straight up to where she is sitting, say "How do you do" to everyone in general, and then ask her as a matter of course, "Are you ready?" If she for the moment loses her wits and asks, "For what?" he says, "That is nice of you! You not only break your date with me but you forget you made it." Then she says, "Oh, I'm sorry," and gets up and goes out with him. Or he might just look at her with a questioning expression and, showing her his watch, say, "If we are going, we'd better get started." And then she answers, "I'm ready!" and goes out with him.

The point to be made clear is that it is entirely proper that she accept his invitation or his attentions, but not even in this day of woman's emancipation can she escape criticism or ridicule if she appears to go after a man and to "pick him up."

THREE IS A CROWD

Another and greater problem to solve is that of the inescapable presence of a third person—sometimes a stranger and sometimes a friend—who cannot see two people evidently interested in each other without wanting to wedge himself (or herself) between them. Sometimes a rival of Mary, liking John's looks, deliberately thrusts herself upon John's notice, believing that she can divert his interest from Mary to herself. Often the persistent third person is just a natural barnacle or bore, but the most difficult third-person situation is that of the intimate friend whom Mary thinks it unfair to leave.

Let us say that Mary is staying with a friend named Mabel, and that as John's and Mary's interest in each other becomes serious, Mabel says, "I know you two want to go out in the canoe by yourselves! I know you two don't want me tagging along," but obviously expects them to contradict her. Or even worse, "Mary, dear, don't worry about leaving me alone; of course any time you want me I'd love to go, but I won't think of it unless you invite me!" After which, what can Mary do except invite her—or let John think she does not even care how cruel she is to her lonely friend?

Therefore, if you are Mabel, you should bear in mind that John is Mary's especial friend and not yours. If you have an especial one of your own, you know very well that you don't want to have Mary overhear and join in every word you and he say to each other. Not that you say anything that can't be overheard, but two are company and a third is a whole neighborhood listening on a party wire!

HOW FAR MAY A GIRL RUN AFTER A MAN?

Cat-like, she may do a little stalking! But "run"? Not a step. The freedom of today allows her to go to meet him halfway, but the girl who runs, runs after a man who runs faster.

To be sure, she can invite him to any sort of party, so long as it is not just a sit-at-home party of two. She can say even to one who has been lately introduced to her, "Come and see me some time! I'm almost always at home after five"—or whenever she is likely to be at home.

She may also say to one she knows at all well, "I'll answer, if you write to me." She may also buy tickets, but not often, for an entertainment and telephone him, "I have two tickets for the game (or the theater). Would you like to go with me?"

It isn't so much *what* she does, as the way she does it. A girl who is apparently impersonal, who is "cat-like" in disguising her intent, may pursue quite actually and with success, where one who bounds in pursuit, like a puppy let loose, has lost the prize at the start. All of which is mere common sense.

LETTERS FROM READERS

HE IS FROM OVER THE TRACKS

My fiancé's parents live just a few blocks from our house, but as yet have not come to see me, or my family. It sounds snobbish to explain, but facts are facts. You see my family is "of society" and his family lives "on the other side of the car tracks." In this town the dividing car tracks are as definite as the boundaries between hostile countries. I know the members of his family hesitate to cross the tracks. I want them to like me and not to think my family or I feel above them in any way, but how can I be conciliatory without seeming patronizing? Should Mother ask them to come to dinner—which might embarrass them—or should I go to see my fiancé's mother?

You may not want them to think that you feel above them, but you DO! Did you not feel above them, you would not fear to seem patronizing. And yet your belief that they would be embarrassed in being invited to your mother's house shows not their lack, my dear, but yours. If you were a truly great lady, it would not even occur to you that anyone could be embarrassed under your roof—ever! To imagine that one or another side of the car tracks can grant a patent of superiority, or furnish proof of inferiority, is to acknowledge that the foundations of your own social position are very wobbly.

I know I am being brutal, but for the sake of your own character, as well as your whole future happiness, go out on those car tracks and take a good look at them! Ask yourself if you are really such a snob that you can't see true values except as some of your friends happen to appraise them for you. And if the car track boundaries still seem to you those of a foreign country, break your engagement. If, on the other hand, you can overcome the car tracks, then forget them now and forever. And go to see the family of the man you love and try to make *them* receive *you!*

SHE IS FROM OVER THE TRACKS

The man I love is from a very prominent family. I have complete confidence in our mental and spiritual compatibility; but as I am of a family that is socially obscure and of meager financial backing, I am appalled at the thought of having the spotlight of criticizing society suddenly turned on me. I know the glare will exaggerate my limitations and I wonder if any love can stand such mortification. Do you know of any such cases that have come through their probation period without losing the high stakes of love? Will you give me your guidance?

If there were really no doubt about your "mental and spiritual qualifications," how could any "glare" produce mortification? There is nothing of importance in the fact that a well-known man is marrying a girl who is unknown to his friends. But it is true that his future happiness (which naturally involves your own) very greatly depends upon your adaptability to his background, your real understanding of his point of view. To assume that you are easily his mental and spiritual equal, meaning that your instinctive standards of taste and of ethics are the same as his own, and then to exaggerate the importance of money and social experience, except as they may give the mental compatibility of which you say you are sure, is the one doubt for your future that your letter inspires. In answering this, I have assumed "prominent family" to mean people of intrinsic quality and not a family that is merely conspicuous because rich.

18

Engagements

FIRST DUTY OF THE ACCEPTED SUITOR

If a young man and his parents are very great friends, it is more than likely that he will already have told them of the seriousness of his intentions. As soon as he and she have definitely made up their minds that they want to marry, it is the immediate duty of the man to go to the girl's father or whoever else is head of her family and tell him (or her) that he and Mary have become engaged, and "ask for his consent." If her father refuses, the young woman is faced with the problem of breaking the engagement or else marrying in opposition to her parents. There are, of course, unreasonable parents; but even so, there is no excuse for the most unfilial act of all—deception. The honorable young woman who has made up her mind to marry in spite of her parents' disapproval, announces to them, if she can, that on such and such a day her wedding will take place. If this is impossible, she at least refuses to give her word that she will not marry. The height of dishonor is to "give her word" and then break it.

THE APPROVED ENGAGEMENT

Usually, however, when the young man goes to see his fiancée's father, the latter has a perfectly good idea of what he has come to say and is probably willing to accept his daughter's choice; and the former, after announcing that he has been accepted, goes into details about his prospects. If the finances are not sufficiently stable, the father may advise him to wait before marrying. Or if they are satisfactory, he makes no objection to an immediate announcement.

HIS PARENTS CALL ON HERS

A troublesome convention which is concerned with the announcement of an engagement is that correctly the mother, father, sisters, brothers, aunts and cousins of the bridegroom-to-be should go at once and call upon the bride and her family. If they do not live in the same city, letters should be written. Much unhappiness—or at least awkwardness—has resulted from not being sure of this convention. However, it is much better that the girl be ready to accept the attitude of her future family (whatever it may be) than that she stand inflexibly upon her own rights. After all, the thing that really counts is the happy relationship between herself and her future in-laws.

THE ENGAGEMENT RING

It is doubtful whether he who carries a solitaire ring in a little square box and produces it from his pocket upon the instant that she says "Yes" ever existed outside comic cartoons! The man should consult the girl's taste—which of course may be gratified or greatly modified, according to the depth of his purse. The most practical thing is for him to go and have the jeweler put aside a selection of rings at the price he can afford, and then bring his fiancée into the store and let her choose from them the one she likes best. A solitaire diamond is the conventional emblem of "the singleness and durability of the one love in his life," but other stones, especially her birthstone, are entirely correct.

In the present day, precious stones having soared out of reach of all but the really rich, fashion rather prefers a larger semi-precious one to a microscopic diamond. "Fashion," however, is merely momentary and local, and the great majority will probably always consider a diamond the only ring to have.

CONCERNING THE ENGAGEMENT RING

The engagement ring is worn for the first time "in public" on the day of the announcement. BUT THE ENGAGEMENT RING IS NOT ESSENTIAL TO THE VALIDITY OF THE BETROTHAL. This is printed in capitals because many, confusing the engagement ring with the wedding ring, believe the former is as indispensable as the latter—which is not the case. The wedding ring is a requirement of the marriage service. The engagement ring is merely "evidence" that HE proposed marriage and that SHE answered, "Yes!"

There have been countless wives who never had an engagement ring at all. Many another has received her ring long after marriage, when her husband was able to buy the ring he wanted her to have.

WHEN SHE GIVES HIM AN ENGAGEMENT PRESENT

It is not obligatory, or even customary, for the girl to give the man an engagement present; but there is no impropriety in her doing so if she wants to. Any of the following articles would be suitable: a pair of cuff links, or waistcoat buttons, or a watch chain, or a key chain, or a cigarette case. Probably because the giving of an engagement ring is his particular province, she very rarely gives him a ring or, in fact, any present at all.

BIRTHSTONES

Birthstones are always suitable adjuncts to, as well as the principal part of, a gift for either a girl or a man.

January	Garnet or Hyacinth
February	Amethyst
March	Bloodstone, Aquamarine or Jasper
April	Diamond
May	Emerald
June	Pearl, Moonstone or Agate
July	Ruby or Onyx
August	Sardonyx, Peridot or Carnelian
September	Sapphire
October	Opal or Tourmaline
November	Topaz
December	Turquoise or Lapis Lazuli

BEFORE ANNOUNCEMENT

Usually a few days before the formal announcement, the girl and man both write to their aunts, uncles, and cousins, and to their most intimate friends, telling of their engagement, asking them not to tell anyone until the determined date.

As soon as they receive the news, all the relatives of the bridegroom-elect properly call on the bride. She must, of course, return all these visits, and as soon as possible.

If his people are in the habit of entertaining, they should very soon ask her with her fiancé to lunch or to dinner, or after the engagement is publicly announced, give a dinner or other party in her honor. If, on the other hand, they are very quiet people, their calling upon her is sufficient in itself to show their welcome.

In case of a recent death in either immediate family, the engagement should be quietly announced by telling families and intimate friends.

THE ANNOUNCEMENT

The announcement should be made by the parents of the bride-elect. This is done intimately by note, and publicly through the newspapers, and verbally to friends individually or collectively. Engraved announcements are not correct.

The public announcement is made by telephoning the society editor of the daily papers, and saying that Mr. and Mrs. John Jones of 100 Park Avenue are announcing the engagement of their daughter, Mildred, to Mr. George Brown, son of Mr. and Mrs. Emerson Brown of New Orleans. If the families concerned are prominent, a photograph of the fiancée will probably be asked for. If she would like to have her picture appear, she should have one ready; but it is not in good taste to send a photograph unless one is asked for.

When a party is given for the purpose of announcement, the news is told by the girl herself or her mother, as the guests arrive and find the fiancé standing beside them. Or perhaps, if the "party" is a dinner, it is told by the father, who rises and proposes the health of his daughter and future son-in-law.

NOVELTY ANNOUNCEMENTS

To those of you who ask about the propriety of inventing a novel way to announce your engagement, convention is not partial to names on balloons, or a sash tying the left arm of the girl to the right arm of the man! And yet there is really no logical objection to whatever may please those most closely concerned. One logical objection, however, does exist: Novelty must have surprise, or it isn't novelty. Therefore, whether you let a cat out of a bag with your names written on a ribbon around its neck, or whether you distribute bouquets and boutonnières tagged with both names, or whether the guests receive the glad tidings in telegrams used as place cards, there is not a rule in the world to hamper the complete freedom of your own imagination. You can literally give any variety of party you choose, invite whom you choose, and serve whatever you choose.

HOW A HEALTH IS PROPOSED

But to return to the conventional announcement made by the father of the bride at a dinner: After directing that all glasses at the table be filled, the host rises, lifts his own glass, and says: "I propose we drink to the health of Mary and the young man she has decided to add permanently to our family, James Smartlington."
Or
"A standing toast: To my Mary and to her—Jim!"
Or
"I want you to drink the happiness of a young pair whose future welfare is close to the hearts of all of us: Mary (holding up his glass and looking at her) and Jim!" (holding it up again and looking at him). Everyone except Mary and Jim rises and drinks a swallow or two (of whatever the beverage may be). Everyone then congratulates the young couple, and Jim is called upon for a "speech!"

Generally rather "fussed," Jim rises and says something like this: "I—er—we—thank you all very much indeed for all your good wishes," and sits down. Or if he is an earnest rather than a shy youth, perhaps he continues, "I don't have to tell you how lucky *I* am; the thing for me to do is to prove, if I can, that Mary has not made the mistake of her life in choosing me, and I hope that it won't be very long before we see you all at our own table with Mary at the head of it and I, where I belong, at the foot."

Or

"I can't make a speech and you know it. But I certainly am lucky and I know it."

WHEN NO SPEECH IS MADE

The prevailing custom in New York and other big cities is for the party to be given on the afternoon or evening of the day of announcement. The engagement in this case is never proclaimed to the guests as an assembled audience. The news is "out" and everyone is supposed to have heard it. Those who have not, cannot long remain ignorant, as the groom-elect is either receiving with his fiancée or brought forward by her father and presented to everyone he does not know. Everybody congratulates him and offers the bride-to-be good wishes for her happiness.

ENGAGEMENT PRESENTS

It is not unusual for a bride-to-be to receive a few engagement presents sent either by her very intimate friends or by members of her fiancé's family as special messages of welcome to her—and as such are very charming. But any general fashion that necessitates giving engagement as well as wedding presents is rightly tabu.

SHOWERS

Engagement showers will be found in Chapter 33; also consult Index.

ENGAGED COUPLE IN PUBLIC

There is said to be still preserved somewhere in Massachusetts a whispering reed through the long hollow length of which lovers were wont to whisper messages of tenderness to each other while separated by a room's length and the inevitable chaperonage of the fiancé's entire family.

From those days to the present unrestricted display of snuggles in public, from which one is made to feel like withdrawing in embarrassment, is a far cry.

Everyone supposes that lovers kiss each other, but people of good taste wince at being forced to play audience to love scenes which should be private.

Great love is seldom flaunted in public, though it very often shows itself in pride—that is a little obvious, perhaps. There is a quality of protectiveness in a man's expression as it falls on his betrothed, as though she were so lovely a breath might break her; and in the eyes of the girl whose love is really deep there is always evidence of that most beautiful look of championship, as though she thought, "No one else can possibly know how wonderful he is!"

This underlying tenderness, this pride which is at the base of the attitude of each, only glints beneath the surface of perfect comradeship. Their frank approval of whatever the other may do or say is very charming; and even more so is their obvious friendliness toward all people, their air of wishing the whole world to be beautiful for everybody because it is so beautiful to them. That is love—as it should be! And its evidence is a very sure signpost to future happiness.

ETIQUETTE OF ENGAGED PEOPLE

It is unnecessary to say that an engaged man shows no attention whatever to other women. It should be plain to everyone, even though he need not behave like a moon-calf, that "one" is alone in his thoughts.

Often it so happens that engaged people are together very little because he is away at work, or for other reasons. Rather than sit home alone, she may, of course, go out with her friends but she must avoid going out with any one man or being seen with any particular man more than with another. In short, she should remain visibly within the general circle of her group.

SHOULD A LONG ENGAGEMENT BE ANNOUNCED?

Whether to announce an engagement that must be of long duration is not a matter of etiquette but of personal preference. On the general principle that frankness is always better than secretiveness, the situation is usually cleared by announcing it.

MEETING OF KINSFOLK

At some time before the wedding, it is customary, when possible, for the two families to meet each other. That is, the parents of the groom dine or lunch or have tea at the house of the parents of the bride to meet the aunts, uncles and cousins. And then the parents of the bride are asked with the same purpose to the house of the groom-elect.

THE ENGAGED COUPLE AND THE CHAPERON

The question of a chaperon differs with locality. It is perhaps sufficient to say that if a man is thought worthy to be accepted by a father as his daughter's husband, he should also be considered worthy of trust no matter how far any situation they might find themselves in may be lacking in propriety.

GIFTS WHICH MAY AND THOSE WHICH MAY NOT BE ACCEPTED

The fiancée of a young man who is "saving in order to marry" would be lacking in taste as well as good sense were she to encourage or allow him extravagantly to send her many flowers and other charming but wasteful presents. On the other hand, however, if the bridegroom-elect has ample means, she may accept anything he chooses to select, except wearing apparel or a car, especially a town car, or a house and furniture. In short, he can give her anything for her adornment but nothing that can be classified as "maintenance."

It is perfectly suitable for her to drive his car, and she may select furniture for their house, which he may buy or have built. But, if she would keep her self-respect, the car must not become hers nor must she live in the house or use its furniture until she is given his name. He may give her all the jewels he can afford; he may give her a fur scarf, but not a fur coat. The scarf is an ornament; the coat is wearing apparel. If she is very poor, she may have to be married in cheesecloth, or even in the dress she wears usually, but her wedding dress and the clothes she wears away must not be supplied by the groom nor, under most circumstances, by his family.

There are, of course, exceptions. If his mother has long known the girl and loves her dearly, there is no reason why she should not give her almost everything she chooses. But it would be starting life on a false basis, and putting herself in a category with women of another class, to be clothed by any man, whether he is soon to be her husband or not.

IF THE ENGAGEMENT IS BROKEN

If the engagement should be so unfortunate as to be broken off, the engagement ring and all other gifts of value must be returned to the giver. A notice reading, "The engagement of Miss Mary Black and Mr. John Doe has been broken by mutual consent" should be sent to the newspapers which announced the engagement.

[Please consult the Index for additional details of any subject treated in this book, as they may belong in some other chapter. For example, "Engagement Showers" will be found in Chapter 33. Recalling Wedding Invitations p. 116.]

19

*First Preparations for a Wedding**

FOR A CHURCH WEDDING OF IMPORTANCE

To begin with, before deciding the date of the wedding, the bride alone, or more probably with her mother, must find out definitely on which day the clergyman who is to perform the ceremony is disengaged, and make sure the church is bespoken for no other service. If it is to be a very important wedding, she must also see that the time available for the church is convenient for the caterer as well.

Having settled upon a day and hour, she next decides on the number of guests that can be provided for; this is determined by the size of the church and the house, and the type of reception intended.

THE INVITATIONS

The bride-elect and her mother then go to the stationer and decide details, such as size and texture of paper and style of engraving, for the invitations. The order is given about two months in advance for the engraving of all the necessary plates, and for a moderate number of invitations or announcements, which may be increased later when the lists are completed and the definite number known.

(For all details of wedding forms, see Chapter 11.)

BOTH MOTHERS MAKE WEDDING LISTS

The bride's mother then consults with the groom, or more likely with his mother, about how the house list is to be divided between them. If the families have long been friends and it is decided that two hundred may be included at the breakfast, Mrs. Smith and Mrs. Smartlington each make a list of one hundred and fifty or more, according to the names likely to be duplicated. But if their friends are in different circles, each would have to limit her list to one hundred.

If the groom's people live in another place, invitations to the house may be sent liberally, as the proportion of guests who will take a long trip seldom exceeds that of the immediate family and such intimate friends as might be asked to the smallest of receptions.

---
* For war weddings, see Chapter 52, p. 624.

CHURCH INVITATIONS UNLIMITED

Invitations to a big church wedding are always sent to the entire visiting list, and often to the business acquaintances of both families, no matter how large the combined number may be or whether they can by any chance be present or not. Even people in deep mourning are included, as well as those who live thousands of miles away, for the invitations not merely proffer hospitality, but are messengers carrying the news of the marriage.

After a house wedding, or a private ceremony where invitations had to be limited to relatives and personal friends of the young couple, general announcements are sent out to the entire visiting list.

THE LIST FOR THE LARGE WEDDING

In the cities where a Social Register or other Visiting Book is published, people find it easiest to read it through, marking "XX" in front of the names of family members and intimate friends who *must* be asked to the house, and "√" in front of those to be asked to the church only, or to have announcements sent them. If the reception list is unavoidably limited, certain names are marked with a single "X," meaning that these are to have house invitations if possible. Names which do not appear in the printed list are added, of course, as "thought of." In country places and smaller cities, or where a published list is not available or of sufficient use, the best assistant is the telephone book.

A word of warning: To leave out old friends because you think them unimportant and to include comparative strangers because they are of great importance, not only shows a want of loyalty and proper feeling, but invites the contempt of those very ones whom such snobbery seeks to impress.

Four lists, therefore, are combined in sending out wedding invitations; the bride and the groom make one each of their own friends, to which is added the visiting list of the bride's family (made out by her mother or other near relative) and the visiting list of the groom's family (made out by his mother or a relative). When the lists have been completed, the bride's mother counts the combined number of double X's, and if she finds that the guests can include, let us say fifty more, she tells the bridegroom's mother that she can change twenty-five single X names into double ones. On the other hand, should the total number of double X's be too many, distress in having to cut the list is the result.

At a typical wedding, friends are asked to the reception as well as to the church, and acquaintances to the church only. If the wedding is to be in the house, or is otherwise very small, so that none but families and intimate friends are invited, announcements are sent to all uninvited acquaintances.

INVITATION ALWAYS A COMPLIMENT

An invitation sent to someone thousands of miles away is entirely proper, since its meaning is, "We would like to have you with us, were it possible for you to be here."

When lists are very long, the compiling is usually done by a professional secretary, who also addresses the envelopes, encloses the proper number of cards, and seals, stamps and posts the invitations. The address of a professional secretary can always be furnished by the stationer. Where lists do not run to great length, the envelopes are addressed and the invitations sent out by the bride herself and some of her friends who volunteer to help her.

THE MOST ELABORATE WEDDING POSSIBLE

Whether in the city or the country, the church is decorated with masses of flowers in some such elaborateness as standards, or sprays tied to the pew ends, as well as the floral embellishment of the chancel. The service is perhaps conducted by a bishop or another distinguished clergyman, with an assistant clergyman, and accompanied by a full choral service, possibly with the addition of a celebrated church soloist. The clothes of the bride and her maids are chosen with seeming disregard of cost.

Later, at the house, there is not only a floral bower under which the bridal couple receives, but every room has been turned into a veritable woodland or garden, so massed are the plants and flowers. An orchestra—or two, so that the playing may be without intermission—is hidden behind palms in the hall or wherever most convenient. A huge canopied platform is built on the lawn or added to the veranda (or built out over the yard of a city house). It is packed with small tables, each seating four, six, or eight, as may be preferred or as space permits.

(For further description, see next chapter.)

THE USUAL FASHIONABLE WEDDING

The more usual fashionable wedding is merely a modification of the one outlined above. The chancel of the church is decorated—but less lavishly—and, except in summer, when garden flowers are to be had in profusion, there is very little attempted in the body of the church other than sprays of flowers at the ends of the ten to twenty reserved pews, or possibly only at the ends of the first two pews and the two that mark the beginning of the ribboned section. There is occasionally a choral service and a distinguished officiating clergyman. Except for the background against which the bride and groom receive, there is very little floral decoration at the reception.

A number of small tables in the dining room may seat perhaps twenty or even fifty guests, or perhaps a hundred are served from a buffet; the bride's table is placed in another room. If the bride has no attendants, she and the groom choose a few best friends to sit at the table with them.

THE WEDDING OF A CINDERELLA

When the bride's family are not particularly well off—and how many families are not in this day!—it is not only inadvisable to attempt expenditure beyond what they can afford, but they would lay themselves open to greater criticism through inappropriate lavishness than through moderate arrangement—which need not by any means lack charm, or even perfection.

Some years ago there was an extremely fashionable wedding which will be remembered always by every witness in spite of, or maybe because of, its utter lack of costliness.

It was in June in the country. The invitations were by word of mouth to neighbors and personal notes to the groom's relatives at a distance. The village church was decorated by the bride and her friends with dogwood, than which nothing is more bride-like or beautiful. The shabbiness of her father's house was smothered with flowers and branches cut—with an eye to pruning and not destroying the trees—far back in the thickets of a neighboring wood. Her dress, made by herself, was of tarlatan covered with a layer or two of tulle, and her veil was of tulle fastened with a spray, as was her girdle, of natural bridal wreath and laurel leaves. Her bouquet was of trailing bridal wreath and white lilacs. She was very young, and divinely beautiful, and fresh and sweet. The tulle for her dress and veil and her thin silk stockings and white satin slippers represented the entire outlay of any importance for her costume. A little sister in smock of pink sateen, with a wreath and tight bouquet of pink laurel clusters, toddled after her and held her bouquet—after first laying her own on the floor!

The breakfast was as satisfying to the taste as the dresses of the bride and bridesmaid were to the eye. A home-made wedding cake, "professionally" iced and big enough for everyone to take home a slice in waxed paper piled near for the purpose, and a white wine cup, were the most pretentious offerings. In addition there were hot biscuits, cocoa, coffee and scrambled eggs, and the "music" was a phonograph. The bride's "going away" dress was of brown Holland linen and her hat a plain little affair as simple as her dress; again her only expenditure was on shoes, stockings and gloves. Later, she had all the clothes that money could buy, but in none of them was she ever more lovely than in her cloud-like wedding dress of tarlatan and tulle, and the plain little frock in which she drove away.

A BIG CHURCH MADE SMALL

A wedding may of course be smaller, much, than this Cinderella one.

If it is to be in church and only the two or three first pews are to be occupied, the effect of emptiness may be entirely overcome by making a hedge of small trees or branches across the pews that form the boundary.

Such a hedge was made by renting a dozen lengths of two-inch lumber, six feet long and four inches wide, from a builder. Tree branches were nailed on one side only of each upright, making flat but wide tree trimmings which were then used to screen in the first eight pews on either side of the center aisle by merely propping them against the backs of the pews in front and against the partitions between the center and side pews. A few extra ones were made to stand alone in Christmas-tree holders. The effect was that of a small, green-hedged chapel which was further accentuated by having the chancel and this chapel interior brilliantly lighted, and putting all the other lights in the church out. The wedding procession came down the center aisle and entered the enclosure through an opening made by the sexton, who lifted a standing tree out of the way and closed it again as soon as the recessional had passed through. The guests came in and went out by a side aisle which led into the improvised chapel.

This arrangement gives to the smallest possible wedding all the solemn beauty of church surroundings, including organ music.

RECEIVING IN CHURCH, A FRIENDLY CUSTOM

When the marriage takes place in a church and there is to be no reception afterward, the bride and groom often follow the friendly and charming custom of waiting after the recessional in the vestibule of the church, in order to receive the good wishes of the congregation as it passes out.

THE EVENING WEDDING

All through the South and generally throughout the West smartest weddings are celebrated at nine o'clock in the evening. There is a reason for the evening wedding in the South. The heat of the day has passed and the coolness of the evening, which lends itself better to festivities and to dancing, which has always been a wedding-supper feature, prevails.

The details are precisely the same as those of morning or afternoon. In fashionable Southern circles the bride and bridesmaids wear dresses that are perhaps more elaborate and "evening" in type, and the bridegroom, as well as all men present, wear full evening clothes and the women dress as though going to a ball. For the church ceremony, the women should wear light scarfs of some sort around their shoulders and over their hair, in compliance with the regulations forbidding the uncovering of women's heads and shoulders in consecrated places of worship.

In simpler communities the guests wear exactly what they would wear to evening service in church—a good dress and hat by the women, and dark daytime suits of clothes by the men.

THE EARLY MORNING WEDDING

Among Catholics, an eight o'clock morning wedding is not unusual, and its details are precisely the same as for later hours. But for others, who are perhaps boarding an early morning train or ship, and who would especially like the informality to which such an hour lends itself, a wedding may be carried out as follows:

The bride could wear any simple dress of plain material. She would wear a veil, of course, but of tulle instead of lace, either falling to the hem of her dress or of finger length. She would, of course, carry a bouquet, but probably of moderate size, and no gloves—unless she carries a prayer-book instead of a bouquet.

Her attendants might wear the simplest sort of morning dresses (with long skirts) and garden hats; the groom and his best man, sack suits or flannels. And the breakfast—really breakfast—might consist of toast and coffee and griddle cakes!

In fact, a small early-morning wedding—where everyone is dressed in morning clothes, and where the breakfast suggests the first meal of the day—can be perfectly enchanting.

A MARRIAGE AT THE PARSONAGE

Marriages are often performed in the clergyman's study or in another room at the parsonage. But such a ceremony is merely a marriage and not a wedding.

On such an occasion the clergyman should be notified ahead of time regarding the hour set. The bride and bridegroom go together and are met at the parsonage by the members of their families and the two or three friends invited. When all are assembled, the bridegroom tells the clergyman they are ready. The clergyman takes his place. The bride and bridegroom stand before him and the service is read. Afterwards those present congratulate them, and that is all. Of course they

LOOKING UP THE BRIDE'S AISLE IN A DOUBLE-AISLED CHURCH

When there are two aisles, any decoration of the pew ends is necessarily duplicated on the groom's aisle.

A BRIDE'S BOUQUET

FIRST PREPARATIONS FOR A WEDDING

may all go to the house of the bride or of a witness, or to a restaurant, and have lunch, or tea, or dinner, together. At such a marriage the bride rarely wears a white wedding dress and veil, but it is entirely proper for her to do so if she chooses—especially if they are going to the home of a friend for a wedding dinner afterwards. If the marriage is performed by a magistrate, however, a wedding dress is entirely out of keeping.

BREACH OF ETIQUETTE FOR BRIDEGROOM TO GIVE WEDDING

No matter whether a wedding is to be large or tiny, there is a supposedly fixed rule that the reception must be either at the house of the bride's parents, or grandparents, or other relative of hers, or else in assembly rooms rented by her family. Etiquette has always decreed that the groom's family may give entertainments of whatever description they choose for the young couple after they are married; but the wedding breakfast as well as the trousseau of the bride must be furnished by her own side of the house!

There might be circumstances, however, when it would be caviling not to break this rule. If, for instance, the bride were without family, she might perfectly well be married in the church or the rectory, and go afterwards to the house of the bridegroom's parents for breakfast, or for a reception. After all, there are few rules that permit no exceptions under extenuating circumstances. (See letters at end of next chapter.) But in the average case—where the girl is known slightly or perhaps not at all by the family of the bridegroom, she would put herself in a false position and bring criticism upon her own family's inability to assume the wedding obligations which properly belong to them.

RECORDING THE WEDDING PRESENTS

And now let us return to the details of the wedding of our particular bride.

The invitations are mailed about three weeks before the wedding—unless it is to be a very small one, in which case the invitations are sent out about two weeks before the day.

(See p. 251 for gift suggestions.)

If the presents, which begin to arrive as soon as the cards are out, are likely to be many, each one should be entered at once in the gift book. There are many published for the purpose, but any ruled blank book about eight to ten inches square will answer the purpose. The usual model spreads across the double page as follows:

Present Received	Article	Sent by	Sender's Address	Where Bought	Thanks Written
May 20	Silver Dish	Mr. and Mrs. White	1 Elm Place	Sterling Co.	May 20
May 21	12 Plates	Mr. and Mrs. Green	2 North Street	Crystal's	May 21

All gifts as they arrive should be put in a certain room, or part of a room, and never moved away until the description is recorded.

THE BRIDE'S THANKS

In return for the many presents showered upon a happy bride, there is a corresponding task which may not be evaded.

On a sheet of note paper—not a folded visiting card—and in her own handwriting, she must send a separate letter for each present she receives—and, if humanly possible, she writes each letter of thanks on the day the present arrives. If she does not, they soon get ahead of her and her whole honeymoon is taken up with note-writing.

(For wording of bride's notes, see Index.)

Notes of thanks can be very short, but they should be written with as little delay as possible. When a present is sent by a married couple, the bride writes to the wife and thanks both: "Thank you for the lovely present you and Mr. Jones sent me."

NEVER SEND AN ENGRAVED CARD OF THANKS

It would not be possible to overemphasize the inexcusable rudeness of the bride who sends a printed or engraved card of thanks for wedding presents sent her. Whoever devised this flagrant affront to the traditions of common decency was, obviously, more concerned with making sales to stationers than with acquiring knowledge of the precepts of polite behavior.

A young woman who had many friends but, as it happened, little knowledge of social usage, was led to send out engraved cards announcing

MISS NOBACKGROUND
HEREBY ACKNOWLEDGES
YOUR KIND GIFT
AND SENDS YOU HER APPRECIATIVE THANKS

It is scarcely necessary to add that appreciative thanks are *not* expressed in this way. In the case of the young woman in question, her presents stopped like a turned-off faucet as soon as the news of her rudeness spread.

Another form which reads, "Miss Sylvia Newrich hereby acknowledges receipt of your gift, for which she will later write you her thanks" is not rude and might be necessary after a sudden war wedding when presents arrive after the bride has left.

In that case, there will probably be a note from the bride's mother saying, "Mary had gone when your lovely present came. She will, of course, write you as soon as she gets back." If Mary is to be gone for months, her mother should write a description from which Mary sends her "thanks for the lovely tray" (or whatever) her mother described.

Ordinarily, an acknowledgment followed later by a note of thanks seems a useless waste of double effort; a minute or two more would complete a note of thanks to enclose in each stamped and addressed envelope instead of addressing and stamping every acknowledgment twice. Also it seems pretentious because it implies that so many presents were expected that special preparations were made in advance to take care of the avalanche. Moreover, this engraved notice, which attracts formal attention to the promised letter, exacts that the letter be longer and better than an unheralded note in which a few sentences could say all that is necessary.

ARRANGING THE PRESENTS

Not so much in an effort to parade her possessions as to do justice to the kindness of the many people who have sent them, a bride should show her appreciation of their gifts by placing each one in the position of greatest advantage. Naturally, all people's tastes are not equally pleasing to the taste of the bride—nor are all pocketbooks equally filled. Very valuable presents are better put in close contrast with others of like quality—or others entirely different in character. Colors should be carefully grouped. Two presents, both lovely in themselves, can be made completely destructive of each other if the colors are allowed to clash.

Usually china is put on one table, silver on another, glass on another, laces and linens on another. But pieces that jar together must be placed as far apart as possible and perhaps even moved to other surroundings. A crudely designed piece of silverware should not be left among beautiful examples, but be put among china ornaments, or other articles that do not reveal its lack of fineness by too direct comparison. For the same reason imitation lace should not be put next to real, nor stoneware next to Chinese porcelain. To group duplicates is another unfortunate arrangement. Eighteen pairs of pepper pots or fourteen sauce boats in a row might as well be labeled: "Look at this stupidity! What can she do with all of us?" They are sure to make the givers feel at least a little chagrined at their choice.

WHEN THE PRESENTS ARE SHOWN

There is absolutely no impropriety in showing the presents at the wedding reception. The only reason for not showing them is lack of space in a small house or, of course, an apartment. If there is an extra sitting room—such as a library—they are shown there. Otherwise a bedroom from which all the furniture has been removed is suitable. Tables covered with white damask (plain) tablecloths are put like counters around the sides of the room.

It is not good taste to display checks—or even to tell people in general of their amounts. It is quite proper, however, to say, "Uncle John gave me a check"—or "a bond."

PRESENTS FROM BRIDEGROOM'S FRIENDS

The bridegroom seldom receives any presents. Even a friend who cares about him in particular and has never met the bride sends his present to her—unless he sends two presents, one in courtesy to her and one in affection to him. Rather often friends of the bridegroom pick out things suitable for him, such as cigar or cigarette box or decanter or rather masculine-looking desk sets, etc., which are sent to her but are obviously intended for his use.

CARDS LEFT ON

The cards that were sent with the gifts are sometimes removed, but there is no impropriety in leaving them on, and it certainly saves members of the family from repeating many times who sent this and who sent that!

If the house is small, so that there is no room available for this display at the wedding, the presents are shown on the day before, and intimate friends are especially asked to come in for tea, and to view them. This is not done if they are to be displayed at the wedding.

Very intimate friends seldom need to be asked; the chances are they will come in often, to see what has come since they were in last!

MARKING SILVER

Wedding presents are all sent to the bride, and are, according to law, her personal property. According to the etiquette of yesterday, when Muriel Brown Jones married John Ross, not a piece of linen or silver in "Ross house" was marked otherwise than "M. B. J." But as this long proved a confusing and senseless custom, it is now recognized as more practical to mark everything with the bride's future initials: "M.J.R."

When she has three initials, the smartest marking is the triangle of block letters—last name at the top:

R
M J

According to present-day taste, all overlong and fancy letters should be avoided. A single initial in old English is always excellent.

USE OF CREST

The one occasion when it is in good taste to use a family's crest is in the marking of silver. *Correctly*, no heraldic device may be used by a woman, except a lozenge (see page 94); but many families have accepted it as reasonable that silver given the bride by her own family (especially when it matches silver which she will inherit) be marked with her father's crest. That which is given by the bridegroom's family is marked with his crest. The coat of arms is sometimes engraved on very large and absolutely plain pieces, but the crest alone—and small in size—is in better taste than anything conspicuous or florid.

EXCHANGING WEDDING PRESENTS

Some people think it discourteous if a bride changes the present chosen for her. But it has been a time-honored custom to permit a bride to exchange all duplicate presents, and no friends should allow their feelings to be hurt, unless they have chosen the present with a particular sentiment. A bride never changes the presents chosen for her by her own family or by the bridegroom's family—unless especially told that she may do so. But to keep twenty-two salt cellars and sixteen silver trays when she has no pepper pots or coffee spoons or vegetable dishes would be putting "sentiment" above "sense."

THE TROUSSEAU

A trousseau, according to the derivation of the word, was "a little trusse or bundle" that the bride carried with her to the house of her husband. In modern times the "little bundle" often requires the services of a van to transport.

At present the extravagant trousseaux of yesterday's daughters of the very rich are dwindling to items of actual requirement. Household linen enough to run an enormous house—and for a lifetime—is probably past for always. The following trousseau listed in former editions of this book is so out of present-day proportion as to seem an absurdity to reprint—except as a factual account of what a completely filled linen closet of yesterday contained:

One to three dozen of the finest quality embroidered, or otherwise trimmed, linen* single-bed sheets, with large embroidered monogram.

One to three dozen of the finest quality single-bed linen under-sheets with narrow hem and no monogram.

Half these quantities for double beds.

Two pillow-cases and also one small pillow-case—for a small down pillow—to match each double upper sheet.

Three blanket covers of crêpe de chine or other washable silk for each bed, white or in colors to match each room, and edged with narrow lace and breadths put together with lace insertion, and monogram in center; or with hemmed or scalloped edge and seams put together with *entredeux*.

Two pair of blankets (one summer and one winter weight) for each bed.

One light wool and—in cold latitudes—one down-filled quilt for each bed.

Two to five dozen finest-quality linen, large face towels, with deep-fringed or embroidered ends or insertion let-in-hems† and embroidered monogram—or initials.

Three to five dozen fine-quality hemstitched linen towels, with embroidered monogram or initials, but otherwise plain.

Three to five dozen small hand towels to match the large ones.

One to two dozen bath sheets, white or colored, with contrasting monograms or initials.

Two to three dozen bath towels of hand size to match.

Two to three dozen wash cloths to match.

Six to twelve bath mats to match pattern or colors.

TABLE LINEN

One or two tablecloths six yards long by two and a half yards wide, or four yards square, of finest but untrimmed white linen damask, with embroidered monogram on each side of center, for dinners of eighteen or twenty. (When counting size, allow 18 inches for each plate, and in addition half a yard margin to fall over on each of the four sides.)

Two dozen dinner napkins, 30 by 36 inches, to match.

Two or four linen damask tablecloths, either white or pastel colored, three and a half to four yards long, for dinners of ten or twelve.

---

* Yard-deep embroidered bed linen, with square French pillow-cases gave way to silk—now passing out; and fashion (after again returning to linen) has now become habituated to percale—rarely trimmed, but often dyed to match the colors of the rooms.

† Fringes unobtainable and lace trimming rarely if ever chosen today.

Eight to twelve linen damask tablecloths, white or colored, two and a half or three yards long.

One dozen napkins, 27 by 30 inches, to match each tablecloth.

One or two dozen fine white damask tablecloths, one and a half yards square, for big dinners at little tables.

Four to eight dozen napkins, 24 by 24 inches to match.

All tablecloths and napkins must have embroidered monogram or initials.

Two to six runners or centerpieces, with place mats and lunch napkins to match. Or, if a modern bare table is preferred, only place mats and napkins.

Four to six tea cloths of filet lace or drawn work or Russian embroidery, with small napkins to match.

Four to six dozen tiny cocktail napkins.

Table pieces and tea cloths have monograms if there is any plain linen where a monogram can be embroidered. Otherwise monograms or initials are put on the napkins only.

Six to twelve linen and needlework breakfast tray covers, with two small napkins to match each.

In addition to the above there are two to three dozen* servants' sheets and pillow-cases, fine quality cotton; four to eight pair of woolen blankets; four to eight wool-filled quilts; four to six dozen towels; one or two dozen bath towels; six to eight damask or other tablecloths, and six to twelve dozen napkins, all marked with machine embroidery. Two to three dozen kitchen cloths and towels, two to four dozen pantry dish-towels, and one to two dozen roller towels complete the list.

MARKING LINEN

It is, of course, essential to perfection that all linen be embroidered with monogram or initials. On napkins a single initial is enough, but on larger articles an initial designed with a few additional lines to give the effect of a monogram is more effective and the expense is less than two initials.

Large tablecloths are marked on either side of center, midway between table center and edge of table. Small yard-and-a-half-square tablecloths—invaluable for those most popular of dinners, big ones at little tables—are marked at one corner about a foot from table center, put parallel with table edge or cross-cornered. Square monograms look well set in line with the table edge; irregular ones look best cross-cornered. The placing of marking is important; therefore

---

* For only one maid, cut list to 8 sheets and pillow-cases, 1 pair blankets, 1 light weight quilt, 1 heavy, etc.

it is best to set the table, or at least make a diagram on cross-bar paper, and then decide.

Very large damask napkins are marked in center; others are marked in one corner—cross-cornered usually, but sometimes straight. To decide about the place for marking the napkins, always fold the napkin exactly as it is to be folded for use, and then make a light pencil outline in the center of the folded napkin.

Sheets are always marked with base of letters toward hem—when on the bed, the monogram is right-side up to a person standing at foot of bed—and it is put at half the depth at which the sheet is turned back. Long American pillow-cases are marked halfway between edge of case and beginning of the pillow. On square French pillow-cases* the monogram is put cross-cornered with top to corner.

Although there is no fixed rule for marking towels other than where you think the device looks best, a safe one to follow is to divide the length of each towel into eighths and center the marking on, or put it directly under, the line that is one eighth from the front lower edge. Then whichever proportion you choose for one set of towels must be followed in the marking of any other variety to be used in the same bathroom.

EACH BRIDE'S ESSENTIAL LINEN LIST

From the overextravagant list given in its completeness above, the bride or new householder should run down the items and choose for herself the articles which are necessary to her own habits of life, and cross off the superfluous.

But certain suggestions can, of course, be given. To one, for example, who is going to have one maid or very likely none, it should be repeated that damask is not very practical for everyday because an accidental spot necessitates a fresh cloth. Moreover, not only do spots necessitate a fresh cloth, but folding and refolding it necessarily mars its freshness.

If there were no danger of spilling a drop of anything, ever, then three or four cloths would be enough. On the other hand, lace mats never muss, and should something be spilled on one piece, it can be washed and pressed out in a moment. In fact, one set of lace place mats can be used indefinitely—and always look the same. But lace won't do for breakfast! Damask, which is the most formal table covering known, is also the most ideal cover for the table at breakfast. Failing damask, use any other variety of linen cover or mats.

If you use a damask cloth on your dinner table, larger napkins will be necessary than for mats or a runner—again a matter that must be

---

* French shape rarely seen today.

considered because of laundering. How many napkins must be included in your supply must be measured by the way you will live. If you are to have one fresh napkin for each person every meal, including afternoon tea, this for a family of two alone would mean forty-nine napkins a week; whereas if you have one napkin for each person a week, the minimum would be three.

Your household linen has less variation; five sheets to each bed, and four pillow-cases for each pillow would be the minimum if top sheet is changed twice a week and laundry is delivered promptly.

One dozen face towels and three bath towels and four wash cloths and two bath mats would be the minimum for each person (the same for the maid).

For the kitchen you should have at least six glass towels, six kitchen towels, and four roller towels—for a family of two and one maid.

To this list add as much more as you need or your means allow.

Remember, too, that big dinners served at little tables are fashionable, because practical. For these you will need one tablecloth and four napkins each for however many small tables you can include.

(For further details see Index.)

THE WEDDING DRESS

It is always proper for a bride to wear a white dress and veil, no matter in what season of the year the wedding is held. It may be of any white material—satin, brocade, velvet, chiffon, or entirely of lace. It may be embroidered with pearls, crystals or silver; or it may be as plain as a slip-cover. It may be anything, in fact, that the bride fancies, and may be made in whatever fashion or period she chooses.

As for her veil—in its combination of lace or tulle and orange blossoms—perhaps it is copied from a headdress of Egypt or China, or from the severe drapery of Rebecca herself, or it may proclaim the knowing touch of the Rue de la Paix. It may have a cap, like that of a lady in a French print, or fall in clouds of tulle from under a diadem made of anything that the art of millinery can contrive.

The origin of the bridal veil is an unsettled question. Roman brides wore "yellow veils," and veils were used in the ancient Hebrew marriage ceremony. The veil as we use it may be a substitute for the flowing tresses, which in old times fell like a mantle modestly concealing the bride's face and form. Or it may be an amplification of the veil which medieval fashion added to every headdress.

In olden days the garland rather than the veil seems to have been of greatest importance. The garland was the "coronet of chastity," and the bride's right to wear it was her inalienable attribute of virtue. Very old books speak of three ornaments that every virtuous bride must wear: "a ring on her finger, a brooch on her breast and a garland on her head." A bride who had no dowry of gold was said nevertheless to bring her husband great treasure if she brought him a garland—in other words, a virtuous wife.

At present the veil is usually mounted by a milliner on a made foundation, so that it need merely be put on. But every girl has her individual idea of what she wishes her wedding veil to be and may choose rather to put it together herself, or have it done by some particular friend whose taste and skill she especially admires.

If she chooses to wear a veil over her face up the aisle and during the ceremony, the front veil is always a short, separate piece about a yard square, gathered on an invisible band, and pinned with a hairpin at either side, after the long veil is arranged. It is taken off by the maid of honor when she gives the bride's bouquet back to the bride at the conclusion of the ceremony.

The face veil is rather old-fashioned, and is appropriate only for a very young bride of a demure type. The tradition is that a maiden is too shy to face a congregation unveiled, and reveals her face only when she is a married woman.

The length of the train of the bride's dress depends somewhat upon the size of the church. In a large church the train should be very long; in a little chapel, short. A moderately short train extends one yard on the ground. A bride's dress should always be on the conservative side of fashion.

If short loose gloves happen to be in fashion, she merely pulls the glove off at the altar, but if she wears elbow-length or longer evening gloves, usually the under seam of the wedding finger of the glove is ripped for about two inches and the bride need only pull the tip off to have the ring put on. Or, if the wedding is a small one, she wears no gloves at all.

Brides have been known to choose a color other than white. Cloth of silver is quite conventional and so is very deep cream. Also permissible is powder pink—this a color so pale as to give the impression of white. But cloth of gold or any other definite color suggests the habiliment of a widow rather than that of a virgin maid—of whom the white and orange blossoms, or myrtle leaf, are the emblems.

If a bride chooses to be married in traveling dress, she has no bridesmaids, though she often has a maid (or matron) of honor. A "traveling" dress is either a "tailor-made," if she is going directly to a boat or train, or a morning or an afternoon dress—whatever she would "wear away" after a big wedding.

WHAT OTHER CLOTHES FOR THE BRIDE'S TROUSSEAU?

It is impossible for anyone but the bride herself to answer the question of what clothes she will need and of what variety. It all depends

FIRST PREPARATIONS FOR A WEDDING

—is she to be in a big city for the winter season, or at a watering place for the summer? Is she going to travel, or live quietly? It is foolish to get more "outside" clothes than she has immediate use for; fashions change too radically.

On the subject of the under things, one can dip into any of the women's magazines devoted to fashion and understand at first sight that the furnishings which may be put upon the person of one young female would require a catalogue as long and varied as a seedsman's. An extravagant trousseau contains every article illustrated—and more besides—and by the dozens! But it must not for a moment be supposed that every bride has a trousseau which requires an outlay possible only to parents who are very rich and also very indulgent.

DISPLAYING THE TROUSSEAU

Household linen, especially if very beautiful, is often displayed with the wedding presents, but in cities such as New York, Washington or Boston, it has never been considered good taste to make a formal display of the bride's personal trousseau. She may, of course, show intimate friends some of her things, but her trousseau is never spread out on exhibition. Objection to her doing so may, however, be removed if it is the custom of the place in which she lives.

WHAT THE BRIDESMAIDS WEAR

The costumes of the bridesmaids—slippers, stockings, dresses, bouquets, gloves and hats—are selected by the bride, without considering or even consulting them as to their taste or preferences. This rule is important to note. On occasion a bride will try to consult them and get all to agree, but long experience has proved that six girls almost certainly quarrel over six opposed ideas. Bridesmaids, therefore, customarily wear—and pay for—what the bride chooses. That is the rule. The only consolation is that, if they are ugly, she gets full blame. If they are lovely, she gets the credit. The bridesmaids are always dressed exactly alike as to texture of materials and model of making, but sometimes their dresses differ in color. The two who follow the ushers might wear pale green, the next two peach, and the next two violet, and the maid of honor yellowish cream; and all carry the same kind of flowers.

The dress of the maid or matron of honor, by the way, never precisely matches that of the bridesmaids, though it is usually similar but reversed in color. For example: If the bridesmaids wear peach dresses with blue sashes and peach hats trimmed in blue and have bouquets of larkspur, the maid of honor wears the same dress in blue, with peach sash, has a blue hat trimmed with peach, and carries talisman roses.

Sometimes the bridesmaids wear the same color, but in graduated value. The first two would wear American beauty rose, the next two a lighter tint, and the next two a still lighter color, while the maid of honor would be in palest flesh pink. Although a bride seldom cares to run the risk of having the white of her attendants detract from the effect of the single whiteness of her dress, an all-white wedding could be entrancing, especially in a garden with a background of dense green, like the high-hedged Italian ones.

The other important item is the selection of a material for the bridesmaids' dresses that will complement the material of the dress of the bride. Perhaps the bride's dress might be of fine white lace (the starched variety) and the bridesmaids' of taffeta; or if in the South, she might wear taffeta and put them in organdy—or organza with broad taffeta sashes. Or they might all wear the same soft lustrous satin and let the bride's veil and train alone make the difference.

FLOWER GIRL AND PAGES

Flower girls and pages are dressed in quaint old-fashioned dresses and suits of white silk or satin of whatever period the bride fancies as being especially picturesque. Or perhaps they are dressed in their ordinary white clothes, with wreaths and bouquets for the girls and white boutonnières for the boys.

BRIDESMAID IN MOURNING

A bridesmaid who is in mourning, may wear colors on this one day, as bridesmaids' dresses are looked upon as uniforms, not individual costumes.

WHAT THE BRIDESMAIDS CARRY

The bridesmaids almost always carry flowers—bouquets sometimes, or baskets, but usually sheaves which they hold on their outside arms. Those walking on the right side hold them on the right arm with the stems pointing downward to the left; and those on the left hold their flowers on the left arm, with stems toward the right. Bouquets or baskets are, however, held in front.

Sometimes bridesmaids carry muffs in winter, or in summer fans or parasols, more often flower-filled baskets or hats made into baskets by tying their wide brims together with ribbons. Flowers matching those in the basket might be worn in the hair (in which case the bridesmaids need not buy either hats or hair ornaments).

As a warning against the too blatant use of cosmetics, it may not be out of place to quote one commentary made by a man of great distinction who, having seen nothing of the society of very young people for many years, "had to go" to the wedding of a niece. It was one of the biggest weddings of the spring season in New York. The flowers were wonderful; the bridesmaids were many and beautiful. Afterwards the family talked long about the wedding, but the distinguished uncle said nothing. Finally, he was asked point blank, "Don't you think the wedding was too lovely? Weren't the bridesmaids beautiful?"

"No," said the uncle, "I did not think it was lovely at all. Every one of the bridesmaids was so powdered and painted and mascaraed that there was not a sweet or fresh face among them. I can see a procession just like them any evening on the musical comedy stage! One expects unrestrained make-up in a theater, but in the house of God it is shocking!"

THE COST OF BEING BRIDESMAID

With the exception of the flowers they carry, which are presented by the bride, every article worn by the bridesmaids, flower girls or pages, although chosen by the bride, must be paid for by the wearers.

It is perhaps an irrefutable condemnation of the modern wedding display that many a young girl has had to refuse the joy of being in the wedding party because a complete bridesmaid's outfit costs a sum that parents of moderate means are quite unable to meet for popular daughters. And it is seldom that the bride herself is in a position to give six or eight complete costumes, much as she may want all her most particular friends with her on her day of days.

Unless her bridesmaids have unusually deep purses, the bride who has a conscience tries to choose clothes that will not be too expensive. Yesterday the tender-hearted bride who, for the sake of their purses, sent her bridesmaids to an average "little woman" to have their clothes made, and to a little hat-place around the corner, was likely to have a rather dowdy little flock fluttering down the aisle in front of her. Today, however, the department stores as well as the specialty shops are prepared to submit enchanting ready-to-wear models that can be ordered in different colors, or even materials, and at almost whatever the budget decided upon may be.

HOW MANY BRIDESMAIDS OR OTHER ATTENDANTS?

This question is answered by: How many friends has she whom she has "always promised" to have with her on that day? Has she a large circle of intimates or only one or two? Her sister is always maid of honor. If she has no sister of suitable age, she chooses her most intimate friend.

In addition to a maid or matron of honor, a bride may have a veritable procession: eight or ten bridesmaids, junior bridesmaids, flower girls and pages and a ring bearer.

At an average New York wedding there are four or six bridesmaids. Half the "maids" may be "matrons." Although it is not very suitable to have young married women as bridesmaids and then have an unmarried girl as maid of honor, this rule is usually broken in the case of a bride's unmarried sister.

Although a bride need have no attendants, it is best that she have at least one. The picture of her father holding her bouquet and stooping to adjust her train would be difficult to witness with gravity.

CHILDREN IN THE WEDDING PROCESSION

The clothes of children who serve as bridal attendants should more or less match those of the bride. Although it is not necessary that flower girls wear long dresses unless the bride wears a period dress, they may, however, wear anything that the imagination of the bride or the mother of the children (with the bride's consent) can design. At many weddings the children are all dressed in white—especially the ring bearer. Ring bearers, as it happens, are unknown in the smart world of New York, but they are very popular in many other American localities. And if the bride would like to have her little brother or nephew perform this office, he is, of course, dressed in white, carries the ring on a white cushion and walks ahead of her.

The ring is either lightly sewed to the cushion or fastened by having an ordinary pearl-headed flower pin thrust into the center of the cushion and the ring encircling this. The best man should be shown beforehand whether he is to pull or lift it off.

TRAIN BEARERS

Train bearers, as the name implies, hold the bride's train. They, too, must be very little boys and dressed in white. The train trailing smoothly by itself is really more assuring than a train in the hands of very little children whose manner of bearing it is uncertain, to say the least. One baby train bearer halfway down an immensely long aisle decided that he had held up the train long enough, so, dropping it, he sat down on it instead and let the bride drag him the rest of the way. He was adorable but a very serious handicap to the bride's ability to walk.

Both boys and girls wear slippers with a strap and white socks. If they are dressed in white, their slippers are of course white; but if they wear color, their slippers are colored, either to match their clothes or of a constrasting color—more often the latter. As everyone knows, children's strap slippers come in several colors; otherwise white ones are easily dyed. Kid is in better taste than satin.

At important weddings little girls often wear picture bonnets. At simpler weddings they wear narrow wreaths on their heads. These should be carefully measured for size and must be neat in outline. Small artificial flowers are far better for this purpose than real flowers, which are likely to be ragged as well as too heavy.

BEST MAN AND USHERS

No matter how small the wedding, the bridegroom always has a best man. It is not an unbreakable rule, but it hints of a family quarrel if the brother of the bridegroom is not best man, or the sister of the bride is not maid of honor, unless, of course, brother or sister is many years senior or junior. When the bridegroom has no brother, his next selection is his most intimate friend; or, if deciding upon this best one is difficult, he perhaps chooses the brother of the bride.

"Groomsmen" is supposedly an obsolete term; it is still used in some parts of the country, but the word generally used today is "ushers." The number of ushers is in proportion to the size of the church and the number of guests invited. At a house wedding, ushers are often merely "honorary," and the bridegroom may have many or none, as he chooses.

As ushers and bridesmaids are chosen from only most intimate friends of the bride and groom, it is scarcely necessary to suggest how to word the asking! Usually they are told at the time of announcing the engagement that they are expected to serve; or they are told whenever one happens to meet them. If school or collge friends who live at a distance are among the number, letters are necessary. Such as:

"Mary and I are to be married on the tenth of November, and, of course, you are to be an usher." Usually he adds, "My dinner is to be on the seventh at eight o'clock at——," naming the club or restaurant.

It is unheard of that a man refuse the honor unless a bridegroom, for snobbish reasons, asks someone who is not really a friend at all.

It is entirely correct for a married man to act as usher, or for a married woman to be matron of honor, when neither the wife of the first nor the husband of the second is asked to take part. In fact—though there is no rule against it—it is most rarely, if ever, that a man and wife both serve at the same wedding. The one not officiating is of course invited to the wedding, but not necessarily invited to sit at the bridal table.

BRIDE'S USHER AND GROOM'S BRIDESMAID

Unless attendants are limited to her sister and his brother, a brother of the bride, or if she has no brother, then her "favorite cousin" is always asked by the groom to be usher out of compliment to her. The bride returns the compliment by asking the sister of the groom who is nearest her own age to be bridesmaid, or if he has no sister, she asks a cousin. If she is to have a number of bridesmaids—especially if the groom has no sister—she very often shows her courtesy by asking the groom to name a particular friend of his. The bride in asking the groom's bridesmaid does not say, "Will you be one of my bridesmaids because Jim wants me to ask you?" If the bridesmaid is not a particular friend of the bride, she knows perfectly that it is on Jim's account that she has been asked. It is the same with the bride's usher. If the groom is choosing six or eight or ten ushers, he often includes one who is an especial friend of the bride, and asks him exactly as he asks the others.

When the homes of the bride and bridegroom are a great distance apart, so that none but the bridegroom's immediate family can make the journey to the wedding, it is not unusual—if he has no brother—that he choose his father or even stepfather as his best man. The ushers are chosen from among the friends of the bride. (It is not unusual that his father serve as best man—at any time.)

BRIDEGROOM'S TROUSSEAU FOR THE HONEYMOON

The clothes the bridegroom will need for his wedding trip depend naturally upon where they are going. He will need two sack suits—not necessarily new, but good as new—and two pair of shoes to wear alternately. He should choose suits which look well with the same overcoat—which let us hope is either blue or dark gray if it is also to be worn with evening clothes.

If they are going on a real journey by train or boat and stopping perhaps at a coast or country resort, then he should take clothes for whatever sport they are likely to follow.

So much for the groom as he appears in public. And now to answer the question, "How important are the groom's clothes to the bride?" The disappointing but truthful answer is that outside of England not one woman in a hundred knows the first thing about men's clothes—or even notices them. It is true that Mary will notice when John, in her opinion, looks particularly well—or not so well—compared with other men. But the chance is very small that she even notices his new suit or hat or shoes, unless they are so strikingly new that they literally shout at her.

But there is one thing that she will notice and that is the attractive neatness or the sloppiness of his personal belongings.

To John, whose budget is probably limited, it is suggested that instead of getting another new suit, which looks exactly like one he has now, that he pay attention to the neatness of his possessions so that when they are laid out on the top of the bureau or the wash-stand shelf, there are no brushes with the bristles looking as though chewed off or matted down, nor any dingy shaving things, nor half-empty toothpaste tubes, twisted and crinkly and smeared.

New slippers and a dressing gown of simplest variety, that is, fresh and washable, is to be preferred to one of silk brocade that is bedraggled. Let his underwear be new, and his pajamas attractive in color and becoming in neckline.

THE WEDDING CLOTHES OF THE BRIDEGROOM

If the wedding is to be a formal one in an ultra-fashionable community and he does not already possess a well-fitting morning coat, often called a cutaway, he must order one. He must also have dark gray-striped trousers. At extremely smart weddings, especially in the spring, a groom and his best man wear white piqué high double-breasted waistcoats, because the more white that can be got into an otherwise sombre costume the more wedding-like it looks. Because the white waistcoat is a needless extravagance, the bridegroom usually wears a black one to match his coat, as do the ushers. As to his tie, he may choose a four-in-hand to match those selected for the ushers, of black silk with a narrow single or broken white stripe at narrow or wide intervals. At many smart weddings the groom and all the men of the wedding party wear bow ties of black silk with small white dots. Ascot ties are somewhat Victorian but proper if preferred and are often worn by the father of the bride.

White buckskin gloves are the smartest; but if the bridegroom prefers gray suède, they should at least be as light a gray as possible. White kid is worn only in the evening. At small country weddings gloves are not worn at all. Spats, if chosen, must fit flat and match the gloves exactly; but they are fast disappearing!

Especially well-dressed bridegrooms have the soles of their shoes blackened with waterproof shoe polish so that when they kneel, their shoes look dark and neat. (One must be sure that the polish is of the kind that will not come off on carpets or rugs.)

WHAT THE BEST MAN WEARS

The best man wears precisely what the bridegroom wears. The groom and best man often wear ties that are different from those worn by the ushers, and occasionally white waistcoats. Otherwise the two principal men are dressed like the ushers.

WHAT THE USHERS WEAR AT A FORMAL WEDDING

It is of greatest importance that in dress each usher be an exact counterpart of his fellows, if the picture is to be perfect. Everyone knows what a ragged-edged appearance is produced by a company of recruits whose uniforms are odd lots.

The smartness of the wedding procession depends solely upon military uniformity. This is so important that fastidious men (especially those who have been in military service) send typewritten instructions to their ushers, covering every detail of the equipment required. Few people may reason why, but it is always just such attention to detail that produces a perfectly finished result. The directions sent by a certain New York bridegroom were as follows:

Wedding rehearsal on Tuesday at St. Bartholomew's Church at 5 P. M.
Wedding on Wednesday at 4 P. M.
Please wear:
Black calfskin low shoes.
Plain black silk socks.
Gray striped trousers—the darkest you have.
Morning coat and single-breasted black waistcoat.
White dress shirt. See that cuffs show three-quarters of an inch below coat sleeves.
Stand-up wing collar.
Tie and gloves are enclosed.*
Boutonnière will be at the church.
Be at the church yourself at three o'clock, sharp.

The above list is for the *most* correct and formal wedding.

CLOTHES OF USHERS AT A SIMPLE WEDDING

If, however, the wedding is to be a very small and informal one—in the country, or in a community where the bridegroom and his friends do not possess cutaway coats—it would be permissible to wear dark blue sack suits, stiff white shirts, wing collars, blue and white ties, white boutonnières and no gloves. White waistcoats always add a wedding-like effect, but are not likely to be useful afterwards.

The principal requirement is that all the men of the wedding party shall be *alike*.

FLANNELS PERMISSIBLE AT MIDSUMMER WEDDING

For a small midsummer wedding in the country, white flannel trousers, blue or gray double-breasted coats (without waistcoats), turned-down collars, bow ties, white buckskin shoes and white flowers in buttonholes are quite perfect. Other clothes might be all right, if all the men had them. Ex-petty officers could wear their ducks, for example, with the insignia taken off.

* Groom had already found out size of gloves and also size of collars, since bow ties had been selected.

THE HEAD USHER

In certain localities courtesy designates the usher who is selected to take the bride's mother up the aisle as the "head" or "first" usher.

Very occasionally, too, a nervous groom appoints an especially reliable friend head usher so as to be sure that all details will be carried out—including the prompt and proper appearance at the church of the other ushers. The ushers divide the arrangements among themselves. The groom decides who goes on which aisle. One volunteers or is asked to look out for the bride's coming and to notify the groom. Another is detailed to take the two mothers up the aisle. But very often this arrangement is arbitrarily decided by height. If one mother is very tall and the other very short, each goes up with a different usher.

THE BRIDESMAIDS' LUNCHEON

In many sections of America, especially in the country and in small towns, brides ask their bridesmaids to a farewell luncheon, just as in other communities the bride is given a shower. (See Chapter 32.)

There is no especial difference between a bridesmaids' luncheon and any other lunch party, except that the table is elaborately decorated—usually in pink with bridesmaids' roses. There is a bride's cake—lady cake with pink icing—and there are favors in the cake, and candies wrapped in pink papers on which are written sentimental verses or "fortunes," and altogether it is a "lovely party."

In any event, the typical scene during the days before a wedding is one of packages arriving and bridesmaids and other intimate friends running in and out of the house at all hours of the day, looking at new presents as they come, perhaps helping the bride to write the descriptions in the gift book or to arrange them in the room where they are to be displayed.

The bride usually goes to oversee the last fittings of the bridesmaids' dresses in order to be sure that they are as she wants them. This final trying-on should be arranged for several days at least before the wedding, so there may be sufficient time to make any alterations that are found necessary. Often the bride tries on her wedding dress at the same time, so that she may see the effect of the whole wedding picture as it will be; or if she prefers, she tries on her dress at another hour alone.

GIFTS FOR THE BRIDE'S ATTENDANTS

Usually her bridesmaids lunch with her, without any "party preparations," or come in for tea, the day before the wedding, and on that day the bride gives each of them "her present," which is always something to wear. The typical bridesmaid's present is a bracelet, a bangle, a pin, a clip or other trinket, which, according to the means of the bride, may have great or scarcely any intrinsic value. The gift to her maid (or matron) of honor may well match those given the bridesmaids or be quite different.

BRIDESMAIDS' AND USHERS' DINNER

If a wedding is held in the country, or if most of the bridesmaids or ushers come from a distance and are therefore staying at the bride's house or with her neighbors, there is naturally a dinner, in order to provide for the visitors. But where the wedding is in the city—especially when all the members of the bridal party live there also—the custom of giving a bridesmaids' and ushers' dinner has gone out of fashion. If the bridal party is asked to dine at the house of the bride on the evening before the wedding, it is usually for the purpose of seeing that they go to the church for rehearsal, which is of all things the most important. More often the rehearsal is in the afternoon, after which they all go to the bride's house for tea, allowing her parents to have her to themselves on her last evening home, and giving her a chance to go early to bed so as to look her prettiest on the morrow.

THE BACHELOR DINNER

Popularly supposed to be a frightful orgy, the bachelor dinner was in truth, more often than not, a sheep in wolf's clothing. As a matter of fact, an "orgy" was never looked upon with favor by any but silly and misguided youths, whose idea of a howling good time was to make a howling noise, chiefly by singing at the top of their voices and breaking glasses. A boisterous picture, but scarcely a vicious one! Especially as a lot of the cheapest glassware was always there for the purpose.

The breaking habit originated with drinking the bride's health and breaking the stem of the wine glass, so that it "might never serve a less honorable purpose." And this same time-honored custom is followed to this day. Toward the end of the dinner the bridegroom rises, and holding a filled champagne glass aloft says, "To the bride!" Every man rises, drinks the toast standing, and then breaks the delicate stem of the glass. The impulse to break more glass is natural to youth, and probably still occurs. It is not hard to understand. The same impulse is seen at every county fair where enthusiastic youths delight in shooting, or throwing balls, at clay pipes and ducks and—crockery!

Aside from toasting the bride and its glass-smashing result, the bridegroom's farewell dinner is exactly like any other "man's dinner."

FIRST PREPARATIONS FOR A WEDDING

GIFTS PRESENTED TO USHERS

The bridegroom's gifts to his ushers are usually put at their places at the bachelor dinner. Cuff links are the most popular gift. Silver or gold pencils, belt buckles, key rings, cigarette cases, bill-folders, or other small and personal articles are suitable. The present to the best man is approximately the same, or slightly handsomer than the gift to the ushers.

VITAL IMPORTANCE OF REHEARSAL

The bride always directs her wedding rehearsal, but never herself takes part in it, as it is supposed to be bad luck. Someone else—anyone who happens to be present—is appointed as understudy.

Most of us are familiar with the wedding service, and its form seems simple enough. But, unless one has by experience learned to take care of details, the effect is hitchy and disjointed. It is not that awkward happenings are serious offenses; but any detail that destroys the smoothness of the general impression is fatal to dignity, which is the qualification necessary above all in every ceremonial observance.

HOW THE PROCESSION IS DRILLED

At an elaborate Protestant wedding with choral service, the choir enters in advance of the hour set for the ceremony, and does not form any part of the wedding procession. But at an important Catholic wedding—in St. Patrick's Cathedral in New York, for instance—the choristers wearing lace-trimmed surplices over cassocks lead the wedding procession, singing as they go. The ushers immediately follow them.

In any event, whether the wedding be Catholic or Protestant, the most elaborate possible or small and simple, the organist must always be at the rehearsal, as one of the most important details is marking the time of the wedding march. Witnesses of most weddings can scarcely imagine that a wedding march is a *march* at all; more often than not, the heads of ushers and bridesmaids bob up and down like something boiling in a pan. A perfectly drilled wedding procession, like a military one, should move forward in perfect step, rising and falling in a block or unit. To secure perfection of detail, the bars of the processional may be counted so that the music comes to an end at precisely the moment the bride and groom stand side by side at the chancel steps. This is not difficult; it merely takes time and attention.

A wedding rehearsal should proceed as follows:

First of all, it is necessary to determine the exact speed at which the march is to be played. The ushers are asked to try it out. They line up at the door, walk forward two and two. The audience, consisting of the bride and a few or many members of the families, decides whether the pace looks well. It must not be fast enough to seem brisk, nor slow enough to be funereal. At one wedding the ushers counted two beats as one and the pace was so slow that they all waddled in trying to keep their balance. On the other hand it is unsuitable to trot up the aisle of a church.

The "audience" having decided the speed, and the organist having noted the tempo, the entire procession, including the bridesmaids and a substitute, instead of the real bride, on her father's arm, go out into the vestibule and make their entry. Remember, the father is an important factor in the ceremony, and must take part in the rehearsal.

The procession is arranged according to height, the two shortest ushers leading—unless others of nearly the same height are found to be more accurate pacemakers. The bridesmaids come directly after the ushers, two and two, also according to height, the shortest in the lead. After the bridesmaids, the maid (or matron) of honor walks alone; flower girls come next (if there are any); and last of all, the understudy bride leaning on the arm of the father, with pages (if she has any) holding up her train. Each pair in the procession follows the two directly in front by four paces or beats of time. In the vestibule, everyone in the procession must pay attention to the feet directly in front; the pacemakers can follow the army sergeant's example and say very softly, "Left, left!" At the end the bride counts eight beats before she and the father put "left foot" forward. The whole trick is starting; after that they just walk naturally to the beat of the music,

FORMATION OF THE WEDDING PROCESSION— KEY: ⊠, USHERS; ⊕, BRIDESMAIDS; MH, MAID OF HONOR; FG, FLOWER GIRL; F, FATHER; B, BRIDE

FIRST PREPARATIONS FOR A WEDDING

GROUPING AT THE ALTAR— KEY: +, MINISTER; B, BRIDE; G, GROOM; MH, MAID OF HONOR; BM, BEST MAN; FG, FLOWER GIRLS OR PAGES; ☒, USHERS; ⊕, BRIDESMAIDS; F, FATHER OF BRIDE

but keeping the ones in front as nearly as possible at the same distance.

At the foot of the chancel, the ushers divide. In a small church, the first two go up the chancel steps and stand at the top, one on the right, the other on the left. The second two go a step or two below the first. If there are more, they stand below again. Chalk marks can be made on the chancel floor if necessary, but it ought not to be difficult, except for very little children who are flower girls or pages, to learn their position.

Or in a big church they go up farther, some of them lining the steps, or all of them in front of the choir stalls. The bridesmaids also divide, half on either side, and always stand in front of the ushers. The maid of honor's place is on the left at the foot of the steps, exactly opposite the best man. Flower girls and pages are put above or below the bridesmaids, wherever it is thought "the picture" is best.

The grouping of the ushers and bridesmaids in the chancel or lining the steps also depends upon their number and the size of the church. In any event, the bridesmaids stand in front of the ushers, half of them on the right and half on the left. They never stand all on the bride's side, and the ushers on the groom's.

CHURCH WITH TWO MAIN AISLES

When the church has two main aisles instead of the more usual center one, it is a matter of choice whether to use one and treat the other as a side aisle, or to use the right one for the processional and the left one for the recessional.

CHURCH WITH TWO MAIN AISLES—KEY: XX, GROOM'S PARENTS; OO, BRIDE'S PARENTS

One aisle is usually chosen if the wedding is very small. But if the wedding is a large one, both aisles are made equally prominent, as indicated in the diagram above. If only one aisle is chosen, the bridesmaids and ushers are grouped on this side of the chancel; if both are used, the wedding group is the same as for a single-aisled church.

ENTRANCE OF THE BRIDEGROOM

The clergyman who is to perform the marriage comes into the chancel from the vestry. At a few paces behind him follows the groom, who in turn is followed by the best man. The groom stops at the foot of the chancel steps and takes his place at the right, as indicated in the preceding diagram. His best man stands directly behind him. The ushers and bridesmaids always pass in front of him and take their places as noted above. When the bride approaches, the groom takes only a step to meet her.

A more effective greeting of the bride is possible—but only if the door of the vestry opens into the chancel, so that on following the clergyman, the groom finds himself at the top instead of the foot of the chancel steps. He goes forward to the right-hand side (his left), his best man behind him, and waits where he is until the bride approaches. He then goes down the steps to meet her—which is perhaps more gallant than to stand at the head of the aisle and wait for her to join him.

At the rehearsal the real bride watches carefully how the substitute bride takes her left hand from the real father's arm, shifts her fan, or whatever represents her bouquet, from her right hand to her left, and gives her right hand to the real bridegroom. In the proper performance the groom takes her right hand in his own right hand and draws it through his left arm, at the same time turning toward the chancel. If the service is undivided, and all of it is to be at the altar, this is necessary, as the bride always goes up to the altar leaning on the arm of the groom. If, however, the betrothal is to be read at the foot of the chancel, which is done at most weddings now, he may merely take her hand in his left one and stand as they are.

THE ORGANIST'S CUE

The organist stops at the moment the bride and groom have assumed their places. That is the cue to the organist as to the number of bars necessary for the processional. After the procession has practiced "marching" two or three times, everything ought to be perfect. The organist, having counted the necessary bars of music, can readily give the leading ushers their "music cue"—so that they can start on the measure that will allow the procession and the organ to end together. The organist can, and usually does, stop short, but there is a better finish if the bride's giving her hand to the groom and taking the last step that brings her in front of the chancel is timed so as to fall precisely on the last bars of the processional.

The bride may select whatever music she prefers, but the wedding march from the opera "Lohengrin" has come to be almost as much a part of the impression of the wedding procession as the bride and her bridesmaids. The recessional, on the other hand, is usually that of Mendelssohn

No words of the service are ever rehearsed, although all the places to be taken by the several participants in the marriage ceremony are rehearsed.

The substitute for the bride takes the bridegroom's left arm and goes slowly up the steps to the altar. The best man follows behind and to the right of the groom, and the maid of honor, or "first" bridesmaid, leaves her companions and moves forward at the left of the bride. The substitute for the bride, in pantomine, gives her bouquet to the maid of honor; the best man, also in pantomine, hands the ring to the groom, this merely to see that they are at a convenient distance for the services they are to perform. The recessional is played, and the procession goes out in reversed order—bride and groom first, then bridesmaids, then ushers, again all taking pains to fall into step with the leaders.

The bridesmaids must not walk either up or down the aisle with the ushers! Once in a while the maid of honor takes the arm of the best man and together they follow the bride and groom out of the church. But it gives the impression of a double wedding and spoils the picture.

THE DOUBLE WEDDING

At a double wedding, the two bridegrooms follow the clergyman and stand side by side, each with his best man behind him; the groom of the older sister nearer the aisle. The ushers—one half, friends of the first, and the others, friends of the second bridegroom—go up the aisle together. Then come the bridesmaids of the older sister followed by her maid of honor, who walks alone. The older sister follows, leaning on her father's arm. Then come the bridesmaids of the younger sister, her maid of honor, and last, the younger bride on the arm of a brother, uncle, or nearest male relative.

The first couple ascend the chancel steps and take their places at the left side of the altar rail, leaving room at the right side for the younger bride and her bridegroom. The father stands just below his older daughter. The brother takes his place in the first pew.

The ceremony is a double one, read to both couples, with the particular responses made twice. The father gives both brides away—first, his older daughter, and then his younger. Then he takes the place which must be saved for him beside his wife in the first pew.

At the end of the ceremony, the older sister and her husband turn and go down the aisle first. The younger couple follows. The bridesmaids of the older are followed by those of the younger; the ushers follow last.

FIRST PREPARATIONS FOR A WEDDING

WHEN BRIDES "ATTEND" EACH OTHER

It is not usual, but it is quite possible, for each bride at a double wedding to serve as maid of honor for her sister. Each in turn holds the other's bouquet during her betrothal ceremony.

But the wise bridegroom, if he dispenses with a best man and uses the services of his brother groom, keeps his own bride's ring in his own waistcoat pocket.

SEATING PARENTS AT A DOUBLE WEDDING

One difficulty of a double wedding is the seating of the parents of the two bridegrooms, who must either share the first pew or draw lots for the occupation of first or second—which questions they must decide for themselves.

Occasionally the brides are cousins, in which case the front pew on the bride's side must be shared by both mothers—the older sister—or sister-in-law—being given the aisle seat.

BUYING THE WEDDING RING—OR RINGS

It is quite customary for the bride to go with the groom when he buys the wedding ring, the reason being that as it stays for life on her finger, she should be allowed to choose the width and style she likes. No ring could ever be in better taste than the band of gold, either yellow or white. A diamond band, no matter how fashionable, is much more suitable as a guard than as a wedding ring, especially for the bride who because of sentiment intends never to take her wedding ring off. This is because the under side of a diamond band must be cleaned constantly and moreover a lost diamond replaced every so often. If the bridegroom wishes to have a ring, the bride buys a plain gold band to match hers but a little wider—or it may be any type of ring he prefers and she is able to buy—at the same time.

MARKING THE ENGAGEMENT AND THE WEDDING RING

The wedding ring may be engraved with whatever sentiment the bridegroom chooses. On the broad rings of yesterday it was not unusual to have a quotation of twenty-five letters or more, as well as the initials A.Y.X. and L.M.N., September 2, 1900. On the rings of today, however, A.B.Z. and L.M.N., Sept. 2, 1941, is invariably chosen.

The mounting of the modern engagement ring is usually so narrow that "A. to L.—4, 16, '41" is the most that space can be found for—and at that a magnifying glass is needed to read the letters.

The bridegroom's ring is also marked with initials or a sentiment, as the bride chooses.

THE BRIDEGROOM'S PRESENT TO THE BRIDE

He is a very exceptional and enviable man who is financially able to take his fiancée to the jeweler and let her choose what she fancies. Customarily the bridegroom goes shopping alone and buys the handsomest ornament he can afford—a string of pearls, if he has great wealth, or a diamond pendant, brooch or bracelet, or perhaps only the simplest bangle or charm. But whether his gift is of great or little worth, it must be something for her personal adornment.

THE BRIDE'S PRESENT TO THE BRIDEGROOM

The bride *need* not give a present to the groom, but she usually does if she can. Her favorite gift is something permanent and personal—ranging from a watch to cuff links or ring.

THE CLERGYMAN'S FEE

The fee of the clergyman may range anywhere from ten dollars to one or two hundred dollars, according to the means of the groom and the importance of the wedding. Whatever the amount, it is enclosed in an envelope and taken in charge by the best man, who hands it to the clergyman in his vestry room immediately after the ceremony.

When the clergyman comes from a distance either because he is a relative or school-master or a friend of the bridegroom's family, his travelling and hotel accommodations are, of course, paid by the groom or his family.

TO THE BRIDE WHO ASKS FOR THE PRETTIEST WEDDING AT LEAST EXPENSE

To the bride who has looked through this chapter in search of the simplest of wedding details and who has found the many directions confusingly elaborate, this postscript is intended to make clear the fact that every wedding—no matter whether it be the largest or the simplest—follows this outline:

(1) The first thing to do is to arrange with the clergyman for a day and hour, either in church or at her home, or in the study at the parsonage, or wherever else the ceremony is to take place.
(2) The bride and groom make a list of their friends and send out their invitations or prepare for sending out the announcements.
(3) She invites her attendants, if any. He selects his best man, also his ushers, if any.
(4) He buys the ring.

FIRST PREPARATIONS FOR A WEDDING

(5) She prepares her trousseau, simple as this may be.
(6) Preparation is made for some decoration of the background against which the ceremony is to take place and they are going to receive.
(7) Refreshments: The essential item is wedding cake and something in which to drink the health of the bride and bridegroom. This last may be a fruit juice.

For other simplest wedding details see "Answers to Readers" at end of next chapter. For expenses of bridegroom see page 251.

20

The Day of the Wedding

No one is busier than the best man on the day of the wedding. His official position is a cross between trained nurse, valet, general manager and keeper.

Bright and early in the morning he hurries to the house of the bridegroom, generally before the latter is up. Very likely they breakfast together. In any event, he takes the groom in charge precisely as might a guardian. He takes note of his patient's general condition; if he is normal and "fit," so much the better. If he is "up in the air" or "nervous," the best man must bring him to earth and jolly him along as best he can.

BEST MAN AS EXPRESSMAN

His first actual duty is that of packer and expressman. He must see that everything necessary for the journey is packed, and that the groom does not absent-mindedly put the furnishings of his room in his valise and leave all his belongings hanging in the closet. He must see that the clothes the groom is to "wear away" are put into a special bag to be taken to the house of the bride, or to wherever the reception is taking place where he, as well as she, must change from wedding into traveling clothes. The best man becomes expressman if the first stage of the wedding journey is to be to a hotel in town. He puts all the groom's luggage into his own car or a taxi, drives to the bride's house, carries the bag with the groom's traveling suit in it to the room set aside for his use—usually the dressing room of the bride's father or the bedroom of her brother. He then collects—according to prearrangement—the luggage of the bride and drives with that of both bride and groom to the hotel where accommodations have already been engaged, sees their bags bestowed and that everything is as it should be. If he is very thoughtful, he may himself have flowers put about as a decorative welcome. He also registers for the newly-weds, takes the hotel key, returns to the house of the groom, gives him the key and assures him that everything at the hotel is in readiness. This maneuver allows the young couple, when they arrive, to go quietly to their own number without attracting the notice of anyone, as would be the case if they arrived with baggage and were conspicuously led by a bell-boy whose manner unmistakably proclaims: "Bride and Groom!"

THE DAY OF THE WEDDING

Or, if they are traveling at once by boat or train, the best man takes the baggage to the station, checks the large pieces, and fees a porter to see that the hand luggage is put in the proper stateroom or parlor car chairs. If they are going by automobile, he takes the luggage out to the garage and personally sees that it is bestowed in the car.

BEST MAN AS VALET

His next duty is that of valet. He must see that the groom is dressed and ready early, and plaster him up if he cuts himself shaving. If he is wise in his day, he even provides a small bottle of adrenalin for just such an accident, so that plaster is unnecessary and that the groom may be whole. He may need to find his collar button or even to point out the "missing" clothes that are lying in full view. He must also be sure to ask for the wedding ring and the clergyman's fee, and put them in his own waistcoat pocket. A very careful best man carries a duplicate ring in case of one's being lost during the ceremony.

BEST MAN AS COMPANION-IN-ORDINARY

With the bride's and groom's luggage properly bestowed, the ring and fee in his pocket, the groom's traveling clothes at the bride's house, the groom in complete wedding attire, and himself also ready, the best man has nothing further to do but be gentleman-in-waiting to the bridegroom until it is time to escort him to the church, where he becomes chief of staff.

AT THE HOUSE OF THE BRIDE

Meanwhile, if the wedding is to be at noon, dawn will not have much more than broken before the house—at least below stairs—becomes bustling.

Even if the wedding is to be at four o'clock, it will still be early in the morning when the business of the day begins. But let us suppose it is to be at noon. If the family is one used to assembling at an early breakfast table, it is probable that the bride herself will come down for this last meal alone with her family. They will, however, not be allowed to linger long at the table. The caterer will be clamoring for possession of the dining room; the florist will by that time have dumped heaps of wire and greens into the middle of the drawing room, if not beside the table where the family are still communing with their eggs. The doorbell has long ago begun to ring. At first there are telegrams and special delivery letters; then as soon as the shops open, come the last-moment wedding presents, notes, messages and the insistent clamor of the telephone.

Next, excited voices in the hall announce members of the family who come from a distance. They all want to kiss the bride, they all want rooms to dress in, they all want to talk. Also comes the hairdresser to do the bride's or her mother's or aunt's or grandmother's hair, or the hair of all these; add, too, anyone else who may have been thought necessary to give final beautifying touches to the female members of the household. The dozen and one articles from the caterer are meantime being carried in at the basement door: made dishes, and dishes in the making, raw materials of which others are to be made; folding chairs, small tables, chinaware, glassware, napery, knives, forks and spoons. It is a struggle to get in or out of the kitchen or through the area doorway.

The bride's mother consults the florist for the third and last time as to whether the bridal couple would not better receive in the library, because of the bay window which lends itself easily to the decoration of a background, and because the room is, if anything, larger than the drawing room. And for the third time, the florist agrees about the advantage of the window, but points out that the library has only one narrow door and that the drawing room is much better, because it has two wide ones, and the guests going into the room will not be blocked in the doorway by others coming out.

The best man turns up and wants the bride's luggage.

The head usher comes to ask whether the Joneses, who are to be seated in the fourth pew, are the tall dark ones or the blond ones; and whether he would not better put some of the Titheringtons, who belong in the eighth pew, also in the seventh, as there are nine Titheringtons, and the Joneses in the seventh pew are only four.

A bridesmaid-elect hurries up the steps, runs into the best man carrying out the luggage. Much conversation and giggling and guessing where the luggage is going. Best man very important, also very noble and silent. Bridesmaid shrugs her shoulders, dashes up to the bride's room and dashes down again.

More presents arrive. The furniture movers have come and are carting lumps of heaviness up the stairs to the attic and down the stairs to the cellar. It is all very like an ant-hill. Some are steadily going forward with the business in hand, but others, who have become quite bewildered, seem to be scurrying aimlessly this way and that, picking something up only to put it down again.

THE DRAWING ROOM

Here, where the bride and groom are to receive, one cannot tell yet what the decoration is to be. Perhaps it is a palm grove, a flowering recess, a screen and canopy of wedding bells—but a flowering background of some sort is gradually taking shape.

THE BRIDE'S TABLE

The sit-down breakfast at a wedding of perfection.

Photograph by H. R. E. Phyfe   Floral decorations by Wadley and Smyths

THE DINING ROOM

The dining room, too, blossoms with plants and flowers. Perhaps its space, and that of a tent which has been put up in the garden or city backyard adjoining, is filled with little tables, or perhaps a single row of camp chairs stands flat against the walls. In the center of the room the dining table, pulled out to its fullest extent, is being decked with trimmings and utensils which will be needed later when the spaces left at intervals for various dishes shall be occupied. Preparation of these dishes is meanwhile going on in the kitchen.

THE KITCHEN

The caterer's chefs in white cook's caps and aprons are in possession of the situation, and their assistants run here and there, bringing ingredients as they are told. Or perhaps the caterer brings everything already prepared, in which case the waiters are busy unpacking the big tin boxes and placing the *bains-maries* (fireless-cooker receptacles in tanks of hot water) from which the hot food is to be served. Huge tubs of cracked ice, in which the ice-cream containers are buried, are standing in the shade of the areaway or in the back yard.

LAST PREPARATIONS

Back again in the drawing room, the florist and his assistants are still tying and tacking and arranging and adjusting branches and garlands and sheaves and bunches, and the floor is a litter of twigs and strings and broken branches. The photographer is asking that the central decoration be finished so he can group his pictures; the florist assures him that he is as busy as possible.

The house is as cold as open windows can make it, to keep the flowers fresh, and to avoid stuffiness. The doorbell continues ringing, and the parlor maid finds herself a contestant in a marathon, until someone decides that card envelopes and telegrams shall be left in the front hall.

A first bridesmaid arrives. She at least is on time. All decoration activity stops while she is looked at and admired. Panic seizes some one! The time is too short, nothing will be ready! Someone else says the bridesmaid is far too early; there is no end of time.

Upstairs everyone is still dressing. The father of the bride—one would suppose him to be the bridegroom himself—is trying on most of his shirts, and the floor is strewn with discarded collars! The mother of the bride is hurrying into her wedding array so as to be ready for any emergency, as well as to superintend the finishing touches to her daughter's dress and veil.

IN THE BRIDE'S ROOM

As the hour approaches, everyone seemingly is in her room: her mother, her grandmother, three aunts, two cousins, three bridesmaids, four small children, two friends, her maid, the dressmaker and an assistant. Every little while the parlor maid brings a message or a package. Her father comes in and goes out at regular intervals, in sheer nervousness. The rest of the bridesmaids gradually appear and distract the attention of the audience so that the bride has moments of being allowed to dress undisturbed. At last even her veil is adjusted and all present gasp their approval: "How sweet!" "Dearest, you are too lovely!" and "Darling, how wonderful you look!"

Her father reappears. "If you are going to have the pictures taken, you had better all hurry!"

"Oh, Mary," shouts someone, "what have you on that is

'Something old, something new,
Something borrowed, something blue,
And a lucky sixpence in your shoe'?"

"Let me see," says the bride. " 'Old,' I have old lace; 'new,' I have lots of new! 'Borrowed,' and 'blue'?" A chorus of voices: "Wear my ring," "Wear my pin," "Wear mine! It's blue!" and someone's pin, which has a blue stone in it, is fastened under the trimming of her dress and serves both needs. If the lucky sixpence—a dime will do—is produced, she must at least pay discomfort for her "luck."

TAKING THE WEDDING PICTURES

Having pictures taken before the ceremony is a dull custom, because it is tiring to sit for one's photograph at best. But to attempt posing at the moment when the procession ought to be starting is as trying to the nerves as it is exhausting, and more than one wedding procession has consisted of very "dragged out" young women in consequence.

At a country wedding it is very easy to take the pictures out on the lawn at the end of the reception and just before the bride goes to dress; this time is always chosen when the bridegroom and his ushers are to be included in the wedding picture. Sometimes in a town house they are taken in an upstairs room at that same hour. But usually the bride is dressed and her bridesmaids arrive at her house fully half an hour before the time necessary to leave for the church; and pictures of the group, as well as several of the bride alone, are taken with special lights against the background where she will stand and receive

PROCESSION TO THE CHURCH

Whether the pictures are taken before the wedding or after, the bridesmaids always meet at the house of the bride, where they also receive their bouquets. When it is time to go to the church, there are several motors drawn up at the house. The bride's mother drives away in the first, usually alone, or she may, if she chooses, take one or two bridesmaids in her car; but she must reserve room for her husband, who will return from church with her.

The maid of honor, bridesmaids and flower girls go in closely following vehicles—either their own or supplied by the bride's family.

Last of all comes the bride's car, which always has a wedding appearance. The chauffeur wears a small bunch of white flowers on his coat, and white gloves, and has all the tires painted white. The bride drives to the church with her father only. Her car arrives last of the procession, and stands without moving, in front of the awning, until she and her husband—in place of her father—return from the ceremony and drive back to the house for the breakfast or reception.

If she has no father, this part is taken by an uncle, a brother, a cousin, her guardian, or other near male connection of her family.

MOTHER TAKES FATHER'S PLACE

If it should happen that the bride has neither father nor any very near male relative, or guardian, she may walk up the aisle alone. At the point in the ceremony where the clergyman asks, "Who giveth this woman to be married?" her mother stays where she is standing in her proper place at the end of the first pew on the left and bows her head very distinctly to indicate "I do." (There is no rule against her going forward as the bride's father would have done, but it is no longer usual.)

It is also unusual, but not unheard of at the small and simple wedding of a bride whose father has died, that her mother walk up the aisle with her in her father's place. But this would be in very bad taste if her father were living and divorced, since it would publicly proclaim his unfitness to exercise his natural right to give his daughter in marriage. To air publicly any disturbance in one's private life is in bad taste, and doubly unforgivable should the repudiation of the father be unjust.

Upon the rare occasion when the mother walks with her daughter, she should choose her dress very carefully so as to avoid detracting from that of the bride. The most appropriate is perhaps absolutely plain gray chiffon, taffeta or velvet with a very small matching hat. Needless to say, there should be no bridal attendants unless perhaps two little children, either pages or flower girls, dressed in white to match the bride.

AT THE CHURCH

Meanwhile, about an hour before the time for the ceremony, the ushers arrive at the church and the sexton turns his guardianship over to them. They leave their hats in the vestry or in the coat room. Their boutonnières, sent by the groom, should be waiting in the vestibule. These should be in charge of a boy from the florist's, who has nothing else on his mind but to see that they are there, that they are fresh, and that the ushers get them. Each man puts one in his buttonhole, and also puts on his gloves. The head usher decides—or the groom has already told them—to which ushers are apportioned the center, and to which the side aisles. Those of the ushers who are the most likely to recognize the various friends and members of each family are invariably detailed to the center aisle. A brother of the bride, for instance, is always chosen for this aisle because he is best fitted to look out for the family's best friends. A second usher should be either a brother of the groom or a near relative who is able to recognize the family and intimate friends of the groom. The parents of the bride always sit in the first pew on the left, facing the chancel. The groom's parents in the first pew on the right. In a two-aisle church her parents sit on the left of right aisle, and his on the right of left aisle. (See page 216.)

IN FRONT OF THE RIBBONS

The first six to twenty pews on either side of the center aisle (depending upon the size of the families) are marked off with ribbons into a reserved enclosure. This is done by fastening a lead sinker or a stone or anything to weigh each end of a length of white satin ribbon, between three or four inches wide and just long enough to reach across the aisle and drop over the ends of the pews and rest on the pew seats, and thus make a barrier across the aisle at this point. The families sit "in front of the ribbons," as do the very few *most intimate* friends. The seats in front of the ribbons are all reserved—not only on usher's lists, but also by cards sent to individuals. As a guest belonging in front of the ribbons is escorted up the aisle, the usher lifts one end of the ribbon from its anchorage, drops it to the floor, and leads the guest to the proper seat. Coming down the aisle again, he picks up the ribbon and drops it over the end of the pew.

The one point confusing to many is the taking of a few pews from one family to give to the other when the one family is very small and the other large. If the bridegroom is from a distant part of the country, it is obvious that few members of his family and almost none of his friends can be present. The bride, let us say, will need eleven pews.

Because a ribbon cannot very well be run from the back of the third pew on his side to the back of the eleventh on hers the fourteen pews needed by both are divided and seven ribboned off on each side, and all beyond the first three on his side filled as though they were hers.

SEATING THE GUESTS

It is the duty of the ushers to show all guests to their places. An usher offers his arm to each lady as she arrives, whether he knows her personally or not. If the vestibule is very crowded and several ladies are together, he sometimes gives his arm to the oldest and asks the others to follow. But this is not done unless the crowd is great and the time short.

If the usher thinks a guest belongs in front of the ribbons, though she fails to present her card, he always asks, "Have you a pew number?" If she has, he then shows her to her place. If she has none, he asks whether she prefers to sit on the bride's side or the groom's, and gives her the best seat vacant in the unreserved part of the church.

At one time, lists of all the guests were given to the ushers, with pew numbers following, for almost the whole church. From every point of view, the typewritten list was bad. First, it wasted time. As everyone arrived at the same moment and every lady was supposed to be taken personally up the aisle "on the arm" of an usher, the time consumed while each usher looked up each name on several gradually rumpling or tearing sheets of paper may be easily imagined. Besides this, one who is at all intimate with either family cannot help feeling in some degree slighted when, on giving his name, he sees the usher look for it in vain.

The present way is simple. Guests having numbered pews are shown to them; those not having them are given the best unnumbered ones available. As no one but the families *expect* numbers, no one's feelings are hurt.

USHERS AND GUESTS ALWAYS TALK

Ushers never escort guests in total silence, even when they are strangers to themselves. A few remarks are made—about the weather or the decorations—in a low voice, but not whispered or solemn.

The deportment of the ushers should be natural, but dignified and quiet in consideration of the fact that they are in church. They must not trot up and down the aisles in a bustling manner; yet they must be fairly swift, as the vestibule is packed with guests all of whom have to be seated as expeditiously as possible.

The guests without reserved cards should arrive first in order to find good places. Members of the families and the few guests who have places in front of the ribbon come later.

THE BRIDEGROOM WAITS

Meanwhile, about fifteen minutes before the wedding hour, the groom and his best man—both in morning coats, top hats, boutonnières and white buckskin (not shiny kid) gloves—walk or drive to the church and enter the side door which leads to the vestry. They sit there, or in the clergyman's study, until the sexton or an usher comes to say that the bride has arrived.

THE PERFECTLY MANAGED WEDDING

At a perfectly managed wedding, the bride arrives exactly one minute after the hour in order to give the last comer time to find a place. Two or three maids or other volunteers have been sent ahead to wait in the vestibule to help the bride and bridesmaids off with their wraps and hold them until they are needed after the ceremony. The groom's mother and father also are waiting in the vestibule. As the carriage of the bride's mother drives up, an usher hurries to tell the groom. Any brothers or sisters of the bride or groom who are not to take part in the wedding procession and have arrived in their mother's carriage are now taken by ushers to their places in the front pews. The moment the entire wedding party is in the church, the doors between the vestibule and the church are closed. No one is seated after this, except the parents of the young couple.

The proper procedure should be carried out with military exactness and is as follows:

The groom's mother goes down the aisle on the arm of the head usher and takes her place in the first pew on the right; the groom's father follows alone and takes his place beside her. The same usher returns to the vestibule and immediately escorts the bride's mother. He should then have time to return to the vestibule and take his place in the procession. The beginning of the wedding march should sound just as the usher returns to the head of the aisle.

To repeat: *No person should be seated after the entrance of the mother of the bride.* Nor must anyone be admitted to the side aisles while the mother of the bride is being ushered down the center one. Her entrance should not be detracted from by late arrivals scuttling into their seats behind her. Guests who arrive late must stand in the vestibule or go into the gallery.

The sound of the music is also the cue for the clergyman to enter the chancel, followed by the groom and the best man. The two latter wear gloves but have left their hats and sticks in the vestry room.

The groom stands on the right-hand side at the head of the aisle; but if the vestry opens into the chancel, he sometimes stands at the top of the first few steps. He removes his right glove and holds it in his left hand. The best man remains always directly back and to the right of the groom, and does not remove his glove.

HERE COMES THE BRIDE*

As already described, the processional advances. First come the ushers two by two, four paces apart; then the bridesmaids—if any—at the same distance exactly; then the maid of honor alone; then the flower girls—if any; then the ring bearer—if any; then, at a *double distance*, the bride on her father's *right* arm. At a wedding of great size, she is dressed, always, in white, with a veil of lace or tulle. She always carries white bridal flowers—usually a bouquet; sometimes only a few orange blossoms fastened to the ends of white ribbon markers in a prayer-book.

THE BRIDEGROOM ADVANCES TO MEET THE BRIDE

As the bride approaches, the groom waits at the foot of the steps, unless he comes down the steps to meet her. The bride relinquishes her father's arm, changes her bouquet from her right to her left arm, and gives her right hand to the groom. The groom, taking her hand in his right, puts it through his left arm—just her finger tips should rest near the bend of his elbow—and turns to face the chancel as he does so. It does not matter whether she keeps his arm or whether they stand hand in hand or merely side by side at the foot of the chancel in front of the clergyman.

HER FATHER GIVES HER AWAY

Her father has remained where she left him, on her left and a step or two behind her. The clergyman stands a step or two above them and reads the betrothal. When he says, "Who giveth this woman to be married?" the father goes forward, still on her left, halfway between her and the clergyman, but not in front of either. The bride turns slightly toward her father and gives him her right hand. The father puts her hand in that of the clergyman, signifying his reply, "I do." He then takes his place next his wife at the end of the first pew on the left.

The clergyman, holding the bride's hand in his own right, takes the bridegroom's hand in his left and very deliberately places the bride's hand in that of the bridegroom.

THE MARRIAGE CEREMONY

A soloist or the choir then sings while the clergyman slowly ascends to the altar, before which the marriage is performed. The bride and groom follow slowly, the fingers of her right hand on his left arm.

* For complete description of bridal dress and flowers, see Index.

The maid of honor, or else the first bridesmaid, moves out of line and follows on the left-hand side until she stands immediately below the bride. The best man takes the same position exactly on the right behind the groom. At the termination of the anthem, the bride hands her bouquet to the maid of honor—or her prayer-book to the clergyman—and the bride and groom plight their troth.

When it is time for the ring, the best man produces it from his pocket.

The wedding ring must not be put above the engagement ring. On her wedding day a bride either leaves her engagement ring at home when she goes to church or she wears it on her right hand. Afterwards she wears it above her wedding ring.

When the bridegroom is also to have a ring, the maid of honor hands it to the bride at the moment that the best man gives her ring to the groom, and the bride puts it on his finger immediately after she has received her ring from him. The ceremony then proceeds.

AFTER THE CEREMONY

At the conclusion of the ceremony, the minister congratulates the new couple. The organ begins the recessional. The bride takes her bouquet from her maid of honor—who removes the bride's veil, if she has worn one over her face. She then turns toward her husband—her bouquet in her right hand—and puts her left hand through his right arm, and they descend the steps.

The maid of honor, handing her own bouquet to a second bridesmaid, follows a short distance after the bride, at the same time stooping and straightening out the long train and veil. The bride and groom go on down the aisle. The best man disappears into the vestry room. At a perfectly conducted wedding he does not walk down the aisle with the maid of honor. The maid of honor recovers her bouquet and walks alone. If a bridesmaid performs the office of maid of honor, she takes her place among her companion bridesmaids, who go next; and the ushers go last.

The best man has meanwhile dashed out of the side entrance and around to the front to give the groom his hat and stick.

Sometimes the sexton takes charge of the groom's hat and stick and hands them to him at the church door as he goes out. But in either case the best man always hurries around to see the bride and groom into their car, which has been standing at the entrance to the awning since she and her father alighted from it.

All the other conveyances are drawn up in the reverse order from that in which they arrived. The bride's car leaves first; next come those of the bridesmaids; next that of the bride's mother and father; next that of the groom's mother and father. Then follow the nearest members of both families, and finally all the other guests in the order of their being able to find their conveyances.

The best man goes back to the vestry, where he gives the fee to the clergyman, collects his own hat and coat (if he has one), and goes to the bride's house or wherever the reception is to be held.

To recur to the ceremony for a moment: As soon as the recessional is over, the ushers hurry back and escort to the door all the ladies who were in the first pews, according to the order of precedence; the bride's mother first, then the groom's mother, then the other occupants of the first pew on either side, then the second and third pews, until all members of the immediate families have left the church. Meanwhile it is a breach of etiquette for other guests to leave their places. At occasional weddings, just before the bride's arrival, the ushers run ribbons down the whole length of the center aisle, fencing the congregation in. As soon as the occupants of the first pews have left, the ribbons are removed and all the other guests go out by themselves, the ushers having by that time hurried to the bride's house to make themselves useful at the reception.

AT THE HOUSE

An awning makes a covered way from the edge of the curb to the front door. At the lower end the chauffeur, or one of the caterer's men, stands to open the motor doors and give return checks to the chauffeurs and their employers. Inside the house the florist has finished, an orchestra is playing in the hall or library, everything is in perfect order. The bride and groom have taken their places in front of the elaborate setting of flowering plants that has been arranged for them.

THE RECEIVING LINE

The only actual receiving line is that of the bride and groom and the bride's attendants. (The ushers and best man have no place in the receiving line ever.)

The bride's mother receives alone at the door of entrance to the room. On the hall side of the doorway within sight of her, her own butler, or one furnished by the caterer, asks each guest his name and then repeats it aloud. The guests shake hands with the hostess, and, making some polite remark about the "beautiful wedding" or "lovely bride," continue in line to the bridal pair. If there is no one announcing, guests unknown to the hostess announce their own names: "Mrs. Samuel Stranger," "Miss Elderly," or "John Brown" or "Muriel Manners."

THE BRIDEGROOM'S PARENTS

Unless the bridegroom's mother is a stranger, in which case she is invited to receive with the mother of the bride, there is no rule as to

KEY
A: MOTHER OF BRIDE, B: MOTHER OF GROOM, C: FATHER OF GROOM,
D: FATHER OF BRIDE, BR: BRIDE, G: GROOM, MH: MAID OF HONOR, X: BRIDESMAIDS,
I: BOUILLON, S: SANDWICHES & CAKE, T: TEA, W: WEDDING CAKE—PROGRESS OF GUESTS

whether the two mothers receive together or whether the groom's mother stands somewhere beyond the bridesmaids—but never as part of the bridal receiving line.

All the guests should shake hands with the groom's mother whether they know her or not, and say a few words of greeting if she is a stranger, or otherwise say something pleasant about the wedding, the bride, or the groom. The bride's father sometimes stands beside his wife, but he usually circulates among his guests just as he would at a ball or any other party where he is host.

The groom's father is a guest and it is not necessary for strangers to speak to him, unless he stands beside his wife, and, as it were, "receives"; but there is no impropriety in telling him how well one knows and likes his son or his new daughter-in-law.

USHERS AT THE HOUSE

At a small wedding the duty of ushers is personally to take guests up to the bride and groom as soon as they have greeted the bride's mother—and anyone receiving with her. But at a big reception where the guests outnumber ushers fifty or a hundred to one, being personally conducted is an honor accorded only to the old, the celebrated or the usher's own best friends. All the other guests stand in a long congested line by themselves.

NO RULE ABOUT WHETHER BRIDE OR BRIDEGROOM IS GREETED FIRST

The bride always stands on the bridegroom's right. The direction of the queque depends upon the plan of the room. If, in the room shown on page 234, the door to the dining room were at the right, the mothers would stand at left and the queque would naturally swing away from that door and approach the line from the opposite direction, and guests would greet the bride first, instead of the bridegroom.

Usually the bride and groom receive against the wall opposite the door of entrance; but this is not a fixed rule, and they choose whichever side of the room will make the most convenient background. This is usually made of leaves and flowers, but may equally well be the closed curtains of a window or other draperies hung from the picture molding.

The bride stands on the bridegroom's right, the maid of honor at the right of the bride. Usually all the bridesmaids stand on the right of the maid of honor, but sometimes (depending on the space) half stand at the right of the maid of honor and the other half on the left of the bridegroom.

WHAT TO SAY TO BRIDE AND GROOM

What you should say in congratulating a bridal couple depends on how well you know one or both of them.

If you know neither of them more than slightly and are in a queue, you merely shake hands with whichever you come to first, and say a formal word or two, such as "All good wishes" or "Best wishes for your happiness" or "All good luck to you both." It is proper to say "congratulations" to the groom, but you do not congratulate the bride, ever. But it is a time-honored custom to kiss her. You may also kiss the groom—if you would like to. An intimate friend, kissing the bride, probably says, "You look too lovely, dear Mary, and I hope you will always be as happy as you look today!" or "Mary darling, every good wish in the world to you!"

A woman relative or old friend of his kisses the groom saying, "All the luck in the world to you, dear Jim; she certainly is lovely!"

To all the above, the groom and bride answer merely, "Thank you."

To a relative or friend of the bride, but a stranger to the groom, the bride always introduces her husband, saying "Jim, this is Aunt Kate!" or, "Mrs. Neighbor, *This* is Jim!" or formally, "Mrs. Faraway, may I present my husband?"

The groom, on the approach of an old friend of his, says, "Mary, this is Cousin Carrie." or, "Mrs. Denver, Mary." or, "Hello, Steve. Mary, this is Steve Michigan." If he is an older man or old-fashioned, Steve says, "How do you do, Mrs. Smartlington!" And Mary says, "How do you do. Jim often speaks of you!" If he is young or modern, he says, "I'm glad to meet you, Mary." And she replies, "I'm glad to see *you*, Steve."

The bride with a good memory thanks each arriving person for the gift sent her: "Thank you so much for the lovely candlesticks" or "The platter is just what we wanted." The person who is thanked says, "I am so glad you like them—or it" or "I hoped you might find it useful" or "I didn't have it marked, so that in case you have a duplicate, you can change it." But these verbal thanks do not lessen her obligation to write an additional "thank you" note.

These fragments of conversation are given merely to indicate the sort of things people usually say. There is, however, one real rule: Do not launch into long conversation or details of yourself, how you feel or look or what happened to you, or what you wore when you were married! Your subject must not deviate from the young couple themselves, their wedding, their future.

Above all, be brief in order not to keep those behind waiting longer than necessary. If you have anything particular to tell them, you can return later when there is no longer a line. But even then any long conversation, especially concerning yourself, is out of place.

THE DAY OF THE WEDDING

The guests, as soon as they have congratulated the bride and groom, go out and find themselves places—if it is to be a sit-down breakfast—at a table.

DETAILS OF A SIT-DOWN BREAKFAST

A sit-down breakfast is the most elaborate wedding "reception" known.

Unless the house is remarkable in size, there is usually a canopied platform built next to the veranda or on the lawn or over the yard of a city house. The entire space is packed with little tables surrounding the big one reserved for the bridal party. At a large breakfast a second table is reserved for the parents of the bride and groom and a few especially invited friends.

Place cards at the bride's table and at the parents' table are of white cardboard embossed in silver to match the monograms on the wedding-cake boxes. Or plain white cards may have a strap cut—like a double button-hole—and small white flowers thrust under the strap.

Place cards are not put on any of the small tables. All the guests, except the few placed at the two reserved tables, sit with whom they like. Sometimes they do so by prearrangement, but usually they sit where they happen to find friends—and room!

The general sit-down breakfast—except in great houses such as a few of those in Newport—is always furnished by a caterer, who brings all the food, tables, chairs, napery, china and glass, as well as the necessary waiters. The butler and footmen of the house may assist or oversee, or be detailed to other duties.

Small *menu* cards printed in silver are usually put on all the tables. Sometimes these cards have the crest of the bride's father embossed at the top, but usually the initials of the bride and groom are stamped in silver to match the wedding-cake boxes.

Example

Bouillon
Lobster Newburg
Suprême of Chicken
Peas
Aspic of Foie Gras
Celery Salad
Ices
Coffee

The "bouillon" is more than likely of clear tomato, or it may be a bisque or clam broth. Instead of the bouillon there may be caviar, melon, or grapefruit. Instead of lobster Newburg there may be soft-shelled crabs or oyster pâté, or another sea food. The main dish may also be broiled chicken—half of a squab or chicken for each guest—sweetbreads and mushrooms, or chicken pâté.

Any variety of aspic with celery salad may be served.

Individual ices are accompanied by little cakes of assorted variety.

At a wedding breakfast of this extreme elaborateness, the only correct beverage has always been champagne. A substitute is at best "a poor thing." Orange juice and ginger ale, or white grape juice and ginger ale, with sugar and mint leaves, are two attempts at a satisfying cup.

THE BRIDE'S TABLE

The feature of the wedding breakfast always is the bride's table. Placed sometimes in the dining room, sometimes on the veranda or in a room apart, this table is always elaborately decorated. There are white garlands or sprays or other white flowers, and in front of the bride, as chief ornament, is a white iced wedding cake. On top it has a bouquet of white or silver flowers, or confectioner's quaint dolls representing the bride and groom. The bride as always cuts the first slice, which she divides to share with the groom.* Then each attendant —coming and standing next the bride—cuts herself or himself a slice. There should be two sets of favors hidden in the cake between the two sections marked as in the illustration with four orange-blossom buds or by match ends wrapped in silver foil or other easily seen markers to distinguish the sections to be cut. The bridesmaids' favors are always on the bride's side, and the ushers' on the side of the groom.

Various articles have either been wrapped in waxed paper and baked in the cake, or each, wrapped in silver foil, has been pushed between the two marked sections through the bottom of the cake at short intervals. The bridesmaids find a ten-cent piece for riches, a little gold ring for "first to be married," a thimble or little parrot or cat for "old maid," a wishbone for the "luckiest." On the ushers' side, a button or dog is for "old bachelor," and a miniature pair of dice is a symbol of a lucky chance in life.

When this is the only wedding cake to be offered at a small wedding, the cake is usually black fruit cake and it is passed to others after purposely narrow sections have been taken by the bridal party.

Ordinarily this is a small lady cake or pound cake, and called "the bride's cake."

THE ARCHITECTURAL WEDDING CAKE

As the centerpiece of interest on an elaborate buffet, the cake is actually the first-story or foundation which supports two or three tiers of colonnades (sometimes made of icing but often made of plaster of paris). This ornamental superstructure is lifted off like a lid when the bride—assisted by the bridegroom—is ready to cut the first piece.

THE TABLE OF THE BRIDE'S PARENTS

The table of the bride's parents differs from other tables in nothing except its larger size and the place cards for those who have been invited to sit there. The groom's father always sits on the right of the bride's mother, and the groom's mother has the place of honor on the host's right. The other places at the table are occupied by distinguished guests, who may or may not include the clergyman who performed the ceremony. If a bishop or dean performed the ceremony, he is always included at this table and is placed at the left of the hostess, and his wife, if present, sits at the bride's father's left. Otherwise only especially intimate friends of the bride's parents are invited to this table.

* Best advice on cutting the cake is to make a straight perpendicular thrust with the point of the knife and follow this with a sequence of similar thrusts. Any attempt to bring the knife blade down as though it were a lever will meet with crumbling resistance on the part of the cake.

A SMALL WEDDING

At the smallest wedding possible, where only the immediate families are present, they very often all sit together at one lunch or dinner table. (See diagram below.)

	BRIDE	GROOM	
BEST MAN			MAID OF HONOR
BRIDESMAID			USHER
USHER			BRIDESMAID
YOUNG GIRL			USHER
RELATIVES AND FRIENDS INCREASING IN AGE			RELATIVES AND FRIENDS INCREASING IN AGE
			GROOM'S FATHER
			BRIDE'S MOTHER
WIFE OF CLERGYMAN			CLERGYMAN
	FATHER OF BRIDE	MOTHER OF GROOM	

At a very simple stand-up breakfast the details would be the same, except that in place of the elaborate cold dishes there would be one hot dish and one salad. If chicken salad is served, there should be a hot dish of eggs or creamed fish. Moreover, if the hot dish is chicken croquettes or chicken à la King, there is a salad of mixed vegetables. The bouillon and ice cream are served as above stated for the big wedding.

Usually, but not always, there is a bride's table, decorated exactly as that described for a sit-down breakfast, and placed usually in the library; but there is no special table for the bride's mother and her guests—or for anyone else.

THE STAND-UP BREAKFAST OR SUPPER

The stand-up breakfast differs from the sit-down breakfast in service only. Instead of numerous small tables at which the guests are served with a course luncheon, a single long one is set in the dining room. The regular table is pulled out to its farthest extent. It is covered with a plain white damask cloth. In the center is a centerpiece of white flowers. On it are piles of plates, (preferably white, or white and gold) stacks of napkins and rows of spoons and forks at intervals.

If there is no sit-down bridal table, the wedding cake (not necessarily—or even usually—an architectural one) is put at the center of one side of the buffet with a centerpiece of white flowers behind it or

THE DAY OF THE WEDDING

two floral pieces flanking it. At an elaborate breakfast there is usually a big urn at one end filled with bouillon, and one filled with chocolate at the other. In four evenly spaced places are two cold dishes, such as an aspic of chicken, or ham. The hot dishes may be creamed crab meat, chicken à la king, or chicken croquettes. Whatever the choice is, there are two or three cold dishes and at least two hot dishes. Also the food selected must be easily eatable with a fork while the plate is held in the other hand. There are also thin sandwiches of two or three varieties or plain bread and butter.

There are dishes filled with fancy cakes, chosen for looks as much as taste, as well as peppermints, caramels, and chocolates. Ice cream is the typical dessert.

After-dinner coffee is put on a side table, as is champagne (or the substitute punch).

MODERN SIMPLIFICATION OF WEDDING COLLATION

In New York eating between meals is distinctly going out of fashion, and even the bridal table is more often eliminated than not. The table is set exactly as for afternoon tea, to which is added the wedding cake, of course, and a white decoration of flowers. Tea is at one end and chocolate at the other. Champagne or fruit punch, a few dishes of thin sandwiches and little cakes are added and that is all.

THE BOXES OF WEDDING CAKE

In addition to the big regulation wedding cake there are, at all weddings of importance, near the front door—so that the guests may each take one as they go home—little individual boxes of wedding cake, "black" fruit cake. Each box is made of white moiré or grosgrain paper, embossed in silver with the last initial of the groom combined with that of the bride and tied with white satin ribbon. At a sit-down breakfast the wedding-cake boxes are sometimes put, one at each place, on the tables, so that each guest may be sure of receiving one, and other "thoughtless" ones prevented from carrying away—sometimes—as many as three or four boxes.

THE BRIDAL PARTY EAT

Recurring to the sit-down breakfast. When it has reached the second course and the queue of arriving guests has dwindled and melted away, the bride and groom decide that it is time they go to breakfast. Arm in arm they lead the way to their own table, followed by the ushers and bridesmaids. The bride and groom always sit next to each other, she at his right, the maid of honor, or matron, at his left. The best man is at the right of the bride. Around the rest of the table are bridesmaids and ushers alternately. Sometimes one or two others —intimate friends who were not included in the wedding party—are asked to the table; when there are no bridesmaids, this is always the case.

The decoration of the table, the service, the food, are exactly the same whether the other guests are seated or standing. At dessert the bride cuts the cake, and the bridesmaids and ushers find the luck pieces.

THE TOAST TO THE BRIDE AND GROOM

At a sit-down bridal table champagne is poured as soon as the first course has been served. The glass of the bride is filled first, then that of the bridegroom, and then on around the table, starting with the maid of honor at the groom's left and ending with the best man seated at the right of the bride. Then someone—it may be anyone (although it is really the duty of the best man) proposes a toast to the bride and bridegroom. All (except the bride and groom) rise, raise their glasses and drink the toast. Then the groom rises and replies with thanks for them both, and that is all. But there is no reason why other toasts may not be drunk should anyone care to propose them, although at a large reception these are necessarily confined to individual groups. People also make speeches, if they feel like it, but these are not at all necessary and should on no account be more than a few seconds long. A speech running into minutes is proper only for a lecture platform.

DANCING AT THE WEDDING

On leaving their table the bridal party join the dancing, which by now has begun in the drawing room where the wedding group received. The bride and groom dance at first together, and then each with bridesmaids or ushers or other guests. Sometimes they linger so long that those who had intended staying for the "going away" grow weary and leave—which is often exactly what the young couple want!

Unless they have to catch a train, they always stay until the "crowd thins" before going to dress for their journey. At last the bride signals to her bridesmaids and leaves the room. They all gather at the foot of the stairs. About halfway to the upper landing as she goes up, she throws her bouquet, and they all try to catch it. The one to whom it falls is supposed to be the next married. If she has no bridesmaids, she collects a group of other girls and throws her bouquet to them.

INTO TRAVELING CLOTHES

The bride goes up to the room that has always been hers, followed by her mother, sisters and bridesmaids, who stay with her while she changes into her traveling clothes. As soon as the bride has gone upstairs, the groom goes to the room reserved for him and changes into the ordinary sack suit which the best man has taken there for him before the ceremony.

THE GOING-AWAY DRESS

A bride necessarily chooses her going-away dress according to the journey she is to make. The bride and groom of good taste try to avoid being noticeably conspicuous in clothes that shout too loudly, "Look, at us! How smart we are!—and all brand NEW!"

But to return to the wedding. The groom, having changed his clothes, waits upstairs until the bride appears in her "going-away" clothes. All the ushers shake hands with them both. His immediate family, as well as hers, have gradually collected. Any that are missing must unfailingly be sent for. The bride's mother gives her a last kiss; her bridesmaids hurry downstairs to have plenty of rice ready and to tell everyone below as they descend, "Here they come!" A passage from the stairway and out the front door, all the way to the motor, is left free between two rows of eager guests, their hands full of rice.

HERE THEY COME!

Down the stairs, out through the hall, into the motor, slam the door, and they are off!

The wedding guests stand out on the street or roadway looking after them for as long as a vestige can be seen—and then gradually disperse.

THOUGHT FOR BRIDEGROOM'S PARENTS

At the end of the wedding there is one thing the bride must not forget. As soon as she is in her traveling dress, she must send a bridesmaid or someone out into the hall and ask her husband's parents to come and say good-by to her.

It is very easy for a bride to forget this act of thoughtfulness and for a groom to overlook the fact that he cannot stop to bid his parents good-by on his way out of the house, and many a mother and father, seeing their son and new daughter rush past without even a glance from either of them, have returned home with an ache in their hearts. One naturally exclaims, "But how stupid of them! Why didn't they go upstairs?" But often the groom's parents are strangers; and if by temperament they are shy or retiring people, they hesitate to go upstairs in an unknown house until they are invited to do so. So they wait, feeling sure that in good time they will be sent for. Meanwhile the bride "forgets"; and it does not occur to the groom that, unless he makes an effort while upstairs, there will be no opportunity in the dash down to the car to recognize them—or anyone.

THE HOUSE WEDDING

A house wedding involves slightly less expenditure but has the disadvantage of limiting the number of guests. The ceremony is exactly the same as that in a church, except that the procession advances through an aisle of white satin ribbons from the stairs down which the bridal party descends, through the drawing room, to the improvised altar. A small space near the altar is fenced off with other ribbons, for the family. Always there is a bench or cushion for the bride and groom to kneel on during the prayers of the ceremony. Often this bench is backed by an altar rail. In this case the bench is usually six or eight inches high, and between three and four feet long; at the back of it an upright on either end supports a crosspiece—or altar rail. It can be made in roughest fashion by any carpenter, or amateur, as it is entirely hidden under leaves and flowers. On the kneeling surface of the bench are placed cushions rather than flowers, because the latter stain. Often the only preparation made is a long thick cushion on the floor. All caterers have the necessary standards to which ribbons are tied, like the wires to telegraph poles. The top of each standard is usually decorated with a spray of white flowers.

At a house wedding the bride's mother stands at the door of the drawing room—or wherever the ceremony is to be—and receives people as they arrive. But the groom's mother merely takes her place near the altar with the rest of the immediate family. The ushers are purely ornamental, unless the house is so large that "pews" have been installed and the guests are seated as in a church. Otherwise the guests stand wherever they can find places behind the aisle ribbons. Just before the bride's entrance, her mother goes forward and stands in the reserved part of the room. In an apartment the procession starts in the foyer or bedroom hall. Otherwise the ushers go up to the top of the stairway. The wedding march begins and the ushers come down two and two, followed by the bridesmaids, exactly as in a church, the bride coming last on her father's arm. The clergyman and the groom and best man have, if possible, reached the altar by another door. If the room has only one door, they go up the aisle a few moments before the bridal procession starts.

A HOUSE WEDDING AT LEAST EXPENSE

When there are no flowers in the family garden, a very pleasing background can be made by drawing heavy curtains or hanging curtains of damask or velvet or any plain fabric from the picture molding across any flat wall space. Against this the colorful clothes of the maid of honor or bridesmaids and, above all, the bride's white dress and veil are entirely effective.

For music, nothing could be more beautiful than the phonograph records of organ and choir purposely made for weddings.

Even at the smallest wedding possible, the clergyman would enter, followed by the bridegroom; the bride would then enter with her father, or alone, and the wedding service would be read.

The collation might consist of nothing but ginger ale or fruit-juice cup, wedding cake and a few sandwiches spread upon a card table, covered with a tea cloth.

HOUSE WEDDING DIFFERS FROM CHURCH WEDDING

The chief difference between a church and house wedding is that the bride and groom do not take a single step together. The groom meets her at the point where the service is read. After the ceremony, there is no recessional. The clergyman withdraws, an usher removes the prayer bench, and the bride and groom merely turn where they stand, and receive the congratulations of their guests,* unless, of course, the house is so big that they receive in another room.

When there is no recessional, the groom always kisses the bride before they turn to receive their guests. At a church wedding the groom does not kiss her at the altar unless the officiating clergyman is the bride's father or other very near relative, who instead of shaking hands with her would naturally kiss her. In this case, of course, the groom kisses her first. It is against all tradition for anyone to kiss the bride before her husband does.

* There is a new and lovely song which is now being sung at many weddings, and is particularly suitable at house weddings, to give a moment's pause at the conclusion of the ceremony and the turning to receive the guests. The music was written by Jennie Prince Black, who chose the beautiful words from the Book of Ruth in the Bible—"Entreat me not to leave thee—" It is called "The Pledge" and is published by G. Schirmer and Sons.

There are seldom many bridal attendants at a house wedding—two to four ushers, and one to four bridesmaids—unless the house is an immense one.

In the country, a house wedding may be performed in the garden, with the wedding procession under the trees and tables out on the lawn—a perfect plan for California or other rainless States, but difficult to arrange on the Atlantic seaboard where rain is too likely to spoil everything.

FLIPPANCY OR RADIANCE

A completely beautiful wedding is not merely a combination of wonderful flowers, beautiful clothes, smoothness of detail, delicious food. These, no matter how pleasing, are external attributes. The spirit, or soul of it, must have something besides; and that "something" is in the behavior and in the expression of the bride and groom.

The most beautiful wedding ever imagined could be turned from sacrament to circus by the indecorous behavior of the groom and the flippancy of the bride. She must not reach up and wigwag signals while she is receiving, any more than she must wave to people as she goes up and then down the aisle of the church. She must not cling to her husband as though unable to stand, or lean against him or the wall, or any person or thing. She must not swing her arms as though they were dangling ropes. She must not switch herself this way and that, and she must not shout; and above all she must not, while wearing her bridal veil, smoke a cigarette. No matter how young or "natural" and thoughtless she may be, she *must*, during the ceremony and the short time that she stands beside her husband at the reception, assume that she has dignity.

It is not by chance that the phrase "happy pair" is one of the most trite in our language, for happiness above all is the inner essential that must dominate a perfect wedding. An unhappy looking bride, an unwilling looking groom, turns the greatest wedding splendor into sham. Without love it is a sacrament profaned, and the sight of a tragic-faced bride strikes chill to the heart.

The radiance of a truly happy bride is so beautifying that even a plain girl is made pretty, and a pretty one, divine. There is something glad yet sweet, shy yet triumphant, serious yet—radiant! There is no other way to put it. And a happy groom looks first of all protective—he, too, may have the quality of radiance, but it is different—more directly glad. They both look as though there were sunlight behind their eyes, as though their mouths irresistibly turned to smiles. No other quality of a bride's expression is so beautiful as radiance—that visible proof of perfect happiness which endears its possessor to all beholders and gives to the simplest little wedding complete beauty.

THE DAY OF THE WEDDING

WHEN PARENTS ARE DIVORCED

When Mary Smith who is about to be married has been living half of the year with her mother who is now Mrs. Jones, and half of the year with her father, who also has re-married, the invitations are sent out only in the name of Mary's mother. Thus:

> Mrs. John Jones
> requests the honor of your presence
> at the marriage of her daughter
> Mary Smith
> to
> (The rest of the invitation as usual)

The wedding breakfast, however, is always given by both Mary's mother and her stepfather, and the invitations worded:

> Mr. and Mrs. John Jones
> request the pleasure of your company
> on Wednesday, the third of April
> at one o'clock

IT IS PREFERABLE THAT WEDDING BE GIVEN BY BRIDE'S MOTHER

When they are divorced, it is always better that the wedding and wedding breakfast be given by the mother rather than by the father of the bride, since it is proper that the father walk up the aisle of the church with his daughter and give her away, even though the invitations are sent out by his former wife. It is also not improper according to present-day convention that he be seen at the house of his daughter's mother, nor does the fact that the wedding is given by her imply that he was at fault in the divorce. On the other hand, should the wedding be given by Mary's father, this reversal of the usual custom might readily imply that the mother had been considered unfit to have the custody of her daughter. Especially would this be true should his second wife insist on taking the front pew.

IF WEDDING IS GIVEN BY FATHER

If, in spite of the objections previously noted, the wedding is given by Mary's father, the church invitations are sent out in the name of her father, but the house invitations include the name of his second wife. The second wife does not go to the church, and Mary's mother does not go to the house. Mary's own mother sits in the front pew with members of her family—but not her second husband. Mary's father gives her away and takes his place in one of the further-back pews on the bride's side.

FRIENDLY MEETING OF DIVORCED CONDONED

Until very lately the friendly meeting of divorced people was considered in very bad taste. But experience has proved that the situation is so much happier for the children when friendliness rather than hatred exists between the separated parents that the ban of bad taste is gradually being lifted. According to modern precept the personal feelings of those concerned are taken into consideration. If friendly relationship has been possible, both of Mary's step-parents are present at the church and even possibly at the house. The one unbreakable tabu is the sending of the wedding invitation by the divorced parents —together!

WHEN BRIDEGROOM'S PARENTS ARE DIVORCED

When all members of divorced families have remained friends, there is no problem to solve other than letting the bridegroom's parents decide where they will sit in church and stand at the reception. But if they are not friendly, his mother and her family should be given the first pew on the bridegroom's side of the church, and the father and his family seated three or four rows behind on the same side. At a large reception their presence need not be conspicuous nor make anyone uncomfortable. However, if the groom's mother is to receive with the bride's mother, she and her ex-husband and his wife can avoid meeting only by having a tall member of the bride's family wait purposely to go ahead of the groom's father and step-mother, and by his talking to the groom's mother form a barrier while the others greet the hostess. After this, they are free to greet the bridal party and stand somewhere beyond this line to receive their own friends.

REFORM AND ORTHODOX JEWISH WEDDINGS*

The Orthodox wedding ceremony differs somewhat from the Reform Jewish ceremony. In the Orthodox ceremony, the bride is veiled and is escorted under a cloth canopy supported by four poles, usually held by hand, by the father and mother. The groom is escorted by his parents. Hats are worn by all men attending the ceremony. Within recent years, the canopy, called "chupa," has been made stationary, that is, the posts rest upon a platform. Sometimes the canopy is made of flowers instead of cloth—the underlying idea being that there must be a covering over the heads of the couple married.

The service is read in Hebrew. The groom places a ring upon the

---

* The Author is indebted for the following material to Rabbi Nathan Krass of Temple Emanu-El, New York.

finger of the bride, repeating the following formula: "Thou art consecrated unto me with this ring, according to the law of Moses and Israel." The officiating minister then makes the benediction over the wine, giving the groom and bride the goblet, from which they drink. A document is read in Aramaic, giving in detail the pledge of fidelity and protection on the part of the groom towards the bride, and also indicating the bride's contribution towards the new household. At the conclusion of the ceremony, a glass is broken, symbolizing the fact that one must never overlook, even at the height of happiness, the possibility of misfortune.

In the Reform Service, the vernacular is used. The canopy is dispensed with. Several of the blessings are pronounced in Hebrew. The groom is usually ushered in by his best man, and the bride is escorted on the arm of her father. The matron of honor, the bridesmaids and the ushers function in the regular way. The groom repeats either the Hebrew formula or its English equivalent. The bride and groom also drink wine out of the same cup, symbolizing the cup of joy. Usually the officiating minister delivers a brief address upon the significance of marriage.

THE SECOND MARRIAGE

The details of a spinster's wedding are the same whether she marries a bachelor or a widower, the difference being that a widower does not give a bachelor dinner. The marriage of a widow is the same as that of a maid, except that she cannot wear a bridal veil, orange blossoms, or a myrtle wreath, which are emblems of virginity; nor does she have bridesmaids, though she may have a maid (or matron) of honor.

A widow usually takes off her first engagement ring as soon as she becomes engaged. Sometimes, however, she transfers the first ring to her right hand. This depends entirely on her own and especially on her new fiancé's feelings. Usually she removes her wedding ring at the same time, but occasionally—if her fiancé does not object—she continues to wear her wedding ring until the morning of her second marriage when she takes it off forever. Usually a widow chooses a very quiet wedding, but this is no reason why she cannot have a lovely wedding. Although she usually chooses a dress and hat of color, she may, if she chooses, wear all white; but of course not a bridal veil, and not orange blossoms.

A wedding in very best taste for a widow is held in a small church or chapel, a few flowers or palms in the chancel the only decoration. There would be two ushers or quite possibly none. There are no ribboned-off seats, as only very intimate friends are invited. Usually the bride wears an afternoon street dress and hat—which may be of color or equally well be white. There may be a family dinner afterwards, or the simplest afternoon tea. In any case the breakfast—or perhaps dinner—is, if possible, at the bride's own house, and the bridal pair may either stay where they are and have their guests take leave of them, or themselves drive away afterwards.

Few people send presents for a second marriage, but there is no objection to anyone's doing so who might care to.

COMPLETE SUMMARY OF WEDDING EXPENSES

All the expenses of a wedding belong to the bride's parents. The invitations are issued by them, the reception is at their house, and the groom's family are little more than ordinary guests. The cost of a wedding varies as much as the cost of anything else that one has or does. A big fashionable wedding can total far up in the thousands, and even a simple one entails considerable outlay if it is to be of any size. This cost can, however, be modified by those who are capable of doing things themselves instead of employing professional service at every point.

THE PARENTS OF THE BRIDE PROVIDE

1. Engraved invitations and announcements.

2. The service of a professional secretary who compiles a single list from the various ones sent her; addresses the envelopes, both inner and outer; encloses the proper number of cards; seals, stamps and mails all the invitations. (This is an item which may be omitted if the work is done by the family.)

3. The biggest item of expense—the trousseau of the bride, which may consist not alone of everything to wear in great variety and lavish detail, but household linen of finest quality—priceless in these days—and in quantity sufficient for a lifetime. Or it may consist of the wedding dress, and even that a traveling one, and one or two others, with pretty, simple underthings and other accessories.

4. Awnings for church and house. This may be omitted at the house in good weather, at the church if the wedding is a very small one, and at all weddings in the country.

5. Floral decorations of church and house. Bouquets for the bride and bridesmaids, and a boutonnière for the father of the bride. This expense can be eliminated by using garden or field flowers.

6. Choir, soloists and organist at church. (Choir and soloists unnecessary.) And a fee to the sexton.

7. Orchestra at house. This may mean fifty pieces with two leaders; or it may mean a piano, violin and drum, or a violin, harp and guitar —or a phonograph.

8. Motors for the bridal party from house to church and back, and for the bride and groom to drive away in, unless they are fortunate enough to be going on their journey in a car of their own.

9. The collation, which may be the most elaborate sit-down luncheon or the simplest afternoon tea.

10. Boxes of wedding cake—also the big one (the former necessary at every wedding of importance; the latter alone indispensable).

11. Champagne, if served, is one of the biggest items of expense; a fruit cup, on the other hand, is of moderate cost.

12. The bride's presents to her bridesmaids. They may be jewels of value or trinkets of trifling cost.

13. A wedding present to the bride from each member of the family—not counting her trousseau, which is merely part of the wedding.

14. The bride gives a wedding present or a wedding ring, or both, to the groom, if she especially wants to. (Not necessary or even customary.)

15. Photographs taken of the bridal party. (Not generally given to attendants.)

THE BRIDEGROOM'S EXPENSES

1. The engagement ring—as handsome as he can possibly afford.
2. A wedding present to the bride—jewels if he is able, always something for her personal adornment.
3. His bachelor dinner.
4. The marriage license.
5. A personal gift to his best man and to each of his ushers.
6. To each of the above he gives their wedding ties and boutonnières; also gloves, if they are to wear them. He buys his own boutonnière.*
7. The wedding ring.
8. The clergyman's fee.
9. From the moment the bride and groom start off on their wedding trip, all the expenditure becomes his.

CHOOSING A WEDDING PRESENT

Announcements require neither reply nor presents, ever. And there is no obligation to send a present or even to reply to an engraved

---

* In many American cities it is customary for the groom to provide the bouquet carried by the bride. In others it is said to be the custom for the bride to send boutonnières to the ushers and for the groom to order the bouquets of the bridesmaids. In New York's smart world, the bride's as well as the bridesmaids' bouquets are looked upon as part of the decorative arrangements, all of which are provided by the bride's parents. If the groom does not give the bride her bouquet, he sends her a corsage to wear away.

invitation to the church only. An invitation by written note requires a reply and also a gift. It is customary (but not obligatory) to send a present if you accept the invitation to the reception. You naturally give a wedding present to the bride who is an intimate friend, or who is the daughter of an intimate friend, whether she has a large wedding or one so small that not even you are invited to it. In many cases you send a present to a bride whom you don't know who is marrying a man who is an old friend. You *must* send a present to one who is marrying into your family.

Typical wedding presents include almost anything ornamental as well as useful for the furnishing of a house or the setting of a dining table, from a piece of silver to a glass ash tray, a picture frame to a clock, a paper cutter to a lamp, a cigarette box to an "occasional" table or chair. Naturally, the less you know about the future living plans of the bride and groom, the more necessary it is to choose a gift that can be used by anyone living anywhere.

OCCASIONAL PRESENT TO BRIDEGROOM

In addition to this wedding gift sent to the bride, a personal present is sometimes given to the groom by his family or a best friend. This is an extra gift, however, that is prompted entirely by personal feeling and has nothing to do with the general present-sending obligation.

NEAREST RELATIVES MAY GIVE CHECKS

Nearest relatives may properly give their gifts in the form of money. A check should be drawn to the bride alone in her maiden name, or in the names of both: John and Mary Smith.

CARDS WITH PRESENTS

A visiting card is usually enclosed with a wedding present, left blank or on which is written "Best wishes" or "All best wishes for your happiness." If you have no visiting card, write the same message on a blank one and sign it. And be sure your address is included—unless you are certain that the bride knows it.

DELAYED PRESENTS

If, because of illness or absence, a present is not sent until after the wedding, a short note should accompany it, giving the reason for the delay.

WEDDING ANNIVERSARIES

The 8 anniversaries known to us all are:

> 1 year, Paper
> 5 years, Wood
> 10 years, Tin
> 15 years, Crystal
> 20 years, China
> 25 years, Silver
> 50 years, Gold
> 75 years, Diamond

Until comparatively modern times, the eight anniversaries were all that were acknowledged. Lately, however, anniversaries have been added until now there is one for each year up to 15, and one for every five years after that. Moreover, several different gifts are considered suitable for a number of these anniversaries. The complete list is as follows:

1 year, paper. 2 years, calico—in some states any cotton. Calico is the more amusing word and suggests, perhaps, a more amusing party. But to say "any sort of cotton" makes present-giving easier. 3 years, leather (or muslin). 4 years, silk. 5 years, wood. 6 years, iron. 7 years, copper or woolen. 8 years, electric appliances (which shows that innovation has supplemented tradition). 9 years, pottery.

10 years, to the "tin" of this year is now added aluminum. 11 years, steel. 12 years, linen. 13 years, lace. 14 years, ivory.

15 years, crystal, as it has ever been, and of course it includes everything made of glass. After this there are four giftless anniversaries and then:

20 years, china. 25 years, the Silver Wedding Anniversary, which has surely been celebrated more often than all the others put together. 30 years, pearls. 35 years, coral and jade. 40 years, ruby. 45 years, sapphire. 50 years, the Golden Wedding Anniversary. 55 years, emerald. 60 years, diamond. 75 years, diamond also.

Suitable parties to celebrate any of the earliest wedding anniversaries are a house-warming or perhaps a stork shower, a calico fancy-dress party, a barn dance, a treasure hunt, or any informal party that appeals to the imagination. For that matter, it can also be a surprise party arranged for the bride and groom by their friends. The shorter years suggest much more informal gatherings than the Silver Wedding, for example, which is perhaps celebrated by a big dinner at little tables, or a general entertainment, such as a musicale or a garden party. The most important anniversary, the golden wedding (50 years), is usually celebrated by a somewhat formal afternoon or evening meal at home, or by a family dinner either in the evening or at midday after which additional relatives, friends and neighbors come in to offer their congratulations. No one must feel that a present is obligatory, especially when the anniversary year is one which suggests an item of value. Intimate friends, however, usually take or send something if possible. Flowers are of course always an appropriate remembrance of such an occasion.

(For wording of anniversary invitations, see Index.)

ANSWERS TO READERS' QUESTIONS

"MISS" BLANK'S INVITATION TO "DAUGHTER'S" MARRIAGE

My father died just before I was born and my mother did not survive my birth. I had not even any grandparents, and my mother's dearest friend adopted me. And since she never married I have always been Miss Blank's daughter, which is of course understood at home. But now comes the question of having my wedding invitations engraved, and "Miss" followed by "her daughter" would look strange to people in my fiancé's town. Mother and I wonder whether you can solve our problem.

Certainly. Word the invitations

>Miss Mary Blank
>requests the honour of your presence
>at the marriage of her adopted daughter
>Margaret

WHEN GROOM'S MOTHER MAY SERVE AS MOTHER TO BRIDE

I know that all the expense of a wedding must be undertaken by the family of the bride. But I wonder whether this rule must apply under my circumstances. My fiancé's family and my own family lived for fifteen years next door to each other. My mother and my mother-in-law were as devoted as sisters—and ever since my own mother's death she has been almost everything that a mother could be. I know that she loves me too. My father died a year ago. The whole situation is this: Having no daughter of her own, my future mother-in-law wants to give me my wedding dress and some of my other things, and to have the wedding breakfast at her house. Do you think this could be criticized? Everyone in town knows the circumstances. I live with a cousin who has a tiny little flat; we could not possibly have any sort of reception there, and I don't want to hire a parlor at the hotel. My uncle is coming to give me away, and the church invitations are to be sent out in his name.

No one could possibly criticise your future mother-in-law for giving you whatever she may want to, including the wedding breakfast. Where the rule really applies is in the case of a girl whose family is not well-to-do and who is herself known slightly or perhaps not at all by the family of

THE DAY OF THE WEDDING

the bridegroom, who puts herself in a false position by publicising her own family's inability to assume the wedding obligations which properly belong to them. But in your personal case I cannot imagine that anyone could fail to appreciate a very beautiful situation!

ANNOUNCEMENT OF SON'S ENGAGEMENT AT OWN ANNIVERSARY

My fiancé's parents are soon to entertain in honor of their twenty-fifth wedding anniversary and they would like to announce our engagement at this time because all their friends will be present. My family think it wrong for them to make the announcement. What do you think?

Your family is right. But there would be no impropriety should your family announce your engagement in the newspapers on the day of the anniversary party. After this you and your fiancé would receive with his parents, who would introduce you to all their relatives and friends.

AN UNTHINKING BRIDE AND THE GROOM'S FAMILY

My fiancé and I have been making plans for our wedding trip and he insists that we must stop over with his family for several days, as our route takes us near their place. I feel that no family can expect this of us on our honeymoon; but when I said as much, he seemed astonished that I could even think of any other plan. Before saying any more, I would like your opinion.

This is one of those replies that can be made only by asking other questions, such as: How long a trip are you taking? What are the chances that he will be able to take you to see his people again? If you can go in a short while, then you are perhaps right. But if it is possible that he may not be able to go home again for an indefinite time, it is natural that he would expect you to show some eagerness to share his background and his people. Perhaps, too, you might remember one thing: a devoted son makes a perfect husband, nine times out of ten. The son who cares nothing about his father and mother is not very likely to care very faithfully for his wife—at least the law of averages does not point that way. A quarter of your honeymoon spent with his people would certainly not be too much to ask of you to give with a gracious heart. If you think this unfair—I hope it will remain fixed in your memory should you some day have a son who marries.

IN BRIDAL DRESS IN HER THIRTIES

Could I, who am small and reasonably young-looking (far into the thirties), dare to choose a real bridal dress—or must I be content with ordinary clothes on this far-from-ordinary occasion? We have been engaged for many years, and instead of being easy, it is doubly hard, I find, to have what you call a wedding frame with no picture in it of the bride in her white dress and veil.

Of course you can wear a bridal dress—and I hope that perhaps you may find the following suggestions useful.

The important detail is that you take pains to choose a white (particularly if satin) of a definitely becoming tint. You know, if you've ever really looked at them, that very few materials are pure white. For a bride beyond her twenties, the right one of these off-white tints is as flattering as the wrong one is cruel.

IF A WEDDING SHOWER, WHY NOT A SHOWER WEDDING?

This is also an answer to a bride who had a runaway impulse. I am including it at the end of these letters because it not only is to me a delighting story, but has in it an idea both practical and new. An intimate friend found out that, believing a wedding impossible, a certain young couple had made arrangements to be married in an empty church. At the hour set they drove up alone and went into the vestry, where the clergyman was waiting. As the door into the church opened, the lights of the Chancel went on and the organ, to the surprise of the principals, softly began the wedding march, and then instead of the somberness of an empty church they saw flowers and faces of friends in the front pews. After the ceremony, everyone went to the rectory for a surprise shower breakfast, which included a white iced wedding cake, and in this instance, champagne. So, to those friends of a bride-to-be who might like to follow this example, I would make one suggestion: It would be better that the bride be given at least a hint in advance, so that if she wants to, she can dress as a bride, or at least not in clothes chosen to wear at a football game, as was the case in the story given above. Otherwise there is, so it seems to me, unending possibility in the question, "If a wedding shower, why not a shower wedding?"

BRIDEGROOM'S FAMILY SHOULD NOT SEND ANNOUNCEMENTS

May the bridegroom's family send announcements of the marriage to their own friends and relatives when the bride's family is not sending any?

When a bride's own family has made no move to send out the marriage announcements the bridegroom's family may properly notify their own friends by telephoning the society editors of the newspapers as well as by writing personal letters to their relatives. But it would be in questionable taste should they send out engraved announcements.

To best friends as well as relatives a very appealing announcement is the sending of a snapshot of the New Mr. and Mrs. ...... taken together.

21

Simplified Wedding Details for a Bride in Everyday Clothes

A WHITE bridal dress and veil, the garden-party effect of bridesmaids' clothes, and the formal black and white of the men of the bridal party—that is still and must ever be the perfect picture. But it is essential that a compromise be made between the too unreasonable conventions of tradition and the situation of the young woman who finds the ruling unfair that all the beauty of wedding preparations— even the propriety of having a few dearest friends take part—shall depend solely upon the bride's ability to afford the extravagance of bridal array.

In short, many a bride is now protesting against the rigid regulations which prevent her spending her trousseau money on a "best dress" that will be useful as well as becoming throughout the coming season, in order to be allowed to have a "real" wedding. This same handicap of having to buy useless dresses, applies also to bridesmaids.

So, in answer to this problem, let us see how, without completely breaking traditional precepts, to suggest a "real" wedding for the bride who is going to wear everyday clothes!

A lovely effect might easily be produced by a bride in a pale and fragile picture dress, preceded by her maid of honor in a costume equally picturesque. But this does not solve the problem. A garden-party type of dress in pink or pale blue is not going to be any more useful for daily wear afterwards than would the far lovelier bridal dress of white.

FIRST ASSET IS UNITY

Therefore, starting with a practical dress, as pretty and as becoming as it can possibly be for future utility, let us consider all the details essential to a perfect wedding and see how many can be considered *suitable*. The first and most important of these is unity. Soldiers on parade are something to look at because each in appearance and in movement is exactly like every other. At the most elaborate of weddings, perfection is always the result of similarity of appearance and of drilled precision. This is why bridesmaids' dresses and ushers' clothes must match; this is why the processional must be perfectly rehearsed, and why it may be possible to have a wedding of satisfying beauty for a bride in everyday clothes—if they have in any way a bride-like effect. She might have accessories of white, a white flower hat—for example, with coarse-mesh hat veiling around it, and she could carry a white bouquet—not a set florist's one suggestive of greenhouse flowers. Let us hope that the skirt of her dress is long but that its design is one which will be equally good if shortened after the wedding. There are many dresses that look equally well long or short, and are in fact offered to customers in both street and evening lengths.

She may, of course, wear any styles and colors that she likes best—but it must be pointed out that the picture she is to make does necessarily affect the frame to be built around her. That is, if she is going to wear a plain dark tailored street dress, no further plans than going with the bridegroom and getting married are possible. Even if she has a maid of honor, she could be no more than a best friend to stand up with her.

A wedding procession must be something more than one young woman in a street dress followed by another young woman also in street dress, walking with a man in a business suit. But let us say that the bride is going to make a sufficiently bride-like appearance to balance a wedding background. The plans that could be made for her are these:

The wedding to be in church—organ music, of course. Decoration of altar with white flowers, but not too much decoration otherwise. That is, no palms and no suggestion of greenhouse flowers. There might very well be a moderate arrangement of white garden flowers on the chancel or a spray tied to the ends of each of the front pews. But she must be careful not to build up too great a feeling of expectation.

In the same way there may be two ushers—even possibly four—but not in cutaway coats. They will wear blue sack suits, probably, with white shirts, blue and white ties, black shoes, no gloves, but of course white boutonnières. In summer, gray flannel trousers with their blue coats would look very well if they all have them. The rule is that the best man is either dressed exactly like the bridegroom or else like the ushers. But at this wedding they should all be alike—except that the boutonnière of the groom may be a little larger.

This same idea of unity, which is always followed where there are many bridesmaids, can do much to overcome the casual unmatching effect of bride and attendant in ordinary clothes, by having the bride's clothes repeated identically by her maid of honor, but in a different color. At this particular wedding, there is no reason why she might not have two bridesmaids dressed alike; and she may, of course, have a flower girl.

AT THE CHURCH

Arriving guests at the wedding are seated as always by the ushers, who should not be too solemn. This does not mean that they may be less than dignified, but it must be remembered that anticipation is likely to be overbuilt by great formality. When the bride arrives, the procedure is the same as always. The groom and best man follow the clergyman and wait at the foot of the chancel. The processional is headed by the ushers, followed by the two bridesmaids, the maid of honor; then the flower girl, but *not* scattering petals. And then the bride on her father's right arm.

One detail of the processional is important: Everyone must of course keep time with the march as played, but the tempo chosen by the organist should be that of a natural walk—meaning not too draggingly slow. As a matter of fact, this same admonition might be given at the rehearsal of every wedding, although when the bride has a very long train, a somewhat slower pace adds dignity.

SIMPLEST RECEPTION REQUIREMENTS

If there is to be no reception, the bride and groom can go out into the vestibule of the church to receive the congratulations of their friends. If there is a reception, midafternoon would be the best time, because only lightest refreshments are necessary. If it were in the morning, followed by a one o'clock noon breakfast, that would mean substantial food; and in the evening one rather expects an elaborate wedding—evening clothes, etc. An afternoon reception can, however, be very simple and much less expensive really than a big dinner for the family. All that is required is a fruit punch in which to drink the bride's and groom's health, and wedding cake. More than this would include either tea or coffee and thin sandwiches.

The decoration of the table at the reception, and the wedding cake, should of course be white. If someone in the family has any manual dexterity, the little bride and groom dolls might be dressed to match the clothes of the real bride and groom: scraps of her dress basted (or pasted) over parts of the doll's dress and a copied effect of her hat. The groom doll's clothes should also be changed from "tails" to look like the groom's uniform if he is wearing one.

One last word about the invitations and announcements: Formally worded announcements sent out after the wedding are, of course, correct. But since engraved invitations are the essence of formality, invitations to the ceremony as well as to the reception (if there is to be one) should be by personal messages from the bride to her nearest relatives and best friends or from her mother to other relatives and neighbors, including those of the groom.

22

The Stranger at a Wedding

A CERTAIN situation of very real importance, even though it occurs but seldom, is the disappointment of a young person who does not dare to accept the invitation to a wedding because of the ordeal of having to go to it alone. A case in point is that of a young business woman—a stranger in a great city—who has written these eager words:

"The daughter of the president of our company has just sent me an invitation to her wedding—to the church and the reception both! I am so surprised—and I do want to go! But to have to go alone, not knowing what a guest is expected to do and say from arriving at the church all the way to leaving the reception—really I can't face it! I don't *dare* accept the most wonderful invitation I shall probably ever have."

So to you who perhaps find yourself in this same situation, the following directions are offered:

Hold your card of admission ready to give to the man who will ask for it at the door. When you enter the church, go as far as the foot of the center aisle; if you get there early there will be plenty of seats. Wait until one of the ushers comes up to you. If you were a member of either family or a very intimate friend of the bride or the groom, you would tell him your name. He would look on his "in front of the ribbons" list in order to seat you. If you say nothing, he will ask you whether you are a friend of the bride or of the groom, in order to seat you on her, or his, side of the aisle. In any case, you put your hand on the inside of his proffered arm, and he escorts you to a seat.

If you have arrived early enough to be given an aisle seat, there is one rule of etiquette which is a seeming contradiction to politeness, and therefore important to know: It is entirely proper that you keep your aisle seat, no matter who or how many enter the pew later. Now and then an inconsiderate late-comer, seeing someone much younger or a stranger sitting on the aisle, unfairly demands, "Move up, please." Nine out of ten well-bred people do so, instinctively, and find themselves pushed along to the sixth seat in. To stand up where you are and to make room for the late-comers to pass you and take their places farther in is all that is required by etiquette, even though the one on the aisle be a young man and the newcomer an elderly woman. In other words, pew seats at a wedding are held exactly as reserved seats are held in a theater.

At a wedding it is also proper to smile and bow slightly to people you know—even to talk briefly in a very low voice to a friend sitting next to you; but when you find yourself among strangers, you just sit quietly until the processional starts. In most of the Protestant churches, the congregation then rises and stands throughout the service. In any case, you merely follow those in front of you; stand if they stand, kneel if they kneel, and sit if they sit.

When the service is over and the recessional has passed by, those in the pews farther back must wait in their places until the immediate families in the front pews have left. When in doubt, therefore, wait until those around you start to leave.

As soon as you leave the church, you are expected to go at once to wherever the reception is to be held. But since you are a lone stranger, it will be better to walk or drive around for fifteen minutes or so, to let the house get crowded and make the fact of your aloneness unnoticeable. Except at out-of-town weddings for which the guests arrive by special train, no provision is ever made for taking any of the guests from the church to the house. You go in your own car, or you call a taxi, or if the distance is short, you walk.

YOUR BEHAVIOR AT THE RECEPTION IN DETAIL

Whether in a house or hotel, you will be met at the entrance by someone who tells you, "Ladies' dressing room to the right" (or wherever it is). You leave your wrap, if you choose to, but you do not take off your hat or your gloves. Since you are not an intimate friend, you add your visiting card to the others on a tray in the hall. And then you go to the door of the room in which the reception is held. (You will see people going in and hear a man announcing their names.) As you approach, he asks you, "What name, please?" And you give your name with title. If he says nothing, you say to *him*, "Miss Pauline Panic" (or Mrs. John Jones). He then repeats in a clear rather than loud voice (though it may sound loud to you), "Miss Pauline Panic." Then you go through the door. The bride's mother will be standing close beside you. She offers you her hand, smiles, and if you are unknown to her, she says, "How do you do." If she knows you, she says whatever is suitable. In the first place, you also say, "How do you do"; in the second, you reply to what she says to you. If she says, "I'm very glad to see you," you answer, "Thank you" or "It was very kind of you to invite me," and add something pleasant about the bride or the wedding in general. If the groom's mother is standing next to her, you must shake hands with her too, whether you are introduced to her or not. (Even if you know both of the mothers very well, there would really be no time to say more than perhaps something such as "What a lovely day Mary and John have for the wedding!" or "How beautiful Mary looks!") You then join the queue of guests who are waiting to "congratulate" the bride and groom. Actually you congratulate the groom, but you wish the bride happiness. Remember, it is a breach of good manners to congratulate a bride on having secured a husband.

If you are in doubt about being known to either of them, you give your name, shake hands with the bride, and add, "I wish you every happiness!" Then you shake hands with the groom and say, "Congratulations, and all good wishes." If the bride does not introduce you because being greeted by someone following you—and the groom knows you well by name, though not by sight—you tell him who you are. Otherwise, you don't.

You greet any of the bridesmaids who are friends of yours. Otherwise you walk on—or smile perhaps if you happen to be looking directly at one of them who also looks at you. But there is no chance to stop and really talk to anyone unless you arrived early, or else so late that no one is waiting behind you.

After greeting the bride and groom, you look around for friends of your own. If you see no one whom you know well enough to join, the best thing to do is to make your way slowly and nonchalantly to wherever refreshments are being served.

You take your time to look at the table and then either ask one of the waiters to serve you, or help yourself to what you want. You can linger and nibble as long as you like, or sit down and watch people; and you may speak to anyone who is alone and looks willing to be spoken to.

A SIT-DOWN BREAKFAST

A sit-down breakfast presents a very awkward situation to you who are a stranger. You cannot very well join a group of people whom you do not know. Therefore, it is best to go into the dining room as soon as you can, and sit down at an unoccupied table, and let others join *you*. If you wait until every table has several people sitting at it, you have no alternative but to run the risk of making yourself an unwelcome intruder.

When you want to leave, you just do so. It is not necessary or even polite to attract attention to your going if it is soon after your arrival.

23

Making One's Position in the Community

THE BRIDE WHO GOES TO LIVE IN HER HUSBAND'S HOME TOWN

THE bride who is a stranger, but whose husband is well known—best of all, whose family-in-law welcome her warmly—has no problem further than making herself liked. The best way to do this is to be ready to like them, to be interested in what interests them and to try to understand and adapt herself to their different points of view. This does not mean that she is to be double-faced, but merely that she is not to chop up the smooth pathway that they have laid down for her by riding roughshod over all of their pet prejudices before she has even found out what they are.

The bride, for example, who comes from New York or Chicago to live in Bright Meadows and rudely criticizes the smaller town's ways, and who in fact insists upon dragging fifty-story skyscrapers into comparison with Bright Meadows' new six-storied building, is being not merely discourteous but stupid in her choice of comparison. But as already noted, the bride of a townsman is not a stranger. Therefore, let us consider the situation of those who are.

YOU WHO ARE STRANGERS

Let us say you are not a bride and groom in whom people are usually inclined to take a sentimental interest, but an unheralded young couple who have come to live in Oldtown because your husband has been sent there by his firm.

He will of course meet men through business. You yourself will find it hard—or easy—to make friends according to a number of circumstances. First of all, the size of Oldtown. If the town is very small and characteristically friendly, you will get to be known by your neighbors, and by the members of the church you go to, quickly. And if they like you—which will mean that you like them—this is almost all there is to the first step. After that then, through the church and other community activities open to you, you quite simply enlarge your acquaintance throughout the town.

A CHILD OR—A PUPPY

A very young, very captivating child is, as we all know, an irresistible attraction! But the really unfailing friendmaker is a puppy not however, if you let it bark or slip through the fence and dig your neighbor's lawn or chase her chickens, or frighten her baby.

YOUR FIRST VISITORS

If before you are settled, neighbors come to see you and you are "caught" in a paint-smattered smock and the house in no way fit to be seen, don't worry! The situation could not be better! The whole picture is so out of key with a formal hostess-visitor scene that the atmosphere is friendly, and before you know it, you are showing two neighbors all the objects you have painted—or intend to paint— and before they know it, they are giving you their best advice (which perhaps you follow or perhaps you don't); in any event, by the time they go they seem like friends—and probably they soon become just that.

APPEARING TO BE A SNOB

The following situation, for example, can easily occur. Let us say that Oldtown is not very small and that the people, while courteously polite, are innately reserved and show you nothing but indifference. You are for the first time in your life horribly lonely, and missing your friends and your family at home. Mrs. Nextdoor is friendly. Perhaps she brings you books or flowers or broth when you are ill. Appreciating her kindness, you keep away from the thought that her topics of conversation don't interest you a bit, and that you and she have not a thing in common. Then you meet other people and gradually get to know them better. You find that while you like Mrs. Nextdoor herself, your husband does not like her husband at all, and that neither of you is in sympathy with the people you meet at their house.

Or let us suppose that you are particularly interested in gardening or in music or books or sports. Naturally you drift toward membership in the Garden Club, or the Symphony Society, the Reading Class, or the Country Club. You naturally join these organizations because they appeal to your taste.

If you drift entirely away from Mrs. Nextdoor, it is not because you do not feel as friendly toward her personally as ever you did. You would be delighted to include her in your activities, but she does not care for your interests; she does not really enjoy the company of your friends any more than you find pleasure in being with hers.

Perhaps she sees all this clearly and remains as friendly a neighbor as ever. But it may very well happen that she resents your desertion, and proclaims you a snob!

A hundred proverbs proclaim the triteness of the fact that like drifts inevitably to like. The objection is not to your going eventually with your own kind, but to having made believe you were other than you are. If you hadn't done this, then no criticism could have been deserved.

"Perfect" society is composed of those who have tastes and thoughts in common—that is exactly what the term should mean. Liking, appreciation and friendliness also exist between those who share some one special interest or activity.

THE CRUELTY OF NEW YORK

Because so many young women, as well as men, have an idea that life in a great city is completely glamorous, this explanation may perhaps serve as a useful antidote at least to the hurt pride that is felt by the bride who comes from a small, neighborly, friendly community into this crushing city of titanic size and inhuman indifference, and has to face a situation that is harder than that of any other newcomer. The unknown wife of no matter how attractive a man, if he have neither strong family backing nor wealth enough to build a background for her, can but find herself bereft of a position such as she had at home—or would have in almost any other community. This is not because New York refuses to accept her—not at all. New York might put her on a pedestal if it knew of her existence—and that is the very point! In a city of nearly eight million people, how *can* one young bride be found, no matter how lovely she is! In a very small town no one can for long be an unrecognized stranger. Walk down Main Street a dozen times, and dozens of people will have seen you twelve times. So let it be said, first of all, DON'T go as strangers to a great city. If you have a few friends to start with, that is one thing; but otherwise live in the suburbs instead. Even if you do this, you will have to leave to fate (or to your judgment of the neighborhood you settle in) the hope of finding your neighbors congenial, and the equal hope that they will find the same quality in you.

24

Christenings

INVITATION TO CHRISTENING

A CHILD can, of course, be christened without any festivity at all. On the other hand, it is the time-honored occasion for a new mother to see her friends and show her baby to them.

Invitations to a christening are usually telephoned, or else friends are asked when seen. But it is both correct and polite to write notes.

Dear Mrs. Kindhart:

The baby is to be christened here at home next Sunday at half past four, and we hope you and Mr. Kindhart—and the children if they care to—will come.

Affectionately,
Mary Meadows

ASKING THE GODPARENTS

Before setting the date for the christening, the godmothers—usually two for a girl and one for a boy—and the godfathers—two for a boy and one for a girl—have, of course, already been chosen. In fact, they are usually asked to serve at the time that the baby's arrival is announced to them—occasionally before.

The Gilding baby, for instance, supposedly sent the following telegram:

Mrs. Richard Worldly,
    Great Estates.

I arrived last night and my mother and father were very glad to see me, and I am now eagerly waiting to see you.

Your loving godson,
Robert Gilding, 3d.

But more usually a godparent at a distance is asked by telegraph.

John Strong,
    Fartown.

It's a boy. Will you be godfather?

Bob

But in any case do *not* write, "My husband and I sincerely hope

CHRISTENINGS

that you will consent to be our son's godmother," etc. Anyone so slightly known as this wording implies could not be asked to fill so intimate a position as that of godmother without great presumption.

One must never ask any person to be a godmother or godfather whom one does not know intimately, as it is a responsibility not lightly to be undertaken and also one impossible to refuse. Godparents should, however, be chosen from among friends rather than relatives, since the sole advantage of godparents is that they add to the child's stock of relatives, so that, if it should be left alone in the world, its godparents become its protectors. But when a child is born with plenty of relatives who can be called upon for advice and affection and assistance in event of its becoming an orphan, godparents are often chosen from among them.

GODPARENT BY PROXY

If a godfather (or godmother) whom the parents particularly want is unable to be present at the christening, a proxy quite simply acts for him (or her) at the ceremony. Consent by the real godparent must have been given.

OBLIGATION OF BEING A GODPARENT

The obligation of being a godparent is essentially a spiritual one. He must see that the child is given religious training and that he shall in proper time be confirmed. Beyond this "obligation" he is expected to take an especial interest in the child—much as a very near relative would do. At the christening he gives the baby as nice a present as he can afford. The typical gift is a silver mug or a porringer marked with full inscription

> Robert Meadows, Jr.
> From his godfather
> John Strong

The next most typical presents are a silver fork and spoon, silver and mother of pearl rattle, a set of bib pins—or, if the godfather is well-to-do, a government bond which is kept with interest intact until a girl is eighteen or a boy twenty-one.

TIME OF CHRISTENING

In other days of stricter observances a baby was baptized in the Catholic or high Episcopal church on the first, or at least second, Sunday after its birth. In the Catholic church the christening still takes place when the baby is very young, and always in church or baptistry (unless its baptism is *in extremis*). In the Protestant churches today the christening is usually delayed until the mother is up and about again. Often it is put off for months, and in some denominations children need not be christened until they are several years old.

THE CHRISTENING IN CHURCH

In arranging for the ceremony the clergyman, of course, is consulted and the place and hour arranged. It may take place at the close of the regular service on Sunday; but if a good deal is to be made of the christening, a weekday is chosen and an hour when the church is not being otherwise used. In either case, the guests invited for the christening seat themselves in the pews nearest to the font.

As soon as the clergyman appears, the baby's coat and cap are taken off and the godmother, holding the baby in her arms, stands directly in front of the clergyman. The other godparents stand beside her, and relatives and friends stand nearby.

The godmother who is holding the baby must be sure to pronounce its name distinctly; in fact it is wise, if the name is long or unusual, to print it on a slip of paper and give it to the clergyman beforehand, as more than one baby has been given a name not intended for it. And whatever name the clergyman pronounces is fixed for life. (The little Towne girl, who was to have been called Marian, is actually Mary Ann!)

As soon as the ceremony is over, the baby and all its relatives and friends go to the house of the parents or grandparents where a caudle party has been arranged.

HOUSE CHRISTENING

Unless forbidden by the church to which the baby's parents belong, the house christening is by far the easier, safer and prettier ceremony —easier, because the baby does not have to have wraps put on and off and be taken out and brought in; safer, because it is not likely to catch cold; and prettier, for a dozen reasons.

The baby in the first place looks much prettier in a dress that has not been crushed by having a coat put over it and taken off and put on and off again. In the second place, a baby brought down from the nursery without any fussing is generally "good," whereas one that has been dressed and undressed and taken hither and yon is likely to be upset and therefore to cry. If it cries in church, it just has to cry! In a house it can be taken into another room and be brought back again after it has been made "more comfortable." It is trying to a young mother who is proud of her baby's looks, to go to no end of trouble to get the prettiest clothes she can for it, and ask all her friends in, and then have it look like a tragedy mask carved in a beet! And you can scarcely expect a self-respecting baby who is hauled and mauled and taken to a strange place and handed to a strange person who pours cold water on it—not to protest. And alas! it has only one means of protest: to turn deep red and scream!

ARRANGEMENTS FOR HOUSE CHRISTENING

The arrangements for a house christening are always quite simple. In the country in summer, flowers, of course, add lovely decoration. Otherwise, the only decoration is that of the "font." This is always a bowl—usually of silver (often borrowed)—put on a small high table. A white napkin on the table inevitably suggests a restaurant rather than a ritual and is, therefore, unfortunate; most people prefer to have the table covered with something dark. Old brocade or velvet is ideal. In the center of the table, flowers are arranged in a flat circle, the blossoms around the outside, the stems toward the center and covered by the base of the bowl, which is set within this circle.

(If the clergyman is to wear vestments, a room must be put at his disposal.)

NO FEE REQUIRED

Baptism is a sacrament of the Church, for which no fee is ever required. A donation may, however, be given.

At the hour set for the ceremony, the clergyman enters the room first and takes his place at the font. The guests naturally make way, forming an open aisle. If not, the baby's father or another member of the family clears an aisle. The godmother carries the baby and follows the clergyman; the other two godparents walk behind her, and all three stand near the font. At the proper moment the clergyman takes the baby, baptizes it and hands it back to the godmother, who holds it until the ceremony is over.

CLOTHES AT THE CHRISTENING

The baby's christening dress is often one that was worn by the baby's mother, father, or even one of its grand- or great-grandparents.

At the christening everything the baby wears is white. But at other times the various colored accessories for a girl are supposed to be pink, and for a boy, blue. But a mother naturally—if she is sensible—chooses the color she prefers.

As soon as the ceremony has been performed, the clergyman goes to the room set apart for him, changes into his ordinary clothes, and then returns to the living room to be one of the guests at luncheon or tea.

The only difference between an ordinary informal tea and a christening tea is that a feature of the latter is a christening cake and caudle. The christening cake is generally a white "lady" cake elaborately iced, sometimes with the baby's initials, and garlands of pink sugar roses. And although, according to cookbooks, caudle is a gruel, the actual caudle invariably served at christenings is a hot eggnog, drunk out of little punch cups. One is supposed to eat the cake as a sign that he partakes of the baby's hospitality, and is therefore its friend, and to drink the caudle to its health and prosperity. But by this time the young host—or hostess—is peacefully asleep in the nursery.

ANNOUNCEMENT OF ADOPTION

So many people are interested in adoption announcements that the following has been chosen as being not only charming but likely to bring reassuring comfort to the child later on, should she ever doubt her place in the hearts of those who chose her to be their own:

>Mr. and Mrs. Nuhome
>have the happiness to announce
>the adoption of
>Mary
>aged thirteen months

Or, if announcements are sent during the legal proceedings, change above form to read:

>have the happiness to announce
>the arrival
>and prospective adoption of

ANNOUNCEMENT OF BIRTH

The conventional announcement is the little card printed with the baby's name: Robert William, Jr., or Robert William Young, Jr., and down in the right corner the date of his birth: June tenth. This is tied to the Mr. and Mrs. card of his parents, generally with white ribbon, but there is no objection to pink or blue. If one of the many enchanting birth-announcement cards is chosen at the stationers, the names of the parents should be signed "Mary and John Young," not "Mr. and Mrs. John Young."

25

Funerals

IN A TIME of bereavement, when we stand baffled and alone, etiquette performs its most real service by smoothing the necessary personal contacts and making sure that the last rites of our beloved shall be performed with beauty and gravity.

NOTIFY PEOPLE

If members of the immediate family are not already present, the first act of someone at the bedside of the deceased is to notify them and one or two intimate friends whose capability as well as sympathy can be counted on.

If the deceased had suffered a long illness, and the family has become attached to the trained nurse, no one is better fitted than she to turn her ministrations from the one whom she can no longer help to those who now have a very real need for her care.

But she, a friend, or a member of the family must look after many details.

NEWSPAPER NOTICE

One of the first things to do is to put into the newspapers a notice of the death and—as soon as it is known—a statement of the time and place of the funeral. The form can be selected from among those appearing in the daily press. If this notice appears in several papers and several times, the person who has charge of the funeral expenses must remember to ask for the total amount, for it can be an appreciable item.

Except for those relatives and intimate friends who received telephoned or telegraphed messages asking them to go to the house at once, everyone is expected to consider this newspaper announcement notification enough.

When the notice reads, "Funeral private" and neither time nor place is given, very intimate friends are given this information; others understand that they are not expected to be present.

The notification of a private funeral is telephoned or written on the personal card of the friend in charge. "Mr. Brown's funeral will be at Christ Church, Monday at 11 o'clock."

When the notice requests that no flowers be sent, the wish should be strictly followed, particularly if the service is being held in a Catholic or very "high" Episcopal church to which flowers are not admitted.

THE FUNERAL DIRECTOR

After consulting members of the family about their wishes in the matter, the friend who is taking charge of arrangements either goes to or accompanies one of the family to a funeral director, who then assumes, subject to the family's approval, the many details of the service and burial.

Because of the criticism of a certain not admirable type of funeral director in the earlier editions of this book, it must at once be said that this was not meant to apply to any of the directors of high reputation who are conscientiously considerate not only of the feelings of the family but also of their pocketbook.

But because what have come to be known as racketeers do exist—and unhappily flourish in this very profession which comes closest to human suffering—it is necessary that the paragraph as formerly printed remain, in order that those few to whom the description applies be recognized for what they are.

First of all, the wrong type of director will refuse to give an itemized list of costs, but will, instead, do his best to hypnotize the family into believing that the more expensive the casket* and the more elaborate the preparations the greater the love and honor shown to the deceased. If not checked, he will bring the most ornate and expensive casket in his establishment. He will perform every rite that his professional ingenuity for expenditure can devise. He will order vehicles numerous enough for the cortège of a President. He will even, if thrown in contact with a bewildered chief mourner, secure a pledge for the erection of an elaborate mausoleum.

Someone, therefore, who has the family's interest at heart and knows their taste and purse, should go personally to the establishment of the funeral director and go carefully into the specification of all details, so that everything necessary may be arranged for, and unnecessary items omitted.

This does not imply that a family which prefers a very elaborate funeral should not be allowed to have one. But the great majority of people have moderate rather than unlimited means, and it is not unheard of that a small estate is seriously depleted by vulgarly lavish and entirely inappropriate funeral expenses. It must be added that this

---

* In spite of the fact the word *coffin* is still preferred by most people of fastidious taste and used in the spoken language of these same people, it seems best to follow present-day commercial usage and admit the word *casket* to these pages—especially since the shape of a modern coffin is undeniably that of a casket.

FUNERALS

situation is quite as often the fault of an incompetent friend as of a conscienceless funeral director. Therefore, unless a member of the family can attend to the details, it is most important that a funeral director of known integrity be chosen, probably by the clergyman, or more likely by the sexton of the church.

THE CLERGYMAN

If the deceased or the family are members of a particular church, the pastor is notified immediately and asked to officiate at the service. If there is no such natural choice of clergyman, a request is made of one who may be a friend, an adviser, a fellow lodge member, a college classmate, or one whose sermons have been a source of inspiration. Occasionally two clergymen are asked, one for the funeral service and one for the burial.

No fee is asked by the clergyman, ever—nor is one expected; but those who would like to give something in appreciation of his services do so. The amount depends entirely upon their means.

A bill rendered by the sexton includes all necessary charges for the church.

HONORARY PALLBEARERS

The member of the family who is in charge will ask either when they come to the house, or by telephone or telegraph if they are at a distance, six or eight men who are close friends of the deceased to be the pallbearers. When a man has been prominent in public life, he may have twelve or more from among his political or business associates as well as his lifelong friends. Members of the immediate family are never chosen, as their place is with the women of the family.

The pallbearers meet a few minutes before the time set for the service, in the vestibule of the church.

Honorary pallbearers serve only at church funerals. They do not carry the coffin. This service is performed by the assistants of the funeral director, who are expertly trained.

HANGING THE BELL

Some indication must be made that there has been a death in the house in order that inadvertent interruptions may be avoided.

In most cases the funeral director hangs streamers on the bell: white ones for a child, black and white for a young person, or black for an older person. People who are well-to-do order flowers from their own florist (or the funeral director will attend to this too): white flowers with white ribbon streamers for a child or very young person, purple flowers with purple ribbons for an older person, and purple flowers with black ribbon for an old person.

A MEMBER OF THE FAMILY IN CHARGE

An intimate friend or male member of the family should be—if not at the door—as near the front hall as possible to see the countless people with whom details have to be arranged, to admit to the family anyone they may want to see, and to give news to, or take messages from, others.

As people come to the house to inquire and offer their services, he gives them commissions the occasion requires. The first friend who hurries to the house—in answer to the telephone message which announced the death—is asked to break the news to an invalid connection of the family, or he may be sent to the florist to order the bell hung, or to the station to meet a child arriving from school.

MOURNING FOR THE FUNERAL

Unless the family is one which does not believe in wearing black even when there is no war, the family who is following the conventions of mourning will surely find among those who come to the house a woman friend or relative whose taste and means of outlay are similar to those of the family. She looks through the clothes they have to see whether there is a black dress or suit that can be used, and makes a list of all the necessary articles only which will have to be procured—or quite possibly borrowed if the family is not going into permanent black.

KEEPING AN ACCURATE LIST

Whoever takes charge of the flowers must carefully collect all the notes and cards. On the outside of each envelope (they have been careful to supply themselves with screw-point pencils because the wood pencils break easily) this friend and those assisting her write a description of the flowers that came with the card. For example:

> Large spray Easter lilies tied with white ribbon
> Laurel wreath with gardenias
> Long sheaf of pink roses—broad pink ribbon

Without such notations, the family has no way of knowing anything about the flowers that their different friends have sent. Moreover, these descriptions are necessary to make the notes of thanks to be sent later more personal and appreciative.

ARRANGING THE FLOWERS

If the family is Protestant, an hour before the time set for the service, one or two women friends go to the church to arrange the flowers which have already been placed in the chancel. If there are many flowers, these friends, especially if they are inexperienced, should have the assistance of a florist. Effective grouping and fastening of the heavy wreaths and sprays is difficult for novices, no matter how perfect their taste may be.

"SITTING UP" NO LONGER CUSTOMARY

Unless the deceased be a prelate or personage whose lying-in-state is a public ceremony, or unless it is the particular wish of the relatives, the solemn vigil through long nights by the side of the casket is no longer essential as a mark of veneration or of love for the departed.

Everything is done to avoid unnecessary evidence of the change that has taken place. In many instances, the person who has passed away is left lying in bed or on a sofa in a negligée, if a woman, or dressing gown, if a man, and with flowers placed about the room. In any event, the last attentions are paid in accordance with the wishes of those most nearly concerned. A general viewing of the deceased at the funeral is not customary in the case of private citizens of fastidious taste, in most localities.

CONDUCT OF FRIENDS

When you hear of the death of a friend, you should go at once to the house, write "With sympathy" on your card and leave it at the door. Or you write a letter to the family. In either case you send flowers, addressed either to the funeral of ——— (name of the deceased) or to the nearest relative. The latter method is preferable, if the relative is a friend. But the former method is followed if the deceased alone was known to you.

On the card accompanying the flowers, and addressed to one of the family, you write "With sympathy," "With deepest sympathy," or "With heartfelt sympathy," or "With love and sympathy." If there is a notice in the papers requesting that no flowers be sent, you send none. On the other hand to any bereaved person who is particularly in your thoughts, a few flowers sent from time to time—possibly long afterward—are especially comforting in their assurance of continued sympathy.

If the notice reads "Funeral Private," you do not go unless you have received a message from the family that you are expected, or unless you are such an intimate friend that you know you are expected.

It is the duty of all members of the family to find out when the funeral is to take place and to go to it without waiting to be notified.

Above all it is heartlessly delinquent not to go to the funeral of one with whom you have been associated in business or other interests, or to whose house you have been often invited, or where you are an intimate friend of the immediate members of the family.

It is no longer considered necessary to wear black when you go to a friend's funeral unless you sit with the family, but you should choose clothes that are dark and inconspicuous.

Enter the church as quietly as possible, and as there are no ushers at a funeral, seat yourself where you approximately belong. Only a very intimate friend should take a position far up on the center aisle. If you are merely an acquaintance, you should sit toward the rear of the church.

CHURCH FUNERAL

The church funeral is the more trying in that the family have to leave the seclusion of their house and be in the presence of a congregation. On the other hand, many who find solemnity only in a church service with the added beauty of choir and organ prefer to take their heartrending farewell in the House of God.

As the time appointed for the funeral draws near, the congregation gradually fills the church. The first pews on either side of the center aisle are left empty.

THE PROCESSIONAL

At most funerals of today, the processional is omitted. The coffin, with one or several floral pieces on it—or covered with a pall of needlework belonging to the church or one of flowers—is placed on a stand at the foot of the chancel a half-hour before the service. The family enter from the vestry and take their places in the front pews, unobserved.

Should the family prefer that there be a processional, it forms in the vestibule. If there is to be a choral service, the minister and the choir enter the church from the rear, and precede the funeral cortège. Directly after the choir and clergy come the honorary pallbearers, two by two; then the coffin covered with flowers; and then the family—the chief mourner being first, walking with whoever is most sympathetic to him (or her).

Usually each woman leans upon the arm of a man. But two women or two men may walk together, according to the division of the family. If the deceased is one of four sons and there is no daughter, the mother and father walk together immediately after the body of their child, and they are followed by the two elder sons and then the younger, and then the nearest woman relative.

Although the arrangement of the procession is thus fixed, it is of greater importance that those in deepest affliction should each be placed next to the one whose nearness may be of most comfort. A younger child who is calm and soothing would better be next to his mother than an older one who is of more nervous temperament.

At the chancel the choir take their accustomed places, the clergyman stands at the foot of the chancel steps, the honorary pallbearers take their places in the front pews on the left, and the casket is set upon a stand previously placed there for the purpose. The actual bearers of the casket, who are always professionals furnished by the funeral director, walk quietly to inconspicuous stations on the side aisles. The family occupy the front pews on the right; the rest of the procession fill vacant places on either side. The service is then read.

THE RECESSIONAL

Upon the conclusion of the service, the procession moves out in the same order as it came in, except that the choir remain in their places. Outside the church, the casket is put into the hearse, the family enter motors waiting immediately behind the hearse, and the flowers are put into a covered vehicle. It is very vulgar to fill open landaulets with floral offerings and make a parade through the streets.

FEW GO TO THE BURIAL

If the burial is in the churchyard or otherwise within walking distance, the congregation naturally follows the family to the graveside. Otherwise, the general congregation no longer expects, nor wishes to go to the interment, which—except at a funeral of public importance—is witnessed only by the immediate family and the most intimate friends. The long line of carriages that used to stand at the church, ready to be filled with mere acquaintances, is a thing of the past.

FUNERAL AT THE HOUSE

Many people prefer a house funeral. It is simpler, more private, and obviates the necessity that those in sorrow face people, for the nearest relatives may stay apart in an adjoining room where they can hear the service yet remain in seclusion.

MUSIC

Earlier editions of this book said there seldom was music at house funerals because nothing could be a substitute for the deep, rich tones of the organ. At present, phonographic reproduction has become so fine that organ and choir records are entirely beautiful and may be used most helpfully.

HOUSE ARRANGEMENT

Arrangements are usually made to hold the service in the drawing room. The coffin is placed in front of the mantel, or between the windows, but always at a distance from the door. It is usually set on stands brought by the funeral director, who also supplies enough folding chairs to fill the room without crowding.

At a house funeral, the relatives either take their places near the casket or stay apart in seclusion. If the women of the family come into the drawing room, they wear hats and veils, as in a church.

All other women keep their wraps on. The men wear their overcoats or carry them in their arms and hold their hats in their hands.

It is unusual for any but a small group of relatives and intimate friends to go to the cemetery. There the grave has been lined with boughs and greens—to lessen the impression of bare earth.

"THE FUNERAL HOME" OR "CHAPEL"

In recent years, because many people live in hotels and small apartments, the establishments of funeral directors have assumed a new prominence. In the more important ones, there is a chapel, actually a small and often very beautiful non-sectarian church. There are also many rest rooms and reception rooms where the families may keep vigil by themselves or receive the condolences of their friends.

A MEMORIAL SERVICE

Under some circumstances, a memorial service is held instead of a funeral.

Notice of this service is put into the obituary column of the paper, or, in a small town, people are telephoned and each given a short list of his own nearest neighbors whom he is asked to notify.

These services are very brief. In general outline, two verses of a hymn are sung. Then follow short prayers and a very brief address about the work and personality of the person for whom the service is held. The service is closed with a prayer and two verses of another hymn.

Usually, no flowers, except a few for the altar, are sent. Sometimes flowers are sent. They are arranged as bouquets (not sheaves) so that they may be put into the wards of a hospital without having to be taken apart and re-arranged.

ACKNOWLEDGMENT OF SYMPATHY

In the case of a very prominent person, where messages of condolence, many of them impersonal, mount into the thousands, the sending of engraved cards to strangers is proper, such as

> The Governor and Mrs. State
> wish gratefully to acknowledge
> your kind expression of sympathy

Or

> Senator Michigan
> wishes to express his appreciation of
> ....'s
> sympathy in his recent bereavement.

A certain nationally important mother who had lost her only daughter sent this printed card:

> "Mrs. X thanks you for your very kind expression of sympathy and *hopes* soon to write you personally."

But under no circumstances should such cards be sent to those who have sent flowers or to intimate friends who have written personal letters.

When someone with real sympathy in his heart has taken the trouble to select and send flowers, or has gone to the house and offered what service he might, or has in a spirit of genuine regard written a personal letter, the receipt of words composed by a stationer and dispatched by a professional secretary is exactly as though his outstretched hand had been pushed aside.

A personal message on a fold-over visiting card is all anyone asks for. It takes but a moment to write "Thank you for your beautiful flowers" or "Thank you for your kind sympathy" or "Thank you for all your kindness." Nor is it much more of an effort to write "Thank you, dear Mrs. Smith, for your beautiful flowers and your kind sympathy" or "Your flowers were so beautiful! Thank you for them and for your loving message" or "Thank you for your sweet letter. I know you meant it!" or "I cannot half tell you how much all your loving kindness has meant to me."

ANOTHER MAY WRITE FOR ONE IN MOURNING

If the list is very long, or the person who has received the flowers and messages is in reality unable to perform the task of writing, some member of the family may write for her, "Mother (or Father) asks me to thank you for your beautiful flowers and kind message of sympathy." No one expects more than a short message of acknowledgment, but that message should be *seemingly personal*.

MOURNING

During the past decade no other changes in etiquette have been so great as those of the conventions of mourning. Until a short time ago the regulations for mourning were definitely prescribed according to the precise degree of relationship of the mourner. One's real feelings, whether of grief or comparative indifference, had nothing to do with the outward manifestation one was expected to show as a sign of respect.

A greater and ever greater number of persons today do not believe in going into mourning at all. There are some who believe, as do the races of the East, that great love should be expressed in rejoicing in the rebirth of a beloved spirit instead of selfishly mourning their own earthly loss. How many can attain this spirit we have no way of knowing. Most of us merely do the best we can to continue to keep occupied and to avoid casting the shadow of our own sadness upon others.

THE CRÊPE VEIL IS NO MORE

It is a very healthy sign that the crêpe veil is no more and that going into complete seclusion for two whole years or more is not encouraged. In all former editions of this book there was a paragraph on the protection which was afforded by a crêpe veil. One sentence reads: "A widow, or mother, in the newness of her heavy veil, has her hard path made as little difficult as possible by everyone with whom she comes in contact, no matter on what errand she may be bent. A clerk in a store will try to wait on her as quickly and as attentively as possible. Acquaintances avoid stopping her with long conversations that could but torture and distress her. She meets small kindnesses at every turn, which save unnecessary jars to supersensitive nerves."

Re-reading this shows plainly how far out into the sunlight of normal behavior we have gone! It is not that we *care* less, but that we are eager to see those we love gain strength, not cotton-wrap them into weakness.

Therefore, the new rules are first of all these:

A crêpe veil is worn by no one except at the funeral—and very rarely even then—nor does one wear a thick veil of any sort after the funeral. Mourning materials are, however, still definitely prescribed as follows:

MOURNING MATERIALS

Cotton, linen, woolen, and all lusterless silks are suitable for deepest mourning. Uncut velvet is as deep mourning as crêpe, but cut velvet is not mourning at all! Nor is satin or anything shiny. The only lace permissible is a plain or hemstitched net known as "footing."

A very perplexing decree is that clothes entirely of white are deepest mourning, but the addition of a black belt or hat or gloves produces second mourning.

Patent leather and satin shoes are not mourning. And stockings of

FUNERALS

beige or any color other than black or white or dark grey (which looks black) are proof that one dressed entirely in black is NOT in mourning.

People in second mourning wear all combinations of black and white as well as clothes of gray and mauve.

Much jewelry with mourning is not in good taste. Habitual jewelry, especially items of utility, such as a watch or a pin that really fastens one's dress, are permissible; and of course one continues to wear one's engagement ring no matter if it be of brightest color. A string of pearls is proper and either pearl or diamond earrings—particularly on older women who have habitually worn then.

A WORD OF ECONOMY

In the first days of stress, people sometimes give away every colored article they possess, and not until later are they aware of the effort, to say nothing of the expense, necessary to procure an entire new wardrobe. Therefore it is well to remember that:

Dresses and suits can be dyed without ripping. Any number of fabrics, for instance, all woolens, soft silks, crêpe de chine, georgettes and voiles, dye perfectly. Buttonholes sometimes have to be reworked, snaps or hooks and eyes changed to black, a bit of trimming covered with braid or dull silk, and the clothes look every bit as well as though newly ordered. All leather shoes can be blackened.

Further than such adjustments, customs of mourning have been radically lightened—in fact, the number of those who do not go into mourning at all after the day of the funeral would seem to be increasing. But, because the majority do go into mourning, the exactions of mourning etiquette will be given.

MOURNING PROPRIETIES GREATLY LIBERALIZED

The liberalizing of mourning conventions is entirely due to the single fact that the crêpe veil no longer exists; therefore, the depth of mourning which it represented no longer exists. Those who are wearing mourning do not now go to balls or other conspicuously formal parties, nor take a leading part in purely social activities. On the other hand, anyone who is in public life or who has a professional career must, of course, continue to fulfill the exactions of his career, whatever these may entail. The fact that many women have gone into business or are following careers may be another cause of the lightening of mourning and the shortening of its duration.

A WIDOW'S MOURNING

A widow, formerly, never wore any but woolen materials, made as plain as possible, with deep-hemmed, turn-back cuffs and collar of white organdy. On the street she wore a small crêpe bonnet with a widow's cap border of white crêpe organdy and a long veil of crêpe that swathed her from head to within a few inches of the ground—and was worn frequently for life. Today this costume, even for one on the far side of eighty, is unimaginable.

A widow of mature years may still—if she chooses—wear mourning for life. On the other hand, deep mourning for a year, followed by another year of second mourning, is now considered conventional.

THE YOUNG WIDOW

The young widow should wear all-black for a year, and then usually second mourning for six months. She should, however, *never* remain in mourning for her first husband after she has decided she can be consoled by a second.

There is no reason why a woman—or a man—should not, in time, find such consolation. But to welcome the attentions of a new suitor before the "year of respect" is up is likely to be thought heartless—especially if the marriage had been a happy one.

MOURNING FOR COUNTRY WEAR

Except for elderly ladies to wear to church, somber black clothes are not appropriate in the country—ever! All grey mixtures with a black band on the left sleeve of the jacket or else clothes in dull materials of white are most suitable. Actual sports clothes may be of any inconspicuous mixture, with black arm band on the left sleeve.

MOURNING WORN BY A MOTHER

A mother who has lost a grown son or daughter wears all-black for a year and second mourning for a second year. All-white or tweeds with arm band in the country. Second mourning is characterized by greys, mauves, black and white mixtures.

A DAUGHTER OR SISTER

wears mourning for a long season and second mourning for one.*

MOURNING FOR BUSINESS WOMEN

Since mourning is the outward evidence of a personal frame of mind which has no place in the impersonal world of business, mourn-

---

* Counting by season is very practical because of clothes. When going into mourning in the spring or summer, wear deep mourning until winter clothes are appropriate; then change to second mourning. Or vice versa: wear deep mourning in the autumn and winter; change to second mourning with lighter summer clothes

ing which attracts attention is as unsuitable in an office as a black uniform would be on a soldier.

Inconspicuous mourning, on the other hand, is entirely proper. The fact that a woman invariably wears a black dress, or a gray mixture suit, attracts no attention if she has a little white at the throat. Too solid black, including a black-bordered handkerchief, would be out of place in the office.

The sleeve band, long worn by men, is now being worn by business women and school girls—for obviously practical reasons of economy.

MOURNING FOR MEN

It is entirely correct for a man to go into mourning by the simple expedient of putting a black band on his hat and on the left sleeve of his clothes. Also he wears black shoes, gloves, socks and ties, and white instead of colored linen. In the country a young man continues to wear his ordinary golf stockings and shoes and sweater—no matter how gay, and without any sleeve band. But he must wear a black tie and a white shirt and carry a white handkerchief.

The sleeve band is from three and a half to four and a half inches in width and is of dull cloth on overcoats or winter clothing, and of serge on summer clothes. The sleeve band of mourning is sensible for many reasons, the first being that of economy. Men's clothes do not come successfully from the encounter with the dye vats, nor lend themselves to alterations; and an entire new wardrobe is an unwarranted burden to most men.

There is one objection to even a sleeve band on business clothes: the implied bid for sympathy, from which men of taste recoil. Many men, therefore, "go to the office" with no evidence of mourning other than a black tie and black socks.

Except for the one black suit bought for the funeral and kept for church on Sunday or some other special occasion, only men who are both well-to-do and elderly go into black clothes. The deep black band on the hat is also rarely seen, because a high silk hat is seldom worn in most communities.

LITTLE CHILDREN NEVER WEAR BLACK

For either of their parents little children may, of course, be kept in white—which is the favorite color to choose for them anyway. But on no account should a child of eight or younger be put into black.

BEHAVIOR EXACTED OF CHILDREN

A question often asked is whether children who are in mourning for a parent may take part in school exercises. entertainments or parties. The answer is that they, of course, take part in sports, in gymnasium exercises, and possibly even in a school concert or play. But they should not go to a dance or other purely social party for a period of from six weeks for children between seven or eight and eleven, of three months for those up to fifteen, and six months for those in the neighborhood of sixteen.

GOOD TASTE IN MOURNING

The more severely plain the mourning dress, the more dignified and appropriate and becoming to its wearer it becomes. Anything that can be labeled an eccentricity of fashion should be avoided.

POOR TASTE IN MOURNING

Mourning observances are of all conventions the most exacting, and any deviation from fixed form is interpreted by the world at large as signifying want of proper feeling.

How often has one heard it said of a young woman, who was perhaps entirely ignorant of the effect of her inappropriate clothes or unconventional behavior: "Look at her! And her dear father scarcely cold in his grave!" or "Little she seems to have cared for her mother—and such a lovely one she had too!" Such remarks are as thoughtless as are the actions of the daughter, but they point to an undeniable fact. Better far not wear mourning at all, saying you do not believe in it, than allow your unseemly conduct to indicate indifference to the memory of a really beloved parent. Better that a young widow should go out in scarlet and yellow on the day after her husband's funeral than wear the latest exaggerations of fashion grotesquely rendered in widow's black.

MOURNING FOR A FAMILY-IN-LAW

A wife always goes into mourning with her husband on the occasion of a death in his family, but to a slightly less degree. A husband also goes into mourning with his wife on a similar occasion. She wears black for her husband's parents, brothers and sisters for from six weeks to three months, then wears second mourning for as long as her husband stays in mourning.

LENGTH OF MOURNING FOR MEN

Although the etiquette is less exacting for a man than for a woman, a widower should not be seen at a dance or any large and solely social entertainment for from six to eight months; a son from four to six months; a brother for three—at least! The length of time a father stays in mourning for a child is from four to eight months.

MOURNING LIVERY

Chauffeurs wear black liveries in town. In the country they wear gray, or even their ordinary whipcord with a black band on the left sleeve. The house footman is always put into a black livery with covered buttons and a black and white striped waistcoat. Maids are not dressed in mourning uniforms.

THEY ALSO MOURN WHO DO NOT WEAR BLACK

So many women, as well as men, follow occupations which preclude the wearing of mourning, that unrelieved black is no longer considered obligatory to those who would show honor to their beloved dead.

Each year the number increases of those who go about their daily tasks in whatever clothes they habitually wear, showing the mourning in their hearts by no means other than the quiet dignity of their lives.

26

The Well-Appointed House

EVERY house has an outward appearance to be made as presentable as possible, and an interior continually to be set in order and incessantly to be cleaned. For those that dwell within it there are meals to be prepared and served, linen to be laundered and mended, personal clothes to be brushed and pressed, and perhaps children to be cared for. There is also a doorbell to be answered, in which manners as well as appearance come into play.

Beyond these fundamental necessities, luxuries can be added indefinitely, such as splendor of architecture, of gardening and of furnishing, with every refinement of service that executive ability can produce. With all this genuine splendor possible only to the greatest establishments, a little house can no more compete than a diamond weighing but half a carat can compete with a stone weighing fifty times as much. And this is a good simile, because the perfect little house may be represented by a corner cut from precisely the same stone and differing therefore merely in size (and value naturally), whereas the house in bad taste and improperly run may be represented by a diamond that is off color and full of flaws, or in some instances merely a piece of glass that, to none but those as ignorant as its owner, for a moment suggests a gem of value.

A gem of a house may be no size at all, but its lines are honest, and its painting and furnishing in good taste. As for its upkeep, its path or sidewalk is beautifully neat, steps scrubbed, brasses polished, and its bell answered promptly by a trim maid with a low voice and quiet, courteous manner; all of which may very well contribute as unmistakably to the impression of "quality" as the luxury of a palace whose bronze door is opened by the smartest of footmen.

But the "mansion" of bastard architecture and crude detail, with its brass indifferently clean, with coarse lace behind the plate glass of its golden-oak door, and the bell answered at eleven in the morning by a butler in an ill-fitting dress suit and wearing a mustache, might as well be placarded, "Here lives a vulgarian who has never had an opportunity to approach the outermost edges of cultivation." As a matter of fact, the knowledge of how to make a house distinguished both in appearance and in service is a much higher test than presenting a distinguished appearance in oneself and acquiring presentable manners.

The personality of a house is indefinable, but there never lived a lady of great cultivation and charm whose home, whether a palace, a farm cottage or a tiny apartment, did not reflect the charm of its owner. Every visitor feels impelled to linger, and is loath to go. Houses without personality are a series of walled enclosures with furniture standing about in them. Sometimes their lack of charm is baffling; every article is "correct" and perhaps even beautiful, but one has the feeling that the decorator made chalk-marks indicating the exact spot on which each piece of furniture is to stand. Other houses are filled with things of little intrinsic value, often with much that is shabby, and yet they have that "inviting" atmosphere, that air of unmistakable rightness, which is an unfailing indication of highly cultivated people.

"BECOMING" FURNITURE

Suitability is the test of good taste always—the manner to the moment, the dress to the occasion, the article to the place, the furniture to the background. And yet to combine many periods in one and commit no anachronism—to put something French, something Spanish, something Italian, and something English into an American house and have the result the perfection of American taste—is a feat of legerdemain that has been accomplished time and again.

A woman of great taste follows fashion in house furnishing, just as she follows fashion in dress, in general principles only. She wears what is becoming to her own type, and she puts into her house only such articles as are becoming to it.

That a quaint old-fashioned house should be filled with quaint old-fashioned pieces of furniture, in size proportionate to the size of the rooms, and that rush-bottomed chairs and rag carpets have no place in a marble hall, need not be pointed out. But to an amazing number of persons, proportion seems to mean nothing at all. They will put a huge piece of furniture in a tiny room so that the effect is one of painful indigestion; or they will crowd things all into one corner so that it seems about to capsize; or they will spoil a really good room by the addition of senseless and inappropriately cluttering objects, in the belief that because they are valuable they must be beautiful, regardless of suitability. Sometimes a room is marred by "treasures" clung to for reasons of sentiment.

THE BLINDNESS OF SENTIMENT

It is almost impossible for any of us to judge accurately of things to which we have been accustomed throughout a lifetime. A chair that was grandmother's, a painting father bought, the silver that has always been on the dining table—are all so much a part of ourselves that we are sentiment-blind to their defects.

For instance, the portrait of a Colonial officer, among others, had always hung in Mrs. Oldname's dining room. One day an art critic, whose knowledge was better than his manners, blurted out, "Will you please tell me why you have that dreadful thing in this otherwise perfect room?" Mrs. Oldname, somewhat taken aback, answered rather wonderingly, "Is it dreadful?—Really? I have a feeling of affection for him and his dog!"

The critic was merciless. "If you call a cotton-flannel effigy a dog! And as for the figure, it is equally false and lifeless! It is amazing how anyone with your taste can bear looking at it!" In spite of his rudeness, Mrs. Oldname saw that what he said was quite true, but not until the fact had been pointed out to her. Gradually she grew to dislike the poor officer so much that he was finally relegated to the attic. In the same way most of us have belongings that have "always been there" or perhaps "treasures" that we love for some association, which are probably as bad as can be, to which habit has blinded us, though we would not have to be told of their hideousness were they seen by us in the house of another. Or perhaps they are not bad. Perhaps they are quite beautiful, but unsuitable to the particular situation and to the things with which they are placed.

It is not to be expected that all people can throw away every esthetically unpleasing possession with which nearly every house twenty-five years ago was filled; but those whose pocketbook and sentiment will permit would add greatly to the beauty of their houses by sweeping the bad into the ash can! Far better have stoneware plates that are good in design than expensive porcelain that is vulgar in decoration. Expense, in other words, is no criterion of taste.

The only way to determine what is good and what is horrible is to study and try to understand the principles underlying what is good in books, in museums, in art classes at the universities, and in the magazines devoted to decorative art.

Be very careful, though. Do not mistake modern eccentricities for "art." There are frightful things in vogue at times—flamboyant and discordant colors, grotesque deformities, designs that cannot possibly be other than bad, because aside from striking novelty there is nothing good about them. By no standard can a room be in good taste that looks like a perfume manufacturer's phantasy, or a gas-pipe and boiler factory that has just gone into partnership with a manufacturer of coffins, or any other ill-balanced design suggestive of the reflections in the distorting mirrors that are mirth-provokers at county fairs.

SERVICE

The subject of appointments, meaning *decoration*, and furnishing of a house is really outside the province of this book, which is that of

A GEM OF A HOUSE
It may be no size at all, but its details are perfect, and its bell is answered promptly by a trim maid with a low voice and quiet, courteous manner.

Photograph by Mattie Edwards Hewitt

THE MODERN IDEAL OF HOSPITALITY

Friendliness rather than formality is expressed in every detail of this enchanting picture.

Photograph by Samuel H. Gottscho

MAIDS' DINING ALCOVE IN AN APARTMENT

Every considerate mistress of the house sees to it that those in her employ have quarters that are convenient and attractive.

neither architecture nor decoration.* The *appointments* of this chapter's concern are, therefore, those related to *service*.

But before going into the various details of service, it may be well to speak of the unreasoning indignity cast upon the honorable vocation of a servant.

There is an inexplicable tendency, in this country only, for working people in general to look upon domestic service as an unworthy if not altogether degrading vocation. The cause may perhaps be found in the fact that this same scorning public, having for the most part little opportunity to know high-class servants, who are to be found only in high-class families, take it for granted that ignorant "servant girls" and "hired men" are representative of their kind. Therefore they put upper-class servants in the same category—regardless of whether they are uncouth and illiterate, or persons of refined appearance and manner who often have considerable cultivation, acquired not merely at school but also through constant contact with the refinements of surroundings, and not infrequently immeasurable advantages through opportunity for world-wide travel.

And yet so insistently has this obloquy of the word "servant" spread that everyone sensitive to the feelings of others avoids using it exactly as one avoids using the word "cripple" when speaking to one who is slightly lame. Yet are not the best of us "servants" in the Church? And the highest of us "servants" of the people and the State?

To be a slattern in a vulgar household is scarcely an elevated employment, but neither is belonging to the lower orders of any other calling.

HOW MANY SERVANTS?

The comments immediately following are from the standpoint of highest-class perfection. Simpler requirements will be taken up later on.

It stands to reason that one may expect more perfect service from a "specialist" than from one whose functions are multiple. But small houses that have a double equipment—meaning an alternate who can go in the kitchen, and two for the dining room—can be every bit as well run, so far as essentials go, as the palaces of the Gildings and the Worldlys, though of course not with the same impressiveness. But good service is handicapped if, when the waitress goes out, there is no one to substitute for her, and if, when the cook goes out, there is no one to prepare a meal.

* Mrs. Post's book which gives every needful detail on these subjects is *The Personality of a House*. Funk & Wagnalls Company, New York.

It seems almost beside the mark to describe the running of a great establishment in detail, since each succeeding year is seeing their number diminish. And yet it is thought best that this chapter be left as originally written, because a book such as this would be incomplete without the inclusion of every detail concerned with the running of a great house.

For what one might call "complete" service (meaning service that is adequate at all times) the minimum number is three; i.e. a cook, a butler (or waitress) and a housemaid. The reason why this number is necessary is that the waitress (or butler) and the housemaid are on alternate shifts in staying in and going out, the waitress being on "duty" to answer bell and telephone and serve tea one afternoon, and the housemaid taking her place the next. One of these also takes the place of the cook on her afternoon and evening out.

HOW CAN ANY HOUSE REQUIRE A DOZEN SERVANTS?

The answer is simple. Each additional chambermaid, parlor maid, footman, scullery maid or useful man is made necessary by the size of the house rather than (as is often supposed) the desire for show. The seemingly superfluous number of men and women employed at Golden Hall and Great Estates is actually needed to do the immense amount of work that houses of such size entail; whereas a simple house can be fairly well looked after by one alone. (This qualification of "fairly" is necessary for only one reason, which is that, when the maid is out, there is no one to take her place.)

THE STAFF OF A LARGE HOUSE

As noted elsewhere, in the present day great houses like Golden Hall are becoming fewer and fewer. None are kept up as they were before the war. Perhaps their luxury will never be seen again and the following details of use only as a record of the past. Or it may be that the record will prove useful to new builders of fortunes. In any case, the material is being left intact.

All house employees and details of their several duties, manners, and appearances, are enumerated below. In the greatest and most complicated establishments possible, the employee of highest rank is the companion.

THE COMPANION

The position of companion, which is always one of social equality with her employer, rarely exists unless the lady of the house is an invalid, very elderly, a widow, or a young girl. (In the last case the "companion" is a "chaperon.")

Her duties cannot very well be set down, because they vary with individual requirements. One lady likes continually to travel and merely wants a companion (usually a poor relative or friend) to go with her. Another, who is a semi-invalid, never leaves her room, and the duties of her companion are almost those of a trained nurse. The average requirement is in being personally agreeable, tactful, intelligent, and—companionable!

A companion dresses as any other lady does—according to the occasion, her personal taste, her age, and her means. If she is expected to go out in public places or to be constantly dressed for company at home, her employer should help her with the expense and not let this burden fall upon her own comparatively small salary.

THE PRIVATE SECRETARY

The most important secretarial position and one that comes into immediate contact with his employer's home and social, as well as public, life is that of resident confidential secretary. By this is especially meant a man—rather than a woman—whose employer is either a diplomat or a governor or of other importance in public life and therefore in need of an assistant who is always on hand. This type of secretary is in every way considered a member of the family. He is always present at business meetings and usually present at social ones as well. He always has a secretary of his own and perhaps several stenographers. In other words, he is a deputy who serves as extra eyes and hands and supplementary brains for his "chief."

The position of an ordinary private secretary is sometimes embarrassingly undefined, since he (or she) is in no sense a servant, nor does he rate as a guest or a member of the family. On the other hand, his own social position may be much higher than that of his employer. Usually, however, a private secretary's position is entirely apart from the social life of his employer.

The duties of a private secretary are naturally to attend to all correspondence, take shorthand notes of speeches or conversations, file papers and documents, telephone personal messages, arrange appointments, and also serve as extra hands and eyes and intelligence for his employer.

THE BUSINESS OR SOCIAL SECRETARY

The position of business or social secretary is an entirely clerical one, and never of itself confers any "social privileges" unless the secretary is also "companion."

Her duties are to write all invitations, acceptances, and regrets; keep a record of every invitation received and every one sent out; and enter in an engagement book every engagement made for her employer, whether to lunch, dinner, to be fitted, or go to the dentist. She also writes all impersonal notes, takes longer letters in shorthand, and writes others herself after being told their purport. She also audits all bills and draws the checks for them; the checks are filled in and then presented to her employer to be signed, after which they are put in their envelopes, sealed and sent. When the receipted bills are returned, the secretary files them according to her own method, where they can at any time be found by her if needed for reference. In many cases it is she, though it may equally well be the butler or waitress or personal maid, who telephones invitations and other messages. (In a house that has men servants it is always the butler who answers the telephone. When he is off duty, a footman answers in his place. Otherwise this substitute is necessarily one of the maids.)

Occasionally a social secretary is also a social manager, devises entertainments and arranges all such details as the decorations of the house for a dance or a program of entertainment following a very large dinner. The social secretary very rarely lives in the house of her employer; more often than not she goes also to one or two other houses—since there is seldom work enough in one to require her whole time.

Miss Brisk, who is Mrs. Gilding's secretary, has little time for anyone else. She goes every day for from two to sometimes eight or nine hours in town, and at Golden Hall lives in the house. Usually a secretary can finish all there is to do in an average establishment in about an hour, or at most two, a day, with the addition of five or six hours on two or three other days each month for the auditing of accounts and the payment of bills.

Suppose she takes three positions. She goes to Mrs. A from 8:30 to 10 every day and for three extra hours on the 10th and 11th of every month; to Mrs. B from 10:30 to 1 (her needs being greater) and for six extra hours on the 12th, 13th and 14th of every month; and to Mrs. C every day at 3 o'clock for an indefinite time of several hours or only a few minutes.

Her dress is that of any business woman. Extremes of fashion that border on the eccentric are out of keeping, as they would be out of keeping in an office; this, however, is no reason why she should not be smart. Well-cut tailor-made effects are the most appropriate, with a good-looking but simple hat, as good shoes as she can possibly afford, and immaculately clean blouses or neck trimmings. These represent about the most dignified and practical clothes. But why describe clothes? Every woman with good sense enough to qualify as a secretary has undoubtedly sense enough to dress with dignity.

The further professional positions of tutor and governess will be found in the children's section of this chapter.

THE HOUSEKEEPER

In a very big house the housekeeper usually lives in the house. Smaller establishments often have a "visiting housekeeper" who comes for as long as she is needed each morning. The resident housekeeper has her own bedroom and bath and sitting room always. Her meals are brought to her by an especial kitchen maid, called in big houses the "hall girl," or occasionally the butler details an under-footman to that duty.

In an occasional house all the servants, the gardener as well as the cook and butler and nurses, come under the housekeeper's authority; in other words, she superintends the entire house exactly as a very conscientious and skilled mistress would do herself if she gave her whole time and attention to it. She engages the servants, and if necessary, dismisses them; she sees the cook, orders meals, goes to the market, or at least supervises the cook's market orders, and likewise engages and apportions the work of the men servants. Ordinarily, however, she is in charge of no one but the housemaids, parlor maids, useful man, and one of the scullery maids. The cook, butler, nurses and lady's maid do not come under her supervision.

It is unnecessary to say that the qualifications of a good housekeeper include tact as well as ability and experience.

The management of a house of greatest size is divided usually into several distinct departments, each under its separate head. The housekeeper has charge of the appearance of the house and of its contents; the manners and looks of the housemaids and parlor maids, as well as their work in cleaning walls, floors, furniture, pictures, ornaments, books, and taking care of linen are her responsibility.

The butler has charge of the pantry and dining room. He engages all footmen, apportions their work, and is responsible for their appearance, manners and efficiency. He is also responsible for silver and wines.

The cook is in charge of the kitchen, under-cook and kitchen maids.

The nurse and the personal maid and cook are under the direction of the lady of the house. The butler and the valet as well as the chauffeur and gardener are usually engaged by the gentleman of the house. When garage or garden requires under-men, the head chauffeur usually, and the head gardener always, engages his assistants.

THE BUTLER

The butler is not only the most important servant in every big establishment, but it is by no means unheard-of for him to be in supreme command, not only as steward, but as housekeeper as well.

At the Worldly's, for instance, Hastings, who is actually the butler, orders all the supplies, keeps the household accounts, and engages not only the men servants but the housemaids, parlor maids and even the chef.

But normally in a great house the butler has charge of his own department only, and his own department is the dining room and pantry, or possibly the whole parlor floor. In all smaller establishments the butler is always the valet—and in many great ones he is valet to his employer, even though he details a footman to look after other gentlemen of the family or visitors.

In a small house the butler works a great deal with his hands and not so much with his head. In a great establishment, the butler works very much with his head, and with his hands not at all.

At Golden Hall, when guests used to come in dozens at a time,* his stewardship—even though there was a housekeeper—was not a job which a small man could fill. He had perhaps twenty men under him at big dinners, ten who belonged under him in the house always; he had the keys to the wine cellar and the combination of the silver safe. He also chose the china and glass and linen as well as the silver to be used each day, oversaw the setting of the table and the serving of all food.

When there is a house party, every breakfast tray that leaves the pantry is first approved by him.

At all meals he stands behind the chair of the lady of the house so that at the slightest turn of her head he need only take a step to be within reach of her voice. (The husband, by the way, is "head of the house," but the wife is "head of the table.")

At tea time he oversees the footmen who place the tea table, and who put on the tea cloth and carry in the tea tray and also the tray of cocktails, if these are served; then Hastings himself places the individual tables—small tables or stands with nothing on them, and intended merely as a convenience on which to put down a cup and saucer, tea plate, or glass and ash tray. When there is "no dinner at home," he waits in the hall and assists Mr. Worldly into his coat, and hands him his hat, which has previously been handed to the butler by one of the footmen.

THE BUTLER IN A SMALLER HOUSE

In a smaller house the butler also takes charge of the wines and silver, and does very much the same as the butler in the larger house, except that he has less overseeing of others and more work to do himself. Where he is alone, he does all the work—naturally. Where he has either one footman or a parlor maid, he always cleans the silver

---

* This has to be considered as written in the past tense because house parties, etc., are over for the duration.

and answers the front door and telephones, and passes the main courses at the table. The assistant passes the secondary dishes and also washes dishes and cleans the dining room and pantry. They take turns in answering the door and serving tea.

The butler is also valet not only for the gentleman of the house but for any gentleman guests as well.

(For useful butler see "Valet-Butler Alone," toward end of this chapter.)

WHAT THE BUTLER WEARS

The *butler never wears the livery of a footman*. In the early morning he wears an ordinary sack suit—black or very dark blue—with a dark, inconspicuous tie. For luncheon or earlier, if he is on duty at the door, he wears black trousers with gray stripes, a double-breasted, high-cut, black waistcoat, and black swallowtail coat without satin on the revers, a white stiff-bosomed shirt with standing collar, and a black four-in-hand tie.

In fashionable houses the butler does not put on his dress suit until six o'clock. Unless he is an old-time colored servant in the South, the butler's evening dress differs from that of a gentleman in a few details only: he has no braid on his trousers, and the satin on his lapels (if any) is narrower; but the most distinctive difference is that a butler wears a black waistcoat and a white lawn tie, and a gentleman always wears a white waistcoat with a white tie, or a white waistcoat and a black tie with a dinner coat, but never the reverse.

It should be unnecessary to add that none but vulgarians would employ a butler (or any other house servant) who wears a mustache! To have him open the door collarless and in shirt-sleeves is scarcely worse!

A butler never wears gloves, nor a flower in his buttonhole. He sometimes wears a very thin watch chain in the daytime but none at night. He never wears a scarf pin or any jewelry that is for ornament alone. His cuff links should be as plain as possible, and his shirt studs white enamel ones that look like linen.

The butler's clothes are usually provided by his employer, but in occasional houses he is expected to provide his own.

THE HOUSE FOOTMAN

All house servants who assist in waiting on the table come under the direction of the butler and are known as footmen. One who never comes into the dining room is known as a useful man. The duties of the footman (and useful man) include cleaning the dining room, pantry, lower hall, entrance vestibule, sidewalk, attending to the furnace, carrying wood to all the open fireplaces in the house, cleaning the windows, cleaning brasses, cleaning all boots, carrying everything that is heavy, moving furniture for the parlor maids to clean behind it, valeting all gentlemen, setting and waiting on table, attending the front door, telephoning and writing down messages, and—incessantly and ceaselessly—cleaning and polishing silver.

In a small house the butler polishes silver, but in a very big house one of the footmen is silver specialist and does nothing else. Nothing? If there is to be a party of any sort, he puts on his livery and joins the others who line the hall and bring dishes to the table. But he does not assist in setting the table, in washing dishes, or in cleaning anything whatsoever—except silver.

The butler also usually answers the telephone—if not, it is answered by the first footman. The first footman is deputy butler and takes his place whenever the butler is off duty.

The footmen also take turns in answering the door. In houses of great ceremony like those of the Worldlys and the Gildings, there are always two footmen at the door when anyone is to be admitted: one to open the door, and the other to conduct a guest into the drawing room. But if formal company is expected, the butler himself is in the front hall with one or two footmen at the door.

THE FOOTMAN'S LIVERY

People who have big houses usually choose a color for their livery and never change it. Maroon and buff, for instance, are the colors of the Gildings; all their motor cars are maroon with buff lines and cream-colored or maroon linings. The chauffeurs and outside footmen wear maroon liveries. The house footmen, for everyday, wear ordinary footmen's liveries, maroon trousers and long-tailed coats with brass buttons and maroon-and-buff striped waistcoats. A house footman wears this same livery no matter what the hour of the day, except of course when he is actually engaged in doing his work, at which time he wears an apron and shirt sleeves and does not appear in the front part of the house.

The regulation livery always has trousers and coat to match, buttons of either brass or silver, stiff starched collar and shirt, white lawn tie, striped waistcoat and white cotton gloves. The number of buttons on the tails of the coats is determined by the employer's personal idea of smartness.

For gala occasions Mrs. Gilding adds as many caterer's men as necessary, but they all are dressed in her livery, cut like the everyday liveries, with silver buttons on which the crest is raised in relief, but with black velvet collars, and black satin waistcoats in place of the everyday striped ones; black satin knee breeches, black silk stockings, pumps with silver buckles. (The "court" coat with frogs and lace cravat and epaulettes and white stockings, etc., has gone completely out of usage. And in most of even the greatest houses everyday liveries and gala liveries are the same.)

To choose servants who are naturally well-groomed is more important than to put them into smart liveries. Men who are smart must have at least moderately slim figures, and hold themselves, not stiffly, but with a suggestion of military bearing. They may, however, be quite elderly. Grey hair is very suitable for a butler. They must, of course, be smooth-shaven and have their hair well cut. Their linen must be immaculate, their shoes polished, their clothes brushed and in press, and their fingernails clean and well cared for. If a man's fingers are indelibly stained, he must wear white cotton gloves.

THE CHAUFFEUR

The position of chauffeur differs from that of the other domestic employees in two respects. The first is that he has no regular days out. Second, he usually finds (and pays for) his own board and lodging. Sometimes a single man eats with the servants in the kitchen, but this is not usual. Sometimes, too, there may be a room over the garage or perhaps a whole apartment—especially above a garage that has been converted from a stable—in which he and his family may live. Although he seemingly gets higher wages than any of the other servants, it must be remembered that living expenses have to be deducted from his pay, whereas the wages of other servants are clear.

When traveling, the employer always pays for the chauffeur's room and lodging for so long as they are away from home.

His uniforms are furnished him by his employer.

His duties are irregular, sometimes extremely so. In a large family, particularly where there are half-grown or grown daughters, a chauffeur's life can be inhumanly strenuous. He can, for example, be expected to take the younger children to school, come back and take the lady shopping, go back to school for the children, drive various members of the family during the afternoon, come back and take his employers out to dinner, go back later to fetch them, and perhaps take them or a débutante daughter to a supper club or ball. Or, if his employers are home that evening, he may perhaps have to stand on the sidewalk to open the car doors of the arriving guests, and be on duty again when they depart.

On the other hand, there are places in which the chauffeur is almost a man of leisure; his employer, perhaps, is an old lady who goes to church on Sunday morning from eleven to half-past twelve, who likes to drive from three to five every afternoon, and who goes out to dinner or to a concert or to the theater perhaps not more than twice a week. Both of these extremes can be encountered in almost every city. The typical schedule is midway between the two. Perhaps he has long driving days intermixed with short ones. But every considerate employer tells his chauffeur as far in advance as he can when he knows he is not going to want the car, since it is only under these circumstances that the chauffeur may himself make any personal engagements.

When the car is in a private garage and the chauffeur has no helper, he must of course wash it and take care of it himself. In a public garage the washing is done for him and the interior of the car is also brushed out by the garage attendant. A lady's town car is usually locked by the chauffeur and he alone takes care of its interior.

No chauffeur ever carries a robe on his arm as a footman does when waiting at the door for his employer. Properly, the lap robe is laid in deep full-length folds on the far side of the seat. As soon as the occupants have taken their places, the chauffeur reaches across and, holding the edge of the fold, draws it toward him across their laps. Upon arriving at destination, if there is a doorman or a chauffeur stationed on the sidewalk, he remains seated; otherwise he leaves his seat and holds open the door for the occupants to alight. In assisting a lady or possibly a gentleman who is elderly, the chauffeur presents his forearm held horizontally with his wrist bent inward so that the person alighting puts her or his hand upon his sleeve as though it were a balustrade.

He touches his hat at the close of any order given him, unless the car is in motion, when he merely nods his acknowledgment.

It is unnecessary to add that a chauffeur may never smoke when seated in his employer's car even though it be unoccupied, nor may he smoke when standing on the sidewalk waiting for his employer.

No employer is expected to show leniency to a chauffeur who has driven while intoxicated.

THE COOK

The cook is always in charge in the kitchen. In a small house, or in an apartment, she is alone and has all the cooking and the cleaning of kitchen and larder to do, the basement or kitchen bell to answer, and the servants' table to set and their dishes as well as her kitchen utensils to wash. In a larger house, the kitchen maid does all cleaning of kitchen and pots and pans, answers the basement bell, sets the servants' table and washes the servants' table dishes. In a still larger house, the second cook cooks for the servants always, and for the children sometimes, and assists the cook by preparing certain plainer portions of the meals, the cook preparing all dinner dishes, sauces and the more elaborate items on the menu. Sometimes there are two or more kitchen maids who merely divide the greater amount of work between them.

In most houses of any size, the cook does all the marketing. She sees the lady of the house every morning and submits menus for the day. In smaller houses the lady does the ordering of both supplies and menus.

SUBMITTING THE MENU

In a house of largest size—at the Gildings', for instance—the chef writes in his "book" every evening the menus for the next day, whether there is to be company or not. (None, of course, if the family are to be out for all meals.) This "book" is sent up to Mrs. Gilding with her breakfast tray. It is a loose-leaf blank book of rather large size. The day's menu sheet is on top, but the others are left in their proper sequence underneath, so that by looking at her engagement book to see who dined with her on such a date and then looking at the menu for that same date, she knows—if she cares to—exactly what the dinner was.

If she does not like the chef's choice, she draws a pencil through the items to be left out and writes in something else. If she has any orders or criticisms to make, she writes them on an envelope pad, folds the page, and seals it and puts the "note" in the book.

If the menu is to be changed, the chef rewrites it; if not, the page is left as it is, and the book is put in a certain place in the kitchen.

The butler always goes down into the kitchen shortly after the book has come down and copies the day's menus on a pad of his own. From this he knows what table utensils will be needed.

The reason for this system is that, in houses where there is a great deal of entertaining, it is much simpler for the butler to be able to go and "see for himself" than to ask the cook—and forget—and ask again; or for the cook to forget, and then—disturbance!—because the butler did not send down the proper silver dishes or have the proper plates ready, or had others heated unnecessarily.

THE COOK'S DRESS

The cook always wears a white dress and usually a high apron with pockets, white stockings and white shoes. She is expected to furnish her clothes herself, but her aprons and uniforms (and her caps if she wears them) are laundered for her. A certain few fastidious cooks wear small white kerchief-shaped caps when they are preparing food. It is to be hoped that this custom may become universal, since nothing in the world is so revolting as even the thought that a sudden breeze is quite likely to blow a hair into the food.

THE KITCHEN MAIDS

The kitchen maids are under the direction of the cook, except the one known colloquially as the "hall girl," who is supervised by the housekeeper. She is evidently a survival of the "between maid" of the English house. Her sobriquet comes from the fact that she has charge of the servants' hall, or dining room, and is in fact the waitress for them. She also takes care of the housekeeper's rooms, and carries all her meals up to her. If there is no housekeeper, the hall girl is under the direction of the cook.

The kitchen maid wears a colored cotton dress to match that of the other maids in the house, but she wears a heavier, larger apron and short sleeves. Her dress is given to her. Sometimes she wears white. It is better that she wear color all the time or white all the time, since to dress her in white in the afternoon and color in the morning really means a double supply of clothes.

THE PARLOR MAID

The parlor maid keeps the drawing room and library in order. The useful man brings up the wood for the fireplaces, but the parlor maid lays the fire. In some houses the parlor maid takes up the breakfast trays; in other houses, the butler does this himself and then hands them to the lady's maid or the housemaid, who takes them into the bedrooms. The windows and the brasses are cleaned by the useful man, and the heavy furniture is moved by him so that she can clean behind it.

The parlor maid assists the butler in waiting at table and washing dishes, and takes turns with him in answering the door and the telephone.

In huge houses like the Worldlys' and the Gildings', the footmen assist the butler in the dining room and at the door—and there is always a "pantry maid" who washes dishes and cleans the pantry.

THE HOUSEMAID

The housemaid does all the chamber work, cleans all silver on dressing tables, polishes fixtures in the bathroom—in other words takes care of the bedroom floors. She also takes care of the rooms of the other servants.

In a larger house, the head housemaid has charge of the linen and does the bedrooms of the lady and gentleman of the house and a few of the spare rooms. The second housemaid does the nurseries, extra spare rooms, and the servants' floors. The larger the establishment, the more housemaids, and the more the work is further divided. The housemaid is by many people called the chambermaid.

THE CLOTHES OF THE WAITRESS, PARLOR MAID AND HOUSEMAID

In all houses of importance and fashion, the parlor maid, the housemaids, and the waitress—where there is no butler—are all dressed alike. Their "work" dresses are of plain cambric and in whatever the "house color" may be, with large white aprons with high bibs, and plain white rolled-back collars, but no cuffs, as they must be able to unbutton their sleeves and turn them up. Those who serve in the dining room must always dress before lunch, and the afternoon dresses vary according to the taste—and purse—of the lady of the house. Where no uniforms are supplied, each maid is expected to furnish herself with a plain black dress for afternoon, on which she always wears thin swiss collars and cuffs as well as aprons. All collars, cuffs and aprons are supplied by the employer.

In some houses they wear caps, but usually they do not. Twenty years ago, every maid in a lady's house wore a cap except the personal maid, who wore a velvet bow or nothing on the head. But when every little slattern in every sloppy household had a small mat of whitish swiss pinned somewhere on an untidy head and was decked out in as many yards of embroidery ruffling on her apron and shoulders as her person could carry, people of taste began taking caps and trimmings off.

If no head-dress is worn, the hair must be faultlessly smooth and neat; and of course, where two or more maids are seen together, they must be alike. It would not do to have one wear a cap and the other not. Hair, whether bobbed or long, must be worn very short. Anything suggesting spaniel ears or curls flying long and loose would be in as shockingly bad taste as a butler wearing a mustache!

THE LADY'S MAID

A first-class lady's maid is required to be a hairdresser, a good packer and an expert needlewoman. Her duty is to keep her lady's clothes in order and to help her dress and undress. She draws the bath, lays out underclothes, always brushes her lady's hair and usually dresses it, and gets out the dress to be worn, as well as the stockings, shoes, hat, gloves, wrist-bag, or whatever accessories go with the dress in question.

As soon as the lady is dressed, everything that has been worn is taken to the sewing room and each article is gone over carefully. Everything mussed is pressed, everything suspected of not being immaculate is washed or cleaned with cleaning fluid, and when in perfect order is replaced where it belongs in the closet. Underclothes as mended are put in the clothes hamper. Stockings are looked over for rips or small holes, and the maid usually washes very fine stockings and handkerchiefs herself, also small pieces of lace trimming, and very often silk underclothes. Ladies who do not change nightgowns every night have them pressed when they are to be put on a second or third time.

Some maids have to wait up at night, no matter how late, until their ladies return; but as many, if not more, are never asked to wait beyond a certain hour.

In other days the maid for a débutante in the height of the season, who used to have an unending amount of "go fetching" at this place and that, and the cleaning of party dresses soiled by a partner's hands on the back, and slippers "walked on" until there was quite as much black part as satin or kid, had no sinecure. But today the chauffeur usually does the "go fetching," and backless dresses, if they have no other virtues, at least make cleaning easier for the lady's maid.

DRESS OF A LADY'S MAID

A lady's maid used to wear a black skirt, a laundered white waist, and a small white apron, the band of which buttoned in the back. But today she is allowed to wear her own clothes, so long as they are quiet in color and plain in design. Usually, in the smartest houses, she wears an all-black dress with or without white collar and cuffs and a small black taffeta silk apron. Mrs. Gilding, junior, puts her maid on "company occasions" when she waits in the dressing room, in light gray taffeta, gray stockings and slippers, and a very small embroidered mull apron with a narrow gray velvet waist-ribbon, and collar and cuffs of mull to match. This uniform is extremely pretty, but equally extravagant. Many ladies dress their maids in black taffeta with cream lace collar, cuffs and apron. Customarily however, and always for ordinary occasions, the lady's maid buys her own clothes, except when those to be discarded by "her lady" are given to her. This is a personal matter. Certain ladies give their maids more than lavish supplies from a scarcely worn wardrobe. Others give them things of small account, or nothing.

THE VALET

The valet (pronounced val-et not vallay) is what Beau Brummel called a gentleman's gentleman. His duties are exactly the same as those of the lady's maid—except that he does not sew! He keeps his employer's clothes in perfect order, brushes, cleans and presses everything as soon as it has been worn, lays out the clothes to be put on, and puts away everything that is a personal belonging. Some gentlemen like their valets to help them dress; run the bath, shave them and hold each article in readiness as it is to be put on. But most gentlemen merely like their clothes "laid out" for them, which means that trousers have belts or braces attached, shirts have cuff links and studs, and waistcoat buttons are put in.

The valet also unpacks the bags of any gentleman guests when they come, valets them while there, and packs them when they go. He always packs for his own gentleman, buys tickets, looks after the luggage, and makes himself generally useful as a personal attendant, whether at home or when traveling.

At big dinners he is often required (much against his will) to serve as a footman—in a footman's livery.

The valet wears no livery except on such occasions. At all hours of day or evening, he wears an ordinary business suit, dark and inconspicuous in color, with a black tie.

VALET-BUTLER ALONE

In a bachelor's quarters a valet is often general factotum, not only valeting but performing the services of cook, butler, and even housemaid. When serving meals, he either wears a jacket like that of a steward, or the clothes of a butler. The latter are smarter, of course, but not very practical for one who works in the kitchen. Because of the danger that spattering grease may get on his sleeves and cuffs, a surgeon's apron is perhaps most practical when he takes the roast out of the oven. At all events it is easier to put a long-sleeved gown over what he wears than to take off coat, undo cuff links, roll up sleeves, and then have to reverse this process—just to handle one roast.

THE TUTOR

The social position of a tutor is similar to that of a resident confidential secretary (see earlier pages of this chapter) in that he is necessarily the constant companion of half-grown pupils and therefore brought into close association with their family. Moreover, he is usually a college man, who is either pursuing special studies of his own or else his position is a summer one during which he is earning the wherewithal to continue his college work.

A tutor often seems to have a higher social rating than a governess —probably because he is an extra man and extra men are always more or less welcome, while extra women are not! Rules for the proper behavior of a tutor are the same as those for a governess, a secretary or the holder of any other professional position in residence. He is expected to be present when wanted and absent when not, to be at all times agreeable and at the same time impersonal, and to remember that so far as his character and ethical behavior are concerned, his job carries on through the hours when he is "off duty" as well as when he is "on."

THE GOVERNESS

The position of governess varies greatly according to her own accomplishments, the ages of the children, and the mode of each family's life. If the house is a large one, she has a sitting room of her own. Otherwise her room should be furnished as an attractive and transformable sitting room, with a day bed, a desk instead of a bureau, easy chairs and good reading light. This is not an excessive amount of luxury but a very plain necessity, because otherwise she has nowhere to sit except in the discomfort of a bedroom or else with the family—a situation as trying for them as for her.

A governess usually comes to the family breakfast and lunch table and to dinner if the children do. But when her charges are half-grown, it is often arranged that they shall dine with their parents while the governess is served in her own sitting room. Arrangement is also made whereby the children and the governess are served elsewhere when formal company is expected. When friends of the family come for lunch or dinner and the governess is to be present, she shows herself ready to be agreeable to anyone inclined to talk to her, but she does not lead the conversation ever. After the meal she withdraws to her own quarters—unless she is asked to stay.

In other words, the requirements of a professional member of a family are much the same as those of the members of an office staff. In an office, an employee does not take part in the conversation of her employer and an associate or a customer, unless brought into the conversation by one or the other. She who is resident in her employer's house must be even more self-effacing than one who works in an office. After all, friends come to see their own friends and not the stranger sitting in the room. That the family like to be together alone is natural. The governess would not want the family to sit with her when she sees friends of her own. The fact that she should make herself invisible does not in any way imply her lack of personal attractiveness, nor should it have its basis in snobbishness—it is merely that professional relationships are more valuable and more enduring when they are left on a purely professional plane.

According to best taste, a governess should not wear unsuitably conspicuous clothes, which does not mean that she cannot wear the latest fashion of the day, but that fashion should be whispered rather than shouted out loud.

THE REGISTERED NURSE

The social position of a registered hospital nurse is, of course, that of a lady. Beyond this her professional position when on duty is much the same as that of a governess or a secretary, or—if on a long case—that of a companion. She eats her meals with the family or else has them served to her on a tray in a sitting room. She NEVER eats in the kitchen unless that is where the family also eat.*

When on duty in her patient's room or anywhere in a private house, she wears her uniform. But when going into the street or going downstairs in an hotel—or travelling—she wears her own clothes. Like those of a governess or companion, they may be in smartest fashion but not conspicuously extreme.

THE CHILDREN'S NURSE

Everybody knows the children's nurse is either the comfort or the torment of the house. Everyone also knows innumerable young mothers who put up with inexcusable crankiness from a crotchety middle-aged woman because she was "so wonderful" to the baby. And here let it be emphasized that such an one usually turns out to have been not wonderful to the baby at all. That she does not actually abuse a helpless infant is merely granting that she is not a "monster."

Devotion must always be unselfish; the nurse who is *really* "wonderful" to the baby is pretty sure to be a person who is kind generally. In ninety-nine cases out of a hundred the sooner a domineering nurse —old or young—is got rid of, the better. It has been the experience of many a mother whose life had been made perfectly miserable through her belief that if she dismissed the tyrant the baby would suffer, that in the end—there *is* always an end!—the baby was quite as relieved as the rest of the family when the "right sort" of kindly and humane person took the tyrant's place. It must never be forgotten that a young child is inescapably imprisoned in the atmosphere made by the disposition of the person in charge of it, and that sunlight is no more necessary to a plant than an atmosphere of sympathetic light-heartedness to a child.

It is hardly necessary to add that one cannot be too particular in asking for a nurse's reference and in never failing to get a personal note from the lady she is leaving. Not only is it necessary to have a sweet-tempered, competent and clean person, but her moral character is of utmost importance, since she is to be the constant and inseparable companion of the children, whose whole lives are influenced by her example, especially where busy parents give only a small portion of time to their children.

Properly a nurse is always dressed in white in the house. On the street she wears a very simple suit and hat of either blue or gray. To dress any nurse in the cloak and cap of the English nurse is suitable only if she herself be British.

* For the registered nurse's immunity to convention see page 554, Unconventional Situations.

COURTESY TO ONE'S HOUSEHOLD

In a dignified house, a servant is never spoken to as Jim, Maisie, or Katie, but always as James or Margaret or Katherine, and a butler is called by his last name, nearly always. The Worldlys' butler, for instance, is called Hastings, not John. In England, a lady's maid is also called by her last name, and the cook, if married, is addressed as Mrs., and the nurse is called "Nurse" by the family and "Mrs." by the other servants whether she is married or not. A chef is usually called "Chef" or else by his last name. In the United States as everywhere, all professional people, secretaries, tutors, governesses and registered nurses are of course called Miss or Mr. or Mrs. Jones.

Every well-bred lady or gentleman says "please" in asking that something be brought her or him. "Please get me the book I left on the table in my room!" Or "Please give me some bread!" Or "Some bread, please." Or one can put politeness into one's tone and say, "I'd like some toast"; but no lady or gentleman barks, "Get me that book," "Gimme th' bread!"

In refusing a dish at the table, one must say, "No, thank you," or "No, thanks," or else one shakes one's head. A head can be shaken politely or rudely. To be courteously polite, and yet keep one's walls up, is a thing every thoroughbred person knows how to do—and a thing that everyone who is trying to become such must learn to do.

A rule can't be given, because there isn't any. As said in another chapter, a well-bred person always lives within the walls of his personal reserve; a vulgarian has no walls—or at least none that do not collapse at the slightest touch. But those who think they appear superior by being rude to others whom fortune happens to have placed below them might as well, did they but know it, shout their own much lower origin to the world at large, since by no other method could it be more widely published. On the other hand a condescendingly "I am *so* sweet" manner is equally hard for a self-respecting person of dignity to bear!

It must also be added that a well-bred servant shows self-respect in a quiet manner, a low voice, and correct behavior, such as is exacted by a well-bred politeness everywhere.

THE MANAGEMENT OF SERVANTS

It is certainly a greater pleasure and incentive to work for those who are appreciative than for those who continually find fault. Everyone who did war work cannot fail to remember how easy it was to work for, or with, some people, and how impossible to get anything done for others. And just as the "heads" of workrooms or "wards" or "canteens" were either stimulating or dispiriting, so must they and their types also be to those who serve in their households.

This, perhaps, explains why some people are always having a "servant problem," finding servants difficult to get, more difficult to keep, and most difficult to get efficient work from. It is a question whether the "servant problem" is not more often an employer problem! It must be! Because, if you notice, those who have woes and complaints are invariably the same, just as others who never have any trouble are also the same. It does not depend on the size of the house; the Lovejoys never have any trouble, and yet their one maid-of-all-work has a far from "easy place," and a vacancy at Brookmeadows is always sought after, even though the Oldnames spend ten months of the year in the country. Neither is there any friction at the Golden Hall or Great Estates, even though the latter house is run by the butler—an almost inevitable cause of trouble. These houses represent a difference ranging from one alone to nearly thirty on the household payroll.

THOSE WHO HAVE PERSISTENT "TROUBLE"

It might be well for those who have trouble to remember a few rules which are often overlooked: justice must be the foundation upon which every tranquil house is constructed. Work must be as evenly divided as possible; one servant should not be allowed liberties not accorded to all.

It is not just to be too lenient, any more than it is just to be unreasonably strict. To allow impertinence or sloppy work is inexcusable, but it is equally inexcusable to show causeless irritability or to be overbearing or rude. And there is no greater example of injustice than to reprimand those about you because you happen to be in a bad humor, and at another time to overlook offenses that are greater because you are in an amiable mood.

There is also no excuse for "correcting" either an employee or a child before people.

And when you do correct, do not forget to make allowances, if there be any reason why allowance should be made.

If you live in a palace like Golden Hall, or any completely equipped house of important size, you overlook *nothing* (except for genuine cause). There is no more excuse for delinquency than there is in the Army. If anything happens, such as the illness or departure of one servant, there is another to substitute. A huge household is a machine, and it is the business of the engineers—in other words, the secretary, housekeeper, chef and butler—to keep it going perfectly.

But in a little house it may not be fair to say, "Selma, the silver is dirty!" when there is a hot-air furnace and you have had company for every meal, and have perhaps sent her on errands between times, so that she has literally not had a moment. If you don't know whether she has had time or not, you may give her the benefit of the doubt and say, trustingly, not haughtily, "You have not had time to clean the silver, have you?" This—in case she has really been unable to clean it—points out just as well the fact that it is not shining, but it is not a criticism. Carelessness, on the other hand, when you know she has had plenty of time, should not be overlooked.

Another type that has "difficulties" is the distrustful—sometimes actually suspicious—person who locks everything tight and treats all those with whom she comes in contact as though they were meddlesomely curious at least, or at worst, dishonest. It is impossible to overstate the misfortune of this temperament. The servant who is "watched" for fear she "won't work," listened to for fear she may be saying what she oughtn't, suspected of wanting to take a liberty of some sort, or of doing something else she shouldn't do, is psychologically encouraged, almost driven, to do these very things.

The perfect mistress expects perfect service, but it never occurs to her that perfect service will not be voluntarily and gladly given. She, on her part, feels responsible for the well-being of all of those in her employ, and shows them the consideration and trust due them as honorable, self-respecting and conscientious human beings. If she has reason to think they are not all this, a lady does not keep them in her house.

ETIQUETTE OF SERVICE

The well-trained, high-class servant is faultlessly neat in appearance, reticent in manner, speaks in a low voice, walks and moves quickly but silently, and is unfailingly courteous and respectful. She (or he) usually knocks on a door, even of the library or sitting room, but opens it simultaneously before there is time to be told "Come in," as knocking on a downstairs door is merely politeness. At a bedroom door she would wait for permission to enter. In answering a bell, she asks, "Did you ring, Sir?" or if especially well-mannered she asks, "Did Madam ring?"

A servant always answers, "Yes, Madam," or "Very good, Sir," *never* "Yes," "No," "All right," or "Sure." Sons and daughters in the house are called "Miss Katharine" or "Mr. Oliver"; half-grown children are generally called by their familiar names with the prefix of Miss or Master (Miss Kitty, Master Ollie), but never by the nurse, who calls them by their first names until they are grown—sometimes always. To demand that the servant call really little children Miss and Master is suggestive of the *parvenu*.

All cards and small packages should be presented on a tray.

THE WELL-APPOINTED HOUSE

TIME "OUT" AND "IN"

No doubt in some regions there are young women who work long and hard and for little compensation, but at least in all cities the compensation has become such that big houses are everywhere being abandoned for apartments which can be run on half or a quarter the number of servants. Then the stage where fewer or none at all will be necessary—in order to tally with a reasonable income—is each year more closely approaching. Servants have their definite time out, and are allowed in humanely run houses to have "times in" when they can be at home to their friends. In every well-appointed house of size there is a sitting room which is furnished with comfortable chairs and sofa if possible, a small radio, good lights to read by, often books, and always magazines (sent out as soon as read by the family). In other words, the employees have an inviting room to use as their own exactly as though they were living at home. If no sitting room is possible, the kitchen table has a cover put on it, and a droplight and a few restful chairs are provided.

ARE MAIDS ALLOWED TO RECEIVE MEN FRIENDS?

Certainly they are! Whoever in remote ages thought it was better to forbid "followers" the house and have Nora or Marie or Selma slip out of doors to meet them in the dark had very distorted notions, to say the least. And any lady who knows so little of human nature as to make the same rule for her maids today is acting in ignorant blindness of her own duties to those who are not only in her employ, but also under her protection.

A pretty young woman whose men friends come in occasionally and play cards with the others, or dance to a not too loud phonograph or radio in the kitchen, is merely being treated humanly. The fact that she works and lives in an employer's house makes her no less a young girl, with a young girl's love of amusement, which, if not properly provided for her "at home," will be sought for in other, and quite possibly dangerous, places.

This responsibility to the unknowing impulses of youth is one that many ladies who are occupied with charitable and good works elsewhere often overlook under their own roof.

To suggest that young maids—or older ones—be allowed the privileges of hospitality means nothing more radical than that they shall not be begrudged a few cups of tea or coffee and a plate of cakes or sandwiches for a small party to their friends. This does not mean that the kitchen should be a scene of perpetual revelry and mirth, or that it should disturb the quiet of the neighborhood or even of the family. Unseemly noise is checked, to be sure, much as it would be checked if young people of the family were disturbing neighbors. Continuous company is not suitable either, and those who abuse privileges naturally must have them curtailed, but the really high-class employee who does not appreciate kindness and requite it with considerate and proper behavior is rare.

SERVICE IN FORMAL ENTERTAINING

For a wedding or a dance there is an awning from curb to front door. A formal dinner is prepared for by stretching a carpet—a red one invariably!—down or up the front steps and across the pavement to the curb's edge. At all important functions there is a chauffeur—or a caterer's man—on the sidewalk to open the door of motors, and another stationed inside the door of the house to open it on one's approach and to direct arriving guests to the dressing rooms.

DRESSING ROOMS

Houses especially built for entertaining have two dressing rooms—one for the ladies and one for the gentlemen—on the ground floor, each with its lavatory. In houses where dressing rooms have not been installed by the architect, the end of the hall, if it is wide, is sometimes supplied with a coat rack, which may be rented from a caterer, for the gentlemen. Ladies in this case either go into the drawing room as they are, or go upstairs to the bedroom put at their disposal.

If the party is very large, coat checks are given exactly as in public "check rooms." Whether downstairs or in the bedroom of the hostess, the ladies' dressing room should be supplied with brushes and combs, hairpins, powder, stacks of individual cotton puffs; also safety pins. In the lavatory there must be fresh soap and plenty of small hand towels.

The maid on duty in the dressing room should always look each arriving guest over for anything that may be amiss. If the drapery of a dress is caught up on its trimming, or a fastening undone, it is her duty to say, "Excuse me, madam (or miss), but there is a hook undone"; or, "The drapery of your gown is caught—just a moment, I'll fix it!" Which she does as quietly and quickly as possible. If there is a rip of any sort, she says, "I think there is a thread loose; I'll just tack it. It will only be a moment." Or she renders any other service that may be necessary.

The well-bred maid instinctively makes little of a guest's accident, and is as considerate as the hostess herself.

In a great house the valet looks after the gentlemen. But in most houses they put their own coats and hats where they find a place, and get them again perfectly well by themselves.

THE ANNOUNCEMENT OF GUESTS

The butler (or caterer's announcer) stands just outside the drawing room, and the hostess stands just within, and as the guests pass through the door, he announces each one's name. When necessary, he asks, "What name, please?" He then says, "Mr. and Mrs. Jones." If Mrs. Jones is considerably in advance of her husband, he says, "Mrs. Jones!" then waits for Mr. Jones to approach before announcing, "Mr. Jones!"

It is now customary in many houses to have waitresses announce people, but this must not be done unless she pronounces names with ease and a dignified but unself-conscious manner.

THE HOUSE WITH LIMITED SERVICE

The fact that you live in a house with two servants, or quite as likely with only one, need not imply that your house lacks charm or even distinction; but, as explained in the chapter on Dinners, if you have limited service you must devise systematic economy of time and labor or you will have disastrous consequences. (If you have none at all, read the chapter devoted to the serviceless problems of Mrs. Three-in-One.)

Every person, after all, has only one pair of hands, and a day has only so many hours, and one thing is inevitable, which young house-keepers tend to forget: a few cannot do the work of many and do it in the same way.

HOUSE RUN BY ONE MAID

The details of just how much, and just what, one maid should do, constitute a subject of importance to tens of thousands, but one which is almost impossible to treat in a general statement, because her work must be adjusted not only to the needs of the particular family by whom she is employed, but also to her own capability.

Out of every twenty-four hours every normal human being should have at least eight hours for sleeping, dressing and undressing, in addition to an hour and a half for eating three meals. This leaves her fourteen hours of the day, out of which she must find the time for recreation as well as for work.

The maid's food and lodging, uniforms and aprons, are part of her pay; and when one considers that the greater part of the average business man's or woman's salary goes for food and clothes and lodging, it is not unreasonable that her hours for housework should—at least on occasions—run to longer than ordinary business hours.

It is impossible to establish a fixed schedule that can apply to time in and time out, because these are in many cases subject to personal requirements and agreements. If there be children, the maid must of necessity stay in when the mother and father go out. In other houses the maid may go out when her employers go out. Normally every maid has her specified afternoons and evenings out. If your requirements be unusually hard or confining, you compensate for this as best you can.

Although no definite schedule exists, the following is intended as a working outline to be adjusted according to your own needs:

WORKING SCHEDULE FOR A ONE-MAID HOUSE

The house has seven rooms: a living room, dining room, porch, kitchen, maid's room and bath, three bedrooms, and two baths.

6:45 A.M.	Wash and dress.
7:00	Downstairs. Put kettle on to boil. Start cereal. Set breakfast table.
7:30	Cook breakfast. Eat own breakfast.
8:00	Serve family breakfast.
8:30	Clear table, wash dishes, pick up living room, sweep dining room, kitchen, halls. Mistress plans meals for the day and orders marketing.
10:00	Go upstairs, make beds, clean bathrooms, sweep, dust, empty wastebaskets.
11:00	Do special work for day. Clean one room thoroughly; if the living room, nothing else that day. If an easily cleaned room, she can polish silver, or make a cake, make dessert for dinner, or prepare vegetables.
12:30 P.M.	Prepare luncheon, set table.
1:00	Serve luncheon.
1:30	Clear table, wash dishes. Go to own room to rest, bathe, and change dress.
3:00	On duty in kitchen. Ready to answer door, etc.
5:00	Prepare meat, vegetables, etc. for dinner. Set table.
5:30	Cook dinner.
6:30	Serve dinner.
7:00	Wash dishes, put dining room and kitchen in order for night.
8:00	Plans for the evening will be adapted to the household needs.

"Special work for the day" schedule

Monday—Clean the three bedrooms.
Tuesday—Clean dining room and polish silver.
Wednesday—Clean sun porch and do extra baking.
Thursday—Clean kitchen and maid's room. (Afternoon and evening out*)
Friday—Clean living room.
Saturday—Polish brass, silver, furniture, etc. Bake cake for Sunday.
    (Every other Sunday afternoon and evening out.)

* Or other times out substituted by mutual agreement.

ADVICE TO THE BEGINNER WHO ENGAGES A GENERAL MAID

If you have never kept house before and do not know what a maid should be able to do, it might be best to go to a reliable intelligence office where the clerk will be glad to tell you about hours and wages and an average working plan. On the other hand, if you advertise in the paper, then you could perhaps ask a friend, whose own house is run most nearly the way you would like your own to be, to give you advice on making a fair and practical schedule.

Interviewing an Applicant

When you interview an applicant, it is a fixed rule of propriety that in your own house she should stand; but if you go to an office, it is proper to invite her to be seated while you talk with her. In either case, the first thing she does—always—is to hand you her written references from her last employer. If she has several, she shows you the last two or three. A good reference should say that she is honest, sober, capable, trustworthy and of good disposition. If one of these items is missing in each of the references shown you, then you should take this shortcoming into consideration.

However, let us say that the references of a certain applicant are good and that the wages you can pay meet her expectations. Let us say, too, that you like her face. (Perhaps this is not a gauge generally used, but it is to be recommended.)

Be Accurate

The next move is to give her briefly but ACCURATELY the schedule of both working and time-off hours. "Accurately" is emphasized because careless misrepresentation of facts or intentions is unfair. It is unfair, for example, to assure the maid that she is to have no care of the baby, and then gradually ask that she do just about everything that would be expected of a special nurse—unless of course her schedule is shifted with her own consent. Plainly, too, it is not fair at the last minute to expect the maid to change her afternoon and evening out because it happens to be inconvenient to you. This lack of consideration is one of the chief causes of domestic trouble.

Another important point is that you should try to visualize what you offer her as well as what you exact of her. Don't say that you are always prompt when you are not; don't say that your meals will be very simple and then expect her to be an expert chef. Don't say that the house is easy to take care of when it couldn't be more inconvenient. Don't say that her work will take a certain number of hours a day without having the vaguest notion of how much work can be reasonably done in this length of time. At the other extreme, it isn't necessary to exaggerate whatever inconveniences there may perhaps be, particularly when there will be much compensating pleasantness that should make her quite happy with you—more so, in fact, than in a house whose shortcomings would be fewer.

As to how much work a general maid can be expected to do, the essential point to consider is that in the working hours of each day one pair of hands can do exactly so much, and you therefore have to adjust your requirements accordingly. If you live in a suburban community where everything stays very clean and the rooms are not too cluttered with ornaments and other time-taking objects, and if your meals are reasonably simple, one maid alone should be able to do all the work of the house without difficulty. This, however, would not mean that she could do all the cleaning and cooking and the waiting on table for no matter how big a family or how much company, or that in addition to her daily routine of housework she can be ceaselessly interrupted. This question of interruption is important, since to call her away from whatever she is doing to do something else and then to reprimand her for not having finished the first work is the very type of thing that unthinking employers do time and again.

Make Her Room Attractive

But meanwhile let us go back to the day of your new maid's arrival. It is obviously important that pains be taken to make her room as attractive as possible. This is after all merely imagining yourself in her place. Surely nothing could be more dispiriting than for any normal young woman—or older one either—to arrive in a strange place, which is actually to be her "home," and to be taken into a drab and comfortless room which all too plainly shows that you have not given so much as a thought to what this complete unattractiveness of surroundings must mean to her. After all, a comfortable bed in as pretty a room as you can supply, and with conveniences in keeping with the standards of the rest of your house, is no more than reasonable. Naturally, if the rest of your house is very simple, much less is expected of you than would be the case if the house were luxurious. The same attention to attractiveness and convenience should be evident in the kitchen—in which she is not only to work and to take her meals, but in which she is also to spend most of her hours of leisure.

Uniforms Furnished by Employer

According to modern usage, a maid's uniform as well as her aprons and collars and cuffs are furnished by her employer. For morning in a perfectly appointed house she wears a cotton dress, either white or colored, and a big apron with a bib. The long sleeves which were once exacted have now been supplanted by those of elbow length, which are not only more practical, but much prettier than rumpled long ones, pulled down, to wait on table as well as go to the door! In a simple house it is also in good taste—because suitable—that her uniform for afternoon and evening have three-quarter sleeves with cuffs just below the elbow. On the other hand, in a house where there is a cook and where the waitress has no heavy work of any sort to do in the afternoon, her uniforms should have long sleeves with cuffs around the wrists. Where the family is very small and the maid's schedule permits her finishing all heavy work before serving the midday meal, she changes for this into her afternoon dress. This dress is usually of alpaca or crêpe de chine or artificial silk, with a small thin apron, with cuffs and collar to match. In the average house where it is not practical that she dress at such an early hour, it is necessary that she wait on table in her morning clothes.

The Heart of the Whole Domestic Problem!

Whether a house runs smoothly or roughly depends entirely upon the personal adjustments made between the lady of the house and the one or many whom she employs. This is the heart of the whole domestic problem. I think we all have certain neighbors whose houses suggest the smoothness, the tranquility, and the beauty of a sun-dappled mountain brook. And we can also name others who live in a storm center of perpetual upheaval. We know, too, that wealth is not the important factor.

Selma at the Joneses and the whole staff of the Oldnames not only like their jobs but plainly like their employers, while the procession of cooks goes unceasingly on at the Flashpans. Selma's position is by no means an easy one, and yet she has three times put off her wedding because she cannot quite bring herself to leave the Jones family.

If we attempt to analyze the spirit pervading these and all other houses like them, I think it will be found in the understanding and fairness that is shown on both sides. Proper pride on the part of every high-minded employee, whether in office or factory or domestic service, exacts of herself that she give fair value for wages received. On the other side, the obligation of the lady of the house is obviously intensified since each of her employees lives, for however many months or years it may be, under conditions which are happy or miserable, developing or blighting, according to the character and personality that she and the other members of her family instinctively show. If she is human in her understanding, if she is fair in what she exacts, if she is just in her point of view, and if, being herself kind and trustable, she naturally believes that those who serve her have the same traits—the chances are very, very small that house-keeping "difficulties" will ever be hers!

27

Flat Silver—Its Choice and Usage— Condensed Table Setting

THE most complete list of flat silver possible in a perfectly equipped house includes the following articles. Those marked with a star are the most important.

    Serving spoon
   *Tablespoon
   *Dessertspoon
   *Teaspoon
   *After-dinner coffee-spoon
    Iced-tea spoon
    Orange spoon
    Salt spoon
    Serving fork
   *Large fork—often called dinner fork
   *Small fork—sometimes called salad or dessert fork
    Fish fork
    Oyster fork
    Fruit fork
   *Large knife—dinner knife with steel blade
   *Small knife—silver blade
    Fish knife
    Fruit knife
    Butter knife—"Butter spreader" is the manufacturers' term.

From the above list may be subtracted as unnecessary all but the asterisked items, but to the list must be added serving implements, noted in detail further on.

THE MOST IMPORTANT RULES FOR CHOOSING SILVER

To the bride who wants to choose silver that will meet the permanent standards of best taste, the following rules are suggested. Because silver is something intended to last a lifetime, the rule of safety is to study the old designs which, having had the approval of time, are certain to endure for many years to come; whereas the new design, no matter how attractive, may prove in a short while to have been but a transient fashion. For one who feels certain of her taste or for one who can again buy new, this precaution is unimportant.

The silver illustrated in this chapter is admirable because it is beautifully simple. Its surface is brilliant; the corners of the forks are smoothly round; the prongs are slim. On inferior silver the fork-corners are sharp, the prongs thick, and something is added to or cut away from what is supposed to be a plain design. For those who do not like plain silver, there are several standard patterns with ornamentation, most notably the "King Pattern." This last is made by almost every silversmith and in plate as well as in sterling.

Silver—as already explained in the chapter on dinners—must be kept brilliantly polished. One should be able to see one's image in it clearly. An oxidized, dulled, or frosted surface is to be shunned.

MIXED PATTERNS TOGETHER

When bought new, silver of one pattern is naturally preferred. Therefore, unless a whole set of flat silver is given her by one person, it is customary that a bride choose the pattern she prefers and that her family and perhaps friends buy forks or knives or spoons, or whatever pieces they choose, of that design. But many, many tables in beautifully appointed houses are set with mixed silver; the reason is obviously that very few can, or want to, discard inherited silver, especially that which has a sentimental association.

QUANTITY OF FLAT SILVER NECESSARY

For the most elaborate service for dinners or lunches of twelve, there should be 36 small forks and 12 of each of the other items starred in the list at the beginning of this chapter. For a small house, cut each dozen to 8 or 6. For a house of extensive hospitality, double or treble individual articles according to your need. Add table- and dessert-spoons, forks and knives in preparation for dinners, or extra dessert-spoons, teaspoons and small forks if afternoon teas or buffet meals are to be frequent entertainments of the house.

EACH PIECE OF FLAT SILVER IN DETAIL

The serving spoon and fork, though correct and convenient, may easily be dispensed with because the dinner spoon and fork may perfectly well be used in place of the serving spoon and fork, which are merely a trifle larger.

The tablespoon must be used for soup that is served in a soup plate. Dip the soup away from you and pour it between your lips silently from the side, not the tip. A soup that is semi-solid, such as a *minestrone* or *petite marmite*, or one that is so thick with rice or vegetables that it is more solid than liquid, may be "eaten" from the end. But in this case the bowl must never be more than half filled because an entire tablespoon must never be thrust into no-matter-how-large a mouth! Young children whose table manners are past the elementary stage feel deeply the humiliation of having small-sized silver. But to give them full-sized forks and spoons entails the undivided attention of someone to prevent their becoming adept in stowing heaped spoon and fork loads into the unsuspected capacities of the young human jaw.

The dessertspoon is midway in size between the table- and teaspoon, and is used for almost everything that is "eaten" with a spoon, such as dessert, fruit, cereal, soup in bowls or in cups that are very wide. For small cups of bouillon use teaspoons. The dessertspoon should not be used for soup in plates. If you have no tablespoons, you must not serve consomme or other thin soup in plates.

The teaspoon is used for all beverages served in cups and for grapefruit, boiled egg, fruit cocktail, etc. One rule to remember: *Never leave a teaspoon standing in a cup.* The instant it is out of your hand, it belongs in the saucer.

The after-dinner coffee-spoon is half the size of a teaspoon and is for the small cup of black coffee and for nothing else. You stir sugar with it and possibly taste the coffee. But you drink the coffee from the cup, leaving the spoon in the saucer.

The iced-tea spoon is the ordinary ice-cream soda spoon of the soda counter now made in most patterns of best table silver and used for beverages served in tall glasses. If there is a plate under the glass, you lay the spoon on it after stirring or tasting. But if there is no plate, you leave it in the glass. If a teaspoon is used for this purpose, you also leave it in the glass, as you can't lay it on a plate used for food and certainly not on a table. At a soda fountain you may lay it on the marble counter or table after tasting—which practically dries the spoon. You should not stir your drink around, however, and then let soda or orangeade run in a wet smear on either table or counter.

The orange spoon is a somewhat narrow, pointed-tip teaspoon. It is not necessary because a teaspoon perfectly—and usually—takes its place.

The serving fork is an extra-large dinner fork and is not necessary.

The dinner or "large" fork is essential for the meat course at dinner and also for any meat served at lunch.

The small fork is the most important fork there is. Its use is for every possible course at breakfast, lunch and dinner except the meat course, for which the large fork is used. The small fork is used literally for *everything* else, and in such great houses as the Worldlys' and Gildings' no other is included in the silver chest.

The special fish fork is wasteful, since it must be bought and kept polished for no other purpose than eating fish. Also it must be added that fretwork trimmings across the prongs are absolutely tabu.

But the plain fork with a flattened first tine and the silver knife with pointed end and saw-tooth edge are not tabu because their designs have tradition.

One rather wonders whether, in bygone days, the slit at the top of the flattened first prong was used to pinch out fish bones. And how the feat was accomplished. The saw-edged knife creates a mental picture of fish with very thick skin, served whole, and each diner who would partake of it sawing himself a chunk.

The oyster fork is a very small, slim fork, about six inches long, the prong end of which is about half an inch wide. It is used for oysters, clams, or any cold shellfish cocktail at the beginning of lunch or dinner. Unless you serve these courses, these forks are unnecessary.

The fruit fork is brought on with the fruit knife, either with or after the finger bowl. See illustration.

The large or dinner knife has a steel blade and is used only for the meat course at dinner, or occasionally at lunch.

The small knife has a silver or silver-plated blade and is used for breakfast, lunch, supper, and every course at dinner except the meat course.

A small, sharp, silver-bladed knife with a pointed end is for fruit. It is often different in pattern from the rest of the silver. Its blade may be of silver or gilt, with a handle of silver, gilt, mother of pearl, ivory, agate or other semi-precious material. Usually there is a fork that matches it.

The butter knife is always used to spread butter or jam or jelly on bread of every description; it is used for nothing else. If there is no special butter knife, the small knife will answer. Butter that is mixed with food and condiments such as accompany different meats is spread on the meat with a fork.

SERVING IMPLEMENTS

In the majority of houses an ordinary tablespoon and dinner fork are used for almost every dish, but in the very complete silver chest the special serving spoon and fork are exactly like the tablespoon and dinner fork, but of a slightly larger size. In other days "Apostle" or other ornate spoons and forks were often used, but today it is preferable that the serving pieces match the silver.

A wooden salad fork and spoon—also a wooden bowl—is admissible, especially at the family table where father or mother is an expert on salad dressing and mixes it personally. But in very formal houses salad is served with the serving spoon and fork that match the silver.

The serving spoon alone is used in a dish of small vegetables, such as peas or mashed potatoes, or a pudding or cereal—anything easily taken with a spoon in the right hand. Otherwise a fork accompanies the spoon, and you are expected to insert the spoon under a piece of meat or fish, or branching vegetable, something on toast, or whatever it may be, holding the food in place with the fork in the left hand, held prongs down.

Sauces are usually ladled. If there is no ladle, you pour the sauce from the sauce boat.

With tongs you help yourself to asparagus by pushing the lower tong under a few stalks, grasping the tongs tightly, and closing them.

A cake or pie lifter is a flat piece of silver with a handle. You lift the griddlecakes or a piece of pie on it and steady them—or it—with the fork. If there is no fork, you lift carefully!

No matter what sort of serving device you encounter, you cut, if necessary, with the edge of a spoon or other broad implement, and then, pushing it under the helping, hold the food in place with the fork-shaped piece.

MISCELLANEOUS IMPLEMENTS

There must be sugar tongs for lump sugar and a spoon for powdered sugar, unless it is in a shaker. Ladles are used for gravy—even if there is a sauce boat. If there is a ladle, you dip it full, stop the drip against the lip of the bowl or sauce boat, empty it on the food for which it is intended, and paying attention to its drip, put it carefully back without letting any drops fall.

The proper way to take salt that is not in a shaker is with a salt spoon, not on the blade of one's knife. If there isn't any salt spoon, then at least be sure the knife blade or fork tip is clean.

Grape scissors are of silver—usually ornamented with a grape design. You cut about half a dozen hot-house grapes off a large bunch —which needless to say no one is supposed to take whole! If there are no scissors, you break off a small cluster or two with your fingers.

Nutcrackers and nutpicks properly belong on the Thanksgiving and Christmas or any home dinner table. But unshelled nuts have no place at a formal lunch or dinner party, and salted ones have no place after the table has been crumbed.

At the seacoast where broiled lobsters are a specialty (and not sufficiently cracked!), nutcrackers and nutpicks are indispensable for breaking the claws and extracting the meat.

Silver handles with prongs to be thrust into the ends of ears of corn on the cob are often included in the silver chest.

WHICH FORK?

One of the fears expressed time and again in letters from readers is that of making a mistake in selecting the right table implements. As a matter of fact the choice of an implement is usually unimportant

FLAT SILVER

But the plain fork with a flattened first tine and the silver knife with pointed end and saw-tooth edge are not tabu because their designs have tradition.

One rather wonders whether, in bygone days, the slit at the top of the flattened first prong was used to pinch out fish bones. And how the feat was accomplished. The saw-edged knife creates a mental picture of fish with very thick skin, served whole, and each diner who would partake of it sawing himself a chunk.

The oyster fork is a very small, slim fork, about six inches long, the prong end of which is about half an inch wide. It is used for oysters, clams, or any cold shellfish cocktail at the beginning of lunch or dinner. Unless you serve these courses, these forks are unnecessary.

The fruit fork is brought on with the fruit knife, either with or after the finger bowl. See illustration.

The large or dinner knife has a steel blade and is used only for the meat course at dinner, or occasionally at lunch.

The small knife has a silver or silver-plated blade and is used for breakfast, lunch, supper, and every course at dinner except the meat course.

A small, sharp, silver-bladed knife with a pointed end is for fruit. It is often different in pattern from the rest of the silver. Its blade may be of silver or gilt, with a handle of silver, gilt, mother of pearl, ivory, agate or other semi-precious material. Usually there is a fork that matches it.

The butter knife is always used to spread butter or jam or jelly on bread of every description; it is used for nothing else. If there is no special butter knife, the small knife will answer. Butter that is mixed with food and condiments such as accompany different meats is spread on the meat with a fork.

SERVING IMPLEMENTS

In the majority of houses an ordinary tablespoon and dinner fork are used for almost every dish, but in the very complete silver chest the special serving spoon and fork are exactly like the tablespoon and dinner fork, but of a slightly larger size. In other days "Apostle" or other ornate spoons and forks were often used, but today it is preferable that the serving pieces match the silver.

A wooden salad fork and spoon—also a wooden bowl—is admissible, especially at the family table where father or mother is an expert on salad dressing and mixes it personally. But in very formal houses salad is served with the serving spoon and fork that match the silver.

The serving spoon alone is used in a dish of small vegetables, such as peas or mashed potatoes, or a pudding or cereal—anything easily taken with a spoon in the right hand. Otherwise a fork accompanies the spoon, and you are expected to insert the spoon under a piece of meat or fish, or branching vegetable, something on toast, or whatever it may be, holding the food in place with the fork in the left hand, held prongs down.

Sauces are usually ladled. If there is no ladle, you pour the sauce from the sauce boat.

With tongs you help yourself to asparagus by pushing the lower tong under a few stalks, grasping the tongs tightly, and closing them.

A cake or pie lifter is a flat piece of silver with a handle. You lift the griddlecakes or a piece of pie on it and steady them—or it—with the fork. If there is no fork, you lift carefully!

No matter what sort of serving device you encounter, you cut, if necessary, with the edge of a spoon or other broad implement, and then, pushing it under the helping, hold the food in place with the fork-shaped piece.

MISCELLANEOUS IMPLEMENTS

There must be sugar tongs for lump sugar and a spoon for powdered sugar, unless it is in a shaker. Ladles are used for gravy—even if there is a sauce boat. If there is a ladle, you dip it full, stop the drip against the lip of the bowl or sauce boat, empty it on the food for which it is intended, and paying attention to its drip, put it carefully back without letting any drops fall.

The proper way to take salt that is not in a shaker is with a salt spoon, not on the blade of one's knife. If there isn't any salt spoon, then at least be sure the knife blade or fork tip is clean.

Grape scissors are of silver—usually ornamented with a grape design. You cut about half a dozen hot-house grapes off a large bunch —which needless to say no one is supposed to take whole! If there are no scissors, you break off a small cluster or two with your fingers.

Nutcrackers and nutpicks properly belong on the Thanksgiving and Christmas or any home dinner table. But unshelled nuts have no place at a formal lunch or dinner party, and salted ones have no place after the table has been crumbed.

At the seacoast where broiled lobsters are a specialty (and not sufficiently cracked!), nutcrackers and nutpicks are indispensable for breaking the claws and extracting the meat.

Silver handles with prongs to be thrust into the ends of ears of corn on the cob are often included in the silver chest.

WHICH FORK?

One of the fears expressed time and again in letters from readers is that of making a mistake in selecting the right table implements. As a matter of fact the choice of an implement is usually unimportant

FLAT SILVER—EACH ARTICLE REDUCED TO ABOUT THREE-EIGHTHS OF ITS ACTUAL SIZE

1. After-dinner coffee spoon. 2. Tea spoon. 3. Dessert spoon. 4. Table spoon. 5. Dinner fork. 6. Small fork. 7. Dinner knife. 8. Small knife. 9. Butter knife. 10. Fruit fork. 11. Fruit knife.

—a trifling detail which people of best position care nothing about.

However, in order that you may make no mistake, you need merely remember that you are to take the outside—that is, the farthest from the plate—spoon or fork first. If the pieces have not been laid in this order, the fault is that of the person who set the table, and not yours. If you are in doubt, wait until your host or hostess has picked up his or her implement, and do likewise.

The statement above, that people of position do not care about which piece of silver to use, has one qualification. They could not use the dinner fork for oysters or a teaspoon for soup, because they instinctively choose an implement suitable for whatever they are about to eat. But if they happen to choose a medium-sized pronged article for fish when it was intended by the manufacturer to be especially helpful for salad or shredded-wheat biscuit, it makes no difference whatever.

[Please make full use of the Index to find additional details on any subject. Advice on Silver, for instance, will be found under "Marking Silver" and "Setting Table" as well as under "Silver."]

DETAILS OF TABLE SETTING

BREAKFAST

Small-sized fork at left of plate.
Small-sized knife at right of plate.
Cereal spoon at right of knife.
Teaspoon for cut-up fruit, but not for coffee, at right of cereal spoon.
Butter knife at left of fork, or across bread and butter plate, which is to the left and above knife. "Butter knife" is the proper word—not butter spreader.
Napkins at left of plates if cut-up fruit at places; otherwise on heated place plates, if table is set with hot food.
Coffee cups with spoons lying at right of saucers, at the right of each plate if coffee is served from pantry. If served by the lady of the house, cups and saucers are included with tea or coffee service at her place.
Food is equally often passed in courses or all put in covered dishes on the table.

LUNCHEON OR SUPPER

Salad fork at left, next to plate.
Meat fork at left of salad fork.
Then outside at left, fork for egg dish or entrée or fish, if there is to be a first course requiring a fork.

Silver salad knife at right next to plate. In spite of the somewhat prevalent idea that salad should be eaten with a fork alone, the salad knife always has had its place on the well-appointed table whenever leafy salad or cheese is to be served.

Next to the salad knife comes a meat knife, and at the right of this knife is a bouillon or fruit spoon. At supper the tea or coffee service is put in front of the hostess.

DINNER

Salad fork at left of plate, then meat fork, and left of that a fork for fish or the entrée.

At right, next to the plate, if three knives are necessary, the salad knife first, then a dinner knife, then a fish knife. Then the soup spoon, then the oyster fork, or fruit spoon.*

In every case, the implements necessary for each course are arranged in order of their use. The one to be used first goes on the outside, where it is reached first; the implement to be used last is put nearest the plate, where it is encountered in turn when the outer articles have been taken away. Dessertspoon and fork are brought in on dessert plate after the table is "cleared." The dessert services are explained on page 346. On the properly set table there may never be more than three forks and two knives, preferably (but, if unavoidable, three). This rule applies only to a strictly formal house. In a simple house, especially one without servants, the hostess necessarily adapts this as well as other rules to her own personal situation.

WHO IS HEAD OF TABLE?

The head of the table is wherever the hostess sits. In other words, the wife is head of the table, though the man is head of the house.

Why then, if this be so (and it *is*) is the table silver always marked with his crest (if he has one) and the household linen always marked with her initials?

The answer is just as senseless as pronouncing through, throo; enough, ennuff; plough, plow;—and just as definite.

*Most correctly the table is set with two knives—a dinner knife always, with either the salad knife next to the plate or the fish knife at the right of the dinner knife. The menu is selected accordingly. But should three knives be necessary, they are permitted.

28

Formal Dinners

ALTHOUGH the trend of the day is away from the formal dinner—or dinner of ceremony—and toward the informal or friendly dinner, it is necessary that this chapter be left as it was originally written because its every detail is a definite part of the complete set of patterns *from which all details* of dinner giving are chosen.

To give a perfect dinner of ceremony is the supreme accomplishment of a hostess! It means not alone perfection of furnishing, of service, of culinary skill, but also of personal charm, of tact.

There are so many aspects to be considered in giving a dinner that it is difficult to know whether to begin upstairs or down, or with furnishing, or service, or people, or manners! One thing is certain: no novice should ever begin her social career by attempting a formal dinner any more than a pupil swimmer, upon being able to take three strokes alone, should attempt to swim three miles out to sea. The former will as surely drown as the latter.

A DINNER IN A GREAT HOUSE

When Mrs. Worldly gives a dinner, it means no effort on her part beyond deciding upon the date and the principal guests who are to form the nucleus. Every further detail is left to her subordinates—even the completion of her list of guests. For instance, she decides that she will have an "older" dinner, and finding that the tenth is available for herself, she tells her secretary to send out invitations for that date on the dinner blank described elsewhere. She then looks through her "dinner list" and orders her secretary to invite the Oldworlds, the Eminents, the Learneds, the Wellborns, the Highbrows, and the Onceweres. She also picks out three or four additional names to be substituted for those who regret. Then turning to the "younger married" list, she searches for a few "amusing" or good-looking ones to give life and charm to her dinner, which might otherwise be heavy. But her favorites do not seem appropriate. It will not do to ask the Bob Gildings, not because of the difference in age but because Lucy Gilding smokes like a furnace straight through dinner and is miserable unless she can play bridge for high stakes and, just as soon as she can bolt through dinner, sit at a card table; while Mrs. Highbrow and Mrs. Oncewere quite possibly disapprove of women's smoking at all and class all playing for money with "gambling." So she adds the Kindharts and the Normans, who "go" with everyone, and approves her secretary's suggestions as to additional names if those first invited should "regret."

The list being settled, Mrs. Worldly's own work is done. She sends word to her cook that there will be twenty-four on the tenth; the menu, which she will probably merely glance at and send back, will be submitted to her later. She never sees or thinks about her table, which the butler will arrange properly.

On the morning of the dinner her secretary brings her the place cards—the name of each person expected is written on a separate card—and she puts them in the order in which they are to be laid on the table, very much as though she were playing solitaire. Starting with her own card at one end and her husband's at the other, she places the lady of honor at his right, the second in importance at his left. Then at either side of herself she places the two most important gentlemen. The others she fits in between, trying to seat side by side those congenial to each other.

When the cards are arranged, the secretary puts the name of the lady who sits at each gentleman's right in the envelope addressed to him. She then picks up the place cards, still stacked in their proper sequence, and gives them to the butler, who will lay them in the order arranged on the table after it is set.

Five minutes before the dinner hour, Mrs. Worldly is already standing in her drawing room. She has no personal responsibility other than that of being hostess. The whole machinery of equipment and service runs seemingly by itself. It does not matter whether she knows what the menu is. Her cook is more than capable of attending to it. That the table shall be perfect is merely the everyday duty of the butler. She knows without looking that her chauffeur is on the sidewalk; that footmen are in the hall; that her own maid is in the ladies' dressing room, and the valet in that of the gentlemen; and that her butler is just outside the door near which she is standing.

So with nothing on her mind—except possibly a jeweled diadem—she receives her guests with the tranquillity attained only by those whose household—whether great or small—can be counted on to run like a smoothly coordinated machine.

HOW A DINNER CAN BE BUNGLED

This is the contrasting picture to the dinner at the Worldlys'—a picture to show you particularly, a bride, how awful a meant-to-be-"formal" dinner can be when undertaken without experience.

Let us suppose that you have a quite charming house, and that your wedding presents included everything necessary to set a well-

FORMAL DINNERS

appointed table. You have not very experienced servants, but they would all be good ones with a little more training.

You have been at home for so few meals you don't quite know how really inexperienced they are. Your cook makes good coffee and eggs and toast for breakfast, and the few other meals she has cooked seemed to be all right, and she is such a nice person!

So when your house is "in order" and the last pictures and curtains are hung, the impulse suddenly comes to you to give a dinner! Your husband thinks it is a splendid idea. It merely remains to decide whom you will ask. You hesitate between a few of your own intimates, or older people, and decide it would be such fun to ask a few of the hostesses who have been most kind to you. You decide to ask Mrs. Toplofty, Mr. Clubwin Doe, the Worldlys, the Gildings, and the Kindharts and the Wellborns. With yourselves that makes twelve, which is really too many, but you decide that it will be safe to ask that number because a few are sure to "regret." So you write notes—since it is to be a formal dinner—and—they all accept! You are a little worried about the size of the dining room, but you are elated by the wonderful evidence of your popularity and you prepare light-heartedly for your dinner. You must get Sigrid a dress that properly fits her; and Marie, the chambermaid, who was engaged with the understanding that she is to serve in the dining room when there is company, has not yet been at table, but she is a very willing young person who will surely look well.

Nora, when you tell her who are coming, eagerly suggests the sort of menu that would appear on the table of the Worldlys or the Gildings. You are thrilled at the thought of your own kitchen producing the same. That it may be the same in name only does not occur to you. You order pink roses and pink cakes and pink candles for the table. You pick out your best tablecloth, but you find rather to your amazement that when Sigrid asks you about setting the table, you have never noticed in detail how the places are laid. Knives and spoons go on the right of the plate, of course, and forks on the left, but which goes next to the plate, or whether the wine glasses should stand nearer or beyond the goblet you can only guess. It is quite simple, however, to give directions in serving; you just tell the chambermaid that she is to follow the waitress, and pass the sauces and the vegetables. And you have already explained carefully to the latter that she must not deal plates around the table like a pack of cards, or ever take them off in piles either. (*That* much at least you do know.) You also make it a point above everything that the silver must be very clean. Sigrid seems to understand, and with the optimism of youth, you approach the dinner hour without misgiving.

Wearing the dress your husband likes, you come downstairs.

The table, set with your wedding silver and glass, looks quite nice. You are a little disturbed about the silver—it does look rather yellow, but perhaps it is just a shadow. Then you notice there are a great many forks on the table! You ask your husband what is the matter with the forks. He does not see anything wrong. You need them all for the dinner you ordered. How can there be less? So you straighten a candlestick that was out of line, and put the place cards on.

Then you go into the living room. You don't light the fire until the last moment, because you want it to be burning brightly when your guests arrive. The room looks a little stiff somehow, but an open fire more than anything else makes a room inviting, and you light it just as your first guest rings the bell. As Mr. Clubwin Doe enters, the room looks charming. Then suddenly the fire smokes, and as the smoke gets thicker and thicker your other guests arrive. Everyone begins to cough and blink. They are very polite, but the smoke, growing each moment denser, is not to be overlooked. Mrs. Toplofty takes matters in her own hands and makes Mr. Doe and your husband carry the logs, smoke and all, and throw them into the yard. The room still thick with smoke is now cheerlessly fireless, and another factor beginning to distress you is that, although everyone has arrived, there is no sign of dinner. You wait, at first merely eager to get out of the smoke-filled room. Gradually you are becoming nervous—what can have happened? The dining-room door might be that of a tomb for all the evidence of life behind it. You become really alarmed. Is dinner never going to be served? Everyone's eyes are red from the smoke, and conversation is getting weaker and weaker. Mrs. Toplofty—evidently despairing—sits down. Mrs. Worldly also sits; both hold their eyes shut and say nothing. At last the door opens with a jerk, and Sigrid, instead of bowing slightly and murmuring gently, "Dinner is served," stands stiff as a poker, and shouts: "Dinner's ready!"

You hope no one heard her, but you know very well that nothing escaped any one of those present. And between the smoke and the delay and your Sigrid's manners, you are already thoroughly mortified by the time you reach the table. But you hope that at least the dinner will be good. For the first time you are assailed with doubt. And then comes the soup. You don't have to taste it to see that it is wrong. It looks not at all as "clear" soup should! Instead of being glass-clear amber, it is a greasy-looking brown. You taste it, fearing the worst, and the worst is realized. It tastes like dish-water—and is barely tepid. You look around the table; Mr. Kindhart alone is trying to eat it.

In removing the plates, Delia, the assistant, takes them up by piling one on top of the other, clashing them together as she does so. You can feel Mrs. Worldly looking with almost hypnotized fascination—

as her attention might be drawn to a street accident against her will. Then there is a wait. You wait and wait, and looking in front of you, you notice the bare tablecloth without a plate. You know instantly that the service is wrong, but you find yourself puzzled to know how it should have been done. Finally Sigrid comes in with a whole dozen of plates stacked in a pile, which she proceeds to deal around the table. Instinct tells you that to try to interfere would only make matters worse. You hold your own cold fingers in your lap knowing that you must sit there, and that you can do nothing.

The fish, which was to have been a *mousse* with *Sauce Hollandaise*, is a huge granulated mound, much too big for the platter, with a narrow gutter of water around the edge and the center dabbed over with a curdled yellow mess. You realize that not only is the food itself awful, but that the quantity is too great for one dish. You don't know what to do next. There is no use in apologizing; there is no way of dropping through the floor, or waking yourself up. You have collected the most knowing and the most critical people around your table to put them to discomfort that you feel they will never forget. Never! You have to bite your lips to keep from crying. Whatever possessed you to ask these people to your horrible house?

Mr. Kindhart, sitting next to you, says gently, "Cheer up, little girl, it doesn't really matter!" And then you know to the full how terrible the situation is. The meal is endless; each course is equally unappetizing to look at, and abominably served. You notice that none of your guests eat anything.

You leave the table literally sick, but realizing fully that the giving of a dinner is not as easy as you thought. And in the living room, which is now fireless and freezing, but at least smokeless, you start to apologize and burst into tears!

As you are very young, and those present are all really fond of you, they try to be comforting, but you know that it will be long—if ever —before any of them will be willing to risk an evening in your house again. You also know that without malice, but in truth and frankness, they will tell everyone, "Whatever you do, don't dine with the Newweds unless you eat your dinner before you go, and wear black glasses so no sight can offend you."

When they have all gone, you drag yourself miserably upstairs, feeling that you never want to look in that dining room again. Your husband, remembering the many bad lunch counters he often eats at, tries to tell you it was not so bad! But you *know!* You lie awake making plans to let the house, and to discharge your awful household the next morning, and then you realize that the fault was yours.

If you had tried the chimney first, and learned its peculiarities; if you yourself had known every detail of cooking and service, of course you would not have attempted to give the dinner in the first place—at least not until, through giving little dinners, the skill of your household had become expert enough to encourage your giving a big one.

On the other hand, suppose that you had had a very experienced cook and waitress. The dinner would, of course, not have been bungled, but it would have lacked something, somewhere, if you added nothing of your own personality to its perfection. It is almost safe to make the statement that no dinner is ever really well done unless the hostess herself knows every smallest detail so thoroughly that, like a proofreader, she is unobserving of perfection, but unfailingly ready to correct a flaw. The perfect housekeeper is not even conscious of paying attention, but nothing escapes her. She can walk through a room without appearing to look either to the right or left; yet if the slightest detail is amiss, her eyes see it at once!

Having generalized by drawing two pictures, it is now time to take up the specific details.

DETAILED DIRECTIONS FOR DINNER GIVING

The requisites at every dinner of perfection, whether a great one of 200 people or a little one of four, are as follows:

Guests. People who are congenial to one another. This is of first importance.

Food. A suitable menu perfectly prepared and dished. Food that is good of its *kind*.

Table furnishing. Faultlessly laundered linen, brilliantly polished silver, and all other table accessories in perfect condition and suitable to the occasion and surroundings.

Service. Expert for *your* requirement.

Living room. Inviting in arrangement (and smokeless).

A cordial and hospitable host.

A hostess of charm. Charm says everything—tact, sympathy, poise and perfect manners—always.

And though for all dinners these requisites are much the same, the necessity for perfection increases in proportion to the formality of the occasion and the importance of the establishment.

(For dinner giving in the less formal American house see Chapter 29 and for the house without servants Chapter 31.)

SELECTION OF PEOPLE

The proper selection of guests is the first essential in all entertaining. Some people have this "sense"—others haven't. The first are the great hosts and hostesses; the others are the mediocre or the failures.

It is usually a mistake to invite great talkers together. Brilliant men

THE PERFECTLY APPOINTED FORMAL DINNER TABLE IN A GREAT HOUSE

Photograph by Mattie Edwards Hewitt

DETAIL OF A FORMAL DINNER TABLE
(Also see illustration on preceding page)

For the purpose of balance the oyster forks have been placed left instead of right as is usual.

CORRECT SETTING OF EACH COURSE AT A FORMAL DINNER

Dinner is served. (There is no bread-and-butter plate at a formal dinner.)

Soup plate (with rim) is put on service plate. The designs differ but plates are of same color.

Fish plate has been exchanged for soup and service plates. Sherry glass to be removed.

The meat plate has now been exchanged for the fish plate.

It is correct that a salad knife be provided for the salad course.

Table cleared before dessert plate, fork and spoon are put down.

DESSERT AND AFTER-DINNER COFFEE SERVICE

The formal service of after-dinner coffee.

The after-dinner coffee tray.

FORMAL DINNERS

and women who love to talk want hearers, not rivals. Very silent people should be sandwiched between good talkers, or at least voluble talkers. Silly people should never be put anywhere near learned ones, nor the dull near the clever, unless the dull one is a young and pretty woman with a talent for listening and the clever is a man with an admiration for beauty and a love of talking.

Most people think two brilliant people should be put together. Often they should, but with discretion. If both are voluble or nervous or "temperamental," you may create a situation like putting two operatic sopranos in the same part and expecting them to sing together.

The endeavor of a hostess, when seating her table, is to put together those who are likely to be interesting to each other. Professor Bugge might bore *you* to tears, but Mrs. Entomoid would probably delight in him, just as Mr. Stocksan Bonds and Mrs. Rich would probably have interests in common. Making a dinner list is a little like making a Christmas list. You put down what *they* will (you hope) like, not what you like. Those who are placed between congenial neighbors remember your dinner as delightful—even though both food and service were mediocre; but ask people out of their own groups and seat them next to their pet aversions, and wild horses could not drag them to your house again!

ASKING SOMEONE TO FILL A PLACE

Since no one but a fairly intimate friend is ever asked to fill a place, this invitation is always telephoned. A very young man is asked by the butler if he will dine with Mrs. Gilding that evening, and very likely no explanation is made; but if the person to be invited is a lady or an older gentleman (except on such occasions as noted above), the hostess herself telephones. "Can you do me a great favor and fill a place at dinner tonight?" The one who receives this invitation is rather bound by the rules of good manners to accept if possible.

IMPORTANCE OF DINNER ENGAGEMENTS

Dinner invitations must be answered immediately; engraved or written ones by return post, or those which were telephoned, by telephone and at once! Also, nothing but serious illness or an utterly unavoidable accident can excuse the breaking of a dinner engagement.

To accept a dinner at Mrs. Nobody's and then break the obligation upon being invited to dine with the Worldlys proclaims anyone capable of such rudeness an unmitigated snob, whom Mrs. Worldly would be the first to cut from her visiting list if she knew of it. The rule is: "Don't accept an invitation if you don't care about it." Having declined the Nobody invitation in the first place, you are then free to accept Mrs. Worldly's, or to stay at home.

There are times, however, when engagements between intimate friends or members of the family may perhaps be broken, but only if made with the special stipulation: "Come to dinner with us alone Thursday if nothing special turns up!" And the other answers, "I'd love to—and you let me know, too, if you want to do anything else." Meanwhile, if one of them is invited to something unusually tempting, there is no rudeness in telephoning her friend, "Lucy has asked us to go to the opera on Thursday!" and the other says, "Go, by all means! We can dine Tuesday next week if you like, or come Sunday for supper." This privilege of intimacy can, however, be abused. An engagement, even with a member of one's family, ought never to be broken without good reason, or it becomes apparent that the other's presence is more a fill-in of idle time than a longed-for pleasure.

THE MENU

It may be this war period, which has accustomed everyone to going with very little meat and to marked reductions in all food, or it may, of course, be merely vanity that is causing even grandparents to aspire to svelte figures; but whatever the reason, people are putting much less food on their tables than formerly. The few very rich, still living in great houses with an imposing array of servants, sit down to three, or at most four, courses.

Under no circumstances does a modern dinner, no matter how formal, consist of more than

1. Soup or oysters or melon or clams.
2. Fish or Entrée.
3. Roast.
4. Salad.
5. Dessert.

After-dinner coffee.

THE BALANCED MENU*

One should always try to choose well-balanced dishes; an especially rich dish is balanced by a simple one. Fish timbale with a thick creamed sauce might perhaps be followed by spring lamb, other plain roast meat or a *filet mignon*. A broiled fish might be followed by boned capon or another elaborate meat dish. It is equally bad to select peculiar food except as a secondary course. Some people love highly flavored Spanish or Indian dishes, but they are not appropriate for a formal dinner. At an informal dinner an Indian curry or Spanish enchillada for one dish is delicious for those who like it; and if there is

* This is of course a pre-war list. It is included because its general advice is practical no matter what dishes may be chosen.

another substantial dish, such as a plain roast, which practically everyone is able to eat, those who don't like East Indian dishes can at least stay their hunger.

It is the same way with Italian dishes. One who abjures garlic and onions would be very wretched if onions were put into each course—and liberally! With curry, a fatally bad selection would be a very peppery soup, fish with green peppers, and then the curry with chutney and other throat-searing ingredients, finishing with an endive salad. Yet more than one hostess has selected exactly these.

Equally bad is a dinner of flavorless white sauces from beginning to end: a cream soup, boiled fish with white sauce, or a *vol-au-vent* of creamed sweetbreads, followed by breast of chicken and mashed potatoes and cauliflower, palm-root salad, vanilla ice cream and lady cake. Or, everything sweet: beet soup, fish with apricot sauce, duck basted with currant jelly, a sweet fruit salad with *Bar-le-duc* jelly, and a sugary dessert. In these examples each dish is good in itself but unappetizing in the monotony of its combination.

Another thing: although a dinner should not be long, neither should it consist of samples, especially if set before men who are hungry!

The following menu—one course too long at that—might seem at first glance a good dinner, but it is one from which the average man would go home and forage ravenously in the icebox:

Clear soup (no substance)
Smelts (one apiece)
Individual croutards of sweetbreads (holding about a dessertspoonful)
Broiled squab, small potato croquette, and string beans
Lettuce salad, with about one small cheese straw apiece
Ice cream

The only thing that had any sustaining quality, barring the potato which was not more than a mouthful, was the last, and very few men care to make their dinner of ice cream. If instead of squab there had been filet of beef cut in generous slices, and the potato croquettes had been more numerous, it would have been adequate. Or if there had been a thick cream soup, and a fish with more substance—such as salmon or shad, or a baked thick fish of which he could have had a generous helping—the squab would have been adequate also. But many women order trimmings rather than food; men usually like food.

SETTING THE TABLE

The one unbreakable rule is that everything on the table must be geometrically spaced; the centerpiece in the actual center, the "places" at equal distances, and all utensils balanced. Beyond this one rule you may set your table as you choose.

If the tablecloth is of white damask, which for a formal dinner is always the best possible style, a "felt" must be put under it. (To say that it must be smooth and white, in other words perfectly laundered, is as beside the mark as to say that faces and hands should be clean.) Damask is the old-fashioned but essentially conservative tablecloth, especially suitable in a high-ceilinged room that is either English, French, or of no special period, in decoration. Lace tablecloths are better suited to an Italian room—especially if the table is a refectory one. Handkerchief linen tablecloths embroidered and lace-inserted are also, strangely enough, suited to all quaint, low-ceilinged, old-fashioned but beautifully appointed rooms, the reason being that the lace cloth partially reveals the bare table. The lace cloth must also go over a refectory table without felt or other lining.

(For bare tables see Index.)

Whenever a damask cloth is used, the middle crease must be put on so that it is an absolutely straight and unwavering line down the exact center from head to foot. If it is an embroidered one, be sure the embroidery is "right side up." Next goes the centerpiece—usually an arrangement of flowers in either a bowl or a vase—but it can be any one of an almost unlimited variety of things: flowers or fruit in any arrangement that taste and ingenuity can devise; or an ornament in silver that needs no flowers, such as a covered cup; or an ornament of glass or china.

Next comes the setting of the places. (If it is an extension table, leaves have, of course, been put in; or if it is stationary, guests have been invited according to its size.) The distance between places at the table must never be so short that guests have no elbow room and that the servants cannot pass the dishes properly; when the dining-room chairs are very high-backed and are placed so close as to be almost touching, it is impossible for servants not to risk spilling something over someone. On the other hand, to place people a yard or more apart so that conversation has to be shouted into the din made by the shouting of all the others is equally trying. About two feet from plate center to plate center is ideal. If the chairs have narrow and low backs, people can sit much closer together, especially at a small round table, the curve of which leaves a spreading wedge of space between the chairs at the back even if the seats touch at the front corners. But on the long, straight sides of a rectangular table in a very large—and impressive—dining room there should be at least a foot of space between the chairs.

SETTING THE PLACES

The necessary number of plates, with the pattern right side up, are first put around the table at equal distances, spaced with a string—if

FORMAL DINNERS

whoever is setting the table has not an accurate eye. Then on the left of each plate, handle toward the edge of the table and prongs up, is put the salad fork; the meat fork is put next, and then the fish fork. The salad fork, which will usually be the third used, is thus laid nearest the plate. If there is an entrée, the fork for this course is placed between the fish fork and that for the roast, and the salad fork is left to be brought in later. On the right of the plate, and nearest to it, is put the silver-bladed salad knife, or if the salad is one for which no knife is necessary, the knife nearest the plate is the steel-bladed meat knife; next the silver fish knife, the edge of each toward the plate. Then the soup spoon and then the oyster fork or grapefruit spoon. Not more than three forks and three knives belong on the table when it is set. Additional forks and knives (when necessary) are put on the table during the dinner.

PUTTING ON THE GLASSES

Which wine glasses shall be chosen depends of course upon the menu, but their table-setting arrangement will have to be according to size, in that little ones cannot very well be hidden behind large ones. Therefore, the goblet (or tumbler) for water is placed directly above the knives at the right of the plate; next to it, at a slight distance to the right, the champagne glass; in front and between these two, either the claret glass or the tall-stemmed glass for white wine. Then, either in front of this, or somewhat to the right again, the sherry glass. If there is to be a glass for burgundy, it would be at the back between the goblet and the glass for champagne.

Such an array as this is scarcely ever seen, except at a semi-public dinner, which is more properly rated as a banquet. At the typical dinner, three glasses in addition to the goblet is the maximum; at an informal dinner, more likely two: one for sherry and one for claret, or possibly one for a very light white wine and one for burgundy. Or, instead of grouping the glasses on the table, some people prefer to have them placed in a straight row slanting downward from the goblet at upper left to the glass for sherry (or possibly chablis) at lower right.

Wines will be considered further on as soon as we finish setting the table.

NAPKIN SHOULD BE PUT ON PLATE

A dinner napkin folded square and flat is laid on each "place" plate; very fancy foldings are not in good taste, but if the napkin is very large, the sides are folded in so as to make a flattened roll a third the width of its height. (Napkins are put at the side or across top of plates only when it is necessary to put food on the table. To put the napkin at the side of the empty plate in order to display it is very much like wearing a ring over a glove—as well as being incorrect for formal table-setting. Bread should not be put in the napkin—not nowadays. Butter plates are never put on a formal dinner table.) The place cards should be put on top of the napkin in the center of the plate.

When the places have been set, two pair of silver candlesticks are placed at the four corners about halfway between the center and the edge of the table, or two candelabra at either end halfway between the places of the host and hostess and the centerpiece. How many candles depends upon whether the dining room is otherwise lighted or not. If the candles alone light the table, there must be a candle a person, at least (two five-branch candelabra and one pair of candlesticks for a dinner of twelve). But if the candles are merely ornaments, four candles will be adequate for a table of eight. Candles are used with or without shades. Fashion at the moment says "without," which means that, in order to bring the flame well above people's eyes, candlesticks or candelabra must be high and the candles as long as the proportion can stand. If the flames shine into the eyes of those at table, the candles must have shades. Shades, by the way, increase the light on the table if they are flaring in shape and of course translucent as well as white or almost white in color.

Dishes, either bowl or basket or paten shaped, are put at the corners, between the candlesticks, or candelabra, and the centerpiece, or wherever there are equally spaced vacancies on the table. These dishes, or compotiers, hold candy, fruit, fancy cakes or other edible trimmings, chosen less for taste than for decorative appearance. Salted nuts do not belong in any dishes which remain on the table after it is crumbed. Properly, nuts are often put on the dinner table, either in two big silver dishes or in small individual ones at each of the places. In any case they are removed with the salt and pepper pots after the salad course. The colloquial description of eating "from soup to nuts" could never apply to a formal dinner. After dessert "nuts and raisins" belong only on the family dinner table—at the Thanksgiving table especially.

On a very large table four compotiers are filled with candy, and perhaps two larger silver dishes or baskets are filled with fruit and put on midway between two of the candy dishes. Flowers are also often put in two or four smaller vases, in addition to a larger and dominating one in the center.

Pepper pots and salt cellars should be put at every other place. For a dinner of twelve there should be six salt cellars and pepper pots.

Olives and celery are passed during the soup course. Each fish or meat or salad has its own accompanying condiment, sauce or relish. Pickles have no place on the correct dinner party menu, because they are never served except as an accompaniment or garnishing for cold meats, which belong especially to lunch, supper, buffets, and picnics.

HAVE SILVER THAT SHINES OR NONE

Many people who would not dream of using a wrinkled tablecloth or chipped glass or china seem totally blind to silver that is jaundiced in color and black in the crevices.

WINES

Since wines have come back to their proper place in the menu of a perfect dinner, let us consider each of them in detail.

Sherry—Customarily this (in a small V-shaped glass) is the first wine served at dinner. It should always be put into a decanter and served at room temperature. (It can stand being decantered indefinitely without spoiling.) All wines are poured at the right of each person at table and without lifting the glass from the table. Sherry is also served at lunch or at supper or as a hospitable refreshment at any time. In olden days it was invariably offered with crackers or cakes to guests arriving from a journey or about to depart on one. At present it is becoming fashionable to include sherry with cocktails as an alternate choice.

White Wine—A certain few epicures have always insisted that chablis, made very cold, be served with oysters. Otherwise white wine is served with fish, possibly with an entrée, or as the only wine at a woman's lunch, or at the family dinner table.

Claret—At a simple dinner party claret is served with meat instead of champagne. Epicures shudder at its appearance before the meat, but at the family dinner table either claret or white wine is drunk plain or in water from the beginning of the meal to its close.

Burgundy is stronger than claret. It is especially suitable with duck and all game. Claret and burgundy should both be of room temperature or a degree or so warmer rather than colder if the vintage be very fine. The decanting of vintage wines is a very delicate as well as important operation. Clarets and white wines have so little alcohol in them that they spoil almost immediately upon contact with the air. They should be lifted as gently as possible, without changing the side on which the bottles are lying, into straw baskets of the sort that they are served from in restaurants.

The white wines are carried carefully to a cool—even cold—place. Red wines are carried with equal care to the dining room or pantry, which has a temperature approximating 68 degrees; and all these wines are left in their baskets until as short a time as practical before they are to be served, and then, with all the care and gentleness possible, decanted. Many epicures put them through filter papers—others believe that filtering robs them of some of their bouquet. At all events, care is taken not to let any sediment, which has settled at the bottom of the wine, get into the decanter.

Champagne—Since this is above all other beverages that of the formal dinner party, it has, like all other formal details, many exigencies. When other wines are included, it is served with the meat course; but, when it is the only wine, it is served as soon as the first course has begun. Its proper temperature depends upon its quality.

Champagne which is not especially good is put in the icebox for a day and then frappéed by putting it into a cooler with a very little salt as well as ice, holding the bottle by the neck, and turning it back and forth a few times. In doing this, take care not to turn it so much that it becomes sherbet! Also be sure to wrap the top of the bottle in a heavy towel as a protection in case it explodes.

A fine vintage champagne, on the other hand, is packed in ice without salt and on no account allowed to frappé.

Champagne glasses ought to be as thin as soap bubbles. Thick glasses do no harm to poor champagne, which should have its poorness disguised; but a thick glass will lower the temperature at which a really fine champagne should be served and spoil its perfection. If thick glasses must be used, the epicurean thing to do is to keep them in the icebox and put them on the table at the moment the champagne is served.

(For advice on serving champagne see page 344.)

Whisky—At an informal dinner party (informal in this sense meaning anything less than a dinner of greatest ceremony) whisky is always proffered, as an alternative, to the gentlemen. Before pouring the champagne, the butler or waitress asks, "Would you prefer Scotch or rye, Sir?" "High ball" is a social tabu. One says "Scotch and soda" or "whisky and soda." A tall glass—the same as that for iced tea—should have one large piece of ice in it (small pieces melt quickly and fail to keep the drink cold). The whisky is poured by the servant until the guest makes a gesture to stop. And then the glass is filled with soda or any other sparkling mineral water.

When only fine vintage wines are served, and an occasional bottle may have turned sour, about a teaspoonful of each bottle opened is first poured in the glass of the host, who tastes it. If the wine is good, the bottle is poured for his guests. If not good, another bottle is opened. For this reason extra bottles should be ready to open.

Port and Liqueurs—English port and especially fine cognac are not likely to be served in the average American house. If they should be, they are brought to the gentlemen alone, who remain seated at table, drinking their coffee and smoking cigars and eating unsalted nuts. Liqueurs, on the other hand, are always proffered the ladies as well as the gentlemen. Three small decanters are proffered on a tray, which also holds a row of very little glasses. The fashionable list includes cognac always, and two others: chartreuse and benedictine, or kümmel or green mint or cointreau.

If mint is chosen, a few of the glasses must be filled with fine crushed ice over which the mint is poured. (White mint is the same. The green is merely prettier.)

THE BUTLER IN THE DINING ROOM

When the dinner guests enter the dining room, it used to be customary for the butler to hold out the chair of the mistress of the house. The theory is that the host himself will hold the chair of the guest of honor—who sits on his right—and all the other gentlemen will hold the chairs of the ladies on their right except the partner of the hostess, whose chair is held by her servant so that the gentleman of honor need not help her. But, whatever the theory, this has always seemed a discourtesy to the guests. And the polite hostess insists on having the butler stand at the chair of the guest of honor instead of her own. This is much more important at a lunch where there are no gentlemen than at a dinner.

If there are footmen enough, the chair of each lady is held for her. Ordinarily, where there are two servants, it is best that they stand at opposite sides of the room and help those who may seem in need of assistance.

In a big house the butler always stands throughout a meal back of the hostess' chair, except when giving one of the men under him a direction or when pouring wine. He is not supposed to leave the dining room himself or ever to handle a dish. In a smaller house, where he has no assistant, he naturally does everything himself; when he has a second man or parlor maid, he passes the principal dishes and the assistant follows with the accompanying dishes or vegetables.

(See Index for further details.)

CORRECT SERVICE OF DINNER

In every formally appointed house, whether there are two at table or two hundred, plates are changed and courses presented in precisely the same manner.

So-called "Russian" service is that of every *formally* appointed house. The term merely means that nothing to eat is ever put on the table except ornamental dishes of fruit and candy. The meat is carved in the kitchen or pantry; vegetables are passed and returned to the side table. Only at breakfast are dishes of food put on the table—or, of course, at a buffet meal of any sort.

THE EVER-PRESENT PLATE

From the setting of the table until it is cleared for dessert, a plate must remain at every place. The plate on which oysters or clams are served is put on top of the place plate, as is also a plate holding fruit or cold fish in a stemmed glass. At the end of the course the used plate is removed, leaving the place plate. The soup place is also put on top of this same plate. But when the soup plate is removed, the underneath plate is removed with it, and the plate for the next course immediately exchanged for the two taken away. The place plate merely becomes a hot fish plate, but it is there just the same.

THE EXCHANGE PLATE

If the first course had been any cold dish that was offered in bulk instead of being brought on separate plates, it would have been eaten on the place plate, and an exchange plate would have been necessary before the soup could be served. That is, a clean plate would have been exchanged for the used one, and the soup plate then put on top of that. The reason is that *a plate with food on it can never be exchanged for one that has held food;* a clean one must come between.

If an entrée served on individual plates follows the fish, clean plates are first exchanged for the used ones until the whole table is set with clean plates. Then the entrée is put at each place in exchange for the clean plate.

DISHES PRESENTED AT LEFT BUT REMOVED FROM RIGHT

Although dishes must be always presented at the left of the person served, and it is better that plates be removed at the left, too, it is permissible, if more convenient, to remove them at the right.

Glasses are poured and additional knives placed at the right, but forks are put on as needed from the left.

TWO PLATES AT A TIME?

The only plates that are regularly brought into the dining room one in each hand are for soup and dessert and, on occasion, a small plate with fruit or canapé or fruit or fish cocktail glass on its plate. Three of these are put down on the service plates which have not been removed, and the dessert plates need merely be put down on the table cloth. But the plates of every other course have to be exchanged and therefore each individual service requires two hands. Soup plates, two

FORMAL DINNERS

at a time, would better not be attempted by any but the expert and sure-handed, as it is while placing one plate and holding the other aloft that the mishap of "soup poured down someone's back" occurs! If only one plate of soup is brought in at a time, the accident at least cannot happen. In the same way, the spoon and fork on the dessert plate can easily fall off unless it is held level. "Two plates at a time," therefore, is not a question of etiquette, but of the servant's skill.

PLATE REMOVED WHEN FORK IS LAID DOWN

Many years ago it was considered impolite to remove any plates until the last guest at the table had finished eating! Then came one or two decades of speed, during which good service required the removal of each plate the instant the fork was laid upon it, so that by the time the last fork was put down, the entire table was set with clean plates and was ready for the service of the next course.

But the protests of the slow eaters were heard throughout the land, and the hostess who a few years ago prided herself on having no used plate left at any place more that a few seconds now does not have the plates removed until the slowest eaters have finished.

MORE THAN ONE SERVICE

At every well-ordered dinner there should be a separate service for each six persons; that is, no hot dish should, if avoidable, be presented to more than six, or seven at most. At a dinner of eighteen, for instance, three dishes, each holding six portions, are garnished exactly alike and presented simultaneously: (1) to the lady of honor, (2) to the lady sitting in the sixth seat to the right, (3) to the lady in the sixth seat—around the end of the table. Study the chart on page 340, which also explains seating precedence and partner arrangement.

THE ORDER OF TABLE PRECEDENCE

This order of seating is rigid and unbreakable. The lady of highest rank is on the host's right. The lady of next highest rank is on his left. The third lady sits on right of man of highest rank. The fourth lady on left of man of the second rank, and so on as marked on chart. The lowest in rank is nearest the center. The "lady of honor" or first rank must be "taken in" by the host and seated at his right. (See page 340.)

At ordinary dinners therefore the hostess goes in to dinner with the man of the second highest rank. But if the man of honor is of such importance that she must go in with him as well as place him at her right, it is necessary to send the seventh lady and the seventh man (or any other two of lesser rank) in to dinner together and then separate them! He sees her to her place, and, discovering his card is not next to her, goes around the table until he finds his own. This is plainly shown on Diagram 1.

At dinners of eight, twelve, sixteen, twenty and twenty-four, where either two ladies or two men must sit at head and foot of the table, the hostess usually relinquishes her place and the host keeps his. At a dinner of twelve it is important that she take the place at her left instead of at her right, because otherwise she, instead of the lady at the right of the gentleman of honor, will be served first.

Diagram 1

FORMAL DINNERS

For an example of this, see Diagram 2.

Serving the host second is unavoidable without too much confusion in skipping and returning to him later.

DINNER OF TWELVE IN THE HOUSE OF A WIDOW

Since it is almost impossible to seat twelve in the house of a widow who appoints a member of her family or a very intimate friend to take the place of host to avoid serving herself from an untouched first dish, it is now considered essential to consider the lady of honor the one who is seated on the right of the gentleman of honor, who sits on the right of the hostess.

Diagram 2

GENTLEMAN OF HIGHEST RANK

HOSTESS
3RD
5TH 2ND
5TH 4TH
GO IN TOGETHER IF HOSTESS GOES WITH GENTLEMAN OF 1ST RANK
4TH 3RD
2ND LADY OF HONOR

HOST

REVERSE DIRECTION EVERY OTHER COURSE

If the dinner is given for a lady and it is therefore important to appoint a deputy host to seat her opposite the hostess, then the only way to avoid serving the hostess first would be to resort to the maneuver shown in Diagram 4.

Diagram 3

This reverses service on the right side of the table and awkwardly returns to the omitted gentleman, but there is no help for it without committing the unforgivable offense of serving the hostess to one set of dishes first.

Diagram 4

*Gentleman who substitutes for host

FORMAL DINNERS

THE COURTEOUS HOSTESS IS NEVER SERVED FIRST

The hostess who has herself served first when another woman is a guest at her table is giving an innocent example of the outstanding rudeness in America at the present day.*

In all first-class restaurants each dish is presented to the host for his approval before it is passed or served to his guests, but he does *not* help himself. Nor should a hostess.

A DINNER OF EIGHT WHEN THERE IS NO HOST

Gentlemen never take the ladies in to dinner at so small a dinner as eight.

Diagram 5

HOSTESS
(H)

1ST GENTLEMAN [G]   [G] 2ND GENTLEMAN

LADY OF MOST IMPORTANCE (L)   (L) LADY

GENTLEMAN [G]   [G] GENTLEMAN
1ST   (L) LADY   6TH
3RD COURSES 5TH 2ND 4TH COURSES

It makes no difference whether or not there is a host, the lady at the foot of the table is generally served first. And the dishes are passed to the right, or passed alternately right and left in order that the same gentleman shall not always get the last piece on a dish. In many houses the lady at the first gentleman's right is served first, if she is really of more importance than the lady at the end of the table. Service goes around to the right as usual, or reverses for alternate courses, as the hostess chooses, so that those served first and last shall be varied.

FILLING GLASSES

As soon as the guests are seated and the first course is put in front of them, the butler goes from guest to guest on the right-hand side of each, and asks, "Apollinaris or plain water?" and fills the goblet ac-

---

* It is only fair, therefore, to give a complete history of the origins of this upstart rudeness, some of them understandable and others not. It will be found at the end of this chapter.

cordingly. In the same way he asks later before pouring wine, "Sherry, Sir?" or "Madam?" Champagne is of course the typical dinner-party wine. In fact, it is to many people the evidence of a party, in contrast to the sherry, white claret or claret of the family table. In France champagne is often not served until dessert, but in the smartest houses elsewhere, sherry is served with the soup (or chablis with oysters), and then champagne is served straight through to the end.

The proper way to serve it is from its own bottle with a napkin around it (put on like a shawl) and wrapped tight. The reason for this is to catch all drops—either of wine or condensed moisture—that might fall.

(For other details regarding wines, see page 335.)

AT TABLE, SHOULD A LITTLE WINE BE POURED?

Whether it is best at table—because least conspicuous—to allow a little wine to be poured into your glass before you check the pouring is open for discussion, because, unless your host happened to be looking at your glass when the wine was poured, he will not notice later on that your almost empty glass had never been filled. On the other hand, if he did happen to notice, he could not feel that much wine was wasted. In any case, to turn your wine glass upside down is a needlessly rude way to say "No."

As to this general subject of saying "No" when we want to, one wonders why so many people who feel embarrassed when refusing cocktails have no hesitation whatever in refusing foods—particularly those to which they are allergic! The reason is probably this: The censorious attitude of those who disapprove of alcohol, no matter how temperate its use, has brought about a connotation of disapproval in its refusal. One may refuse to eat bread or fish or strawberries, and this may cause regret on the part of the hostess who knows that her biscuits are superlatively good or the fish caught but a few hours before the meal, or the strawberries picked at just the right hour of the day in the garden, but no disapproval can possibly be implied on the part of the guest who says, "No, thank you."

Not no many years ago, when diet fads had not come into fashion, and the scientific study of balanced rations, vitamins, and allergies and so on was unknown outside the laboratories, it was considered very discourteous to refuse whatever one's host or hostess proffered. A well-behaved guest took at least a little of everything passed and ate or drank that little. Today no one is ever expected to eat any items to which he is personally antipathetic. In fact, the increasing present use of the word "allergic" has been more helpful to the acceptance of the phrase "No, thank you" than anything that ever happened.

FORMAL DINNERS

BREAD

As soon as soup is served, dinner (finger) rolls are passed in a flat dish or a basket. An old-fashioned silver cake basket makes a perfect modern bread basket. Or, most popular of all, a shallow wicker basket that has a fringed napkin laid in it and several sorts of breads displayed. (Finger rolls, crescent rolls, melba toast and rye or whole wheat crackers are typical.) A guest helps himself with his fingers and lays the roll or bread on the tablecloth, always. No bread plates are ever on a table where there is no butter, and no butter is ever served at a formal dinner. Whenever there is no bread left at anyone's place at table, more should be passed. The glasses should also be kept filled.

PRESENTING DISHES

Dishes are presented held flat on the palm of the servant's left hand; every hot one must have a napkin placed as a pad under it. An especially heavy meat platter can be steadied if necessary by holding the edge of the platter with the right hand, the fingers protected from being burned by a second folded napkin.

Each dish is supplied with whatever implements are needed for helping it. In a formally appointed house both a serving spoon (somewhat larger than an ordinary tablespoon) and a fork of large size are put on all dishes. In a simpler house the spoon alone is used except on the dishes that are hard to help. String beans, braised celery, spinach en branche, etc. need a fork and spoon. Asparagus has various special lifters and tongs, but most people use the ordinary spoon and fork, putting the spoon underneath and the fork prongs down, to hold the stalks on the spoon while being removed to the plate. Corn on the cob is taken with the fingers, but this dish, delectable though it be, is *never* served at a *formal* dinner party. For this occasion it should be cut off, buttered, seasoned and served in a vegetable dish. A galantine or mousse should have both fork and spoon, but peas, mashed potatoes, rice, etc. are offered with a spoon only—except at a formal table.

THE SERVING TABLE

The serving table is usually an ordinary table placed in the corner of the dining room near the door to the pantry, and behind a screen, so that it may not be seen by the guests at table. In a small dining room, where space is limited, a set of shelves like a single bookcase is useful; best of all are shelves, made by a carpenter, and fitted to the folds of the screen.

The serving table is a halfway station between the dinner table and the pantry. It holds stacks of cold plates, extra forks and knives, and the finger bowls and dessert plates. The latter are sometimes put out on the sideboard, if the serving table is small or too crowded.

At little informal dinners all dishes of food after being passed are left on the serving table in case they are called upon for a second helping. But at formal dinners, dishes are never passed twice, and are therefore taken directly to the pantry after being passed.

CLEARING TABLE FOR DESSERT

At dinner always, whether at a formal one or whether a member of the family is alone, the salad plates, or the plates of whatever course precedes dessert, are removed, leaving the table plateless. The salt cellars, pepper pots, unused flat silver, and nut dishes are taken off on the serving tray (without being put on any napkin or doily, as used to be the custom), and the crumbs are brushed off each place at table with a tightly folded napkin onto a tray held under the table edge.

DESSERT SERVICE

There are two methods of serving dessert. The first, which used to be known as the "hotel method" but has within the last few years become the accepted one everywhere, is to put the fork and spoon on a china plate. Some people put a glass plate for ice cream on this but most use china. After the dessert the finger bowl is brought in on a plate by itself. In the other service, which used to be that of all private houses, the entire dessert paraphernalia is put on at once. (See full page illustration.)

This single service may sound as though it were more complicated than the two-course service, but actually it is simpler unless fruit is served. People dip their fingers in the finger bowls (which they have put above their own places) and leave the table. Otherwise each plate has to be exchanged for a finger bowl on its separate plate.

When fruit is to be served, it is passed immediately after ice cream; and last are passed decorative sweets. Usually these include chocolates, caramels, peppermints, candied orange, or whatever one chooses for decoration as well as taste.

Before leaving the subject of dessert, it may be well to add that the finger bowl is less than half filled with cold water; and at dinner parties a few violets, sweet peas, or occasionally a gardenia may (or may not) be put in it. A slice of lemon is never seen in a well-appointed house in an after-dessert finger bowl. After broiled lobster, lemon in *hot* water (or soapy hot water) is excellent.

Black coffee is never served at a formal dinner table, but is brought afterwards with cigarettes and liqueurs into the drawing room for the ladies, and with cigars, cigarettes and liqueurs into the library for the gentlemen.

If there is no library or similar man's room, coffee and cigars are brought to the table for the gentlemen after the ladies have gone into the drawing room.

(For full descriptions of the several varieties of coffee serving, see Index.)

MENU CARDS

Small, standing porcelain slates, on which the menu is written, are seen on occasional dinner tables. Most often there is only one which is placed in front of the host; but sometimes there is one between every two guests.

Menus on fashionable tables never include obvious accessories, such as celery, olives, rolls, peppermints, radishes, currant jelly, chocolates, fruit, any more than they include ice water or butter.

PLACE CARDS

The place cards are usually plain, about an inch and a half high by two inches long, sometimes slightly larger. Fancy cards, while suitable on special occasions, such as Christmas or a birthday, have gone out of fashion on a formal table.

SEATING THE TABLE

As has already been observed, the most practical way to seat the table is to write the names on individual cards first, and then "place" them as though playing solitaire; the guest of honor on the host's right, the second lady in rank on his left; the most distinguished or oldest gentleman on the right of the hostess, and the other guests filled in between.

WHO IS THE GUEST OF HONOR?

The guest of honor is the oldest lady present, or a stranger whom you wish for some reason to honor. A bride at her first dinner in your house, after her return from her honeymoon, may be given, if you choose, precedence over older people. The guest of honor is *always* she who is taken in to dinner by the host and placed on his right, whether she is one for whom the dinner is given or merely one who was selected at random. This place at table makes her the guest of honor.* The lady of next greatest importance sits on the host's left and is taken in to dinner by the gentleman on whose right she

---

* In Washington, for instance, even though the dinner be given for a guest of medium rank, the ladies of highest rank have the honor-places on either side of the host. The lady for whom the dinner is actually given is merely "among those present," unless those of higher rank agree to waive precedence.

sits. The hostess is always the last to go into the dining room at a formal dinner unless the President of the United States or the Governor at a dinner in his own State be present. In these exceptional cases the hostess would go in to dinner with the guest of honor, who leads the way, and the wife of the President or Governor would follow immediately with the host.

THE ENVELOPES FOR THE GENTLEMEN

In an envelope addressed to each gentleman is put a card on which is written the name of the lady he is to take down to dinner. This card just fits in the envelope, which is an inch or slightly less high and about two inches long. When the envelopes are addressed and filled, they are arranged in two neat rows on a silver tray and put in the front hall. The tray is presented to each gentleman just before he goes into the drawing room, on his arrival.

THE TABLE DIAGRAM

The new and exceedingly practical method of telling each gentleman where he is to sit at a very large table is to choose a small fold-over card instead of the usual one in an envelope. His name is on its front fold and his partner's name inside, and below her name in the lower half of the fold is a small engraved diagram showing the table and the door of entrance and the location he is to find marked with pen strokes.

[diagram: Mrs Neighbor — ENTER arrow, table with location marked "A"]

Or if it is so big a dinner that there are many separate tables, the tables are numbered with standing placards (as at a public dinner) and the table number written on each lady's name-card. (Do not say escort-card!)

THE HOSTESS AT THE SIDE

When the number of guests is a multiple of four, the host and the hostess never sit opposite each other. It would bring two ladies and two gentlemen together if they did. At a table which seats two together at each end, the fact that the host is opposite a gentleman and the hostess opposite a lady is not noticeable; nor is it ever noticeable at a round table. But at a narrow table which has room for only one at the end, the hostess invariably sits in the seat next to that which is properly her own, putting in her place a gentleman at the end. The host usually keeps his seat rather than the hostess because the seat of honor is on his right; and in the etiquette governing dinners, the host and not the hostess is the more important personage!

When there are only four, they keep their own places, otherwise the host and hostess would sit next to each other. At a dinner of eight, twelve, sixteen, twenty, etc., the host keeps his place, but at supper for eight or twelve, the hostess keeps *her* place and the host moves a place to the right or left because the hostess at supper pours coffee or chocolate. And although the host keeps his seat at a formal dinner in honor of the lady he takes in, at a little dinner of eight, where there is no guest of honor, the host does not necessarily keep his seat at the expense of his wife unless he carves, in which case he must have the end place; just as at supper she has the end place in order to pour. (See Diagram No. 2, page 341.)

SIDEWALK, HALL, AND DRESSING ROOMS

In other days very big or formal dinners often had an awning, especially at a house where there was much entertaining; but dinners of this importance have been gradually growing fewer, until an awning now suggests a wedding at least. In any case the man on the pavement must, if it is raining, shelter each arriving guest under his doorman's umbrella from motor to door. If it does not rain, he merely opens the doors of vehicles. Checks are never given at dinners, unless the guests number fifty or more. "Mr. Worldly's car" is called to the chauffeur on duty at the front steps, and he notifies Mr. Worldly's chauffeur.

In all modern houses of people who do much entertaining, there are two rooms on the entrance floor, built sometimes as dressing rooms and nothing else, but more often they are small reception rooms, each with a lavatory off of it. In the one given to the ladies, there is always a dressing table with toilet appointments on it, and the lady's maid should be on duty to give whatever service may be required. When there is no dressing room on the ground floor, the back of the hall is arranged with coat hangers and an improvised dressing table for the ladies, since modern people—in New York at least—never go upstairs to a bedroom. In fact, nine ladies out of ten drop their evening cloaks at the front door, handing them to the servant on duty, and go at once without more ado to the drawing room. A lady arriving in her own closed car can't be very much blown about, in a completely airtight compartment and in two or three minutes of time! Gentlemen also leave their hats and coats in the front part of the hall.

ANNOUNCING GUESTS

A gentleman always falls behind his wife in entering the drawing room. If the butler knows the guests, he merely announces the wife's name first and then the husband's. If he does not know them by sight, he asks whichever is nearest to him, "What name, please?" And whichever one is asked answers, "Mr. and Mrs. Lake."

The butler then precedes the guests a few steps into the room where the hostess is stationed, and, standing aside, says in a low tone but very distinctly, "Mrs. Lake," a pause and then, "Mr. Lake." Married people are usually announced separately as above, but occasionally people have their guests announced "Mr. and Mrs.——."

ANNOUNCING PERSONS OF RANK

All men of high executive rank are not only announced first, but take precedence of their wives in entering the room. The President of the United States is announced simply, "The President." His title needs no qualifying appendage, since he, and he solely, is *the* President. He enters first, and alone, of course; and then "Mrs. Roosevelt," being announced, follows. The Governor of a State is in courtesy announced as "His Excellency" but the correct announcement would be "the Governor of (name the state)" and then "Mrs. Goodland." He enters the room and Mrs. Goodland follows. "His Honor the Mayor and Mrs. Lake" observe the same etiquette; or in a city other than his own he would be announced "The Mayor of Chicago and Mrs. Lake."

Other announcements are "The Honorable the Chief Justice and Mrs. Law," "The Secretary of State and Mrs. Eminent," "Senator and Mrs. Washington"; but the senator allows his wife to enter the room first, because his office is not executive. An ambassador must be announced, "His Excellency the British Ambassador" and then "Lady Howard!" He enters the room first. A minister plenipotentiary is announced, "His Excellency the Swedish Minister."* He enters

---

* "Excellency," though strictly a title belonging to none but an ambassador, is always granted by courtesy to a minister plenipotentiary. In many of our embassies and legations, we Americans make ourselves absurd in the eyes of Europeans by exacting that counselors, first secretaries—almost everyone in the service—be addressed by subordinates and strangers as "Excellency," which is *not* correct. The only exception is made in favor of a chargé d'affaires. This courtesy is, however, temporary and ceases upon the return of his chief.

and a moment later "Mrs. Ogren" follows. But a first secretary and his wife are announced without other title than their own, "Count and Countess European," or "Mr. and Mrs. American."*

The President, the Vice-President, the governor of a state, the mayor of a city, the ambassador of a foreign power—in other words, all executives—take precedence over their wives and enter rooms and vehicles first. But senators, representatives, secretaries of legations and all other officials who are not executives, allow their wives to precede them, just as they would if they were private individuals.

Foreigners who have hereditary titles are announced by them. "His Grace the Duke" or "Her Grace the Duchess of Overthere," "The Marquis and Marchioness of Landsend," or "Sir Edward and Lady Blank," etc. Titles are invariably translated into English. "Count and Countess Lorraine," not "M. le Comte et Mme. la Comtesse Lorraine." Archbishops have heretofore been called Your Grace, but they are now addressed as Your Excellency instead.

HOW A HOSTESS RECEIVES AT A FORMAL DINNER

On all occasions of formality, at a dinner as well as at a ball, the hostess stands near the door of her drawing room, and as guests are announced, she greets them with a smile and a handshake and says something pleasant to each. What she says is nothing very important; charm of expression and of manner can often wordlessly express a far more gracious welcome than the most elaborate phrases (which as a matter of fact should be studiously avoided). Unless a woman's loveliness springs from generosity of heart and sympathy, her manners, no matter how perfectly practiced, are nothing but cosmetics applied to hide a want of inner beauty; precisely as rouge and powder are applied in the hope of hiding the lack of a beautiful skin. One device is much like the other; very pleasing unless brought into comparison with perfection of the real.

Mrs. Oldname, for instance, usually welcomes you with some such sentence as, "I am very glad to see you" or "I am so glad you could come!" Or if it is raining, she very likely tells you that you were very unselfish to come out in the storm. But no matter what she says or whether anything at all, she takes your hand with a firm pressure and her smile is really a *smile* of welcome, not a mechanical exercise of the facial muscles. She gives you always—even if only for the moment—her complete attention; and you go into her drawing room with a distinct feeling that you are under the roof, not of a mere

* Should a woman be appointed Ambassador or Minister, she would receive the title of Her Excellency the American Ambassadress—or Minister—and of course enters the room before her husband.

acquaintance, but of a friend. Mr. Oldname, who stands never very far from his wife, always comes forward and, grasping your hand, accentuates his wife's more subtle but no less vivid welcome. And either you join a friend standing near, or he presents you, if you are a man, to a lady; or if you are a lady, he presents a man to you.

Some hostesses, especially those of the Lion-Hunting and the New-to-Best-Society variety, are much given to explanations, and love to say, "Mrs. Jones, I want you to meet Mrs. Smith. Mrs. Smith is the author of *Dragged from the Depths*, a most enlightening work of psychic insight." Or to a good-looking woman, "I am putting you next to Mavro Bey—I want him to carry back a flattering impression of American women!"

But people of good breeding do not exploit their distinguished guests with embarrassing hyperbole, or make personal remarks. Both are in worst possible taste. Do not understand by this that helpful explanations cannot be made; it is only that they must not be embarrassingly made, or overdone. Nor must a "specialist's" subject be forced upon him, like a pair of manacles, by any power-displaying hostess who has captured him. In illustration of the helpful explanation as indicated above, Mrs. Oldname might perhaps, in order to assist conversation for an interesting but reticent person, tell a lady just before going in to dinner, "Mr. Traveler, who is sitting next to you at the table, has just come back from two years alone with the cannibals." This is not to exploit her "traveled lion," but to give his neighbor a starting point for conversation at table. And although personal remarks are never good form, it would be permissible for an older lady in welcoming a very young one, especially a débutante or a bride, to say, "How lovely you look, Mary dear, and what an adorable dress you have on!" But it would be objectionable to say to an older lady, "That is a very handsome string of pearls you are wearing." And never anywhere or at any time may one ask, "How much did it cost?"

THE DUTY OF THE HOST

The host stands fairly near his wife, so that if any guest seems to be unknown, he can present him to someone and not let him stand alone. At formal dinners introductions are never general, and people do not as a rule speak to strangers, except those next to them at table or in the drawing room after dinner. The host therefore makes a few introductions if necessary. Before dinner, since the hostess is standing (and no gentleman may therefore sit down), and as it is awkward for a lady who is sitting to talk with a gentleman who is standing, the ladies usually also stand until dinner is announced.

WHEN DINNER IS ANNOUNCED

It is the duty of the butler to "count heads" so that he may know when the company has arrived. As soon as he has announced the last person, he notifies the cook. The cook being ready, the butler, having glanced into the dining room to see that windows have been closed and the candles on the table lighted, enters the drawing room, approaches the hostess, bows, and says quietly, "Dinner is served." Or if she happens to be looking at him, he merely bows.

The host offers his right arm to the lady of honor and leads the way to the dining room. All the other gentlemen offer their arms to the ladies appointed to them, and follow the host, in an orderly procession, two and two; the only order of precedence is that the host and his partner lead, while the hostess and her partner come last. At all formal dinners, place cards being on the table, the hostess does not direct people where to sit. If there was no table diagram in the hall, the butler usually stands just within the dining room door and tells each gentleman as he approaches "Right" or "Left." He has plenty of time to reach the chair of the hostess before her, as she always enters the dining room last.

WHEN THERE IS NO HOST

A hostess who is either a widow or unmarried asks the man she knows best—a relative if there is one present—to "act as host." He gives his arm to the guest of honor and leads the way to the dining table, where he sits opposite the hostess. After dinner he leads the men to the smoking room and later to the drawing room to "join the ladies."

THE MANNERS OF A HOSTESS

First of all, a hostess must show each of her guests equal and impartial attention. Also, although engrossed in the person she is talking to, she must be able to notice anything amiss that may occur. The more competent her servants, the less she need be aware of details herself, but the hostess giving a formal dinner with uncertain dining-room efficiency has a far from smooth path before her. No matter what happens, if all the china in the pantry falls with a crash, she must not appear to have heard it. No matter what goes wrong, she must cover it as best she may, and at the same time cover the fact that she is covering it. To give hectic directions merely accentuates the awkwardness. If a dish appears that is unpresentable, she as quietly as possible orders the next one to be brought in. If a guest knocks over a glass and breaks it, even though the glass be utterly irreplaceable, her only concern must seemingly be that her guest has been made uncomfortable. She says, "I am sorry!" But the glass is *nothing!* And she has a fresh glass brought (even though it doesn't match) and dismisses all thought of the matter.

Both the host and hostess must keep the conversation going, if it lags, but this is not as definitely their duty at a formal as at an informal dinner. It is at the small dinner that the skillful hostess has need of what Thackeray calls the "showman" quality. She brings each guest forward in turn to the center of the stage. In a lull in the conversation she says beguilingly to a clever but shy man, "John, what was that story you told me——" and then she repeats briefly an introduction to a topic in which "John" particularly shines. Or later on, she begins a narrative and breaks off suddenly, turning to someone else, "*You tell them!*"

These examples are rather bald, and overemphasize the method in order to make it clear. Practice and the knowledge of human nature, or of the particular temperament with which she is trying to deal, can alone tell her when she may lead or provoke this or that one to being at his best, to his own satisfaction as well as that of the others. Her own character and sympathy are the only real "showman" assets, since no one "shows" to advantage except in a congenial environment.

THE LATE GUEST

Fifteen minutes is the established length of time that a hostess may wait for a belated guest. To wait more than twenty minutes, at the outside, would be showing lack of consideration to many for the sake of one. When the late guest finally enters the dining room, it is she who must go up to the hostess and apologize for being late. The hostess remains seated and the guest merely shakes hands quickly in order that all the men at table need not rise. The hostess must never take the guest to task, but should say something polite and conciliatory such as, "I was sure you did not want us to wait dinner!" In other days the newcomer was always served with dinner from the beginning unless she was considerate enough to direct the servant who held her chair, "Let me begin with this course." But today so many of the younger people are carelessly—on occasion even wilfully—late that it has become proper to bring no dish back after it has left the dining room.

ETIQUETTE OF GLOVES AND NAPKIN

Ladies always wear gloves to formal dinners and take them off at table. Entirely off. It is hideous to leave them on the arm, merely turning back the hands. Both gloves and bag are supposed to be laid across the lap, and one is supposed to lay the napkin, folded once in half across the lap too, on top of the gloves and wrist bag and possibly fan, and all three are supposed to stay in place on a slippery satin skirt on a lap that more often than not slants downward.

FORMAL DINNERS

It is all very well for etiquette to say "They stay there," but every woman knows they don't! And this is quite a nice question. If you obey etiquette and lay the napkin on top of the bag and fan and gloves loosely across your satin-covered knees, it will depend merely upon chance whether the avalanche starts right, left or forward onto the floor. There is just *one* way to keep these four articles (including the lap as one) from disintegrating, which is to cover the fan and gloves, and wrist bag too, with the napkin put cornerwise across your knees and tuck the two side corners under like a lap robe, with the gloves and the fan tied in place, as it were.

This ought not to be put into a book of etiquette, which should say you must do nothing of the kind, but it is either do that or have the gentleman next you groping under the table at the end of the meal; and it is impossible to imagine that etiquette should wish to conserve the picture of "gentlemen on all fours" as the concluding ceremony at dinners.

A vanity case can be put on the table or added to the lap collection, as you choose, but a bag of even small size has no place on a dinner table.

THE TURNING OF THE TABLE

The turning of the table is accomplished by the hostess, who merely turns from the gentleman (on her left probably) with whom she has been talking through the soup and the fish course to the one on her right. As she turns, the lady to whom the "right" gentleman has been talking turns to the gentleman further on, and in a moment everyone at table is talking to a new neighbor. Sometimes a single couple who have become very much engrossed refuse to change partners, and the whole table is blocked, leaving one lady and one gentleman on either side of the block staring alone at their plates. At this point the hostess has to come to the rescue by attracting the blocking lady's attention and saying, "Sally, you cannot talk to Professor Bugge any longer! Mr. Smith has been trying his best to attract your attention."

"Sally" being in this way brought awake, is obliged to pay attention to Mr. Smith, and Professor Bugge, little as he may feel inclined, must turn his attention to the other side. To persist in carrying on their own conversation at the expense of others would be inexcusably rude, not only to their hostess but to everyone present.

At a dinner not long ago, Mr. Kindhart, sitting next to Mrs. Wellborn and left to himself because of the assiduity of the lady's farther partner, slid his own name-card across and in front of her, to bring her attention to the fact that it was "his turn." Other hostesses have been known to send a note by a servant saying, "Please talk to Mr. Jones on your right."

ENEMIES MUST BURY HATCHETS

One unbreakable rule of etiquette is that you must talk to your next-door neighbor at a dinner table. You *must;* that is all there is about it!

Even if you are placed next to someone with whom you have had a bitter quarrel, consideration for your hostess, who would be distressed if she knew you had been put in a disagreeable place, and further consideration for the rest of the table which is otherwise "blocked," exacts that you give no outward sign of your repugnance and that you make a pretense, at least for a little while, of talking together.

At dinner once, Mrs. Toplofty, finding herself next to a man she quite openly despised, said to him with apparent placidity, "I shall not talk to you—because I don't care to. But for the sake of my hostess I shall say my multiplication tables. Twice one are two, twice two are four——" and she continued on through the tables, making him alternate them with her. As soon as she politely could, she turned again to her other companion.

MANNERS AT TABLE

It used to be an offense, and it still is considered impolite, to refuse dishes at the table, because your refusal implies that you do not like what is offered you. If this is true, you should be doubly careful to take at least a little on your plate and make a pretense of eating some of it, since to refuse dish after dish cannot fail to distress your hostess. If you are "on a diet" and accepted the invitation with that stipulation, your not eating is excusable; but even then to sit with an empty plate in front of you throughout a meal makes you a seemingly reproachful table companion for those of good appetite sitting next to you.

ATTACKING A COMPLICATED DISH

When a dinner has been prepared by a chef who prides himself on being a decorative artist, the guest of honor and whoever else may be the first to be served have quite a problem to know which part of an intricate structure is to be eaten and what part is scenic effect!

The main portion is generally clear enough; the uncertainty is in whether the flowers are edible vegetables and whether the things that look like ducks are potatoes or trimming. If there are six or more, the chances are they are edible, and that very few of a kind are embellishments only. Rings around food are nearly always to be eaten; platforms under food seldom, if ever, are. Anything that looks like pastry is to be eaten; and anything divided into separate units should be taken on your plate complete. You should not try to cut a section from anything that has already been divided into portions in the kitchen. Aspics and desserts are, it must be said, occasionally Chinese puzzles; but if, in taking what looks like something eatable, you do help yourself to part of the decoration, no great harm is done.

Dishes are *never* passed from hand to hand at a formal dinner—or even at an informal one in a formally appointed house. Often people pass salted nuts to each other, or an extra sweet from a dish near-by, but not circling the table.

(For service in a servantless house see Chapter 31.)

LEAVING THE TABLE

At the end of the dinner, when the last dish of sweets has been passed and the hostess sees that no one is any longer eating, she looks across the table, and catching the eye of one of the ladies, slowly stands up. The one who happens to be observing also stands up, and in a moment everyone is standing. The gentlemen offer their arms to their partners and conduct them back to the drawing room or the library or wherever they are to sit during the rest of the evening.

Each gentleman then bows slightly, takes leave of his partner, and, with the other gentlemen, follows the host to the room where their after-dinner coffee, liqueurs, cigars, and cigarettes are being served. It is perfectly correct for a gentleman to talk to any other who happens to be sitting near him, whether he knows him or not.

At the end of twenty minutes or so, the host must take the opportunity of the first lull in the conversation to suggest that they "join the ladies" in the drawing room.

In a house where there is no extra room to smoke in, the gentlemen do not conduct the ladies to the drawing room, but stay where they are (the ladies leaving alone) and have their coffee, cigars, liqueurs and conversation sitting around the table.

In the drawing room, meanwhile, the ladies are having coffee, cigarettes, and liqueurs passed to them.* There is no modern New York hostess, scarcely even an old-fashioned one, who does not have cigarettes passed after dinner.

At a dinner of ten or twelve, the five or six ladies most often sit in one group, or possibly two sit by themselves, and three or four together; but at a very large dinner they inevitably fall into groups of

* Coffee is served three ways: 1. The footman proffers a tray of cups, saucers and sugar; the butler follows with coffee pot alone and pours into the cup held in the guest's hand. 2. A tray—for illustration, see Index—is proffered by the butler or the waitress to guests who help themselves. 3. The tray of cups and sugar is held on servant's left hand. The guest puts sugar into one of the cups and the servant pours coffee with the right hand. Liqueurs are offered exactly as coffee in No. 2 and No. 3. The guests pour their own, or saying "Chartreuse" or "Mint, please," their choice is poured for them. Cigarettes are arranged on a tray with matches, or a lighter which is burning. (For the informal service of coffee—and for café brûlot—see page 366.)

four or five or so each. In any case, the hostess must see that no one is left to sit alone. If one of her guests is a stranger to the others, the hostess draws a chair near one of the groups and, offering it to her single guest, sits beside her. After a while, when this particular guest has at least joined the outskirts of the conversation of the group, the hostess leaves her and joins another group where perhaps she sits beside someone else who has been somewhat left out.

When there is no one who needs any especial attention, the hostess nevertheless sits for a time with each of the different groups in order to spend at least a part of the evening with all of her guests.

THE GENTLEMEN RETURN

When the gentlemen return to the drawing room, if there is a particular lady whom one of them wants to talk to, he naturally goes directly to where she is and sits down beside her.

Usually, the ladies on the ends, being accessible, are more likely to be joined by the first gentlemen entering than is the one in the center, whom it is impossible to reach. This is, however, quite simply done. When John Jones particularly wants to talk with Miss Smith, he goes up to her, bows, and asks, "Will you come and talk to me?" Whereupon she leaves her sandwiched position, and goes to another part of the room and sits down wherever there are two vacant seats.

Needless to say, gentlemen should not continue to talk together after returning to the drawing room, as it is not courteous to those of the ladies who are thus necessarily left without partners.

At informal dinners, and even at many formal ones, bridge tables are set up in an adjoining room, if not in the drawing room. Those few who do not play bridge spend half an hour (or less) in conversation and then go home, unless there is some special diversion.

TAKING LEAVE

That the guest of honor must be the first to take leave was in former times so fixed a rule that everyone used to sit on and on, no matter how late it became, waiting for her whose duty it was to go! More often than not, the guest of honor was an absent-minded old lady, or celebrity, who very likely was vaguely saying to herself, "Oh, my! are these people *never* going home?" until by and by it dawned upon her—or someone reminded her—that the obligation was her own!

But today, although it is still the obligation of the guest who sat on the host's right to make the move to go, it is not considered ill-mannered, if the hour is growing late, for another lady to rise first. In fact, unless the guest of honor is one *really*, meaning a stranger or an elderly lady of distinction, there is no actual precedence about her being the one first to go. If the hour is very early when the first lady rises, the hostess always rises too.

The guest merely says, "Good night. Thank you so much." The hostess answers, "I am so glad you could come!" She has already pressed a bell for the servants to be in the dressing rooms and halls. When one guest leaves, they all leave—except those at the bridge tables. They all say "Good night" to whomever they were talking with and shake hands, and then going up to their hostess, they shake hands and say, "Thank you for asking us" or "Thank you for a very pleasant evening."

"Good night!" and "Thank you so much!" is the usual expression. And the hostess answers, "It was so nice to see you again" or "I'm glad you could come."

In the dressing room, or in the hall, the maid is waiting to help the ladies with their wraps, and the butler is at the door. When Mr. and Mrs. Jones are ready to leave, he goes out on the front steps and says, "Mr. Jones's car!" The host's chauffeur signals to Mr. Jones's chauffeur and then reports to the butler, who in turn says to Mr. Jones, "Your car is at the door, Sir" and they go out.

The bridge people leave as they finish their games; sometimes a table at a time or most likely two together. (Husbands and wives are never, if it can be avoided, put at the same table.) Young people in saying good night say, "Good night. It has been too wonderful!" or "Good night, and thank you *so* much." And the hostess smiles and says, "So glad you could come!" or "Good night!"

THE "STAG" OR "BACHELOR" DINNER

A man's dinner is sometimes called a "stag" or a "bachelor" dinner, and as its name implies, is a dinner given by a man and for men only. A man's dinner is usually given to celebrate an occasion of welcome or farewell. The best-known bachelor dinner is the one given by the groom just before his wedding. Other dinners are more likely to be given by one man (or a group of men) in honor of a noted citizen who has returned from a long absence, or who is about to embark on an expedition or a foreign mission. Or a young man perhaps gives a dinner for a friend's twenty-first birthday; or an older man gives one merely because he has a quantity of game which he has shot and wants to share with his special friends.

Nearly always a man's dinner is given at the host's club or in a private room in a hotel. But if a man chooses to give a stag dinner in his own house, his wife (or his mother) should *not* appear. For a wife to come downstairs and receive the guests for him cannot be too strongly condemned as out of place. Such a maneuver on her part, instead of impressing his guests with her gracious hospitality, is far more likely to make them think what a "poor worm" her husband must be to allow himself to be hen-pecked. And for a mother to appear at a son's dinner is, if anything, worse. An essential piece of advice to every woman is: No matter how much you may want to say "How do you do" to your husband's or your son's friends—*don't!* (In the house of Mrs. Three-in-One even she may not wait at table. She must hire someone on that occasion.)

CHAIRMAN (OR TOASTMASTER) AT A PUBLIC DINNER

The chairman, or toastmaster or master of ceremonies, sits at the center of the most prominent table, usually on a dais.

After the dessert is served, the chairman rises and makes a few remarks, or perhaps a very short address on the association or object of the dinner, and ends with a reference to the first speaker, telling

```
    x  x  x  x  D  B  A  C  E  x  x  x
   ┌─────────────────────────────────────┐
   │                                     │
   │           SPEAKERS' TABLE           │
   │                                     │
   └─────────────────────────────────────┘

        ( 1 )    ( 2 )    ( 3 )    ( 4 )
```

KEY: A: THE TOASTMASTER'S PLACE; B: GUEST FOR WHOM DINNER IS GIVEN, OR MOST PROMINENT PERSON PRESENT; C: THE NEXT MOST PROMINENT; THEN D, THEN E AND XXX: ALL THOSE WHO ARE TO BE CALLED ON TO SPEAK; AND OTHER PARTICULARLY HONORED GUESTS. 1, 2, 3, 4, ETC.; GENERAL GUESTS' TABLES

what he (or she) has accomplished, or is trying to accomplish, and then adds, "I have great pleasure in introducing Mr. Smith" or "It gives me great pleasure to introduce Mr. Smith" (or Miss Jones).

The chairman sits down and the speaker stands up.

When the first speaker sits down, the chairman again stands, thanks the first speaker and says something pleasant about his talk—that it was interesting or delightful or instructive or whatever most aptly describes it—and then introduces the next speaker—probably with a brief reference to his especial qualifications. Or possibly he says, "Our next speaker is one who is known to, and loved by, us all: Professor Bugge." And so on throughout the list. The principal speaker is usually last on the program.

TOASTS

It is impossible to suggest definite toasts because they ought to be personal and spontaneous. Usually they are scarcely longer than the toast at the bridegroom's dinner: "To the bride!" "To the Professor! may he live to be a hundred and his teaching endure a thousand years." "To the team! whether it win or lose, may it always be glorious."

At a dinner given by a group of young women in honor of their mothers, the chairman might give this toast: "To those to whom we owe all that we are, and for whom we would like to be all that they believe we are—Our Mothers!" Or, on the other hand, a group of mothers at a dinner given for their daughters might say: "To those of the newer generation who, in blazing new trails, carry our faith, our hopes and our hearts' encouragement—a toast to our daughters!"

But as noted above, each toast ought to express the sentiment of the person proposing it. And on general principles, the shorter it is, the better.

The subject purposely saved for the conclusion of this chapter is one the importance of which cannot be overemphasized. In fact, it has, within the last ten years, become known almost throughout the civilized world.

THE GREAT AMERICAN RUDENESS

The outstanding rudeness in America is that of the hostess who helps herself first when a woman guest is seated at her table. In fact, if such a custom is to be allowed to continue spreading, what possible meaning remains in the word "courtesy"? Since consideration of those who are her guests is the very first rule of courteous behavior, the hostess who helps herself to the fresh and untouched dishes and then lets her only —or her most important—woman guest take her leavings is either unthinking (which is quite likely), or she is intentionally rude (which cannot be likely).

Although less threatening than it was a few years ago, the hostess who permits herself to be served before any woman guest at her table is still encountered in sufficiently numerous localities to make it of importance to trace the behavior to its separate origins.

Example No. 1—This goes back to the days of the Borgias, when hosts invited enemies to their tables with the intention of poisoning them. It, therefore, became the duty of every innocent host or hostess to partake of each dish or flagon first, to assure his guests that neither food nor drink was poisoned. It is customary when fine vintage wines are served, to pour about a teaspoonful into the host's glass to see whether the wine is good. If not good, he orders another bottle. But his glass is never filled until the last at table.

Example No. 2—In the crude days when frontier towns were rough, many of the guests invited to a gentlewoman's table were quite unversed in table manners. Their hostess, therefore, put them at ease not only by helping herself to each dish first, but by eating first as well, so that they who might know little about the use of table implements could follow her example. But this behavior, which was proper then, is not—and never has been—proper when the guests are quite as skilled as their hostess in the use of a serving fork and a spoon. This "showing their guests how" is the reason most often given by those who defend the hostess-first practice. It would be hard to imagine a reason less polite.

Even if the dish is an architectural masterpiece like those of the nineties, nothing is simpler for one who is served first than to say to whoever is waiting at table, "Do I take this?" prodding lightly with the fork—or "Do I cut here?" This is done every day! In fact, many New Yorkers can well remember an old-time butler whose dishes were about three parts ornament to one part food, and who frequently advised one who had taken a dab of pink hominy foundation and a raw-turnip rose, "The brown piece at the right, Madam, is very tasty." Or if a hostess had reason to suppose her guest of honor may be embarrassed—an old lady perhaps who does not see very well—then the dish might be cut into and the serving spoon inserted beneath the first helping and the fork at the hand above it, in the way a dish is prepared for a child who does not otherwise know what or how much to take.

Example No. 3—There is a line of American tradition which traces back to the patriarchal system where three or even four generations lived at the old homestead when great-grandmother sat in her high-backed, cushioned armchair at the head of her table, and first dishes and first courtesy were shown to her because she was the matriarch. When visitors came to meals, they were not likely to be as old as she, for roads were too rough to entice old ladies from their firesides or gardens. But this deferential practice of first serving a hostess who was very old became an example of impropriety when copied by her newly married granddaughter, who, without taking the trouble to think, jumped to the conclusion that what Grandmother did was right. Quite true! But what was right for a great-grandmother surrounded by members of her own family, is far from right for a hostess of twenty—or even of fifty, at whose table sit neighbors or strangers. There is no difference whatever between the rudeness of a hostess who chooses the piece she prefers and gives second choice to a guest, and the rudeness of a child who helps herself to her own choice pieces of candy and then hands the discarded pieces to the child who has come to play with her.

Example No. 4—Royalty, when seated with the nobility or commoners, is served first (for that matter, is served from set-apart dishes). This has nothing to do with us unless it points out the presumption of one who considers herself royalty and her friends of a lower class!

Example No. 5 is the occasional discourtesy in the house of the well-born but absent-minded hostess who is carelessly unaware of what her badly trained butler or waitress is doing! This does not affect those who, knowing better, neither care nor notice, but it does affect Mrs. Littletown, whose worldly experience has not been very wide, and who goes home and unquestioningly copies what she has seen young Mrs. Smartan Careless is letting her butler do. A number of her friends in turn copy her. And so it goes!

Example No. 6—This is not really so much an example as a contributing cause. Exactly as it is the natural instinct of an office employee to devote his energies to his employer rather than to anyone else, this same impulse is characteristic of the domestic employee. Today wages are paid usually by the lady of the house; therefore those in her employ will be inclined to serve her first unless otherwise directed—and on occasion persistently directed.

Example No. 7—And perhaps the principal offender against good taste is the self-styled "School" for domestic employees who teach (so it is said) this misbehavior. When a pupil from this school serves the first meal in the house of Mrs. Fastidious, this first rudeness is the last. But a new employer who is perhaps for the first time engaging a butler, hesitates to criticize his manner of serving, no matter what it may be; and this adds still another link to the chain of rudeness, as she does not dare to insist that he serve another lady first. (When only gentlemen are present, the hostess is of course served first.)

29

Modern Dinner Giving

THE EVERYDAY DINNER

IN the preceding chapter every inflexible requirement of a dinner which according to etiquette is alone correctly formal was given in detail. This was NOT meant to discourage dinner giving by those whose houses (and purses) are not equipped to comply with its exactions, but was intended merely as the complete pattern from which each hostess selects or adapts as many details as are practical to her personal use. Perhaps in time the term "formal dinner" may come to mean nothing more exacting than company at dinner, but correctly the term "formal dinner"—or dinner of ceremony, which means the same thing—can be applied only to the most exacting and most ceremonious social function that exists. Correctly, too, the word "formal" has nothing to do with charm or hospitality or any quality of delightful entertaining.

THREE CLASSIFICATIONS OF TABLE SERVICE

Accurately speaking, there are three classifications of table service: first, formal or European service—described in the preceding chapter and permitting no deviation from ceremonious forms; second, American service—permitting great flexibility; and, third, hostess-alone service, which, as the term implies, is the most difficult as well as most important service, since it is practiced in by far the greatest number of American homes.

The one detail that, at one end of the scale, separates formal service from semi-formal American service is any carving or serving by the host or hostess at table; and the one detail that, at the other end of the scale, separates American service from hostess-herself service is having no servant to wait even partially in the dining room.

THE SERVICE KNOWN AS AMERICAN

American service can be quite as formal—in so far as having many servants and following an exacting ritual is concerned—as that in the most formally run house. Or it can, on the other hand, be adapted to whatever is most practical for each family's particular needs.

The formal aspect of American service is perhaps best illustrated by considering that in the house of the Squires. Mr. Squire, for instance, carves at table, and Mrs. Squire pours after-dinner coffee in the living room. Otherwise every detail of table setting is formal.

Mr. Squire's practice of carving at table, which is otherwise formally served, is more complicated as well as slower than completely formal service. In the latter case the carving is all done in the kitchen, while the soup or fish is being eaten. Plates are exchanged, and at once the platter of cut and arranged meat is proffered each person, who helps herself or himself. But in the almost-formal house of Mr. Squire there is an obstructingly long ritual—preceding the meat course—of exchanging used fish plates for clean plates all around the table; and then putting one hot plate in front of Mr. Squire, waiting for it to be filled, taking it up with the right hand, putting a fresh hot plate in front of Mr. Squire with the left hand, picking up the plate of the one to be served and putting down the filled plate; going to the side table, leaving the exchanged plate, getting a fresh hot plate, returning to Mr. Squire, and repeating the same procedure. Each time a plate is filled, the waitress (or butler) takes the plate with the serving on it where she (or he) is told—"For Mrs. Jones," "For Miss Mary," "For Mr. Jones," and so on.

Happily, a much simpler method of service is to put a stack of hot plates in front of the one who serves, and let the maid lift each plate as it is served and take it to the one for whom it is intended. When all have been served, she passes the vegetables.

At the Neighbors' at the opposite end of the scale, the family of eight are "waited on" by one maid, who sets a stack of soup plates in front of Mrs. Neighbor and then the soup tureen. Mrs. Neighbor ladles the soup and the maid carries it to each in turn, and then goes back to the kitchen. (Water is in each glass and bread and butter on each bread and butter plate when the family sit down.) When she is rung for, the maid takes away the plates two at a time, stacks them QUIETLY on the serving table behind the screen, and then carries out the tureen. Then she brings in the stack of hot dinner plates and sets them in front of Mr. Neighbor, who puts a piece of meat—also gravy, stuffing or condiment—on the plate at the top of the pile, and then, when it is filled, hands it either right or left in the nearest direction toward the person for whom it is intended (in front of whom no formal place plate stands); meanwhile the maid brings in the vegetables (a double or triple dish is most practical) and proffers this to each person who has been served the meat. She also proffers bread and pours water as necessary. As she returns to the kitchen, she carries out the used soup plates. Dessert or salad is served by Mrs. Neighbor and passed by the maid, who then carries the coffee tray into the living room.

(For details of dinner giving in a house that has no servant, see **Chapter 31**, also Index.)

AMERICAN SERVICE TABLE SETTING

The table must be larger than the table set for formal service, because room must be left for the tea service or the soup tureen at one end, and for the meat or fish platter at the other, and quite probably for the vegetable dishes in between. Otherwise the setting is much the same. Table cover of what you please—damask or runners or doilies, or bare table with place mats—centerpiece, candlesticks or candelabra for evening light.

The first change from the formal arrangement is that, instead of limiting forks to three, all flat silver to be used is put at each place. As always, the implement to be used last is put nearest the plate, the one to be used first on the outside. The service plate, which is an inseparable item of formal service, is put on the informal table only when it is to be used. Otherwise each place at the table is left plateless.

In many houses of notable hospitality, the salad ingredients are attractively arranged in a set of bowls and bottles that fit on a tray, and the tray is brought in with the salad bowl and put in front of the hostess, who mixes the dressing herself. In one of the loveliest old houses in the South, salad-mixing is a veritable ritual—and goodness only knows what goes into the mixture. A few drops of this, or shakes of that, or spoonfuls of the other, all stirred and stirred with a wooden fork and spoon. It is quite wonderful! And—who knows?—perhaps its deliciousness is accented by the display of its making.

The same idea exactly has made certain restaurants in Paris famous—all because the chef, or the proprietor himself, cooks and mixes something before your eyes. The ducks of the "Tour d'Argent," the Crêpes Suzette of Joseph seem to acquire an added allure by the visible process. In short, preparing a dish at the table (which many servantless hostesses think of as a handicap) may easily become an especially appreciated feature of hospitality.

INFORMAL SERVICE OF COFFEE

The most popular informal way of serving coffee is to place a good-sized tray on a coffee table or stand. On the tray is a percolator or other coffee-making machine—most pleasingly one of glass, which is enticing to watch, whereas an opaque one merely emphasizes the time you have to wait for the coffee to be made. You, when you are hostess, sit near this tray, turn on the switch or light the lamp, make the coffee, pour it—with much sugar, little sugar, no sugar, as each guest directs—and hand it exactly as at afternoon tea. If the cups are large, cream is always offered. This is now also done when the cups are small.

CAFÉ BRÛLOT

In many great houses of the South of yesterday, making café brûlot was an established ritual. On a huge silver tray was arranged a collection of little dishes and boxes holding slivers of lemon rind, cloves, allspice, aloes, granulated sugar, cinnamon, a decanter of brandy, a pot of very black, freshly made coffee, and a deep silver bowl and ladle. Into the bowl went a variety of spices, and over these brandy was poured, lemon rind was squeezed, and the brandied spices pressed and stirred. The brandy was then lighted, and while it blazed high the coffee was poured in little by little and all the time the ladle, stirring and dipping and pouring back, kept the alcohol burning. Often the lamps were momentarily carried out of the room so that the beauty of the blazing coffee was accentuated. When the alcohol had burned out, the lights were brought back and the coffee was ladled into cups. Like salad-making, it was a charming custom. It is almost unknown today, and is added only for old times' sake. Perhaps, though, the description of this enticing ritual may encourage its coming back into fashion.

DISHES THAT HAVE ACCOMPANYING CONDIMENTS

But let us return to further details concerned with the subject of informal dinners in a house with limited equipment. In other words, let us consider the expert choice of dishes which do not require accessories.

Nothing so delays the service of a dinner as dishes that must immediately be followed by gravy, condiment or other dishes. If there is only one person to do the serving, no dish must be included on the menu—unless you are only two or three at table—that is not complete in itself.

For instance, fish has nearly always an accompanying dish. Broiled fish, or fish meunière, has ice-cold cucumbers sliced as thin as Saratoga chips, with a very highly seasoned French dressing, or a mixture of cucumbers and tomatoes. Boiled fish always has mousseline, Hollandaise, mushroom or egg sauce, and even if covered with sauce when served, is customarily followed by additional sauce and round scooped boiled potatoes sprinkled with parsley.

Many meats have condiments. Roast beef is never served at a dinner party—it is a family dish and generally has Yorkshire pudding or roast potatoes on the platter with the roast itself, and is followed as soon as possible by pickled or spiced fruit.

Turkey likewise, with chestnut stuffing and accompanying cranberry jelly and giblet sauce, is not a "company" dish, though excellent for an informal dinner. Saddle of mutton is a typical company dish—all mutton has currant jelly. Lamb has mint sauce—or mint jelly.

Partridge or guinea hen must have two sauce boats—presented on one tray—browned bread crumbs in one, and hot bread sauce in the other.

Apple sauce goes with barnyard duck.

The best assurance of an epicure's enjoyment of wild duck is the precisely timed 16 minutes in a quick oven! Celery salad is the accompaniment of all "game"—wild or "tame."

SPECIAL MENUS OF UNACCOMPANIED DISHES

One person can wait faultlessly on many people if dishes which need no supplements are chosen. The fewer the dishes to be passed, the fewer the hands needed to pass them. And yet many housekeepers thoughtlessly order dishes within the list above, and then wonder why the dinner is so hopelessly slow when their waitress is so good!

The following suggestions are merely offered in illustration; each housekeeper can easily devise further for herself. It is not necessary to pass anything whatever with melon or grapefruit, or a macédoine of fruit, or a canapé. Oysters, on the other hand, should be followed by tabasco and buttered brown bread or layered brown and white bread. Soup needs nothing with it (if you do not choose split pea, which needs croutons, or petite marmite, which needs grated cheese). Fish dishes which are "made" with sauce in the dish, such as sole au vin blanc, lobster Newburg, crab ravigote, fish mousse, especially if in a ring filled with plenty of sauce, do not need anything more. Tartar sauce for fried fish *can* be put in baskets made of hollowed-out lemon rind—a basket for each person—and used as a garnishing around the dish though it is preferable, when possible, to garnish the dish with pieces of lemon and pass the sauce separately.

Filet mignon, or fillet of beef, duly surrounded by little clumps of vegetables, shares with chicken casserole the distinction of being the dinner-party life-saver of the hostess who has no one to help her one servant in the dining room. Another dish, but more appropriate to lunch than to dinner, is of French chops banked against mashed potatoes or purée of chestnuts, and surrounded by string beans or peas; or a crown roast of lamb with peas in the center, mint jelly in small pastry cups, and potato croquettes as a garnish. None of these dishes require any following dish whatever, not even a vegetable.

Fried chicken with corn fritters on the platter is almost as good as the two beef dishes, since the one green vegetable which should go with it can be served leisurely, because fried chicken is not quickly eaten. And a ring of aspic with salad in the center does not require accompanying crackers as immediately as plain lettuce.

Steak and broiled chicken are fairly practical since neither needs gravy, condiment, nor sauce—especially if you have a divided vegetable dish so that two vegetables can be passed at the same time.

If a hostess chooses not necessarily the above dishes but others which approximately take their places, she need have no fear of slow service.

(For perfect dinner giving with service done by the hostess herself, see what Mrs. Three-in One does in Chapter 31 and also read Buffet Suppers and Big Dinners at Little Tables in Chapter 32.)

THE POSSIBILITIES OF THE PLAIN COOK

In giving informal or little dinners, you need never worry because you cannot set the dishes prescribed for a formal dinner (see page 330) before your friends or even strangers, so long as the food that you are offering is good of its kind.

It is by no means necessary that your cook should be able to make the "clear" soup that is one of the tests of the perfect cook (and practically never produced by any other); nor is it necessary that she be able to construct comestible mosaics and sculptures. The essential thing is to prevent her from attempting anything she can't do well. If she can make certain dishes that are attractively dished as well as good to taste, so much the better. But remember, the more pretentious a dish is, the more it challenges criticism.

If your cook can make neither clear nor cream soup, but can make a delicious clam chowder, better far to have a clam chowder! And the same way throughout dinner. Whichever dishes your own Nora or Selma can do best are the ones you must have for your dinners.

Another thing: it is not important to have variety. If you gave the Normans chicken casserole the last time they dined with you, that is no reason why you should not give it to them again—if it is the "specialty of your house," as the French say.

A late, and greatly loved, hostess whose Sunday luncheons at a huge country house just outside Washington were for years one of the outstanding features of Washington's smartest society, had clam broth, fried chicken and pancakes, week after week, year after year. Those who went to her house knew just as well what the dishes would be as they did where the dining room was situated. At her few enormous and formal dinners in town, her chef was allowed to be magnificently architectural; but if you dined with her alone, the chances were ten to one that Sunday chicken and pancakes would be served.

This illustrates a point that most hostesses fail to take advantage of. Most people like "specialty" dishes and look forward to them when dining again in the same house.

DO NOT EXPERIMENT FOR STRANGERS

Typical dinner-party dishes are invariably the temptation no less than the downfall of ambitious ignorance. Never let an inexperienced

A LOVELY DINNER SERVICE WITHOUT SILVER DECORATION

cook *attempt a new dish* for company, no matter how attractive her description of it may sound. Try it yourself, or when you are having family or most intimate friends who will understand, if it turns out all wrong, that it is a "trial" dish. In fact, it is a very good idea to share the testing of it with someone who can help you with suggestions, if they are needed for its improvement.

Or suppose you have a cook who is rather poor on all dinner dishes, but makes delicious bread and cake and waffles and oyster stew, scrambled eggs, or even hash! You can make a specialty of asking people to "supper." Suppers are necessarily informal, but there is no objection to that. Formal parties play a very small rôle anyway compared to informal ones.

PROPER DISHING

The "dishing" is quite as important as the cooking; a smear or thumb-mark on the edge of a dish is like a spot on the front of a dress!

Water must not be allowed to collect at the bottom of a dish. That is why a folded napkin is always put under boiled fish and sometimes under asparagus. And dishes must be hot; they cannot be too hot! Meat juice that has started to crust is nauseating. Far better have food too hot and let people take their time eating it than make them suffer the disgust of cold victuals!

Sending in tepid food is about the worst fault (next to not knowing how to cook) that a cook can have.

BLUNDERS IN SERVICE

If an inexperienced servant blunders, you should pretend, if you can, not to know it. Never attract anyone's attention to anything by apologizing or explaining, unless the accident happens to a guest. Taking her to task makes the situation worse, for the original trouble was probably due to nervousness. Speak, if it is necessary to direct her, gently as well as kindly; your object is to restore confidence, not to increase the disorder. Beckon her to you and say quietly, "Mrs. Smith has no fork." Never let her feel that you think her stupid, but encourage her as much as possible; and when she does anything especially well, tell her so.

THE ENCOURAGEMENT OF PRAISE

Nearly all people are quick to censure but rather slow to praise. Admonish, of course, where you must, but censure only with justice; and don't forget that whether of high estate or humble, we all like praise—sometimes. When a guest tells you your dinner is the best he has ever eaten, remember that the cook cooked it, and tell her it was praised. Or if the dining room service was silent and quick and perfect, then tell whoever served it how well it was done. If you are entertaining all the time, you need not commend your household after every dinner you give; but if any especial willingness, attentiveness, or tact is shown, don't forget that a little praise is not only merest justice, but is beyond the purse of no one.

GIVING A SUCCESSFUL DINNER

What do we mean by a successful dinner? Does it mean the snob's satisfaction in the importance of those who came to break bread at his table? Or does it mean the perfectionist's satisfaction in the knowledge that every detail was smoothly flawless? Or does it mean that every minute of the evening sped by gaily, and that everyone lingered late and at that was loath to go?

DO WHATEVER YOU CAN DO WELL, AND DON'T WORRY

The last-named success is the real success. The first requirement for successful dinner giving is skill in selection of a few (or many) friends who find each other amusing or entertaining, or at least agreeable. And this costs not a cent. A second requirement is provision of food and service, which, since the dinner is not a formal one, can be whatever you choose or whatever you can provide.

The failing that no party can overcome is the combination of an ill-at-ease hostess, a host who behaves as though he were a stranger, and guests who have nothing in common. The only salvation of such a party is a host or hostess of genius who can make these guests believe, at least temporarily, that they HAVE something in common.

ANSWERS TO READERS' QUESTIONS

ORDER OF TABLE-SETTING

Will you please give me a list of important factors for my waitress to remember when setting the table for a dinner party?

The items of a properly equipped dinner table include:
1. A tablecloth, or place mats, or whatever is to be the foundation of the setting.
2. A centerpiece of fruit or flowers, or an ornament complete in itself.
3. A place plate (often called a service plate) marking the center of each place set for each person at table.
4. Flat silver: implements necessary for the courses to be served—three forks, three knives and soup spoon, and either fruit spoon or oyster fork maximum amount.
5. Never less than four candlesticks or two candelabra. Two candles are absurdly out of proportion to any table larger than a card table.

6. Two dishes of sweets on a refectory table, four dishes on a round or square table.

7. Glasses for whatever you serve. (Never put on glasses or pieces of flat silver that are not to be used.)

8. Salt cellars and pepper pots between every two places.

9. A napkin on each place plate.

At a family dinner, bread and butter plates are allowed, but never at a dinner party. Place cards are never used for dinners of less than ten persons or for lunches of less than eight. If you like place favors, there is no reason why you should not have them—especially at Christmas or Thanksgiving or birthday or wedding anniversaries or other intimate dinners. On more formal occasions, plain place cards are best.

Salted nuts are put either in small individual dishes above each plate or in a pair of dishes, one at either side or end of the table. Certain hostesses always include them and others never do.

NOT A FORMAL MENU

Would it be dreadful to serve steak smothered in onions, mashed potatoes and brussels sprouts at a formal dinner? This followed by apple pie is my husband's favorite dinner and he says we can't provide anything better.

If you are using the word "formal" in its proper sense—meaning a dinner of ceremony—the menu must be limited to definitely prescribed dishes, which include steak only when cut into small rounds of tenderloin. But if you are actually having a small friendly dinner (of less than ten) to which you are inviting intimate friends, there is only one objection—that of the pentrating odor of frying or any cooking of the cabbage or onion families. The one thing every hostess tries to avoid is the risk of the smell of cooking. But if your kitchen is so shut off, or the draught above your range so efficient that you can avoid this handicap, or if you are sure that the robust appetites of those coming will not mind having your menu announced to them as they come in the front door, then that is all right. In fact, I have said many times that the best menu to provide is that which your kitchen does best.

DINNER OR SUPPER?

Is the evening meal more properly called dinner or supper? I have heard people in best circles refer to this meal as supper when I know they really have their dinner (or their heaviest meal) at this time.

It depends upon what is served. At dinner, soup is always served in plates (with rims) and eaten with a tablespoon. Coffee is served in half-sized cups after dinner. At lunch soup is served in bouillon cups or bowls and eaten with a teaspoon (or bouillon spoon) or a dessertspoon. Cups and saucers for coffee with cream, or tea or chocolate, are put at the places. There is also a difference in the menu, such as a roast with dinner and mince or hash or other made-over meat or else cold meat for supper.

30

Luncheons,* Breakfasts and Suppers

THE INVITATIONS

ALTHOUGH the engraved card is occasionally used for an elaborate luncheon, especially for one given in honor of a noted person, formal invitations to lunch in very fashionable houses are nearly always written in the first person, and rarely sent out more than a week in advance. For instance:

Dear Mrs. Kindhart (or Martha):
    Will you lunch with me on Monday the tenth at half after one o'clock?
    Hoping so much for the pleasure of seeing you.
                    Sincerely (or affectionately),
                             Jane Toplofty.

If the above luncheon were given in honor of somebody—Mrs. Eminent, for instance—the phrase "to meet Mrs. Eminent" would have been added immediately after the word "o'clock." If it is a very large luncheon for which the engraved card might be used, "To meet Mrs. Eminent" is written across the top of the card or invitation. It is by no means necessary to give either a dinner or lunch for anyone. In fact, the average for a guest of honor is certainly not once in a thousand invitations.

THE FORMAL LUNCHEON OF TODAY

Luncheon, being a daylight function, is never so formidable as a dinner, even though it may be every bit as formal and differ from the latter in minor details only. Luncheons are generally given by and for women, but it is not unusual, especially in summer places or in town on Saturday or Sunday, to include an equal number of men.

But no matter how large or formal a lunch may be, the hostess, instead of receiving at the door, sits usually in the center of the room in some place that has an unobstructed approach from the door. Each guest coming into the room is preceded by the butler to within a short speaking distance of the hostess, where he announces the new arrival's

---

* The word "lunch" is used in best society much more than luncheon. "Luncheon" is rarely if ever *spoken*, but it is written in third-person invitations, and in books like this one.

name and then stands aside. A waitress does the same only if she can announce names distinctly and with ease and dignity. Otherwise the guests greet the hostess unannounced. The hostess rises, or if standing, takes a step forward, shakes hands, says, "I'm so glad to see you" or "I am delighted to see you." She then waits for a second or two to see whether the guest who has just come in speaks to anyone; if not, she makes the necessary introduction.

When the butler or waitress has "counted heads" and knows the guests have arrived, he or she enters the room and merely approaches the hostess and slightly bows. But if it is necessary to attract the hostess's attention, he (or she) says, "Luncheon is served."

If there is a guest of honor, the hostess leads the way to the dining room, walking beside her. Otherwise, the guests go in twos or threes, or even singly, just as they happen to come, except that the very young make way for their elders, and gentlemen stroll in with those they happen to be talking to, or, if alone, fill in the rear. The gentlemen *never* offer their arms to ladies in going in to a luncheon—unless there should be an elderly guest of honor, who might be taken in by the host, as at a dinner. But the others follow informally.

THE TABLE

Candles have no place on a lunch or breakfast table, and are used only where a dining room is unfortunately without daylight. Also a plain tablecloth, which must always be put on top of a thick table felt, is correct for dinner but not for luncheon. In other words, *we dine and breakfast on damask, but we lunch on lace*. We also lunch on damask if it be colored. Traditionally the lunch table is "bare"—which may perhaps mean bare between the place mats which may be made in literally unrestricted varieties of linen, needlework or lace.

Or if the table is a refectory one, instead of place mats and a bare center, the table is set with a runner not reaching to the edge at the side, but falling over both ends. Or there may be an embroidered tablecloth made to fit the top of the table to within an inch or two of its edge.

The decorations of the table are practically the same as for dinner: flowers or an ornament in the center, and two or four dishes of fruit or candy where they look best. If the table is very large and rather too bare without candles, four slim vases with small sprigs of flowers to match those in the centerpiece—or any other glass or silver ornaments—are often added.

The places are set as for dinner, with a place plate, three forks, two knives and a small spoon. The lunch napkin, which should match the table linen, is much smaller than the dinner napkin, and is not folded quite the same: it is folded like a handkerchief, in only four folds (four thicknesses). The square is laid on the place plate diagonally, with the monogrammed (or embroidered) corner pointing down toward the edge of the table. The upper corner is then turned sharply under in a flat crease for about a quarter of its diagonal length; then the two sides are rolled loosely under, making a sort of pillow effect laid sideways; with a straight top edge and a pointed lower edge, and the monogram displayed in the center. Or it can be folded in any simple way one prefers. If, as in the house of Mrs. Three-in-One (see Chapter 31), it is not practical to put the napkin on the service plate, the best way to fold it when it is to be laid on the table is to fold its square of four thicknesses once again, perpendicularly, like a narrow book.

Another feature of lunch service, which is always omitted at a formal dinner, is the bread and butter plate.

THE BREAD AND BUTTER PLATE

The bread and butter plate is part of the luncheon service always—as well as of breakfast and supper. It is put at the left side of each plate just above the forks. Butter is sometimes put on the plate before the meal, but usually it is passed. Hot breads are an important feature of every luncheon; hot crescents, soda biscuits, bread biscuits, dinner rolls, or corn bread, the latter baked in small shallow pans like pie plates three to four inches in diameter. At all events several breads are passed as often as necessary. Butter is also passed throughout the meal until the table is cleared for dessert. Bread and butter plates are always removed immediately before the dessert, with the salt and pepper pots.

THE SERVICE OF LUNCH

The formal service is identical with that of dinner. Carving is done in the kitchen and no food set on the table, except ornamental dishes of fruit, candy and nuts. The plate service is also the same as at dinner. The places are never left plateless, except after salad, when the table is cleared and crumbed for dessert. The dessert plates and finger bowls are arranged as for dinner.

Flowers are often put in the finger bowls, a little spray of any sweet-scented flower, but "corsage bouquets," complete with pins and laid at the places, are for official, semi-public and débutante luncheons.

If, in local communities, corsage bouquets are acceptable, it is of course proper to include them—in those communities. But in New York a group of women with flowers pinned on proclaims, "Politics" or "The Stage" or a "Débutante's Luncheon."

THE LUNCH MENU

Five courses at most (not counting the passing of ornamental sweets or after-dinner coffee as a course), or more usually four actual courses,

LUNCHEONS, BREAKFASTS AND SUPPERS

are sufficient for the longest and the most elaborate luncheons possible. For example:

1. Fruit, or soup in cups
2. Eggs or shell fish
3. Fowl and vegetables
4. Salad
5. Dessert

In New York the menu for lunch eaten in a private house is seldom more than four courses and would eliminate either Nos. 1, 2, or 5.

The most popular fruit course is either melon, grapefruit or a mixture of fresh orange and grapefruit or a little pineapple; any sort of fruit cut into very small pieces, with sugar and maraschino or rum or ordinary preserved apricots for flavor, served in special bowl-shaped glasses that fit into long-stemmed and much larger ones, with a space for crushed ice between; or it can just as well be put in "champagne" glasses, after being kept as cold as possible in the icebox until sent to the table.

Soup at luncheon, or at a wedding breakfast or a ball supper, is never served in soup plates, but in two-handled cups, and is eaten with a teaspoon or a bouillon spoon, or drunk from the cup. It is limited to a few varieties: either chicken or clam broth, with a spoonful of whipped cream on top; or bouillon, or green turtle, or strained chicken, or tomato broth; or in summer, cold chicken, beef or tomato bouillon.

Lunch-party egg dishes must number a hundred varieties. (See any cookery book!) Eggs that are substantial and "rich," such as eggs Benedict, or stuffed with pâté de foies gras and a mushroom sauce, should then be "balanced" by a simple meat, such as broiled chicken and salad, combining meat and salad courses in one. On the other hand, should you have a light egg course, like "eggs surprise," you could have meat and vegetables, and plain salad; or an elaborate salad and no dessert. Or with fruit and soup, omit eggs, especially if there is to be an aspic with salad.

The menu of an informal luncheon, if it does not leave out a course, at least chooses simpler dishes: a bouillon or broth, shirred eggs or an omelette; or scrambled eggs on toast which has first been spread with a pâté or meat purée; then chicken or a chop with vegetables, a salad of plain lettuce with crackers and cheese, and a pudding or pie or any other "family" dessert. Or broiled chicken, chicken croquettes, or an aspic is served with the salad in very hot weather. While cold food is both appropriate and palatable, no meal should ever be chosen without at least one course of hot food. Many people dislike cold food, and it disagrees with others; but if you offer your guests soup (or at supper tea or chocolate), it would then do to have the rest of the meal cold.

LUNCHEON BEVERAGES

At women's lunch parties in very conservative houses, cocktails are seldom proffered, and if they are, there are always non-alcoholic as well as stronger ones; but a light rhine wine or claret or a fruit cup is served at table. If men are present, cocktails are passed in most communities; but always—at no matter what sort of party—there must be tomato or fruit juice for those who do not like alcohol. Nothing is in worse taste than forcing any guest either to take alcohol or else to sit conspicuously empty-handed.

At the family lunch table it is a widespread American custom for the lady of a house to have the tea-set put before her at the table, not only when alone, but when having friends lunching with her, and to pour tea, coffee, or chocolate. Such hot beverages are served only in old-fashioned communities and at the family table, but iced tea, coffee, and chocolate are admitted to summer lunch tables everywhere.

Iced tea at lunch is prepared like a "cup" with lemon and sugar, and sometimes with cut-up fresh fruit or a little squeezed fruit juice, and it is poured into glasses at each place. But coffee should be passed around in a glass pitcher on a tray that also holds a bowl of powdered sugar and a pitcher of cold milk, and another of cream as thick as possible. The guests pour their coffee to suit themselves into tall glasses half full of broken ice, and furnished with very long-handled spoons.

A BRIDGE LUNCH AT THREE TABLES

If you are one of those who have a very small dining room or perhaps no dining room at all, but have a large living room or perhaps a wide veranda, or if you live in a rainless climate that permits tables to be set either in a patio or out on the lawn, a luncheon of twelve, followed perhaps by bridge, is not only one of the nicest parties imaginable, but not beyond the possibilities of a simple house.

Preparations are much the same as those for a big dinner at little tables (see Index). Each card table should be set with a damask cloth, either white or pastel color, a yard and a half square, which is much the best covering for lunch as well as dinner on small tables. Any other style of small tablecloth will of course do, but they should, if possible, be exactly alike. Better to have simple matched ones than assorted elaborate ones. You set your places as at every table, the amount of silver depending upon your menu.

If you were giving a formal lunch and had two servants to wait at table, there would be no food at the places. But under the usual circumstances of having only one maid to wait on as many as eight, it would be much easier for her to put the cold soup in a cup (or hot soup in little individual pots with covers) at each place before people were seated. While they are eating their soup, she passes the rolls first,

Photograph by Samuel H. Gottscho

THE CORRECTLY SET EVERY-DAY LUNCH TABLE

Even when the lady of the house lunches alone, the table in a formally appointed house is set with four places.

Luncheon is served. (Note the presence of the bread-and-butter plate.)

The bouillon cup* has been exchanged for a service plate.

Plate for entrée follows bouillon. It is almost unheard of to serve two courses before the meat.

Meat plate takes place of entrée.

Salad plate follows meat course. The bouillon cup and saucer were brought in on a matching plate, since the service plate was of a different color.

Place cleared of everything except glasses before dessert service is put down as illustrated. Finger bowl same as for dinner (see illustration between pp. 328 and 329).

CORRECT SETTING OF EACH COURSE AT LUNCHEON

Photograph by Whitman   A SEATED BUFFET SUPPER TABLE OF UNUSUAL BEAUTY   *From Arts and Decoration*

and then pours iced tea from a big pitcher into the glasses which are on the table. A great saving in service would be to have your service plates hot, so that when the maid carries away the last soup cup on its saucer, the service plates are all ready to be used for the main course, which she then passes.

At card tables, the formal requirements of the dinner table may be relaxed and the main course plates removed one in each hand, before a salad course previously arranged on each plate, as well as before dessert. At the end of lunch, you and your guests go elsewhere for coffee, which you make and pour.

While you are drinking your coffee, the maid clears the tables and resets them with two packs of unopened new cards, three sharpened pencils (one extra one in case a point breaks), and two score pads.

(For other bridge parties, see Index.)

THE AFTER-MEAL ICE WATER

On a hot summer day when people have been playing cards for an hour or a little over, the maid should bring in a tray with a large pitcher of ice water and perhaps another pitcher of iced tea and put it down on a convenient table. The one thing that hostesses tend to forget is that five people out of six long for a drink of water in the afternoon more than anything else. In occasional very hospitable houses sandwiches and cookies are brought in in addition to the iced tea, but these are not necessary when bridge is following a luncheon. If you were inviting people to come at three and play for the afternoon, light refreshments would be considered necessary between half-past four and five o'clock.

The Buffet Supper, "Stand-up" Lunch, Dinner or Supper—Also Bridge Luncheons at Little Tables—will be found in Chapter 32 ("Simple Party Giving").

"BREAKFAST"

A hunt breakfast is just such a stand-up luncheon. It is a "breakfast" by courtesy of half an hour in time. At twelve-thirty it is breakfast, at one o'clock it is lunch.

Regular weekly stand-up breakfasts are given by hospitable people who have big places in the country and encourage their neighbors to drive over on the day when they are "at home"—Saturday or Sunday generally—and friends are always prepared for.

SUPPERS

Supper is the most intimate meal there is, and since none but family or nearest friends are ever included, invitations are invariably by word of mouth.

The atmosphere of a luncheon is often formal, but informal lunches and suppers differ in nothing except day and evening lights, and clothes. Strangers are occasionally invited to informal luncheons, but only intimate friends are bidden to supper.

THE SUPPER TABLE

The table is set, as to places and napery, exactly like the lunch table, with the addition of candlesticks or candelabra or both, as at dinner. The supper table differs from the usual lunch table, however, in this: in front of the hostess is a big silver tea tray with full silver service for tea or cocoa or chocolate or breakfast coffee, most often chocolate or cocoa and either tea or coffee. At the host's end of the table there is perhaps a chafing dish—that is, if the host fancies himself a cook!

Many hospitable people, whose houses are run with plenty of servants, love to give informal Sunday-night suppers on their servants' Sundays out, and forage for themselves. And in the thousands of houses which have no servants at all, this same Sunday-night custom is equally possible. The table is left set; a cold dish of something and salad are left in the icebox; the ingredients for one or two chafing-dish specialties are also left ready. At supper time a member of the family and possibly an intimate friend or two carry the dishes to the table and with a few electric cooking utensils prepare almost anything they fancy.

For the serious aspects of cooking parties given by chef-hosts, see page 407.

31

Mrs. Three-in-One Gives a Dinner Party

THE hostess who is not troubled by any of the exactions of formal dinner giving—whose friends will pay no attention to her leaving her seat at table as often or for as long as she likes, may follow whatever directions in this chapter she finds pleasing. But its especial intention is to answer the problem of the hostess who has to serve her dinner without ever leaving the table, because at the first gesture she makes to rise, every man instantly springs to his feet. No matter how earnestly she asks them to stay where they are, up they jump and after her they go!

The following directions are therefore especially written for you, Mrs. Three-in-One, who must be cook and waitress and apparently unoccupied hostess, and whose principal problem is the serving of a dinner for six or even eight without ever leaving the table.

TO YOU WHO ARE MRS. THREE-IN-ONE:

To begin with, you set your table according to the formal pattern exactly! Centerpiece of flowers or fruit or a permanent ornament of silver or china, candlesticks or candelabra. You set the places with whatever flat silver and glasses will be needed for your menu. The only differences are that you probably lay the dessertspoon and fork horizontally above each of the places, and above these, finger bowls. If they have a flower or two in each and no plates under them, they look quite surprisingly like decoration rather than waiting utility.

Service plates, (even hot ones which are very useful when the first course is to be passed by a waitress) must be omitted. It is much better that Mrs. Three-In-One set her table with a napkin folded attractively.

The principal items of equipment that you cannot do without are two sturdy serving tables: one to stand at the side of your husband's chair and the other next your own, to be used for supplies and discards.* The bottom shelves are to put the used dishes on, and the middle shelves for supplies and later-used dishes. On the top of your own table you probably put the dessert, while the salad goes on the

---

*Easiest to find are the plain, early American oblong sofa-end tables from 10" to 12" deep by 22" to 25" wide. They have two shelves below the top and come in every sort of wood and are for sale in every furniture department.

top of your husband's table. (Half of the salad plates on top of half of the dessert plates on your second shelf. The duplicate half of both on your husband's shelf.) Also on top of your table, finger rolls and melba toast in a bread basket; (for these no butter is necessary). Sherry, claret or port is of course decanted and put on the table. White wine is left in its napkin-wrapped cold bottle in a silver coaster on the table. Water in thermos pitchers (which don't drip) on either side of the table.

FLOOR STANDING SUSANS

If you live in an early American or Georgian house and have a fairly large dining room, a pair of floor standing Lazy Susans are really lovely. The 18th Century cabinet-makers called them "dumb waiters". A big round tray at the bottom with two or three others diminishing in size above revolve on a pole that has widespread claw feet and a little finial at the top—it looks like a tall, thin or short, fat Christmas tree.

Old ones are rare, even in museums, but any competent cabinet-maker could make a pair without difficulty and in the height and circumference best suited to your needs.

The pattern of tray for either type of Susan is that of any Chippendale or Sheraton pedestal table.

YOU DECIDE ON THE MENU

If you happen to own a silver roast-beef platter with a huge silver cover, you can perfectly well include both soup and roast in your menu, because the silver cover which is also ornamental—if polished—will keep the roast out of sight (and hot!) during the eating of a soup course. Otherwise you will probably find it best either to omit the soup, or choose a meat course other than a roast.

For example, if you begin with soup, the meat course is perhaps a veal and ham pie, or chicken casserole, or sliced turkey with mushrooms or chicken à la king—kept HOT in a chafing dish in front of your husband's place—perhaps a second dish of baked macaroni, or scalloped potatoes and a green vegetable in a covered dish on your husband's (or your) second shelf.

IF YOU BEGIN WITH SOUP

If your first course is to be soup, the most practical soup dishes are the individual pots on matching plates with heat-holding lids, put on at each place just before you announce dinner. After the soup has been eaten, you remove the soup plates from the guests on either side of you. (If you are eight at table you also remove the plates from the one beyond the guest at your left.) At his end, your husband does the same.

BEGINNING DINNER WITH AN UNCOVERED ROAST

If you have no roast beef cover (very few of us have), and your meat course is to be a roast, it will be best to begin your dinner with this, and provide the equivalent of a first course in the living room by serving plenty of substantially satisfying canapés with cocktails, which should include at least one of vegetable or fruit juices to take the place of a first course at table.

You receive your guests and stay with them until all have arrived; then you leave them with your husband and go into the kitchen, take the roast out of the oven, put it at your husband's place and the vegetable dishes beside it and then invite everyone to "Come in to dinner."

Your husband carves the roast. Perhaps he also serves the vegetables. Or perhaps the dishes are handed around.

At the end of the meat course, your husband puts the meat platter on the lowest shelf of his table and the vegetable dishes beside it. He then removes the plates of the two guests sitting on either side of him (and if you are eight, of the second beyond, on his left). You do the same at your end of the table, putting the used plates on the lowest shelf of your table. You both place fresh plates for salad in front of those next to you; implements are all at the places.

If you were only six at table then you would have no trouble, but the one snag at a dinner of eight is that unless you have an uneven number of men and women, you have to sit at the left of your own place at table. If you take the seat at the right of your place, you will have to reach three persons on your left to keep plates from crossing the "guest of honor" on your husband's right—which you avoid if you can.

The same plate-changing procedure follows each course.

THE SALAD COURSE

Salad should be arranged in a bowl or on a platter, not only because that which is arranged on individual plates takes up too much room on the side tables (they would be incorrectly placed on the dining table) but plates already served are likely to give one person a much larger helping than he will eat, or another not as much as he would like, nor of his choice.

Salad dressing mixed at table is a ritual in many houses; but unless it is a specialty, it is best to have it already mixed and to pass the bowl so that people can help themselves. Each one, in turn, holds the bowl for the next.

Dessert is probably served by you and handed down the table exactly as your husband carved and handed the meat course.

COFFEE IN THE LIVING ROOM

At the end of dinner after your guests are seated in the living room, you go to the kitchen, take the cream out of the icebox and put it on the coffee tray—which has otherwise been prepared—and carry it into the living room; you put it down on your coffee table, sit beside it and make the coffee.

Probably you use a glass coffee-maker which, being interesting to watch, never seems to take half as long to wait for as the unseen coffee in a percolator.

When it is ready, you pour it. When everyone has finished, you collect the cups and saucers and carry the tray back into the kitchen, where you can then take a few moments to put away "spoilable" foods.

OTHER DINNER-GIVING DETAILS

All other details are the same as at every dinner. The less pretense made, the less risk of criticism.

In selecting your menu, remember that a good dinner is much more dependent upon its preparation than upon selection. It doesn't really matter whether you give people dinner-party saddle of lamb or corned beef hash—what does matter is that it shall be *good* of its kind.

YOUR UNANSWERABLE FRONT DOOR

One of the real problems is that of answering your front door. You can scarcely say you are "not at home"; and unless your really intimate friends have a special ring, they, as well as strangers, meet an unopened door at such times as you are unable to see "visitors."

Of course, if you are giving a party, either you leave your front door open—except in very cold weather—and stand near enough to greet those coming in, or else you have to ask a relative or friend to open the door for you.

For a really big party, it is usually possible to hire a special cook, waitress or waiter who can cook and serve for every sort of entertainment. But in a small house or apartment that everybody knows is normally run by you alone, suddenly to acquire an impressive staff is likely to give an impression of over-great effort.

RULES OF ESCAPE FOR HELPLESS HOSTESSES

There is a very real need for new rules which can politely effect the escape of a hostess from an interrupting visitor who refuses to listen to the hostess who plainly explains she is in the middle of her work. Often it is true the visitor says, "Don't let me interrupt you!" and then just sits—leaving the hostess helpless!

And yet nearly all the things we do and say seem polite or rude, proper or questionable, according to the *way* they are done or said. For example, Mary Warmhart can greet a visitor, "Oh, I'm so sorry! I have to go to Cora's for bridge in five minutes, but I *do* want to see you even for these few moments." Or at another time she can say to someone who stays on and on, "I hate to interrupt our talk, but I *have* to meet the 2:15." Or "Oh, I can't believe it's ten minutes *past* eleven! And we have Board meeting at eleven."

There are many situations from which every well-bred visitor instinctively tries to protect her (or his) otherwise helpless hostess. When a hostess happens to appear in full view, so that she can't possibly be "not at home," but when it is perfectly clear that she is very busy, the considerate visitor says at once, "I'll come again soon!" The quite proper thing for the hostess to answer is, "Oh *will* you? *Please* do! Because I can't ask you to wait until (whatever it is that is demanding her time) is finished." But if the hostess replies, "I'm not at all busy; do come in!" then it is her fault if the visitor interrupts her.

A LITTLE JACK HORNER SHELF OF WELCOME

This term is intended merely as a suggestion. It may so happen that you and your husband love people and that your friends are inclined to swarm into your house late in the afternoon, on holidays especially, when markets are shut, and stay until supper time. John, your husband, shows symptoms which you know very well mean, "I'm hungry"—and still your friends stay. In your own mind you go over the contents of the icebox. Your perfectly good supper for two might do for three, but at the moment you are seven or nine.

The answer to you who are often in this predicament is to have a supply of ever-ready preparations which you call your LITTLE JACK HORNER SHELF OF WELCOME.

This is a shelf of provisions sealed in by having paper pasted across it like a Jack Horner pie so that its contents shall never be depleted. Fill this shelf with foods put up in cartons or tins, ready to eat as they are or as soon as heated. Also, on this shelf, keep stacks of paper cups and plates and napkins—and perhaps even paper spoons and forks. Then, when the party is over, all you need to do is to take off the little remaining food, a few platters, dishes, and pitchers, and dump everything else into the fire or garbage can.

In stocking your Shelf of Welcome, be sure to remember that a man's idea of a meal is something substantial and hot!

This description has nothing to do with etiquette other than to make it possible to say at any time to any number, "Do stay! We can have a picnic supper ready in a few minutes."

HOSPITALITY NOT DEPENDENT UPON WEALTH

The fact that one is able to spend very little is no bar at all to hospitality. A young couple living in a single room that has a folding sofa-bed, so that the room can be made into the semblance of a sitting room, may ask friends they care for—and others are of no importance—to come to their "home-in-a-room."

Where people do things with modest hospitality, and fail, it is not because of their stinted means, but because of their own attitude. They mentally if not actually apologize, which is fatal. They entirely overlook the fundamental fact that hospitality is far more dependent upon personality than upon lavishness of provision.

The real secret of successful party giving is simply the gift of never outgrowing a child's imagination. In other words, the spirit of "let's pretend," which enters into the play of all children, is the very spirit that animates the subconscious mind of every ideal hostess.

Unless you really love the game of hospitality, unless you delight to have the friends you like share your festival, your party, even though it be given in a palace with rows of lacqueys and a ton of choicest viands, will be but a heavy procession of over-richly laden minutes. Whereas, if the enthusiasm of your welcome springs from innate friendliness—from joy in furthering the delight of good-fellowship beneath your own roof—you need have little doubt that those who have accepted your hospitality once will eagerly look forward to doing so again and again.

(Solutions to other problems of Mrs. Three-in-One will be found in many chapters of this book, particularly the chapters "Simple Party Giving" and "Modern Dinner Giving.")

32

Simple Party Giving

To all who live in simple unpretentious houses, successful party-giving amounts to little more than the friendly enthusiasm of the host or hostess! Practically all of us fall naturally into one of two categories. In the first belong those to whom the thought of giving any sort of party is as full of delight (and as empty of qualm) as the prospect of a visit to the circus is to a child. In the second are all those who are literally panicked at the thought of inviting anybody in. They are sure people won't want to come; they are sure they will be bored if they do; they are sure, in fact, that "company" is a synonym for "failure"—with the result that these fears all too often come true.

On the other hand, those who love to give parties usually give them with ease, which means an unworried attitude of mind. Even if a dozen things go wrong, they know that few of their friends will notice, and fewer still will care, and after all why should things go wrong?

The point is that sometimes the hostess seems to imagine she is asking enemies to her house, a condition brought about perhaps by those two formidable words, hostess and guest. Perhaps if she would forget that she was to be hostess and that guests were coming, and would think instead, "John and I are going to be at home, and Mary, Jane, Jim and Bob are coming in," the entire situation would clear. At all events, this is given as a suggestion.

GIVING A BRIDGE PARTY

In giving a bridge party, whether of two tables or of ten, the first thing to do is to make a list of those to be invited. And then divide those who accept into groups of four; that is, seat at each table only those who like to play together. They can play one type of game at one table and another type of game at another, but you must do your best to put those who play about the same game at the same table. Apart from ability as players, it is important to remember characteristics of temperament. Don't put people who take their game seriously with others who unceasingly chatter. Don't put one who plays rapidly at a table with hesitators and dawdlers who take a whole minute to decide upon which card they'll play—and who even then take half a minute more in daring to lay an intended finesse face up on the table!

We all know hostesses who apparently seat players by drawing names out of a hat without the slightest regard to who plays well and who plays badly. At an evening party the unthinking hostess will put two men who are the best players in town at a table with one woman who, imagining herself a wit, thinks of nothing but the next bright remark she can make, and another woman who is beautiful to look at but who knows scarcely more than a child of eight about contract. A man will be delighted to find a pretty woman next to him at the dinner table, but at the bridge table he hopes for an expert partner. If she is pretty or charming, or both, so much the better, of course, but these attributes are secondary. The real point is that one poor player spoils the whole evening—or afternoon—for the three who play well, and what she (or he) does to an unfortunate partner who perhaps cuts her (or him) more than once can be left to your imagination.

And now your preparations. It seems scarcely necessary to say that the two packs of cards on each table must be fresh, and that the pencils laid beside the score pads must be sharpened and the leads not broken under the edge of the wood. On each table you leave a slip of paper on which you have written distinctly the names of the four players who are to play there together. They, of course, cut for their seats and partners. It is also of importance to see that each table is comfortably lighted, because poorly placed light that is reflected from the shiny surface of the cards is just as bad as darkness so deep that red cards are indistinguishable from black ones. If you have any doubt about light, sit in each place, hold cards in your hands, lay a few on the table and see!

If it is customary in your community to play for prizes, then you, of course, select a first prize for the highest score to be made by a woman and a first prize for the highest score to be made by a man; but at a party to which no men are invited, a second prize is usually given. In any case, all prizes are attractively wrapped before being presented. Those who receive the prizes must, of course, open the packages at once and show some evidence of appreciation when thanking the hostess. Needless to say, a well-behaved person does not show disappointment upon receiving a prize that happens not to please her, nor does she "forget" to take it home. If the hostess chooses to give a present to her guest of honor, this should neither be called nor treated as a guest prize. (See page 405.)

REFRESHMENTS AT A BRIDGE PARTY

At a bridge party given, let us say, at three or half past three in the afternoon, hot tea or chocolate or coffee or else cold beverages—and with any of these sandwiches and cake—should be served at about five o'clock, and nothing else whatsoever. At a very large party the table is set in the dining room exactly as at a formal tea, but under typical circumstances the everyday afternoon tea table is set in a corner of the living room. Sometimes a member of the hostess's family pours tea, or perhaps at the finish of a rubber the hostess herself pours tea. This is always the case when the party is to be concluded at tea time and when prizes are given. Very often enthusiastic bridge players playing for stakes and not for prizes play straight through until six o'clock or later. They need not stop playing. One by one, as each becomes dummy, she goes to the tea table, drinks a cup of tea or a glass of iced tea or coffee, eats a sandwich or two, and returns to the rubber. She perhaps repeats these nibblings several times as she becomes dummy.

If a few neighbors come in to play bridge in the evening, have a tray brought in with one or two cold beverages and a few thin sandwiches. On the other hand, if you are giving a party and the weather is cold, set a light buffet—in the dining room—of welsh rarebit or scrambled eggs and sausage, hot chocolate or coffee, or both, with buttered finger rolls.

BUFFET PARTIES

There are three delightful things about buffet suppers that appeal to nearly all of us. First, there is no handicap in lack of service. Second, no distress is caused by the yesterday-minded hostess who keeps a dozen courteously prompt guests waiting for those Never-On-Times. On the other hand, and third, for those of us whose training in deportment included awareness of the essential courtesy of never keeping others waiting, an invitation to a stand-up (buffet) supper allows us to dress without constantly looking at the clock, and to arrive more or less at our leisure without running the risk of being either rude or breathless.

Those who arrive promptly and like to eat promptly, do so. Those who come late fare almost as well, and no one is made to do anything he (or she) doesn't want to—and that seems to be the ultimate in present-day hospitality.

THE PEOPLE YOU INVITE

Since every informal party is at its best when people know each other well, it is essential either that you confine your invitations to people in one group or that you ask a reasonable number from each different group so that none can find themselves without friends to sit with.

The invitation is usually written across the top of the face of your double visiting card.

> *Tuesday, March sixth,*
> *Buffet supper at 7 o'clock.*
>
> Mr. and Mrs. John Newhouse
>
> *Please answer if not coming.*

If request for a reply is added in the lower corner, the invitation should be answered, for otherwise the hostess has no idea how many to provide for. The answer can be telephoned or sent on a return card saying merely "Sat. Oct. 2 with pleasure."

Very often the invitation is telephoned. "Will you come to a buffet (or picnic or stand-up) supper next Tuesday?"

SETTING A BUFFET

In preparation, the chairs are taken away from the dining table, which often, but not necessarily, is placed against a wall.

There are no especial directions for setting the table. The one difference in the principle of buffet and ordinary table setting is that objects of utility are of first importance, and unless there be ample space for both, objects that are solely for ornament are omitted. Flowers in the center of the table are lovely, of course, but if it is a question of choosing between flowers and fruit, a centerpiece of fruit is preferable.

In the same way, if the table be crowded and candles are not needed to see by, they would better be left off. If candles are needed, candelabra are better than candlesticks—always—and for two reasons: first, they give better light; second, they contribute height.

In setting a buffet table the important dishes of food are placed down the length of the table as close to the centerpiece as possible. The two most important items of equipment are placed precisely in the center of each end. A large tea and coffee set on its tray, or a soup tureen, or other container of size, at one end is balanced by platters of hot food at the other.

Sometimes cider is poured into big pitchers and claret or white wine is decanted and put on the table. A punch bowl is sometimes put at the end opposite the tea and coffee service, and the platters or chafing-dishes of hot foods are put in the center of one side of the table and cold dishes on the other, but as a rule cold drinks are put on the sideboard. Beer should be left in its cans or bottles on the sideboard.

Color plays an enormous part in the beauty of a modern buffet table. If you have copper bowls or dishes or a samovar or a copper-bound beer keg, red-cheeked peaches, apples, pears, purple grapes, bananas and oranges, even a few tomatoes to add to the coppery red, are effective—especially if you live far from the sea and cannot include the ubiquitous platter of lobster decorated with its claws!

With copper, keep all the autumn tints in mind: green, red, russet and yellow on a bare table. Or if you prefer, a red or green or yellow tablecloth will make a warm and inviting combination. Coarse white damask tablecloth and napkins dyed a fairly strong color make an ideal foundation for a table that you prefer not to have bare. Especially suitable for the buffet table are strong colors like eggplant, russet brown, lobster red, leaf green and dark blue; or if you are setting your table with chromium, additional colors of tablecloths to choose from include turquoise blue, emerald green and magenta.

In a modernistic house you perhaps go to the smartest of colorless extremes and have every item black or white or silver, black or white glass, or else everything in brilliant chromium. Or during the holidays, if you are setting your table with pottery and pewter, nothing is nicer than an old-fashioned red damask tablecloth with holly or poinsettia and plenty of colorful fruit. But there is no rule about how you place things other than choosing the way that seems to you most inviting.

THE MENU

It does not matter which dishes you happen to choose, so long as they are good of their kind and easy to eat with fork alone—or possibly with a spoon. Otherwise, merely use a reasonable amount of common sense in selecting dishes that will be satisfying to the people invited. In other words, don't feed hungry men bouillon, dabs of hors-d'œuvre, samples of fruit salad and meringues. For women alone, food might be trifling; but for normal men with normally good appetites you should provide three or four dishes that are substantial, and at least two of these should be hot.

Substantial dishes, for example, include all thick soups, eggs, meat, starch, vegetables, puddings and pie. Nearly everything made in a baking dish is ideal for a buffet meal, not only because it is substantial, but because it is easily kept hot. Olives, radishes and celery are nothing but trimmings. Olives and other relishes are typically served with cocktails before dinner in the living room. This statement is added because hundreds of hostesses seemingly believe that an olive is the first essential—the symbol, as it were—of a party. Have them, of course, if you like, but count them out as items of food.

Buffet menus include such acceptable combinations as these.

(1) Fish baked in pudding dish (hot); a variety of cold meats (cut into narrow strips to eat without a knife; even roast beef can be managed if strips are not only narrow, but thin); vegetable salad; hot pudding. (If expense is important, plenty of stuffed hard-boiled eggs can take the place of cold meats.)

(2) A thick Italian soup; curry of lamb cut in small pieces with noodles or wild rice; vegetable salad; two varieties of pie.

(3) Spaghetti Milanaise; beef and kidney or veal and ham pie; baked macaroni and mixed green salad; macedoine of fruit and apple betty.

It is true that men are prone to turn up their noses at any menu that lacks a hot roast, but a good Irish stew or goulash or meat pie will be found acceptable if nothing is said to them about the missing roast! The hostess who tactlessly apologizes for not supplying this essential dish will find herself in the same position as that of anyone who tells a child that the circus is in town but tickets are not to be had.

Of course, buttered rolls, party sandwiches, a fruit cup and coffee, and perhaps hot chocolate, should be included with each menu.

Each dish should have a stack of plates beside it and the proper implements to eat with in a row beside the plates; cups and saucers or glasses should surround the container of each beverage. But other than using ordinary practical common sense in considering convenient arrangement, there are no table-setting rules.

It is very important that hostesses who give buffet parties collect a supply of small tables so that each guest can put down extra plates, glasses, and cups and saucers. But, of course, if it is not practical to store so many tables, though they come in compact nests of four, people naturally have to hold their plates in their hands and put their cups and saucers and glasses down wherever space can be found—even on the floor.

THE BUFFET PARTY BEGINS

So let us say that the table is set with all the cold foods and the dining room lights are lighted and the hot foods are ready to be brought in from the kitchen, or else that they are already in their hot-water-heated chafing-dishes or other containers, and let us go with the host and hostess into the living room (or drawing room) and wait for the guests to arrive.

As people enter the room, the host and hostess go forward to greet them and perhaps introduce any who may for the moment find themselves alone. It must, of course, always be remembered that at every small and particular party (as distinguished from a huge and general one) the roof of a friend's house serves as an introduction, and one talks with those whom one finds near-by, whether he knows them or not.

When the majority of those expected have arrived, the doors into the dining room are opened and people in more or less of a queue file around the dining table and the women as well as the men help themselves. Or perhaps, as at a dance, the men fill plates and take them to the women.

A man seeing a woman sitting and not eating naturally asks her (whether he knows her or not), "Can't I get you something to eat?" If she says, "Yes, please," he fills a plate and a glass and takes them to her. But most likely she says, "Thank you, but I'm going into the dining room in a moment." If people continue to sit and wait to be served, the hostess has to direct them as she would direct children at a party, saying, "Please go into the dining room and help yourself to what you like." Then, if they stand blockading the table, she has to say, "Won't you please take your plate and go into the other room again and sit down?"

If there are no little individual stands or tables and guests must put their glasses on the floor (there being no other place), it is rather better to have the iced drink in goblets which are raised on high but substantial stems, because these are easier to reach than low tumblers which sit flat on the floor. They are also better than tumblers because less likely to make rings wherever they are set down. The cup, saucer and spoon necessary for the coffee, tea or chocolate must be managed as best one can under the circumstances.

Important item: plenty of ash trays. For a buffet supper recently a New York hostess went to a ten-cent store and bought a hundred ash trays. She put two of them on each step of her staircase—one next to the wall and one on the outer edge. She put all the others in every space that could possibly serve as a cigarette parking place.

The only serving detail of importance in a buffet meal is the clearing away of used dishes and the unceasing emptying of ash trays. In a house with servants every plate is removed as soon as put down and filled ash trays constantly replaced. Also, if there are servants, the glasses of those seated are refilled from time to time, and the main dishes are often proffered. But the only thing the servantless hostess can do is to ask one or two members of her family—or her most intimate friends—to help her put used dishes in several spaces provided, from which she can stack them and take them away as easily and unobtrusively as possible.

But the fact that guests must do their own serving is no handicap, since people do exactly the same thing in a great house. In fact, it is thought that sitting for awhile here, then going again into the dining room and foraging for themselves, then coming back to the same place or finding a place with others is one of the very things that make buffet parties the informal and popular gathering that they are. If people are not sitting beside those they find particularly congenial, women as well as men are free to move elsewhere. An attractive woman can even escape the most persistent bore by going to the table and then joining whomever she chooses. So if you have never given a buffet lunch, dinner, or especially supper, you can't begin too soon to discover the charm of this delectable form of entertaining.

BIG DINNERS AT LITTLE TABLES

A big dinner or supper at little tables is the buffet party's only serious rival in modern popularity, because it is equally suitable for indoors in winter or outdoors in summer, as well as for those who have many servants and for those who have one or none! Since those who have many servants merely follow the directions fully given in other chapters, let us consider the best method of serving a supper of twenty or possibly thirty with no one to serve it but the hostess and anyone she can requisition as an aide: husband, perhaps, but more likely sister or friend.

IF YOU ARE A HOSTESS ALONE

To begin with, the number of guests you can have depends upon the number of tables that can be fitted into your dining room and wherever else you choose. If your dining table is a big one, take it away if you can. But if you can't, push it flat against the wall. Don't forget, if you are setting tables in your living room, to leave plenty of space in which to receive your guests—even though they may not be able to sit down until they take their places at the tables. The smallest and cheapest card tables are excellent unless their legs wabble!

Have each table set with a small damask tablecloth, if you have damask tablecloths; if not, use what you have. At each place put a napkin and the amount of flat silver necessary for your menu, and a glass for water or for fruit cup. And if your dinner is really a supper, put a breakfast cup and saucer at each place too. Also put on a salt cellar and a pepper pot. Put a hot-plate mat in the center of each table and leave it clear. Seat the tables with place cards, because many people, without place cards to guide them, are rather at a loss.

The menu must be short and simple, but substantial. For example, don't waste energy, dishes and implements on a cold nothing-to-eat first course of fruit or canapé that leaves everyone even hungrier than when he sat down. Begin at once with a substantial hot dish such as

Photograph by Peter A. Nyholm
From House and Garden

THE BUFFET SUPPER APPEALS TO ALMOST EVERYONE

Photograph by Dana B. Merrill

AT TEA TIME IN A CITY YARD
The inviting charm of a garden setting — even that of a city yard — is all too often overlooked.

chicken à la king with rice around it, or macaroni with meat balls and a rich tomato sauce, or a real goulash. Second course, put a mound of vegetable salad on a big platter and surround it with plenty of stuffed eggs. Third course, pie or any other equally practical dessert.

And now the problem of serving three tables each seating four—six tables if you have room and your sister, for example, to help. Using three tables as our one-person unit: a dish of buttered rolls and four hot plates would be put on each of your own three tables before guests sit down, and your sister would supply her three tables in the same way. Therefore, for the sake of clearness, let's think only of your own three-table unit (of which your sister's is a duplicate). As soon as your people are seated, you put the hot course on the place-mat in the cleared center of the first table. Then you put a pitcher of fruit cup, or since this type of dinner may equally well be called supper, a pitcher of cocoa or a pot of coffee on a tray with sugar and cream, in the center of the second table. By this time those at the first table have served themselves to the hot dish, which you now carry to the third table. Then those at the second table having served themselves to coffee or whatever the beverage may be, you place the coffee tray or the fruit-cup pitcher on the first table. The second table in turn is given the hot course from the third table, at which you now take your own place. Each course is served the same way.

The one difficulty is in finding platters deep enough to supply twelve persons, and at the same time be put in the center of a card table, because otherwise the platters must be refilled. In taking off the used dishes and plates, this is one occasion when a service wagon is practical and therefore proper.

(For Bridge Lunch at Small Tables see page 376.)

A DANCE CAN BE SIMPLE

A successful dance at least expense rather implies that it will be given at home, though it might perhaps be given at a golf club, an inn or a tea room. But let us say that when all the furniture is out of your own living room, the space will be large enough to dance in. Decorations and supper can be as simple as you like, but one item that must be considered, before deciding definitely to send out invitations, is good music.

INVITATIONS

Invitations, by the way, are written across the top of the visiting card of the young girl's mother, or whoever is hostess—"Jan. 6. 9 p. m. Small dance"—or possibly, if only her own friends are invited, across the young girl's own card. If a holiday dance is given by a young boy, his name is written on his mother's card. But a man giving a dance writes on his own card.

MUSIC AND PARTNERS

But to return to the question of good music. By this is meant music that is gay and with perfect rhythm, and not necessarily many pieces. Heavy or feeble music will guarantee a complete failure, no matter what all other preparations may be. A perfect dance from a young girl's point of view is *wonderful* music and—lots and lots of partners! In fact, one ought to put partners before the music, since the best orchestra is wasted if there are not plenty of young men. Ideally there should be about three men (or boys) to every two girls. But a hand-picked collection of young men who dance with enthusiasm is infinitely more helpful to the success of the party than twice the number, most of whom spend the entire evening propped against the walls.

DANCE USHERS

The best plan for a successful party—meaning that every girl shall have plenty of partners—is for the hostess to appoint a sufficient number of young men as floor committee or ushers, as they are sometimes called. Ushers wear white boutonnières or other badges so that they may be easily recognized. An usher needs no introduction to ask a girl to dance. His principal duty is to see that every girl has a partner—and no partner for too long. If he notices that one boy and girl are dancing time and again, he looks questioningly first at one and then at the other and says with his lips, "Want to change?" If both signal "No," he pays no further attention; but if one signals "Yes, *please!*" he cuts in and dances with the girl until he signals to a stag. No stag may refuse the signal from the usher.

Another of the uses which a boy can make of the floor committee is to tell one of its members beforehand when he is going to undertake an obligation dance. This means dancing with someone whom he knows very slightly. Within a reasonable time that member of the floor committee will see that he is relieved. There should be one usher for every ten girls at every big dance.

One might ask why a young man is willing to be an usher. First, because there is a certain social honor in being chosen for that function, much as in being usher at a wedding. And there are also advantages in being an usher! He can dance with anyone he chooses, and the moment he no longer chooses, he signals to a stag to whom he hands his partner.

DANCE HOSTESSES

When a sorority or other girls' club gives a dance—and also at the best-known junior dances given during the holidays in the great cities—a certain number of girls are sometimes appointed as dance hostesses. Their duties are similar to those of the boys who serve as floor committee (or ushers) at other dances. When a hostess sees a girl stranded, she quite possibly takes her own partner to the girl. If her partner is an especial friend of hers and one she wants to continue dancing with, she goes to the stag line and takes one of the stags by the arm and asks him to cut in on her own partner, and she then dances with him again. Possibly she has to do the same thing over again. At all events, whenever she introduces a man to the stranded girl, she must see that he is relieved.

SUPPER AT A SIMPLE DANCE

As previously said, supper can be very simple. A punch bowl kept filled with some sort of thirst-quenching ice-cold fruit juice to drink between dances is, of course, important; but sandwiches and hot chocolate passed around on trays are really quite enough for refreshments. Or if you would add more, then have bouillon instead of chocolate with the sandwiches, and add ice cream and cake. Beyond this you can add as much as you may choose. At all events, for a really simple party, something hot to drink, something cold, sandwiches (not sweet), cakes (sweet) would be ample.

ABOUT MANNERS

Dancing and smoking at the same time is in very worst taste. All awkwardness seems exaggerated at a dance, because the traditions of grace and elegance are centered rather especially in the setting of a ballroom, and bad manners therefore become exaggeratedly uncouth. A method of dancing not infrequently seen in public places, whereby the girl hangs her arm around her partner's neck, puts her head on his shoulder, and then pretends she is a broken-spined horse backing out of a stall, is unspeakable. Fortunately it is unknown in best society. It is mentioned merely because very young people are inclined to like anything that suggests fun, and this grotesque clownishness may very well have started as someone's idea of fun.

When it is time to end the party, the orchestra plays "Home Sweet Home" or "Good Night, Ladies" and stops; which, of course, means that everyone should say good-night to the hostess and go home.

PICNICS

From earliest spring until latest autumn the very proposal, "Let's give a party," is almost certain to suggest a picnic of one sort or another. In its essential outline "going on a picnic" means the packing of a lunch basket—possibly several baskets—with things to eat and drink, and then either walking or sailing, paddling or motoring to some pleasant outdoor spot and eating this lunch or supper.

But, although picnics can be utterly delightful when well done, they can be altogether awful when bungled! Therefore it may perhaps be convenient to list a few general directions for the benefit of those who want to give a party of one or another picnic variety.

The first thing to decide is whether you are going to give what is merely an outdoor lunch or supper, meaning you take only things that are ready to serve, or whether you are going to build a fire and cook.

If the latter, what are you going to cook and who is going to do the cooking? And what about each and every other preparation that must be made? In short, it is important to make as careful preparations as you would were you inviting people to dine or to lunch with you at home.

You wouldn't ask people to lunch at one o'clock and then think it quite all right to serve at three; nor would you be blissfully content to give them fish or steak or chicken, one side of which is raw and one side charred to a cinder. Nor would you tranquilly proffer greasy and black-edged scrambled eggs, or ice cream in cups because it had turned to soup.

BUILDING YOUR PICNIC FIRE

But for your definite picnic example let us choose a grill supper, because this is the sort of picnic every man likes.

Your first preparation includes acquiring some sort of picnic broiler. There is an especial one with folding legs that can be bought; but if you haven't one of these, any ordinary broiler will do just as well. A really excellent suggestion is that you take two lengths of iron tubing. Don't let the children borrow the brass curtain poles or metal closet ends or bars from an old-fashioned brass or iron bed, all of which answer only too well; but give them two three-foot lengths of similar metal tubing for their own.

If the picnic is to be on a beach where wood for a fire is likely to be scarce, buy a bag of charcoal at the grocer's and take along some excelsior or prepared fire-lighter which will quickly start the fire. You must provide whoever is going to do the real cooking with the best cooking fire that can be built!

This is, of course, made by digging a basin-shaped hole something less than a foot deep, and wide enough to allow for sloping sides that won't cave in. Put your lighting material on the bottom and then your charcoal; stoke it until it is red-hot, then spread out its embers evenly.

SIMPLE PARTY GIVING

Put your two iron rods across the sand—at the surface, or sunk down a little way. Set your broiler across them, and cook!

PACKING FOR THE PERFECT PICNIC

The perfect picnic manager, like the perfect traveler, has made simplification an exact science. She knows very well that the one thing to do is to take the fewest things possible and to consider the utility of those few.

Fitted hampers, tents and umbrellas, folding chairs and tables are all very well in a shop—and all right if you have a trailer or a station wagon to take the things in—but the usual flaw of picnics is that there are too many things to carry and to look after, and to clean and pack up and take home again.

Plainly, therefore, the rule of safety is to take one big pot of something easily heatable—for example, Irish stew, creamed chicken or corned-beef hash—rather than raw meat and potatoes and vegetables to cook. But this, of course, depends entirely upon who is going to cook. For cold foods, stuffed eggs, each wrapped in wax paper, are better than plain cold boiled ones. Sandwiches of about three varieties, in addition to some of plain bread and butter, seem necessary unless you know the tastes of those who are going. And by all means label each variety. Don't attempt to take bread and fillings separately and let people make their own. The messiest picnic that can be imagined is one at which knives and plates and bread and butter and a half-dozen jars of jams and meat pastes are all blown around together and flavored with sand. Also take everything you possibly can in containers that can be burned, and use nothing but paper plates and forks and spoons and cups that can all be burned too.

The best recommendation for a picnic is everything neatly wrapped and labeled, and then everything that has been used burned. And don't leave anything behind you. And be sure that the fire is out!

DON'T TRY OUT A STRANGE PLACE

Advice scarcely necessary to offer is that for your picnic you select a site that you know something about—because you have picnicked there before and know that the ground is not swampy, or that it is not more mosquito-infested than anywhere else, or that it is not a dangerous snake country. If it is to be on a beach, it is well to remember to make some preparation to shield both your guests and the food they are to eat from sand. For this nothing is better than a few ordinary five-foot garden stakes and a few yards of ticking with a hem at each end of each length, through which a stake is inserted and then thrust into the sand, with another stake or two on the lee side. These make effective sand- and wind-breaks of the least weight and size to carry. Or you might use a double thickness of unbleached muslin with a lapover opening across the center, and make each end serve also as a bag in which to carry such things as paper napkins, cups and plates (the center hung over the shoulder and the bags balancing each other).

By the way, if you are giving a large picnic and including a number of people of average variety—by this is meant not picnic addicts—it is important to select a site that is easy to get to or away from. This suggestion is made because of a picnic once given on a far-away beach. When the tired company from the city wanted to leave, they found that their hosts had chosen a place surrounded by a sandbar which could be crossed only at high tide. And the tide was then low!

Nothing is so dampening to the enjoyment of a picnic as the presence of one or more fault-finders who never lift a finger, sit and complain of the heat, of the sun, or the chill of the wind, or the danger of sitting on the ground, or of their personal sufferings caused by mosquitoes or black flies, as though their tender skins were alone sensitive to these trials. On the other hand, if you select your company from among those who have a genuine passion for picnics, not only will they make everyone forget blowing sand and inquisitive ants or hungry mosquitoes, but most likely they will work like beavers.

CLAMBAKE

The preparations for a clambake are more specialized; but if you know how a seaweed oven is made (practically, as well as theoretically), or if someone on your beach has had long experience in making it and timing the baking of corn on the cob and potatoes and the clams, nothing is more in keeping with a holiday at the seaside than a clambake.

HOSPITALITY IN A BACK YARD IN TOWN

To the many who overlook the possibilities of the smallest of gardens as a setting for charming hospitality, the following description is offered. In a certain great city there is a certain little house less than eighteen feet wide. Its back yard is naturally the same width by about twenty feet deep. Against the fence surrounding it the vines are tacked flat, and at the far end a painted vista gives an illusion of distance. There is a flagged space next to the open double glass doors of the ground-floor rear room, and an awning drops down, hiding the surrounding buildings and showing only the walls of vines at either side with the painted vista at the end. While the early spring flowers are blooming in the beds in front of the vines, the owners of this garden are at home in it, every afternoon late, to friends who drop in for a glass of iced tea or other beverage, and who find the setting the most attractive in town.

SIMPLE PARTY GIVING

In the country a dooryard garden needs neither recommendation nor praise. Preferably the space in which one sits is paved with flagstones or brick, but it may very well be of grass. Always, of course, it is close to a door leading into the house. Sometimes it is covered with a pergola or other type of overhead trellis, supported by vine-covered posts and furniture that is cool but comfortably cushioned with waterproof material to withstand the rain. An awning that can be pulled across a foot or more above the trellis, or that takes the place of any other roof, grants protection from either rain or a too-hot sun.

DANCING PLATFORM IN THE GARDEN

A garden in which there is a permanent dance platform affords perhaps the greatest pleasure that can be devised for summer evenings. Such a platform, moreover, can easily be built in any garden where there is an available patch of level ground. For example, in their garden, which is not one of unusual size nor of especial beauty, the Littlehouses have built a permanent dancing floor, painted with four coats of deep blue paint and polished with wax. Around the edge of the floor is a protecting rail hidden by a clipped hedge unbroken except for an entrance on either side. The dance floor can be seen only from the upstairs windows of the house—from which it looks like a pool.

Impromptu dances at the Littlehouses' are as much the center of the summer social life of their neighborhood as are the outdoor swimming pools elsewhere. And since flood lighting, which is necessary to bring out the particular beauties of the garden and to light the dance floor, is part of the permanent fixtures, all the actual preparation necessary when their friends want to dance is to turn on the light switch—or perhaps not, if there is bright moonlight—and find a dance program on the radio or choose dance records for the phonograph.

THE FRIENDLIEST OF SIMPLE PARTIES

Let us say you want to give the very simplest and friendliest party possible. For supper preparations nothing could make your party more thoroughly friendly than to cook something yourself in one or more chafing-dishes. What you happen to have to eat isn't important. The point is choose whichever dish you can make exceptionally well and serve it with very little else. Before supper what you do depends, of course, upon the tastes, and perhaps the ages, of your guests. Quite possibly you just sit about and talk, or perhaps you choose the evening and the hour on purpose to tune your radio in on an especially favorite program. Or perhaps you tune in on dance music—if there are any spare inches of floor space there are always those who will dance—or perhaps you play games.

IF YOU WANT TO GO TO BED, DON'T BEGIN GAMES

It is true that most people beyond their teens are likely to put on an expression suggestive of eating lemons when anyone proposes playing games; but if you can make them begin playing clumps or consequences (or with any talent in the party, charades), you'll probably find that nothing short of the appearance of breakfast can stop them.

Of course, if in your own heart you don't want to play games, you won't be able to make anyone else want to—and that is in fact the secret of successful entertaining!

In proof of this, an occasion may be cited when the Normans gave what Mrs. Norman called a "haphazard party" in her cottage at the seashore. Without any regard to who liked or disliked whom, she asked merely those whom she happened to meet in the village post office while the mail was being sorted. The result was one of those nightmare evenings where the quarreling neighbors and the one divorced couple found themselves seated together, and the inflexible conservatives were next to the violent radicals, the highbrows next to morons, the snobs next to those who most despised them.

Fifteen minutes after their arrival everyone was occupied with the problem of how to leave without being rude, when suddenly an irrepressible young man—we'll call him Jonesy—exclaimed, "Let's all play Going to Jerusalem!" Everybody, looking glum, muttered, "Oh, no!" But whether they said it out loud or to themselves mattered nothing to Jonesy, who ordered, "Stand up, please" and took all the chairs of those who stood and put them down the middle of the room. Then he commanded a usually unapproachable pianist to "strum a march," and to Jerusalem half of those present went. The next turn included everyone, and in less than fifteen minutes a stiff, dull and utterly unmixable party had become almost a children's romp. Going to Jerusalem was followed by charades, and all those who had been contemplating going home at nine were still, at two in the morning, guessing or illustrating syllables.

Behind the trifling story of this evening lies something of real importance—something akin to a rule for happiness, which might be supposed to read: Let's not pretend that we are old while we are still young. And above all, let us not get actually old, ever, by being lazy or overcritical and always ready to protest, "Oh, no!" It's a thousand times better to encourage the frame of mind that exclaims, "Oh, yes, let's!"—whether we happen to have lived fifteen years or fifty. In short, between the young voice that responds enthusiastically "Oh, yes!" and the old voice that mumbles, "Oh-h-h, no-o-o!" lies the whole road of life.

33

American Neighborhood Customs

ASIDE from the fixed rules for speech and manner and deportment, which are the same for all well-bred persons, people living in this neighborhood or that follow the customs of the locality in which they live. In other words, to *do exactly as your neighbors do* is the only sensible rule.

SHOWERS

Showers are friendly neighborhood gatherings held usually in honor of a bride-to-be, or in welcome of a new clergyman or of new house-owners, or in expectation of the arrival of the stork. In fact, one may give a shower of almost any variety that imagination can invent. Presents given at a stork shower include everything for a new baby. A larder shower includes everything eatable. The shower for a bride is sometimes specified as a linen shower or a kitchen shower, or a silk-stocking shower or a general shower, to which each person brings what appropriate item she chooses.

The setting for a shower can be almost anything—a luncheon, a dinner, an afternoon tea, an evening party, or even a morning sewing circle.

Invitations to showers are either telephoned—"I'm having a kitchen shower for Mary on Tuesday at three o'clock"—or written on a visiting card—"Larder shower for Dr. Smythe" or "Stork shower for Mrs. Newlywed" or "Shower for Miss Mary Bride" and then the day and hour. Or, if you prefer, any shower card that appeals to you is equally proper.

It is not supposed to be quite appropriate for the invitations to be sent out by the immediate family of the bride, because each person who accepts must "shower" Mary with a present. It is true that gifts are usually sent by those who accept an invitation to a wedding reception or breakfast, but even so they are not obligatory. Moreover, a wedding is an outstanding social event and present-giving a secondary consideration, whereas the sole object of a shower is the showering of presents upon Mary.

If the invitation specifies "linen" or "kitchen utensils" or "silk stockings," the gifts should be those indicated. Sometimes the "showered" presents are given in place of wedding gifts. Sometimes they are an extra expression of generosity. Sometimes they are the donation of a small sewing circle of the bride's most intimate friends who have been busy throughout a number of months hemming or embroidering a set of "friendship" table linen, each piece of which is embellished and "signed" by the sewer. For those who in this busy age have time for such expressions of affection, such gifts have certainly a charming and personal sentiment that a bride can scarcely fail to appreciate.

Wedding presents are sent from the shop where they are bought, but gifts for a shower are given personally—usually upon arrival; but sometimes the packages are taken at the door and put with the others on a table in another room.

Or another and more effective way of giving the presents is to have them all sent to the hostess several days beforehand. She leaves the packages wrapped as they are, but puts each in a uniform outer wrapping so that the whole stack of packages shall be attractively alike. For this purpose nothing could be prettier for a bride's shower than a roll of wallpaper—something in green and white suggestive of orange blossoms under transparent cellophane, no matter what variety of gifts they may contain. (Or a blue and white paper for a kitchen shower for a new householder, or one of the colored cellophanes for a larder shower, or pink or blue tissue paper for a stork shower.) When all are wrapped, the presents are piled on a table, perhaps in another room or behind a screen, or perhaps in full view against one wall of the living room.

A suggestion to make a few presents go far is to treat each present as a treasure in a treasure hunt and tell Mary to look for them. When she finds one, she will find instructions—but not too obvious—for finding the next present.

When everyone—or almost everyone—expected has arrived, Mary opens the package one by one and thanks each giver. "Thank you, Susie—how lovely!" "Oh, Margaret, this is just what I need!" "Jane, dear, I never saw anything prettier!" It is rather safer that the cards of donors be enclosed. But if not, the given waits and as her present is unwrapped says, "That's from me."

After that, if the party is at tea time, the guests are offered light refreshments of tea or coffee and cakes; if in the evening, coffee and cakes and ice cream are served; or if at meal time, a buffet luncheon or supper is served first.

A shower for a bride may be given at any hour of the day or evening. Evening is chosen when the shower presents take the place of wedding presents, because in this case men as well as girls are invited.

Whether or not a wedding present is sent in addition to a shower gift depends upon the custom of one's own community; it also depends upon how well one knows and how much one cares for Mary. And most of all it depends upon the depth of one's purse.

The shower for a clergyman is usually given in the early evening. A stork shower is always given in the early afternoon and only intimate girl or women friends of the mother invited—that is, when the shower is an anticipation shower. Sometimes a stork shower and surprise party combined is given at the house of the mother when the baby is five or six weeks old. Although a surprise party, this is one occasion when it would be excusable for someone to give her a hint at least half an hour in advance, so that both she and the baby will be found waiting for company and not asleep. Also, usually the guests bring light refreshments with them as at all typical surprise parties. This is always the case with a surprise shower for a clergyman.

SURPRISE PARTY

Popular now as it ever was is a surprise party, given usually to new householders but equally suitable for any neighbors or friends. The general plan of a surprise party is, as everyone knows, the arriving by surprise at a friend's house in the eager hope of routing all those to be surprised out of their beds!

The ways to make preparation are two. One is to find out an evening when John and Mary Neighbor are giving a dinner at home. In this case the company who are to surprise them meet in a house near-by and then troop in a procession, with quite possibly a band leading the way, to storm the house. The second way is to choose an evening when John and Mary are dining with the Greens. In this case the Greens are, of course, in the know; and while dinner at the Greens is progressing, those who are giving the surprise take possession of John and Mary's house. When they return, a dance is in full swing. In any case, provisions for supper are always brought by the unexpected guests.

Such parties, needless to say, always consist of a group of intimate friends and usually take place on John's or Mary's birthday or some other suitable anniversary, particularly the wedding anniversaries that are celebrated in paper, wood, tin or crystal.

WARNING AGAINST GOLDEN SURPRISE

A word of warning for those who might be inclined to celebrate a golden wedding anniversary with a surprise party. If the bride and groom are young for their ages and likely thoroughly to enjoy this type of party, then this would be entirely suitable. But if life has not dealt quite so kindly, or if they were not married in their earliest youth, the disturbance of too great a surprise might very well have the opposite of happy results.

SINGING AND SEWING CIRCLES

Singing circles meet usually in the evenings and include men as well as women. They sing for a while and then have a buffet supper or more light refreshments such as coffee and sandwiches, or welsh rarebit and beer, or perhaps merely doughnuts and cider. Very often they give a concert at the end of the year. Otherwise there are no rules for singing circles—except to ostracize those who can't keep in tune.

The hostess at whose house a sewing circle meets should have an extra supply of different-sized thimbles, and of needles and several pair of scissors and spools of thread. Usually a member with a good reading voice and clear enunciation is chosen to read aloud while the others sew. What they sew depends upon the purpose of the class, which may be to make garments for a nursery or hospital or other organization; or, having no object other than meeting socially, the members sew for themselves—which perhaps means making needle-point, or darning socks, or, most likely of all, knitting. Very often a sewing circle or a reading class is also a lunch club which meets weekly or fortnightly at the houses of the various members. They sew from eleven until about one and then have a sit-down or buffet luncheon.

In many of the oldest communities, membership in the sewing circle rates as the hall-mark of highest social position. But apart from its social stamp, nothing could be more encouraging to the continued friendship of classmates.

DESSERT BRIDGE PARTY

As an innovation intended to eliminate tea-drinking and cake-eating late in the afternoon, dessert bridge parties are becoming popular in many neighborhoods. This is a back-to-husband movement especially intended for Mrs. Three-in-One, who should go home and get husband's dinner, but who stays on and on, and then eats and eats, and, wanting no dinner herself, sets a very poor one before tired and hungry husband. Each guest goes to the dessert bridge party without having eaten midday dessert at home. At the house of the hostess the dining table is set for the dessert course only: a china dessert plate and a lunch napkin on the plate (as though it were any place plate), the fork on the table at the left of the plate and the spoon at the right. Or if preferred, because rather more decorative, each place is set with a china plate and on that a glass dessert plate and on that a finger bowl and in it a few flowers, and the napkin at the left of the fork. The table covering would be the same as for a luncheon, with centerpiece and candy dishes at either side. The table should, furthermore, be set with a coffee tray in front of the hostess; while her friends are finishing their dessert, she pours the coffee, and it is handed around the table.

After coffee, they begin playing on tables already set out in the living room. The game ends at four or half past, or five at the latest. Mrs. Three-in-One goes home hungry and provides a substantial dinner. (At least this is the theory.)

(For Conventional Bridge Party Details, see Index.)

HEAVY AFTERNOON MEAL AT A CARD PARTY

Although a heavy afternoon meal served at a card party is customary in certain American localities, this practice has never been adopted in what, for want of a better word, we call the smart world, where not one in a hundred would risk her slimness of outline by eating between meals anything more than a sliver of a sandwich with her cup of sugarless tea. But for those who can stay slim and lovely no matter how much mayonnaise and chocolate and whipped cream they eat, or for those whose husbands think them more beautiful the plumper they get—what can it matter how long the menu be?

But even so, this food-on-card-table procedure sounds awkward and unpleasant. For instance, if you go into a crowded dining car on a train and have to sit at a table that has been used while the waiter clears away, lays a cloth and resets the places, you put up with it amiably, but it is not a thing that you would choose. To have this same thing done in reverse at home, certainly sounds less pleasant than the correct service of afternoon tea on a table of its own.

THE TROUBLESOME GUEST PRIZE

The prize that in many American neighborhoods is known as the "guest prize" is really not a prize at all, because it is received and not won. Should the guest for whom it is intended chance also to be "high score," she can ask that the next highest receive first-score prize and the third highest receive the second prize. If she choose, however, she is entirely within her rights to take both "guest" and "first" prize home. She must on no account give away her guest prize.

To avoid the troublesome situation of this "guest prize" complication, it is much better either that the presentation of it be made before the other guests come, or that it be put at her place at table. The point is that it should not be given at the same time nor confused with the prizes awarded for high scores.

HOURS FOR PARTY GIVING

The hour chosen for a meal or a party or a game or a visit should always be that of neighborhood custom. To invite friends to dine two hours later than their habitual meal hour is far more likely to distress than impress them with what may be intended as a fashionable innovation. People dine in London at nine, but this is no reason for upsetting the digestions of those of us who prefer to dine at seven. If weddings in the evening are customary in your neighborhood, then have your wedding in the evening too. If, on the other hand, a nine o'clock dinner hour and a noon wedding are customary, then even though you forage in the icebox an hour or more before the dinner hour, at nine you dine and at noon you marry, even though a moonlight wedding is the one that has ever been your especial fancy.

If neighbors pay visits in the evening—or if morning is the hour preferred—you take your protesting husband with you in the evening, or go by yourself in the morning, no matter how inconvenient to you personally either hour may be.

IDENTICAL PATTERN FOR EVERY SORT OF PARTY

Every sort of party, whether it be a tea, a wedding, a christening, a silver wedding, a supper, a dance, a meeting of a sewing or book club, an engagement party, a shower, house-warming, tea for some one person or for the hostess alone, is governed by the same rules.

The hostess—usually alone, but on occasions with a daughter or a guest of honor who may be receiving with her—always stands in the principal room of the house, or within easy view of the entrance, and shakes hands with each arriving guest. The guests then exchange greetings. After this they may devote the time to dancing, or playing cards, or listening to music or a speaker, if it is that kind of party being given; or they congratulate the bride and groom, or are shown over the house, or watch the unwrapping of the showered presents. But eventually they always go into the dining room and help themselves or are helped—to light or substantial refreshments set out upon the dining table.

For a between-meal hour the refreshments consist of sandwiches, cake, and tea in the afternoon; or chocolate and cake, or ice cream and cake, or bouillon and sandwiches at night. It might be noted that thick soups are an appreciated substitute for bouillon whenever other refreshments are to be light.

After the refreshments are concluded, the guests go home or continue dancing or playing cards or games, as the case may be.

34

Hospitable Hosts

To the old saying that man built the house but woman made of it a "home" might be added the modern supplement that woman accepted cooking as a chore but man has made of it a recreation. Whether it is true that to man go the laurel-wreaths for raising cookery to the heights of a fine art is a question that would be interesting to debate. That, however, is quite apart from the newest of subjects—that of party-giving by the men of the family, who might properly be called chef-hosts.

WHEN THE HOST DONS A CHEF'S CAP

It is true that the cooking of an especial concoction in a chafing-dish at table, or the cooking—or perhaps supervising—of terrapin or canvas-back ducks in the kitchen by the host himself has been the practice of many a host of past generations. But yesterday's occasional chef-hosts, who prepared a specialty to the delight of a particular few appreciative friends, are now being replaced by scores of men who have taken to the organization of supper clubs in winter and clambake clubs in summer, and who at the present moment would seem to be leading the world of Society (with a capital S) into the kitchen!

In other words, this new interest in cooking by expert amateurs has led to the organization of a number of supper clubs whose members are taking the art of cooking as a new form of competitive sport. The bi-monthly parties given at one of the latest and smartest of these clubs may perhaps be interesting not only to those who are organizing similar ones, but to every owner of a simple house that has an attractive kitchen.

But first the Club.

LET US CALL IT THE "GRILL AND SAUCE-PAN CLUB"*

Its thirty members consider themselves connoisseurs as well as expert chefs. The club house is an old barn which one of the members donated; then together they bought a small piece of land on a roadside in the country. They then had the barn hauled to its new site, and this is what they did with it.

*This name as well as the following description is purposely fictionized.

They took out the partitions, leaving one big, open, raftered room. A board sub-floor was laid, and on that linoleum, strong blue in color. Into the opening at one end that used to frame the double doors they built a big chimney of field stone; and at the opposite end a perfectly equipped kitchen was divided from the room proper by a zinc-topped work table that ran across the entire space like a counter. The face of this table was painted blue like the floor. The walls of the main part of the room, which were the soft mousy brownish color of old chestnut wood, were left unpainted. There was no furniture in the center of the room, but all along both side walls, around the corners and stopping on either side of the big fireplace, were built benches, like those in French restaurants, with backs and seats upholstered in bright red leather fabric. In front of these long benches were set wood tables neatly covered with bright blue oilcloth. The wooden chairs, ranged on the opposite sides of the tables, were painted the same bright red as the bench upholstery. Two chandeliers designed to look like candles set on wagon wheels ornamented with tin, were hung from the rafters. There were also six side brackets, matching the tin ornament. The side brackets as well as the chandeliers have hidden bulbs in addition to those in the candles, so that the choice between moderate or brilliant light is a mere question of turning it on.

The feature of the club is, of course, the kitchen end of the room. This is divided into three spaces. A door on one side leads into the men's coat room, and on the other side into the ladies' powder room. In the center space between these two rooms is a large alcove which forms the kitchen and is divided from the main room by the zinc-topped counter. The kitchen, in contrast to the weathered-wood color of the main room, is all white, bright red and chromium. The range, the icebox and cupboards are all white; the grill alone is black. The sauce pans are bright red lined with white, and all other receptacles used are of red and white china or of glass or of chromium.

GENTLEMEN COOK; LADIES LOOK ON

Suppers are given throughout the winter on the first and third Saturdays of every month, and three members are always hosts together. Each "chef" prepares one course, and each has his own apportioned section of the counter. Behind the counter are three sinks with receptacles underneath them into which all pots or dishes can at once be put out of sight until they are washed later. At one end of the counter is a lifting section like that in the counter of every store.

The guests are invited to arrive half an hour before supper, and they either stand or draw up chairs on their side of the counter to watch the chefs display their talents. Cocktails are offered them, but not in over-liberal quantity nor accompanied by appetizers, since nothing must take away from the full appreciation which "hunger lends" to the dishes in preparation.

When supper is ready, the cook of the first course beats a gong. All women guests hurry to their places at the tables and the men line up in front of the counter and carry this first course to their partners. Later, when the gong strikes for the second course, each man carries his partner's and his own dishes to one end of the counter, and then again stands in line for the second course. This is all repeated for the third course. By the time this has been eaten, the fire has purposely been encouraged to burn down to embers, so that no bright flame will detract from the ceremonial of the café brûlot* with which each supper party closes.

COFFEE CEREMONY

For this ceremony the chef-hosts come into the supper room. The first places a small high table in the center of the room. On this another places a big bowl; the third fills the bottom of it with spices. The first again pours in the brandy. All the lights in the room are turned off and the brandy and spices lighted. Then carefully, little by little, so as not to quench the flame, the coffee is poured into the mixture, which is continuously lifted with a silver ladle whose every motion intensifies the flame until finally it burns out. The lights of the room are then turned up again, logs thrown on the fire, and the coffee ladled into cups. While the lights are out, one of the hosts draws the curtains (of coarse red cotton damask) that run on a rod in front of the kitchen alcove. Women hired for the occasion then do the dishwashing and putting in order behind the scenes.

Just how far this fad—if it is a fad—will go, no one can say, but the subject seems well worth considering from several angles. One of these is that clubs of this sort are growing in popularity, but of greater importance is the undeniable fact that men like to cook—*sometimes!*

THE KITCHEN FINDS ITSELF IN SOCIETY

The popularity of these men's clubs naturally suggests to the owners of all houses which have attractive kitchens that they make a feature of the actual preparation, not of a whole dinner, but of a single supper dish or possibly two. In short, instead of always leaving the kitchen behind the scenes, why not make it (on occasion only) the company room of the house?

It is true that all-time occupancy of the kitchen by the family is possible only in the house of Mrs. Three-in-One, whose kitchen is her own. In the house of Mrs. One-Maid, the kitchen should be consid-

*See café brûlot, p. 366.

ered available only when the maid is out. And in the house of one who has many servants, the kitchen, of course, belongs to them as entirely as the front of the house belongs to the family—unless a family, happening to belong to the cooking brotherhood (or sisterhood), prefers to let its household, no matter how many, go out on the same Sunday instead of, as is usual, letting half go one Sunday and half the next.

AN OBLIGATION OF COURTESY TO THE SERVANTS

In any case, there is one exaction which every family should practice without fail: The kitchen should be returned to its rightful tenant, the cook, in just as good order as it was turned over to the family when she went out. The same is true of the pantry and even the dining room. Leaving a few pots and pans filled with water in an otherwise clean sink in an otherwise tidy kitchen is reasonable. But it would not be fair to the cook, any more than it would be to the maid alone, to leave her a kitchen that requires hours of scrubbing and polishing to get back in order.

It should be added for the benefit of the many to whom the thought of cleaning up afterward is dismal enough to take all glamour away from the kitchen, that a behind-the-scenes supper party is the one most suitable time (except an outdoor picnic) to use paper plates and napkins, which need only be gathered together and disposed of.

THE WHEN, WHERE, AND HOW OF DINING OUT-OF-DOORS

The outstanding problem of the modern day is the happy adjustment of the family which is divided on the subject of eating outdoors or indoors. Such a family is, let us say, violently separated into one group of outdoor worshipers who find no heat too great, no rain too wet, no wind too strong, and an equal number of discomfort-haters who wilt in blistering sun or grow cross in tearing wind and who have, moreover, an antipathy to insects. The joy of the first group is all too often spoiled by the obvious suffering of the second. In such a case, nothing can be done except to let the outdoor members go picnicking by themselves while the indoor lovers remain tranquilly at home.

OUTDOOR FURNISHINGS

There are many outdoor terrace, porch, and penthouse furnishings of painted iron and glass, and glass-like substances, that are having an undoubted effect upon the present popularity of eating on loggias or on terraces or in the gardens. But, for true outdoor lovers and families or parties numbering more than six, it is doubtful whether anything can ever take the place of a dining table of painted boards, either permanently nailed or removably hooked to "horses." If you intend to give big suppers or lunches and want to make sure of their success, make your table as long as you like but no more than thirty—or better, twenty-eight—inches wide. Its effect of friendliness upon the whole company is magical. A person at a very wide table talks only to the one on his right and then to the one on his left. But at a very narrow table one talks not only to one's neighbors on either side, but also to those across the table.

There is always something friendly and completely informal in the mere fact of setting a table out-of-doors. But there are certain factors essential to comfort which those who are for the first time choosing outdoor dining equipment should know. Even if you belong to a united salamander family and can stand any amount of unshaded sun no matter how broiling or brilliant, you should at least give thought to the eyes of your guests, to say nothing of your own. Do not, therefore, put a white cloth on your table, and do not use white iron and glass or white china except in the shade. To most people, the sun shining down on their heads from above and the white light shining up into their eyes from below is torturing, to say nothing of being really dangerous to sight. A table painted green or a soft green tablecloth is of course the natural color to think of; but since there is green in every direction, a deep blue is perhaps more appealing.

Wind is the greatest problem in setting an outdoor table. Even an ordinary summer breeze will blow away flowers and everything else blowable. For an ordinary outdoor table made of boards, a flower box sunk into the center of it, planted—and transplanted frequently—like a flower-shop window box, works perfectly. If you use a tablecloth, don't forget that its four corners must be weighted in case there is a wind. (For this, sew pockets in the corners—also one or two in between—and into these drop lead weights.) If the table top is of ordinary planks, either plain or painted place mats can be secured with thumb tacks. To keep small, lightweight napkins on the plates where they belong is practically impossible; therefore, the obvious thing to do is to put the napkin half under the plate instead of on it. For those who smoke at table, deep ash receivers that are half filled with water and have trap tops are essential. Otherwise, ashes blow on everything even when the breeze is otherwise scarcely perceptible.

It is absolutely necessary on a lawn (even more so on a beach) to have cross stretchers at the bottoms of both chairs and tables, even when these are of wood, since chairs sink down in the earth or sand to wherever their rungs are placed.

Every dish should, of course, have a cover. Candy and salted nuts should be put in glass-covered urns. Flowers, if not growing in a box, must be tied or wired into a bouquet and then tied to a heavy sinker.

The endless gadgets for use or for beauty on outdoor tables to be seen in the advertising pages are just one irresistible temptation after another. Among the most practical are the keep-hot (or keep-cool) dishes made of two thicknesses of aluminum with an air space between. For outdoors they are perfect, or for whenever the food is left long on the table. They are heated in the oven (or frozen in the icebox) before the food is put into them; then they are brought to the table and everything in them stays hot (or freezing cold) for an hour at least.

35

The Country House and Its Hospitality

THE difference between the great house of a few years ago with its twenty to fifty guest rooms, all numbered like the rooms in an hotel, and the farmhouse or small cottage which has but one "best" spare chamber is much the same as the difference between the elaborate and simple wedding—one merely of degree, and not of kind. In other words, all people of good taste follow the same standard pattern of living, no matter whether it is followed intact or must be greatly adjusted to fit personal needs. Ill-mannered servants, incorrect liveries or service, sloppily served food, carelessness in any of the details that to fastidious people constitute the well-run house are no more tolerated in the smallest cottage (even though it be that of Mrs. Three-in-One who has no one to wait on her but herself) than in the palace. But, because the largest houses are those which not only establish the complete pattern but challenge most criticism, suppose we begin our detailed description with them.

HOUSE PARTY OF MANY GUESTS

A week end means from Friday afternoon or from Saturday lunch to Monday morning. Everyone arrives about five o'clock on Friday or on Saturday at lunch time. Many come in their own cars; others are met at the station.

No hostess should fail to send a car to the station or boat-landing for everyone expected. If she has no conveyance of her own, she must order public ones and have the fares charged to herself.

If she is staying home to welcome those coming by motor, she tells her chauffeur whom he is to meet—or she describes them to the garage chauffeur, so that each one is greeted by name. "Mrs. Town?—Mr. Doe?—Mrs. Neighbor sent me to meet you."

GREETING OF THE HOST

The host always goes into the front hall and shakes hands with everyone who arrives. He asks the guests if they want to be shown to their rooms, and, if not, sees that the men who come give their keys to the butler or valet, and that the ladies without maids of their own give theirs to the maid who is on duty for the purpose.

GREETING OF THE HOSTESS

As soon as her guests appear in the doorway, the hostess at once rises, goes forward, shakes hands and tells them that she is glad to see them. This is one of the occasions when everyone is introduced. If at tea time, the newly arrived are supplied with tea and whatever else may be offered.

After tea, people either sit around and talk, or perhaps play bridge. About an hour before dinner the hostess asks how long each one needs to dress, and tells them the time. If any need a shorter time than she must allow for herself, she makes sure that they know the location of their rooms, and goes to dress.

A ROOM FOR EVERY GUEST

It is almost unnecessary to say that in no well-appointed house is a guest, except under three circumstances, put in a room with anyone else. The three exceptions are:

1. A man and wife, if the hostess is sure beyond a doubt that they occupy similar quarters when at home.

2. Two young girls who are friends and have volunteered, because the house is crowded, to room together in a room with two beds.

3. On an occasion such as a wedding, a dance, or an intercollegiate athletic event, young people don't mind for one night—that is spent for the greater part "up"—how many are doubled; and house room is limited merely to cot space, sofas, and—not unheard of—the billiard table.

But she would be a very clumsy hostess, who, for a week end, filled her house like a sardine box to the discomfort and resentment of everyone.

In the well-appointed house, every guest room has a bath adjoining for itself alone, or shared with a connecting room—and used only by a man and wife, by two women or by two men. A bathroom should never be shared by a woman and a man. The perfect accommodation for a man and wife is a double room with bath and a single room next.

THE GUEST ROOM

The perfect guest room is not necessarily the last word of a decorator. In fact, a room "to be looked at" is what it is NOT. Its perfection is the result of nothing more difficult than painstaking attention to detail.

It is by no means idle talk to suggest that every hostess be obliged to spend twenty-four hours in each room that is set apart for visitors. If she does not do this, she should at least make occasional tests. She should periodically go into the guest bathroom and draw the water in every fixture, to see that there is no stoppage and that the hot water faucets are not seemingly jokes of the plumber. If a man is to occupy the bathroom, she must see that the hook for a razor strop is not missing and that there is a mirror by which he can see to shave both at night and by daylight. Even though she can see to powder her nose, it would be safer to make her husband bathe and shave both a morning and an evening in each bathroom and then listen to what he says about it.

She may have a perfect housemaid, yet it is not unwise occasionally to make sure herself that every detail has been attended to; that in every bathroom there are plenty of bath towels, face towels, a freshly laundered wash rag, bath mat, a new cake of unscented bath soap in the bathtub soap rack, and a new cake of scented soap on the washstand.

It is not expected, but it is often very nice to find violet water, bath salts, listerine, talcum powder, almond or other hand or sunburn lotion in decorated bottles on the washstand shelf. But to cover the dressing table in the bedroom with brushes and an array of toilet articles is more of a nuisance than a comfort. A good clothesbrush and whiskbroom are usually acceptable, because guests almost invariably forget these.

A comforting adjunct to a spare room that is given to a woman is an electric heating pad with a plug for it beside the bed, or a hot-water bottle with a woolen cover, hanging on the back of the bathroom door. If the water does not run sufficiently hot, a card also on the back of the door might read, "Please ring bell three times for hot water to fill this."

HOSTESS SHOULD SLEEP IN HER OWN SPARE ROOM

In the bedroom the hostess should make sure—by sleeping in it at least once—that the bed is comfortable, that the sheets are long enough to tuck in. Nothing is easier than sewing a half yard wide strip of strong muslin to the botton of each sheet. She must see, too, that there are two pillows—one medium hard and one especially soft, so that one may make one's choice. There must also be plenty of covers. Besides the blankets there should be a wool-filled or an eiderdown quilt of a color to go with the room, laid across the foot of the bed.

There must, of course, be a night light at the head of the bed. Not just a decorative glow-worm effect, but a 60-watt light with an adjustable shade that is really good to lie in bed and read by. Moreover, if there are twin beds, there must be a light for each bed that is shaded from the other bed. And always there should be books—chosen more to divert than to strain the reader's attention. The sort of selection appropriate for a guest room might best comprise two or three non-fiction books of the moment, a light novel or a mystery novel, a book of essays or poetry, another of short stories, and a few of the latest magazines. It is very important that this selection be revised for each guest, for even though one may not guess accurately the taste of another, one can at least avoid making the guest room either a waste basket or a catch-all for books selected because their bindings look pretty!

There should be a candle and a box of matches, for even though there is electric light, it has been known to go out! There should also be cigarettes, matches and ash receivers on the desk and a scrap-basket beside it. In hot weather, every guest should have an electric or at least a palm-leaf fan, and in August, even though there are screens, a fly "swatter."

DRESSING TABLE AND DESK

A bedroom sofa is very important—if the room is a large one—with a sofa pillow or two and a light-weight quilt across the end of it.

The hostess should do her own hair in each room to learn whether the dressing table is placed where there is a good light over it, both by electric light and by daylight. A very simple expedient in a room where massive furniture and low windows make the daylight dressing table difficult is the European custom of putting an ordinary small table directly in the window and standing a good-sized mirror on it; or, if you have no standing mirror, any small mirror hung on the window frame will answer the purpose of comfort even better.

And the pincushion! It is more than necessary to see that the pins are usable and not rust to the head. There should be black ones and white ones, long and short; also safety pins in several sizes. Three or four threaded needles of white thread, black, gray and beige silk are an addition that has proved many times welcome. And supply a thimble of usable size—or better, two or three sizes—instead of the habitual No. 12 into which any woman whose fingers are tapered can put two together. One must also examine the writing desk to be sure that the ink is not a cracked patch of black dust at the bottom of the well, and the pens solid rust, and the writing paper textures and sizes at odds with the envelopes. There should be a fresh blotter and a few stamps. Again thoughtful hostesses put in some convenient place a card giving the post-office schedule and saying where the mail bag can be found. And a calendar, and a clock that *goes!* Is there anything more typical of the average spare room than the clock that is at a standstill?

Photograph by Samuel H. Gottscho

SITTING-ROOM CONVERTIBLE INTO BEDROOM

When the eight cushions are removed, the mattress beneath is made up as a bed. The box spring occupies the full depth of space behind pleated valance. A small table turns into a dressing table. The room has large closets and its own bath.

THE TRAY FOR A GUEST WHO BREAKFASTS IN BED
This tray should be adequately as well as attractively set, and the morning newspaper not forgotten.

PLENTY OF HANGERS

There must be plenty of clothes hangers in the closets. For women a few hat stands, and for men trouser hangers and the coat hangers that have a bar across the shoulder piece.

It is unnecessary to add that every bureau drawer should be looked into to see that nothing belonging to the family is filling the space which should belong to the guest, and that the white paper lining the bottom is fresh.

In a hunting country, there should be a bootjack and boot-hooks in the closet.

People who like strong perfumes often mistakenly think they are giving pleasure in filling all the bedroom drawers with pads heavily scented. Instead of feeling pleasure, some people are made almost sick! But all people—hay-fever patients excepted—love flowers, and vases of them beautify rooms as nothing else can. Even a shabby little room, embellished with a few wild flowers, loses all effect of shabbiness and is inviting instead.

When bells are being installed in new houses, they should be on cords and hung at the side of the bed. Light switches should be placed at the side of the door going into the room and bathroom, but the bedlight should be on its separate plug.

BUT NO SHUTTERS THAT BANG!

Guest rooms should have shutters and dark shades for those who like to keep the morning sun out. The rooms should also, if possible, be away from the kitchen end of the house and the nursery.

A shortcoming in many houses is the lack of a newspaper, and the thoughtful hostess who has the morning paper sent up with each breakfast tray, or has one put at each place on the breakfast table, deserves a halo.

At night a glass and a thermos pitcher of water should be placed by the bed.

THE GUEST CARD

Needless to say, guest cards are used only in huge houses that are now almost unknown. But the questions on it are and always have been asked by every competent hostess, though the guests may not readily perceive the fact. At bedtime she always asks, "Would you like to come down to breakfast, or will you have it in your room?" If the guest says she would like to have it in her room, she is asked what she would like to eat. She is also asked whether she cares for milk, or fruit or other light refreshment at bedtime, and whether there is a special book she would like to take up to her room.

The guest card at the Gildings' is as follows:

PLEASE FILL THIS OUT BEFORE GOING DOWN TO DINNER

What time do you want to be awakened? ....
Or, will you ring? ....
Will you breakfast upstairs? ....
Or down? ....

UNDERSCORE YOUR ORDERS

Coffee, tea, chocolate, milk,
Oatmeal, hominy, shredded wheat,
Eggs, how cooked?
Rolls, muffins, toast,
Orange, pear, grapes, melon.

AT BEDTIME WILL YOU TAKE

Milk, orangeade, grape juice?
Cookies, crackers?
Apple, pear, grapes?

Besides this list, there is a catalogue of the library with a card clipped to the cover, saying, "Following books for room No. X." Then a few blank lines and a place for the guest's signature.

AT THE DINNER HOUR

Everyone goes down to dinner at a country house party as promptly as possible, and the procedure is exactly that of all dinners.

BEDTIME

At the end of the evening, it is customary for the hostess, rather than the guests, to suggest going upstairs; but etiquette is not strictly followed in this matter. If, at a reasonable time after dinner, anyone is especially tired, he or she quite frankly says, "I wonder whether you would mind very much if I went to bed?" The hostess always answers, "Why, no, certainly not! I hope you will find everything in your room. If not, will you ring?"

It is not customary for the hostess to go upstairs with one guest if others are still sitting in her living room. She does, of course, go with an only woman guest to make sure that everything has been thought of for her comfort.

THE LITTLE HOUSE OF PERFECTION

As a complement rather than a contrast to the house party in a great house like that of the Gildings (most of which are one by one being razed to the ground), the attributes of the completely perfect house cannot be better represented than by Brook Meadows Farm, the all-the-year home of the Oldnames. Nor can anything better illustrate its perfection than an incident that actually took place there.

A great friend of the Oldnames had married a widow from a distant state. Because her husband was a man of gregarious habits and indiscriminating tastes, the new wife had no way of guessing what the Oldnames might be like nor what kind of clothes to pack. So she asked her husband to tell her something about their hosts and their house.

"Oh," said he, "they're wonderful! Their house? It's just a little farmhouse. Oldname wears a dinner coat of course; his wife wears—I don't know what—but I've never seen her dressed up a bit!"

"Evidently plain people," thought his wife. And aloud, "I wonder what daytime dress I have that I could wear in the evening! The grey voile might do. Perhaps I had better put in my cerise satin . . ."

"The cerise?" asked her husband. "Is that the red you had on the other night? It is much too handsome, much! I tell you, Mrs. Oldname never wears a dress that you could notice. She always looks like a lady, but she isn't a dressy person at all."

So the bride packed her plainest clothes, but at the last minute she put in the "cerise."

When she and her husband arrived at the railroad station, she found *that* at least primitive enough; and Mr. Oldname in much-worn tweeds might have come from a castle or a cabin. Country clothes are no evidence. But her practiced eye noticed the perfect cut of the chauffeur's coat, and that the car was beautiful.

"At least they have good taste in motors and accessories," thought she, and was glad she had brought her best evening dress.

They drove up to a low white-shingled house, at the end of an old-fashioned brick walk bordered with flowers that were a harmony in color and all in perfect bloom. She knew no inexperienced gardener produced that apparently simple approach to a door that has been chosen as frontispiece in more than one book on Colonial architecture. The door was opened by a maid in a silver-gray taffeta dress, with organdie collar, cuffs and apron, white stockings and silver buckles on black slippers. The guest saw a quaint hall and vista of rooms that at first sight might easily be thought "simple" by an inexpert appraiser. But Mrs. Oldname, who came forward to greet her guests, was the antithesis of everything the bride's husband had led her to believe.

To describe Mrs. Oldname as "simple" in her environment is about as apt as to call a pearl "simple" because it doesn't dazzle. Nor was there an article in the apparently simple living room that would be refused were it offered to a museum.

The tea table was Chinese Chippendale and set with old Spode on a lacquered tray over a mosaic-embroidered linen tea cloth. The soda biscuits and cakes were light as froth; the tea a special blend sent from China. There were three other guests besides the bride and groom: a United States Senator, and a diplomat and his wife who had lately been liberated from long internment in enemy country. Instead of bridge there was conversation.

When the bride went to her room—which adjoined that of her husband—she found her bath drawn, her clothes laid out, and the dressing-table lights lighted.

That night the bride wore her cerise dress to one of the most perfect dinners she had ever gone to.

When at last they went upstairs and she saw her husband alone, she took him to task. "Why in the name of goodness didn't you tell me the truth about these people?"

"I did tell you it was a little house. It was you who insisted on bringing that red dress. I told you it was too handsome!"

"Handsome!" she cried in tears. "I don't own anything to compare with the least article in this house. And that 'simple' little woman, as you call her, would make almost anyone seem provincial. As for her clothes, they are priceless—just as everything is in this little gem of a house!"

These two houses are extremes, but each an extreme of luxury—from which, however, is derived the perfect pattern that is to be followed only so far as it is useful and to be discarded the moment it is not. As a matter of fact Mrs. Three-in-One could perfectly well follow every detail described.

GUEST-ROOM SERVICE

Unless a visitor brings her own maids, the personal maid of the hostess (if she has one; otherwise, the housemaid) unpacks the luggage, lays toilet articles on the dressing table and in the bathroom, puts folded things in the drawers and hangs dresses on hangers in the closet. If, as she unpacks, the maid sees that something of importance has been forgotten, she tells her own lady; or, in case she has been long employed, she knows what selection to make and supplies the guest, without asking, with such articles as comb and brush or clothes brush or tooth brush. (This last article is afterwards packed in the guest's luggage.)

Whoever looks after the host's clothes performs the same service for the men. In small establishments, where there is no lady's maid or valet, the housemaid is always taught to unpack guests' belongings and to press and hook up ladies' dresses, and to send gentlemen's clothes to a tailor to be pressed.

In big houses, breakfast trays for the ladies are usually carried to the bedroom floor by the butler—some butlers delegate this service to a footman—and are handed to the lady's maid or else the housemaid, who takes the tray into the room. In small houses they are carried up by the waitress.

Trays for men visitors are rare, but when ordered are carried up and into the room by the butler. If there are no menservants, the waitress carries up the tray.

BREAKFAST TRAY ADVANTAGES

Unless breakfast is at a set time and everyone comes down promptly, the advantage of having one's guests choose breakfast upstairs is that no delayed breakfast prevents the dining room's being put in order or the lunch table set. Trays, on the other hand, can stand all morning "all set" in the pantry and interfere much less with the dining room work.

Every china store carries breakfast sets, of course, but only in "open" stock patterns can one buy extra dishes or replace broken ones—a fact it is well to remember. A set always comprises a coffee or teapot, a hot milk pitcher, a cream pitcher and sugar bowl, a cup and saucer, two plates, an egg cup and a covered dish. A cereal is usually put in the covered dish, toast in a napkin on a plate, or eggs and bacon in place of cereal. This with fruit is the most elaborate "tray" breakfast ever provided.

TRAY SERVICE

When a guest rings for breakfast, the housemaid goes into the room, opens the blinds, and in cold weather lights the fire, if there is an open grate in the room. Asking whether a hot, cool or cold bath is preferred, she goes into the bathroom, spreads a bath mat on the floor, a big bath towel over a chair, and draws the bath. As few people care for more than one bath a day and many people prefer their bath before dinner instead of before breakfast, this office is often performed at dinner time.

TIPS

Fortunately, in the United States, when you dine in a friend's house, you do not tip anyone—ever. But when you go to stay as a house guest, you do give a tip. If you have ample means, you naturally tip more generously than you do if you have very small means. A fixed schedule is really impossible to prepare, because each occasion varies.

To an average servant in an average house, two dollars is about right for a week end. Mrs. Lavender, staying with the Littlehouses and not making more work than the least possible, might quite acceptably give no more than a dollar for a week. Intimate friends in a medium-sized house send tips to all the servants—perhaps only a dollar apiece, but no one is forgotten. In a very big house, this is never done; you tip only those who have served you. If you have your maid with you, you always give her about two dollars to give the cook—often the second one—who prepared her meals and one dollar for the kitchen maid who set her table.

A gentleman (very unfairly) scarcely ever remembers any of the women (except a waitress) and tips only the butler and the valet, and sometimes the chauffeur. The least he can offer any of the menservants is two dollars and the most ever is five. No woman gets as much as that, for such short service. If a gentleman brings his own valet, he gives him money for his tips exactly as a lady gives tipping money to her maid.

In a few houses the tipping system is abolished, and in every guest room, in a conspicuous place either on the dressing table or over the bathtub where you are sure to read it, is a sign saying:

> Please do not offer tips to my employees. Their contract is with this special understanding, and proper arrangements have been made to meet it. You will not only create "a situation," but cause the immediate dismissal of anyone who may be persuaded by you to break this rule of the house.

The notice is signed by the host. The arrangement referred to is one whereby every guest means a bonus of so much per day added to the wages of all employees. This system is much to be preferred for two reasons. First, self-respecting servants dislike the demeaning effect of tips—an occasional few won't take them. Secondly, they can count that so many visitors will bring them precisely such an amount.

HOW TIPS ARE GIVEN

Just before the time for saying good-by to your hostess, when the maid has finished packing your bag and the chambermaid is probably doing up your room, you give each her tip. And you give the butler his—or the waitress hers—in the front hall. You may always give the butler a tip for any other menservants.

In a small house, if the waitress is not in the hall, you go to the pantry and put the money into her hand. If you are an habitual visitor and know her name, you say, "Good-by, Anna, and thank you." Then you go into the kitchen and do and say the same thing or you may, after giving Anna her own tip, hand her a second sum of money saying, "Please give this for me to the cook." If Anna has pressed your dress, let us say, or sewn something that had ripped or done any special service, you give her fifty cents or a dollar or two extra—and when you say good-by, you add "Thank you"—for whatever the service was.

HOUSES WE LIKE TO STAY IN

In houses where visitors like to go again and again there is always a happy combination of some attention on the part of the host and hostess, and the perfect freedom of the guests to occupy their time as they choose. In other words, while we of the modern day like to have some attention paid to us at least now and then, the majority of us—at least those on the far side of our teens—would rather go to stay with one who lets us quite alone than ever again go to stay with one who is over-energetic.

THE ENERGETIC HOSTESS

The energetic hostess is she who fusses and plans continually, who thinks her guests are not having a good time unless she rushes them, Cook's-tourist fashion, from this engagement to that, and crowds with activity and diversion—never mind *what* so long as it is something to see or do—every moment of their stay.

She walks them through the garden to show them all the nooks and vistas. She dilates upon the flowers that bloomed here last month and are going to bloom next. She insists upon their climbing over rocks to a summer-house to see the view; she insists on taking them in another direction to see an old mill; and, again, everyone is trouped to the cupola of the house to see another view.

She insists on everyone's playing croquet before lunch, to which she gathers in a curiously mixed collection of neighbors. Immediately after lunch everyone is driven to a country club to see some duffer golf—for some reason there is never "time" in all the prepared pleasures for any of her guests to play golf themselves.

After twenty minutes at the golf club, they are taken to a church fair. The guests are introduced to the ladies at the booth and those who were foolish enough to bring their purses with them from now on carry around an odd assortment of fancy work.

There is another entertainment that her guests must not miss! A flower pageant of the darlingest children fourteen miles away! Everyone is dashed to that. On someone's front lawn, daisies and lilies and roses trip and skip—it is all sweetly pretty, but the sun is hot and the guests have been on the go for a great many hours. Soon, however, their hostess leaves. "Home at last!" think they. Not at all. They are going somewhere for tea and French recitations. But why go on? The portrait is fairly complete, though this account covers only a few hours and there is still all the evening and tomorrow to be filled in just as liberally.

THE ANXIOUS HOSTESS

The anxious hostess does not insist on your ceaseless activity, but she is no less persistent in filling your time. She is always asking you what you would like to do next. If you say you are quite content as you are, she nevertheless continues to shower suggestions. Shall she turn on the radio or shall she play the phonograph to you? Would you like her to telephone to a friend who sings too wonderfully? Would you like to look at a portfolio of pictures? If you are a moment silent, she is sure you are bored, and wonders how to divert you!

DON'TS FOR HOSTESSES

When a guest asks to be called half an hour before breakfast, don't have him called an hour and a half before because it takes you that long to dress, nor allow him a scant ten minutes because the shorter time is seemingly sufficient. Too often the summons on the door wakes him out of sound sleep; he tumbles exhausted out of bed, into clothes, and downstairs, to wait perhaps an hour for breakfast.

If a guest prefers to sit on the veranda and read, don't interrupt him every half page to ask if he really does not want to do something else. If, on the other hand, a guest wants to exercise, don't do everything in your power to obstruct his starting off by saying that it will surely rain, or that it is too hot, or that you think it is senseless to spend days that should be a rest to him in utterly exhausting himself.

Don't, when you know that a young man cares little for feminine society, fine-tooth-comb the neighborhood for the dullest or silliest young women to be found.

Don't, on the other hand, when you have an especially attractive young woman staying with you, ask a stolid middle-aged couple and an octogenarian professor for dinner because the charm and beauty of the former is sure to appeal to the latter.

Don't, because you personally happen to like a certain young girl who is utterly old-fashioned in outlook, and different from ultra modern others who are staying with you, try to "bring them together." Never try to make any two people like each other. If they do, they do; if they don't, they don't, and that is all there is to it. But it is of vital importance to your own success as hostess to find out which is the case and collect or separate them accordingly.

THE PERFECT HOSTESS

The ideal hostess must have so many perfections of sense and character that were she described in full, no one seemingly but a combination of seer and angel could ever hope to qualify.

She must first of all consider the inclinations of her guests; she must not only make them as comfortable as the arrangements and limits of her establishment permit, but she must subordinate her own inclinations utterly. At the same time, she must not fuss and flutter and get agitated and seemingly make efforts in their behalf. Nothing makes a guest more uncomfortable than to feel his host or hostess is being put to a great deal of bother or effort on his account.

A perfect hostess like a perfect housekeeper has seemingly nothing whatever to do with household arrangements, which apparently run in oiled grooves and of their own accord.

Certain rules are easy to observe once they are brought to attention. A hostess should never speak of annoyances of any kind—no matter what happens! Unless she is actually unable to stand up, she should not mention physical ills any more than mental ones. She has invited people to her house, and as long as they are under her roof, hospitality demands that their sojourn shall be made as pleasant as lies in her power.

If the cook leaves, then a picnic must be made of the situation as though a picnic were the most delightful thing that could happen. Should a guest be taken ill, she must assure him that he is not giving the slightest trouble; at the same time nothing that can be done for his comfort must be overlooked. Should she herself or someone in her family become suddenly ill, she should make as light of it as possible to her guests, even though she withdraw from them. In that event she must ask a relative or intimate friend to come in and take her place. Nor should the deputy hostess dwell to the guests on the illness, or whatever it is that has deprived them of their hostess.

36

Whether You Are Hostess or Guest

IN other days when slow traveling made distances distressingly fatiguing, no limit was set upon a guest's visit. In fact, one young woman who went to spend a fortnight with friends in Virginia stayed thirty years—until she died. But in the present day and age, a hostess always says definitely, "Will you come on Friday for over Sunday?" or "Will you come on the sixth for a week?" or "Will you come for the month of September?"

The guest who accepts may shorten her visit, but she must not stay beyond the time she was asked for, unless especially urged to do so. Even then it is generally wiser to go and be missed than to run the risk of outstaying her welcome.

THE ART OF BEING A HOUSE GUEST

Having accepted the invitation, there are four details which demand your attention: selection of clothes to be taken, selection of luggage to put them in, selection of trifling gifts, and selection of the ideal guest's frame of mind—assuming that you want to be an ideal guest!

It is not necessary, but it is always courteous to take your hostess a gift—or better, if she has children, to take presents to them. The conventional list of flowers, fruit, candy, or a book is really not a best choice, unless you *know* of a book she wants, or that she *eats* candy, has no flowers in her garden or fruit on her trees. As to the children, if they are young, a collection of small articles from a ten-cent store often gives them more pleasure than a single gift of value.

Your first concern when going on a visit is to condense your luggage in both quantity and size—particularly size. If you are to need many things, it will be better to take several small pieces rather than one giant wardrobe trunk.

It is sometimes impossible to go for a week end without a good deal of luggage. An athletic man, who is likely to ride and play golf and tennis and perhaps polo, might easily be taken for a vaudeville star carrying his properties with him. Otherwise a dinner coat, colloquially known as a tuxedo, and one or, at most, two country suits with the necessary shirts, shoes, ties, etc., will suffice.

TAKE YOUR OWN SPORTS CLOTHES

If you are going where you are to swim or ride or play games, be sure you take your own bathing suit, riding habit, racket or golf clubs, and your own warm coat. What long-suffering hostess is not familiar with the bathing suit wet and mildewed, the rotted rubber cap stuck tight as a plaster, the tennis racket left out on the grass overnight, the golf clubs broken, the polo coat spotted with machine oil.

THE GUEST NO ONE INVITES AGAIN

It too often follows that the borrower is likewise an abuser of the lender's property. The guest no one invites a second time is the one who runs a car to destruction and a horse to a lather, who "dog ears" books, who burns cigarette trenches on table edges, who uses towels for boot rags, who stands wet glasses on polished wood, who tracks muddy shoes into the house, and leaves his room looking as though it had been through a cyclone. Nor are men the only offenders. Women have been known to commit every one of these offenses and more besides.

Perhaps the greatest damage that most of us are ever asked to bear is that caused by a lap dog which is taken everywhere and allowed to run free because of its owner's bland unawareness that, although it may be house-trained in its own home, all strange places are outdoor places to it, and the chairs and sofas in a strange house are all "trees in the street."

Besides these actually destructive shortcomings, there are evidences of the bad upbringing of modern youth, whose lack of consideration is scarcely less annoying. Those who are late for every meal; cheeky others who invite friends of their own to meals without the manners or the decency to ask their hostess's permission; who help themselves to a car and go off and don't come back for meals at all; and who write no letters afterwards, nor even take the trouble to go up and speak to a former hostess when they see her again! This abuse of hospitality is of course more often met with by hostesses of great estates who have general week-end parties than by the hostess of a little house who seldom has anyone staying with her except a really intimate friend.

Needless to say, a young person who is considerate is a delight immeasurable—such a delight as only a hostess of much experience can perhaps appreciate. A young girl who tells where she is going, first asking whether it is all right, and who finds her hostess as soon as she is in the house at night to report that she is back, is the one who very surely will be asked again and often. A young man, of course, is much freer, but a similar deference to the plans of his hostess and to the hours and customs of the house will result in repeated invitations for him also.

The lack of these things, showing want of common civility and decency, reflects not only on the girls and boys themselves, but on their parents, who failed to set proper examples of good manners to their children at home.

THE IDEAL HOUSE GUEST

The laws governing the behavior of the ideal guest are by no means easy to follow—at least not for some people. Whether easy or not, you as a guest must conform to the habits of the family with which you are staying. You take your meals at their hour, you eat what is put before you, and you get up and go out and come in and go to bed according to the schedule arranged by your hostess. *And no matter how much the hours or food or arrangements may upset you, you must appear blissfully content.*

When the visit is over, you need never enter that house again; but while you are there, you must like it. You must like the people you meet and the things they do. That is the first and the inviolable law for the guest. If you neither understand nor care for dogs or children, and both insist on climbing all over you, you must seemingly like it, just as you must be amiable and polite to your fellow guests, even though they be of all the people on earth the most detestable to you. You must, with the very best dissimulation at your command, appear to find the food delicious though they offer you all of the viands that are especially distasteful to you or to which you are allergic. You must disguise your hatred of red ants and scrambled food, if everyone else is bent on a picnic. You must pretend that six is a perfect dinner hour though you never dine before eight, or, on the contrary, you must wait until eight-thirty or nine with stoical fortitude, though your supper hour is six and by seven your chest seems securely pinned to your spine.

YOU CAN SEND YOURSELF A TELEGRAM

If you go to stay in a small house in the country, and they give you a bed full of lumps in a room of mosquitoes and flies on a floor over that of a crying baby, under the eaves with a temperature of over a hundred, you *can* the next morning walk to the village and send yourself a telegram and leave! But though you feel starved, exhausted, wilted, and are mosquito bitten until you resemble a well-developed case of chickenpox or measles, by not so much as a facial muscle must you let the family know that your comfort lacked anything that your happiest imagination could picture—nor must you confide in anyone afterwards (having broken bread in the house) how desperately wretched you were.

TO BE ALWAYS IN DEMAND

If you know anyone who is always in demand, not only for dinners, but for trips on private cars and yachts, and long visits in country houses, you may be very sure of one thing—the popular person is first of all unselfish or else extremely gifted; very often both.

The ideal guest not only tries to wear becoming clothes, but tries to get into an equally becoming frame of mind. No one is ever asked out very much if she is in the habit of telling people all the misfortunes and ailments she has experienced or witnessed, though the perfect guest listens with apparent sympathy. Another attribute of the perfect guest is never to keep people waiting. She is always ready for anything —or nothing. If a plan is made to picnic, she likes picnics above everything and proves her liking by enthusiastically making the sandwiches or the salad dressing or whatever she thinks she makes best. If, on the other hand, no one seems to want to do anything, the perfect guest has always a book she is absorbed in, or a piece of sewing she is engrossed with, or else beyond everything she would love to sit in an easy chair and do nothing.

This ideal guest is an equally ideal hostess; the principle of both is the same: a ready smile, a quick sympathy, a happy outlook, consideration for others, tenderness toward everything that is young or helpless, and forgetfulness of self, which is not far from the ideal of womankind.

HOW THE EXPERT VISITOR LOOKS AFTER HIS OWN COMFORT

The most trying thing to people of very set habits is an unusual breakfast hour. When you have the unfortunate habit of waking with the dawn, and the household you are visiting has the custom of sleeping on Sunday morning, the long wait for your coffee can quite actually upset your whole day. On the other hand, to be aroused at seven on the only day when you do not have to hurry to business, in order to yawn through an early breakfast and then sit around and kill time, is quite as trying. The guest with the "early" habit can in a measure prevent discomfort. He can carry in a small case (locked if necessary) a very small solidified alcohol outfit and either a small package of tea or powdered coffee, sugar, powdered milk, and a few crackers. He can then start his day all by himself in the barnyard hours without disturbing anyone, and in comfort to himself. Few people care enough to "fuss," but if they do, this equipment of an habitual visitor with incurably early waking hours is given as a suggestion.

Or perhaps the entire guest situation may be put in one sentence. If you are an inflexible person, very set in your ways, don't visit! At least don't visit without carefully looking the situation over from every angle to be sure that the habits of the house you are going to are in accord with your own.

A solitary guest is naturally much more dependent on his host (or her hostess), but on the other hand he or she is practically always a very intimate friend who merely adapts himself or herself like a chameleon to the customs and hours and diversions of the household.

WHEN YOU STAY IN A LITTLE HOUSE

When you are visiting in a house run by one maid, it is inconsiderate to make your visit a burden through the extra "picking up" that your careless disorder entails. Even should you be staying in a house where there are many servants, it should be remembered that each has her share of work to do. If the housemaid offers to press a dress that has become mussed in packing, you can accept her offer with gratitude and later give her a gratuity—but you should hesitate to ask this service.

WHEN YOU HAVE TO LEAVE BEFORE A PARTY IS OVER

At a musicale or other performance, when you cannot stay until the conclusion of the program, you should sit as near the door as possible. It is discourteous to the performers to leave before the conclusion of their offering.

THE GUEST ON A YACHT

The sole difference between being a guest at a country house and a guest on a yacht is that you put to a very severe test your adaptability as a traveler. You live in very close quarters with your host and hostess and fellow guests, and must therefore be particularly on your guard against being selfish or out of humor. If you are on shore and don't feel well, you can stay home; but off on a cruise, if you are ill you have to make the best of it, and a seasick person's "best" is very bad indeed! Therefore, let it be hoped you are a good sailor. If not, think very, very carefully before you embark!

WHEN YOU ARE THE HOSTESS

When you are the hostess, you must see that no guest is left standing alone. You must—if there is to be more than one table—decide beforehand who are to play at each and put a list of four names on each table. Also take much more trouble to be sympathetic and agreeable than when you are a guest. As a guest, it is not your fault that a shy person sits pinched together in a corner. But if you have invited her to your own house, it is your duty to dispel her shyness, either by sitting beside her or by bringing her into the circle in which you are sitting.

"POT-LUCK" HOSPITALITY

A rather typical husband's idea of hospitality is to bring an unannounced friend home with him. And his typical complaint is that his wife's idea of hospitality is to invite people to "dine on the eighteenth" and have everything so brought in for the occasion that he hardly knows his own table and certainly doesn't know the hired waiters walking around it. This inclines most of us to sympathize strongly with the man.

Of course, if the day is one when there happens to be just enough dinner for two, and really not enough for three, and there is nothing in the house to make an extra portion with—and the husband then brings in a friend with a full-sized appetite—his wife would have cause for distress because there is not enough to eat.

The only thing she can do is to say good-naturedly to the unexpected guest that if he doesn't mind "short rations" this once, he shall have extra long ones next time! Thereupon she at least tries to make the friendliness of her welcome disguise the dinner's shortcomings. If a course consists of two "individual" dinners, there is nothing to do but to pretend she is "on a diet" of whatever she may have found in the larder.

On no account may she let the guest feel that his presence is an inconvenience to her. If necessary to make any comment, it must be done light-heartedly. And, unless the menu is so meager that he actually gets up from the table as hungry as when he sat down, the chances are that he will never notice the dinner's shortcomings.

DETAILS OF INTEREST TO THE HOSTESS

If your guests are invited to an entertainment at any time between meal hours, the refreshments are served afterwards. But if the invitation is for an hour between twelve-thirty and one, or six and eight, breakfast, lunch, dinner or supper is served first and the entertainment takes place afterwards—with the exception of a wedding, at which refreshments follow the ceremony.

FIRST AID TO A SUCCESSFUL HOSTESS

To be able to remember the certain dishes that your friends like, or more especially the ones they avoid, is a wonderful asset that can be acquired by anyone willing to take a little trouble. If you haven't a talent for remembering—and few of us have—then keep a "like and dislike" notebook in which you index: "John Allen—cannot eat shellfish, red meat, or strawberries. Favorite dishes, chicken Maryland and roast turkey. Took two helpings chocolate ice cream. Likes coffee very strong." Opposite John Allen's food page you might note that he dislikes Susie Long, dislikes bridge with Major Case. And so on indefinitely with each person you are likely to ask to your house.

Nothing is a greater help to your success than the use of just such information. The unobserving, uncaring hostess will time and time again invite John Allen and give him crabs, red meat, strawberries, and tastelessly weak coffee, seat him at table next to Susie Long, and at the bridge table with Major Case. John Allen is evidently a dyspeptic, but he illustrates the idea!

When inviting a stranger to your house, you offer him the best you can provide, and if your choice be unfortunate for him, it can't be helped. But there is no excuse for not remembering that a friend persistently refuses certain dishes—that is, if you would be a perfect hostess.

THE GIVE AND TAKE OF HOSPITALITY

It is true that a return invitation should, when possible, be paid for every first invitation. This modifying clause "when possible" indicates the difference between the reasonableness of today in contrast to the fixed exactions of yesterday. Today we return hospitality when and as we can. And if we can't return it—at least, in kind—no great harm is done.

For instance, let us say that the Greathouses invite their friends the Onerooms first to dinner, then to lunch, then to dinner again throughout every month in the year. It is entirely possible that the Onerooms proffer no return invitations whatsoever, and yet the Greathouses may very well feel themselves repaid many times over. Mary Oneroom perhaps puts herself out to do a dozen kindnesses of one sort or another, or quite possibly she and her husband repay the hospitality only with themselves, with their good looks, their amiability, their tact, their wit or their sympathy. This "payment-of-oneself," as the French say, is an important phase of hostess-and-guest obligation which many people overlook!

Mrs. Greathouse, who likes nothing better than giving parties, cannot possibly give them without guests, can she? The unthinking may imagine that mere money will do. But let us draw the picture of a beautiful background, a splendid house, a perfect butler, a row of smart footmen, floral decorations, an orchestra, beautiful table appointments, a perfectly prepared menu, Mr. and Mrs. Greathouse in flawless evening clothes waiting in a flawless drawing room—for whom? That's it, exactly! For their guests. And the quality of their party depends first and last upon the people who are coming. It is the guests who make the party a brilliant success or a dull failure. Every prominent hostess knows that she must more or less depend upon a few especially adaptable and tactful and personable aides, such as the Gaylings who are always smart and amusing, and the Lovejoys who have good looks, tact and charm, found only in those who are keenly interested in people and things in general, and not especially interested in themselves.

Obviously a hostess who says, "We have had the Gaylings four times this year and the Lovejoys time and again, and I'm not going to ask them until they invite us back" is without any sense of values. No wonder her parties are failures. Naturally no hostess continues sending invitations to those who repeatedly decline, or to those who show no appreciation or who make no return in whatever they can. But a hostess of talent would never put the Gaylings or the Lovejoys or the Onerooms on the debtor side of her ledger any more than she would put flowers or music or professional entertainers there.

This does not mean that those who can make "material" return are not under any obligation to do so. To keep the scales balanced, it is necessary that we contribute something. But that "something" can be anything that opportunity suggests—a cup of tea with someone especially interesting, a trifling present now and then, or the payment made with the cooperative effort of our own talents—whatever they may be.

COURTESY TOWARD ARTISTS AND ENTERTAINERS

Apart from the courtesies that every really well-bred hostess instinctively shows alike to friends, acquaintances or strangers who are admitted to her house, particular rules that should apply in reference to professional artists do not go very far because so much depends upon circumstances. Generally speaking, all entertainers should be admitted at the front door, of course.

Musicians who play at a dance or at a wedding reception necessarily arrive long before the guests, and are shown at once to a dressing room and then to the place where they are to play. They should be greeted briefly by whoever is in charge of arrangements. Ginger ale or other iced drinks of simple variety should be taken to them from time to time. Refreshments should also be taken to them at the time that fits in best with their program.

Soloists or actors who are to make their entrance from behind scenes on a stage should be shown to dressing rooms and then to the best "green room" the house can provide. They should be greeted as soon after their arrival as possible by the host or hostess or both, who naturally asks whether there is anything that would add to their comfort. Whether after their performance they meet many of the guests or none depends upon their own standing no less than upon their personality. When musicians or actresses or actors are especially charming or talented—or both—guests are likely to ask to meet them.

When several concert artists, lecturers, or other performers make up the program, they are usually shown to front-row places in the music room or ballroom by their host or by a member of the family.

COURTESY TO A CELEBRITY

A real celebrity, whether a star in the musical world or a notable person who is to lecture, is usually the guest of honor and treated as such in every particular—except that he (or she) does not take his place in the receiving line and meet the guests as they arrive. Since the hostess cannot leave her place at the door, the host or another member of the family is delegated to greet the celebrity upon his arrival and to conduct him to whichever is the most suitable room in which to wait until it is time to make his entrance. The host or delegate remains with the artist or speaker until the hostess herself appears. She greets the celebrity, and conducts him to the music room or to the platform and introduces him to the audience. At the end of the program the hostess stands beside the celebrity and introduces those of her guests who come up to be introduced.

But no matter in which category an artist belongs, there is a certain purely business matter-of-factness to the situation of a professional fulfilling an engagement. He goes prepared to do to the best of his ability what he has agreed to do, and at the close of his performance he receives the sum that has been agreed upon. Whether in addition to this he has a delightful evening or a trying one is, so far as his business contract goes, beside the mark.

INEXCUSABLE BEHAVIOR TO FRIENDS WHO ARE PROFESSIONALS

For this reason a far more inexcusable example is that of a hostess who considers the talents of professional friends—and even bare acquaintances—as assets to which she has proprietary rights. Don't we know Mrs. Hi Wayman, who invites Mr. Barrytone Tops or Mr. Hit-on-Broadway to dine on Sunday evening! After dinner she coyly announces that she just knows that Mr. Tops will be delighted to sing, or that Mr. Hit-on-Broadway will of COURSE do that delicious scene which is the only reason why the theater is packed to bursting every night in the week except this—his one evening of rest!

It is true that at a party of considerable size a star professional can (or possibly must) decline on the plea that contracts prohibit his appearance. But at an informal dinner at which one or two others of lesser talent have contributed their part, it is often embarrassing to refuse because it seems ungenerous to all those present who so eagerly look toward him. But actually it is unfair to expect someone to return the courtesy of a little food and a place at table between no matter how pleasant companions with an entertainment commercially valued at something approaching—or possibly surpassing—four figures!

FAVORS TOO MUCH TAKEN FOR GRANTED

Much might be said about the unthinking casualness with which numberless people ask favors of their professional friends. Put bluntly, one would not go to a bank and ask for money, nor to the shop of a milliner and ask to be given a hat, and yet the friends of a professional artist will think nothing of asking for a sketch or a recital. And the work of every professional is his bank account. If he gives to one person, how can he refuse to give to the next—and who will want to buy what is given so freely?

Of much less importance, but merely illustrating the point: The barest acquaintances of an author think nothing of asking him for his books. Almost all people imagine that books grow like daisies in the field and that an author need merely pick them at random. Doctors and lawyers are constantly asked for professional advice by people they meet casually in the houses of their friends. As for people of the theater, no others in all the professions in the world are so persistently asked to give their time, their vitality and their talent. And in nearly all cases they are delighted to give generously to someone they care for or to a cause in which they are interested; but when they are asked to give, a conventional "I'm so sorry" should be respected without forcing them into a position that seems (to them) ungracious.

If musicians are amateurs, however, their friends can perfectly well ask them to play at a musical. But they should not be asked to provide a background accompaniment to chatter as a certain quartette was expected to do at a wedding reception. No one with any sensibility would invite first-class artists to play or sing and then make no effort to preserve silence during their performance. On the other hand, professional dance orchestras and other party musicians who play at dances and at weddings do not expect, or even want, to face a room full of completely silent people sitting in neat rows on gilt chairs.

RECEIVING GUESTS IN A CLUB OR RESTAURANT

When giving a lunch or any party in a club or hotel, the hostess takes her place as near the entrance as she conveniently can, without dominating the public room. As her guests arrive, they join her and stand or sit near her.

If the room is filled with others, she herds her own group, as it were, a little apart. When their number is complete, they go to the dining room and to the table, which must always have been prepared in advance for them.

GUESTS AT A BANQUET

It is only at a semi-public lunch or dinner, at which there is a separate speakers' table, that the guests take their places without waiting for the arrival of the principal guest.

HOSTESS ENTERS LAST

If entering a room or her house with a guest, a hostess goes first only when necessary to show the way. And then she usually says, "Excuse me for going first."

DON'T!—WHEN YOU ARE HOSTESS

Don't pretend to be other than you are. In other words, don't dress the chore-man as butler, or the grocery boy as a footman in the hope of impressing your neighbors. To make too much effort is always a mistake.

On the other hand, don't lazily and incompetently think that no provision at all is "plenty good enough."

DO!—WHEN YOU ARE A GUEST

It is not necessary to be told, when going out on the street, to put on a hat and perhaps a coat and gloves, or when going to swim to wear a bathing suit, or when going to a dinner party to wear evening dress.

But there are lots of people who, taking great pains to put on becoming clothes, never for an instant think of putting on a becoming frame of mind. When going to a party, it is far more important to put a headache or a worry out of view than to wear a new dress.

ANSWERS TO READERS' QUESTIONS

EXPLAINING THE TERM "GUEST OF HONOR"

In answering the inquiry of a society reporter, I mentioned that Mrs. Prominent was the guest of honor. The paper reported that the party was "given for Mrs. Prominent." I had not wanted to create this impression because, since Mrs. Prominent is very important and not an especial friend, it might suggest the motive of a climber, whereas to say that she had the honor place at table seemed to me only courteous. I called the newspaper to register a complaint but they would not agree with my reasoning. Will you tell me whether the guest of honor is necessarily one for whom a party is especially given?

The term "guest of honor" is ambiguous in that it may mean the lady for whom the party was given, or equally well mean that she merely sat in the place of honor at table—which automatically bestows the right to be served first and the obligation to leave first. But when you described Mrs. Prominent as "the guest of honor," the reporter was right in assuming that the party was given for her.

CONSIDERATION FOR THOSE WHO ARE AFFLICTED WITH ANTIPATHY TO CATS

We have recently moved to a new community where everyone is making us feel at home. But a serious problem threatens to spoil everything. Last evening, at the house of a new friend, we were having a pleasant time until suddenly my husband turned deathly pale and trembled as with a violent chill. No one could have failed to notice that he was very ill. I knew immediately that he was suffering from a genuine illness, but one which I can hardly hope strangers will understand. I made excuses, explaining that it must be the fish we had for supper. Everyone was kind and helped him into our car, and I drove him home. But what happened was that our hosts had a cat, and a cat always affects my husband this way. If a cat should jump on him, I'm afraid he might even die. What CAN *we do about this, Mrs. Post? We like these people so much! And yet we can't have this same thing happen in other houses?*

It seems to me that frankness is the only way to meet this problem. Tell others who invite you that you *have* to ask whether they have a cat, because your husband is affected with a perfectly well-known nervous antipathy to cats—a cat phobia, in fact. They will surely understand, as everyone did at home, and keep their cats out of his way. In fact, your husband's situation is much less difficult for your friends to protect him from than that of the victims of another phase of cat antipathy which causes a serious attack of asthma—coming on in a moment but lasting for days after the slightest contact with a cat. Even contact with cat's hairs produces the same suffering as that caused by the actual presence of the animal.

37

Telephoning, Smoking, and Out-In-Company Manners

SOMEONE PUTS IN A CALL FOR YOU

PROBABLY the most discourteous habit on the telephone is that of the man who tells his secretary to call Mr. Jones and is then not waiting to take the receiver. The secretary, for example, dials the number; a voice announces, "A. B. Jones Company"; the secretary says, "Mr. Brown is calling Mr. Jones." Promptly Mr. Jones says, "Hello, Brown!" but instead of Brown's voice, that of his secretary explains, "Mr. Brown will be here in a moment. Please hold the wire." Mr. Jones listens good-temperedly—a few seconds, and more seconds. Mr. Brown is evidently unaware that seconds seems minutes to a busy person listening to a dead receiver.

It is quite all right, of course, to have someone call a number for you, if you are ready to pick up the receiver immediately. Usually this annoyance applies to an executive who has several telephones on his desk—one of which rings just as Mr. Jones is about to reply. In this case the secretary—while continuing to listen to the Jones wire—should reply, "Mr. Brown is talking on another telephone. Will you wait or may I call you?" If a new voice says, "I'll wait," they all wait for Mr. Jones. The moment he replies, she hands the telephone to Mr. Brown and keeps the other wire waiting. As soon as the Jones' conversation ends, she tells the waiting caller, "Mr. Brown is here now" and hands him the telephone.

The point is that the person who has been called has the right of way—even though he has not yet come to the telephone. It is picking up the second telephone after putting in a call on the first that results in rudeness to the one who, having been called to the telephone, is asked to wait! Usually this "absentee telephone calling" comes from an office, but it is not at all unheard of at home.

THE BUSINESS OFFICE "GOOD MORNING"

There is considerable doubt about the business office salutation, "Smith, Brown Company—good morning!"

This salutation is still that of most business firms as well as hotels, and there is great hesitation about criticizing it because it is polite and pleases many. And yet—when we are pressed for time, it is not as pleasing as it ought to be, to be held up even by a voice with a smile—in fact, the lovelier the smile, the more likely is it to impel us to reply, "Good *morning*—er, eh—I'd like to speak to Mr. Smith please. This is Mr. Jones." All of which is more time-taking than "A. K. Jones calling Mr. Smith." Moreover, it can happen that Aunt Jane from Bright Meadows, hearing the operator's friendly, "Blank Company. Good morning!" replies, "Why, good *morning*. Who is this I'm speaking to?" The operator explains briefly and Aunt Jane explains at length, "I'd like to talk to Mr. Jones—he's my nephew, you know—he's my sister Sarah's oldest boy. She told me to be sure to let him know—" Aunt Jane purrs on, hampering—if not disrupting—the reception desk.

All of this leads to the advice of putting "Good-morning" at the beginning of the salutation, which works quite well. A brisk "Good-morning, Smith Jones Company" is without discourtesy answered, "Mr. Jones, please," whereas "Smith Jones Company" and then a smiling "Good morning" impels a "Good-morning" in reply.

"HELLO" CORRECT AT HOME

The correct way to answer a house telephone is still "Hello." This is because it is like looking out through the shutters, as it were, to see who is there. To answer, "This is Mrs. Jones' house" leaves the door standing open wide, and to answer, "Mrs. Jones speaking" leaves her without chance of retreat.

This is not nonsense. It is a really important angle of modern telephone etiquette. In all great cities, telephones are rung so persistently by every type of stranger who wants to sell something to Mrs. Householder, or ask a favor of Mrs. Prominent, or to get in touch with Mr. Official (having failed to reach him at his office) that many persons of prominence are obliged to keep their personal telephones unlisted. The last thing that they want to do, therefore, is to announce to strangers, "Miss Star speaking." It is far more practical to say "Hello" and let the one calling ask, "Is this Miss Star's house?—Mr. Director would like to speak to her." Or if she answers herself, a friend recognizing her voice says, "Hello, Mary. This is Kate."

In a doctor's office it is proper, of course, to announce, "Dr. Squill's office."

"WHO IS CALLING, PLEASE?"

Everywhere it is correct that the person answering the telephone ask, "Who is calling, please?" If the person says, "I want to speak to Mrs. Brown personally—never mind my name!" whoever answers the telephone replies, "I'm sorry but I can't interrupt Mrs. Brown unless I tell her your name." Those who refuse to send a message or give their names have obviously no claim on Mrs. Brown's attention.

GIVING ONE'S NAME

A question often asked is whether to give one's name with or without title.

In business, and also when talking with strangers, titles are always used. Socially, many people like being called by their first names; others dislike it intensely.

The following rules hold good:

An older person announcing herself (or even himself) to one who is younger says, "This is Mrs. Elder" or "Miss Spinster" or "Mr. Elder."

Mrs. Worldly, who is middle-aged, says, "This is Mrs. Worldly" always, except to those who actually call her Edith.

A younger one, or one of the same age, whether married or single, says, "This is Marie Manners." In fact, she makes this same announcement to everyone whom she knows socially, whether that person calls her Marie or Mrs. Manners. (The phrase "this is" is more impersonal —and also less pompous—than "I am . . . ")

Socially, a young man always says, "This is Dick Jones." In business when telephoning a woman customer he says, "This is Mr. Jones of Blank and Company." But when telephoning a man he says, "Jones of Blank and Company speaking."

In business, it would be in very worst taste for a salesman to announce himself to a customer—a lady—as Sam Sales. Correctly he says, "This is Mr. Sales of the Blank Company." But to a gentleman he leaves off the "Mr."

A young woman in business also says, "This is Miss Shepard of the New York Travel Bureau" or "Transcontinental Railroad—Mr. Train's secretary speaking."

In business, names must be given as briefly, but as explicitly, as possible.

INVITATIONS BY TELEPHONE

If Mrs. Smith and Mrs. Jones are themselves telephoning, there is no long conversation, but merely

Mrs. Jones: "Is that you, Mrs. Smith (or Sarah)? This is Mrs. Jones" (if she is elderly), or "Alice Jones" (if she is fairly young), or "Alice" (if an intimate friend). "Will you and your husband (or John) dine with us tomorrow at eight o'clock?"

Mrs. Smith: "I'm so sorry we can't. We are dining with Mabel."

Or "We'd love to," or "Yes—with pleasure."

Invitations for a week-end visit are as often as not telephoned.

"Hello, Ethel! This is Alice. Will you and Arthur come on the sixteenth for over Sunday?"
"The sixteenth? That's Friday. We'd love to!"
"Will you drive out, or do you want to come by train?" etc.

DON'T ASK "WHAT ARE YOU DOING SATURDAY?"

A bad habit which should be avoided is the prefacing of an invitation with, "Hello, John. What are you doing Saturday night?" Or "Are you going to be busy Monday afternoon?" This maneuver puts John in the position of finding it embarrassing to refuse after having answered "nothing" and then being told that he is expected to dine with the Borings or to play bridge with the Revokes. On the other hand, if he answers, "I have an engagement" and is then told that he would have been invited to something he likes very much, it is disappointing not to be able to go—without seeming rude to the person whose invitation he at first refused. If this situation is bad for a man, however, it is still worse for a woman. A man can perhaps be excused for changing his mind when he hears Louise Lovely is going to be at the dinner or playing at the same table with him. But a young woman who says she has an engagement and is then told, "Too bad you can't come, because John Brilliant was looking forward to meeting you" can't very well change her mind and say, "In that case I'll come after all!"

COURTEOUS CONSIDERATION OF THE OPERATIONS ANGLE

Since lack of courtesy is almost always due to lack of understanding, a few of the operating angles of telephone service should be explained.

We know (if we think about it) that every time we talk on the telephone we use a certain amount of equipment that cannot be released to anyone else until we hang up. Plainly, of course, the longer the distance of our call, the greater the amount of equipment involved in holding the connection.

In other words, if the whole process of telephoning were visible and we could see our operator putting in her plugs over and over again and asking for our line, we would not be as impatient as we are.

A very important point to make is that when she finally calls us only to ask whether we still want that line, we ought to know that were she to put our long distance call through and then find we had walked away, a difficulty would be created. In other words, the obligation asked of us is that we answer, "Yes, please" politely.

An acute sense of timing has been a war requirement in our personal use of the telephone.

LONG DISTANCE

To those who have asked for special efficiency rules, the following suggestions are offered:

When calling long distance, keep on the tip of your tongue what you have to say, and say it promptly. Receiving the reply, say "Goodbye" and hang up. If you have several things to say, write them down and read them off. Best of all, use a stop-watch if you have one; if not, any clock (with minutes clearly marked on it) will prevent your thinking a ten-minute talk was three. You should, of course, always keep a pad and two sharpened pencils beside the telephone. To exclaim, "Wait a minute until I find something to write on!" doesn't give a picture of a well-ordered house—or mind.

If you have to refer to something that you can't put your hand on instantly, don't leave the telephone while you search for the address or the letter (or whatever it is), but say that you will call back in a few minutes. Or, if not pressing (or needed to conclude your conversation), say that you will mail the information.

A detail to remember is that people who have moved to a new address are likely to be without extension telephones and that you should wait long enough to permit someone to come from quite a distance before concluding that no one is home.

TWO IMPORTANT DON'TS

When the number you get is evidently wrong, don't ask, "What number is this?"—Ask instead "Is this Main 2-3456?"

Don't answer and then say "Wait a minute" and keep whoever called you waiting while you vanish on an errand of your own. If you can't listen at that moment, say "I'll call you back in a few minutes!" And do so.

DON'T LET YOUR SMALL CHILD ANSWER THE TELEPHONE

A custom that is satisfactory to few of us is that of letting a tooyoung child answer the telephone. A lot of time is wasted trying to make the child understand a message and bring an answer that leaves you in no doubt as to its mother's meaning. If there comes a long silence, there is no way of knowing whether the child is hunting for Mother or playing with a friend or a dog, quite forgetful of the telephone which, being off the hook, can no longer ring.

OUR POOR WEAK YOUNGER GENERATION!

It is not this book's intention to be intolerant of our younger generation, but if it is to be of any use as an aid to good manners, it must say what it can to make both boys and girls realize that it is not the feebly old or the weakly ill who call upon "Information" to a degree that is literally crippling to the service. Investigation has proved that the principal offenders are the lazy young who have seemingly neither the strength of muscle nor the sense of fairness to lift themselves off their spines long enough to look up a number in a city telephone book; they ask "Information" to do it for them.

TELEPHONE PAYMENT BY VISITORS

A cause of embarrassment to many is the question of payment for a telephone call by a visitor—usually a house guest. Many are embarrassed because they fear their hostess may resent proffered payment. The definite rule is this: Should one be obliged to make a single local call, one would not ordinarily offer payment for it, but it is absolutely *required* that one pay for every long distance call. Moreover, it is the only way a house guest can feel *free* to telephone as often as he or she may want to. One should always call the operator as soon as one has finished speaking and ask for "the toll charge on XY-23 Great Town" and then leave this amount with a slip, giving date and number called. Or if one has made many during a long stay, the complete list of telephone calls and telegrams sent, with the amounts of each and their total, should be handed to the hostess when one says goodbye.

This is not humiliating—it is the *correct* way to pay this, or any other, incurred debt.

A special message to those who live where local calls are not counted! It does not occur to those who go to stay with friends in New York, for example, that a minimum number of calls a month are all that are allowed each subscriber, and that each additional call over that number means an extra charge added to the bill. It is only fair to the Towns, therefore, that their visitors, the Countrys, who come to stay with them, shall know that each talk they have on the telephone with their many friends will appear on the next month's bill of the Towns. Moreover, a new tax is now being added to the normal rate of 5 cents for each three minutes of conversation—meaning that the amount charged to the Towns will be somewhat higher.

This is written because the Towns *can't* tell the Countrys—and it is certain that the Countrys would like to know!

PAYING FOR CALLS ON NEIGHBOR'S TELEPHONE

In all the instances where newcomers are still unable to get telephones, careful track should be kept of toll calls and also the taxes on calls—which although very trifling considered call by call, can amount to quite a sum at the end of the month—especially when several families have to share one neighbor's telephone.

OUR CONSIDERATION OF EQUIPMENT

A few words about the consideration which we should show to the Telephone Company by taking care of the instrument itself:

Don't stand it where it may be easily knocked off, or too near a radiator, or in the very hot sun or where it can be rained on.

Don't let the cord get snarled tight! Material so treated becomes destroyed and is therefore wasted.

SMOKING ETIQUETTE

The ever-increasing custom of smoking in nearly all places at nearly all hours and by nearly all people has made it necessary that the politeness of smoking be defined within at least reasonable limits.

The first point that must be made is that in all large cities the odds are against those of us who do not like to smoke. If ten people hated it to every one who liked it, that would be one tning; but in nearly all great cities where the smokers outnumber the non-smokers possibly 100 to 1, about the only thing we who also live in these cities can do is to profit by the song sung at the sneezing pig-baby in that pepper-filled kitchen in *Alice in Wonderland:*

> I speak severely to my boy,
> I beat him when he sneezes,
> For he can thoroughly enjoy
> The pepper when he pleases.

In other words, at this present time we are all going to have to enjoy "the pepper" or stay in our own homes—and even there admit none but non-smokers.

MORE SMOKING IN WARTIME

A war-encouraged as well as most trying situation for non-smokers is the encounter with smokers on trains. A lifting of rules permits smoking in all cars, including parlor cars; at present the crowds are so great that seats have to be sold in smoking cars and observation cars and bars. A certain elderly and smoke-hating lady who had to take a six-hour journey found her seat in a "parlor car" to be in a "bar" where the dense eye-smarting cigar smoke was further tainted with the smell of whiskey and beer—a combination that made her car-sick and miserable.

Advice to non-smokers: If your purse is deep travel only in a drawing-room. If not very deep then second choice is by bus.

SMOKING CAN BE AVOIDED

Since smokers are allowed only on the rear seats or on the upper deck of double deckers, sitting up in front on a bus is, up to the present, as comfortable as ever. As a matter of fact, those whose families and dearest friends are not chain smokers and who do not themselves care about going into smoke-filled lobbies, cafés, night clubs and mezzanines find very little discomfort. (It is true, of course, that those who *never* encounter smoking anywhere are in the position of the old lady on the journey, and are made wretchedly sick when they do meet it.) But in ordinary pleasures and pursuits the non-smokers need suffer only on occasion.

There is not a breath of smoke in church, or at the opera, concert, or theatres, or even in orchestra seats at movies. If one *chooses* to go out between the acts at a theatre and stand among the smokers, he has certainly no right to complain of an atmosphere which could easily have been avoided. Also if one chooses to sit in the mezzanine where a neighbor's cigar can be more nearly asphyxiating than under any other circumstance—that too is one's own choice—even though its discomfort is due to the fact that the smoker is not noticing that the thin column of smoke from his cigar is blowing directly into his neighbor's face.

WHEN GUESTS SMOKE

But while it may be just to agree that the few have no right to interfere with the pleasure of the many, there are certain requirements of propriety and of consideration for others that those who smoke should be careful to observe. It is entirely proper that a hostess —or even a host—ask that they do so.

The answer to the hostesses who ask how they can protect their possessions from careless guests is that hospitality need not be helpless. It is true that after a guest has burned a hole in the upholstery or a groove on a table edge, nothing can be done about it. But when a hostess sees a smoker pick up an ornament of value to use— why no one knows—in place of an ash receiver, she can certainly take it away and put an ash receiver in its place. Perhaps she says nothing or perhaps she smiles and says, "Let me give you *this* ash receiver." In other words, frankness taken as a matter of course does not mean being tactlessly fussy or rude.

SMOKING DON'TS

First of all, it is unforgivable to lay a cigarette (or cigar) on the edge of a table or other piece of furniture—ever! Forgetting it and letting it burn a charred groove on a table edge, or a brown scar on a marble mantel, is merely the result of putting it down on wrong places to begin with. Find an ash tray to lay it on—or ask for one.

Striking a match directly at someone—most often outdoors and "with the wind"—belongs in the category with a pointed gun, should the head of the match fly off and land—or sparks blow—on a woman's inflammable dress.

Never press a cigarette out without being sure that the object pressed on is intended for that purpose. Cigarettes put out against lamp bases, ornaments, and almost any surface that presents itself to an unthinking smoker, may mar or destroy objects of value.

Lighted cigarettes should not be thrown into fireplaces. A roaring fire started on a hot July day is a rather marked example of misplaced pleasantness, though such a result may be preferable to having a cigarette tossed out the window upon an awning or the clothes of someone passing.

CIGARETTES AT TABLE

Until the last few years, smoking at a really formal dinner was unthinkable, but today cigarettes are passed at the end of the salad course even in the houses of those conservatives who have heretofore held out against any smoking before or during dinner. It is true that in all great cities there are numberless women who light their own cigarettes the moment they have entered the room and greeted their hostess, and again as soon as they are seated at table—some of them even greet their hostess cigarette in hand! It is also true that others, following their example, are as likely as not to give the impression that smoking is approved by the most conservative.

When young Mrs. Inconsiderate lights her cigarette even before laying her napkin across her knees and greets the man on her right from beneath an ascending veil of smoke, all others at table, including the men next to her, feel free to follow her example. And there is really nothing that the conservative hostess can do.

Whether it is proper to smoke at table depends upon the setting of the places. If each place is set with cigarettes, naturally people may smoke as soon as they choose. But in the houses of those who do not put them on the table—or who have them passed at dessert—it is bad manners to light one's own cigarette and smoke throughout the meal.

It is also very bad manners to pay no attention to whether smoke is blowing in the face of someone who is not smoking.

INEXCUSABLE UNTIDINESS

Other don'ts include all the untidinesses of average smokers, such as spilling ashes on the floor and into any and all the parlor ornaments. Surely you can look around for something that is obviously an ash receiver, or, failing to find it, ask your hostess. If she seems reluctant to provide you with an ash tray, or tells you she has none, stop smoking and carry the offending object outdoors, if possible, or wherever you can best destroy its odor. (Remember: just putting it out does not help at all. Nicotine nausea, which affects non-smokers, is greatest when caused by cigars or cigarettes *that have been put out*. Dead butts are the sick-making ones.)

WHEN SKINS ABSORB

Another detail—difficult but important to write about—is that of the person whose skin seems to absorb the odor of nicotine. On the other hand, it is true that others can smoke incessantly and yet never carry a trace of it with them. Their secret is probably that of counterbalancing their smoking habit with an equally persistent addiction to the toothbrush and nailbrush, to the use of long holders incessantly cleaned—or much better a continual supply of fresh holders made of paper.

TIMES WHEN NO ONE MAY SMOKE

One may not smoke in a church or during any religious service or ceremonial proceedings. One may not smoke in a sick-room. One should not smoke in the room of a convalescent unless the convalescent himself is smoking. Good taste forbids smoking by a woman on a city street. To these obvious exceptions should be added those in business (regulated by the rules of each firm) and those of consideration for the customs of the community in which you may find yourself, or for the prejudices of the people with whom you personally come in contact.

RADIO COURTESY
S O S FROM SYMPHONY FANS

The following paragraphs are addressed especially to visitors who uncaringly interrupt one's favorite radio programs. So many pages in this book emphasize the courtesy that a hostess is obliged to show her guests that it is really high time to think a little of the courtesy that a chance visitor owes to the friend she (or he) goes to see.

Let us say it is a Saturday afternoon and your favorite orchestra is on one of the networks, or the outstanding baseball or football game is on; it really doesn't matter what the program may be, as long as it is a program that you and perhaps your whole family especially care to hear. Let us even say that your husband and the children have stayed at home on a beautiful afternoon in order to listen to the game play by play.

Or suppose it is a complete opera or a great symphony orchestra. You have let the family go to the motion picture without you because you don't want to miss this special program. Just as you hear the opening bars without a trace of static, and you settle yourself in blissful anticipation of complete enjoyment, in come two visitors.

You turn down the sound, hoping against hope that they will say, "Oh, please don't interrupt the music; we want to hear it." Do they? You know very well they don't.

If one of them is an intimate friend, she very likely exclaims, "Oh, Mary, shut that thing off; we can't hear ourselves think." And if they are not intimate friends, you will have been forced by courtesy to give your attention to conversation such as:

"Well, have you been well?"

"I've been very well, thank you."

"And how's your husband?"

"He's well."

"And your mother?"

"She's well, thank you."

"Did she go to see your sister?"

"Yes. She is staying with her now."

"Will she be back soon?"

"Oh, yes, I think so."

"Lovely weather we've been having, though it's really been too hot for this season of the year!"

Meanwhile your mind is achingly aware that locked away behind the silence of your turned-off radio the second movement of Beethoven's Fifth Symphony is melting into a lost opportunity that will never come back. The tortures of Tantalus were not half as great. Of course, if to us musical programs are nothing more than an accompaniment to shouted conversation, then that's all right so far as our own radios are concerned. But when we go to the houses of friends and find the radio on—no matter how uninteresting to us the program may seem—we should really try to notice the expressions of the different members of the family after the host or hostess has in politeness shut off the sound.

ONE RADIO FAN'S SOLUTION

The following story is told in all seriousness in the hope that it may prove of use in solving your own situation as well as it did that of Miss Neighbor. She is an invalid whose one great joy is good music. She lies on a sofa with a radio close beside her, and an electric clock that automatically turns on the station at the hour she is waiting for. As she is a charming person, neighbors flock to see her, frequently interrupting an hour that she loves. Finally, after missing two long-awaited symphonies, she was interrupted at the beginning of a third. It was too much to bear and she burst into tears. Happily a relative who understood sent the visitors away and turned on the music. The next day this same relative produced a slate on which she had lettered in white,

> RADIO PROGRAM ON THE AIR
> FROM ...... TO ...... O'CLOCK

A wide space was left in the center for the name of the program to be written in chalk, and at the bottom in white painted letters: "Please enter silently."

At first people were inclined to resent this slate message, but at present it is becoming an accepted custom not only in that community but in several others. It really is not rude, because all are invited to come in and listen, and the hour written on the slate tells how long the radio will be on. Those who also like music often make it a habit to go at a regular symphony hour, and sit quietly, as they would at any concert. Of course this same slate can be used no matter what broadcast you may want to hear.

WHY CAN'T A RADIO ENGAGEMENT BE VALID?

To most people appreciation of radio programs is not even understandable, an attitude which makes a very difficult situation for those who do. Mary Littlehouse, for example, invited by the Onthehills to Sunday-night supper refused. Mrs. Onthehill persisted in wanting to know why Mary could not come, until finally she said, "I'll be delighted to go to supper, but I have to leave at ten minutes to nine." As she was leaving at the time she had said, Mrs. Onthehill, still very much intrigued, insisted, "I must know where you are going!" Mary answered, "To listen to a concert on the radio." Her hostess, instantly offended, retorted, "Do you mean to tell me you're leaving my party to go home and listen to nothing but the radio? I have never heard of anything so rude." Said Mary, "If I were going to the opera, you wouldn't think me rude. Why isn't it equally forgivable to want to hear opera stars—in the only way I can?"

THE IMPORTANCE OF TIMING

IT'S NOT SMART TO BE LATE

Let no one believe such nonsense as that it is smart to be late. It is true that lateness is on occasion tolerated in those whose compensating assets of talent or charm are sufficiently great. But even so, very few of us find amiability unstrained and our enthusiasm undimmed after repeated experiences with those who are never on time.

Moreover, we all know people who are good-looking, amusing—attractive as they can be. And yet when we think of asking them to lunch or dine—to play bridge or go to a play—we hesitate, simply because we know that half an hour after every other guest has arrived, the careless one will blandly appear.

"Oh, am I late? So glad you didn't wait for me." If you are a very polite hostess, you say, "No, I thought you wouldn't want us to." But you long to tell her frankly, "We waited half an hour and then came in." This same person, arriving an hour late for a bridge game, will greet three people sitting at a card table with complete self-satisfaction. "Three-handed bridge? Do you want to go on with it, or would you like me to play?" Hostess, with patience: "Of course we want you to play. We started a three-handed game because we thought you had forgotten." "Oh, no! Of course I hadn't *forgotten!*" But not a glimmer of regret for the annoyance to the three players who waited, and waited, and finally started to play as best they could without a fourth.

It is true that all of us have on some occasion been late—unless we have the other habit of arriving everywhere too soon! But the *won't-think-about-others* person is always late—with the sort of lateness that spoils the tranquillity or pleasure of everyone else. It is all very well for the hostess not to wait beyond the fifteen-minute allowance required by etiquette; but even so, there is a gap at the table, an empty chair; there is confusion when the delinquent arrives, and a check in the smooth service of dinner while dishes are served over again for her alone.

A certain social leader who was the first to take a drastic stand against the habitual late-comer's injustice to the skill of his chef, no less than rudeness in keeping others waiting, is old Mr. Gilding. A striking clock in his drawing room announces dinner. A connoisseur of wines, he has never served cocktails. Therefore, no time allowance is made for them. At exactly three seconds after the last stroke of eight o'clock has sounded, he offers his arm to the lady who is to sit on his right and leads the way to the dining room. Late guests—no matter who they may be—are shown to their places at table, but no dish is ever brought back, once the course has been passed. One young woman (whose face is familiar to all who look through the illustrated magazines devoted to society and sports) arrived one evening just as everyone was leaving the dining room. "Oh, dear Mr. Gilding, am I late?" "You are," said he, "very." "And I am so hungry!" "Oh, are you?" he answered. "Well, coffee will be served immediately in the drawing room."

Repeating this incident is not recommending that we be lacking in courtesy to guests made late by accident—but it is high time to protest against the misplaced courtesy all too often shown the callously tardy at the expense of those to whom first consideration is due. It is unfairly showing favor to the one who is at fault, and being unfair to those who are courteously prompt, to make them wait indefinitely for a dinner often spoiled by standing. It is certainly not fair to miss the whole first act of an opera or a play just because young Mrs. Vanity Selfish didn't happen to feel like getting there on time; or, worse yet, wilfully sat at home until she was sure that hers would be the last, and therefore the most effective, entrance.

In other days when it was taken for granted that no well-bred person could ever be late unless for an unavoidable circumstance, the fifteen-minute grace was established to save them from the humiliation of being proved so rude as not to have arrived promptly. But because of the increasing carelessness of certain younger people, there is a decided inclination toward the exaction of promptness by the more important hostesses of today. Those who serve appetizers have them passed as soon as most of the guests have arrived, and dinner or luncheon is announced as soon as the number expected is complete, or after waiting until fifteen minutes past the hour of the invitation, for one who is late.

WHEN SHE KEEPS HIM WAITING

In other days, when life was slow-paced, a man who was attentive to a girl seemed not to mind standing around and waiting for her for half-hours on end. In fact, waiting for her was one of the evidences of his devotion that romance rather exacted. Moreover, etiquette of yesterday did not find it proper that a lady wait for a gentleman, anywhere, ever. Today, too, for that matter, a gentleman is instinctively very prompt in keeping an appointment with a lady, since years of tradition have told him that he, and not she, should be the one to get to their meeting-place first. Ideally she should be there on the stroke of time and he a minute or two before. When going to lunch in a great city like New York, one may find it difficult to get through traffic and arrive with the exactness of a perfect watch, but this is the ideal that she, as well as he, should strive for.

Most women think that they alone hate to be kept waiting—but how many hate it as much as a man does? It would be amusing to know in just how many cases the reason his evident admiration so suddenly cooled is found in the statement, "She kept him waiting!"

If you, therefore, are a young woman who would like to be pleasing to a man and you are lunching with him at one o'clock, walk into the hotel lobby on the stroke of one. Who was it, one wonders, who first suggested to the feminine mind that it is effective to "keep him in suspense!" The idea is that in five minutes he will wonder eagerly, "Where is she?" In fifteen minutes he will ask himself anxiously, "Where can she be?" In half an hour he will be verging on despair lest he is not to have the happiness of seeing her at all! Perhaps this idea began in the imagination of the lady novelists of fifty years ago, but it is certain that the young woman who tries any such tactics in the present day will find that HE has looked at the clock and gone back to his office. Not always, of course; but it would be interesting to know how many romances have died on the suspicion that Louise Lovely is in truth Tilly Tardy.

PLEASE KEEP YOUR GERMS TO YOURSELF

How often do we hear Mrs. Cravin Praze explain at length, "I got out of bed to come (a-choo! sniffle, snuffle). I thought I'd never be able to get into my clothes I had such a chill (snuffle, sniffle, cough, cough). My temperature is over 103. I really ought to have a medal for bravery! But I did not think it fair to give out." Helpless hostess says, "Oh, my dear, I'm so sorry! You ought to go straight back to bed." Unhappily, politeness does not let her say what she thinks, which is, "How could you be so thoughtless of others as to come here and breathe flu germs on everybody!"

Therefore, although there is a fixed rule which makes it very discourteous to break a dinner engagement, this rule is canceled when there is any danger of scattering infectious germs.

Even at home one member of the family who has tonsillitis or a bad cold will go and sit close enough to another to breathe in his face—and then protest violently later, "I *know* Jimmy did not get the grippe from *ME!*" Far more considerate to stay quarantined in one's room alone unless nose and mouth are both covered with a protecting mask of gauze. Feeling utterly miserable themselves, they would try to keep others from feeling likewise—you'd think!

The business angle of this subject is unhappily not so easily solved. A clerk or stenographer or saleswoman or even a school teacher cannot stay at home because of slight ailment. But she *can* do her best—by gargling and inhaling antiseptic medication and by trying not to breathe in close contact with anyone except through a piece of fresh gauze or a fresh handkerchief—to keep her germs to herself.

ANSWERS TO READERS' QUESTIONS
PARTY-LINE COURTESY

Whenever I try to telephone, I cut in on a conversation, and everyone complains about never getting me. There are six families on our line! Even so, aren't there rules that give us each definite rights?

The usual number on a party line is four; the maximum ten! And for so long as one person is talking, no outside call can reach any other on that line. One on the same line *can* overhear or interrupt but should not ordinarily do so.

The rule of courtesy when you find the wire in use, is to hang up for three minutes before signalling. If there is an emergency, you of course say *"Emergency!"* in a loud voice, and then "Our barn is on fire," or "Johnny's had an accident"—or whatever it is. But unless all on the line hang up, your telephone is cut off.

I know of a soldier who tried to say a few last words to his wife before sailing. For fifty minutes the long distance operator repeatedly received a "busy-wire" signal. He had to go without a word to her.

Upon telling this to an executive of the Telephone Company he gave this advice: While the "operator" is not permitted to cut in on a busy wire, her supervisor can. In this case the husband could have asked for the supervisor of the station called, and have briefly explained. At her discretion, she could then have cut in and announced a long distance call for Mrs. Soldier, would those talking hang up and permit her to take it?

PAYING FOR CALLS ON A NEIGHBOR'S TELEPHONE

We don't mind letting neighbors use our telephone. We know they can't get their own. However, we find the question of paying for calls very awkward. One neighbor frequently calls long distance. Often she leaves the amount, other times she asks me to let her know when we get the bill. Later we discover she did not give us enough for her calls and I end by feeling too self-conscious to tell her. The trouble is the bills are more than we can pay.

To the many like you who hesitate to remind their neighbors of telephone charges owed them, it can not be said too plainly that it is just as correct for a subscriber to send in a bill for toll charges owed him, as to send a bill for eggs or chickens.

For an occasional short distance call, he might let it go, but for those who make many long distance calls, it is simplest as well as most accurate that the subscriber show the users of his telephone the toll list sent him by the Company, and let each check his calls and pay the totals.

It is important that those who live where local calls are not charged for remember, when they are visiting in New York or other cities where every call in excess of the two-a-day allowance is added to the subscriber's bill, to leave five cents for each city call, beside the telephone.

38

The Clothes of a Lady

CLOTHES not only add to our appearance; they *are* our appearance. The first impression that we make upon others depends entirely upon what we wear and how we wear it. Manners and speech are noted afterward, and character is discerned last of all.

In the community where we live, character is the fundamental essential; but for the transient impression that we make everywhere in public, two superficial attributes are alone indispensable—good manners and a pleasing appearance. And such an appearance is utterly impossible—at least in fashionable communities—without an average degree of smartness.

In Europe, where a high title serves in lieu of gold brocade, or in the intellectual circles where talent alone is said to count, or in small communities where people are known for what they really are, appearance is of esthetic rather than essential importance.

But in the world of smart society, clothes represent not only our ticket of admission but our contribution to the effect of a party. What makes a brilliant party? Clothes. Good clothes. A frumpy party is nothing more nor less than a collection of badly dressed persons.

Not even the most beautiful background could in itself suggest a brilliant gathering if the majority of those present were frumps—or vulgarians! Rather be frumpy than vulgar! Much. Frumps are often celebrities in disguise—but a person of vulgar appearance is pretty sure to be vulgar all through.

DO YOU KNOW HOW TO WEAR CLOTHES?

The woman who knows how to wear clothes is a stage director who skilfully presents—herself. This skill in presentation is something for which it is difficult to write directions, because it is a talent rather than a formula. Naturally she who is young and whose skin is clear, whose figure is model "16," can literally put on any hat or dress she fancies and have both become her to perfection. And yet another girl, lacking the knack of personal adjustment, will find the buying of a becoming hat an endless search through such trials of unbecomingness that she buys, not one she likes, but the one she dislikes least, because she must put *something* on her head!

The sense of what is becoming and the knack of putting clothes on well are the two greatest assets of smartness. And both are acquirable by anyone willing to look at herself as she really is!

FOLLOWING FASHION HAS LITTLE IN COMMON WITH BEAUTY

Fashion has the power to appear temporarily in the guise of beauty, though it is the antithesis of beauty as often as not. If you doubt it, look at old fashion plates. Even the woman of beautiful taste succumbs occasionally to the epidemics of fashion, but she is more immune than most. All women who have any clothes sense whatever know more or less the type of things that are their style—unless they have such an attack of "fashionitis" that they are irresponsibly delirious.

There is one unchanging principle which must be followed by everyone who would be well dressed—SUITABILITY.

VULGAR CLOTHES

To define differences between clothes that are notable because of their smartness and clothes that are merely conspicuous is to define something that is very elusive. However, there are certain rules that seem to be established.

Vulgar clothes are those which, no matter what the fashion of the moment may be, are always too elaborate for the occasion; they are too exaggerated in style, or have accessories out of harmony with the dress and the wearer.

Beau Brummel's remark that, when one attracted too much notice, he could be sure of being not well-dressed but over-dressed, has for a hundred years been the comfort of the dowdy. It is, of course, very often true, but not invariably. A person may be stared at for any one of many reasons. A woman may be stared at because she is ill-behaved, or because she looks like a freak of the circus or because she is enchanting to behold.

If you are much stared at, what *sort* of stare do you usually meet? Is it contemptuous or curious or is it admiring? If the first, change your behavior; if the second, wear more conventional clothes and make-up; if the third, you may be left as you are. But be sure of your diagnosis.

THE SHEEP

Frumps are not very typical of America; vulgarians are somewhat more numerous; but most numerous of all are the quietly dressed, unnoticeable men and women who make up the representative backbone in every city, who buy as good clothes as they can, but not more than they need, and whose ambition is not to be strikingly noticeable but to fit in suitably with their background, whatever that may be.

Less numerous, but far more conspicuous, are the dressed-to-the-minute women who, like sheep exactly, follow every turn of latest fashion blindly and without the slightest sense of distance or direction. As each new season's fashion is defined, all the sheep run and dress themselves each in a replica of the other; their own types and personalities have nothing to do with the case. Fashion says: "Wear a three-cornered handkerchief instead of a bodice," and daughter, mother, grandmother, and all the neighbors wear the same. If emerald green is fashionable, all the yellowest skins will be framed in it.

Wherever shorts are tolerated, every cornered and cushioned and nubbined knee-cap is hinged in plain view. While evening dresses are cut to the last limit of daring, the ample billows of the fat will continue to vie blandly with the marvels of anatomy exhibited by the thin. Utility, becomingness, suitability, and beauty are of no importance. Fashion is followed to the letter—therefore they fancy, poor sheep, they are the last word in smartness. Those whom the fashion suits *are* "smart," but they are seldom, if ever, distinguished because—they are all precisely alike.

THE WOMAN WHO IS CHIC

The woman who is chic is always a little different. Not different in being behind fashion, but always slightly apart from it. "Chic" (pronounced sheek) is a borrowed adjective, but unfortunately no word in our language expresses its meaning. Our adjective "elegant"—which, before it was vulgarized, most nearly approached it—rather suggested the mother of the young woman who was chic. Its nearest description today is a combination of sophistication (in its intentionally deceptive meaning) combined with fastidious taste.

An example of chi-chi (pronounced she-she) is not a synonym for chic, but a flashy imitation of it.

The woman who is chic adapts the fashion to her own personality. This is in contrast to the average woman who will merely buy the latest hat or dress and adapt herself to it, whether this adaptation is suited to her or not. When it is conspicuously NOT, it is likely to be "chi-chi."

HOW MANY JEWELS

It has always been the rule of the well bred not to wear too many jewels in public places, because public display is considered poor taste in the first place and in the second, a temptation to a thief. But in the present vogue for costume jewelry, the New York smart world has developed a veritable mania for covering itself in public, as well as at home, with pearls, rubies and emeralds—of glass! Since jewelry is, after all, ornamentation, glass makes quite as effective trimming as gems—and, like all other trimming, can be over-done.

In best society, women wear their rings at breakfast, lunch or dinner without the least discrimination in their size or value. A "dinner ring" is an article unheard of and unknown. What is *meant* is probably a large ring.

DON'T EXCHANGE A FACE FOR A MASK

To the modern generation it must seem fantastic that not so very long ago all make-up was considered wicked. Today the only restraint in the use of every item manufactured is the answer to the question: Are you sure you are not exchanging a face for a mask?

For example, a fad of the moment is the painting on of a wide, square mouth as false as that of a clown or a black-face comedian. Smudged eyelids often look like those blacked in a prize ring.

In addition to saying "Don't" to these practices, one might add: Don't daub on rouge until you look as though you had inflammation of the cheek bones. Don't plaster your face with powder until it no longer has any semblance of skin.

Remember that a mask can never take the place of a face. The face of a clown is grotesque—it is meant to be. If cosmetics are to add to beauty, they must be the allies, not the enemies, of nature. For those whose eyebrows are too heavy or straggling, a little plucking is to be commended, because neat edges tidy the face just as clipped borders tidy garden paths.

HAIR DRESSING

Hair tumbling loose to the shoulders is all very well on the very young, but on an older woman it is as grotesque as though she wore a baby's cap and bib. Moreover, a flowing mane that makes the head disproportionately huge, while becoming to a lion, is scarcely conducive to the distinction of a woman.

WHEN THE INCOME IS LIMITED

No one can dress well on nothing a year; that must be granted at the outset. But a woman who has talent, taste, and ingenuity can be suitably and charmingly dressed on little a year, especially at present.

First of all, for a woman to mind wearing a dress many times because it indicates a small bank account is to exhibit a false notion of the values in life.

True, it is tiresome everlastingly to wear black on every formal occasion, but nothing looks so well and nothing is so unrecognizable. A very striking dress cannot be worn many times without making others as well as its owner feel bored at the sight of it. "Here comes the zebra" or "the cockatoo" is inevitable if a dress of stripes or flamboyant color is worn often. She who must wear one dress whenever she goes out would better choose black or very dark blue or possibly gray, with fresh white blouses or with accessories of one sort or another that go together so that they can be made to do double service.

One who would be well dressed on a moderate budget should be chary of buying dresses fashioned in the whim of the moment, if these must be worn after the whim has become a freak.

To buy things at sales is very much like buying things at an auction. If you really know what you want and something about values, you can often do marvelously well; but if you are easily bewildered and know little of values, you are likely to spend your money on trash.

WHAT TO WEAR IN A RESTAURANT

Day clothes—tailored suit or dress—with hat and gloves are the proper dress for lunch in the smartest restaurants—also to matinées. Hatless heads and toe-less shoes are still worn by the lagging sheep, but their number is said to be diminishing.

In times of peace dinner clothes are customarily worn to the best restaurants, as they are during the first months' run of a notable play when one is sitting in front orchestra seats or going to a supper club afterward.

CLOTHES FOR THE AFTERNOON

The hours between one and six are occasions when important day dresses are appropriate. If you have few clothes, you may perfectly well wear the simplest sort of day dress in which you look well.

You need never worry because you are not "dressed" as much as the others. The time to worry is when you are over-dressed.

At a formal lunch party in town, people usually wear worsteds or dull silks made with tailored simplicity. The same is true for an afternoon tea or concert. For a cocktail party day dresses are correct. A dinner dress is permissible only when worn by an intimate friend who has stopped in quite late, on her way to a dinner party.

DON'T GET TOO MANY CLOTHES

Choose the clothes which you must have, carefully, and if you must cut down, cut down on elaborate ones. There is scarcely anywhere that you cannot fittingly go in plain clothes. Very few, if any, people *need* fancy things; all people need plain ones.

A very beautiful Chicago woman who is always perfectly dressed for every occasion has worked out the cost of her own clothes this way: On a sheet of paper, thumb-tacked onto the inside of her closet door, she puts a complete typewritten list of her dresses and hats and the cost of each. Every time she puts on a dress, she makes a pencil mark after its notation. By and by, when a dress is discarded, she divides the cost of it by the number of times it has been worn. In this way she finds out accurately which are her cheapest and which her most expensive clothes. When getting new ones, she has the advantage of very valuable information, for she avoids the kind of dress that is seldom put on—which is a bigger handicap for the medium-sized allowance than many women realize.

WHEN IN DOUBT

There is one rule that is fairly safe to follow: When in doubt, wear the plainer dress. If you don't know whether to put on a ball dress or a dinner dress, wear the dinner dress; or whether to wear wool or velvet to a lunch party, wear the wool.

SHALL I WEAR A HAT?

Notwithstanding the continued practice of younger women to go hatless on all occasions, best taste still exacts that in town a hat be worn with street clothes in the daytime—especially in church. (In many churches, head-covering is obligatory.) With an evening dress, a hat is incorrect; therefore a flower or ornament takes its place.

Although women in street clothes without hats are seen in our cities, the really well dressed woman wears one except when going into the dining room of her own hotel, particularly for breakfast. But when going to lunch in a restaurant a hat *should* be worn.

The older generation hostesses usually wear hats at lunch even in their own houses. It is always best, however, in each community to do what others do.

GLOVES

Always wear gloves, of course, in church, and also on the street. A really smart woman wears them outdoors always, even in the country. Always wear gloves in a restaurant, in a theater, when you go to lunch, or to a formal dinner, or to a dance. Always take them off when you eat.

A lady never takes off her gloves to shake hands, no matter when or where, and *never apologizes* for wearing gloves when shaking hands. On formal occasions she should *put gloves on* to shake hands with a hostess or with her own guests. The only exception is when she is wearing earth-stained gardening gloves, or possibly golf or riding gloves, which might seem marring to the hand or the fresh glove of another. In that case she would pull off her glove or say, "I can't shake hands."

CLOTHES IN THE COUNTRY

In the country, as everywhere else, very young women wear, on the country-club veranda or at a lunch, every variety of simple one-piece dress or sports clothes with skirts. Hats and gloves are optional except at church and other especial occasions. Slacks are proper on a boat or on the beach or at picnics.

Shorts proper (for the young and slim) are permitted on tennis courts and for occasions when utility gives them an excuse. Women not so young—especially those inclined to rotundities—should avoid both, except in the wilds. On a beach, very abbreviated bathing dresses can be quite all right on the young and slim. And certainly there is nothing more beautiful than a very young girl or boy dressed principally in sunburn; but the reason for undress, which is unhampered freedom in swimming, would not be lost even if bathing trunks had an inch or two added, and "swimming skin-tights" should observe a few decencies.

That older women should choose bathing suits that are ample enough to be becoming can not be too strongly advised.

Bare-toed sandals with evening dresses are often too revolting to mention. Otherwise, there are no directions for summer evening clothes except that the simpler they are, the prettier.

For a garden party, a country dress is entirely suitable; but, if you have a very elaborate summer day dress, such as a bridesmaid's dress, this is one of the few times when you can wear it!

No one has to be told what to wear to church. In a small country church or one at the seashore, people wear country clothes. Otherwise, as everyone knows, one puts on "town" clothes and, of course, a hat and gloves.

GUESTS AT A WEDDING*

Because typical wedding preparations today are very simple, wedding guests are also wearing simpler clothes than they used to do. General directions are: Day dresses should be worn up to six o'clock in the evening. At an early morning hour these should be of street length; at noon or at afternoon hours they may be long if the wedding is to be very large. The mothers as well as the grandmothers may

---

*For the clothes of the bride, groom, and their attendants, see chapter on Weddings. Always consult the Index, please. Other items of the subject you are interested in may be printed elsewhere than in the chapter dealing with its main phase. Clothes, for instance, are discussed in eleven different chapters.

wear long dresses at no matter how small a wedding or how early an hour. At an evening reception, so-called dinner dresses are best.

Children always wear best party clothes.

The tendency among civilian men is to wear plain everyday suits at all hours; but semi-formal grey-striped trousers with a plain black sack coat and waistcoat in the daytime, and in the evening a dinner jacket (tuxedo), are not out of place with the wartime uniforms which dominate in today's scene.

The hardest question to decide is what to wear at a half-past-five-o'clock wedding that is to be followed by a reception. Such an invitation should specify "afternoon dress" or "evening dress," in small letters in the lower left corner, for the especial benefit of the men who otherwise have no idea whether in broad daylight they should wear tails and be right later on, or wear cutaways and be right at the ceremony.

The problem of this between-day-and-night hour is simple enough for a woman in this present-day fashion of an evening dress that is turned into a day dress by a jacket and a hat that later on can be taken off. But a man can't turn day clothes into evening ones by any means yet invented. (This may give the tailors something to think about.)

THE WELL-DRESSED GIRL AT COLLEGE

The girl who would like to know what clothes to take to college and how to be well-dressed on a reasonable sum of money should first of all pay particular attention to practicality.

As a tentative list from which you may subtract if you must, or to which you may add as you please, it is safe to suggest one or two suits of tweed or other useful wool material, and several sweater blouses of varying weights. Knit skirts with matching blouses are very good; but skirts of tweed or serge will give better service, because knit skirts require a fairly long rest, lying flat on a shelf, to straighten the bagging knees or sitting-down bulge to which they are inclined, even though they be turned front side back every other time they are worn. The closely knit cotton jersey skirts and sweaters hold their shape much better than the more expensive hand-knitted woolen or bouclé ones. In addition to sweater clothes, which you wear day after day in classes or on the campus, you should have a dress or two to wear under a coat to church on Sundays, to town for lunch on Saturdays and for dinner in the dining room.

For evening clothes there is little to suggest except the practical idea of buying evening dresses that have accompanying jackets or capes. With its jacket such an evening dress can serve many purposes.

Remember that both fussy dresses with trimmings which must be continually cleaned and pressed, and materials which wrinkle like tissue paper or are spotted by a drop of rain are obviously impractical. The type of dress for a moderate budget is one that is plain in cut and that does not scream to go to the cleaner's if anything touches it. Test whatever you are in doubt about by squeezing it into a ball in your hand and then seeing whether the wrinkles stay in or disappear when smoothed out between your fingers.

In addition to dresses, you will also need a heavy country coat—of fur, perhaps—a thinner polo coat, and a raincoat. Hats or caps, though unusual on the campus, depend upon your clothes—and you. Gloves for warmth in a cold climate and other gloves for church and for town are all that you need. But, whatever else you choose, do have sensible shoes for daytime use. Wear fancy slippers or sandals with stilt heels in the evening, if you like, but don't walk about the campus in silly shoes.

You will need a wrapper and slippers, of course; and pajamas and underthings simply tailored are in best taste. A lot of nightgowns and other things deeply trimmed with lace are all very well in the trousseau of a bride, but neither practical nor suitable in a college dormitory.

CLOTHES FOR THE BUSINESS WOMAN

The first requirement is neatness. The unfailing directions for clothes worn in an office are that they be tailor-made, smart to the last degree and in perfect taste, but in nothing conspicuous. Above all, avoid wearing clothes that need constant arranging. If you have to keep fussing at your belt or your neck or your wrists, if anything dangling drips into things or catches on knobs or typewriter keys, discard the distracting detail quickly. It is not necessary to sacrifice prettiness to exaggerated sleekness as on horseback, but the nearer you can come to avoiding everything that interferes or catches, or keeps getting out of place, the better.

Also wear clothes that properly cover you. Scant attire may be very alluring in a musical revue, but men do not look for, nor want to find, that *allure* in their offices. Many a man has asked that a girl who was inclined to dress in transparencies be transferred. Conspicuous clothes are entirely out of place in business. In hot weather, very short sleeves are permissible, but not cut-out armholes or low back. Deep-mourning clothes are not suitable in an office, but you can wear black and white or gray. Also, it is not unusual for women to wear mourning bands on tailored coats, but not on dresses.

Neat, beautifully done hair, but no little-girl effect of hair hanging loose, is in best taste.

One important accessory for beautiful business clothes is a pair of plain sensible shoes of best quality, designed to give proper support to the foot. High-heeled, fancy sandals and slippers not only are inappropriate and extravagant, but ruinous to any foot that must be much stood upon. The hospital regulation for properly supporting shoes were not made to keep nurses from looking pretty, but to preserve toes and arches from blemishes and collapse.

One can't say to everyone, "Wear flat-heeled, laced boots." To those who have a broken arch, a flat heel is agony, and to anyone with a "Morton" toe, a laced or any high boot is torture. But a French-heeled sandal for long hours of walking or standing will not only in time be painful but make a bare foot look horrible.

ON MOTOR OR TRAIN TRIP

On a motor or train trip, for example, the best foundation color is brown with its dilutions of tan, fawn, beige and cream. Nothing is so dust-proof, or goes so long without valeting, as a dust-colored tweed tailor-made skirt and jacket with a gay print blouse, a buttonhole flower of its dominating color, and a swagger coat to match the tone of the suit, with well polished brown leather shoes and a serviceably big wrist bag of the same leather as the shoes (and sent to be polished again and again, so that it too gleams as though varnished, and yet plainly declares it isn't). A brown hat with enough brim to shade your eyes—but otherwise a small hat that not only looks comfortable but IS comfortable—couldn't be smarter. With this brown theme you can have any number of blouses or sweaters. You can have hats of the soft, uncrushable variety, as easy to pack in odd corners of your bag or trunk as are stockings.

ON A BOAT

But for shipboard, blue would probably be a better foundation theme than brown: a navy blue tailored suit, or a blue-mixture tweed, either of these worn with a white blouse. A warm country coat of blue or bluish mixture (to be used also as an evening wrap), a blue hat, bag and shoes and white wash-fabric gloves would be your foundation. Then white knit or cotton dresses, with white—or white and blue—sports shoes, would be all you could need for any wear. In addition to this, two very simple semi-evening dresses, or an evening dress with one or two jackets.

Unless you are dancing or there is a Ritz restaurant in which you are dining, it is not necessary to dress in the evening on any ship unless you feel like it.

CLOTHES FOR A CRUISE

But now let us consider an approximate list of things to take on a definite cruise. Whether it is to be a short one of five days or a longer one of eighteen or more, you must first of all have something in which to travel from wherever you live to where you board the ship. Then you must, of course, take with you steamer clothes for cold days and other things for hot days, and something to wear in the evening. To these add a rain coat and a bathing suit, and that is about all.

For going on board, or for going ashore in a city, the plainest tailor-made coat and skirt of light-weight wool in a dark neutral color is the smartest thing you can wear. Or if you are very young, a bright or light-colored suit with blouse or thin sweater that will look well on the ship as well as on shore. A skirt and coat are more useful for traveling than a dress and coat because the skirt worn with different blouses or thin sweaters, and perhaps hats, will serve the purpose of several costumes. A second lighter-weight, lighter-colored skirt is also useful to wear with the same blouses or sweaters. For hot weather the simplest tailored dresses, either of cotton or possibly foulard are best.

Wear on a steamer in summer the same sort of clothes that are worn in the country anywhere, as they are most practical and suitable.

On shore as well as on shipboard one-piece knit dresses are ideal daytime clothes. If you have these in different weights, you will need nothing else whatsoever for daytime—or for evening, either, if you do not choose to dress. But remember that knit clothes are only for the shingle-thin. One who is inclined toward plumpness should NEVER wear a knit dress without a sweater coat—a coat, moreover, which hangs loose enough not to cling around the line of the equator across the back! Or, as a change from knit dresses, nothing is more practical either for ship or shore in very hot weather than simplest short-sleeved dresses of cotton, such as seersucker or a thinner cotton print. At home white linen or China silk tub dresses couldn't be nicer, but not away from an ironing board and not out on the sea!

For the somewhat older woman, thin foulard—the kind that slithers through your fingers, and that no amount of squeezing can crease—is perfect. Dark neutral-colored ones for town and light or gay ones for coast resorts or on the boat.

Gay colors may sound unconservative for the not-so-young, but it is quite possible to wear a dress and hat of vivid color against the vivid background of a tropical scene and not seemingly imitate either a clown or a cockatoo. But even so, one who is tempted by anything that could be called flamboyant should remember that in any public place to be the most conspicuously dressed is all too likely to be the most vulgar. A ship (unless a yacht) is a public place.

RIDING CLOTHES

A riding habit, no matter what the fashion happens to be, is the counterpart of an officer's uniform; it is not worn to make the wearer look pretty! To look well in a habit a woman must be *smart* or she is a sight! And nothing contributes so much to the "sights" we see at present as the attempt to look pretty instead of correct. The criticism is not intended for the woman who lives far off in the open country and jumps on a horse in whatever she happens to have on, but for those who dress "for looks" and ride in the parks of our cities, or walk on the stage and before the camera, in scenes meant to represent smart society!

A habit is good or it is bad. Whatever the present fashion may be, have your habit utterly conventional! Don't wear checks or have slant pockets, or eccentric cuffs or lapels. Don't have the waist pinched in. Choose a plain dark or "dust" color. A night blue that has a few white hairs in the mixture does not show dust as much as a solid dark color, and a medium-weight close material holds its shape better than a light loose weave.

You may wear a single white carnation or a few violets in your buttonhole—but no other trimming. Get boots like those of a man, low-heeled and with a straight line from heel to back of top. Don't have the tops wider than absolutely necessary not to bind, and don't have them curved or fancy in shape. Be sure that there is no elbow sticking out like a horse's hock at the back of the boot. Don't have a corner on the inside edge of the sole. And don't try to wear too small a size!

Gloves must be of heavy leather and at least two sizes larger than those ordinarily worn.

A hat must fit the head and its shape must be conventional. Never wear a hat that would be incorrect on a man, and don't wear it on the back of your head or over your nose.

Wear your stock as tight as you comfortably can, not *too* tight! Tie it smartly so as to make it flat and neat, and anchor whatever you wear so securely that nothing can possibly come loose.

If you want to see examples of perfection in riding clothes, look at the pictures of any of the smart meets in the London illustrated weeklies or at our own Hartford or Myopia meets, as shown in the magazines devoted to sports and society.

PRINCIPLES OF TASTE APART FROM FASHION

Suppose, since clothes suitable to the occasion are the first requisite of good taste, we take up a few details that are apart from fashion. A formal dinner dress is the handsomest type of evening dress that there is. A ball dress may be exquisite in detail, but it is often merely effective. The perfect ball dress is one purposely designed with a skirt that is becoming when dancing. A long wrapped type of dress would make Diana herself look like a toy monkey-on-a-stick, but might be dignified and beautiful at a dinner. A dinner dress differs from a ball dress only in that it is not necessarily designed for freedom of movement.

Hair ornaments always look well at a ball but are not especially appropriate—unless universally in fashion—on other occasions. A lady in a ball dress with nothing added to the head looks a little like being hatless in the street. This sounds like a contradiction of the criticism of the vulgarian. But because a diadem or a jeweled filet or other ornament is beautiful at a ball, it does not follow that all these should be put on together and worn in a restaurant—which is just what the vulgarian would do. Whether to wear a headdress, however, depends not alone upon fashion but upon the individual. If the type of hair ornament in fashion at the moment is becoming, wear it, especially to balls and in a box at the opera. But if it is not becoming, don't.

FASHION AND FAT

Two things the fat woman should avoid: big patterns and the tailor-made. Fat women look better in feminine clothes that follow in the wake, never in advance, of modified fashion. Fat women should never wear eccentric clothes or clothes in light colors. Clothes that are what the French call "vague" are always better for any bad figure than those which reveal its outline precisely.

The tendency of fat is to detract from one's refinement; therefore, anyone inclined to be fat must be ultra conservative—in order to counteract the effect. Very tight clothes make fat people look fatter and thin people thinner. Satin is a bad material, since high lights are too shimmeringly accentuated. Dull-surfaced, soft materials, and models that have some sort of loose-hanging drapery, are best. Heavy ankles, needless to say, should be clothed in the darkest stockings possible—or at least a slipper to match the stocking. When above-ankle-length evening dresses are in fashion, a hem line running into points or in other ways irregular is more flattering than a straight edge.

THINNESS CAN BE UGLY

There is certainly no beauty in a washboard chest backed by nubbined spine between protruding oyster-shell shoulder blades. Almost rather zeppelin arms than those chicken-wing examples with hollow socket joining at the shoulders. The too thin have furthermore an element of hopelessness in their situation, in that they cannot put on weight and smoothness no matter how hard they try. Whereas the fat *can* get thin if they care enough—by taking the most important of all exercises: shaking their heads violently "no" to a second helping.

THE CLOTHES OF A LADY

DRESSES TO WEAR AT HOME

It is doubtful that the younger generation knows that the "tea gown" of the put-on-for-company variety was a cross between a ball dress and a coronation robe, and nothing at all like a wrapper. Of late years, the word "tea gown" has been given to a wrapper-like house-gown worn to rest in rather than to see company in.

Today's substitute for a tea gown is either a house coat, Sunday-night dress, or a hostess gown. All these, including the house coat (if of beautiful material) are suitable for wear at any very informal gathering at home.

HOSTESS LESS DRESSED THAN GUESTS

A hostess should be less elaborately dressed than her guests and her clothes may be more informal in type. For example, she would wear any distinctly at-home dress that could not possibly be worn on the street when she is giving a cocktail party or a tea to which other people come in street clothes.

CHILDREN SHOULD BE DRESSED LIKE THEIR FRIENDS

Clothes of children need no comment because children should be allowed to dress like their friends. Nothing makes a child, especially a boy, more self-conscious than to look "strange" to the children he plays with. In other words the mother who dresses a boy —or even a girl—in noticeably different clothes, may make the child not merely temporarily unhappy but can very easily set him so far apart, as to warp his whole future life.

TEEN-AGE FADS

As noted in the foregoing paragraph, it is the impulse of all young persons to try to be as exactly like each other as biscuits in a pan. The girl who is a leader for example, starts a fashion and all copy! Sometimes the leader is admirable; sometimes less so.

During the war, groups of teen age girls across the entire country have taken to the sloppiest of over-sized boys clothes worn in the sloppiest way.

How long it will be before a new craze—perhaps for extreme loveliness—takes its place, no one can say. It can only be hoped that the behavior that goes with pants and shirt tail out will not have been found ineradicable.

39

The Clothes of a Gentleman

LET us say at the start that, although the clothes a man chooses (especially his evening ones) are almost as certain to reveal his background as his speech, fashion is not important. How old a suit may be doesn't matter a bit. The conventions of taste, on the other hand, are very important. Wrong clothes, whether new or old, are like illiteracies of speech. By which is meant that the clothes and the speech of an elderly gentleman might suggest yesterday rather than today, and both be most distinguished. But any offenses to taste in details, however small, would be much the same as saying "I seen it" or "drapes" or "pardon *me*."

If you would dress like a gentleman, you must study the subject of a gentleman's wardrobe by paying close attention to the clothes of men of about your own age whom you know to be reliably conservative, until your judgment is sufficiently trained to pick out good suits from freaks.

FORMAL EVENING CLOTHES

Your tail coat is the last thing to economize on. It must be perfect in fit, cut and material, and this means a first-rate tailor. At least this has always been the rule. In the present day this advice must be qualified, because in the better American stores ready-to-wear clothes have reached such a high degree of excellence that a man with a good average figure can be fitted admirably—even to a tail coat. At all events it must be made of a dull-faced worsted, either black or more likely night blue, on no account of broadcloth. Aside from the silk facing of the lapels and wide braid on the trousers, it must have no trimming whatever, and must hang open.

Have all your linen faultlessly clean—always—and your tie of plain white lawn, or piqué, tied so it will not only stay in place but look as though nothing short of a backward somersault could disarrange it.

Your handkerchief must be white, of very fine linen preferably; gloves if any, white; flower in buttonhole, if any, white. White kid gloves are supposed to be obligatory both at the opera and at balls, but it must be confessed that very few New Yorkers ever wear them.

When you go out on the street, wear either an English silk hat or an opera hat. The opera hat is now more generally worn, probably because of its obvious convenience not only at the opera or theater or in coat rooms; but it also does away with the need for a hat box when packing. Wear your hat on your head, not on the back of your neck, or over one ear. Evening coat should be black, but if you choose an overcoat of plain midnight blue, it can be worn both afternoon and evening—that is, if it looks black at night and blue by day.

If you carry a stick, it should be of plain Malacca or other wood, with either a crooked or straight handle. The only ornamentation allowable is a plain silver or gold band, or top; but perfectly plain is best form. The reason why a band on a crooked Malacca is allowed is that the cost of a single length of wood is prohibitive. The less expensive sticks are made with a joining which is hidden by the band. Avoid carrying a stick with a ball top, ever. Above all, avoid an ebony cane with an ivory top as you would avoid wearing a "zoot suit" anywhere in good society.

Lastly, wear patent leather pumps or ties, and plain black silk socks.

THE DINNER COAT OR "TUXEDO"

The tuxedo is merely the English dinner coat, which was first introduced in this country at the Tuxedo Club in the early nineties to provide something less formal than the swallowtail; and the nickname has clung ever since. To a man who cannot afford to get two suits of evening clothes, the tuxedo is of greater importance. It is worn every evening and nearly everywhere, whereas the tail coat is necessary only at balls, formal dinners, and in a box at the opera. Tuxedo clothes are made of the same materials and differ from full-dress ones in only three particulars: the cut of the coat, the braid on the trousers, and the use of a black tie instead of a white. The dinner coat has no tails and is cut like a sack suit except that it is held closed in front by one button at the waist-line. The lapels are silk or satin faced, and the collar left in cloth; or if it is shawl-shaped, the whole collar is of satin. The shawl collar is supposed to be less formal than lapels.

The double-breasted dinner coat is always an extra, since it can be worn only on very informal occasions in summer and for the special purpose of going without a waistcoat. The trousers are identical with full-dress trousers except that the braid should be narrower.

"Cuffed" trousers are of course impossible on all evening clothes. The reason for the turned-up cuff is to keep clear of mud.

Evening ties of fancy silks are bad form. A "butterfly" bow shape is correct in plain black silk or satin.

With dinner coat, no super-fashionable New Yorker, unless short of funds to pay his laundress, wears any but a white waistcoat. Black ones are seen, however, on many who care less for smartness, and on the past-middle-aged who do not care to advertise an expanded waist line. But never, except in vaudeville, wear a gray one or a yellow one, or any tie except a black one.

As noted in a foregoing paragraph, the most practical hat for town wear in winter, both for full-dress and dinner coat, is an opera hat which collapses, instead of the regular high silk one. In summer a straw is usual, but at the present time a black Homburg is proper in summer and is worn on most occasions in winter as well.

Since even Newport, which is the only summer resort in America that is formal enough to make the wearing of full evening dress suitable, has during the last few years practically given it up, there is now no occasion when fashionable New York can possibly wear full dress between the months of May and November, because neither opera nor formal dinners, nor balls are given then, and in New York society an evening wedding is unknown. In San Francisco or Atlanta or other cities where evening weddings *are* fashionable, or elsewhere if balls are given, the full dress is, of course, correct.

THE SILK HOUSE SUIT

The house suit is an extravagance that may be avoided, and an "old" tuxedo suit worn instead. For many generations a gentleman has always been expected to change his clothes for dinner, whether he might be going out or dining at home alone or with his family; and for this latter occasion some inspired person evolved the house or lounge suit, which is simply a dinner coat and trousers cut somewhat looser than ordinary evening ones, made of an all-silk or silk-and-wool fabric in some dark color, and lined with either satin or silk. Nothing more comfortable—or luxurious—could be devised for sitting in a deep easy chair after dinner, in a reclining position that is ruinous to best evening clothes.

A house suit is distinctly what the name implies, and is never worn except at the smallest family dinner or when receiving intimate friends at home. The accessories are a silk or cheviot unstarched soft shirt, with turndown stiff collar, or with a soft collar attached—white of course—and a black bow tie. The coat is either double-breasted or made with two buttons instead of one, so that no waistcoat need be worn with it.

The silk house suit which is worn almost solely by men of fashion must not be confused with the velvet jacket that has no trousers to match, and is typical of studios and Bohemian quarters, nor with the dressing gown that seems to be the moving-picture producer's idea of what a gentleman is supposed invariably to wear at home!

FORMAL AFTERNOON DRESS

Formal afternoon dress consists of a black cutaway or morning coat with black cloth waistcoat to match the coat, and gray-and-black striped or black with white line cashmere trousers. A white piqué waistcoat is fashionable at a spring wedding, especially for the bridegroom, best man, and ushers. The coat can be bound with braid but, in somewhat better taste, it is plain. A satin-faced lapel is wrong, although it is the correct facing for the more formal and elderly frock coat.

Very fashionable is a black sack coat instead of cutaway but with other details the same. The cutaway is still correct, however, for members of the bridal party. The black sack coat is equally smart, but not as formal, since it is worn with a derby hat, which is impossible with a cutaway.

Either a cutaway or a frock coat is accompanied by a silk hat, and worn with plain black waistcoat and a black or black and white or gray bow tie, or a black and white or grey four-in-hand tie. A gray silk ascot worn with a frock coat is still supposed to be the correct wedding garment of the bride's father.

Black calfskin oxford ties are correct in best fashion. Spats are not popular with very smart men except at weddings, and rarely even then. Also they must never be in any color except sand or white, or of any material except linen. White spats are for the wedding party. Cloth spats, like the black evening waistcoat, mean merely a man without knowledge of, or at least indifferent to, smartness—like a woman's ankle-length skirt in this knee-length period.

At a spring wedding or other formal occasion a sand-colored double-breasted linen waistcoat with sand linen spats looks very well on a man who is slim-waisted and young. Old men can wear ankle-warming spats or whatever other muffling is necessary, of course.

THE SACK SUIT

The business or three-piece sack suit is supposed to be an everyday inconspicuous garment and should be. A few rules to follow are:

Don't choose striking patterns or materials; suitable woolen stuffs come in endless variety, and any which look plain at a short distance are "safe."

Don't get too light a blue, too bright a green, or anything suggesting a horse blanket. Trousers may be made with a cuff; sleeves are not. Lapels are moderately small. Padded shoulders are an abomination. Skirt-wide trousers are equally bad. If you must be eccentric, save your efforts for the next fancy dress ball, where you may wear what you please, but in your business clothing be reasonable.

It is better taste not to wear silk socks in winter, except in the evening; but above everything, don't wear white ones—except wool or cotton ones with white tennis shoes. Don't cover yourself with chains, fobs, scarf pins, lodge emblems, etc.; and don't wear "horsey" shirts and neckties. You will only make a bad impression on everyone you meet. The clothes of a gentleman are always conservative; and it is safe to avoid everything that can possibly come under the heading of "novelty." If a salesman offers you anything that has "never been seen before," the rule of good taste is "shun it" unless your judgment is very experienced.

THE FLANNEL SACK SUIT IN SUMMER

Summer clothes are lighter in color as well as weight, and their accessories can be much less conservative. Colored socks are entirely proper not only in browns and grays, but in light bluish colors as well. White socks are worn only with white flannel trousers, and *must* be woolen or cotton. Ties of printed foulard or handkerchief silks can be very gay in coloring but the pattern should be small. The patterns on handkerchiefs themselves may include whole scenes in brightest color and ornamenting the entire border.

JEWELRY

In your jewelry let diamonds be conspicuous by their absence. Nothing is more vulgar than a display of "ice" on a man's shirt front, or on his fingers.

There is a good deal of jewelry that a gentleman may be allowed to wear, but it must be chosen with discrimination. Large pearl shirt studs, real ones, are correct for full dress only. One alone can be worn with a dinner coat! but two, only if quite small. Otherwise you may wear white mother-of-pearl, or black onyx with a very inconspicuous pattern in diamond chips, but so tiny that they cannot be told from a threadlike design in platinum—or others equally moderate.

Waistcoat buttons, studs and cuff links, worn in sets, constitute an American custom that is permissible. Both waistcoat buttons and cuff links may be jeweled and valuable, but they must not have big precious stones nor be conspicuous.

A watch chain should be very thin—in the evening, of platinum—and a man's ring is usually a seal ring of plain gold. If a man wears a jewel at all, it should be sunk into a plain "gypsy hoop" setting that has no ornamentation, and worn on his "little," not his third, finger. When a man wears a wedding ring, it should be worn on his little finger too.

When a bow tie is worn with a cutaway which necessitates a stiff shirt without wash buttons, the one stud that shows above the waistcoat must be of plain gold.

Cigarette case: gold or platinum or mixture, and if with monogram or crest in diamonds, it must be minutely small.

An amusing European fashion is to have innumerable small devices, each given by a friend, *appliquéd* on a plain gold or silver case. Such devices are minute monograms or crests of donors, or designs illustrating a nickname or personal event, executed in enamels or platinum. In the days of our great prosperity they were sometimes in powder-small diamonds.

IN THE COUNTRY

Gay-colored socks and ties are quite appropriate with flannels or golf tweeds. Only, in your riding clothes you must again be conservative. Boot tops must be high on the leg, and snug fitting. And remember that all leather must be polished until its surface is like glass. There is nothing a really smart man abominates more than any leather that *looks* new.

Have your breeches fit you. The coat is less important; in fact, any odd coat will do. Your legs are the cynosure of attention in riding.

In the country men wear either knickerbockers and golf stockings, with a sack or a belted or semi-belted coat, and any variety of homespuns or tweeds or rough worsted materials; or long-trousered flannels with sweaters over a soft shirt—and any sort of coat they happen to have. Coats are of the polo or ulster variety. Shirts are of cheviot or flannel, all with soft collars attached and to match.

On the golf course, "slacks" are now universal—though golfers will tell you nothing is really so practical as knickerbockers, especially on a wet fairway.

The main thing is to dress appropriately. If you are going to play golf, wear golf clothes; if tennis, wear flannels. For instance, do not wear a yachting cap ashore unless you are living on board a yacht, or riding clothes unless about to get on a horse.

If some semi-formal occasion comes up, such as a country tea, the time-worn conservative blue coat with white or gray flannel trousers is perennially good.

A serious breach of etiquette is frequently made by those who are ignorant of the fact that nearly all two- or three-color hat bands are not patterns chosen at random, but emblems to be worn by special privilege. If you choose a fancy ribbon instead of a plain black one, you must be very sure that it has no significance; to announce by your hat band that you played on a certain "Varsity" team, or that you are a member of such a club or association, when you didn't and are nothing of the sort, is precisely the same as wearing the emblem of a fraternity to which you do not belong.

The well-dressed man is always a paradox. He must look as though he gave his clothes no thought and as though literally they grew on him like a rabbit's fur, and yet he must be perfectly groomed. He must be close-shaven and have his hair cut and his nails in good order (not polished). His linen must always be immaculate, his clothes "in press," his shoes perfectly "done." His brown shoes must shine like old mahogany, and his white buckskin must be whitened like a prize bull terrier at a bench show.

THE ESSENTIAL VALUE OF VALETING

One reason—a very great one—why the English gentleman is so often better dressed, on less money usually, than the American, is that the former is perfectly valeted (even though he perform this office himself), while the latter more often than not hasn't much idea what proper valeting means. First of all, how typical is it of the American man to put trees in his shoes the instant he takes them off? And does he carefully pull his trousers flat and fold them straight and hang them smooth over the trouser bar of a hanger (or the back of a chair), and hang his coat carefully, too; or does he fling his clothes any old way upon a chair, and even let his trousers fall into their "natural folds"?

Even let us say he hangs his suit up neatly. Does he perhaps wear the same things day after day until the shoes turn up at the toes like a wrinkle-faced duck and his suit grows balloon-shaped at the knees and sags despondently at the pockets? And then, after wearing his clothes completely out of shape, even if he sends them to a tailor, does he send them to a chosen tailor who will skilfully restore them or to one of another variety who would seem to operate a scorching steam roller rather than an accurately heated pressing iron?

The well-dressed man never wears the same suit or the same pair of shoes two days running. He may have only two suits, but he wears them alternately; if he has four suits, he should wear each every fourth day. The longer time they have "to recover" their shape, the better.

THE SLOPPY HUSBANDS OF VAIN WIVES

Another cause for the general dejection of many a man's clothes is the all-too-typical wife who lets her husband look like a tramp. We can all name women who are themselves walking advertisements of the "beauty specialist," the hair dresser, the manicurist, and whose clothes bear every evidence of unceasing attention as well as frequent bandboxes from the dressmaker's or the milliner's, but whose husbands' clothes loudly bewail the fact that cleaning fluid, pressing iron and mending basket have never been within aid-giving distance.

One wonders sometimes what sort of impression Marie Vanity Jones THINKS she is making upon those who see her always so perfectly appointed, so smart and trig and manicured, while that button is still missing on John's brown suit, and the pockets sag, and the knees bag more and more. Even if Marie is selfish—even if she thinks of herself as alone of interest to observing eyes—wouldn't you think she would consider how his appearance detracts from her own, to say nothing of the impression of her inefficiency as a housekeeper?

THE CLOTHES OF A VERY YOUNG MAN

As already said in this chapter, no man of inexperience should buy anything the salesman assures him is the newest thing out. This means that—if it looks unlike anything he has ever beheld—he should leave it severely alone. This is, of course, a rule of safety. The man who knows a lot about clothes buys what he chooses, but the young man who does not know anything except that violet as a color appeals to him will quite possibly dress himself like a chorus man in the perfume ballet, in utter unconsciousness of his crashing through every tenet of good taste.

One might make a rule that not only symphonies in violet, but all color combinations, such as socks and handkerchief and tie of precisely the same shade, are a little too studied.

There is a certain effect of casual negligence that, especially in the country or at college, is the best sort of dressing. It is a suggestion of ease of movement or lack of vanity. The best description of a college boy's clothes would be that they were *those which suit his type*. In its best expression it is merely the result of rather loosely fitted clothes that have a comfortably worn look, a collar not too high nor too tight, tie neither too thick nor too stiff, comfortable woolen socks and thick-soled shoes.

Country wear allows all sorts of colors; the loudest of golf stockings and sweaters, the most cubistic handkerchiefs and ties, all are perfectly permissible to the boy or man *whose type can absorb them*. This question of absorption is an entirely individual one. Fair-haired, loose-jointed or thin men can absorb strident violences that on thick-set or dark-haired men (particularly those with mustaches or even "blue" chins) look vulgar.

In the city and in the world of work, it must be remembered that the untidy man has a down-and-out appearance, and it may be cruel, but it is true, that good, conservatively chosen clothes ask for better consideration than shoddy ones. Remember, however, a man's clothes need never be new to look well, and happily there are no changes—that matter—in Fashion.

A YOUNG MAN BUDGETS HIS CLOTHES

A man who has plenty of money buys what he chooses and when he chooses; if certain items prove not very useful, they can stay on their hangers or on the shelves and no great harm is done. But the young man of the smart world whose pay envelope is as small as his popularity is great must give serious thought to make his limited means provide him with clothes that will look reasonably well in the environment to which he belongs.

Let him consider, then, what he must spend much money on, what he may save on, and what he can do without:

At the top of the list go good shoes. Therefore, spend money on the quality of leather and of workmanship in shoes; then *take care of them*. Putting trees into them the minute they are taken off is more important than polishing. Polishing can be done at any time, but trees should restore shape while the leather is still warm from the foot. *Never* (if you own two pair) wear the same shoes two days in succession.

In these informal days, a very young man, even in New York society—unless the exactions of formality return to the opera and he is likely to be often in a box—can easily do without a tail coat, for the dinner coat with a white waistcoat takes the place of full evening dress almost everywhere.

For formal day clothes, nothing is smarter than a black sack coat and waistcoat with gray striped trousers, a combination which should enable you to do without a cutaway—at least until your friends begin marrying and you have to serve as an usher. Even so, you can perhaps persuade your bridegroom friends to match your equally smart though somewhat less formal black sack coat and striped trousers. Unless you buy a cutaway, a high silk hat is useless, for the proper hat with a black sack coat is a derby—or black Homburg. With your dinner coat ("tuxedo") you wear an opera hat (collapsible high hat) or black Homburg or, in summer, a straw or Panama.

For daytime clothes, the dark blue sack suit is always put at the head of the list because it looks well on perhaps more occasions than any other type of suit; but for hardest wear, it is not as good as a brownish or grayish or greenish tweed which is much less inclined to grow dusty, to show spots or to acquire a highly polished shine.

Let us say a young man has two sack suits, one gray-brown and the other olive-brown, to be worn alternately. With both he wears brown calf shoes, polished as many times as possible to darken as well as to shine; plain brown socks and a darkish tie, either plain or with an inconspicuous pattern; a brown felt hat, and an overcoat that is brownish. If his overcoat is dark blue or gray, he would do better to choose navy blue or grayish suits and wear black calfskin shoes.

As already said, it is always better that his clothes look utterly unthought-of rather than to risk their looking thought of too much. And the question of how really well dressed he can dare to be without

THE CLOTHES OF A GENTLEMAN

looking over-dressed is the crux of the whole subject. The moment a man's clothes even faintly cry out, "Look at us! Are we not perfection? See how our colors blend; see how well we're pressed?" it is fairly safe to label their wearer "All wrong!"

To say that clothes make a gentleman is a flippant sophistry, but clothes of the sort that a gentleman ought to wear do make a gentleman look the way he ought to look!

WHAT TO WEAR ON VARIOUS OCCASIONS

The appropriate clothes for various occasions are given below. If ever in doubt what to wear, the best rule is to err on the side of informality. Thus, if you are not sure whether to put on your dress suit or your tuxedo, wear the latter.

Full Dress (Tail Coat)

1. At the opera
2. At an evening wedding
3. At a dinner to which the invitations are worded in the third person, and dinners given in winter season by certain formal older hostesses, even though invitations are telephoned
4. At a ball, or formal evening entertainment
5. At certain state functions on the Continent of Europe in broad daylight. Never in daylight in the United States, and never in New York in summer

"Tuxedo" (Dinner Coat)

1. At the theater
2. At most dinners—especially those given by young people
3. At all informal parties
4. Dining at home
5. Dining in a restaurant
6. Every evening everywhere except when you wear full dress as listed above. But *never in the daylight hours*—except when starting in daylight to go to an evening party

A Cutaway (Morning Coat) with Striped Trousers

1. At a noon or afternoon wedding
2. On Sunday for church (in the city)
3. On all daytime occasions of ceremony, such as taking part in a dedication, unveiling, review of a parade, or when accompanying a royal or ecclesiastical or civic personage, or when in any way appearing as an official in public
4. In England to business
5. As usher at a wedding
6. As pallbearer. Or black sack coat with striped trousers, dull black silk tie, and black kid gloves.

Frock Coat

For middle-aged men, who prefer it to a cutaway

Black Sack Coat

Slightly less formal substitute for cutaway

Business (Sack) Suits

1. For every ordinary everyday occasion in town
2. Traveling
3. The coat of a blue flannel suit can be worn with white flannel or duck trousers for a lunch, or to church, in the country
4. A navy blue sack suit will do in place of a cutaway at a small or country wedding (see Index)

Country Clothes

1. Only in the country
   To wear golf clothes or tennis flannels—even coats with belted backs—in town is entirely inappropriate. Not as much so, however, as town clothes in the country.

ACCESSORIES AT A GLANCE

With Full Evening Dress (Tail Coat)

Shirt: Stiff-bosomed, made for one or two studs as preferred. Some men have shirt, tie and waistcoat all of the same piqué
Collar: Wing
Tie: White lawn or piqué
Waistcoat: White piqué with or without revers, single- or double-breasted
Handkerchief: Fine white linen or batiste with white monogram
Socks: Thin black silk with black or open-work clocks
Shoes: Patent leather pumps or patent leather oxford ties
Jewelry: Pearl studs, otherwise studs that are as inconspicuous as possible; cuff links of platinum or white gold or some simple combination such as mother of white pearl with thin platinum rims
Boutonnière: White, conservative. Red, a permissible fashion
Hat: Silk or opera
Stick (if carried): Plain Malacca smartest, but if necessary to hide joining, plain gold band permitted. Ebony tabu. Gold or ivory knob the hallmark of the "imitation gentleman" and never carried by a real one
Gloves: White buckskin with overcoat. White kid evening gloves only for a ball or when usher at a wedding
Overcoat: Should be black (not Inverness) but night blue useful because possible to serve both purposes of afternoon and evening wear
Muffler: White silk

THE CLOTHES OF A GENTLEMAN

Dinner Coat (Tuxedo)

Shirt: Stiff white or plaited
Collar: Wing or turn-down (in very hot weather soft shirt and collar permitted)
Waistcoat: White piqué whenever dinner coat substitutes for full dress; otherwise black is proper; never colored. White worn always by fashionable New Yorkers, Newporters, etc.
Tie: Black satin or silk
Handkerchief, socks, shoes, also boutonnière and stick (if any): Same as for full dress
Gloves: None
Jewelry: Variety less restricted than for full dress. Studs, cuff links, waistcoat buttons and all to match or in different sets of mother of pearl, with platinum or onyx or any jewelry or other variety in conservative taste
Hat: Opera hat or felt (stiff straw or Panama in hot weather)
Coat: Same as for full dress, or any tailored coat. In country, any coat—"polo," etc.

White Dinner Coat

Intended only for hot weather, it should be double-breasted so as to avoid waistcoat; trousers, shirt, tie, socks and shoes: same as with dinner coat (all white articles of clothing must be immaculate and perfectly ironed)
Hat: Stiff straw or Panama or none

White Mess Jacket

Trousers: Black
Waistcoat: White (kummerbund not in as good taste, but black one permissible). Other details same as for white dinner coat

Business, Lounge or Sack Suit

Shirt and Collar: Anything you like except polo
Shoes: Any of brown or black leather (not patent leather)
Socks: Wool, silk and wool or lisle, plain or patterned, but avoid striking mixtures of color
Ties: Plain or figured (avoid flowered designs and stiff satin textures)
Handkerchief: Linen or silk or cotton, white or colored
Jewelry: Very little and for utility, not ornament

Country Clothes

Sports clothes suitable to each particular sport or game
General details: Avoid all clothes that suggest town. Country clothes look better when not too new and too pressed

Shirts: All soft shirts, white or colored, with collars attached. "Polo" type of shirt worn without coat or tie outdoors everywhere in the "real" country; but coat and tie should be put on before going into dining room for lunch or dinner.

Shorts: Very bad on the old or fat or tall or beefy! But all right in the country on the young and thin

Boys' Clothes

The following list of clothes is considered complete for a boy going to a representative preparatory (boarding) school:

Suits: Three sack suits (long trousers): two of tweed for everyday, one navy blue for Sunday and dress occasions

Shoes: Two brown or black pairs for everyday and one pair of black to wear with navy blue suit

Socks: Thin wool smartest, or else cotton. Plain black for blue suit; otherwise subdued colors

Shirts: Cheviot, collars attached; solid colors, light blue or tan, etc. If climate very cold, flannel with fine striped lines. For Sunday and dress, a few white shirts with detachable starched turn-down collars. Polo shirts and shorts for special occasions, such as hikes or scout work of any sort

Ties: Plain dark blue for blue suit; others of mixed colors not too gaudy

One or two pairs old trousers and sweaters of different weights. Windbreaker leather coat, also polo coat and raincoat

For train and in city: Overcoat and felt hat. At school: A knit cap or nothing

In New York every boy home from boarding school for the holidays wears a tuxedo with a white waistcoat to all big holiday parties and dances

College Clothes

The same as for preparatory school with the addition of evening clothes

THE CLOTHES OF THE PROTESTANT CLERGY

For services in which ecclesiastical vestments are not worn, old-fashioned ministers still wear a frock coat at all hours of day or evening—in church or otherwise—either double- or single-breasted, with a lay coat collar and waistcoat, or the clerical coat with a low standing collar. For formal services, certain clergymen wear long single-breasted coats buttoned all the way up to the collar, showing no waistcoat; but the majority of younger clergymen choose a frock coat made to be open in the front, for the full length, over a cassock waistcoat or clerical waistcoat. A cassock waistcoat is without buttons in the front and made either with or without a low band collar of its own material about half the height of the straight white collar fastened at the back and worn underneath the waistcoat. A clerical waistcoat is buttoned down the front and has a short standing collar which has an open space in front showing the full depth of the plain white collar beneath. The clerical waistcoat is always made of cloth to match the coat. The cassock waistcoat is of cloth in the daytime but of ribbed black silk for evening wear. Most modern clergymen choose the cutaway coat in preference to the frock coat, and a clerical waistcoat of cloth and black trousers. But by many others, gray trousers that are almost black are considered permissible.

For everyday wear, the younger clergymen have ordinary sack suits—of black—with a clerical waistcoat; but many high-church Episcopalians prefer a clerical standing collar, forming a notch where the collar fails to meet the top edges of the coat fronts. All these clothes are worn by Episcopal clergymen at home and in public, and during services by clergymen of denominations which do not prescribe vestments.

In the evening many clergymen wear exactly the same clothes that they wear in the daytime. Others merely exchange the cloth waistcoat for a cassock waistcoat of silk. Others, whose parishes happen to be very fashionable, wear evening dress.

At a large evening wedding, for example, at which all men present wear full evening dress, a clergyman, to be suitably in the picture, wears—for the ceremony if he has no vestments, or at the reception after he has removed his vestments—an evening tail coat and trousers and a cassock waistcoat of black ribbed silk. Or at a small evening wedding he wears a tuxedo coat with the same black silk waistcoat.

Not long ago, clergymen wore black clothes always—in the country as well as in town. But the modern love of outdoor sports has brought clergymen as well as laymen out upon the golf links and the tennis courts, and during his recreation hours in the country or at the seaside a clergyman wears the same type of clothes exactly that every other man does who follows these pursuits.

40

Table Manners

WHEN CHILDREN COME TO THE TABLE*

THE distance from the table at which it is best to sit is a matter of personal comfort. A child should not be allowed to be so close that his elbows are bent like a grasshopper's, nor so far back that food is likely to be spilled in transit from plate to mouth.

No child under five can be expected to use a napkin instead of a bib. No matter how nicely behaved he may be, there is always the danger of his spilling something, some time. Soft-boiled egg is hideously difficult to eat without ever getting a drop of it down the front, and it is much easier to supply him with a clean bib for the next meal than to change his clothes for the next moment.

Very little children usually have "hot water plates" that are specially made like a double plate with hot water space between, on which the meat is cut up and the vegetables "fixed" in the pantry, and brought to the children before other people at the table are served, not only because it is hard for them to be made to wait, when their attention is attracted by food not for them, but because they take so long to eat. As soon as they are old enough to eat everything on the table, they are served, not last, but in the regular rotation in which they come at table.

When they are learning to help themselves, they must especially guard against "flinging" the serving spoon and spattering the table. In fact, this principal cause for a spotted tablecloth is something to which even occasionally grown people should pay attention.

TABLE TRICKS THAT MUST BE CORRECTED

To pile mashed potato and other vegetables on the convex side of the fork on top of the meat for two or more inches of its length is an unpleasant habit dear to the hearts of schoolboys and sometimes of their fathers—a habit that is more easily prevented than corrected. In fact, taking a big mouthful (next to smearing the face and chew-

*Parents interested in teaching table manners to very young children will find complete directions in "Children Are People", Emily Post's book of Junior Etiquette.

482

ing with mouth open) is the worst offense at table. To prevent this was perhaps the object of zigzag eating. At least it sounds reasonable.*

To sit up straight and keep their hands in their laps when not occupied with eating is very hard for children, but should be insisted upon in order to prevent a careless attitude that all too readily degenerates into flopping this way and that, and into fingering whatever is in reach. The child must not be allowed to warm his hands on his plate, or drum on the table, or screw his napkin into a rope or make marks on the tablecloth. If he shows talent as an artist, give him pencils or modeling wax in his playroom, but do not let him bite his slice of bread into the silhouette of an animal, or model figures in soft bread at the table. And do not allow him to construct a tent out of two forks, or an automobile chassis out of tumblers and knives, or tie the corners of his napkin into bunny-rabbit ears. Food and table implements are not playthings, nor is the dining room table a playground.

Children should be taught from the time they are little not to talk about what they like and don't like. A child who is not allowed to say anything but "No, thank you" at home will not mortify his mother in public by screaming, "I hate spinach. I won't eat potato. I want ice cream and cookies!"

Older children should not be allowed to jerk out their chairs, to flop down sideways, to flick their napkins by one corner, to reach out for something, or begin to eat candy, fruit or other table decorations. A child as well as a grown person should sit down in the center of his chair and draw it up to the table (if there is no one to push it in for him) by holding the seat in either hand while momentarily lifting himself on his feet. It makes no difference whether he approaches the chair from the left or the right. The only rule is to take his place quietly, and not "jump" or "rock" his chair into place at

* The procedure called "zigzag eating" is this: With knife in right hand and fork in left, the diner cuts a piece of meat. Then instead of lifting the piece to the mouth with fork in left hand—or at least cutting several pieces—the knife is at once laid down, the fork transferred to right hand, turned over, prongs up, and the piece of meat speared and conveyed to mouth. Then the fork is zigzagged back into the left hand and turned over, prongs down, while the knife is picked up again and another piece of meat cut. Again the knife is laid down, fork turned over and zigzagged to right hand—don't let us even picture it. One wonders whether it is considered wrong by the zigzag eaters (whoever they may be) to go up and down stairs left foot, right foot; or do they go down right foot, stop, bring down left, right foot, stop, bring down left? The only serious objection to making the right hand do all the work is that no form of limping, whether it be of foot or hand, expresses effortless ease. And why an able-bodied person should like to pretend that the left hand is paralyzed and cannot be lifted more than three or four inches above the table is beyond understanding.

the table. In getting up from the table, again he must push his chair back quietly, using his hands on either side of the chair seat, and *not* by holding onto the table edge and giving himself, chair and all, a sudden shove!

EMBARRASSING DIFFICULTIES

If food is too hot, quickly take a swallow of water. On no account spit it out! If food has been taken into your mouth, no matter how you hate it, you must swallow it. It is offensive to take anything out of your mouth that has been put in it, except dry fish bones and fruit pits. If you choke on a fish bone, leave the table quickly. To spit anything whatever into the corner of your napkin is too nauseating to comment on. It is horrid to see anyone spit skins or pits on a fork or into the plate, and is excusable only if you get a bad clam or something similar into your mouth. Even then the best—because least noticeable—method is to take it from your mouth in your fingers—thumb underneath and four other fingers forming a screen over whatever it is, from lips to plate.

Peaches or other very juicy fruits are peeled and then eaten with knife and fork, but dry fruits, such as apples, may be cut and then eaten in the fingers. *Never* wipe hands that have fruit juice on them on a napkin without first using a finger bowl, because fruit juices make injurious stains.

WHEN HELPING YOURSELF, REMEMBER—

When helping yourself, the first rule is to pay attention to what you are doing and not fling the serving fork or spoon in such a way as to scatter particles of food over either floor, table or yourself.

Anything served on a piece of toast is usually lifted off on the toast, unless you don't want the toast, in which case you may take the quail or help yourself to asparagus and leave the toast in the dish. Sweetbreads, or mushrooms on toast—you take the toast and all on the spoon and hold it in place with the fork. If there is only **one** implement in the dish, you balance the food as carefully as you can.

WHEN YOU HELP YOURSELF TO CONDIMENTS, GRAVY, PICKLES, JELLY, ETC.

Gravy should be put *on* the meat, and the condiment, pickles and jelly *at the side* of whatever they accompany. Olives, radishes, or celery are put on the bread and butter plate if there is one; otherwise on the edge of the plate from which one is eating. Salted nuts are put on the tablecloth.

When helping yourself, you say nothing; but when declining a dish, you say, "No, thank you." Your voice is barely audible and in fact a negative shake of the head and "Thanks" more nearly describes the usual refusal.

WHEN PASSING PLATE FOR SECOND HELPING

Leave knife and fork on plate when passing it. Be sure the handles are far enough on not to topple off.

THE GRADUATING TESTS IN TABLE MANNERS

A young person is supposed to have graduated from the school of table etiquette when she, or he, is able to sit at a formal lunch or dinner table and find no difficulty in eating properly any of the comestibles which are supposed to be "hurdles" to the inexpert. But the real test of perfect table manners is never to offend the sensibilities of others. Never chew with the lips open; never eat or drink audibly; and never make a mess of either food or implements.

In addition to the directions already given for young children, it may perhaps be useful to list perplexing details.

FORKS OR FINGERS

All juicy or "gooey" fruits or cakes are best eaten with a fork, but in most cases it is a matter of dexterity. If you are able to eat a peach in your fingers and not smear your face, let juice run down, or make a sucking noise, you are the one in a thousand who *may*, and with utmost propriety, continue the feat. If you can eat a napoleon or a cream puff and not let the cream ooze out on the far side, you need not use a fork; but if you cannot eat something—no matter what it is—without getting it all over your fingers, you must use a fork, and if necessary, a knife also!

GOOD TABLE MANNERS AVOID UGLINESS

All the rules of table manners are made to avoid ugliness. To let anyone see what you have in your mouth is repulsive; to make a noise is to suggest an animal; to make a mess is disgusting. On the other hand, there are a number of trifling decrees of etiquette that are merely finical, unreasonable, and silly. Why one should not cut one's salad in small pieces if one wants to, makes little sense, unless one wants to cut up a whole plateful and make the plate messy! Until stainless steel was invented, a steel knife was not permitted for salad or fruit, because it turned black; but silver-bladed knives have always been used for salads as well as for fruits in best-appointed houses.

To condemn the American custom of eating a soft-boiled egg in a glass or cup because it happens to be the English fashion to scoop it through the ragged edge of the shell is about as reasonable as though we were to proclaim English manners bad because they tag a breakfast dish, called a "savory" of fish-roe or something equally inappropriate, after the dessert at dinner.

Many other arbitrary rules for eating food with a fork, spoon or fingers are also stumbling-blocks rather than aids to smoothness. As said above, one eats with a fork or spoon "finger foods" that are messy and sticky; one eats with the fingers those which are dry; and one eats dessert with fork or spoon as one prefers. It is true that one should not eat French fried potatoes or—strictly—Saratoga chips in fingers, because they belong to the meat course. Although separate vegetable saucers are never put on a fashionable table, if a man in his own house likes a saucer for his tomatoes, he is certainly within his rights to have it. But if children are taking daddy as their pattern, let us hope if he insists on eating a chicken wing or a squab leg in his fingers that he asks for a finger bowl. The real objection to eating with the fingers is getting them greasy or sticky, and to suck them or smear one's napkin is equally abominable.

LEAVING FOOD ON ONE'S PLATE NOT GOOD MANNERS

The suggested saving to be made by eating everything on one's plate and leaving no food "for manners" is evidently a confusion of the word plate with platter. To leave a portion on the platter (or in the dish) because a guest might like another helping was good manners. But deliberately to leave a portion of food on one's own plate was never accepted etiquette. In fact, the maxim of frugality is, "Food left on your plate is wicked waste, because it must be thrown away. Food left in the dish is saved for another day."

The one food-saving rule of importance brought about by the war is to serve small portions and then pass every dish a second time. Instead of cutting a broiled chicken in four pieces (or, if small, in only two) as was formerly done at lunch parties, it is now cut in eight pieces (or four) and the platter passed again (as was not the former practice).

ON THE SUBJECT OF ELBOWS ON THE TABLE

Although elbows on the table are seen constantly in highest fashionable circles, a whole table's length of elbows planted like clothes-line poles and hands waving glasses or forks about in between, is certainly not an attractive dinner-table picture. And yet there are occasions when elbows are not only permitted but are actually necessary—especially on tables in restaurants when people are lunching or dining at a small table of two or four, and it is impossible to make oneself heard above the music, and at the same time not be heard at other tables near-by, without leaning far forward. And in leaning forward, a woman's figure makes a more graceful outline supported on her elbows than doubled forward over her hands in her lap as though she were in pain! At home, when there is no reason for leaning across the table, there is no reason for elbows. And at a dinner of ceremony, elbows on the table are rarely seen, except at the ends of the table, where again one has to lean forward in order to talk to a companion at a distance across the table corner.

Elbows are *never* put on the table while one is eating. To sit with the left elbow propped on the table while eating with the right hand —unless one is alone and ill—or to prop the right one on the table while lifting the fork or glass to the mouth—should be avoided.

RUDE TO WIPE OFF TABLEWARE

Sometimes in restaurants one sees people wiping knives, forks and spoons on their napkins. This is an act insulting to any reputable proprietor and usually inexcusable. If it should happen, however, that you are obliged to eat in a really dirty restaurant and must wipe the tableware, do so as inconspicuously as you can under the table's edge so that the attention of others is at least not attracted.

OTHER TABLE DON'TS

Don't encircle a plate with the left arm while eating with the right hand.

Don't push back your plate when finished. It remains exactly where it is until whoever is waiting on you removes it. If you wait on yourself, get up and carry it to the kitchen.

Don't lean back and say "I'm through." The fact that you have put your fork or spoon down shows that you have finished.

Don't *ever* put liquid into your mouth if it is already filled with food—this really means "filled." You might have a little bread in your mouth when you drink your coffee, if it be so little as to be undetectable to others.

Don't dunk, although it is an approved practice in lunch wagons—according to the movies. "Dunking" a whole doughnut into coffee is rated very little above eating with a knife. If you MUST soften your doughnut or slice of toast, at least break it in half and dip an end, or cut the toast into one-inch strips and dip them lightly, or better, break a small piece at a time into your coffee, milk, or soup, and eat it with your spoon.

Don't apologize and thus *call attention* to anything so unpleasant as having to blow your nose at table. The only thing to do is to end it as quickly as possible.

THE KNIFE AS A PUSHER

The knife used as a pusher is proper—*if* properly used. Held in the left hand in the same position as it is when held in the right hand, with the tip of the blade helping to guide and hold each mouthful for the fork to lift, it is not even noticed by most people.

A more conspicuous way of using the knife as a barricade is often dexterously and unobjectionably done by well-mannered men (though rarely practiced by women) by holding the whole length of the knife blade sharp edge down as a barrier and then eating subsequent mouthfuls by pushing the fork against it.

CERTAINLY YOU CAN SOP BREAD INTO GRAVY

But it must be done properly—by putting a small piece down on the gravy and then eating it with knife and fork as though it were any other helping on your plate.

NO EXCUSE FOR EATING CHOPS IN THE FINGERS

The wartime excuse for holding chops, as well as chicken legs, in the fingers as a food-saving measure has no excuse—not even that of food-saving. It is, on the contrary, wasteful. At home, the conscientious carver cuts all the meat on these bones as close as he can—and serves bones to no one. All bones are set aside on a clean plate. After the meal they are broken apart and put into the soup pot. This is a 100 per cent saving. Letting the children chew them (quite apart from the harm done to their manners) wastes 50 per cent of this nutritive value.

Foods That Are Sometimes Difficult to Eat

ARTICHOKES

Artichokes are always eaten with the fingers; a leaf at a time is pulled off and the edible end dipped in the sauce, and then bitten off. When the center is reached, the thistle part is scraped away with a knife, the edges are cut, and the "heart" eaten with a fork.

ASPARAGUS

By reputation this is a finger food, but the ungraceful sight of seeing a bent stalk of asparagus dripping like a fountain into some-

Push the spoon under the toast and hold with fork.

—make cut on right side and lift out the portion. And then help yourself to the food in the center.

Dish always presented with spoon and fork.

When being first to cut into a mousse, or aspic, or vol-au-vent, or any dish of this type, turn spoon and cut left side of the portion this way. And then—

CORRECT CHOICE AND USE OF TABLE IMPLEMENTS

Tablespoon must be used for consommé in a plate. The spoon should be dipped away and soup sipped *silently* from side.

This proves that bacon need NOT be eaten in the fingers.

CORRECT CHOICE AND USE OF TABLE IMPLEMENTS *(Continued)*

Bread should be held against rim of plate while being buttered.

When plate is handed to carver for second helping, implements should be placed at side to make room.

The expert way of eating is to lift mouthful on fork in left hand (without "zigzagging.")

When necessary it is permissible to use knife as pusher. Note: Fork should be pushed against knife which is held steady—as a barricade.

Typical use of knife and fork—hold with fork, cut with knife.

Eating with fork alone.

It is absolutely correct to cut salad with a knife —if the blade be of silver or stainless steel.

When napkin is not to be used again, it is laid loosely folded at side of plate.

CORRECT CHOICE AND USE OF TABLE IMPLEMENTS (*Continued*)

—eat as though it were a piece of meat; pushing it down under sauce with fork and lifting sauce over it with knife.

Use of finger-bowl.

To sop the bread in the sauce lay it in center of sauce and—

Correct use of dessert fork and spoon. Hold with fork; cut and eat with spoon.

one's mouth, and the fact that water is also likely to drip from the end, has been the reason why most fastidious people invariably eat it —at least partially—with a fork. That is, cut the stalks with the fork to where they become harder, and then pick up the ends in the fingers if you choose. But don't squeeze the stalks, or hold your hand below the end and let the juice run down your arm.

Hothouse asparagus, or any other that has no hard end, is eaten entirely with a fork. All hard ends should be cut off asparagus before serving it at a dinner party, since picking up stalks in the fingers is scarcely compatible with formal table manners.

BAKED POTATO

Baked potato—white or sweet—is usually eaten by breaking it in half with the fingers, scooping all the inside of the potato onto the plate with a fork, and then mixing butter, salt and pepper in it with a fork.

Another way to eat baked potato is to break it in half with the fingers and lay both halves, skin down, on the plate. Mix a little butter in a small part of one half—with a fork—and eat that. Then mix a little more, and so on, always eating it out of the skin without turning it out on the plate.

A third way to eat baked potato—for those who eat the skin as well as the inside—is to cut the two halves through in pieces with the knife and fork. This avoidance of the knife probably resulted from the tendency of silver or steel to stain. There is no sensible reason why a stainless steel knife blade should be banned. Then cut them again into pieces of eatable size. Butter the pieces with the fork alone, and eat, of course, with the fork held in right hand, tines up. Later on, cut a few more pieces.

BACON

Breakfast bacon should, when possible, be eaten with a fork. But when it is so very dry and crisp that it scatters into fragments when broken by the fork, fingers are permitted, as they are also for dry Saratoga chips. But French fried potatoes must be eaten with a fork.

BIRDS

Birds are not eaten with the fingers. You cut off as much meat as you can and leave the rest on your plate. If you know how to manage very small bones, such as joint or wing or second joint of a squab, you put the piece of bone with meat on it in your mouth.

BONES, PITS, AND SEEDS—REMOVING FROM MOUTH

Fish bones or other accidental bones are taken between finger and thumb and removed between compressed lips. Pits and seeds must be eaten quite bare and clean in the mouth and dropped into the cupped fist and then into the plate. The pits of stewed prunes or cherries that are eaten with a spoon are made as clean and dry as possible in the mouth (with the tongue and teeth) and then dropped into the spoon with which you are eating, and conveyed to the edge of the plate. But it is horrid to see anyone spit skins or pits into a spoon or into the plate unless really dry and with lips compressed. And even so, people with best manners usually drop the pits even of stewed prunes or cherries into the cupped hand, held close to the lips.

BONES—REMOVING FROM FISH

Lift the end of the bone with a fork, and then lift it all the way out pinched between the knife and fork together, or with the fingers. Do not let the fingers touch the fish.

BOUILLON

Drink any thin soup that is in a cup, or sip it from a spoon, as you prefer (sipping must, of course, be silent). Usually you sip a few spoonfuls and then, when it is cool enough, drink from the cup, holding both handles or one as you choose. Remember not to hold your fingers curled in exaggerated cockscombs. Imagine the double-curled effect, holding two handles.

BREAD AND BUTTER

Bread should always be broken into moderate-sized pieces—but not necessarily single mouthful bits—with the fingers before being eaten. If it is to be buttered, a piece is held on the edge of the bread and butter plate, or the place plate, and enough butter spread on it for a few mouthfuls at a time, with a butter knife. If there isn't a butter knife, use any other knife you choose.

This buttering of bread is not an important rule. There are always commonsense exceptions. For instance, little hot biscuits can of course be buttered immediately, since they please most palates only when the butter is quickly and thoroughly melted. Bread must never, however, be held flat on the palm of the hand and buttered in the air. If the regular steel knife is used, care must be taken not to smear food from the knife's side on the butter. Jellies and jams as well as butter are spread on bread with a knife, never with a fork, though you do put butter on vegetables and jelly on meat with a fork. It is always permissible to use a piece of crust for a "pusher."

BUTTER

Every sort of bread, biscuit, toast, and also hot griddlecakes and corn *on* the cob are buttered with a knife. But corn that has been cut *off* the cob, or rice, or potato—or anything else on your plate—has seasoning or butter mixed in it with a fork.

CANAPÉS

Canapés served before a meal are eaten in the fingers (with cocktails in the living room). At table they are eaten, as are other hors-d'oeuvres, with a fork.

CHEESE

Cheese is one thing that may be spread with either a knife or a fork. If eaten with a salad, with which one is using no knife, one may break off a piece of cheese and put it on lettuce or a cracker with one's fork. Cheese such as Camembert is always spread with a knife, because it is impossible to cut off its crust with a fork. (A hostess must remember this and, if unable to provide salad knives, choose another variety of cheese.)

CLAM CHOWDER

Clam chowder is one of the soups that should be served in a soup plate. You should be able to drink cup soups easily.

CONDIMENTS

The thought of smearing condiments with a knife on food already impaled on a fork is very unpleasant if more than a small amount is taken. The proper way to manage a quantity of cranberry sauce, dressing, jelly, pickle, etc. is to lift it onto the fork and either eat it as a separate mouthful or impale a very small piece of meat on the tips of the tines.

CORN ON THE COB

To attack corn on the cob with as little ferocity as possible is perhaps the only direction to be given, since from the point of view of grace a series of ferociously snatching, teeth-bared bites that can be heard as well as seen, to say nothing of butter and corn fragments sprinkled on chin and cheeks, while delectable to the palate, is horrible to the sight. The only maxim to bear in mind when eating this pleasant-to-taste but not-very-easy-to-manage vegetable is to eat it as neatly as possible. It doesn't matter whether you break the ear in half, or whether you hold it by its own ends or by silver handles. The real thing to avoid is too much buttering all at once, and eating it greedily. If you like much butter, then spread it across only half the length about two rows at a time. If you take a moderate amount of butter, you can spread it across the whole length of two rows, add salt and pepper, hold the ends in both hands and eat it—quietly!

Cutting corn off the cob is chiefly a question of the sharpness of the knife. Considerate housekeepers should supply small sharp vegetable knives to those who like to cut the corn off. When corn is served for a dinner party, it should be cut off the cobs in the kitchen, creamed or buttered.

CRACKERS OR CROUTARDS WITH SOUP

Croutards, which are part of the garnishing of the soup, are scattered on the soup after it has been ladled into the plate to be served. Croutons are either put on the soup or else passed separately in a dish with a small serving spoon and each person puts a spoonful in his soup. Oyster crackers, as well as any others, are put on the bread and butter plate, or on the tablecloth—and two or three pieces at a time dropped into the soup.

FRUIT

Plums and bananas are eaten in fingers; also apples if you choose, but most people quarter them with a knife, cut out the core, peel and eat in fingers; pears the same, or if very juicy hold and eat with fork; peaches (if you dislike the skin) hold with fork, peel and eat with fork. When served at table, all fruits should be accompanied by a fruit knife and fork. These implements are very small; the blade of the knife is silver (or gold plated) and has a sharp point for removing seeds.

LOBSTER, BROILED

This is called a finger food because otherwise the meat in the claws cannot be eaten, unless the claws have been not only cracked but literally broken in half. Properly, a big paper napkin and a finger bowl with hot, slightly soaped water should be put at the side of each place at table as soon as people are served, and carried away, of course, as soon as the plates are removed.

OLIVES

Eat with your fingers. Bite off, but don't nibble around the stone! Bite a stuffed one in half. Put only a very small stuffed olive in your mouth whole.

OLIVES AND CHERRIES IN COCKTAILS

Drink the liquid, and when the glass is drained it is easy enough to tip the glass and drop the cherry or small olive into your mouth. Since a large olive is too much of a mouthful, lift it out and eat it in two or three bites.

SALAD WITHOUT A KNIFE

In well-appointed houses a silver-bladed knife should be given you with all leafy salads; but if you happen to be given none, you do the best you can by cutting each leaf into very small pieces and eating it in postage-stamp samples. At all events, beware of rolling the fork and wrapping springy leaves around the tines in a spiral. Remember what a spring that lets go can do!

SALT

If there is no spoon in the salt dish, use a clean knife. If the salt dish be for you alone, use your knife, or pinch it with your fingers.

SALT ON THE TABLECLOTH

Putting salt on the tablecloth and then pinching it between the fingers to put on food is a very old custom and therefore not tabu if it so happens that a salt cellar is not on one side or the other of one's plate. But dipping celery or radishes into this salt on the table is never permitted. Salt that is to be dipped into should be put on the bread and butter plate or on the rim of whatever plate is before you.

SANDWICHES

All ordinary sandwiches not only at picnics but everywhere are eaten in the fingers. Club sandwiches and other inch-thick and wholemeal sandwiches are best cut in smaller portions before being picked up and held tightly in the fingers of both hands. If you are not sitting at table and you have no knife, you bite into an overlarge and hugely thick piece as nicely as you can—or, quoting former advice in the matter of eating corn on the cob—attack it with as little ferocity as possible.

ANSWERS TO READERS' QUESTIONS

DOES NAPKIN UNFOLDING MATTER?

Does it matter how much a napkin is unfolded at table?

The only thing that matters is that a napkin shall stay on your lap out of sight. In addition to the suggestion on page 354 for keeping a large dinner napkin in place, one who has a shelving lap might go around with a few paper clips and clip a little napkin to her dress—or to the edge of his waistcoat. After all, it isn't of much use on the floor!

MUST IDLE HAND LIE IN LAP?

Must you sit up straight at table, not even bending your head to eat soup? When one hand is not in use, must the other be held in your lap? Our governess has taken all the joy out of eating!

Perhaps your governess is trying to break you of the habit of getting your chin almost down to your plate, or to keep you from propping your cheek on one hand while you eat with the other, or hugging your plate with your left arm, or other serious faults. Normally one does bend forward slightly, and usually both hands are occupied. Children are always taught to sit up straight and keep their unoccupied hands in their laps because this is best training. By and by they can eat without thinking—after they have had enough of this training to check sloppiness instinctively.

LUNCH OR LUNCHEON

Is the word lunch ever permitted, or must we say luncheon?

Pretentious people always say luncheon. Most of us prefer to say lunch. The meaning is the same.

HOW DO YOU EAT AN ORANGE?

Must I eat an orange with a knife and fork? I like to cut a hole in one end and put a lump of sugar in, and suck the juice; but I didn't know if this was correct at a restaurant table.

Oh, dear! No! Do *not* suck an orange in a restaurant, or at table anywhere—unless at a picnic. You can peel it and divide sections and eat it in your fingers; or cut it in half and eat with a spoon, or cut it in any way you like best. My own favorite way is to cut off the rind with a sharp knife, then, holding the fork in the left hand and the knife in my right, cut the peeled orange in half crossways and cut it piece by piece and eat with both knife and fork.

FINICAL TABLE-MANNER ABSURDITIES

A friend who has been studying a book of etiquette has made me unhappy by pointing out all the mistakes I make. She says it is rude not to set four places at table when there are only three to eat. She says the hostess must be served first. She says it is bad manners to speak while you are holding a fork or a spoon or a knife in your hand—you must lay them down and then speak.

I wonder whether your friend is not purposely misleading you—to tease you just a little? Less than four places would be *incorrect* in a formally appointed house, but there could be no rudeness in fewer places if fewer persons are to sit at table. Serving the hostess first is the greatest breach of courtesy possible to commit—unless the food is likely to be poisoned, in which case it would probably be her duty to see whether she dies first! The suggestion that you lay down knife and fork before speaking is an amusing idea for a "low comedian." Imagine a dinner: Down knives and forks, "Oh, I think so, Mrs. Smith"; up knives and forks, eat. Down knives and forks, "I lost what you said, Mrs. Smith"!

41

Formal Correspondence

THE letter you write, whether you realize it or not, is always a mirror which reflects your appearance, taste and character. A "sloppy" letter with the writing all pouring into one corner of the page, badly worded, badly spelled, and with unmatched paper and envelope—even possibly a blot—proclaims the sort of person who would have unkempt hair, unclean linen and broken shoe laces; just as a neat, precise, evenly written note portrays a person of those characteristics. Therefore, while it cannot be said with literal accuracy that one may read the future of a person by study of his handwriting, it is true that if a young man wishes to choose a wife in whose daily life he is sure always to find the unfinished task, the untidy mind and the syncopated housekeeping, he may do it quite simply by selecting her from her letters.

HOW TO IMPROVE A LETTER'S APPEARANCE

Some people are fortunate in being able to make graceful letters easily, to space their words evenly, and to put them on a page so that the picture is pleasing; others are discouraged at the outset because their fingers are clumsy and their efforts crude; but no matter how badly formed each individual letter may be, if the writing is consistent throughout, the page as a whole looks fairly well.

You can *make* yourself write neatly and legibly. You can—with the help of a dictionary if necessary—spell correctly; you can be sure that you understand the meaning of every word you use. If it is hard for you to write in a straight line, use the lined guide that comes with nearly all stationery; if impossible to keep an even margin, draw a perpendicular line at the left of the guide so that you can start each new line of writing on it. You can also make a guide to slip under the envelope. Far better to use a guide than to send envelopes and pages of writing that slide up hill and down, in uncontrolled disorder.

CHOICE OF WRITING PAPER

Suitability should be considered in choosing note paper, just as in choosing a piece of furniture for a house. For a handwriting which is habitually large, a larger sized paper should be chosen than for writing which is small. The shape of paper should also depend somewhat upon the spacing of the lines which is typical of the writer, and whether a wide or narrow margin is used. Low, spread-out writing looks better on a square sheet of paper; tall, pointed writing looks better on paper that is high and narrow. Whether the paper is rough or smooth is entirely a matter of personal choice—so that the quality be good, and the shape and color conservative.

FACSIMILES, REDUCED IN SIZE, OF LETTER AND ENVELOPE GUIDES

Paper should never be ruled, or highly scented, or odd in shape, or have elaborate or striking ornamentation. Many people use smaller paper for notes, or correspondence cards, cut to the size of the envelopes. Others use the same size for all correspondence and leave a wider margin in writing notes.

GOOD TASTE   GOOD TASTE   GOOD TASTE   BAD TASTE   BAD TASTE

The flap of the envelope should be plain and the point neither skimpy nor unduly long. If the flap is square instead of pointed, it may be allowed greater length without being eccentric. Envelopes with colored linings, with monogram or address stamped on the paper to match the lining, are at present in fashion. Young girls may be allowed quite gay envelope linings, and the device on the paper may be gay to correspond, but must not be so large or loud as to be in bad taste. Oblong envelopes are excellent for business, but those more nearly square are smartest for personal use.

Linings for Christmas-card envelopes may be as gay as the ornaments that go on a Christmas tree. But unrestrained masses of red and gold, swirls of purple and green or other striking colors, are abominations at any other time.

Metal-edged paper is not good form. Ragged-edged paper is always suggestive of a studio and for that reason appropriate for artists, but not as good as cut edges for most of us.

PAPER FOR A MAN

Writing paper for a man should always be conservative. Plain white or cream, or gray or granite, or a deep blue (not turquoise) paper of medium or larger size, and stamped with his address or his initials or, for social correspondence, with his crest, is in good taste. The color of the stamping (or printing) should be black or gray, navy blue, or brick red. Ink should be black or Navy blue but not green.

PAPER FOR A WOMAN

White, cream, all blues, grays, and mauves are in best taste. Pink is on the fringe of admittance; green is still a tabu. Paper should be of small or medium size, single or double sheets, plain or with any colored border—even green or red if it be narrow—and stamped with either a monogram, initials, address, or both in color to match the border. Ink may be violet as well as any blue but not green.

FIRST NAME ALONE FOR YOUNG GIRL

A girl's name—either "Elizabeth" in full or "Betty"—embossed in color is popular for all personal correspondence of a young girl. But it should not be used by an older woman except when writing to her intimate friends.

PAPER SUITABLE FOR EVERYONE IN FAMILY

A paper suitable for the use of all the members of a family has the address stamped—or perhaps printed—in plain letters at the top of the first page. Frequently the telephone number is put in small letters under the address, or in the upper left-hand corner under a small telephone device, with the address in the center—a necessary convenience in the present day of telephoning. For example:

350 PARK AVENUE
TELEPHONE PLAZA 4-7572

or

RHINELANDER 4-1988

39 EAST 79ᵀᴴ STREET

DEVICES FOR STAMPING

As heraldry is not an institution in America, the use of a coat of arms is as much a foreign custom as the speaking of a foreign tongue; but in certain communities where old families have used their arms continuously since the days when they brought their device—and their right to it—from Europe, the use of it is proper, but even so, rather conspicuous at the present time.

A WOMAN ALONE MAY NEVER USE A CREST

Notwithstanding the ornamental beauty of a crest and the utter ugliness of a lozenge, a widow has no right to use her husband's crest on her letter paper. Properly she may use the device on the shield of his coat of arms, transferred to a diamond-shaped device called a lozenge. She may also, if she chooses, divide the lozenge perpendicularly into two parts and crowd the device from her husband's shield into the left half and the device from her father's shield into the right half, making a combination such as that in the example below:

A spinster uses her paternal arms on a lozenge without crest or motto. A crest is used only by the male member of the family, and therefore its appearance on the paper of a widow or a spinster is as absurd as it would be to put esquire at the end of her name. Surprisingly few Americans, however, seem to be aware of this heraldic rule.

POST OFFICE REQUIRES RETURN ADDRESS ON ENVELOPE

It has always been customary to place a return address at the top left-hand corner on the face of a business envelope; and when necessary to use one on a personal letter, to put it on the flap. Whatever the real reason for making this distinction, it did separate the two types of letters in our mail. Today (in response to requests made by the United States Post Office) it is considered permissible and even advisable to put *all* return addresses on the face of the envelope.

PRINTING AS WELL AS DIE STAMPING

There are certain definite and fairly inflexible rules about marking. Not many years ago, the paper used by a gentlewoman was either die-stamped (engraved) or left plain. This was in the era when the mystery of operating a typewriter was still the special province of the professional stenographer. But today the writing equipment of a busy woman is almost as certain to include a typewriter as to employ modern pens instead of quills. In the same way the convenience of paper upon which one's full name and address are printed has become indispensable to everyone who must write those unending letters on unending subjects that are part of the daily task of every person of normally diversified interests. In short, the few quires of die-stamped paper—at unavoidably higher cost—have gradually given way to dozens of quires of printed papers—though one should have a few die-stamped quires for formal letters and notes.

COUNTRY HOUSE STATIONERY FOR A BIG HOUSE

In selecting paper for a country house we go back to the subject of suitability. A big house, in important grounds, should have very plain, very dignified letter paper. It may be white, or tinted blue or gray. The name of the place should be engraved, in the center usually, at the top of the first page. A single device slanting across the upper corner, or as many as may be necessary, are put in a column at the upper left side. Many persons use a whole row of small outlines—the engine of a train and beside it Stirlington, meaning that Stirlington is the railroad station; a telegraph pole, an envelope, a telephone instru-

        Stirlington, New York
        Ringwood, New Jersey
        Sloatsburg, New York 732

ment—and beside each an address. Instead of (or in addition to) the engine, there may be a boat or an airplane, or perhaps a bus. These devices are suitable for all places, whether they are great or tiny, that have addresses different from the railroad, post office, telephone, or telegraph.

FOR THE LITTLE COUNTRY HOUSE

On the other hand, farmhouses and little places in the country may have very bright-colored stamping, as well as gay-lined envelopes. Places with easily illustrated names quite often have them pictured. The "Birdcage," for instance, may have a bright blue paper with a birdcage in supposed red lacquer; the "Bandbox," a fantastically decorated milliner's box on oyster gray paper, the envelope lining of black and gray pin stripes; and the "Doll's House" might use the outline of a doll's house in grass green on green-bordered white paper, and white envelopes lined with grass green. Each of these devices loses its

charm unless it is as small as the outline of a cherry pit and the paper is of the smallest size that comes. (Envelopes 3½ x 5 inches or paper 4 x 6 and envelopes the same size to hold paper without folding.)

OFFICIAL WRITING PAPER

An Ambassador or Minister has the coat of arms of his country— in gold usually—stamped at the top of writing paper and on cards of invitation for official or formal use. For his personal use and for the use of all who live at the embassy or the legation, note paper is engraved merely

American Embassy
London

The letter paper of a governor is stamped

Executive Mansion
Albany
N. Y.

and is usually surmounted by the coat of arms of the State.*

This same paper, but without the coat of arms, may be used by his

---

* The letter paper used for social correspondence by a governor's family as well as himself is engraved "Executive Mansion." But "Executive Office" is often chosen as the heading for official letters.

family if the address is also that of their home. Otherwise their paper is stamped with their personal address.

It is unnecessary to add that the wife of a senator has no right to stationery headed "The Senate," nor may the wife of a Congressman write on paper engraved "House of Representatives."

MOURNING PAPER

The wide borders of former days have been discarded for those which customs of yesterday would have called second mourning. An over-heavy border (from 3/8 to 1/2 inch) is unknown in the United States today.

One-fourth of an inch is considered deepest mourning, and 3/16 used as deep mourning by all who are young; 1/16 and 1/32 of an inch are suitable width for second mourning.

DATING A LETTER

Usually the date is put at the upper right-hand side of the first page of a letter, or at the end, and to the far left of the signature, of a note. It is far less confusing for one's correspondent to read January 9, 1945, than 1-9-45.

At the end of a note "Thursday" is sufficient unless the note is an invitation for more than a week ahead, in which case write as in a letter, "January 9." The year is not necessary for it can hardly be expected that a year will be required for a letter's delivery.

SEQUENCE OF PAGES

If a note is longer than one page but shorter than three, the third page is customarily used next, as this leaves the fourth page blank and prevents the writing from showing through the envelope. With heavy or lined envelopes, the fourth is used more often than the third. In letters one may write first, second, third, fourth, in regular order; or first and fourth, then, opening the sheet and turning it sideways, write across the two inside pages as one. Many prefer to write on first, third, then sideways across the second and fourth. Certain people have the habit of repeating the last word on a page at the top of the next. It is undoubtedly a good idea, but makes a stuttering impression upon a reader not accustomed to it.

FOLDING A LETTER

To fold a letter in such a way that the recipient shall be able to read the contents without having to turn the paper is giving too much importance to nothing. It is sufficient that the paper be folded *neatly* —once, of course, for the envelope that is as deep as half the length of the paper, and twice for the envelope that is a third as deep. The paper that folds twice, by the way, should be used only for business purposes. Social letter paper should fold only once and be fitted into a square envelope. Note paper which is smartest at the moment goes into the envelope without folding.

SEALING WAX

Although sealing wax—like the title Esquire—is no longer generally used in America, both look very nice when properly placed. In short, if you use sealing wax, let us hope you are an adept at making an even and smoothly finished seal, and that you choose a plain-colored wax which can be persuaded to pour smoothly and colorfully and not to look like a black streaked blob of dough.

SALUTATIONS

The most formal beginning of a social letter is "My dear Mrs. Smith." The fact that in England "Dear Mrs. Smith" is more formal does not greatly concern us in America. "Dear Mrs. Smith," "Dear Sarah," "Dear Sally," "Sally dear," "Dearest Sally," "Darling Sally" are increasingly intimate.

Business letters begin

Messrs. Smith, Johnson & Co.
  20 Broadway
     New York 4, N. Y.

Dear Sirs:

In this modern day of informal business letters one written to an individual begins

Messrs. Smith, Johnson & Co.
  20 Broadway
     New York 4, N. Y.

My dear Mr. Johnson:

THE COMPLIMENTARY CLOSE

It is too bad that, for personal letters and notes, the English language does not permit the charming and graceful closing of all letters in the French manner, with those little flowers of compliment that leave such a pleasant fragrance after reading. But ever since the eighteenth century English-speaking people have been busy pruning away all ornament of expression; even the last remaining graces, "kindest regards," "with kindest remembrances," are fast disappearing, leaving us nothing but an abrupt "Sincerely yours."

FORMAL CORRESPONDENCE

The close of a business letter should be "Yours truly" or "Yours very truly." "Respectfully" is used only by a tradesman to a customer, by an employee to an employer, or by an inferior, *never* by a person of equal position. No lady should ever sign a letter "Respectfully," except as part of the long, formal "have the honor to remain" close of a letter to the President of the United States or, of course, to a Bishop or a Mother Superior.

The best ending to a formal social note is "Sincerely," "Sincerely yours," "Very sincerely," "Very sincerely yours," "Yours always sincerely," or "Always sincerely yours."

"I remain, dear madam," is no longer in use, but "Believe me" is still correct when formality is to be expressed in the close of a note.

Believe me
Very sincerely yours,

Or

Believe me, my dear Mrs. Worldly,
Most sincerely yours,

This last is an English form, but it is used by quite a number of Americans—particularly those who have been much abroad.

APPROPRIATE FOR A MAN

"Faithfully" or "Faithfully yours" is a very good closing for a man when writing to a woman or for any uncommercial correspondence, such as a letter to the President of the United States, a member of the Cabinet, an Ambassador, a clergyman, etc.

THE INTIMATE CLOSING

"Affectionately yours," "Always affectionately," "Affectionately," "Devotedly," "Lovingly," "Your loving" are in increasing scale of intimacy.

"Lovingly" is much more intimate than "Affectionately" and so is "Devotedly."

"Sincerely" in formal notes and "Affectionately" in intimate notes are the two adverbs most used in the present day. Between those two there is a blank; in English we have no expression to fit sentiment more friendly than the first and yet less intimate than the second.

NOT GOOD FORM

"Cordially" was coined no doubt to fill this need, but its condescension puts it in the category with "residence" and "retire," and all the other offenses of pretentiousness.

"Yours in haste" or "Hastily yours" is not bad form, but is rather carelessly rude.

"In a tearing hurry" is a termination dear to the boarding-school girl; but its truth does not make it any more attractive than the vision of that same young girl rushing into a room with her hat and coat half on, to swoop upon her mother with a peck of a kiss, and with a "——by, Mom!" whirl out again!

OTHER ENDINGS

"Gratefully" is used only when a benefit has been received, as to a lawyer who has skilfully handled a case, to a surgeon who has saved a life dear to you, to a friend who has been put to unusual trouble to do you a favor.

In an ordinary letter of thanks, the signature is "Sincerely," "Affectionately," "Devotedly"—whatever your usual close may be.

The phrases that a man might devise to close a letter to his betrothed or his wife are limited only by the extent of his imagination and do not belong in this, or any, book.

THE SIGNATURE

Abroad, the higher the rank, the shorter the name. A duke, for instance, signs himself Wellington, nothing else, and a queen her first name, Elizabeth.

But in America, it is not customary for a man to discard any of his names. So John Hunter Titherington Smith, finding that name too much of a penful for the one who unendingly signs letters and documents, chooses J. H. T. Smith instead, or perhaps, at the end of personal letters, John H. T. Smith. And in addressing him others naturally follow his lead. (That he is likely to become "J. H." to everyone is another story.)

A married woman should always sign a letter to a stranger, a bank, business firm, etc. with her baptismal name, and add, in parentheses, her married name. Thus:

>   Very truly yours,
>   Mary Jones Smith
>   (Mrs. John Smith)

If for all general purposes her writing paper is marked with her full name and address, her signature, Mary Jones Smith, needs no explanation.

NEVER SIGN A LETTER "MRS."

Although this rule is fully explained on page 526, it is actually the most important rule in this book and cannot be too strongly emphasized.

Thousands upon thousands of well-bred, courteously intentioned American women writing to those whom they admire and respect unthinkingly sign themselves

>Sincerely,
>Mrs. John Jones

>or

>Mrs. Mary Jones

This second signature is lacking in good taste, but it is no ruder than the first.

A lady writing to another lady, or to a gentleman, should sign her name this way to every friend and acquaintance who perfectly well knows her married name:

>Sincerely,
>Mary Jones

To acquaintances who may not know which Mrs. or possibly Miss Jones she is, she signs her name

>Sincerely,
>Mary Jones
>(Mrs. John Jones)

An unmarried lady signs her name

>Sincerely,
>(Miss) Mary Jones

Those who fear to sign their names "Mary" because they think someone might then feel privileged to call them "Mary" can write clearly beneath their signature, "Kindly reply to Mrs. John Smith." And they can moreover sign their name "M. J. Smith" instead of "Mary Jones Smith."

Never under any circumstances sign a letter with "Mr.," "Mrs." or "Miss" as an unseparated part of one's signature unless one is willing to be considered *both* ignorant and rude.

WHEN THE PREFIX "MR." IS CORRECT

As unconventional as it may sound, it is at times permissible that a man prefix "Mr." in parentheses to his signature to explain that such a name as Leslie, Sidney, Shirley, or Marion is not that of a woman. On the other hand, if he is enclosing a self-addressed envelope, this prefix is not necessary.

CORRECT USE OF ESQUIRE

The superscription Esq. has gone almost out of general use in the United States—except among the conservative members of the older generation. Its correct use is, furthermore, confusing. For example, formally engraved invitations are always addressed to Mr. Stanley Smith. Written invitations, as well as all other *personal* letters may be addressed to Stanley Smith, Esq. The title of Esquire is of British origin and formerly used to denote the eldest son of a knight or members of a younger branch of a noble house. Later all graduates of universities, professional and literary men, and important landholders were given the right to this title, which even today denotes a man of education—a gentleman. John Smith, Esquire, is John Smith, gentleman. Mr. John Smith may be a gentleman or may not be one. And yet, as noted above, all engraved invitations are addressed "Mr."

CORRECTLY A WIDOW KEEPS HER HUSBAND'S NAME

According to best taste no note or social letter should ever be addressed to a married woman, even if she is a widow, as Mrs. Mary Town. Correctly a widow keeps her husband's name for *always*. If her son's wife should have the same name, she becomes Mrs. James Town, Senior, or simply Mrs. Town, if there is no other with the same name.

Of course if, in a certain community, it is customary for widows to prefix Mrs. to their Christian names and they themselves have no objection, their names are certainly their own to use as they choose. But to those of you who want to keep your husband's name, best taste and truth agree that the man gave his name when he gave the wedding ring—both were for life, or until the woman marries again.

NAME OF DIVORCÉE

A divorced woman takes her own surname in place of her ex-husband's Christian name. Supposing her to have been Mary Simpson, she calls herself Mrs. Simpson Smith.

DAUGHTERS, SONS AND CHILDREN

The eldest daughter is Miss Smith; her younger sister, Miss Jane Smith. In the present day this right to Miss Smith is considered rather suggestive of a spinster of uncertain age, and the moderns prefer Miss Alice and Miss Jane Smith.

Envelopes to children are addressed Miss Katherine Smith and Master Robert Smith.

Do not write "The Messrs. Brown" in addressing a father and son. "The Messrs. Brown" is correct only for unmarried brothers.

(For further details, see Index)

WRITE ADDRESS PLAINLY

Write the name and address on the envelope as precisely and as legibly as you can. If your writing is poor, PRINT. Remember that the post office has enough to do in deciphering the letters of the illiterate without being asked to do unnecessary work for you!

BUSINESS LETTERS

Preferably a business letter is typewritten; anything bordering on the unconventional is out of place. The correct beginning for an impersonal business letter is

Mrs. Richard Worldly
   257 Park Avenue
      New York 17, N. Y.

Dear Madam:

A personal business letter, meaning a letter from a business or professional man to a customer or client whom he knows personally, begins

Mrs. Richard Worldly
   257 Park Avenue
      New York 17, N. Y.

My dear Mrs. Worldly:

Business letters written by a customer or client differ very little from those sent out from a business house. A business letter should always be as brief and explicit as possible. For example:

                   Tuxedo Park
                   New York
                                 May 17, 1941

H. J. Paint & Co
   22 Branch St
      New York 7, N. Y.

Dear Sirs:
   Your estimate for painting my dining room, library, south bedroom, and dressing room is satisfactory, and you may proceed with the work as soon as possible.
                  Very truly yours,
                     C. R. Town
                (Mrs. James Town)

An order letter to a store should contain precisely this information:
1. Name or description of article. Including—
2. Quantity or size or color and necessarily—
3. Price.
4. How paid for. (C. O. D., check enclosed, or charge account.)
5. How sent, if necessary.
6. Address.

Example

Brown, Green and Company
Dear Sirs: (the "Dear Sirs" is often omitted)
Please forward by American Express C. O. D. to

Mrs. J. B. Greatlake
20 Lakeshore Drive
Chicago, Ill.

3 jars Black's Clensen Cream—50c size
2 yards silk to match enclosed sample
1 chair (No. 4433 in your catalogue) price $36.50
1 quilt (No. 1746) in "rose," price $12.00

Yours truly,
A. K. Greatlake

LETTER OF INQUIRY TO A HOTEL

101 Park Avenue
New York

Proprietor of Ocean House
   Beach Haven, Maine
Dear Sir:

I would like to know what accommodation you can offer me for the month of August. I require one double room with bath for my husband and myself, a single room for my daughter, and a single room for my son.

Your hotel was recommended to me by Mrs. Arthur Norman.

If you will send me floor plan and prices, I will let you know my decision by return mail.

Very truly yours,
Mary Newhouse
(Mrs. John Newhouse)

THE SOCIAL NOTE

The formal social note is always written by hand.

There should be no more difficulty in writing a social note than in writing a business letter; each has a specific message for its sole object and the principle of construction is the same.

* Date

Address (on business letter only)
Salutation
    The statement of whatever is the purpose of the note.
Complimentary close,
Signature

* Or date here.

The difference in form between a business and a social note is that the full name and address of the person written to is never printed on the paper; the address, if given, is die-stamped. Better-quality stationery is used, and the salutation is "My dear ——" or "Dear ——" instead of "Dear Sir."

Example

350 Park Avenue

Dear Mrs. Robinson,
    I am enclosing the list I promised you.
    I do hope the addresses will be of some use to you, and that you will have a delightful trip.
Very sincerely,
Martha Kindhart

Thursday.

SIRS OR MADAMS

The salutation "Dear Sir" or "Sirs" is in much better form than "Gentlemen." When writing to a firm or organization composed of women the salutation is "Dear Madams." Never write "Mesdames," since it is just as ludicrous as writing "Messieurs" instead of "Sirs."

THE NOTE OF APOLOGY

Examples
I
Broadlawns

Dear Mrs. Town,
    I do deeply apologize for my seeming rudeness in having to send the message about Monday night.
    When I accepted your invitation, I stupidly forgot entirely that Monday was a holiday and that all of my own guests, naturally, were not leaving until Tuesday morning; Arthur and I could not therefore go out by ourselves and leave them!

We were disappointed and hope that you know how sorry we were not to be with you.

Very sincerely,
Ethel Norman

Tuesday morning.

II

Dear Mrs. Neighbor,

My gardener has just told me that our chickens got into your flower beds and did a great deal of damage.

The chicken netting is being built higher at this moment and they will not be able to damage anything again. I shall, of course, send Patrick to put in shrubs to replace those broken, although I know that ones newly planted cannot compensate for those you have lost. I can only ask you to accept my contrite apologies.

Always sincerely yours,
Katherine de Puyster Eminent

LETTERS OF THANKS

In the following examples of letters intimate and from young persons, such profuse expressions as "divine," "awfully," "petrified," "too sweet," "too wonderful" are purposely inserted, because to change all of those enthusiasms into "pleased with," "very," "feared," "most kind" would be to change the validity of the "real" letters into smug and self-conscious utterances at variance with anything ever written by young men and women of today. Even the letters of older persons, although they are more restrained than those of youth, avoid anything suggesting prolixity, pedantry or affectation.

Do not from this suppose that well-bred people write poorly! On the contrary, perfect simplicity and freedom from self-consciousness are possible only to those who have acquired at least some degree of cultivation. Pretentiousness in a letter of thanks or sympathy is an infallible sign of insincerity and lack of taste. For simplicity of expression, such as is unattainable to the rest of us, but which we can at least strive to emulate, read the Bible first, then at random such authors as Robert Louis Stevenson, John Galsworthy, Max Beerbohm, Somerset Maugham—or A. A. Milne! E. V. Lucas has written two novels in letter form—which illustrate the best type of present-day letter-writing.

LETTERS OF THANKS FOR WEDDING PRESENTS

Although all wedding presents belong to the bride, she generally words her letters of thanks as though they belonged equally to the groom, especially if they have been sent by friends of his.

TO INTIMATE FRIENDS OF THE BRIDEGROOM

Dear Mrs. Norman,
 To think of your sending us all this wonderful glass! It is simply divine! Jim and I both thank you a thousand times!
 The presents are, of course, to be shown on the day of the wedding, but do come in on Tuesday at tea time for an earlier view.
 Thanking you again, and with love from us both,
Affectionately,
Mary

FORMAL

I

Dear Mrs. King,
 It was more than sweet of you and Mr. King to send us such a lovely clock. Thank you very, very much.
 Looking forward to seeing you on the tenth,
Very sincerely,
Mary Smith

Sometimes, as in the two examples above, thanks to the husband are definitely expressed in writing to the wife. Usually, however, "you" is understood to mean "you both."

II

Dear Mrs. Potter,
 All my life I have wanted a piece of jade, but in my wanting I have never imagined one quite so beautiful as the one you have sent me. It was wonderfully sweet of you and I thank you more than I can tell you.
Affectionately,
Mary Smith

III

Dear Mrs. Eminent,
 Thank you for these wonderful prints. They go too beautifully with some old English ones that Jim's uncle sent us, and our dining room will be quite perfect—as to walls!
 Hoping that you are surely coming to the wedding,
Very sincerely,
Mary Smith

INTIMATE

Dearest Cora,
 That you should have taken days and days to make this marvelous

needlepoint for ME—really, darling, I can't tell you how much I love it, and appreciate it, and *thank* you!

Sally

FOR A PRESENT SENT AFTER THE WEDDING

Dear Mrs. Chatterton,

The mirror you sent us is going over our drawing-room mantel just as soon as we can hang it up! It is exactly what we most needed and we both thank you ever so much.

Please come in soon to see how becoming it will be to the room.

Yours affectionately,
Mary Smith Smartlington

THANKS FOR CHRISTMAS OR OTHER PRESENTS

It was too adorable of you, dear Lucy, to have a chair like yours made for me. Jack says I'll never get a chance to sit in it if he gets there first. In fact we both thank you ever and ever so much.

Affectionately,
Sally

Dear Uncle Arthur,

I know I oughtn't to have opened it until Christmas, but I couldn't resist the look of the package, and then putting it on at once! So I am all dressed up in your beautiful clip. It is one of the loveliest things I have ever seen and I certainly am lucky to have it given to me! Thank you a thousand—and then more—times for it.

Rosalie

Dear Kate,

I am fascinated with my utility box—it is too beguiling for words! You are the cleverest one anyway for finding what no one else can—and everyone wants. I don't know how you do it! And you certainly were sweet to think of me. Thank you, dear.

Ethel

THANKS FOR PRESENT TO A BABY

Dear Mrs. Kindhart,

Of course it would be! Because no one else can sew like you! The sacque you made the baby is the prettiest thing I have ever seen, and is perfectly adorable on her! Thank you, as usual, you dear Mrs. Kindhart, for your goodness to

Your affectionate
Sally

Dear Mrs. Norman,

Thank you ever so much for the lovely afghan you sent the baby. It is by far the prettiest one he has; it is so soft and close—he doesn't get his fingers tangled in it.

Do come in and see him, won't you? We are both allowed visitors (special ones) every day between 4 and 5:30!

Affectionately always,

Lucy

THE BREAD AND BUTTER LETTER

When you have been staying over Sunday, or for longer, in someone's house, it is absolutely necessary that you write a letter of thanks to your hostess within a few days after the visit.

"Bread and butter letters," as they are called, are the stumbling-blocks of visitors. Why they are so difficult for nearly everyone is hard to determine, unless it is that they are often written to persons with whom you are on formal terms, and the letter should be somewhat informal in tone. Very likely you have been visiting a friend and must write to her mother, whom you scarcely know; perhaps you have been included in a large and rather formal house party and the hostess is an acquaintance rather than a friend; or perhaps you are a bride and have been on a first visit to relatives or old friends of your husband's, but strangers, until now, to you.

As an example of the first, where you have been visiting a girl friend and must write a letter to her mother, you begin "Dear Mrs. Town" at the top of a page, and nothing in the forbidding memory of Mrs. Town encourages you to go further. It would be easy enough to write to Pauline, the daughter. Very well, write to Pauline then—on an odd piece of paper, in pencil—what a good time you had, how nice it was to be with her. Then copy your note composed to Pauline off on the page beginning "Dear Mrs. Town." You have only to add, "Love to Pauline, and thank you again for asking me," sign it "Very sincerely," or better, "Affectionately" and there you are!

Don't be afraid that your note is too informal; older people are always pleased with any friendly and spontaneous expressions from the young. Never think, because you cannot write a letter easily, that it is better not to write at all. The most awkward note that can be imagined is better than none—for to write none is the depth of rudeness, whereas the awkward note merely fails to delight.

EXAMPLES

TO A FORMAL HOSTESS AFTER AN ESPECIALLY AMUSING WEEK END

Dear Mrs. Oldname,

Every moment of the week end was a perfect delight! I am afraid my work at the office this morning was down to zero in efficiency; so perhaps it is just as well, if I am to keep my job, that the average week end in the country is different—very. Thank you all the same, for the wonderful time you gave us all, and believe me

Faithfully yours,
Frederick Bacheior

Dear Mrs. Oldname,

Again I realize that there is no house to which I always go with so much pleasure, and leave on Monday morning with so much regret, as yours.

Your party over this last week end was simply wonderful! And thank you ever so much for having included me.

Always affectionately,
Constance

Dear Mrs. Oldname,

Thank you more than I can tell you for my very happy week end.

I enjoyed every minute of it, and think you were very kind to include me in such a delightful house party.

Very sincerely,
John Huntington Smith

FROM AN OLD BACHELOR TO A YOUNG RELATIVE

Dear Mary and John,

Why do I so much like to stay with you? I thought of this as the train of this morning carried me unwillingly away.

I like to stay with you—because I love you both. But that is not quite enough. I love other members of the family but I abhor staying with them. Either they fuss too much—or they rigidly exact that I force my lifelong habits into a pattern strictly theirs. But you have the art (the h is silent—maybe this is the whole trick) of effortless adjustments that are exceedingly soothing to the crotchets of

Your affectionate
Uncle John

FROM A BRIDE TO HER NEW RELATIVES-IN-LAW

A letter that was written by a bride after paying a first visit to her husband's aunt and uncle won for her at a stroke the love of the whole family. This is the letter.

Dear "Aunt Annie,"

Now that it is all over, I have a confession to make! Do you know that when Dick drove me up to your front door and I saw you and Uncle Bob standing on the top step—I was simply *paralyzed* with fright!

"Suppose they don't like me," was all that I could think. Of course, I knew you loved Dick—but that only made it worse. How awful, if you *couldn't* like me! The reason I stumbled coming up the steps was because my knees were actually knocking together! You remember, Uncle Bob sang out it was good I was already married, or I wouldn't be this year? And then—you were both so perfectly adorable to me—and you made me feel as though I had always been your niece—and not just the wife of your nephew.

I loved every minute of our being with you, dear Aunt Annie, just as much as Dick did, and we hope you are going to let us come soon again.

With best love from us both,
Your affectionate niece,
Helen

This type of letter would not have served perhaps if Dick's aunt had been a forbidding and austere woman; but even such a one would be far more likely to take a new niece to her heart if the new niece herself gave evidence of having one.

AFTER VISITING A FRIEND

Dear Kate,

It was hideously dull and stuffy in town this morning after the fresh coolness of Strandholm. The back yard is not an alluring outlook after the beauty of your garden.

It was good being with you and I enjoyed every moment.
Devotedly always,
Caroline

FROM A MAN WHO HAS BEEN CONVALESCING AT A FRIEND'S HOUSE

Dear Martha,

I certainly hated taking that train this morning and realizing that the end had come to my peaceful days. You and John and the children, and your place, which is the essence of all that a "home" ought to be, have put me on my feet again. I thank you much—much more than I can say—for the wonderful goodness of all of you.
Fred

FROM AN OLD FRIEND TO HER HOSTESS

Dearest Mary,

You were simply wonderful to me! I can see you look up from your *petit-point* and smile and shake your head and say, "But, my dear, I did nothing!"

All right, then, let us leave it at that—that "nothing" is to listen without ever a sag of interest, with never less than complete understanding.

So thank you, dear Mary, for the nothing which is everything to your

Devoted
Clara

Dearest Sally,

Words can't tell you how comfortable you made me and how happy I was the whole time I was there. It was all so nice! And such a lovely, lovely holiday! for which I thank you *much*.

Affectionately and appreciatively,
Helen

Lucy, darling,

You know I loved staying with you—I always do!
I hated to go—as always, too!
Thank you and best love to you both.

Devotedly,
Caroline

Darling Lucy,

We both had a wonderful time!

You were good to ask us so soon again, and we thank you very, very much.

Mary

TO AN ACQUAINTANCE

After a visit to a formal acquaintance or when someone has shown you especial hospitality in a city where you are a stranger:

My dear Mrs. Duluth,

It was more than good of you to give my husband and me so much pleasure. We enjoyed, and appreciated, all your kindness to us more than we can say.

We hope that you and Mr. Duluth may be coming East before long and that we may then have the pleasure of seeing you at Strandholm.

In the meanwhile, thanking you for your generous hospitality, and with kindest regards to you both, in which my husband joins, believe me,

Very sincerely yours,
Katherine de Puyster Eminent

AN ENGRAVED CARD OF THANKS

An engraved card of thanks is proper only when sent by a public official to acknowledge the overwhelming number of congratulatory messages he must inevitably receive from strangers when he has carried an election or otherwise been honored with the confidence of his State or country. A recent and excellent example follows: *

EXECUTIVE MANSION

My dear........

I warmly appreciate your kind message of congratulation which has given me a great deal of pleasure, and sincerely wish that it were possible for me to acknowledge it in a less formal manner.

Faithfully,

(signed by hand)

THE LETTER OF INTRODUCTION

A letter of business introduction can be much more freely given than a letter of social introduction. For the former it is necessary merely that the persons introduced have business interests in common—which are much more easily determined than social compatibility, the necessary requisite for the latter. It is, of course, proper to give your personal representative a letter of introduction to anyone to whom you send him.

On the subject of letters of social introduction there is one chief rule:

Never *ask* for letters of introduction, and be very sparing in your offers to write or accept them.

Seemingly few persons realize that a letter of social introduction is actually a draft for payment on demand. The form might as well be, "The bearer of this has (because of it) the right to *demand* your interest, your time, your hospitality—liberally and at once, no matter what your inclination may be."

* Executive Mansion is the established name of the house in which a governor lives. But if he prefers, all professional letters may be sent from the Executive Office.

Therefore, it is far better to refuse in the beginning than to hedge and end by committing the greater error of unwarrantedly inconveniencing a valued friend or acquaintance.

When you have a friend who is going to a city where you have other friends and you believe that it will be a mutual pleasure for them to meet, a letter of introduction is proper and very easy to write; but sent to a casual acquaintance—no matter how attractive or distinguished the person to be introduced—it is a gross presumption.

THE MORE FORMAL NOTE OF INTRODUCTION

Dear Mrs. Marks,

Julian Gibbs is going to Buffalo on January tenth to deliver a lecture on his Polar expedition, and I am giving him this note of introduction to you. He is a very great friend of ours, and I think that perhaps you and Mr. Marks will enjoy meeting him as much as I know he would enjoy knowing you.

With kindest regards, in which Arthur joins,
                                        Very sincerely,
                                            Ethel Norman

If Mr. Norman were introducing one man to another, he would give his card to the former, inscribed as follows:

Introducing Julian Gibbs

Mr. Arthur Lees Norman

Also, Mr. Norman would send a private letter by mail, telling his friend that Mr. Gibbs is coming.

Dear Marks,

I am giving Julian Gibbs a card of introduction to you when he goes to Buffalo on the tenth to lecture. He is delightfully entertaining and a great friend of ours. I feel sure that Mrs. Marks would enjoy meeting him. If you can conveniently ask him to your house, I know he would appreciate it; if not, perhaps you will put him up for a day or two at a club.

                                                  Faithfully,
                                                 Arthur Norman

INFORMAL LETTER OF INTRODUCTION

My dear Catherine,

I am giving this letter to Arthur Newling, a great friend of ours, who is going to be in Chicago the week of January seventh.

I want very much to have him meet you, and hope that this will find you in town.

Affectionately,
Martha Kindhart

At the same time a second and private letter of information is written and sent by mail.

My dear Catherine

I have sent you a letter introducing Arthur Newling. He is young (35 or so), good-looking, very good company and an altogether likable person.

He has only one flaw. He does not play a very good game of bridge—which is not important; but, knowing the game you play, it is only fair to him, as well as to you, to ask you to invite him to something other than cards.

I know you will like him (you would like *him* even at the card table, for that matter, but less than otherwise).

Affectionately,
Martha Kindhart

INTRODUCTION BY LETTER

An introduction by letter is far more binding than a casual spoken introduction, which commits you to nothing. Obviously therefore, you should never ask anyone not a really intimate friend of yours, to put a friend of his under the obligation which such a letter imposes.

A letter of introduction is handed you unsealed, always. It is correct for you to seal it at once in the presence of its author. You thank your friend for having written it and go on your journey.

If you are a man and your introduction is to a lady, you go to her house as soon as you arrive in her city, and leave the letter with your card at her door, without asking to see her. She should—unless prevented by illness—at once invite you to tea or to lunch or to dinner or at least name an hour when she will receive you.

If your letter is to a man, you mail it to his house, unless the letter is a business one. In the latter case you go to his office, and send in your card and the letter. Meanwhile you wait in the reception room until he has read the letter and calls you into his private office.

If you are a woman, you mail your letter of social introduction and do nothing further until you receive an acknowledgment. If the recipient of your letter leaves her card on you, you in return leave yours on her. But the obligation of a written introduction is such that only illness can excuse her not asking you to her house—either formally or informally.

When a man receives a letter introducing another man, he calls the person introduced on the telephone and asks how he may be of service to him. If he does not invite the newcomer to his house, he may put him up at his club, or have him take luncheon or dinner at a restaurant, as the circumstances seem to warrant. But it is absolutely necessary that he show this stranger what courtesy he can.

THE INDIRECT LETTER OF INTRODUCTION

When the Newcomers go to live in Strangetown, an indirect letter of introduction is better than a direct one. By indirect is meant a letter written by Mrs. Neighbor at home to a friend of hers in Strangetown. As already explained, a letter of introduction presented by Mrs. Newcomer to Mrs. Oldhouse puts Mrs. Oldhouse in a position where she *must* do something for the Newcomers, no matter how inconvenient or distasteful it may be. Her neglect of them can be construed as nothing less than a repudiation of friendship for the writer of the letter and an unforgivable rudeness to the Newcomers.

If, on the other hand, Mrs. Neighbor merely writes to Mrs. Oldhouse, "My friends, the Newcomers, are going to live in your neighborhood," the former is free to make advances only so far as she feels inclined.

Mrs. Newcomer, knowing nothing about this letter and expecting nothing in the way of hospitality, is far more likely to be pleased when Mrs. Oldhouse calls on her, and to feel that it is because she is liked for herself, than when she is invited to whatever it may be because Mrs. Neighbor made the invitation obligatory. A letter of introduction is usually an inconvenience and on occasions a very real burden. If you are ill or in mourning—the only excuses possible—you *must* send a note explaining your lack of hospitality, and even then, if possible, send a deputy. Your husband or your sister or even your nearest friend goes to explain—and in so far as possible to take your place.

A transient visitor is soon gone again and your obligation quickly ended; but when someone comes to live in the neighborhood permanently, it is obvious that a letter of introduction involves you in a sponsorship that can become irksome and even embarrassing.

With the indirect letter, you and the Newcomers have the same opportunity to know each other well, if you like each other, but you are bound only by inclination.

THE LETTER OF RECOMMENDATION

A letter of recommendation for membership in a club is addressed to the secretary and should be somewhat in this form:

To the Secretary of the Town Club.

My dear Mrs. Brown,
  Mrs. Titherington Smith, whose name is posted for membership, is a very old friend of mine.
  She is a person of much charm and distinction and when you meet her I am sure you will agree with me in thinking that she will be a valuable addition to the club.
Very sincerely,
Ethel Norman

LETTER OF RESIGNATION FROM A CLUB

Mrs. James Town
Secretary Colonial Club, New York
My dear Mrs. Town,
  It is with great regret that I find it necessary to resign from the club, and to ask you therefore to present my resignation at the next meeting of the governors.
Very sincerely,
Mary Smartlington

RECOMMENDATION OF EMPLOYEES

Although the written recommendation that is given to the employee carries very little weight compared to the slip from the employment agencies where either "yes" or "no" has to be answered to a list of specific and important questions, one is nevertheless put in a trying position when reporting on an unsatisfactory servant.

Either a poor reference must be given—possibly preventing the employee from earning his or her living—or one has to write what is not true. Consequently it has become the custom to say what one truthfully can of good, and leave out the qualifications that are lacking (except in the case of a careless nurse, where evasion would border on the criminal).

That solves the poor recommendation problem pretty well; but unless one is very careful, this consideration for the "poor" one is paid for by the "good." In writing for a very worthy servant, therefore, it is of the utmost importance in fairness to her (or him) to put in every merit that you can think of, remembering that omission implies demerit in each trait of character not mentioned. All good references should include honesty, sobriety, capability, and a reason, other than their unsatisfactoriness, for their leaving. The recommendation for a nurse cannot be too conscientiously written.

A lady does not begin a recommendation: "To whom it may concern" nor "This is to certify," although housekeepers and head servants writing recommendations are very partial to both these forms.

A lady in giving a good reference should write:

Two Hundred Park Square

Selma Johnson has been in my employ as cook for two years and a half.

I have found her honest, sober, industrious, neat in her person as well as her work, of amiable disposition and a very good cook.

She is leaving—to my great regret—because I am closing my house. I shall be very glad to answer personally any inquiries about her.

Josephine Smith
(Mrs. Titherington Smith)

February, 1945

The form of all recommendations is the same.

....has been in my employ...................... months/years as.....................I have found him/her .... He/She is leaving because ....

(Any special remark of added recommendation or showing interest)

....
(Mrs............................)

Date.

LETTERS OF CONGRATULATION ON AN ENGAGEMENT

Dear Mary,

While we are not altogether surprised, we are both delighted to hear the good news. Jim's family and ours are very close, as you know, and we have always been especially devoted to Jim. He is one of the finest—and now luckiest—of young men, and we send you both every good wish for all possible happiness.

Affectionately,
Ethel Norman

Just a line, dear Jim, to tell you how glad we all are to hear of your happiness. Mary is everything that is lovely, and of course, from our point of view, we don't think her exactly unfortunate either!

FORMAL CORRESPONDENCE 523

Every good wish that imagination can think of goes to you from your old friends,

Ethel and Arthur Norman

All the good wishes in the world to you, dearest Mary. Give Jim my love and tell him how lucky I think you both are, and how much I hope all good fortune will come to you.

Lovingly,
Aunt Kate

FROM A CLASSMATE TO A GROOM-TO-BE

Dear Bob,

So she's yours! Best news ever! I know how crazy you have always been about her—and moreover, I think she's something to be crazy about.

In short, I think it's great, and send congratulations to you *both*.

George

Dear Mary and John,

So *that's* why you had no interest in the Junior Assemblies! You were preferring a little assembly of two in front of the fire, or motoring up hill and down dale, or skating off by yourselves down at the ice-house end of the lake! (I did notice this last, and wonder now that I was not awake to all the other evidence!)

Anyway—having taken breath after the surprise of your letter—I am enchanted. That the nicest girl I know is going to marry pretty much the nicest man, is very, very good news. And if you are half as happy as I wish you, life will be all silver, not only as a lining, but on every cloud—all around.

Much love to you both, in which May and Arthur join.

Always affectionately,
Caroline

Tuesday, Jan. 8.

OTHER LETTERS OF CONGRATULATION

Dear Mrs. Brown,

We are so glad to hear the good news of David's success; it was a very splendid accomplishment and we are all so proud of him and happy for you. Please give him our love and congratulations, and with full measure of both to you.

Affectionately,
Martha Kindhart

Another example

Dear Michael,

We all rejoice with you in the confirmation of your appointment. The State needs just such men as you—if we had more of your sort, the ordinary citizen would have less to worry about. Our best congratulations!

John Kindhart

THE LETTER OF CONDOLENCE

Intimate letters of condolence are like love letters in that they are too sacred to follow a set form. One rule, and one only, should guide you in writing such letters. Say what you truly feel. Say that and nothing else. Sit down at your desk; let your thoughts dwell on the person you are writing to.

Don't dwell on the details of illness or the manner of death; don't quote endlessly from the poets and Scriptures. Remember that eyes filmed with tears and an aching heart cannot follow rhetorical lengths of writing. The more nearly a note can express a handclasp, a thought of sympathy, above all, a genuine love or appreciation of the one who has gone, the greater comfort it brings.

Write as simply as possible and let your heart speak as truly but as briefly as you can. Forget, if you can, that you are using written words. Think merely how you feel—then put your feelings on paper —that is all.

Suppose it is a young mother who has died. You think how young and sweet she was—and of her little children, and, literally, your heart aches for them and her husband and her own family. Into your thoughts must come some expression of what she was, and what their loss must be!

Or maybe it is the death of a man who has left a place in the whole community that will be difficult, if not impossible, to fill, and you think of all he stood for that was fine and helpful to others, and how much and sorely he will be missed. All you can think of is "Dear Steve—what a prince he was! I don't think anything will ever be the same again without him." Say just that! Ask if there is anything you can do at any time to be of service to his people. There is nothing more to be said. A line, into which you have unconsciously put a little of the genuine feeling that you had for Steve is worth pages of eloquence.

A letter of condolence may be abrupt, badly constructed, ungrammatical—never mind. Grace of expression counts for nothing; sincerity alone is of value. Do not say to one whose life has been made forever desolate by the loss of one of outstanding character or genius, "I remember the big brimmed hat she wore" or "seeing him reading his paper on the train"! Nothing more unappreciative can be imagined. The only things of the least comfort at such a time are letters which show appreciation of the character, talent, charm or any quality whatsoever that was actual and outstanding in the personality of the one mourned.

The letters from friends and associates, expressing genuine affection for a man's personality or admiration for his character and unreplaceable ability, are the only ones that *share* a widow's or a mother's grief.

An occasional letter from one who has suffered an undeniably equal loss, who in sincerity writes words of encouragement and assurance that in time the pain will grow less instead of greater, is of genuine help. But such a letter must never be written by anyone whose own suffering has not been equally devastating. Glibly listed qualities that did not exist are as meaningless as attributes of true greatness entirely overlooked.

EXAMPLES OF NOTES AND TELEGRAMS

As has just been said, a letter of condolence must, above everything, express a genuine sentiment. A few examples are inserted here merely as suggestive guides for those at a loss to construct a short but appropriate message.

My dear Mrs. Neighbor,
  We are so very much shocked to hear of the sorrow that has come to you.
  If there is anything that either I or my husband can do, I earnestly hope that you will ask someone to call upon us.
                                        Alice Rivington Blake

Or

My dear Mrs. Neighbor,
  I know how little words written on a page can possibly mean to you at such a time. But I must at least tell you that you are in our thoughts and in our hearts, and if there is *anything* that we can do for you, please send us a message—whatever it may be.
                    With deepest sympathy,
                                        Mary Newling

Or this to a near relative or friend:

Darling!
  Words are so empty! If only I knew how to fill them with love and send them to you. All my thoughts.
                                        Mary

LETTER WHERE DEATH WAS RELEASE

The letter to one whose loss is "for the best" is difficult in that you want to express sympathy but cannot feel sad that one who has long suffered has found release. The expression of sympathy in this case should not be for the present death, but for the illness, or whatever it was that fell long ago. The grief for a paralyzed mother is for the stroke which cut her down many years before, and your sympathy, though you may not have realized it, is for that. You might write:

Your sorrow during all these years—and now—is in my heart; and all my thoughts and sympathy are with you.

REPEATED DETAILS OF GREAT IMPORTANCE

NEVER under any circumstances sign a personal letter "Mr.," "Mrs." or "Miss." The proper signature for a married woman is "Mary Smith," and then underneath or to the left in parentheses "(Mrs. John Smith)." The name in parentheses is for information only, and is not a signature. The proper signature for an unmarried woman is "Helen Jones" and when necessary put (Miss) in parentheses to the left. The proper signature for a man is John Smith. If he has a title it can be added underneath, "Mayor of the City of New York" or "Captain U. S. N."

The only times when a lady of quality signs her name "Mrs." are these: in a hotel register, to a business telegram, to a servant in her own employ, or to an order letter *possibly* to a tradesman. And then it must be "Mrs. *John* Smith."

LETTER FROM MOTHER TO SON'S FIANCEE

When it is impossible for a mother to pay the conventional visit upon her son's new fiancee, a letter should be written to her. The general outline is:

Dear Mary,

John has just told us of his great happiness which, of course, brings joy to us. Our one distress is that we are so far away (or whatever else) that we cannot immediately welcome you in person.

We do, however, send you our love and good wishes.

Martha Jones

42

How to Address Important Personages

At the present time when members of the Reigning Families as well as those of lesser degree, have taken refuge in this Country, knowledge of correct forms of address has become more than ever important.

These paragraphs in fact, are in answer to requests from the many who do not want to be thought ill-mannered by our Foreign Visitors.

The very first requirement of proper behavior is to learn enough about rank to know the difference between Royalty, Nobility, and titles that are personal honors, but not inheritable. The most conspicuous as well as inexcusable mistake made by us in America is that of believing a Baron and a Count and their American wives, Royalty.

A study of the last page of the chart and its footnotes should make the divisions clear enough to know that Royalty is set quite above and apart from all others. It is plain, therefore, why etiquette requires that special deference be shown them.

Even so, the exactions of courtesy are merely these: If you are a man, you bow over a hand given to you. If you are a woman, you perhaps curtsy. If you have lived much abroad you probably will; but it is not expected that you do more than bow very much as a man does. Further than this we must wait for Royalty to speak first; to choose the topic of conversation and to invite us to be seated.

If we were their subjects we would address them in the third person. But since this form of speech is not used by us, we are permitted to say "you".

It should be added that persons of Royal birth have themselves the simplest, most unselfconscious manners imaginable. They accept the perfection of the accomplished, or the awkwardness of the untutored with equal grace. Even so, it is pleasanter to be the former than the latter.

Our manners to all members of Nobility are precisely the same as those we show to our own citizens.

ETIQUETTE

HOW TO ADDRESS

PERSONAGE	IF YOU ARE SPEAKING TO HIM YOU SAY	ENVELOPE ADDRESS (including wife or husband) ∧ shows where wife's name is to be inserted	FORMAL BEGINNING OF LETTER
The President [1]	Mr. President, and occasionally throughout a conversation, Sir	(If the letter is sent from abroad) The President of the United States of America (If the letter is sent from within the United States) The President ∧, Washington, D. C. (and Mrs. Roosevelt)	Sir:
The Vice-President	Mr. Vice-President, and then, Sir	The Vice-President ∧, Washington, D. C.	Sir:
The Chief Justice of the Supreme Court	Mr. Chief Justice, and then, Sir	The Honorable, The Chief Justice, ∧ Washington, D. C. (and Mrs. Court)	Sir:
Associate Justice of the Supreme Court	Mr. Justice	The Hon. C. K. Fairplay, Justice of the Supreme Court, ∧ Washington, D. C. (and Mrs. Fairplay)	Sir:
Member of the President's Cabinet	Mr. Secretary (If necessary to differentiate) Mr. Secretary of State	The Secretary of State, Washington, D. C. *or* The Hon. ∧ David C. Eminent, Secretary of State, Washington, D. C. (and Mrs.)	Sir: *or* Dear Sir:
(If a woman)	Madam Secretary (Whether Mrs. or Miss)	Same *or* ∧The Hon. Mary Onerown (Mr. John and)	*or* Madam
United States (*or* State) Senator	Senator Widelands A servant or subordinate says: Mr. Senator (Same if woman)	Socially: Senator ∧ Chester H. Widelands (His house address) On official business: The Hon. Chester H. Widelands, Senator from Texas, Washington, D. C. (and Mrs.) *or* Hon. Mary Widelands	Sir: *or* Dear Sir: *or* Madam
Member of Congress (*or* of a State Legislature)	Mr. Wellcome (Mr. Congressman is not correct) *or* Mrs. *or* Miss	The Hon. ∧ H. C. Wellcome, House of Representatives, Washington, D. C. (and Mrs.) *or* The Hon. ∧ H. C. Wellcome, State Assembly, Albany, New York (and Mrs.)	Sir: *or* Dear Sir: *or* Madam
Governor	Governor Goodland (The Governor is rarely called Excellency when spoken to and when he is announced except in States where this title is official. But in all States letters are addressed and begun with this title of courtesy)	His Excellency the Governor, ∧ Lansing, Michigan *or* The Honorable L. G. Goodland, Governor of Michigan (and Mrs.) (*or* Her Excellency the Governor)	Your Excellency *or* Sir: Your Excellency *or* Madam

All footnotes are on last pages of this chart.

IMPORTANT PERSONAGES

INFORMAL BEGINNING	FORMAL CLOSE	INFORMAL CLOSE	CORRECT TITLES OF INTRODUCTION
My dear Mr. President:	I have the honor to remain, Most respectfully yours, *or* I have the honor to remain, sir, Yours faithfully,	I have the honor to remain, Yours faithfully, *or* I am, dear Mr. President, Yours faithfully,	Only the name of the person introduced is spoken
My dear Mr. Vice-President:	Same as for the President	Believe me, Yours faithfully,	The Vice-President
Dear Mr. Chief Justice:	I have the honor to remain, Yours respectfully,	Believe me, Yours faithfully,	The Honorable, The Chief Justice
Dear Mr. Justice Fairplay:	Believe me, Yours very truly, *or* I have the honor to remain, Yours very truly,	Believe me, Yours faithfully,	Mr. Justice Fairplay
My dear Mr. Secretary:	Same as above	Same as above	The Secretary of State
Madam Secretary	Same	Same	Same
Dear Senator Widelands:	Same as above	Same as above	Senator Widelands (On very formal and official occasions, Senator Widelands of Texas)
Dear Mr. Wellcome: Do *not* write Dear Congressman or Dear Representative	Believe me, Yours very truly,	Yours faithfully, Sincerely yours,	Mr. Wellcome (If the introduction is official you add) Congressman from Ohio *or* Mrs. *or* Miss
Dear Governor Goodland:	I have the honor to remain, Yours faithfully,	Believe me, Yours faithfully,	The Governor (in his own State) (*or*, out of it:) The Governor of Michigan

HOW TO ADDRESS

PERSONAGE	IF YOU ARE SPEAKING TO HIM YOU SAY	ENVELOPE ADDRESS (including wife or husband) ∧ shows where wife's name is to be inserted	FORMAL BEGINNING OF LETTER
Mayor (Mayoress is English, not American)	Mr. Mayor (or Madam Mayor)	His Honor the Mayor ∧, City Hall, Chicago (and Mrs.) (or Her Honor)	Dear Sir: or Sir: (or Madam)
Officers of the Navy with grade of Commander or higher and officers of the Army and Marines with grade of Captain or higher	Admiral Highseas Captain Greenwave	Admiral ∧ Highseas Captain ∧ Greenwave (and Mrs.)	Dear Sir: or Sir:
Junior officers in Navy, Army and Marines	Mr. Ripple Mr. Gun	Ensign Arthur Ripple 2nd Lieutenant John Gun	Dear Sir:
Cardinal	Your Eminence	His Eminence Michael Cardinal Angelus, Archbishop of Baltimore, Baltimore, Md.	Your Eminence:
Roman Catholic Archbishop (There is no Protestant Archbishop in the United States)	Your Excellency (In England Your Grace)	The Most Reverend John Kindhart, Archbishop of San Francisco, San Francisco, California But letter to British Archbishop, His Grace the Right Honourable The Archbishop of Canterbury	Your Excellency: or Most Reverend Sir:
Bishop (Whether Roman Catholic or Protestant)	Bishop Churchleigh	To the Right Reverend Thomas A. Churchleigh, or the Bishop of Rhode Island, Providence, R. I.	Right Reverend and dear Sir:
Priest	Father or Father Matthew or Your Reverence	The Rev. John Matthew [3]	Reverend and dear Sir:
Mother Superior	Reverend Mother	Reverend Mother Superior or Reverend Mother Mary and the initials of her order	Reverend Mother:
Member of Sisterhood	Sister Angelica	Sister Angelica O.S.D. (or whatever her order is)	My dear Sister:

All footnotes are on last pages of this chart.

ADDRESSING IMPORTANT PERSONAGES

IMPORTANT PERSONAGES

INFORMAL BEGINNING	FORMAL CLOSE	INFORMAL CLOSE	CORRECT TITLES OF INTRODUCTION
Dear Mayor Lake:	Believe me, Very truly yours,	Yours faithfully,	Mayor Lake
Dear Admiral Highseas, etc.	Same as above	Same as above	Admiral Highseas Captain Greenwave of the Navy (When introducing a Captain of the Navy, it is important to add "of the Navy" because his rank equals that of a Colonel in the Army)
Dear Mr. Ripple: Dear Mr. Gun:	(In Great Britain junior officers are always introduced as Mr. except when wearing civilian dress. But in the United States best custom tolerates the use of their titles in introductions and on place cards at table)		Ensign Ripple Lieutenant Gun
Your Eminence:	I have the honor to remain, Your Eminence's humble servant,	Your Eminence's humble servant,	One is presented to His Eminence, Cardinal Angelus
Most Reverend and dear Sir:	I have the honor to remain with high respect, Your Excellency's humble servant	Same as formal close	One is presented to The Most Reverend, The Archbishop of San Francisco
My dear Bishop Churchleigh:	I have the honor to remain, Your obedient servant, *or* to remain Respectfully yours, I have the honor to remain, (To the Bishop of the Church of England) Your Lordship's obedient servant,	Faithfully yours,	Bishop Churchleigh
Dear Father Matthew:	I beg to remain, Yours faithfully, *or* I remain, Reverend Father, with high respect, Yours faithfully,	Faithfully yours,	The Reverend Father Matthew
Dear Reverend Mother Mary:	Yours respectfully,	Yours faithfully,	Reverend Mother, may I present Mrs. Jones
Dear Sister Angelica:	Same	Same	Sister Angelica, same

HOW TO ADDRESS

PERSONAGE	IF YOU ARE SPEAKING TO HIM YOU SAY	ENVELOPE ADDRESS (including wife or husband) ∧ shows where wife's name is to be inserted	FORMAL BEGINNING OF LETTER
Monsignor	Monsignor Ryan	The Right Reverend Monsignor Ryan [4]	Right Rev. and dear Monsignor Ryan:
Protestant Clergyman	Mr. Saintly (If he is D.D. or LL.D., you call him Dr. Saintly; or Pastor Nordic if he is a Lutheran)	The Rev. George Saintly (If you do not know his first name, it is better to assume that he is a D.D. than to commit the bad taste of writing The Rev. Saintly without his Christian name)	Sir: or My dear Sir:
Rabbi	Rabbi Temple (If he holds a Doctor's degree, he is called Dr. Temple)	Dr. J. A. Temple, or Rabbi J. A. Temple, or Rev. J. A. Temple	Dear Sir:
University Professor	Professor within the University or College. Mr. elsewhere — or, Dr. always if he holds a degree	Professor, or Associate Professor or Assistant Professor ... or Dr. if holding degree	Dear Sir:
Instructor	Mr. Book — or, if he holds a degree, Dr. Book	Mr. or Dr. Book	Dear Sir:
Ambassador [1] Same for woman (Ambassador preferable to Ambassadress)	Your Excellency or Mr. Ambassador Madam Ambassador (meaning she herself was appointed)	His Excellency The American Ambassador ∧, American Embassy [5] or Embassy of the United States of America,[6] London (and Mrs. Plum)	Your Excellency:
Minister [1] Plenipotentiary	In English he is usually called "Mr. Lovejoy" though it is not incorrect to call him "Mr. Minister" or, if you know him well, "Minister." The title "Excellency" is also used by courtesy, though it does not belong to him. In French he is always called Monsieur le Ministre	His Excellency, The American Minister, ∧ Copenhagen, Denmark (and Mrs. Lovejoy) The Hon. ∧ J. D. Lovejoy,[7] Legation of the United States of America (and Mrs.) or Her Excellency	Sir: is correct but Your Excellency is customary by courtesy
Consul	Mr. Smith or Mrs. or Miss	John Smith, Esq., American Consul, Rue Quelque Chose, Paris, France	Sir: or My dear Sir:
High Federal official	Mr. Jones or Mrs. or Miss	The Honorable* James J. Jones official or home address	Sir: or My dear Sir:

*He himself should never use this title either on his stationery or visiting cards.

ADDRESSING IMPORTANT PERSONAGES

IMPORTANT PERSONAGES

INFORMAL BEGINNING	FORMAL CLOSE	INFORMAL CLOSE	CORRECT TITLES OF INTRODUCTION
Rev. (*or* Very Rev.) and dear Monsignor Ryan:			Monsignor Ryan
Dear Dr. Saintly: (*or* Dear Mr. Saintly if he is not a D.D.)	I have the honor to remain, Yours faithfully, *or* sincerely,	Faithfully yours, *or* Sincerely yours,	Dr. (*or* Mr.) Saintly (If a Lutheran, Pastor Nordic)
Dear Dr. Temple: *or* Dear Rabbi Temple:	Same as above	Yours sincerely,	Dr. Temple *or* Rabbi Temple
Dear Professor Learned *or* Dear Doctor Learned:	Believe me, Sincerely,	Yours sincerely,	Professor, *or* Dr. Learned
Dear Mr. Book (*or* Dr. if he holds a degree)	Sincerely,	Same	Mr. *or* Dr.
Dear Mr. Ambassador: Dear Madam Ambassador:	I have the honor to remain, Yours faithfully, *or* Yours very truly, *or* very formally: I have the honor to remain, sir, (*or* madam) Respectfully yours,	Yours faithfully,	The American Ambassador
Dear Mr. Minister: *or* Dear Mr. Lovejoy: Dear Madam Minister: *or* Dear Mrs. *or* Miss Lovejoy:	Same as above	Yours faithfully,	Mr. Lovejoy, the American Minister, *or* merely The American Minister (Everyone is supposed to know his name or find it out) *or* Mrs. *or* Miss Lovejoy
Dear Mr. Smith: *or* Mrs. *or* Miss	I beg to remain, Yours very truly, *or* Yours very sincerely,	Faithfully,	Mr. Smith *or* Mrs. *or* Miss
Dear Mr. Jones: *or* Mrs. *or* Miss	Faithfully yours, *or* Yours sincerely,	Faithfully,	Officially The Honorable James J. Jones. Otherwise Mr. Jones.

Other footnotes are on last pages of this chart.

ETIQUETTE

HOW TO ADDRESS

PERSONAGE	IF YOU ARE SPEAKING TO HIM YOU SAY	ENVELOPE ADDRESS (including wife or husband) ∧ shows where wife's name is to be inserted	FORMAL BEGINNING OF LETTER
A reigning Sovereign	Your Majesty Throughout a conversation, Sir (or Ma'am—*not* Madam)	His Most Gracious Majesty, The King	May it please Your Majesty
Member of a Royal Family	Your Royal Highness (In long conversation) Sir *or* Ma'am	To His Royal Highness the Duke of Realm (or Crown Prince Olan of Nordia, or Grand Duke Paul, or Prince Berwin, etc.) Each name prefixed by H.R.H. or H.I.H. or H.S.H. as required.	Your Royal Highness:
Duke[9] and Duchess[1]	Duke (or Duchess) (Your Grace is for servants and retainers)	To His Grace the Duke of Overthere (*or* Her Grace the Duchess)	Officially, My Lord Duke: *or* Sir: Socially, Dear Duke of Overthere:
Marquis[9] and Marchioness	Lord Greystone *or* Lady Greystone	Officially: To the Most Honourable The Marquis of Greystone Socially: The Marquis of Greystone (*or* The Marchioness)	My Lord, *or* Sir: *or* Madam:
Earl[9] and Countess Viscount[9] and Viscountess	Lord Alwin Lady Alwin[2] Lord Blunt Lady Blunt	The Earl of Alwin Officially: The Right Honourable The Earl ... The Countess of Alwin	Sir: *or* Madam:
Baron[9] Lowest rank in the Peerage always called Lord	Lord Heath Same as above[2]	Lord Heath Lady Heath	Dear Sir: *or* Dear Madam:
Baronet[9]	Sir Cecil	Sir Cecil Brown, Bt. and Lady Brown[2]	
Knight[9]	Sir Samuel	Sir Samuel Shillings and Lady Shillings[2]	

TITLES OF CHILDREN OF PEERS

Eldest son of a Duke is in courtesy called by his father's second title—whether Marquis or Earl.
All younger sons of Duke or Marquis have Lord prefixed to given name not surname. Envelope addressed to The Lord John Jones, ordinarily called Lord John. His wife is called Lady John (not Lady Alice).
All daughters of either Duke or Marquis are The Lady Mary.
All sons of an Earl are called The Honorable John. Daughters The Honorable Mary.

[1] A wife never shares her husband's official titles. The wife of every American is Mrs.—"The President and Mrs. Roosevelt." "His Excellency the American Ambassador and Mrs. Toplofty." Also the wife of a Duke or a Lord, who may be "His Excellency," is addressed and announced as "The Duchess of this" or "Lady that." She is "Excellency" or "Ambassadress" only occasionally and by courtesy unless she herself received the appointment.

[2] The wife of a Peer, a Baronet or a Knight is NEVER Lady Mary unless she is the daughter of a Duke, a Marquis or an Earl. A serious mistake often made is giving an American woman the title of Lady followed by her own Christian name, which is proper only when she herself is the daughter of a Duke, a Marquis or an Earl. For example: Lady Mary Broadlands could not possibly have been Mary Green, daughter of an American.

When the daughter of a Duke, Marquis or Earl marries a commoner they are called Mr. George and Lady Mary Doe.

Mary followed by Lady is under many circumstances correct. A widow is called Mary, Lady Broadlands. Or Mary, Duchess of Overthere.

It is important that "The" be put before "Lady" as the title of a wife of a Peer exercising his own Peerage to distinguish her from the wife of a Baronet or even the wife of a Knight.

IMPORTANT PERSONAGES

INFORMAL BEGINNING	FORMAL CLOSE	INFORMAL CLOSE	CORRECT TITLES OF INTRODUCTION
There can be none	I remain, Sir, with the greatest respect, Your Majesty's most obedient servant, [8]	There can be none	Only the name of the person introduced is spoken
Sir: (or Ma'am) "Dear Sir" only by a friend to whom this special permission has been given personally,	I remain, Sir, with the greatest respect, Your Royal Highness's most obedient servant, [8]	The same as formal with "Sir" or "Ma'am" in place of Royal Highness	Your Royal Highness, may I present Mrs. Worldly
Dear Duke: Dear Duchess:	I have the honour to remain,	Same as to any friend	Mrs. Worldly, may I present the Duke of Overthere Duchess, may I present Mrs. Worldly
Dear Lord Greystone:	I remain yours very sincerely, Sincerely yours,	Same as to any friend	Mrs. Worldly, Lord Greystone Lady Greystone, Mrs. Worldly

(Beginning, Close and Introduction same for remainder of peerage.)

> Letters and introductions same as above.
> In the world of society all persons of title below Duke and Duchess are spoken to and of as Lord and Lady. To speak of the Marquis or Marchioness, The Earl or Countess announces the speaker as ignorant of social usage. This mistake is made by many writers.
> Honorable is used only on envelopes and place cards; never on visiting cards or spoken.
> IN ALL COUNTRIES NOT BRITISH, the wife of a Marquis, or a Count or a Baron is called Marquise, Countess or Baroness. Lord and Lady are British titles.

Dear Sir or Dear Sir Cecil—never Sir Brown.

Same as above.

[3] When a priest is a member of a religious order the envelope is addressed: Rev. John Matthews, S. J. or O. P., according to the initials of the order of which he is a member.

[4] There are two classes of Monsignori in the Roman Catholic Church: Right Rev. Monsignor Ryan and Very Rev. Monsignor Ryan. Right Rev. takes precedence.

[5] In South America alone, where out of courtesy to those who also consider themselves "Americans," the Embassies and Legations of our country are known as those of The United States of America. But in all other countries of the world we are known simply as "Americans"—it is the only name we have. We are not United Staters or United Statians—there is not even a word to apply to us! To speak of the American Minister to this country or that, and of the American Embassy in Paris, for instance, is correct.

[6] Although our Ambassadors and Ministers represent the United States of America, it is customary both in Europe and Asia to omit the words United States and write to and speak of the American Embassy and the American Legation. In addressing a letter to one of our government representatives in countries of the Western Hemisphere, "The United States of America" is always specified.

[7] Federal usage bestows the title "Honorable" first, officially, and then by courtesy for life, on the following persons: The President, Vice-President, U. S. Senators, U. S. Congressmen, Members of the Cabinet and Federal Judges, Ministers Plenipotentiary, Ambassadors and Governors of all States. But this title is not used by the person himself on his visiting card, on his letterhead or in his signature. The people, in the State address the State Senators as "The Honorable Lawrence Hamilton, State Senator" as a form of courtesy, but officially his title is "Lawrence Hamilton, Esq., State Senator."

[8] This form of closing address to a Sovereign or a Royal Prince is varied according to the social and personal status of the writer.

[9] An official title is given precedence over a title of rank, such as Major Viscount.

43

Longer Letters

The art of general letter writing in the present day is shrinking to such an extent that the letter threatens to become a telegram, a telephone message, or just a post card. Since the events of the day are transmitted by newspapers with far greater accuracy, detail, and dispatch than they could be by the single effort of even Voltaire himself, the circulation of general news, which formed the chief reason for letters of the stage-coach and sailing-vessel days, has no part in the hurried correspondence to today.

Of course, love letters are probably as numerous as need be, though the long-distance telephone must have lowered their number, too. Young girls write to each other as much and as imprudently as they have always done, and letters between young girls and young men flourish like unpulled weeds in a garden where weeds were formerly never allowed to grow.

It is the letter from the friend in this city to the friend in that, or from the traveling relative to the relative at home, that is gradually dwindling. As for the letter which younger relatives used dutifully to write—it has gone already with old-fashioned grace of speech and deportment.

Still, people *do* write letters in this day and there are some who possess the divinely flexible gift for a fresh turn of phrase and delightful keenness of observation. It may be, too, that in other days the average writing was no better than the average of today. It is naturally the letters of those who had unusual gifts which have been preserved all these years.

Nevertheless, to you who find letter writing an utterly impossible chore, it might be just as well to say that, if you are quite content to believe that you are lacking in all power of thought, or humor, observation, or facility of expression, you may be quite right in joining the ever-growing class of people who frankly confess, "I can't write letters to save my life!" and confine your literary efforts to picture post cards with the engaging caption "X is my room," or "Beautiful weather. Wish you were here."

THE TYPEWRITER FOR PERSONAL CORRESPONDENCE

The practicality of the typewriter has created a certain amount of confusion concerning the occasions when it may or may not be used for personal letters.

First of all, the typewritten letter is not only proper but *preferred* for all personal letters of any length. Yesterday's objection to the typewritten letter was the result of the practice of dictating such letters to a stenographer. But today, when almost everyone uses a typewriter himself, the objection no longer holds.

Moreover, the ease with which a typed page can be read is, for most of us, compensation for handwriting that is difficult to decipher.

Whether the letter is written by hand or on the machine, the manner of composition is the same.

THE DIFFICULTY IS BEGINNING

For most people, the difficult parts of a letter are the beginning and the end. Once they are started, they go along smoothly enough, until they face the problem of the closing. The instruction of a professor of English to "Begin at the beginning of what you have to say, go on until you have finished, and then stop" is very like that of a celebrated artist for successful painting: "You simply take a little of the right color of paint and put it on the right spot."

HOW NOT TO BEGIN

Even one who "loves the very sight of your handwriting" could not be expected to find pleasure in a letter beginning, "I know I ought to have written sooner, but I haven't had anything to write about." Or one saying, "I suppose you have been thinking me very neglectful, but you know how I hate to write letters."

These sentences are written time and again by persons who are utterly unconscious that they are expressing an unfriendly and unloving thought. If one of your friends were to walk into the room and you were to receive him stretched out and yawning in an easy chair, no one would have to point out the rudeness of your behavior; yet countless kindly intentioned people begin their letters mentally reclining and yawning in just such a way.

HOW TO BEGIN A LETTER

Suppose you merely change the wording of the above sentences, so that instead of slamming the door in your friend's face, you hold it open.

"Do you think I have forgotten you entirely? You don't know, dear Mary, how many letters I have written you in thought." Or

"Time and time again I have wanted to write you but each moment that I saved for myself was always interrupted by—*something*."

One of the difficulties frequently encountered in beginning a letter is that the answer has been so long delayed that it must be begun with an apology, always a lame duck. These examples show how even an opening apology may be attractive rather than repellent.

If you take the trouble to write a letter, you have remembered someone in a friendly way, or you would not be writing at all.

It is easy to begin a letter if it is in answer to one that has just been received. The news contained in it is fresh and the impulse to reply needs no prodding.

Nothing can be simpler than to say, "We were all overjoyed to hear from you this morning" or "Your letter was the most welcome thing the postman has brought for ages" or "It was more than good to have news of you this morning" or "Your letter from Capri brought all the allure of Italy back to me" or "You can't imagine, dear Mary, how glad I was to see an envelope with your writing this morning." And then you take up the various subjects in Mary's letter, which should certainly launch you without difficulty upon topics of your own.

Remember to answer any of her specific questions. It is certainly not only unflattering to be given the impression that you read them hurriedly, but often very upsetting to have long-awaited news completely overlooked.

ENDING A LETTER

Just as the beginning of a letter should give the reader an impression of greeting, so should the end express friendly or affectionate leave-taking. Nothing can be worse than to seem to scratch helplessly around in the air for an idea that will effect your escape.

"Well, I guess you've read enough of this" or much worse "You're probably bored by now so I'd better close" are stupid.

HOW TO END A LETTER

When you leave the house of a member of your family, you don't have to think up an especial sentence in order to say good-by. Leave-taking in a letter is the same.

"Good-by, dearest, for today.

                                                          Kate"

Or

"Will write again in a day or two.

                                                      Martin"

Or

"Lunch was announced half a page ago! So good-by, dearest, for today.

Mary"

LETTERS NO ONE CARES TO READ

Even in so personal a matter as the letter to an absent member of one's immediate family, remember not to write *needlessly* of misfortune or unhappiness. To hear how ill or unhappy those we love are, is to have our own distress intensified in direct proportion to the number of miles by which we are separated from them.

LETTERS OF GLOOMY APPREHENSION

Letters of the chronic calamity writers seem to wait until the skies are darkest, and then, rushing to their desks, luxuriate in pouring all their troubles and fears of troubles out on paper to their friends.

"My little Betty ["my little" makes it so much more pathetic than saying merely "Betty"] has been feeling miserable for several days. I am worried to death about her, as there are so many sudden cases infantile appendicitis. The doctor says the symptoms are not alarming, but doctors see so much of illness that they don't seem to appreciate what anxiety means to a mother," etc.

Another writes: "The times seem to be getting worse and worse. I always said we would have to go through a long night before any chance of daylight. You can mark my words, the night is hardly more than begun."

THE BLANK

The writer of the "blank" letter begins fluently with the date and "Dear Mary," and then sits and chews his penholder or makes little dots and squares and circles on the blotter—utterly unable to attack the cold, forbidding blankness of that first page. Mentally, he seems to say, "Well, here I am—and now what?" He has not an idea! He can never find anything of sufficient importance to write about. A murder next door, a house burned to the ground, a burglary or an elopement could alone furnish material; and that, too, would be finished off in a brief sentence stating the bare fact.

A person whose life is a revolving wheel of routine may have really very little to say, but a letter need not be long to be welcome.

Dear Lucy

"Life here is as dull as ever—duller if anything! Not even a fire engine out or a new face in town, but this is to tell you that I am thinking of you and longing to hear from *you*."

THE DANGEROUS LETTER

A pitfall that those of sharp wit have to guard against is the thoughtless tendency toward writing ill-natured things. Ridicule is a much more amusing medium for the display of a subject than praise, which is always rather bromidic. The amusing person catches foibles and exploits them, and it is easy to forget that wit flashes all too irresistibly at the expense of other people's feelings, and the brilliant tongue is all too often sharpened to rapier point. Admiration for the quickness of a spoken quip somewhat mitigates its cruelty. The exuberance of the retailer of verbal gossip eliminates the implication of scandal, but both quip and gossip become deadly poison when transferred permanently to paper. For all emotions, written words are a bad medium. The light jesting tone that saves a quip from offense cannot be expressed; and remarks that, if spoken, would amuse can put pique and even insult their subject. Without the interpretation of the voice, gaiety becomes levity, raillery becomes accusation. Moreover, words of a passing moment are made to stand forever.

Anger in a letter carries with it the effect of solidified fury; the words spoken in reproof melt with the breath of the speaker once the cause is forgiven. The written words on the page fix them for eternity.

Love in a letter endures likewise forever.

Admonitions from parents to their children may very properly be put on paper—they are meant to endure and be remembered—but momentary annoyance should never be more than briefly expressed. There is no better way of insuring his letters against being read than for a parent to get into the habit of writing in an irritable or fault-finding tone to his children.

THE LETTERS OF TWO WIVES

Do you ever see a man look through a stack of mail and notice that suddenly his face lights up as he seizes a letter "from home"? He tears it open eagerly, his mouth up-curving at the corners, as he lingers over every word. You know, without being told, that the wife he had to leave behind puts all the best she can devise and save for him into his life as well as on paper!

Do you ever see a man go through his mail and see him suddenly droop—as though a fog had fallen upon his spirits? Do you see him reluctantly pick out a letter, start to open it, hesitate and then push it aside? His expression says plainly, "I can't face that just now." Then by and by, when his lips have been set in a hard line, he will doggedly open his letter to "see what the trouble is now."

If for once there is no trouble, he sighs with relief, relaxes, and starts the next thing he has to do. Usually, though, he frowns, looks worried, annoyed, harassed, and you know that every small unpleasantness is punctiliously served to him by one who promised to love and to cherish and who probably thinks she does!

THE LETTER EVERYONE LOVES TO RECEIVE

The letter we all love to receive is one that carries so much of the writer's personality that she seems to be sitting beside us, looking at us directly and talking just as she really would, could she have come on a magic carpet, instead of sending her proxy in ink-made characters on mere paper.

Let us suppose we have received one of those perfect letters from Mary, one of those letters that seem almost to have written themselves, so easily do the words flow, so bubbling and effortless is their spontaneity. There is a great deal in the letter about Mary, not only about what she has been doing, but what she has been thinking, or perhaps feeling. And there is a lot about us in the letter—nice things that make us feel rather pleased about something that we have done, or are likely to do, or that someone has said about us. We know that all things of concern to us are of equal concern to Mary, and though there may be nothing of it in actual words, we are made to feel that we are just as secure in our corner of Mary's heart as ever we were. And we finish the letter with a very vivid remembrance of Mary's sympathy, a sense of loss in her absence, and a longing for the time when Mary herself may again be sitting on the sofa beside us and telling us all the details her letter can but leave out.

THE LETTER NO WOMAN SHOULD EVER WRITE

The mails carry letters every day that are so many packages of TNT should their contents be exploded by falling into wrong hands. Letters that should never have been written are put in evidence in courtrooms every day. Many cannot, in any way, be excused; but often silly girls and foolish women write things that sound quite different from what they innocently, but stupidly, intended.

Of course the best advice to young girls who feel impelled to pour out their emotions in letters to men can be put in one word, *don't!*

However, if you are a young girl—or even a not-so-young woman—and are determined to write a letter to a man (who is neither your husband nor your betrothed) that contains any possibility of emotion, then at least put it away for "an overnight" in order to re-read it and make sure that you have said nothing that may "sound different" from what you intended to say. Remember this above all:

Never write a letter to anyone—no matter who—that would embarrass you were you to see it in a newspaper above your signature. Not that this means *you*, but thousands upon thousands of women, inspired by every emotion known, have poured words on paper, but few of the many made public have had beauty. There were, as many may remember, a certain few letters read in a Pacific Coast divorce court not long ago, which revealed a woman's character of unforgettable loveliness. But such characters—as well as letters—are rare.

A point to remember, then, is that written words, unless destroyed, are permanent, and that thoughts carelessly put on paper can exist for hundreds of years.

PROPER LETTERS OF LOVE OR AFFECTION

If you are engaged, of course you should write love letters—the most beautiful that you can—but don't write baby-talk and other sillinesses that would make you feel idiotic if the letter were to fall into strange hands.

There is no objection to the natural, friendly, and even affectionate letter from a girl to a man she knows well. Instead of "Dear Jim" it perhaps begins "Dearest Jim" (but not "Dearest!"). Then follows all the "news" she can think of that might possibly interest him—about the home team's new players, Betty and Tom's engagement, the political disagreement between two otherwise friendly neighbors, who won the horse-shoe pitching tournament, how many trout Bill Henderson got at Duck Brook—etc.

Probably she also tells him, "We all missed you at the picnic on Wednesday—Ollie made the flapjacks and they were too awful!" Or

"... We all hope you'll be home in time for Kate's birthday. She has at last inveigled Mother into letting her have an all-black dress which we suspect was bought with the purpose of impressing you with her advanced age! Mother came in just as I wrote this and says to tell you she has a new recipe for chocolate cake that is even better than her old one. Carrie will write you very soon, she says, and we all send love.

     Affectionately, (or Ever Devotedly)
           Ruth"

THE LETTER NO GENTLEMAN WRITES

One of the fundamental rules for the behavior of any man who has the faintest pretension to being a gentleman is that he never writes a letter that can be construed, even by a lawyer, as damaging to any woman's good name.

DETAILS OF GENERAL IMPORTANCE

Although long letters to friends may, and all business letters should, be typewritten,

Never typewrite an invitation, acceptance, or regret.

Never typewrite a formal social note.

Be chary of underscoring and postscripts.

Do not carry paper economy to such lengths that you write over the same sheet twice—once horizontally, and then vertically.

Do not use unmatched paper and envelopes or write with a pencil (if you can help it).

Never send a letter with a blot on it.

Never sprinkle French, Italian, or any other foreign words through a letter written in English. You give an impression, not of cultivation, but of ignorance of your own language. Use a foreign word if it has no English equivalent, but not otherwise unless it has become Anglicized. If hesitating between two words, always select the one of Saxon rather than Latin origin.

The Bible is of course the pure example of Saxon speech.

44

Etiquette in Business

ETIQUETTE may not seem to play an important part in business, and yet no man can ever tell when its knowledge may be of advantage, or its lack may turn the scale against him. The man who remains "planted" in his chair when a lady (or an older man) speaks to him, who receives customers in his shirt sleeves, who does not take off his hat when talking with a lady nor take his cigar out of his mouth when bowing or when addressing her, impresses others, not so much by his lack of good manners, as by his bad business policy, because of the incompetence that his attitude suggests.

THE WELL-RUN OFFICE

In the well-run business office, the more important the executive, the greater courtesy does he seem to show to those who go to see him. In the office of a certain president of a great industry, for example, it has often been noted that this man employs several assistants chosen purposely because of their tact and good manners. If an unknown person asks to see Mr. President, one of these deputies goes out to find out what the visitor's business is; and instead of telling him bluntly that the boss can't see him, the deputy not only says, "Mr. President is in conference just now," but adds, "I know he would not like you to be kept waiting. Can I be of service to you? I am his junior assistant." If the visitor's business is really with the president, he is admitted to the chief executive's office, since it is the latter's policy to see everyone that he can.

He has a courteous manner that makes everyone feel there is nothing in the day's work half so important as what his visitor has come to see him about! Nor is this manner insincere; for whatever the hour, he gives the visitor his undivided attention. Should his time be short and the moment approach when he is due at an appointment, his secretary enters, a purposely arranged few minutes ahead of the time necessary for the close of the present interview, and apologetically reminds him, "I'm sorry, Mr. President, but your appointment with the 'Z' committee is due." Mr. President, with seeming unconcern, uses up most of these few minutes, and his lingering close of the conversation gives his visitor the impression that he must have been late at his appointment, and wholly because of the unusual interest felt in the subject that his visitor brought before him.

This is neither sincerity nor insincerity, but merely bringing social knowledge into business dealing. To make a pleasant and friendly impression is not alone good manners, but equally good business. The less experienced man would quite likely show his eagerness to be rid of his visitor, and after offending the latter's self-pride by the discourtesy of inattention, be late for his own appointment! The man of skill saw his visitor for fewer actual minutes, but gave the impression that circumstances over which he had no control forced him unwillingly to close the interview. He not only gained the good will of his visitor, but was able to arrive at his own appointment in plenty of time.

GOOD MANNERS AND "GOOD MIXERS"

When one thinks of a man who is known in politics and business as a "good mixer," one is apt to think of him as a rough diamond rather than a polished one. A good mixer among uncouth men may quite accurately be one who is also uncouth; but the best "mixer" of all is one who adjusts himself equally well to finer as well as to plainer society. Education that does not confer flexibility of mind is an obviously limited education; the man of broadest education tunes himself in unison with those in whose company he finds himself, whoever they happen to be. The more subjects he knows about, the more people he is in sympathy with, and therefore the more customers or associates or constituents, as well as the more friends, he is sure to have.

RULES OF POKER ARE GOOD IN BUSINESS

There are times when it is wise to "show how much you know," as you show what you have when "called" in a poker game; but there are many more times when you sit tight and hold your cards and mask your expression. To your employer, your partner, your co-worker, you give frankly the best of your ability to think or to do. But to a man whose knowledge is inferior to your own, it is a far better policy to lessen the distance between you than to make his disadvantages plain to him.

In fact, to find himself among men who are superior to himself inevitably reacts upon Mr. Inferiority's own nerves, making him self-conscious, abashed, and finally on the offensive.

THE SELF-MADE MAN AND WORLD-MADE MANNERS

It is not in order to shine in society that grace of manner is an asset; comparatively few people in a community care a rap about "society" anyway! A man of affairs whose life is spent in doing a man's work in a man's way is not likely to be thrilled at the thought of putting on "glad" clothes and going out with his wife to a "pink" tea or a ball.

But what many successful men do not realize is that a fundamental knowledge of etiquette is no less an asset in business or public life, or in any other contact with people, than it is in society.

Just as any expert, whether at a machine bench, an accountant's desk, or at golf, gives an impression of such ease as to make his accomplishment seemingly require no skill, a bungler makes himself and everyone watching him uneasy if not fearful of his awkwardness. And as inexpertness is quite as irritating in personal as in mechanical bungling, so there is scarcely anyone who sooner or later does not feel the need of social expertness. Some day he will see the folly of scorning as "soft" those men who have accomplished manners and of consoling himself with the thought that his own crudeness is strong, manly, and American!

THE "X" MARKERS

But let "success" come to this same untutored man. Let him be appointed to high office. Let him then shuffle from foot to foot, never knowing what to do or say; let him meet open derision or ill-concealed contempt from every educated person brought in contact with him; let opprobrium fall upon his State because its governor is a boor; and let him as such be written of in the editorials of the press and in the archives of history! Will he be so pleased with himself then? Does anyone think of Theodore Roosevelt as "soft" or "effeminate" because he was one of the greatest masters of etiquette who ever bore the most exalted honor that can be awarded by the people of the United States? Washington was completely a gentleman—and so was Abraham Lincoln. Because Lincoln's etiquette was self-taught, it was no less mastered for that! Whether he happened to know a lot of trifling details of pseudo-etiquette matters not in the least. Awkward he may have been; but the essence of him was courtesy. No "rough, uneducated" man has command of perfect English, and Lincoln's English remains supreme.

One thing that some Men of Might forget is that lack of polish in its wider aspects is merely lack of education. They themselves look down upon a man who has to make an "X" mark in place of signing his name—but they overlook entirely that to those of cultivation they are themselves in degree quite as ignorant.

BUT THE SON OF A SELF-MADE MAN—!

And yet many a self-made man changes his attitude completely when his own son is growing up. Almost invariably he takes special pains to make sure the boy will not be handicapped by the disadvantages which the father has never acknowledged but knows very well are his.

In fact, no one can miss the pride of Mr. Self-made, sitting in his office with a visitor—one whom he considers a great man, the governor of the state or the head of a big industry or of a railroad, or a senator—when his son comes into the room with an entire lack of self-consciousness. As his father introduces him as "My son!" he puts out his hand in a frank and easy way and yet with deferential friendliness. Then, having quickly and easily said whatever he came to say, as quickly and easily he makes his way out again. Is Mr. Self-made sorry that the big man thinks, "Fine boy, that!" Does he regret having sent his son to college?

BUSINESS WOMEN

The president of a great manufacturing concern supported his objection to women employees by the following criticism: "A man comes into the office at nine sharp, hangs his hat on a peg, and sits down at his desk ten seconds after coming in the front door. A woman comes in just as conscientiously at a minute to nine, goes into the dressing room and it is anywhere from ten to twenty minutes before she has finished brushing her dress, and fixing her hair, and powdering her nose—and heaven alone knows what!"

If a big concern were to take time out for every moment the women spend fussing with their hair and dabbing at their faces, the total hours wasted would be a surprise to the treasurer.

Then, too, women waste more time in conversation than men. A remark now and then seems too unimportant to note, but a minute now and another then reduces efficiency not alone by the minutes spent in talking but by many more that deflect the mental machinery from its job.

Nevertheless women have gone to stay into not only every branch of business, but every profession as well. Women are heads of their own offices in many businesses and in almost all the professions.

SEX BANNED IN BUSINESS

A woman who goes into an office because she thinks herself pretty and hopes to meet romance in the form of her employer or at least to rise quickly because of her physical charm has clerkship and chorus work mixed. Sex is one thing that has no place in business. Much as a man may admire a pretty or magnetic or amusing woman in his leisure hours, in his hours of work he wants someone to help him with that work. The more help she can give him, the more he values her and the more salary he is willing to pay.

Naturally he likes one whose personality is attractive, rather than one who is strikingly the reverse—but business personality and leisure personality are two different things. They are sometimes combined in one person, and sometimes romance is an outcome of business, but so seldom as to be negligible.

Of course every man likes a woman who is beautifully neat, impersonal, efficient, and polished, just as he likes a motor that is valve-ground and shining and ready to go any distance without boiling over—or breaking down because of broken parts or rust. A successful business personality has as its first attribute *efficiency*.

THE PERFECT SECRETARY

The perfect secretary should forget that she is a human being, and be the most completely efficient aid at all times and on all subjects. Her object is to coordinate with her employer's endeavor, and not make any intrusions which would be more likely to affect him as hurdles than as helps.

She should respond to his requirements exactly as a machine responds to the touch of lever or accelerator. If he says "Good morning," she answers "Good morning" with a smile and cheerfully. She does not volunteer a remark—unless she has messages of importance to give him. If he says nothing, she says nothing, and she does not even mentally notice that he has said nothing. In fact, when she notices his preoccupation, she waits, if possible, holding back irrelevant messages until he has finished the letters he wants to dictate or whatever business it was that made him ring for her.

Needless to say, a secretary must not betray the secrets of her employer. His business dealings must be regarded as professional secrets that it would be dishonorable to divulge—no matter how inconsequential they may seem.

THE CORRESPONDENCE OF HER EMPLOYER

Business training surely teaches every secretary to know everything she can that will be of service to her employer, but to know as little about the things that are not her concern as possible. When sorting his mail, she leaves unopened the obviously private letters—envelopes written by hand on stationery not suggestive of business—and having opened his other letters and clipped them in whatever order he likes to have them, she should then clip a sheet of blank paper on the top of each pile so that visitors—or others who have access to his office and who may accidentally stand behind his desk—will not have the contents of letters displayed before them.

THE GENERAL STENOGRAPHER

When a stenographer enters a man's office in response to his summons—or because it is the hour set for her appearance—she should take a chair and place it near enough to hear him easily. Where she sits depends very much on the office—where the light comes from, and where she can best hear his voice. It is not expected that he get up and offer her a chair or show her the sort of personal attention that a man in social life shows to a woman.

THE IDEAL BUSINESS WOMAN

The ideal business woman is accurate, orderly, quick and impersonal, whether she is a typist or manager of a great concern. By "impersonal" is meant exactly that! Her point of view must be focused on the work in hand not on her own reactions to it, or to anyone's reactions to her.

At the very top of the list of women's business shortcomings is the inability of many of them to achieve impersonality. Mood, temper, jealousy, especially when induced by a "crush on" her employer—these are the chief flaws of the woman in business and a constant source of annoyance in every office where she exists. The greatest handicap to woman's advancement in business is her inability to leave her personal feelings at home! An anonymous expert on business gave as the recipe for success: "The ability to work efficiently and pleasantly with other people." The recipe is perfect—there is nothing to add except to acknowledge that it takes no small amount of will and self-control to "get on" with any constant companion under the daily friction of an enforced relationship that is unrelieved day after day, week after week. It is wonderful that human nature stands the strain as well as it does, especially in situations where one's own work is dependent upon the cooperation of others for its complete efficiency. One would need a disposition made in heaven not to become surly when another's lagging makes one's own energy futile. One horse in a team always pulls better than the other. It is pretty hard on the better one, especially when the lazy one seemingly prevents the better from getting ahead. But just as the driver of a team knows the better horse, the foreman or the manager or the president will almost surely know the better worker in time—even though he may not appear to.

THE UNEXPLAINED REASON FOR MANY LOST POSITIONS

The surest way to lose your position—in at least nine cases out of ten—is persistently to announce your presence to others by any of the odors of the careless—whether from eating garlic and onions daily, or neglecting frequent bathing, or because of digestive or chemical defects. The inexplicable reason why such a condition exists ever is that those who are afflicted are themselves completely immune to their own odor—precisely as the small black and white striped animals of equal, but not greater, nostril-assailing power are probably immune. This is written in all seriousness: If you ever have the slightest impression that others withdraw at your approach, ask someone—or more than one—for the truth. And if you are an odor-maker, ask your doctor or a druggist—and use—what is necessary for a cure.

The reason why no one ever tells another of this failing is that it is supposed to be lack of bathing and sufficient laundering of clothes. On occasion both of these are true, particularly the latter; but the actual cause is almost always a physical condition, curable with the simplest sort of astringent or lotion or gargle.

OFFICE DISCIPLINE

A business organization is, or should be, like a military one. You should take as much pride in helping to keep up the tone of the office you work in as you take pride in your own efficiency.

In preparatory schools boys are always taught to honor the spirit of the school. An employee ought to have that same feeling for the spirit of the organization or the office he works for. He and his associates, his superiors, his inferiors, are fellow members who add to the firm's importance—and their own—or undermine it and themselves.

The possession of tact whereby you know how to please people and make them pleased with your firm is one of the surest ways of getting an increase of salary. To put on airs and think yourself too good for your job is pretty close to "asking for" a job not half as good as the one you hold.

No matter how well her employer may know her out of business hours, he must in the office call his stenographer "Miss Jones" and not "Katie." It is still more necessary that she address him as "Mr. Smith," and that, when she enters his office and is asked a single question, she either say "Yes, Sir," or "No, Sir," or if she objects to "Sir," "Yes, Mr. Smith," or else follow her monosyllable with a short sentence. Certainly nothing makes a poorer impression on a visitor than a dialogue such as the following:

A young woman (or man) answers the president's bell. President: "Haven't my railroad tickets come yet?" Young Woman: "No!" Exit.

When a young woman who holds a subordinate position meets an officer of the company, she does not speak unless spoken to. When a woman clerk meets her department manager in the hallway or in the main offices, when he does not seem preoccupied, she would naturally say "Good morning," but not herself invite any longer conversation.

LUNCHING WITH ONE'S EMPLOYER

A young woman in a subordinate position does not go out to lunch with her employer. But if she holds a responsible position and has matters of business to discuss, there is no reason—unless her own—why she should not on occasion lunch with him. But under average circumstances it would be courting criticism should their going out together become a habit.

THE TELEPHONE IN AN OFFICE

Personal messages over the telephone are at times unavoidable, but long chatty conversations are not only out of place, but wasting time which does not belong to the employee.

BUSINESS GIFTS

Gifts from a firm are usually in the form of a bonus or a proportion of one's salary. At Christmas a man may give his own secretary a present. Candy is conventional; although, when she has been with him for some time, he might choose something more original. It is hardly necessary to add that wearing apparel is NOT suitable. A private secretary known well to a man's wife is sometimes, but not usually, remembered by the wife at Christmas. Occasionally employees give presents to their employers, but it is not usual or correct, or really sound. The exception is when there is a wedding in the employer's family. Then his employees—if they want to show their liking or their appreciation—all contribute and send a wedding gift. They also send flowers to a funeral.

CHARACTER AND TACT WITH CUSTOMERS

A tactful person at the reception desk in an office is of great importance. Neither a condescending nor gushing attitude is suitable —anywhere! A pleasant, quiet but cordial attitude can do much to further the business of the firm for which you work.

When a recumbent, gum-chewing office-boy flings at you from behind a locked gate—, "Who d'ja wanna see?" then shuffles off and returns with: "Mr. Brown's busy. Can't see ya t'day! Y' c'n try t'morrer if ya like!"—the customer will *not* unless seeing Mr. Brown and no other is unavoidable. Many offices—especially those which have many personal contacts—are putting middle-aged women and men at the reception desk because it has been found that people do not resent being refused admittance by a tactful older person as they resent being barred by one who is young—and callous!

A woman going to a man's office sends in her visiting card, or her business card if she has one. This is one of the few occasions when a woman leaves her card upon a man.

A man does not rise when a stenographer or other woman employee comes into his office. But he must stand to receive a woman visitor, and stand until she is seated. He stands again when she prepares to leave and usually goes with her to the door, opens it for her and "bows her out."

SHOULD A STENOGRAPHER RISE?

A question often discussed is whether a stenographer should rise when visitors to the office approach her desk. Many a young woman thinks it very rude not to meet the friendliness of such persons as she would do were she at home.

The answer to this is that unless the visitors are persons of importance to her employer—so that the time she takes from her work is spent in her employer's interest—it would not be expected of her, or even proper, to greet them in such a way as to encourage their talking to her at length. On the other hand, if she were the private secretary of an executive and it were part of her job to make a pleasant impression on behalf of her employer, or perhaps to act as his deputy, she would naturally leave her desk to greet a stranger or a very occasional customer; but not (if she is otherwise busy) to greet one who comes into the office constantly. A secretary's duties do not ordinarily include helping a visitor off and on with his coat.

ANNOUNCING NAMES ON TELEPHONE

A man calling a woman on business says, "This is Mr. Smartling of Dash & Sons." If he were calling a business man, he would be more apt to say, "This is Smartling of Dash & Sons."

A young woman (no matter how young) calling a lady (no matter how old) would say, "This is Miss Jones of Blank & Company."

SPORTSMANSHIP IN GIVING AND TAKING

A situation often met in business is the following: In Oldclerk's department Noohire is given a piece of work to do and he tells the former frankly that he is unable to cope with it. Oldclerk generously takes the sorry mess and works it out. Noohire then writes it into final form and presents it to his employer for approval. When he is congratulated, he remains silent about Oldclerk's part in the matter. The question is, should Oldclerk be sport enough to help him again?

Should he be inclined to make an issue of the incident, or should he consider it better to say nothing and let the final tally speak for itself?

The answer to this is that John Noohire could hardly be expected to announce his own incompetence—perhaps even lose his job—nor, let it be hoped, did Oldclerk help him in order to have him laud the former's ability and generosity. Generosity is not so expressed! A kind and outgiving person would help him, and of course say nothing. If later on he presumes to take full credit to himself for what Oldclerk did, he would certainly be justified in letting Noohire meet his own handicaps in the future.

TO WHAT DEGREE MAY A SECRETARY PROTECT HER EMPLOYER'S INTEREST?

Frankness which springs from tact and loyalty to one's employer must not be confused with the ordinary and despicable habit of talebearing. For example, let us say Miss Bright is secretary to Mr. Brilliant, a man of rare ability and character. She learns that a glib-tongued colleague whom her employer trusts implicitly, and with whom he frankly discusses his ideas, is taking these ideas as fast as he can to the partners of the firm as his own, in the hope of getting Mr. Brilliant's place. Mr. Brilliant is beginning to notice that things are not going well for himself, but he does not suspect that his supposed friend is to blame. Should Miss Bright tell Mr. Brilliant about his friend's treachery or go to his employers? In this specific case, the wisest course would be to do neither until she has collected evidence exactly as she would were she a prosecuting attorney preparing a case for trial in court. What she merely suspects, or believes, or has been told, is not evidence. But if she knows that on such a day Mr. Cheater showed the X representative an outline of Mr. Brilliant's plan, and that on another day he casually suggested to the head of the firm that they handle the Y account in the way Mr. Brilliant was at that moment trying to perfect before submitting it himself, loyalty to her own employer demands that she lay these facts before him in order that he shall be able to act in his own defense. In other words, collecting definite facts in her employer's interest must, of course, not be confused with ordinary talebearing.

A somewhat similar situation, but one far more difficult to handle, would be one involving her employer's wife. Should she find out that his young and beautiful wife is having, or at least on the road toward having, a serious affair with another man, the answer to "What can the secretary do?" is *nothing!* She has no right to tell her employer anything about his wife, and certainly she can't go to the wife. On the other hand, if it were his daughter who was falling in love with a man of whom her father disapproved, and if Miss Bright has worked long enough in the office to be well known by the daughter, she might perhaps go to her, and if she has enough force of character she might influence her against him. But this imaginary ending is too highly improbable to make a sensible alternative to the only answer to cases entirely removed from business situations, which is that wise advice to see no evil, hear no evil, and speak no evil.

BUSINESS WOMEN IN UNCONVENTIONAL SITUATIONS

Situations which women of other days were never called upon to meet have made it evident that something in the way of a modern code of propriety for young women following business or professional careers is essential. Certain jobs—particularly those of responsibility leading to the heights of success—carry with them the paradoxical responsibility of upholding a moral code of unassailable integrity while smashing to bits all rules of old-fashioned propriety.

The young woman who is a confidential secretary to an executive may very well on occasion be required to stay late into the evening working with him alone; or if the nature of his business or profession requires that he go on long tours of investigation or conference with firms in distant cities, it may quite possibly be necessary that she accompany him on this purely business trip. Theoretically and according to the normal conventions of etiquette, nothing could be more improper than that a young woman—an attractive and personable one, no doubt—should go traveling about the country with a man alone. But practically, and according to the exactions of the modern business world, it is necessary that every professional or business woman shall write her own code of propriety. She must! In the case of Miss Secretary, no one in the world can advise her as well as she can advise herself. She knows exactly how necessary she is—or is not —to the work her employer must do; she knows his attitude toward her, and certainly she knows her own attitude toward him. Therefore, she knows beyond the shadow of a doubt whether she must, or whether she need not—or whether she should not—go with him.

The point to be made is that, between breaking conventions in pursuit of a good time and breaking them only in so far as her profession exacts, lies the whole width of the moral code. The most conspicuous illustration is that of the trained nurse who is necessarily called upon to break many rules of the social proprieties, and yet gossips would stoop low indeed to criticize the unconventional exigencies of her profession. If her own attitude is above reproach, no scandal can touch her, no matter how unconventional the circumstances.

It is true that a nurse is set apart—more so than the business woman; but even so, both are free from criticism—unless they themselves give cause for it. It isn't the bald fact of taking trains and staying in hotels and being off in a furthermost state alone with Mr. Employer that will hurt Miss Secretary's good name. Nothing will hurt her good name except her own or Mr. Employer's unprofessional and therefore improper attitude of mind. If his attitude of mind is IMPERSONAL, as it should be, everyone will know it; if it isn't, then that is another story, since by some inexplicable waves of mental wireless everyone will know that too.

A SECRETARY MAKES PREPARATIONS FOR JOURNEY

And now having said that Miss Secretary may defy convention, it is necessary to add a fairly formidable array of qualifying exactions that the critical world expects her to follow.

In preparation for the journey, she orders whatever accommodations he always expects. On trains she engages a drawing room or a section for him, and a section or a lower berth for herself in the same car; but in hotels she engages a suite for him, "and a room and bath for his secretary on another floor." To put herself in another car or in another hotel would be a serious mistake, because she will make her employer conscious of the fact that she is conscious of him.

The only question likely to prove embarrassing is the question what she should do if, upon being shown to their rooms at a hotel, she is given one that communicates with his.

Should she at once refuse the room and perhaps make an awkward scene that would annoy her employer, or worse yet, make it evident that she is thinking of hereslf as a young woman and not a piece of office furniture? Or should she for these reasons stay where she is and let Mrs. Grundy's spies make what account they can of those side-by-side room numbers?

The answer to this is that, since she herself has written or telegraphed the hotel to "reserve parlor, bedroom and bath for Mr. John Employer, and a single room with bath for secretary," rooms together are not likely to be given. For that matter, in no highest class American hotel would the management permit a man and a woman not of his immediate family to occupy communicating rooms—even if they wanted to.

IF SECRETARY IS SHOWN INTO ROOM IN
EMPLOYER'S SUITE

But if she should by unusual chance find herself shown into an adjoining room, the question of what to do depends somewhat upon the type of man he is. Perhaps she says as a matter of fact, "This is not what I ordered. I'm sorry!" Or maybe she says, "This is stupid; I'll go and change it." She then goes down to the desk and tells the clerk that her room is not the one that was ordered, and tries to get another.

To those who may think it stupid as well as prudish to do anything about this at all, since everyone must know as well as she does that the relationship between Mr. Employer and herself is one of professional necessity, the worldly answer is that much more is at stake than a question of social gossip. The greater his prominence, the more seriously could carelessness of propriety endanger his career, and this not at the moment but years later when exaggeration can without limit distort fact.

HER BEHAVIOR OUTSIDE BUSINESS HOURS

Questions concerned with whether Miss Secretary may lunch or dine or dance or go to the theater or a movie with her employer are over the line where professional propriety crosses into dangerous territory. It is almost certain that she will lunch with him or have dinner with him—especially on trains or boats or in hotels in smaller towns. On rushed days she may have to eat in his rooms where they are working; in other words, she takes eating alone or eating with him as incidental to convenience. The danger mark is when the pleasure of dining becomes purely social.

This sounds overstrict perhaps, but these are the rules that even a business woman must consider when she writes her code.

IMPORTANCE OF SUITABLE APPEARANCE WHEN TRAVELING ALONE WITH EMPLOYER

As noted in the chapter on The Clothes of a Lady, the best directions for clothes are—tailor-made. Smart to the last degree and in perfect taste, but in nothing conspicuous. Neat, beautifully done hair, but no spaniel ears and no little-girl effect of hair hanging loose down to the shoulders. Little girls do not go on business trips! Nor does a young professional woman, who keeps her reputation unassailable, go dining and dancing with an employer she travels with. No barebacked evening dress, no dangling bracelets, no obvious make-up, no too-brilliantly colored fingernails, no strong perfume, and no champagne. In short, she must be obviously what she is: an attractive, competent, intelligent and impersonally likable secretary.

STORE ETIQUETTE

The technical aspects of salesmanship are much too specialized to be discussed by anyone who has not learned the subject at first-hand and practiced it with success—success, moveover, that is measured by the tangible proof of satisfactory sales slips, and best of all, an increasing number of customers who ask for Mrs. Keen or Miss Personable when they come again to buy.

But the aspects of salesmanship that depend for their success upon tactful and pleasing manners belong very decidedly in a book such as this. Also very decidedly belong good manners that are to be expected of all customers who make any pretense to being well-bred.

SALESWOMEN VERSUS CUSTOMERS

The behavior of the customer is a far more responsible matter than that of the saleswoman. The distress inconsiderate customers can inflict, or the pleasure considerate ones can give, is plainly of greater concern to one who waits on them than any annoyance or satisfaction that may be felt by the customer.

To the customers nothing is at stake further than the satisfaction or irritation—or most often the completely negative impression—that is made upon them by the woman who waits on them during a few moments of time, the length of which the customers themselves control. But a saleswoman is, so to speak, at the mercy of any customer who is ill-bred or unreasonable, for so long as that customer chooses to keep her in attendance.

Moreover, every displeased customer is a mark against a saleswoman's value, heavy or light according to the evidence of the customer's rightness, as well as to the importance of the customer's account. But, whether heavy or light, many such marks mean loss of a job.

FROM THE CUSTOMER'S POINT OF VIEW

First, however, let us consider the point of view of a customer, since this is something that we all know from personal experience. Whether we all agree as to the type of saleswoman we like or dislike is doubtful. A clever saleswoman must, no doubt, have different methods with different customers. After all, if customers were identical, perfect salesmanship would not be the difficult accomplishment it is. It is quite possible that methods which are unendurable to some of us are acceptable to others. But one does wonder to what degree high-pressure salesmanship pays in the long run. One wonders how many customers who have been high-pressured into buying what they did not really want or into spending more than they could afford have ever afterwards not only avoided getting within range of that particular sales person, but have avoided that particular store.

THE SUCCESSFUL SALESWOMAN

Really great saleswomen have cultivated not only an expert knowledge of the commodities they sell, but an equally expert ability to appraise the customers to whom they sell.

It is essential to know, therefore, whether a customer likes to be "dearied" or "madamed," or chatted to about every topic under the sun to camouflage the sales talk; and whether she is one who likes to have her mind made up for her; or whether she is one who, knowing exactly what she wants, prefers to have her own questions answered intelligently but does not want any unasked-for advice.

But above all saleswomen, the one an intelligent customer is certain to like best—the one in fact to whom she always returns—is one who listens to what she says and tries to give her what she wants, instead of trying to sell her what the store seems eager to be rid of.

For example, when you ask for something she can't supply, the ideal saleswoman would listen attentively to what you say and answer, "I am very sorry we have nothing at all like that in the color you want; but I could give you something in a small pattern of yellow," and then with certain eagerness she would ask, "Have you time to let me show it to you?"

You are pleased, because the saleswoman showed eagerness to help you find what you want, and you as a customer would be very lacking in courtesy not at least to let her show you what she so much hopes may please you. When she brings it, you are inclined to be pleased because, though you know it is not just what you want, you are sure it is not going to be thrust upon you. And the chances are—at least within the range of possibility—that you will take it if you can make it do.

A POOR SALESWOMAN

Of all the varieties of poor saleswomen, the worst is she who simply brushes aside what you say you want and blandly spreads before you something that is exactly what you have explained to her you do NOT want, at the same time trying to force you to like it by extolling its beauties or its bargain values, and capping the climax by telling you that Mrs. Uppity thinks this is exquisite! That kind of saleswoman would try to tell Mr. Kreisler that "they" are not using violins this season!

We can all understand seeking to guide a customer who doesn't know what she wants. But what can result except irritability against a clerk—and, because of the clerk, against the store—when a customer of intelligence is treated as a moron?

A particular illustration would not really be valuable because politeness or rudeness depends so much upon the manner in which a thing is said or done.

TACT ESSENTIAL TO CUSTOMERS AND CLERKS ALIKE

In social life tact is an asset, but in business, almost as much as in diplomacy, tact is essential. Why tact and good temper and courteous consideration of others is exacted of one who sells is simple enough to understand. But why the one who buys is ever led to imagine that the precepts of courtesy need not apply to her own behavior is to be explained only as a point of view of an upstart and snob. The test of a lady is nowhere greater than in situations where the advantage is her own. It isn't possible to advertise lack of quality more blatantly than does the overbearing, inconsiderate shopper who rudely criticizes everything a saleswoman shows her, who treats her as though she were of a completely inferior class, who keeps her in the decorating department for an entire morning or afternoon pulling material about, and then buys nothing.

THE INCONSIDERATE CUSTOMER

At a guess, one might say that the greatest strain upon a saleswoman's sportsmanship and good temper might be in the ready-to-wear dressmaking department, where making a sale is likely to exact a greater amount of time and salesmanship as well as specialized knowledge than would be necessary in a department, for example, where merchandise is sold over a counter.

And what a careless customer often does to model dresses does not always go on the right side of the ledger. Perhaps she smears the fronts of the dresses with lipstick as she pulls them on or off. Or, if the day is very hot and she wears scant underclothes, she dampens them with perspiration. Perhaps she tears them in haste or sheer carelessness; perhaps she scorches one with her cigarette—but rarely does she think *she* did the damage. And in the end she orders none or perhaps she buys and then returns everything looking still more shop-worn the next day.

It is true that we all at some time buy something which for one reason or another we are obliged to send back. But this is not the chronic practice of any considerate person; and neither is being inconsiderate of sales people nor of the merchandise belonging to the store.

Another lack of consideration is shown by those who go to a store ten minutes before closing time.

Another fault—but probably only belonging to women of leisure who have had no business experience—is to think it fair to expect favors from their friends who are no longer women of leisure and who are unable to make below-cost prices, or to put all other customers aside and spend their time in gossiping with a friend.

Is the customer always right? It would not seem likely. Unfailing patience and good temper are qualities exacted of every saleswoman, whereas there is nothing to restrain the ill humor or unreasonableness of a customer—except her own good breeding.

45

Clubs and Club Etiquette

A SOCIETY is an organization composed of persons who band together for a common purpose and are not infrequently obligated to one another by bonds of brotherhood. A club is an organization composed of persons who have no obligation toward one another, but join the group for their individual convenience or pleasure.

A club's membership, whether composed of men or women or both, may be limited to a dozen or may include several thousands, and the procedure in joining may be easy or difficult, according to the type of club and the standing of the would-be member.

Membership in many athletic associations may be had by walking in and paying dues; also many country golf clubs are as free to the public as country inns. But joining a purely social club of rank and exclusiveness is a very different matter. To be eligible for membership in such a club a man must have among the members friends who like him enough to be willing to propose him and second him and write letters for him; furthermore he must be disliked by no one—at least not sufficiently for any member to object seriously to his company.

There are two ways of joining a club: by invitation and by making application or having it made for you. To join by invitation means that you are invited when the club is started to be one of the founders or charter members, or if you are a distinguished citizen, you may at the invitation of the governors become an honorary member; or in a small or informal club you may become an ordinary member by invitation or at the suggestion of the governors that you would be welcome. A charter member pays dues, but not always an initiation fee. An honorary member pays neither dues nor initiation fee; he is really a permanent guest of the club. A life member is one who pays his dues for twenty years or so in a lump sum, and is thereafter exempted from dues even though he lives to be a hundred. Few clubs have honorary members and none have more than half a dozen; so this exceptional type of membership may as well be disregarded.

The ordinary members of a club are either resident—meaning that they live within fifty miles of the club—or non-resident—living beyond that distance and paying smaller dues but having the same privileges.

In certain of the London clubs, one or two New York ones, and the leading club in several other cities, it is not unusual for a boy's name to be put up for membership as soon as he is born. If his name comes up while he is a minor, it is laid aside until after his twenty-first birthday and then put at the head of the list of applicants and voted upon at the next meeting of the governors. In the same way an ex-member who puts his name up for re-election always precedes new applicants.

HOW A NAME IS "PUT UP"

Since no well-bred man is likely to want to join a club in which the members are not his friends, he says to a member of his family or an intimate friend, "Do you mind putting me up for the Nearby Club? I will ask Dick to second me." The friend answers, "Delighted to do it!" and Dick says the same.

It is still more likely that the suggestion to join comes from a friend, who remarks one day, "Why don't you join the Nearby Club? It would be very convenient for you." The other says, "I think I should like to," and the first replies, "Let me put you up, and Dick second you."

It must be remembered that a gentleman has no right to ask anyone who is not really one of his best friends to propose or second him. It is an awkward thing to refuse in the first place; in the second it involves considerable effort, and on occasion a great deal of annoyance, to say nothing of responsibility.

For example let us suppose that Jim Smartlington asks Donald Lovejoy to propose him and Clubwin Doe to second him. Jim's name is written in the book kept for the purpose and signed by both proposer and seconder:

Smartlington, James
        Proposer: Donald Lovejoy
        Seconder: Clubwin Doe

Nothing more is done until the name is posted—meaning that it appears among a list of names put up on the bulletin-board in the club house. It is then the duty of Lovejoy and Doe each to write a letter of endorsement to the governors of the club, to be read by that body when they hold the meeting at which Smartlington's name comes up for election.

Example:

Board of Governors,
The Nearby Club.

Dear Sirs:
    It affords me much pleasure to propose for membership in the

Nearby Club Mr. James Smartlington. I have known Mr. Smartlington for many years and consider him qualified in every way for membership.

He is a graduate of Yalvard, class of 1941, and rowed on the Varsity crew. He is now in his father's firm (Jones, Smartlington & Co.).

Yours very truly,
Donald Lovejoy.

CANDIDATES MUST MEET GOVERNORS

Lovejoy must also at once tell Smartlington to ask about six friends who are club members (but not governors) to write letters endorsing him. Furthermore, the candidate cannot come up for election unless he knows several of the governors personally so they can vouch for him at the meeting. Therefore, Lovejoy and Doe must take Smartlington to several governors (at their offices generally) and personally present him, or very likely they invite two or three of the governors and Smartlington to lunch.

Even under the best of circumstances it is a nuisance for a busy man to have to make appointments at the offices of other busy men. And since it is uncertain which of the governors will be present at any particular meeting, it is necessary to introduce the candidate to a sufficient number so that at least two among those at the meeting will be able to speak for him.

In the example we have chosen, Clubwin Doe, having himself been a governor and knowing most of the present ones very well, has less difficulty in presenting his candidate than might many other members who, though they have for years belonged to the club, have used it so seldom that they know few, if any, of the governors even by sight.

At the leading woman's club of New York, the governors appoint an hour on several afternoons before elections when they are in the visitors' rooms at the club house on purpose to meet the candidates whom their proposers must present. This would certainly seem a more practicable method, to say nothing of its being easier for everyone concerned, than the masculine etiquette which requires that the governors be stalked one by one, to the extreme inconvenience and loss of time and occasionally the embarrassment of everyone.

As already said, Jim Smartlington, having unusually popular and well-known sponsors and being also very well liked himself, is elected with no difficulty.

IMPORTANCE OF GOOD LETTERS OF ENDORSEMENT

But take the case of young Breezy. He was put up by two not well-known members who wrote half-hearted endorsements themselves and did nothing about getting letters from others. They knew none

CLUBS AND CLUB ETIQUETTE

of the governors, and trusted that two who knew Breezy slightly "would do." His casual proposer forgot that enemies write letters as well as friends—and that, moreover, enmity is active where friendship is often passive. Two men who disliked his "manner" wrote that they considered him "unsuitable." As he had no friends strong enough to stand up for him, he was turned down. A man is rarely "black-balled," as such an action could not fail to injure him in the eyes of the world. (The expression "black ball" comes from the custom of voting for a member by putting a white ball in a ballot box, or against him by putting in a black one.) If a candidate is likely to receive a black ball—two disqualify him—the governors do not vote on him at all, but inform the proposer that the name of his candidate would better be withdrawn. Later on, if the objection to him is disproved or overcome, his name can again be put up.

QUALIFICATIONS FOR ELECTION

The more popular the candidate, the less work there is for his proposer and seconder. A stranger—if he is not a member of the representative club in his own city—would have need of strong friends to elect him to an exclusive club in another community, and an unpopular man has no chance at all.

However, in all but very rare instances, events run smoothly; the candidate is voted on at a meeting of the board of governors and is elected.

A notice is mailed to him next morning, telling him that he has been elected and that his initiation fee and his dues make a total of so much. The candidate at once draws his check for the amount and mails it. As soon as the secretary has had ample time to receive the check, the new member is free to use the club as much or as little as he cares to.

THE NEW MEMBER

The new member usually, but not necessarily, goes to a club for the first time with his proposer or his seconder, or at least an old member. The reason is that in exclusive clubs visitors living in the same city are never given the privilege of the club; therefore, none but members can know their way about. Let us say he goes for lunch or dinner, at which he is host, and his friend imparts such unwritten information as, "That chair in the window is where old Gotrox always sits. Don't occupy it when you see him coming in or he will be disagreeable to everybody for a week." Or "They always play double stakes at this table, so don't sit at it, unless you *mean* to." Or "That's Double coming in now. Avoid him at bridge as you would the plague." "The roasts are always good and that waiter is the best in the room," etc.

A new member is given—or should ask for—a copy of the Club Book, which contains, besides the list of the members, the constitution and the by-laws or "house rules," which he must study carefully and be sure to obey.

COUNTRY CLUBS

Country clubs vary greatly in both characteristics and expense. A few, like the Myopia Hunt, the Tuxedo, the Saddle and Cycle, the Burlingame, and countless others in between, are more expensive to belong to than any clubs in London or New York, and are precisely the same in matters of membership and management. It is also quite as difficult to be elected to them as to any of the exclusive clubs in the cities—more so if anything—because they are open to the family and friends of every member, whereas in a man's club in a city his membership gives the privilege of the club to no one but himself personally. The test question always put by the governors at elections is, "Are the candidate's friends as well as his family likely to be agreeable to the present members of the Club?" If not, he is not admitted.

Nearly all country clubs have, however, one open door—unknown to city clubs. People taking houses in the neighborhood are often granted "season privileges"; that is, on being proposed by a member and upon paying a season's subscription, new householders are accepted as transient guests. In some clubs this subscription may be indefinitely renewed; in others a man must come up for regular election at the end of three or six months or a year.

Apart from what may be called the few representative and exclusive country clubs, there are hundreds—more likely thousands—which have very simple requirements for membership. Merely having one or two members vouch for a candidate's integrity and good behavior is sufficient.

Golf clubs, hunting clubs, political or sports clubs, as well as business and professional clubs, have special purposes and membership qualifications. All good golf players are, as a rule, welcomed at all golf clubs, all huntsmen at hunting clubs, and yet the Myopia would not think of admitting the best rider ever known if he were not socially eligible. But this is unusual. As a rule, the great player is welcomed in any club devoted to the sport in which he excels.

WOMEN'S CLUBS

Except that the luxurious women's club has an atmosphere that a man rarely knows how to give to the interior of a house, no matter how architecturally perfect it may be, there is no difference between women's and men's clubs.

In every State of the Union, there are women's clubs of every kind and grade: social, political, sports, professional. Some are housed in enormous and perfect buildings constructed for them, and others in only a room or two.

When the pioneer women's club of New York was started—a club that aspired to be in the same class as the most important men's club—various governors of the latter were unflatteringly outspoken. Women could not possibly run a club as it should be run—it was unthinkable that they should be foolish enough to attempt it! And the husbands and fathers of the founders expected to have to dig down into their pockets to make up the deficit, forgetting entirely that the running of a club is merely the running of a house on a large scale, and that women, not men, are the perfect housekeepers. Today, no clubs anywhere are more perfect in appointment or more smoothly run than the representative women's clubs. In fact, some of the men's clubs have been forced to follow their lead and to realize that a club in which members merely sit about and look out the window is a dull place to the kind of younger members they most want to attract. The combination of the comfort and smartness of a perfectly run private house and extensive equipment for athletics is becoming the ideal in club life and club building today.

GOOD MANNERS IN CLUBS

Good manners in clubs are the same as good manners elsewhere—only a little more so. A club is for the pleasure and convenience of many; it is never intended as a stage setting for a "star" or "clown" or "monologist." There is no place where a person has greater need of restraint and consideration for the reserves of others than in a club. In every well-appointed club there is a reading room or library where conversation is not allowed. There are books and easy chairs and good light for reading both by day and night, and it is one of the unbreakable rules not to speak to anybody who is reading—or writing.

When two people are sitting by themselves and talking, another should on no account join them unless he is an intimate friend of both. To be a mere acquaintance, or, still less, to have been introduced to one of them, gives no privilege whatever.

The fact of being a club member does not (except in a certain few especially informal clubs) grant anyone the right to speak to strangers. If a new member happens to find at the club no one whom he knows, he goes about his own affairs. He either reads, writes or "looks out the window" or plays solitaire or occupies himself as he would if he were alone in a hotel.

It is courteous of a governor or habitual member, on noticing a new member or a visitor—especially one who seems to be rather at a loss—to go up and speak to him; but the latter must on no account be the one to speak first. Certain New York and Boston clubs, as well as those of London, have earned a reputation for snobbishness because the members never speak to those they do not know. Through no intent to be disagreeable, but just because it is not customary, New York people do not speak to those they do not know. It does not occur to them that strangers feel slighted, until they themselves are given the same medicine in London, or, going elsewhere in America, appreciate the courtesy and kindness of the South and West.

The fundamental rule for behavior in a club is the same as in the drawing room of a private house. In other words, heels have no place on furniture; ashes belong in ash receivers; books should not be abused; and all evidence of exercising should be confined to the courts or courses and the locker room. Many people who wouldn't think of lolling around the house in unfit attire, come trooping into country clubs with their steaming faces, clammy shirts, and rumpled hair, giving extremely unpleasant evidence of recent exertion and present fitness for the bath.

THE PERFECT CLUBMAN

The perfect clubman never allows himself to show irritability to anyone. He makes it a point to be courteous to a new member or an old member's guest. He scrupulously observes the rules of the club. He discharges his card debts at the table. He pays his share always, with an instinctive horror of sponging. And lastly, he treats everyone with the same consideration he expects—and demands—from them.

THE INFORMAL CLUB

The informal club is often more suggestive of a fraternity than a club, in that every member speaks to every other—always. In one of the best known of this type, the members are artists, authors, scientists, sportsmen and other thinkers and doers. Every day a long table at which the members gather and talk, everyone to everyone else, is set for lunch. There is another dining room where solitary members may sit by themselves or bring in outsiders if they care to. None but members sit at the "round" table—which isn't "round" in the least!

The informal clubs are always comparatively small, but the methods of electing members vary. In some there is no list of applicants, and membership is gained only by invitation as the result of the spontaneous vote of the whole club; in others members are elected by the governors first, and then asked to join. In either case no man may ask to have his name put up.

THE VISITORS IN A CLUB

The best known and most distinguished club of New England has an "Annex" housing dining rooms to which ladies as well as gentlemen who are not members are admitted; and this annex plan has since been followed by other clubs elsewhere.

CLUBS AND CLUB ETIQUETTE

All men's clubs have private dining rooms where members can give stag dinners, but the representative men's clubs absolutely exclude women from ever crossing their thresholds.

In every club in the United States a member is allowed to "introduce" a stranger—living at least fifty miles away—for a varying length of time determined by the by-laws of the club. In some clubs guests may be put up for a day only; in others the privilege extends for two weeks or more.

Many clubs allow each member a certain number of visitors a year; in others visitors are unlimited. In many city clubs the same guest cannot be introduced twice within the year. In country clubs members may usually have an unlimited number of visitors.

As a rule, when a member introduces a stranger, he takes him to the club personally, writes his name in the visitors' book, and introduces him to those who may be in the room at the time—very possibly asking another member whom he knows particularly well to "look out" for his guest. If for some reason it is not possible for the stranger's host to take him to the club, he writes to the secretary of the club for a card of introduction.

Secretary
The Town Club

Dear Sir:

Kindly send Mr. A. M. Strangleigh of London, a card extending the privileges of the Club for one week.

Mr. Strangleigh is staying at the Ritz-Carlton.

Yours very truly,
Clubwin Doe.

The secretary then sends a card to Mr. Strangleigh.

The Town Club

Extends its privileges to

Mr. *Strangleigh*

from *Jan. 7.* to *Jan. 14.*

Through the courtesy of

Mr. *Clubwin Doe*

Mr. Strangleigh goes to the club by himself. A visitor who has been given the privileges of the club has, during the time of his visit, all the rights of a member except that he is not allowed to introduce others to the club and he cannot give a dinner in the private dining room. Strict etiquette also demands that, if he wishes to ask several members to dine with him, he take them to a restaurant rather than into the club dining room, because the club is their home and he is a stranger in it. He may ask a member whom he knows well to lunch with him in the club rooms, but he must not ask one whom he knows only slightly. As accounts are sent to the member who put him up—unless the guest arranges at the club's office to have his charges rendered to himself—he must be punctilious about asking for his bill upon leaving, and pay it *without question.* Putting a man up at a club never means that the member is "host."

The visitor's status throughout his stay is founded on the courtesy of the member who introduced him, and he should try to show an equal courtesy to everyone about him. He should remember not to obtrude on the privacy of the members he does not know. He has no right to criticize the management, the rules or the organization of the club. He has, in short, no actual rights at all, and he must not forget that he hasn't.

CLUB ETIQUETTE IN LONDON, PARIS AND NEW YORK

"In a very smart London club" (the words quoted are Clubwin Doe's) "you keep your hat on and glare about! In Paris you take your hat off and behave with such courtesy and politeness as seems to you an affectation. In New York you take your hat off and behave as though the rooms were empty, but as though you were being observed through loopholes in the walls."

In New York you are introduced occasionally, but you may never ask to be introduced, and you speak only to those you have been introduced to. In London, you are never introduced to anyone; but if the member who has taken you with him joins a group and you all sit down together, you talk as you would after dinner in a gentleman's house. But if you are made a temporary member and meet those you have been talking to when you are alone the next day, you do not speak unless spoken to. In Paris, your host punctiliously introduces you to various members and you must just as punctiliously go the next day to their houses and leave your card upon each one! This is customary in the strictly French clubs only. In any which has members of other nationalities—especially with Americans predominating, or seeming to—American customs prevail. In French clubs a visitor cannot go to the club unless he is with a member, but there are no restrictions on the number of times he may be taken by the same member or another one.

UNBREAKABLE RULES

Failure to pay one's debts, or behavior unbefitting a gentleman, is cause for expulsion from every club, a disgrace that is looked upon in much the same light as expulsion from the Army. In certain cases expulsion for debt may seem unfair, because one may find himself in unexpectedly straitened circumstances, and the greatest fault or crime could scarcely bring down upon a man a more severe penalty than being expelled from his club.

If a man cannot afford to belong to a club, he must resign while he is still "in good standing." If later on he is able to rejoin, his name is put at the head of the waiting list; if he was considered a desirable member, he is reelected at the next meeting of the governors. But a man who has been expelled—unless he can show that his expulsion was unjust—can never again belong to that, or be elected to any other, club.

Membership in a club must never be used as a business asset or introduction. A man's club, like his wife, is not talked about to strangers. A member may, of course, in a club where visitors are allowed, receive his business associates and talk over whatever they please. But the club must not be brought into publicity, nor must business letters be written on club stationery.

A CLUB MEETING—IN BRIEFEST OUTLINE

Since parliamentary procedure is much too formidable to include in a book so general in scope as this, it is suggested that those who are interested in the subject—especially those who are elected club officers—study one of the textbooks on rules of parliamentary order. The following, therefore, is intended merely as an outline by which a member may know enough about the procedure at an ordinary club meeting to put a question or make a suggestion or cast a vote.

At all meetings, whether they be large or very small, the general order is as follows: When the members have taken their places and it is time for the meeting to begin, the chairman or president raises his (or her) voice slightly—at a very large meeting he raps with a gavel—and says, "The meeting will now come to order."

After this, he directs the recording secretary to read the minutes of the previous meeting. When the secretary finishes, the president asks, "Are there any corrections?" If no one speaks, he then says, "There being none, the minutes stand approved as read." Or if a member has found an error in the secretary's report, he rises and says, "Mister (or Madam) President, there is a mistake in such or such a statement." The president then orders that the secretary change the statement, unless there are objections from other members. He then approves the minutes as amended.

After the reading of the minutes, the president takes up the most important reports, usually those of the treasurer and corresponding secretary. Or perhaps the president asks an investigating committee to submit its report. The president should have a list of the committees so that he may call upon the chairman of each. After each report, there is a discussion. Always, when a member has an opinion to express, he should rise and say, "Mister President" or "Mister Chairman," and then wait until the president answers, "Mr. Smith," after which he says what he has to say. At the end of the discussion, one member says, "I move that we accept the contract (or that we appoint a committee to investigate—whatever it may be). Another member says, "I second the motion." The president states the motion. It is then open to further debate. If the members are not in agreement, he puts it to vote by asking, "Will all in favor (of accepting the contract or appointing the committee) say 'aye'?" Then he waits, and those who approve say, "Aye." Then the president says, "Those not in favor say 'no,' " and these answer, "No." He then announces, "The 'ayes' have it" (or "The motion is carried") or "The 'noes' have it" (or "The motion is denied"), as the case may be.

After reports have been made and discussed and all business left over from the previous meeting taken care of, the new business is called for.

At the conclusion of the business of the meeting, the president asks, "Is there no further business for discussion?" and makes a slight pause to give someone a chance to make a suggestion. Then the meeting is adjourned.*

ANSWERS TO CLUB WOMEN'S QUESTIONS

PROBLEMS OF DELEGATE TO WOMAN'S CLUB CONVENTION

I have been chosen by the members of our local woman's club to go as a delegate to the national convention. But I am dismayed by the formidable list of sessions and entertainments and worried about my clothes. I can't possibly get new ones for all these occasions. What shall I do to make a good appearance for the credit of our club?

Don't be too much impressed by the frightening list of sessions and entertainments. To imagine that you must put on a different dress three times a day, or even each day, is nonsense. You can perfectly well wear the same day clothes to every session and the same semi-evening dress every evening. Have your hair well done and your nails well manicured. And don't put on a too obvious amount of make-up. On the other hand, if you

*A simple and most helpful little book on this subject is *The Club Woman's Handybook on Parliamentary Law*, compiled by Kate Louise Roberts and Ruter William Springer. Funk & Wagnalls Company, New York.

are old-fashioned to the point of believing that a shiny nose and pale lavender lips are the evidence of a lady, you may rest assured that it is entirely possible to be unmistakably a lady and be pretty at the same time by helping nature at least a little. In all hotels pressing is expertly done, so don't leave your prettiest dress at home because it does not pack well.

ARRANGEMENT FOR GUEST SPEAKERS

What special preparation for receiving guest speakers should the committee on arrangements make?

The committee should appoint a sufficient number of ushers so that a definite one may be detailed to each speaker or guest of honor at each session and at each entertainment. These ushers should wait at the door of entrance. Each greets her own particular charge and stays beside her (or him) throughout the meeting—or at least until she is seated in her place on the platform or at table.

FLOWERS FOR GUESTS

What sort of flowers should be given and to whom at the speakers' table?

Flowers are always sent to past presidents and guests of honor at luncheons and at banquets. Properly, smaller corsage bouquets are put at the places of the speakers, for it is rather slighting to see one person—no matter how prominent—covered with flowers, and others with none. If there is only one woman guest of honor, someone on the committee should ask her beforehand what colors she is going to wear and choose flowers accordingly. Purple orchids look well with very few colors and even white gardenias do not look well with everything. Moreover, many people find their perfume oversweet.

PLACE CARDS

When are place cards proper at a semi-public banquet?

There are place cards, of course, at the speakers' table, and when possible it is better that the committee take pains to have place cards for all people expected, because a general scramble to sit where one can find room is unpleasantly confusing.

LABELS SERVE AS INTRODUCTIONS

How is it possible to promote friendliness among strangers at such large gatherings that individual introductions are impractical?

If possible, at a very large convention, the really efficient committee should devise the best means whereby every member may wear, on a plainly-to-be-read badge, her name, official position (if any), and her home town and state, so that members may talk to each other with intelligence. As it is, we perhaps make a remark to Miss or Mrs. Total Blank from Nowhere; instead, we might be thrilled to find ourselves sitting next to someone with whom we have long corresponded, or someone whose work we admire, or someone from our own old home, about which we'd like so much to hear. Or, even if we sit among strangers, labels take the strangeness away and enormously increase fellowship.

HOW TO MAKE A SPEECH

I am going to make my first speech away from home at the coming national convention and any hints you can give me either as to behavior or to making an effective speech will be appreciated.

A suggestion of first importance is not to contradict the speech of the chairman who graciously introduces you. To say, "I'm afraid the chairman has greatly exaggerated my abilities" is a very natural impulse of modesty, but actually it repudiates the speech which she probably took pains to prepare. A speaker of grace should bow and smile. "How kind of you to say all that" is what the smile and possibly the words "thank you" should imply.

Very brief advice on making a speech is to try to present your subject as clearly and as simply as you can. The delightful speaker is never one who is trying to make an impression or, as a matter of fact, thinking about herself at all.

46

Games and Sports

THE popularity of bridge whist began almost half a century ago and has increased slowly but steadily until it is scarcely an exaggeration to say that those who do not play "contract" are seldom asked out. And the epidemic is just as widespread among girls and boys as among older people.

BRIDGE PLAYERS, PLEASANT AND UNPLEASANT

That no one likes a poor partner—or even a poor opponent—goes without saying.

The ideal partner is one who never criticizes or seems even to be aware of your mistakes; on the contrary, he recognizes a good maneuver on your part, and gives you credit for it whether you win the hand or lose. The inferior player is likely to judge you merely by what you win, and blame your "make" if you "go down," though your play may have been exceptionally good and the loss occasioned by wrong information which he himself gave you. Also, to be continually found fault with makes you play your worst; whereas appreciation of your good judgment acts like a tonic and you play seemingly "better than you know."

There is nothing which more quickly reveals the veneered gentleman than the card table, and his veneer melts equally with success or failure. Being carried away by the game, he forgets to keep on his company polish. If he wins, he becomes grasping or overbearing because of his "skill"; if he loses, he sneers at the "luck" of others and seeks to justify himself for the same fault that he criticized in another a moment before.

A trick that is annoying to moderately skilled players is to have an overconfident opponent throw down his hand, saying, "The rest of the tricks are mine!" and often succeed in "putting it over," when it is quite possible that they might not have been his if the hand had been played out. Knowing themselves to be poorer players, the others are not likely to question the move; but they feel none the less that their "rights" have been taken away.

A rather trying partner is the nervous player who has no confidence in his own judgment and will invariably pass a good hand in favor of his partner's bid. If, for instance, he has six perfectly good diamonds he doesn't mention them because, his partner having declared a heart, he thinks to himself, "Her hearts must be better than my diamonds." But a much more serious failing—and one that is far more universal—is the habit of overbidding.

OVERBIDDING

In poker you play alone and can therefore play as carefully or as foolishly as you please; but in bridge your partner has to suffer with you, and you therefore are in honor bound to play a sound game the best you know how—and the best you know how keeps you as far as you can possibly get from overbidding.

Remember that your partner, if he is a good player, counts on you for certain definite cards that you announce by your bid to be in your hand, and raises you accordingly. If you do not have these cards, you not only lose that particular hand, but destroy your partner's confidence in you, and the next time, when he has a legitimate raise for you, he will fail to give it. He disregards you entirely because he is afraid of you! You *must study the rules for makes* and *never under any circumstances give your partner misinformation*. This is the most vital rule there is, and anyone who disregards it is detested at the bridge table. No matter how great the temptation to make a gambler's bid, you are in honor bound to refrain.

The next essential, if you would be thought "charming," is never to take your partner to task, no matter how stupidly he may have "thrown the hand."

DONT'S FOR THOSE WHO WOULD BE SOUGHT AFTER

Don't hold a "post-mortem" on anybody's delinquencies (unless you are actually teaching).

If luck is against you, it will avail nothing to sulk or complain about the "awful" cards you are holding. Your partner is suffering just as much in finding you a "poison vine" as you are in being one—and you can scarcely expect your opponents to be sympathetic. You must learn to look perfectly tranquil and cheerful even though you hold nothing but yarboroughs for days on end, and you must on no account try to defend your own bad play—ever. When you have made a play of poor judgment, the best thing you can say is, "I'm very sorry, partner," and let it go at that.

Always pay close attention to the game. When you are dummy, you have certain duties to your partner, and so do not wander around the room until the hand is over. If you don't know what your duties are, read the rules until you know them by heart and then—begin all over again! It is impossible to play any game without a thorough

GAMES AND SPORTS 575

knowledge of the laws that govern it, and you are at fault if you make the attempt.

Don't be offended if your partner takes you out of a bid, and don't take him out for the glory of playing the hand. He is quite as anxious to win the rubber as you are. It is unbelievable how many people regard their partners as third opponents.

MANNERISMS AT THE CARD TABLE

Mannerisms must be avoided like the plague. If there is one thing worse than the horrible "post-mortem," it is the incessant repetition of some jarring habit by one particular player. The most usual and most offensive is that of snapping down a card as played, or bending a "trick" one has taken into a letter "U," or picking it up and trotting it up and down on the table.

Other pet offenses are drumming on the table with one's fingers, making various clicking, whistling, or humming sounds, massaging one's face, scratching one's chin with the cards, or waving the card one is going to play aloft in the air in Smart Alec fashion as though shouting, "I know what you are going to lead! And my card is ready!" All mannerisms that attract attention are, in the long run, equally unpleasant—even unendurable—to one's companions.

Many people whose game is otherwise admirable are rarely asked to play because they have allowed some such silly and annoying habit to take its hold upon them.

THE GOOD LOSER AT CARDS

The good loser makes it an invariable rule never to play for stakes that it will be inconvenient to lose. The neglect of this rule has been responsible for more "bad losers" than anything else, and needless to say a bad loser is about as welcome at a card table as rain at a picnic.

Of course there *are* people who can take losses beyond their means with perfect cheerfulness and composure. Some few are so imbued with the gambler's instinct that a heavy turn of luck, in either direction, is the salt of life. But the average person is equally embarrassed in winning or losing a stake "that matters" and the only answer is to play for one that doesn't.

PLAYING FOR MONEY

There is one point of consideration which every hostess owes her guests: protection from being forced into playing for stakes which can embarrass them. Giving a guest a chance to decline her invitation beforehand is really much more important in the case of a man than in the case of a woman. A woman usually feels free to say, "I'm sorry, but I never play for more than so much." But a man is made to feel that his refusal is an embarrassing confession of financial failure—a position into which no hostess of good breeding would ever put him. If people coming to her house, for instance, are known to play together, nothing need be said; but if strangers are invited to play with others who play for certain stakes, the hostess should say when she invites them, "The Smiths, and Browns and Robinsons are coming. They all play for a cent. Is that all right?" The one invited can either say, "I'm sorry. I don't play for money" or "My limit is a tenth of a cent"—or for some other reason decline the invitation.

There is one hardship sometimes met in a certain few communities of the very well-to-do; the more expert players set stakes that bar one who plays a first-class game but has a small income from meeting first-class opponents. This, however, applies only to those who want to play with those who in New York, for example, rank as top class. Further down the scale, stakes grow smaller and parties with prizes instead of stakes more numerous. It might be said that it is difficult for most of us to see the ethical difference between playing for prizes and playing for sums usually much less than the cost of a prize.

THE POOR PLAYER WHO INSISTS ON PLAYING

The breaking of the rule that a poor player must not thrust himself into a game made up of good players is the one unceasing annoyance that the good player—especially in a game such as bridge—is forced to endure. The inexpert bridge player will unperceivingly spoil evening after evening for three other players, blandly believing that he is merely having bad luck. Of course, the best player can have a long run of poor cards, but the player who persistently loses about twice as much as he wins would be wise—and more popular—if he took accurate note of his game instead of fixing his attention on the fickleness of luck.

(For further details about bridge stakes, bridge prizes and bridge parties, see Index.)

GOLF

Golf is a particularly severe strain upon the amiability of the average person, and in no other game, except bridge, is serenity of disposition so essential. No one easily "ruffled" can keep a clear eye on the ball, and exasperation at "lost balls" seemingly bewitches successive ones into disappearing with the completeness and finality of puffs of smoke. In a race or other test of endurance a flare of anger might even help, but in golf it is safe to say that he who loses his temper is pretty sure to lose the game.

Golf players, of course, know the rules and observe them; but it quite often happens that idlers, having nothing better to do, walk out over a course and "watch the players." If they know the players well, that is one thing; but they have no right to follow strangers. A player who is nervous is easily put off his game, especially if those watching him are so ill-bred as to make audible remarks. Those playing matches of course expect an audience; therefore, erratic and nervous players ought not to go into tournaments—or at least not into two-ball foursomes where they are likely to handicap a partner.

In following a match, onlookers must be careful to stand well back of the play and neither talk nor laugh nor do anything that can possibly distract the attention of the players.

The rule that you should not appoint yourself mentor holds good in golf as well as in bridge and every other game. Unless your advice is asked for, you should not instruct others how to hold their clubs, which ones to use, or how to make the shot.

A young woman must on no account expect the man she happens to be playing with to make her presents of golf balls or to caddy for her, nor must she allow him to provide her with a caddy. If she can't afford to hire one of her own, she must either carry her own clubs or not play golf.

OTHER GAMES AND SPORTS

There are fixed rules for the playing of every game—and for proper conduct in every sport. The details of these rules must be studied in the "books of the game," learned from instructors, or acquired by experience. A small boy perhaps learns to fish or swim by himself, but he is taught by his father or a guide—at all events, by someone—how and how not to hold a gun, cast a fly, or ride a horse. But apart from the technique of each sport, or the rules of each game, the etiquette—or more correctly, the basic principles of good sportsmanship—are the same.

In no sport or game can any favoritism or evasion of rules be allowed. Sport is based upon impersonal and indiscriminating fairness to everyone alike, or it is not "sport."

SPORTSMANSHIP

The training schools for sportsmanship are three: first, easiest, and best, the nursery; secondly, school and college; thirdly, the adult school of competitive tournaments. "Heart-break school" the latter might be called, because a young woman or man is often irrevocably broken and labeled "yellow" when lack of knowledge, and not weakness of character, is the sole cause.

The quality which perhaps more than any other distinguishes true sportsmanship is absence of temper. It must not be temper brought along and held in check, but temper securely locked and left at home.

The usually accepted pattern of a sportsman is the stoic who never by expression or gesture betrays either satisfaction or chagrin. Although this type of player is by all means the one which every beginner should emulate, he is admirable but not supreme. Stoicism is often a means, not an end. The imperfect sportsman, whether he has traits of character that he cannot otherwise control or whether he is a child or other novice still uncertain of his own reactions, learns that stoicism is the "rule of safety." Following the old saying in bridge, "When in doubt, lead trumps," the sportsman's rule is "When in doubt, play wooden Indian to the death!"

Very often the "wooden Indian," therefore, is merely "playing safe," whereas the Perfect Sportsman meets every situation with easy grace. In fact, only when a player's long-tested impulses can be trusted to take care of themselves does he attain to such innate serenity that he can seemingly break all fundamental rules. He shows chagrin; he shows elation; apparently has never heard of the rules of sportsmanship in his life. But in truth his skill is of such supreme perfection that it has become effortless. Those who notice accurately will find him dependably perfect in every ethical test of situation or impulse. The onlookers always choose him their favorite because he is "human." Every now and then his expression lights with a quick smile, a distinctly happy grin, or creases into a grimace at a bit of bad luck or a bungled play. There is no reason whatever why a player may not on occasions smile, unless the smile broadens into triumphant affront or verges on the smugness of conceit. When he wins, he takes his satisfaction lightly, or perhaps the better term is transiently. If he loses, he takes it good-naturedly—and still more transiently. Furthermore, when the game is over, the subject is finished. And the "why" he won or lost, or how he felt or played, is apparently gone out of mind.

It is entirely proper, even advisable, for the tournament player to win popularity if he can. One often notices that a player does almost "better than he knows" when the public is cheeringly friendly—no champagne is equal to it. On the other hand, silence for himself and cheering for his adversary are quite as real a handicap as extra pounds strapped upon his back—a weight that every player must at least sometimes steel himself to bear.

For the benefit of those who seem to believe that a man is rated a good sport because he spends money freely, it should be stated clearly that they have confused the term "sportsman"—one who competes fairly in any contest—with "sporting-man," a man of far from admirable habits. A player's reputation as a good sportsman is the one thing that money can *not* buy. Neither by giving away boxes of tennis and golf balls, nor by offering colossal silver cups, nor even by a million-dollar endowment, can the richest man that ever was increase by the thickness of a sheet of beaten gold-leaf his rating in sportsmanship.

This "bribery" impulse of the untutored is met with at every club, except the most exclusive few where his kind are not admitted to membership. Being more or less snubbed by those he wants to impress, even *his* not-too-keen perceptions are made gradually aware that a somewhat iced atmosphere surrounds him. Instead of trying to find out what he has done—and is undoubtedly continuing to do—to induce this chilling atmosphere, he attempts to buy the approval of players, or directors, or critics with the impulse of a savage who believes that a string of beads can make friends.

As a matter of fact, an admirable sportsman is merely one who, having thoroughly learned the rules of each game that he attempts to play, can be counted on in every test of character or of play to behave like a gentleman.

FRANKNESS OF TODAY

A young man playing tennis with a young girl a generation ago would have been forced patiently to toss her gentle balls and keep his boredom to himself, or he would have held her chin in his hand, while he himself stood shivering for hours in three feet of water, and tried his best to disguise his opinion as to the hopelessness of her ever learning to swim.

Today he would frankly tell her she had better play tennis for a year or two with a "marker" or struggle at swimming by herself, and any sensible girl would take that advice!

RULES OF SPORTSMANSHIP

After all, if you can't take sports with grace and good temper, don't go in for them. Cursing out your faults or your luck, excusing, complaining, protesting against unfairness won't get you anywhere—except "in wrong." You win or you lose; that is all there is to it! Whether from cowardice or from temper, to throw down your clubs or racket is to throw down your chances of ever holding them again without penalty. Never to display ill humor is the first rule of sportsmanship.

The second rule is always to give your opponent the benefit of the doubt! Nothing is more important to your standing as a sportsman, though it cost you the particular point in question.

Among the lesser shortcomings of an unsportsmanlike player is his practice of understating his ability before a match. It is not necessary to point out the lack of fair play of this procedure before the handicaps are given out; but it is a commonplace occurrence to hear from a man who is perfectly satisfied with his skill, "I am not much of a player" or "I know I'll make a poor showing; I've got a 'bad' arm!" The motive is not necessarily dishonest—though on many occasions it is difficult to see it as anything else—but is often a "show-off" impulse to create admiring surprise should he play brilliantly and "save his face" should his game be "off." The only time a player may declare himself unskilled is when he really is and would otherwise be a source of annoyance in a game beyond his class.

For instance: A poor player, upon being invited by experts to make the fourth, whether at tennis or golf or bridge, refuses, saying, "Thank you, but I don't play well enough." If the experts persist, because no other fourth is available, the poor player says nothing further, either then or later. He does his bungling best, and that is all there is to that—except that he must never himself volunteer to play with them again. If they invite him, he can, if he cares to, accept, and because they know how he plays, he says nothing.

One last and earnestly urged "Don't" is the loser's practice of complaining of illness after having lost a match. This is one real flaw in the average woman's sportsmanship. "I had such a pain in my side, or knee, or back, that I don't know how I ever got through the match!" is heard so frequently that one consciously resists the temptation to taunt every woman loser, "I'm *sure*, poor dear, you were in such pain you could not see the ball!"

Sportsmanship can be very well acquired by following a few simple rules. Keep your mind on the game, but not on your feelings. If you win, don't at once begin to fancy yourself a star in the firmament, above and apart from everybody else. A gloating winner is far more detested than a bad loser. But when you lose, don't sulk, or protest, or long-windedly explain. If you are hurt, whether in mind or body, don't nurse your bruises. Get up and light-heartedly, courageously, good-temperedly get ready for the next encounter. This is the only way to take life—this is also "playing" the game!

47

Manners for Motorists

SOCIAL RATING—BY CAR VALUE

How often have we noticed—perhaps with secret wonder—that John Citizen, who is courteous in all his daily contacts with people, becomes suddenly transformed into a bad-mannered autocrat when driving his car, particularly his *new* car! Is it because, by virtue of the highly reputable make of his car and its horsepower, he feels that he has become automatically the equal of every owner of a similar car, and the superior of the owners of all cars of less importance? One wonders. Is this importance—according to the car—perhaps the reason why so often the man in moderate circumstances will stint himself in every way to buy a car actually beyond his means, thus to gratify his desire to go one better than his neighbor?

GOOD AND BAD DRIVERS

There is another effect that ownership of a high-class car produces upon John Citizen: it makes him believe that his rating as a great driver is above question. Really great drivers do exist, and very good ones are not uncommon; and, moreover, both of these are fully aware of their own expertness. But this chapter is certainly not for either of these, but for the tens of thousands who in ever-increasing numbers swarm out upon the roads to have their lives saved time and again (though they don't know it) by the experts who step in between the Grim Reaper and the bad driver. And if we seriously think of the power in all of these machines running loose upon our highways and realize that no examination in driving courtesy is required of one applying for a license, the wonder is not that there are accidents, but that there are so few.

BAD MANNERS LEAD TO ACCIDENTS

Of course the type of driver who ought to be given a nice long time to think it over in jail is the one who, when the road is crowded, pulls out of a solid line of cars to steal his way forward. Finding himself in sudden danger of a head-on collision, he makes a frantic effort to push his way back into the line he has left—possibly forcing some one off the side of the road, or at least marring fenders. Or perhaps the newspapers carry one more story of a fatal motor crash—caused by the bad manners of a driver who shoves to get ahead, or tries to beat the lights, or crowds another off the road, never considering anybody's rights but his own.

THE AUTOCRAT OF THE DRIVER'S SEAT

The point to be made—because so hard to understand—is that these same drivers are under other circumstances perfectly behaved people. The man who tried to force his way ahead of the line of cars would not think of trying to force his way ahead of others in a box-office queue; nor would he shove a fellow pedestrian off the sidewalk. Or should he by unhappy accident do such a thing, he would be abject in his apology, and mortified by his own rudeness. But in his car he is quite likely to swear roundly at his victim for getting in his way.

DRINK AND DRIVING

It is unnecessary to emphasize the menace of the drunken driver; certainly there is nothing to be said in his defense, nor can anyone want him to escape the full penalty of the law. And furthermore, not half enough emphasis is laid on the exhilarated driver who with overjoyful recklessness takes chances that he would not think of taking when he has had nothing to drink.

THE SNAIL

In contrast to the dangerous driver might be noted the annoying snail—long known by other unflattering sobriquets because of his insistence upon crawling along in the mid-center of the road. Behind him horns can blow and another car nose up to the left of him. He does not budge an inch. Or if he does, beware of his pet trick of starting for his proper side and then not going there, but continuing along the middle of the road, so that the passing car is forced either to swerve perilously near the left edge or else to put on brakes and hold back and perhaps be rammed by a third car whose driver is not expecting him to jerk to a stop. And yet this same snail, when he is walking on the street, does not refuse to let another pass him. Needless to say, courtesy demands of one who likes to crawl that he stay far over on the right side to let faster cars go by; and if he won't, there ought to be a special truck of largest size detailed to push him—and keep him pushed.

HEADLIGHT MENACE

At night—until polaroid glass has become required by law—a not only annoying but dangerous driver to meet is one who will not dim his headlights, although knowing perfectly well that other drivers facing him are helplessly blinded by the blaze of light in their eyes.

ADVICE TO A NOVICE DRIVER

A certain driver whose rating is at the very top told a novice, whom he was teaching, to keep the idea firmly fixed in mind that every car he had to pass or meet was being driven by a fool. At the time, the pupil thought this remark exaggerated. But since then he has realized that it is the very best possible advice on driving, because trusting to the other man's quickness and skill to get out of the way, or to understand an erratic signal or worst of all a sudden change of mind, is a most prolific cause of accident. This driver did not mean that all others were really fools, but that one must think so in order to realize that the responsibility was entirely one's own, and that one could not depend on another to save him from the consequences of his own "fool driving" should one ever be less completely "on the job."

And this means not only paying attention to what you are doing but remembering to tell others what you intend to do. In short, don't take it for granted that the driver of the car behind you is psychic and able to guess what you are going to do, unless you signal to him with sufficient distinctness and deliberation. To jab your hand out as though it were a hen pecking and draw it quickly in again is scarcely enlightening. And whatever you do, don't let the man behind you think you are going to do one thing and then change your mind. Of course, there is always the contingency of the countless drivers who disregard signals and heedlessly dash forward.

SIGNALS

Practically all cars now have an automatic stop-light to warn a following car when the brake pedal is depressed. Cars built in recent years have, in addition, electric turn signals which permit a driver to indicate the direction in which he is going to turn. It is up to all drivers to get the habit of invariably using these signals.

The point to emphasize is that hand signals unfortunately differ in different states. The two most common systems are as follows: Left hand straight out means "I am turning to the left." Hand pointing up means a right turn and hand pointing down means a stop. In the second system the hand held up also means a right turn but, the hand straight out means stop and the hand pointing down is for a left turn. Before using these or any other system, find out which is understood by motorists in the state in which you are driving.

DON'T MAKE FALSE SIGNALS

This means, don't put your arm down outside the car and shake ashes off your cigarette. Don't put your hand out when you throw away your cigar. Don't put your hand out and point at the scenery, and don't let anyone else in your car wave his hand out of a window. All these actions are confusing to drivers who follow.

STOP LIGHT

Although you have a stop light, remember that it does not go on until your brakes are applied; therefore, put your hand out the moment you know you intend to apply the brakes.

DISCOURTEOUS HORN BLOWERS

Trumpet horns—those raucous, penetrating signals designed for use on the open road—are as out of place in city driving as hobnailed shoes in a ballroom. Another impoliteness is the unnecessary blowing of a horn in a traffic line when it can do no good and is merely annoying to others.

If more people realized that the horn, as the voice of the car, is in reality the voice of the driver, there would be less raucous thoughtlessness in its use. People who would never dream of bawling a vocal protest at a moment's delay, blast away on their motor horns at every hesitancy of the car ahead. No young man of good taste would announce his arrival to a lovely lady by standing at the curb outside her door and "yoo-hooing." Yet this is the identical offense which so many commit who, arriving by motor, sit at the wheel and blast away at the horn. A well-mannered visitor will alight and ring the bell.

CITY DRIVING MANNERS

When driving in a city, remember that discourtesy to pedestrians can turn out to be manslaughter. Don't rush traffic lights. A gentleman will no more "cheat the lights" than cheat at cards. Don't fail, at a crossing where the lights have turned against you, to stop far enough back to be sure that you are not blocking the proper path of pedestrians crossing the street. Don't, if you can possibly help it, run through puddles and splash pedestrians or other cars. Don't almost run over someone who is trying to signal a bus or a trolley car when a little consideration requires only a few seconds. Courteous drivers should, before starting on the green light, give pedestrians who are caught in the middle of the street a chance to get across.

DRIVERS WE LIKE—AND DISLIKE

The best-known test of a perfect driver is one with whom you never find yourself driving the car. When you see a passenger involuntarily tensing his muscles and pressing his own feet on an imaginary control, this evidence subtracts by just so much from the driver's rating. Certainly the outstanding characteristic of an abominable driver is that of showing no courtesy to his passengers at all, almost jerking their heads off every time he stops, scaring them half to death, and frequently getting into a position that makes the next move he should have been preparing for impossible.

We are all made nervous by the driver who keeps looking out all the time, expatiating on the view and paying no apparent attention to what is happening on the road. Or the one who turns around to talk to those on the back seat (who can't hear what he says because they are so busy praying that the car will stay on the road). Or the one who carelessly lets go of the wheel while he lights a cigarette or screws the windshield up or down, meanwhile letting his car meander toward the ditch or else cut over toward the wrong side of the road.

Another bad-mannered driver is the one in a hurry. Among the thousands of motor accidents listed on the police blotters, at least half are said to be made by people who have not learned to discipline themselves to be on time. The driver, suddenly becoming conscious that he should have left home earlier, flings his good driving manners to the wind, starts weaving in and out of lines, clipping red lights, pushing his way, and taking chances which he would never take if he were not in a hurry!

CERTAIN BAD MANNERS OF WOMEN DRIVERS

There are, of course, thousands of women drivers who are on every count first-class, but there are certain others who deserve all the criticism that can be given them. Among the worst of these should be put the window-shopper—she who crawls along a crowded thoroughfare with her gaze fastened upon the store windows. In a taxi, the other day, an army pilot followed close behind one of these for about twenty blocks. His taxi driver pointed her out. Said he, "Those window-shoppers are the worst we come up against! Why they don't get killed is God's mercy; they could never be saved merely by man. When I look ahead and see a woman driving her car with her head turned profile, I give her the widest berth I can."

A not unfamiliar sight, in the smaller towns, are the stop-to-talkers who park side by side and hold long conversations while other cars wait or maneuver their way past the blockade as best they can. There is no reason why Cissy Chatter may not talk with Penny Prattle as long as she chooses, but one of them must draw over close to the curb and wait. The other must park her car in a proper place and then come back to the first car and either stand on the sidewalk or get into the car.

DRIVING SPORTSMANSHIP

The good sportsmanship of all well-bred drivers is indicated in the following exactions:

It is just as unfair and unsporting to lag when the traffic light turns green (holding up the cars behind you) as to beat the lights by starting while it is still red.

The fair-minded driver—if not in a hurry—keeps well over to the right so that another, who may be anxious to get somewhere, may overtake him safely. On clover-leaf turns, it is not much to ask of a driver to turn the steering wheel enough to enable him to stay on the right when he turns right and on the left when he turns left. The boorish driver who swings to the left before a right turn, and vice versa, shows plainly a person so selfish or lazy that he would rather risk his own and the following driver's life, than turn the steering wheel the little extra required to make the sharper turn from the proper lane.

Well-bred people neither monopolize space for two parked cars nor park so close to others that they are prevented from pulling out. In marked parking places, well-bred people stay within the marks.

AS TO THE MANNERS OF PEDESTRIANS

When anyone is run over by an automobile, the driver's guilt is *invariably* taken for granted. Often the blame belongs to him, but often again it does not. In other words, motor manners are every bit as important to those who want to escape being injured as for those who want to avoid injuring others. First rules for pedestrians include:

Don't cross in front of green light. Don't cross street in middle of block. Don't dart forward after hiding behind a parked car and imagine that an oncoming driver, whom you yourself could not see, could know by means of clairvoyance that you were there! Don't, when the lights change while you are in the middle of the street, turn and run back to the side you started from. If you keep on going exactly as you were, drivers will automatically wait and give you time to pass in front of their cars. But not one of those you have already passed can possibly be prepared to have you about-face and suddenly dash in front of his wheels.

48

The Code of a Gentleman

FAR more important than any mere dictum of etiquette is the fundamental code of honor, without strict observance of which no man, no matter how "polished," can be considered a gentleman. The honor of a gentleman demands the inviolability of his word, and the incorruptibility of his principles. He is the descendant of the knight, the crusader; he is the defender of the defenseless and the champion of justice—or he is not a gentleman.

DECENCIES OF BEHAVIOR

A gentleman does not, and a man who aspires to be one must not, ever borrow money from a friend except in unexpected circumstances, and money so borrowed must be returned promptly. All money borrowed without security is a debt of honor which must be paid without fail and as promptly as possible. The debts incurred by a deceased parent, brother, sister, or grown child are assumed by honorable men and women as debts of honor.

A gentleman never takes advantage of the poor or the helpless.

One who is not well off does not "sponge," but pays his own way to the utmost of his ability.

One who is rich does not make a display of his money or his possessions. Only a vulgarian talks ceaselessly about how much this or that cost him.

A well-bred man intensely dislikes the mention of money and never speaks of it (out of business hours) if he can avoid it.

A gentleman never discusses his family affairs either in public or with acquaintances, nor does he speak more than casually about his wife. A man is a cad who tells anyone, no matter who, what his wife told him in confidence, or describes what she looks like in her bedroom. To impart details of her beauty is scarcely better than to publish her blemishes; to do either is unspeakable.

Nor does a gentleman ever criticise the behavior of a wife whose conduct is scandalous. What he says to her in the privacy of their own apartments is no one's affair but his own, but he must never treat her with disrespect before their children, or a servant, or anyone.

A man of honor never seeks publicly to divorce his wife, no matter what he believes her conduct to have been; but for the protection of his own name, and that of the children, he allows her to get her freedom on other than criminal grounds. No matter who he may be, whether rich or poor, in high life or low, the man who publicly besmirches his wife's name besmirches still more his own, and proves that he is not, was not, and never will be, a gentleman.

It has for generations been an exaction of best society that no gentleman goes to a lady's house if he is affected by alcohol. One who is addicted to the use of too much alcohol need not be discussed, for inevitably his invitations follow the decline of his behavior.

A gentleman does not lose control of his temper. In fact, in his own self-control under difficult or dangerous circumstances lies his chief ascendancy over others who impulsively betray every emotion which animates them. Exhibitions of anger, fear, hatred, embarrassment, ardor or hilarity are all bad form in public. And bad form is merely an action which "jars" the sensibilities of others.

A gentleman does not show a letter written by a lady, unless perhaps to a very intimate friend if the letter is entirely impersonal and written by someone who is equally the friend of the one to whom it is shown. But the occasions when the letter of a woman may be shown properly by a man are so few that it is safest to make it a rule never to mention a woman's letter.

A gentleman does not bow to a lady from a club window. According to the 'code,' ladies are never discussed in a gentleman's club!

A man whose social position is self-made is likely to be detected by his continual cataloguing of prominent names. Mr. Parvenu invariably interlards his conversation with, "When I was dining at the Bob Gildings' " or even "at Lucy Gilding's," and quite often accentuates, in his ignorance, those of rather second-rate though conspicuous position. "I was spending last week end with the Richan Vulgars" or "My great friends, the Gotta Crusts." When a so-called gentleman insists on imparting information that is of interest only to the Social Register, *shun him!*

The born gentleman avoids the mention of names exactly as he avoids the mention of what things cost; both are an abomination to his soul.

A gentleman's manners are an integral part of him and are the same whether in his dressing room or in a ballroom, whether in talking to Mrs. Worldly or to the laundress bringing in his clothes. He whose manners are only put on in company is a veneered gentleman, not a real one.

A man of breeding does not slap strangers on the back nor so much as lay his finger-tips on a lady. Nor does he punctuate his conversation by pushing or nudging or patting people, nor take his conversation out of the drawing room! Notwithstanding the advertisements in the most dignified magazines, a discussion of underwear and toilet articles and their merit or their use is unpleasant in polite conversation.

All thoroughbred people are considerate of the feelings of others no matter what the station of the others may be. Thackeray's climber, who "licks the boots of those above him and kicks the faces of those below him on the social ladder," is a very good illustration of what a gentleman is *not*.

A gentleman never takes advantage of another's helplessness or ignorance and assumes that no gentleman will take advantage of him. And lastly, a gentleman not only respects the reserves of others, but demands that others respect those which are his.

SIMPLICITY AND UNCONSCIOUSNESS OF SELF

These words have been liberally sprinkled through the pages of this book, yet it is doubtful that they convey a clear idea of the attributes meant.

Unconsciousness of self is not so much unselfishness as it is the mental ability to extinguish all thought of oneself—exactly as one turns out the light.

Simplicity is like it, in that it also has a quality of self-effacement, but it really means a love of the essential and of directness. Simple people put no trimmings on their phrases nor on their manners. But remember: simplicity is not crudeness nor anything like it. On the contrary, simplicity of speech and manners means language in its purest, most limpid form, and manners of such perfection that they do not suggest "manner" at all.

THE INSTINCTS OF A LADY

The instincts of a lady are much the same as those of a gentleman. She is equally punctilious about her debts, equally averse to pressing her advantage, especially if her adversary is helpless or poor.

As an unhappy wife, her dignity demands that she never show her disapproval of her husband, no matter how publicly he slights or outrages her. If she has been so unfortunate as to marry a man not a gentleman, to draw attention to his behavior would put herself on his level. If it comes actually to the point where she divorces him, she discusses her situation, naturally, with her parents or her brother or whoever are her nearest and wisest relatives, but she shuns publicity and avoids discussing her affairs with anyone outside her immediate family. One cannot too strongly censure the unspeakable vulgarity of the woman who, unfortunately obliged to go through divorce proceedings, confides to reporters the details of her private life.

THE HALL-MARK OF THE CLIMBER

Nothing more blatantly proclaims a climber—woman as well as man—than the repetition of prominent names, the owners of which she must have struggled to know. Otherwise, why so eagerly boast of the achievement? Nobody cares whom she knows—nobody, that is, but a climber like herself. To those who were born and who live, no matter how quietly, in the security of a perfectly good ledge above and away from the social ladder's rungs, the evidence of one frantically climbing and vaunting her exalted position is merely ludicrous.

All thoroughbred women, and men, are considerate of others less fortunately placed. One of the tests by which to distinguish between the woman of breeding and the woman merely of wealth is the way she speaks to dependents. Queen Victoria's duchesses, those great ladies of grand manner, were the very ones who, on entering the house of an intimate friend, said, "How do you do, Hawkins?" to a butler, and to a sister duchess' maid, "Good morning, Jenkins." A Maryland lady, still living on the estate granted to her family three generations before the Revolution, is quite as polite to her friends' servants as to her friends themselves. When you see a woman in mink and diamonds speak to a little errand girl or any other untrained helper as though they were the dirt under her feet, you may be sure of one thing: she hasn't come a very long way from the ground herself.

49

What We Contribute to the Beauty of Living

THE OLD HOUSE COAT HABIT

How many times has one heard someone say, "No one is coming in. That old dress will do!" Old clothes! No manners! And what is the result? One wife more wonders why her husband neglects her! Curious how the habit of careless manners and the habit of old clothes go together! And how many women really lovely and good—especially good—commit esthetic suicide by letting themselves slide down to where they "feel natural" in an old house coat, not only actually but mentally.

She who dresses for her children and "prinks" for her husband's home-coming is sure to greet them with greater charm than she who thinks whatever she happens to have on is "good enough." Any old thing good enough for those she loves most!

So many people save up all their troubles to pour on the one they most love, the idea being, seemingly, that no reserves are necessary between lovers. Nor need there be really. But why, when their house looks out upon a garden that has charming vistas, must she insist on his looking into the clothes yard and the ash can?

She who complains incessantly that this is wrong or that hurts, or that some other thing worries or vexes her, so that his inevitable answer to her greeting is, "I'm so sorry, dear" or "That's too bad" is getting mentally into an old house coat!

If something is seriously wrong, if she is really ill, that is different. But of the petty things that are only remembered in order to be told to gain sympathy—beware!

There is a big deposit of sympathy in the bank of love, but don't draw out little sums every hour or so—so that by and by, when perhaps you need it badly, it is all drawn out and you yourself don't know how or on what it was spent.

It should be unnecessary to add that a man and his wife who quarrel before their children or the servants deprive the former of good breeding through inheritance, and publish to the latter that they do not belong to the "better class" through any qualification except the possession of a bank account.

DIVORCE

No change in the rules of established conventions of propriety have been greater than those which formerly required all divorced people to meet as unspeaking strangers. The reason for the strictness of this convention was that, until recently, such an upheaval of home and family as divorce was unthinkable unless there was irreparable injury or antipathy that made tranquil encounter impossible.

Experience has, however, made it plain that serious readjustment of rules must be made—particularly in those cases where conventions and humanities are in conflict. Certainly no thinking person could rate the former above the latter. In the thousands of cases where children are involved, it is far, far better that the parents make every effort to remain on friendly terms. Nothing in all the world is so devastating in its destruction of character and of soul as hatred. Anything is better for children than *that!*

The most bitterly unhappy situation that can come to a child is to be the victim of a court decree which condemns it to the continual shifting, like a human shuttlecock, between parents who hate each other, or—even worse in its emotional effect—to feel that one parent has inflicted unmerited cruelty on the other. Emotional disturbance such as this should not be the portion of any child.

There are cases, of course, where divorce is the best—sometimes the only—solution for everyone concerned. If two persons are truly mismated they certainly—perhaps their children too—are better off if they part. The only consideration of vital importance is that they shall not part because of a transient "love-for-another" attack, and that they shall honestly consider the price to be paid by their children. When children greatly love both parents, the price is almost too much ever to ask. Where they love only one and remain in the care of that one, it can be possible that no payment is made.

Even so, the epidemic of divorce which has been raging in this country for the past ten or fifteen years must be rated with floods, dust-storms, tornadoes and other catastrophes.

One wonders what part divorce has played in the point of view of many of the now-grown younger generation. Their brittle hardness, their lack of consideration for any opinions but their own, and their indifference toward family obligations! How many of the thousands of children who have lived through this experience have suffered spiritual injury, and to what degree? No one can know for certain. Nor can one know to what degree other children, who have been witnesses to the broken homes of their playmates, live in fear of the same thing happening to them.

At present the breaking up of homes is so widespread it may be that those who grow up never having known the completeness of home will find it inessential! Or perhaps it will be the other way around! Perhaps the children of the divided houses will be doubly earnest in their efforts to provide their own children-to-be with the priceless security of a father and mother together in one place called HOME!

RESPECTING THE PRIVATE LIVES OF OUR NEIGHBORS

We should never walk into the house of another as though it were our own unless such behavior is encouraged. And even so, we should try to acquire sufficient alertness to notice whatever cause might make our presence inopportune.

Should we, for instance, find a visitor at Mary's—especially a visitor who is an intimate friend of hers but not of ours—we should leave promptly. This is easily done by saying, "Mary, would you lend me . . . ?" whatever we can think of that will imply that we have not come to stay. Or if we find evidence of family discussion, any situation indicating that the family would like to be alone, we should make an excuse or even say, "I'll be back later!" and withdraw.

Out in public it seems scarcely necessary to add that if we see two people engrossed in a discussion, we must not interrupt unless they make a motion that invites us to join them.

TACT

Certainly we've all been thankful—at times—that other people could not read our thoughts—thoughts such as "How very ill you look!" or "How old you've grown!"—thoughts to be locked away quickly in the silence of our own minds. The tactless person seems compelled to say exactly such things as these out loud.

Of all the qualities that make us likable, none is greater than tact. If there were no tact, there would be little friendship in the world —certainly none between nations. There would be very little accord in business. And social life would revert to the stone-age crudeness. Tact, of course, means quick awareness of the feelings of others, and consideration for them. There is only one flaw in this otherwise most charming of human attributes, the possibility of insincerity. We don't know where we stand with one who diplomatically tells us only what he thinks we'd like to hear, instead of giving us a frank, straightforward answer. In society this person is called a climber, because he too seeks only to please (never mind by what means) those who can help further his ambitions.

The tactless person causes nothing but distress wherever he goes. At this point it may be well to explain that, as in the case of many other attributes, excellence is dependent upon motive. The motive of real tact is kindness. When the motive is self-advantage, tact and truth are apt to part company.

It must be agreed that it's often more than hard to be tactful and truthful at the same time. Let us say you go to see a friend who has just refurnished her house. You think she has spoiled it completely. And WHAT do you say? You can only distress your friend if you tell her, "Well, I think the room is hideous." It's finished; she has to live in it, and criticism would be wanton rudeness! On the other hand, if she had told you about it before re-doing it, you would have been lacking in interest not to give her your thoughtful opinion.

There may be people who, suffering from some personal bitterness or unhappiness, uncaringly say things that hurt the feelings or the pride of others. But most tactless people are merely those who won't stop and think. There are certain people whose minds seem to be drawn as by a magnet to the very subject they ought to avoid.

"Of course," they say, "everybody but you knows your husband is crazy about Laura Lovely!" Or "Well! your daughter didn't marry the Gilding boy after all!" It sounds unbelievable, but these two remarks have actually been heard.

Tact, which is merely appreciation of other people's sensibilities, is just as important to each of us in every contact of life as it is to every member of the diplomatic corps. A few rare persons are born with quick perception and innate kindness; but in greatest measure tact, like most of the social graces, is the result of training. At least half the rules of etiquette are maxims in tact. But don't make the mistake of thinking that tact means veering like a weather vane with each breeze that blows. It means trying to cultivate the habit of paying attention and making the effort to find the pleasant or the encouraging side of truth.

IN-LAW SITUATIONS

One is likely to overlook the fact that when John Jones marries Mary Smith, a number of Smiths and Joneses are suddenly forced into the closeness of family relationships. Even when a bride or bridegroom has no family, he or she becomes son or daughter, sister or brother, to those who often have hitherto been total strangers.

The two difficult situations to meet happily and successfully in the foursome of man, wife, mother-in-law and father-in-law are those of the father-in-law of the husband and the mother-in-law of the wife. The other positions are so easy that there is little reason for failure.

But, in any case, the very first rule that every father-in-law—and especially every mother-in-law—must learn is DON'T INTERFERE. Never mind what small blunders your daughter or your daughter-in-law or your son or your son-in-law may make; remember that it is their right to live and do and think as they please. If you are ASKED what you think, answer truthfully, of course; but don't, upon being given one opening, cram in every item of good advice that you've been storing up for just this chance.

YOUNG WAR WIFE WHO LIVES WITH MOTHER-IN-LAW

The young wife who must live with her husband's people while her husband is overseas (she must adapt herself to their ways without his companionship and guidance) is expected to take her place as a member of the family; she cannot behave as though she were staying in a hotel. She must adapt herself not only to their mode of living, but also to the disposition of the various members of the family; only in this way can she herself be happy. On the other hand, it is essential that the mother-in-law show encouraging appreciation of the younger woman's efforts to become adjusted to completely new surroundings, rather than exhibit constant irritation over her shortcomings.

PARENTS WHO MUST LIVE WITH THEIR CHILDREN

When a mother (or father) MUST live with a married child, the situation demands the wisdom of Solomon, the tact of Récamier, and the self-control of a Stoic. Moreover, she (or he) must conscientiously practice the art of "invisibility" at frequent and lengthy intervals. This does not mean that the mother, for example, must scuttle out of sight like a frightened mouse, but that she shall have or make occupations of her own which keep her from being idly, plaintively or forcefully present—especially when there are younger visitors.

On the other hand there is no excuse for the ruthless unkindness which certain wives show when they are obliged to have a parent-in-law live in their house. This attitude, did they but know it, is not only distressing to the helpless victim of their cruelty, but is unfailingly resented by witnesses.

THE PERFECT IN-LAW RELATIONSHIP

A perfect in-law relationship must be unhampering, uninterfering, uncriticizing.

Whether we be mother or father, bride or groom, the safe rule for our own happiness is to take things as we find them, take pleasure in the assets, not go searching for flaws and not ever for a single second permit ourselves the weakness of feeling sorry for ourselves.

If we who are of yesterday (or the day before that) would have the affection of those of today given to us freely, we must ourselves be free in the sense of being impersonally independent. We all know that nothing is harder to build than this impersonality of mind and one moment's relaxed indulgence in self-pity will bring it all crashing down. The first step in the achievement of impersonality is keeping our thoughts away from every trend that is sentimentally focussed upon ourselves by thinking of something else—never mind what.

The one great struggle that each and every one of us who belongs alone—by that is meant all those who are widowed or single and whose children or sisters and brothers have married—must make is never to give clinging impulses a chance to develop. We hear much about dieting and taking daily dozens and doing all sorts of other irksome things to preserve physical beauty, and relatively little about the unrelaxing exercise of plain common sense in achieving mental beauty by adjusting the capital I to its relative proportion.

FRIENDLY FLOWER GIVING

How many charming, friendly and sympathetic impulses have been smothered under that mania of America for the superlative! Why must the flowers we send be the largest and the finest that many dollars can buy—or else none at all? The poets sing of "a rose," but young John America cannot think of roses as fewer than a dozen!

This does not mean that a big box of the most gorgeous flowers is not an enthralling gift. But why must it be supposed that we haven't the spirit or the sentiment to appreciate *the loveliness of little things?* If we had all the money in the world, would we send a dearest friend who lives in the tiniest of apartments a constant supply of sweet little roses and other short-stemmed flowers? Or once in a year or so would we crowd her small, low-ceilinged room with a twenty-blooms' plant of Easter lilies?

On the other hand, we know that when Lucy Oneroom wants to send flowers to Mrs. Richling, who has shown her repeated kindness, to *have* to choose a little pot of pansies is disheartening. But we know, too, that Mrs. Richling is one person to whom a large box of four-foot stemmed roses is not one bit more welcome than the fewest little buds with four-inch stems. In fact, nothing could distress her so much as evidence that too large a part of Mary's weekly income had gone into long stems—that will quite possibly be cut off in the pantry in order to go into a vase of reasonable height.

WHEN HE GIVES HER FLOWERS TO WEAR

Why does every man take it for granted that the only flowers possible to send are gardenias? Why doesn't He at least find out whether She might prefer something else? Why can't He at some time ask Her casually whether it is true that every woman's idea of flowers to wear begins and ends with gardenias? And then why can't He listen to Her answer? This is added purposely because the other day a certain young man asked this question, and the young woman told him she loved purple violets best of all flowers, and purple sweet peas next. Two evenings later he was taking her to a dance and sent her gardenias!

For the benefit of the man who believes that less than half a dozen gardenias (or two hundred violets) would be too few to think of, it might be well to explain that, according to *best taste*, two gardenias worn on an evening dress are perfection. Three are possible only if they are very small. On the street dress, one gardenia is correct. Therefore, three gardenias are the very most a really smart woman can possibly wear—ever. And yet, unless Mary manages to let John know that two flowers are a perfect number and not thought skimpy by anyone except a "gold-digger," the chances are that he will go on wishing to send a dozen—which means probably none.

WHEN A WOMAN SENDS FLOWERS TO A MAN

It is always proper that a woman send flowers to any man she knows when he is seriously ill or convalescing. Cut ones or plants are equally suitable. A Japanese garden is particularly good, and if her purse is deep enough to send one of considerable size, it might be especially pleasing if arranged to suggest a fragment of a golf course rather than a rock garden in Japan. But sometimes she sends him flowers that have far more sentiment. Should John Strongheart be convalescing, let us say, Louise Lovely might send him a very few flowers—perhaps only one especial flower—every day at the same hour, and tied to it a note or a message or a daily collection of clippings of whatever might interest or amuse him. The value of this suggestion, it must be acknowledged, does depend upon his sentiment for her. So in a situation where there is doubt, a young woman might confine her efforts to clippings sent occasionally, and only one offering of flowers or a plant.

WE MUST SEND FLOWERS IF WE CAN

There are certain occasions when sending flowers is really obligatory unless lack of wherewithal makes this impossible. We must send flowers to the funeral of a friend, or a member of an intimate friend's family. We also send flowers to an intimate friend who is—or has been—seriously ill, to a débutante on her coming out, to neighbors who give an anniversary party, to a guest speaker when we are hostess, and on anniversaries—either joyous or tragic—of our nearest friends.

Certain thoughtful people are constantly sending flowers; others who would like to be thoughtful seldom do. Certainly the majority of us send them much less often than we might, usually because we think those we can afford to buy or those growing in our garden are not good enough.

In a certain neighborhood a certain flower lover has an entrancing habit of sending flowers arranged in containers which are also donated with the flowers. They are usually inexpensive, but her expert eye is constantly on the lookout for small containers becoming to flowers. Some are of glass; some are of pottery; but often they are ten-cent kitchen utensils of tin—even tin cans and boxes from her own kitchen turned into "tole" with the simplest amount of painting done by herself. She also keeps a supply of dried moss and small lead flower holders. Then in winter she buys—or in summer she picks—a careful selection of flowers, puts a holder in the bottom of pot or bowl or box, arranges the flowers, and covers the holder and the stems with soaking-wet moss. Later the person who receives it adds as much water as the container can hold.

A lovely Easter present that can be afforded by almost everyone is a bowl of pebbles in which lily bulbs have been started. These, bought dormant, are not expensive, and plain pottery bowls that cost only a few cents are to be found everywhere.

Only those who have greenhouses can give the very real pleasure that a certain thoughtful old gentleman gives to a number of his younger neighbors every Easter, but it is worth including here—just in case! He sends one or two flats of small seedlings grown in his greenhouse. These are to be kept indoors, of course, until the weather permits their being transplanted in the garden. Heliotrope, snapdragons, annual phlox and lupins are his favorite selection.

Another thoughtful person's favorite gift to a young hostess is a credit account at a florist's—to be used for herself or for her house whenever she may choose. Or, of course, a lovely gift—but not very inexpensive—is a box to be sent by a florist every week, or even oftener.

At all events, there is scarcely any situation in which flowers are not the most suitable as well as the most beautiful messengers of friendship or sympathy or love that can be sent.

50

Traveling Etiquette

TO do nothing that can either annoy or offend the sensibilities of others is the principal rule of conduct under all circumstances—whether staying at home or traveling.

SPECIAL DIRECTIONS FOR NOVICE TRAVELERS

Whether you are going on a long journey or a motor trip, or merely spending a week end with a friend, your first concern is your luggage, which should look nice and give little trouble. Nothing makes a worse impression than broken-down bags and numerous carry-alls and bundles.

TRAIN MANNERS

In a dining car on a day's journey—especially on the Atlantic seaboard—you do not usually speak to your companion at table, beyond a possible "May I have the salt, please?" But in a country hotel, or on a transcontinental journey, if you happen to sit next to the same person for a number of meals, it is extremely snobbish and bad-mannered to sit in wooden silence.

During the day in a sleeping car, the seat which faces forward belongs to the occupant of the lower berth; the occupant of the upper berth rides backward. It would be an act of courtesy for the lady who has the right to the seat facing forward to ask her companion whether she minds riding backward—and if she does, to make a place at her side. The window seat would naturally belong to her—unless she prefers the other.

GOING TO BED IN A PULLMAN

Whether you have a drawing room, compartment, or "bedroom," a section or a berth, you ring for the porter to make up your berth when you are ready to go to bed. If you have a drawing room, compartment or bedroom, you shut your door and go to bed. In every variety of room, all dressing facilities are included so that you do not go to the public dressing room at all. If, however, your berth is in the open car, you finish for the night in the dressing room while the porter makes up your bed. This is especially necessary if you have an upper berth, so that when you have gone up the stepladder the porter brings for you, you will not have to come down again. In the morning when you want to get down, you ring the bell inside your berth and ask for the stepladder. You dress as much as you can in your berth, because there is no privacy—and less space—in the dressing room.

CHILDREN ON TRAINS

Any number of people not only let small children eat continuously so that the car is filled with food odors, but some mothers have been known to let a child with smeary fingers clutch a near-by passenger by the dress or coat and seemingly think it cunning! Those who are sufficiently well-to-do usually take a compartment and keep the children in it. Those who are to travel in seats should plan diversions for the children ahead of time; it is unreasonable to expect little children to sit quietly for hours on end and just "be good."

Two little girls on the train to Washington the other day were crocheting doll's sweaters with balls of worsted in which "prizes" were wound. The amount of wool covering each might take perhaps half an hour to use up. They were allowed the prize only when the last strand of wool around it was used. They were then occupied for a while with whatever it was—a little book, or a puzzle, or a game. When they grew tired of its novelty, they crocheted again until they came to the next prize. In the end they had also new garments for their dolls.

TRAVEL BY AIR

Travel by air has become commonplace. Transport and Clipper planes leave their airports—bad storms alone preventing—with the regularity of trains and steamships. General rules of courtesy are, of course, the same in a plane as in a Pullman—or a bus.

It is well to make your reservations early, for space on a plane is limited. If you are obliged to cancel the trip, the money will be refunded. Unless you have booked the "honeymoon suite" in a Clipper, you are not given a seat number as you are in a Pullman. The space sold you merely assures you that a chair or a berth will be reserved for you. If you are the first comer, you have first choice. You must not, however, claim one which has a card marked "occupied" on it, for this indicates that it belongs to a passenger who has temporarily left the plane. To hold your own place at future stops, ask the stewardess for a similar card.

If you are traveling alone, it is courteous—if one be vacant—to choose a single seat rather than to plump yourself down into one of a pair of seats, thus preventing others who are traveling together from taking these adjoining places. In fact, if you have made part of the journey in one of the double seats, and two people enter the plane together—man and wife, or mother and child particularly—who can find single seats only, you would be very discourteous not to move into a single seat, offering them the double one. This is because many air travelers are inclined to be nervous at first, and likely to be upset if separated from whomever they are with.

This especial consideration for the feelings of others, which shows itself in a general spirit of friendliness among the passengers, is so characteristic of air travel that it has, in fact, brought about certain newly accepted rules of traveling etiquette. The on-the-ground custom of paying no attention to fellow travelers is not observed in the air. Those who are willing to talk—and in a plane nearly all are— are entirely free to do so. On the other hand, if one wishes to be left alone, he can avoid the continuous conversation of a neighbor by arriving at the airport early enough to secure a single seat. But just as friendliness is expected, the explanation "I'd rather not talk" or "I'm very tired" is never resented, for it can so easily happen that a passenger has hurriedly taken the plane in answer to disturbing news.

SPECIAL ASPECTS OF AIR TRAVEL

There are a few ways in which travel by plane is different from travel by train. The member of the crew whom you will see most is the stewardess, a registered nurse who is prepared to do everything possible for the passengers' comfort, even to helping mothers with the care of babies or young children. She is not given a tip—ever. In fact, tipping is strictly forbidden by airline regulations. On the Pan-American Clippers, passengers are looked after by stewards. On the domestic airlines, the stewardesses alone are in charge.

Meals on planes are always included in the price of the ticket, and are served by the stewardess or steward.

On an overnight flight, a woman prepares for bed in the "powder room"—up-in-the-air name for a dressing room. But whatever its name, good manners in it are the same as in the dressing room on a train. When there are many passengers, you must wait patiently for your turn, and when it comes, try to take as short a time as possible— unless you are the last. Even so, you should leave the washstand and the dressing table in perfect order. When you have finished washing, wipe out the basin thoroughly with your used towel, which you then throw into the towel basket. Before combing your hair, lay a fresh towel over the shelf of the dressing mirror. Leave it there until you have finished your hair-do and your face powdering. Then gather up that towel and throw it into the towel basket. Complete neatness is a first essential of good manners. Never leave any unpleasant trace of untidiness *anywhere!*

THE YOUNG GIRL TRAVELING ALONE

In America, a young girl can go thousands of miles by rail, bus, boat, or airplane without the slightest criticism if she behaves herself with sufficient reserve. The difference between the general good fellowship among all the passengers in a plane and the inclination of a man to "scrape acquaintance" with a girl on a train is very great. She should therefore be careful about entering into a conversation with any strange man who seats himself beside her. Above all, she MUST NOT be persuaded by the kindness of a stranger, whether man or woman, to get into a car to be driven to her destination. If a stranger on the train offers to open a window for her, or to get her a chair on the observation platform, he has the right to no more than a civil "thank you."

TO ASSURE ACCOMMODATIONS IN HOTELS

It is well to write or telegraph to a hotel in advance for accommodations. A typical telegram reads:

Please reserve outside single room with bath afternoon December third
                                              Mrs. John Hawkins.

(Another of the few occasions when "Mrs." belongs with a woman's signature.)

A letter is a little more explicit.

Proprietor of the —— Hotel,
  Chicago, Ill.

Dear Sir:
  Please reserve two single rooms with baths or with a bath between for my daughter and me. We are due to arrive in Chicago at five o'clock on the afternoon of December sixth, and shall stay a week.

I prefer average-priced outside rooms not higher than the fourth floor.

                            Very truly yours,
                                    G. K. Smith.

Kindly confirm reservation to
  Mrs. Arthur L. Smith, Brightmeadows, Ill.

Both letter and telegram should state clearly the hour of your arrival, number of persons, whether rooms are to be with or without bath, and the approximate length of your stay.

THE ARRIVAL AT A HOTEL

Your arrival at a hotel is always precisely the same unless you walk in without baggage. Otherwise, a doorman opens the door of your car or taxi and deposits your luggage on the sidewalk. If the hotel is crowded, this individual will ask, "Have you engaged rooms?" If you say "Yes," all is well; but if you say "No," the reply is, "Very sorry, but there is not a room left." This means that you have to go to another or maybe to several other hotels. So you should not only wire or write, but ask for a reply!

Usually a day or two is sufficient notice, but at the time of a political convention or a big football game, or any other occasion of crowded hotels, you must sometimes write months in advance, and not think of going to the hotel unless you receive word that you will be accommodated.

However, let us suppose it is an ordinary occasion and that you have your room. A bellboy dashes or saunters out, takes your bags from the sidewalk and carries them into the lobby and deposits them not far from the desk. In a typical hotel there is a counter with one man or two behind it. In the gigantic city hotels there are divisions of desks, labeled "Rooms," "Accounts," "Inquiry," etc.

In either case you go to the desk, or to the division marked "Room Clerk," and say, "I am Mrs. Arthur Smith. I telegraphed you Friday." If you have had no answering telegram, there is always the chance that the clerk may say, "Very sorry, but we have not had a vacancy. The Bakers' Convention is meeting here. We would have telegraphed you but you gave us no address." Which means that you will probably have to go hunting for a place to sleep.

However, let us suppose your room is waiting for you. The clerk turns the register round—or more probably in a modern hotel he presents a form—for you to sign.

REGISTERING IN A HOTEL

A gentleman writes in the hotel register:

"John Smith, New York."

Never under any circumstances "The Hon." (meaning the American title) and not "Mr." if he is alone. But if his wife is with him, the prefix to their joint names is correct.

"Mr. and Mrs. John Smith, New York."

He should not add his street and house number. If instead of a book he has been given a registration form, he fills in the blank, which usually includes the house address. But his signature is exactly the same whether written in a book or on a card. Neither "John Smith and Wife" nor "John Smith and Family" is good form. If he does not like the "Mr." before his name, he can sign his own without the title on one line and then write "Mrs. Smith" on the one below. The whole family should be registered.

John T. Smith	New York
Mrs. Smith,	"
and maid (*If she has brought one*)	
Miss Margaret Smith,	New York
John T. Smith, Jr.,	"
Baby and nurse.	"

Or, if the children are very young, he writes:

Mr. & Mrs. John T. Smith, New York, 3 children and nurse.

"Miss" is prefixed to the names of girls over five, but small boys are registered John or Henry. "Master" is used sometimes but it is rather suggestive of a parvenu who fears that a small child may not be accorded the respect which his self-aggrandizing father (or mother) believes due to his own importance.

One exceptional occasion when a lady signs her name "Miss" or "Mrs." is in a hotel register.

"Miss Abigail Titherington" is correct, or "Mrs. John Smith"; never "Sarah Smith."

Returning now to "you," whom we are personally conducting: You sign your name, Mrs. Arthur L. Smith, Brightmeadows, Ill. As soon as you have registered, the clerk hands the key, not to you, but to the bellboy, who again gathers up your bags and starts in the direction of the elevators. You follow. (If you have many bags, there will be two boys.) In some hotels they send a maid as well as a bellboy upstairs with each woman guest. (Whether the guest is to be protected from entering a room alone with a bellboy, or the bellboy protected from being left alone with the guest, has never been explained.) In any case, the bellboy having jerked all the shades up, and the maid having pulled them down, each receives a quarter and departs.

Any service that you really require you telephone for. You tell the operator to give you "The Desk" if you want to ask about mail or give the name of a visitor you are expecting. You call "The Porter's Desk" if you have any inquiries about luggage or trains—a hotel will always send for luggage, also dispatch it. You call the "Starter" if you want a taxi at a certain hour, the "News Stand" for magazines, newspapers or theater tickets, and "Room Service" when you want food sent up to you.

BREAKFAST IN YOUR ROOM

In the morning, for instance, if you want to breakfast in your room, you say, "Room Service, please." Then, when this answers, you say, "Please send a waiter to room one one one seven"; or, if you know exactly what you want, you say, "Please send coffee and buttered toast and orange juice for one." Presently the waiter brings in a tray with your order. In a first-class hotel he carries in a long, narrow table that fits between twin beds or stands beside a single one. It is completely set: damask cloth, china, glass, silverware and thermos pitchers, and possibly lamp-lighted dishes to keep the food hot.

It is entirely proper to receive the waiter when you are sitting up in bed or clad in a wrapper. Waiters are used to carrying breakfast trays into the presence of all varieties of pajamas and negligées, and it is not necessary for even the most old-fashioned lady to be completely dressed to receive him.

He places the table between twin beds or in a small hotel puts the breakfast tray on the bed, and then immediately leaves the room. He returns later for the table and check, which can be paid in cash or at the desk when the room is paid for. The room waiter receives from twenty-five to fifty cents, according to the amount of the breakfast check and whether it is for one or two. In addition to this the hotel makes an extra charge for meals served in your room.

OTHER ITEMS OF SERVICE

To have your clothes washed, telephone that you want your laundry sent for. Pressing is usually done by the regular valet or lady's maid. In a small hotel, a woman's dress as well as a man's suit is sent out to a tailor. It is against the rules in most hotels to use your own iron; therefore, when you don't know where to have any pressing done, you ask a chambermaid tactfully, "Where can I have my dress pressed?" She answers, "I will do it for you," or tell you who will.

HOTEL STATIONERY

In Europe only the most luxurious hotels furnish stationery gratis for guests to write on, but all American hotels, the smallest as well as the greatest, give their guests as much writing paper as they need. It is exceedingly bad manners—in fact, not honorable—to take it away in bulk or to waste it.

HOTEL RULES OF PROPRIETY

It is strictly against the rules of every reputable hotel for a guest to receive a visitor of the opposite sex in a bedroom. If you have a private sitting room, you can have everyone you please take a meal in it with you, or you can receive whomsoever you please, so long as you break none of the ordinary conventions of behavior. Noisy parties, men visitors at unconventionally late hours, or anything that suggests questionable behavior is not permitted in any high-class hotel.

The woman staying alone in a hotel and having no sitting room of her own receives her men visitors in any one of the public sitting rooms that all hotels provide. She is also free to ask whom she will to the restaurant or dining room. There is not the slightest reason why a woman—even though she be very young and very pretty—may not stay in a hotel by herself and have men come to see her and be invited by her to lunch or to dine. It is not so much a question of suitable age as of suitable behavior. A girl who is dignified, whose friends are the sort that pass that sharpest of character readers, the House Detective, will never even approach an uncomfortable moment. The woman, on the other hand, who thinks a hotel is a brier-patch where she can hide away all the things she oughtn't to do, will find that she might as well have chosen to hide in a show window.

TIPS

The usual tip for a waiter in a restaurant is ten per cent of the bill, but never less than twenty-five cents in a restaurant with tablecloth on table. If you are staying in an American-plan hotel, you give the waiter or waitress at the end of each week about five per cent of the week's board if for one person, but less if the family is large. When going to stay in a hotel, you give from two to ten dollars to the head-waiter, if you would like a table in a particular location. And you tip him, when you leave, in proportion to the service rendered. You give him one or two dollars a week, if he has done nothing, and five dollars a week for a family that he has been especially attentive to.

The room waiter receives the regulation ten per cent of the bill, but his fees are slightly larger than those of the dining-room waiters, because a small amount is usually added to the prices on the room-service menu.

In an American-plan hotel, a set sum of twenty-five or fifty cents is charged for each meal taken to a room.

The chambermaid in a first-class hotel is given about one dollar a week a room, fifty cents a week in a small inexpensive hotel, or a dollar a month in a boarding house. If you stay one night only, fifty cents for each room in a large hotel, or twenty-five cents in a small one, is left on the bureau—in the hope that the chambermaid and not an inquisitive bellboy will get it!

Other tips: (Nothing to the doorman for putting bag on sidewalk.)

Twenty-five cents if the bellboy carries baggage to room; fifty cents if the bags are many or very heavy.

Twenty-five cents for paging.

Twenty-five cents to a porter for bringing a trunk to the room, or fifty cents if there is much baggage.

TRAVELING ETIQUETTE

Ten cents for ice water, newspapers, packages, telegrams, etc.

Ten cents for checking a man's coat and hat.

Twenty-five cents for checking a woman's wrap in the dressing room of a high-class hotel or restaurant, or ten cents for the coat rack at the entrance to the dining room.

Fifty cents or one dollar to the elevator starter when you leave, or fifty cents a week to an individual elevator man. If staying long in a hotel that has many elevators, a dollar a month for each operator.

Taxi drivers are tipped about ten cents for a fifty-cent drive, fifteen cents for a dollar drive, and ten per cent for a long wait or distance.

On a train or a boat, twenty-five cents is given to the porter for carrying an ordinary amount of baggage an ordinary distance. A larger sum for extra weight or distance. For instance, one dollar is the established tip for carrying a suitcase from a Hudson Tube entrance in New York all the way to a train on the Erie Railroad in Jersey City. This is a journey down two flights of steps, twenty minutes in the tube, an underground walk of a quarter of a mile, then up a flight of steps and into a train.

The porter in a Pullman car is given twenty-five to fifty cents for a day, and fifty cents a berth a night.

Bootblacks are tipped five cents, and barbers, manicures and beauty-parlor specialists on the basis of ten per cent of the bill.

For other lists of tips see Index.

Smart-looking people, who frequent expensive hotels and take drawing rooms on trains, are expected to give larger tips than people traveling economically. The latter may easily be richer, but tips are expected according to appearance.

One piece of advice: You will not get good service unless you tip generously. If you do not care to order elaborate meals, that is nothing to your discredit; but you should not go to an expensive hotel, hold a table that would otherwise be occupied by others who might order a long dinner, and expect your waiter to be contented with a tip of ten cents for your dollar supper! He will be enchanted to serve you a ten cent supper if you will give him the dollar tip!

Tipping is undoubtedly an undesirable system, but it happens to be in force; and that being the case, travelers who like the way made smooth and comfortable have to pay their share of it.

IN A RESTAURANT ALONE*

A hotel guest—whether a woman or a man—going down to the dining room alone, usually takes a book or newspaper, because nothing is duller than to sit eating bread and butter and looking at the

* For complete restaurant details see Chapter 8.

tablecloth—which is scarcely diverting—or at other people—which is impolite—while waiting for one's "order."

It is always proper for a woman to wear a hat in a restaurant, but she may go into the dining room without one if she is staying in the hotel. In the evening she goes without a hat unless she wears street clothes.

CALLING ON PEOPLE IN A HOTEL

When calling on people stopping at a hotel, you ask for them at the desk and the clerk telephones to their rooms. If they are receiving you upstairs, you are told the number of the room you are to go to, and you go up in the elevator alone and find it yourself. You can ask the elevator boy which floor 616 is on, but in practically every hotel this would be the sixth floor.

If the friends you are waiting to see answer that they are "coming down," you sit in the lobby or the lounge until they join you.

LEAVING A HOTEL

The courteous guest tells the management when he arrives that he intends to stay over night only, or several days or a week or two, as the case may be. When he is ready to leave, he goes to the cashier—or telephones—asking that his bill be made out. When he has finished packing, he telephones for a bellboy to carry down his luggage. Then he goes to the desk, pays his bill, and leaves his key and a forwarding address if he wishes any mail sent after him, and departs.

THE USEFULNESS OF A TRAVEL BUREAU

Every prudent traveler should get an expert to lay out and budget his itinerary for him. One of the best ways is to go to a travel bureau. If there isn't one in your own town, write to one that has been recommended, such as my personal choice mentioned in the footnote*. Tell them just where you want to go and when and how—in fact, give all the details you can, and let them work out the best possible plan for you. This is their business, and they can do it not only better but much more economically than you can, and at no extra cost to you, except for railroad tickets and pullman reservations for which there is a regulated charge.

There is one important point that should be explained to a novice traveler. He probably knows that a competent travel bureau will engage best rooms in de luxe hotels and secure automobiles by the week

---

*For many items in this chapter, grateful acknowledgment is made to Miss Dorothy Shepard of the Mayfair Travel Service, Inc., N. Y., whose efficiency has been the outstanding cause of unmarred delight on every journey taken under her personal care.

or month, either with or without chauffeurs, or provide any other service, but he is quite likely unaware that they will, with equal interest, provide the same quality service for those traveling on a limited budget.

The value of the service of a reliable and competent travel bureau cannot be too strongly emphasized. It is almost indispensable in these days of increasingly complex conditions of travel.

PREPARATIONS FOR SAILING

Let us say that your plans are made to sail on such a day. If you are going to foreign countries, your last preparations before sailing include the following items (if you have gone to a travel bureau, it will have attended to the first two things for you).

First: Your passport. Be sure to apply for this as early as possible, to have plenty of time to have it viséd at the consulate of each country you pass through, including the country of destination.

Second: Get a moderate amount of foreign money to have in your pocket when you land. It is also important to take our money in express checks. Even though you have a letter of credit, there are many occasions when it is inconvenient or impossible to go to a bank, and express checks are received everywhere as readily as cash.

Third: Whether you are going to a foreign country or traveling at home, make your list of clothes, not only with utility and becomingness in mind, but with serious attention to the utmost elimination of bulk and weight.

Fourth: See that your luggage is suitable and either new or in perfect repair.

On the day you sail be sure to arrive at the steamer in plenty of time to make sure that your baggage is on board. Then you probably go directly to your cabin.

SELECTING YOUR TRAVEL CLOTHES

The first thing to remember on the day you select your clothes is not to let the weather upset your judgment. Unless you remember about this, should the day you pack be freezing and stormy, you are as likely as not to start to the tropics with rubbers and galoshes, a slicker and a rain coat as well as an ulster, and very little for days which are warm and sunny. On the other hand, should the day on which you go out to get clothes for a trip to the North be torrid, you will be a very unusual person if you remember that a wardrobe selected solely for the tropics may result in your having to go around wrapped in a steamer blanket on more than a few occasions.

Another mistake made by all novice travelers is taking too many things. It is true that knowing how to select the most practical minimum possible is an achievement that is the result of long experience and rather special skill.

(For detailed list of traveling clothes see Chapters 38 & 39.)

AMOUNT OF BAGGAGE

For ordinary travel, having only a few pieces of luggage is an important consideration. But when going on a ship where you will occupy the same cabin the entire time, particularly if you are to have it alone, the number of pieces you take does not matter. On the other hand, if you are sharing a cabin, you must limit your luggage to one steamer trunk and possibly a bag or box that can go under your berth. In other words, you have no right to expect your cabin-mate to live in a baggage room.

TIPPING

There are definite minimum amounts that cabin passengers are expected to give. Give five dollars to your cabin steward, if you are a man; if you are a woman, divide the five dollars between the steward and the stewardess. If you have exacted much service of the stewardess, you should give her five dollars.

The dining-room steward receives five dollars and his assistant—if he has one—two and a half or possibly three.

The smoking-room steward is given from ten cents to a quarter at the time you order anything from him, or if he presents his bill at the end of the voyage, you tip him about as you would have at separate times—between fifteen and twenty per cent, depending upon the amount of service he gave you. If you only bought cigarettes or cigars at the counter, you add ten per cent to his bill.

Ten per cent of the amount on the bill is given to the dining-table wine steward.

To the bath steward you give a dollar.

To anyone on the ship who has been attentive to your wants and taken pains to please you, you show by your manner in thanking him that you appreciate his efforts, as well as by giving him a somewhat more generous tip when you leave the ship.

It should be unnecessary to add that you must on no account attempt to tip a ship's officer! Thank the purser as you would any other acquaintance for courtesy. If you go to see the doctor, or if he is brought to see you for a slight ailment, you merely thank him too. But if you have a real illness, it is proper to send him in an envelope, when you leave the ship, the amount that probably would have been charged by your own doctor.

WHEN TRAVELING FOR PLEASURE SHALL BE RESUMED

One great change that the war has made inevitable is that good manners must increase as world distances decrease. Although it will be some time before any great amount of traveling will be done by ordinary private citizens, the requirements of courtesy are going to be much more exacting than ever before. The continual shortening in the time required for encircling the globe has made the people of the farthest reaches of the earth our neighbors. And it is as such that international etiquette becomes essential in achieving neighborly understanding and friendship.

For us, the first step toward this understanding is the realization that, while our own accepted rules of etiquette are excellent so far as they go, they do not go far enough. *Perfect* American behavior—meaning that which is flexible and sensitive and tactful—will, of course, pass requirements everywhere.

Behavior which is NOT going to be very helpful in building international friendship is that which presumes to set itself up as the pattern to be followed, instead of trying courteously to acquire an understanding and appreciation of the general point of view of the people of each country we visit.

KNOWLEDGE OF LANGUAGE ESSENTIAL TO UNDERSTANDING

It is obvious that the etiquette of each country differs as does its language. We Americans have for years been greatly criticized for our ignorance of both. Not even our diplomats have been required to learn to speak fluently the languages of the countries to which they are accredited. It is really amazing! And then we naïvely believe that wherever we go we will be loved on sight "because we are Americans!"

We don't love all the foreigners who come to our shores. We do love those individuals who are appreciative of our country and courteous to us. It is quite plain, then, that similarly complimentary requirements are exacted of us in the countries where we are foreigners.

It is, of course, true that good manners are good manners everywhere, except that in Latin and Asiatic countries we must, as it seems to us, exaggerate politeness. We must, in France and Italy, bow smilingly; we must, in Spain, South America and the East, bow gravely; but in any event, it is necessary to *bow*—though your bow is often little more than a slight inclination of the head, and a smile—and to show some ceremony in addressing people.

EVEN WHEN WE ALL SPEAK ENGLISH

At first thought, it would seem that there could be no difficulties of understanding between us and those whose language is the same as ours—especially by the Australians and New Zealanders who are said to be so much like ourselves. But slight frictions which developed during the war suggest that thoughtful observance of other people's reactions to the things we do and say would be helpful.

It has been said of our soldiers, for example, that not only have they more money than those of other nations, but that the American troops looked upon foreign currency as being make-believe money—of no value at all.

To our credit it can be said—we are straightforward; we honor our obligations; we keep our word. But sometimes we make over-optimistic promises, and tact is not one of our virtues. Sensitive perception of the feelings of others is something that few of us possess instinctively. It is necessary, therefore, that we train ourselves to perceive the point of view of the people of each country we visit, remembering that it is always the stranger who must adapt himself, just as the visitor does to the ways of the house in which he is a guest.

The English, the Scots, the Welsh and the Irish are like us in so many ways we can easily be thrown out of balance by a few differences. The best type of Britisher, for example (it is his point of view which we most want to understand), has just as keen an appreciation of his own ability as we have, but the code of a British gentleman exacts understatement and personal reserve. Therefore, if you would be liked by the well-bred Britisher, DON'T be a show-off or a braggart or a back-slapper. He detests all three. Also, you might remember not to make the mistake of thinking that he hasn't any sense of humor. (Read "Punch"—at least until you have changed your mind on this.)

COURTESY IN THE FAR EAST

But of much more seriousness is the respect which you must show for the religious exactions of all Orientals. In North Africa, for example, to smoke or let a pet dog run loose near a mosque, to enter a house either in shoes or barefoot, to let bread fall to the ground or to cut it with a knife or to hold it in the left hand—above all to stare at or attempt to talk to a veiled woman—are all not merely discourteous, but grave offences against the religion of a deeply devout people.

In the Far East, the principal advice is this: *Never* lose your self-control. Only by showing unfailing dignity, tranquillity, and poise combined with good nature can you hope to take the first steps toward earning liking and respect.

51

In Official Washington

To most of us who lead quiet private lives, countless conventions of manners and behavior are of comparatively slight importance. But to the few who enter the official world at Washington, and especially abroad, knowledge and observance of even trifling rules of etiquette become vitally necessary.*

Etiquette in Washington is more exacting than in a State capital. While the behavior of every State official reflects upon his office, his shortcomings at home are between himself and his neighbors. But the knowledge or ignorance of a man sent by his State to either Washington or a foreign country reflects credit or discredit upon the dignity of the United States.

THE NEW ARRIVAL IN WASHINGTON

Although most people are kind, and those who have been long in service instinctively try to help the inexperienced, it is imperative that each new arrival in Washington, whether an official or a private citizen, who expects to take part in the social life of the Capital learn first of all the proper title by which each diplomat, government official and military officer is addressed and the order of his rank. When a man has been promoted to high position, he does not take lightly having the respect due his office overlooked; and placing a foreign representative below his proper seat at a dinner table, or in any way showing less than proper concern for the rank which is his due, is actually to endanger diplomatic feeling between nations.

---

* Of social life as it was originally described in this chapter, there is at present scarcely a trace. As one of the younger Washingtonians put it:

"Your whole plan of living is timed so as to avoid standing in line. You dine in mid-morning or early afternoon or late evenings—you do everything at the most inconvenient hour possible because your unceasing plan is to stand the shortest time waiting for a table, a seat at the lunch counter, or supplies at the market. If you go to a movie, you know you have to go in the middle of the picture possibly to view it from that point, or else to be well up near the head of the line when it ends. No matter what you want to get, the approach is by way of a queue, a blocking crowd, a wait for an unfilled taxi, or a bus that will stop."

PRECEDENCE

Precedence is the bane of the Washington hostess; it is as difficult as a cryptogram, and social death if not strictly observed. It is easy enough to know that a general outranks a lieutenant, a duke a count, or a member of the President's Cabinet a State assemblyman. The difficulty begins, for instance, in determining whether a General of the Army should rank the Governor of a State, or whether a Rear-Admiral or a Mayor or a Justice of a State court should go in to dinner first, or where to seat the Archbishop of X and the Duke of Y.

Before giving a dinner to which any persons of conflicting rank have accepted, a Washington hostess should submit her list to the Chief of Protocol at the State Department, whose office replies to such inquiries. The following list must therefore be considered only approximate—although it is as authoritative as possible.

THE ORDER OF PRECEDENCE IN THE UNITED STATES

In an American house the ranking foreigner should insofar as possible be given precedence.

1. The highest possible rank is that of a foreign sovereign or president.
2. Next comes the President of the United States.
3. The Vice-President, in the absence of the President.
4. A special ambassador directly representing his sovereign on a special mission. Or by courtesy a Cardinal. In Catholic houses the archbishop who is the Apostolic Delegate might properly precede the ambassadors.
5. The foreign ambassadors in the order of their length of residence in the country.
6. The Chief Justice.
7. The Vice-President when the President is present.*
8. The Speaker of the House of Representatives.
9. Associate Justices of the Supreme Court.
10. The Secretary of State.
11. The Secretary of the Treasury.
12. Foreign Ministers Plenipotentiary.
13. Secretary of War.
14. Attorney General.
15. Postmaster General.
16. Secretary of the Navy.
17. Secretary of the Interior.
18. Secretary of Agriculture.

* When the Vice-President is not representing the President he ranks as head of the Senate and is placed necessarily below the Chief Justice, who as head of the Supreme Court of the United States outranks the Senate.

19. Secretary of Commerce.
20. Secretary of Labor.
21. Senators. (Each Senator ranks according to his length of service. When elections are of the same date, they are ranked according to the date of the admission of their respective States to the Union, or in case of the Thirteen Original States, according to their population.)
22. House of Representatives.
23. Chief of Staff of Army.
24. Chief of Naval Operations.
25. General of the Army (5 stars).
26. Fleet Admiral (5 stars).
27. General (4 stars).
28. Admiral (4 stars).
29. Governor of State.
30. Lieutenant General.
31. Vice-Admiral.
32. Major General.
33. Rear Admiral, Major General Commandant of Marine Corps.*
34. Chargé d'Affaires.
35. The Solicitor General.
36. Brigadier General.
37. Commodore.
38. Under-Secretaries and Assistant Secretaries.*
39. Lieutenant-Governor of a State, President of a State Senate, Speaker of a State Assembly, all of equal rank.*
40. State Justice, Mayor, State Senator, equal rank.*
41. Counselors, Military, and Naval Attachés.*
42. Assemblymen.
43. Foreign First Secretaries.
44. Federal Reserve.
45. Interstate Commerce Commission.
46. Secretary of the Smithsonian Institution.
47. Director of the Pan-American Union.
48. Foreign Second and Third Secretaries.

Rank is always official. This means that plain Mr. Smith who has become "His Excellency the Ambassador" ranks above a Prince or a Duke who is officially a Secretary of Embassy.

IN A FOREIGN EMBASSY—OR LEGATION

In a foreign embassy the ranking American, or any other stranger is given precedence. The President of the United States takes precedence over the representative of the country which is receiving

* All officials of equal rank would be placed according to length of office.

him. In the President's absence, the Vice-President, the Chief Justice or the Secretary of State—whichever represents the United States—outranks all foreign Ambassadors. In the diplomatic service, the dean or highest ranking Ambassador is he who has been longest in residence, not longest in service of his country, but in Washington. Next come the Ministers in the same order, then the Counselors, First Secretaries, then the Second and the Third Secretaries. The Consul ranks as representative of his country if no member of his embassy or legation is present.

ECCLESIASTICAL PRECEDENCE

As the presence of the Pope is not to be considered, Cardinals are of the highest ecclesiastical rank. Archbishops rank next, then bishops, then monsignori, and last, priests. Next to the Cardinals, the archbishop resident in Washington is of highest rank and the Archbishop of Baltimore second. Otherwise precedence is determined by priority of promotion.

At specifically ecclesiastical gatherings the Catholic clergy rank above all secular personages, and even at social gatherings in the houses of Catholics the higher clergy have precedence over all other notables except the President. In high-church Episcopalian families, clergymen and priests should be accorded the especial respect of rank, in acknowledgment that "the spiritual is superior to the material"; but under all circumstances decency as well as deportment demands that we show deference to priests and clergymen.

UNIVERSITY AND COLLEGE TITLES

The title "Professor" is given within the university or college grounds, but in the social world outside he is addressed as "Mister." Assistant professors and instructors are called "Mister" when introduced or addressed socially. But a man, regardless of scientific distinction, who does not have a doctor's degree—even some who hold a Ph.D.—always resents being addressed as "Doctor."

THE USE OF TITLES

In addition to the information given in chart (Chapter 42) the following sentences indicate the way persons in the diplomatic world are introduced, announced and spoken of and to.

"Mr. Ambassador, may I present Mr. Worldly?" (Mr. Worldly finds out, if he does not know, *which* ambassador.)

But in the case of Mrs. Worldly the order is reversed.

"Mrs. Worldly, may I present The Speaker?"

"Mrs. Worldly, may I present Mr. Justice Law?"

"Mrs. Worldly, may I present the British Ambassador?" or more formally "—his Excellency the British Ambassador."

"Mrs. Worldly, may I present the Governor of Colorado?"

"Mrs. Worldly, may I present the Secretary of the Interior?"

Unless she herself holds a diplomatic position, a woman is never introduced to a man lower in rank than a sovereign or president, member of a reigning family, or a high prelate. A man of lesser rank is always introduced to one of greater.

The governors of certain States, such as Massachusetts, for example, have the official right to the title of "Excellency." But even in States which do not confer this title upon their governors, it is courteous, in speaking about him, to say, "His Excellency has just remarked—"

Speaking of the governor on a single or formal occasion: "Does your Excellency think—" (The title is not repeated throughout a long conversation.)

"May I ask you, Mr. Speaker."

"How do you do, Mr. Chief Justice."

"I am so glad to see you, Mr. Secretary."

"I appreciate the honor, Mr. President."

"Thank you, Mr. Vice-President."

"Thank you, Mr. Ambassador." Or about him: "As his Excellency has explained—" (In this case "Excellency" is his official right.)

"Have you met Senator Brown?" ("The Senator from New Jersey" is used only in the Senate.)

When introducing or addressing a letter to one who has both an inherited and military title, military rank is put first, thus: Colonel, Lord London.

It is utterly improper to call a governor "Mr.," no matter how informal and simple his own inclinations may be. Only those who know him very well say "Governor." In public and before others, he must be addressed as "Governor Jones." And on really formal occasions, "Excellency!!" (As already explained, this last is not said repeatedly, but in presenting him or announcing him or referring to him, "His Excellency, the Governor" is correct, whether his State gives him the title officially or whether it is his merely in courtesy.)

It is very important to remember that no matter how well you may have known a man out of office, you must treat his office with unfailing respect. To slap a governor on the back in public and call him "Jim," is belittling to his office, to him and to you.

In illustration of the traditional dignity of office: One of the justices of the United States Supreme Court was President McKinley's lifelong and most intimate friend. But after Mr. McKinley's inauguration, this friend, whose own office was an exalted one, always addressed him, even when they were alone, as "Mr. President." It was only in grief upon hearing of his death that he cried out: "Bill! Oh, Bill!"

Members of the Cabinet are usually "Mr. Secretary," but if several are present, one is designated "Mr. Secretary of State," the other "Mr. Secretary of the Navy." And you say, of course, "Mr. Chief Justice" or "Mr. Justice Law"—even after he has retired. You also say "General Pershing" and "Admiral Sims" and "Senator Lake," and not merely "General," "Admiral," or "Senator." You should also say "Doctor Brown" rather than just "Doctor," and never under any circumstances "Doc."

Officers below the grade of captain in the Army and commander in the Navy are written to by their titles, but spoken to as "Mr." Captains and commanders and those of higher rank are addressed by their title and name: Captain Brown, Commander Gray, Colonel Steel. To call them by title alone is not objectionable, as it would be in the case of a governor.

Military and naval titles are used only by officers in active service or retired "regulars." It is extremely poor form for reserve officers who held commissions only during the war to continue having their cards engraved Captain, Major or even Colonel. Often a man is affectionately called "Colonel" by his friends, but he should not have the title engraved on his visiting cards, nor should he use it as his signature. A civilian staff officer, such as a colonel on a governor's staff, shows very poor taste in using his title, or rank, when his political chief is out of office.

Announcement or official introduction (or when called upon for an address or speech):
"His Excellency, the French Ambassador."
"The Honorable, the Chief Justice."
"The Secretary of Agriculture."
"The Speaker."
"Count Torla, the military attaché of the Swedish Legation."
"His Honor, the Mayor of New York."

OFFICIAL DINNERS AND FORMS

An invitation to lunch or dine at the White House is a command and automatically cancels any other engagement.

The acceptance must be written—by hand of course. Furthermore, it must be left at the door and not sent by mail. It may be folded once in the ordinary way and not fitted to a full-page-size envelope as is necessary in answering court invitations abroad.

IN OFFICIAL WASHINGTON

AN EXAMPLE OF BEST TASTE

Mr. and Mrs. Richard Worldly
have the honor to accept
the kind invitation of
the President and Mrs. Washington
for dinner on Thursday, the eighth of May
at eight o'clock

The following form is to be avoided:

Mr. and Mrs. Notquite
present their respects (or compliments) to
the President and Mrs. Washington
and beg to express
the great pleasure it will afford them
to be present at dinner
on Thursday, May the eighth
at eight o'clock

It is ardently to be hoped that one who aspires to social distinction will not write as follows:

Mr. and Mrs. X
present their compliments to their Excellencies
the Ambassador of France and Mme. Bonnet
and are most happy to accept their courteous invitation
for dinner on Thursday, May eighth
at eight o'clock at the French Embassy

This form is actually being received in Washington embassies. The proper form is

Mr. and Mrs. Richard Worldly
have the honor to accept
the kind invitation of their Excellencies
the French Ambassador and Madame Bonnet
for dinner on Thursday, the eighth of May
at eight o'clock

The note to a deserted hostess.

Mr. and Mrs. Richard Worldly
regret extremely
that an invitation to the White House
prevents their keeping
their previous engagement for
Tuesday the first of December

DETAILS OF WHITE HOUSE ETIQUETTE

Although customs vary somewhat during succeeding administrations, the following details represent the conventional pattern from which each administration necessarily adapts its own procedure.

When you are invited to the White House, you must arrive several minutes at least before the hour specified. No more unforgivable breach of etiquette can be made than not to be standing in the drawing room when the President makes his entry.

Exactly as at a European court, the President, followed by his wife, enters at the hour set and makes a tour of the room, shaking hands with each guest in turn. When your turn comes, you bow deeply and address him—if he talks to you—as "Mr. President." In a long conversation it is proper occasionally to vary "Mr. President" with "Sir." You call the wife of the President "Mrs. Washington," and treat her as you would any formal hostess. You do not sit down while either the President or his wife is standing. No guest, of course, ever leaves until after the President has withdrawn from the room.

DINNER DETAILS AT WASHINGTON

When seating her table, the Washington hostess addresses the dinner cards of the following notables by titles alone:

The President
The Vice-President
The Archbishop of ......
The .... Ambassador
The .... Minister
The Chief Justice
The Speaker
The Secretary of............ (For members of the Cabinet)

Other notables have their names in addition to their titles:

Mr. Justice Fair
Senator Essex
Governor Lansing
Bishop Chair
Rev. Father Stole
Dr. Saintly

All other names on place cards are prefixed merely by "Mr." at dinners given by a fashionable host and hostess in their own house. The object of a dinner card is double: first, to show the owner of the name where he is to sit; second, to give his neighbors at table (if they have a chance to read the card) a clue to how to address him.

A certain noted lawyer who, being a man of unusual charm, dines much in society makes it a habit, when sitting between strangers, to lay his place card on the table at his right and later at his left. There is no rule for this, but it is an act of consideration for which the neighbors of most officials would often be grateful.

To write on a place card "The Chargé d'Affaires of Great Britain" or to address him as "Mr. Chargé d'Affaires" is preposterous. Also impossible would be "The Assistant Secretary" of this or that. Imagine trying to address your dinner neighbor as "Mr. Second Assistant Secretary of Agriculture!"

The wives of members of the nobility are always addressed by title—"Lady This,"* "Countess That," "Princess the Other." But the wives of men holding official titles, no matter how exalted, remain "Mrs." if British or American, and "Madame" if of another nationality.

At public dinners place cards are inscribed exactly as envelopes would be addressed (see Chapter 41): "His Grace the Archbishop of New York," "His Honor the Mayor of Chicago," "The Assistant Secretary of the Navy."

At a private dinner, the hostess writes the names of her guests as she would if she were speaking to them. "Governor Sweet, will you sit here? Father Stole, will you sit there?"

As already said, the Washington hostess who is in doubt about the rank of her guests should either submit her dinner list to the State Department or avoid asking those of conflicting importance. If she is giving a dinner in honor of some guest of lower rank than another, it is imperative that she ask the latter to waive his right for this one occasion. The one requested cannot very well refuse—and does not as a rule object—but if he is unwilling to cede his right, he can send word that he is prevented for some reason from being present at the dinner. As a matter of fact, giving a party in honor of an average friend is extremely difficult in official circles, for no one may be invited "to meet" another of inferior rank.

After a dinner or lunch in Washington each guest must wait his turn—according to rank—and not take leave until after all those "above him" have departed. A recognized exception is made after a lunch that is not too formal, for the benefit of government officials whose duties demand their return in the early afternoon. A busy man, therefore, can quite properly plead necessary work and go—whether lunching in the house of Americans or of foreigners.

*Lord and Lady are British titles. In all other countries the wife of a Baron or a Count is Baroness or Countess—never Lady.

OFFICIAL VISITS AND DAYS AT HOME*

In Washington, as in Europe, it is the newcomer's place to make the initial visit. Every official's first duty is to call at the White House. But neither the President nor the President's wife ever returns visits, and leaving one's card at the White House is merely a form of respect. After leaving cards at the White House the wife of a new official goes to call upon the wives of all those who rank above her husband. As practically all visits are made upon regularly fixed "reception days," the President's wife is the only one whom a visitor does not ask for at the door, or expect to see.

The order of a visit-paying list varies slightly. The newly arrived wife of a Naval or Marine officer, on the first Monday of visit-paying, hastens to call upon the wife of the Commander at the Navy Yard or the Marine Barracks. But the wife of a Senator or a Congressman spends her first Monday at the houses of the Judiciary.

On Tuesday, the latter goes first to see the wives of the Congressmen from her own State. On following Tuesdays she gradually completes the entire Congressional list. Wednesday, every newcomer goes to leave cards upon the wife of the Vice-President, the wife of the Speaker of the House, and the wives of all the Cabinet officers.

On Thursday, as on Tuesday, all newcomers call first upon the wives of their own Senators and continue calling upon Senators' wives, beginning at the top of the list—ranked always according to length of office—until the list is exhausted.

The wife of an Army officer must go on Friday to call upon the wives of the commanding officers. Otherwise on Friday the newcomer starts out upon the very delightful but—unless she has been much abroad—supposedly difficult mastery of etiquette in the foreign embassies and legations. But diplomats have notably gracious manners or they wouldn't be diplomats. After all, anyone who is innately well-bred has not so very much to learn, and nothing whatever to fear.

WHEN PAYING VISITS IN WASHINGTON

Except that you may be—unless prepared—at a loss to know how to address each official and foreigner, and except that precedence is a thing that must never be lost sight of, you behave in diplomatic and official circles as you do in "best society" everywhere. A man calling upon an ambassador or a minister asks at the door whether "His Excellency" is at home; but a lady going to see his wife asks whether

---

* People who go to Washington as private individuals may leave their cards at the White House if they so choose, but otherwise they follow the procedure of strangers in all other towns and do not call upon those whom they do not know, or to whom they have brought no letter of introduction.

"Madame Telque" or "Lady London" or "Countess Thatone" is at home. Upon being told that she is, the visitor lays her cards—one of her own and two of her husband's—upon the tray offered her and follows the servant to the drawing room. Her hostess greets her and indicates where she is to sit. In New York a visitor would merely take any available seat, but in Washington a visitor should not, with others of higher rank present, sit upon the empty chair on the hostess's right vacated perhaps by a departed "Ambassadress"* but finds a place less obviously prominent.

For those who are at the bottom or very near the top, it is comparatively easy to remember the rank of the very few below or the equally few above; but for the wife of a new official of medium rank the strain upon her memory for faces and names duly classified is heavy. In fact, at first this mastery of the rank list seems nearly impossible. To some it remains so, and they are social failures. To others, practice soon makes perfection.

An invaluable aid, if your memory is not especially good, is to carry a sheet of thin writing paper folded into a note-book with an attached pencil—the whole so small that it can be cupped in the palm of your left hand, and whenever an unobserved chance comes, write quickly the names just heard; or later perhaps you can ask someone present to tell you the titles you did not hear. It is a good idea to add if possible *something* to fix each one in memory:

"Senator Brown, Montana: very tall, thin, gray beard, black eyes."

"Madame Jamand: wife of Finnish Minister, small, round, ash blond, pretty dimpled hands."

"Mrs. Mumford: wife of Congressman from New York, tall, thin, dark, wears glasses, nice smile."

Then when you go home, you find where each belongs on the official list. After a little while your mind gets into the habit of classifying names with appearances. After that, if you have a "talent for people," you elaborate your mere "identification" to a "personality" list.

"Senator Brown: great love of justice. Convince him a thing is right, and he will stand by it through thick and thin."

"Madame Jamand: talks amusingly about people. But not too accurate in what she says."

This last habit of testing and listing people's traits of character is of great value to anyone in any branch of public life.

* Ambassadress is not a correct title, but is occasionally used in courtesy.

52

Concerning Military and Post-War Etiquette

BECAUSE in us Americans flows the blood of every race and creed, there is no other country in the world where there is so great a need of wise appraisal, of sensitive understanding of our countrymen.

The Janus-faced difficulty of this most important aspect of post-war as well as war-time etiquette is, on the one side, the need for alertness lest subversive elements take us unawares, and on the other the equally great need to avoid mistrusting those who are completely loyal to the principles of our Founding Fathers.

When we encounter one whose behavior causes doubt of his loyalty, censorship of our impulses is only fair play, both now and in the years after the war.

There is, however, this warning which must be given: If someone does or says something definitely threatening to our government, write a letter to the F.B.I. or to the governor of your State, or the mayor, or to the sheriff of your township. Or, if you prefer, you can telephone. In any case make your evidence definite and brief.

For example, say, "A group called the Junior Revolutionists who meet regularly Monday evenings at 40 X Street is distributing handbills" (enclose sample). This information can do an innocent person no harm—it might in fact protect one who is unwittingly misled! On the other hand, it is the way to bring a guilty one to justice.

KNOWLEDGE OF MILITARY RANK A PERMANENT REQUIREMENT

Because a knowledge of military etiquette will in the future, as well as the present, probably be required of every well-informed citizen, the following rank lists are of obvious importance.

ON THE SHOULDER STRAPS OF THE ARMY

Rank in the Army is indicated by the insignia on the shoulder straps and upon the collar. A star always means a General; the more stars the higher the rank.

General of The Army	5 Stars in circle		
General	4 Stars	Lieutenant Colonel	Silver Oak Leaf
Lieutenant General	3 Stars	Major	Gold Oak Leaf
Major General	2 Stars	Captain	2 Silver Bars
Brigadier General	1 Star	First Lieutenant	1 Silver Bar
Colonel	Silver Eagle	Second Lieutenant	1 Gold Bar

ON THE SLEEVES OF THE NAVY

By the stripes on the sleeves of the blue uniforms or on the shoulder marks of white or khaki uniforms the rank of commissioned officers is most quickly read. (The insignia on the khaki shirt collar are not so easily seen at any distance.*) The more (and wider) the striping the higher the rank. A two-inch gold stripe (with any additional striping above it) around the sleeve of a blue uniform means "Admiral"; higher rank is indicated by other half-inch stripes. On the solid gold "lace" shoulder mark worn on white uniforms and on overcoats rank is indicated by the number of stars, from Commodore with one star, Rear Admiral with two stars, Vice-Admiral with three stars, full Admiral with four stars, to Fleet Admiral with five stars.

Below the Admirals in order of rank:

Commodore	1 two-inch Stripe
Captain	4 half-inch Stripes
Commander	3 half-inch Stripes
Lieutenant Commander	2 half-inch Stripes plus narrow one between
Lieutenant	2 half-inch Stripes
Lieutenant (jg)	1 half-inch Stripe plus narrow one above
Ensign	1 half-inch Stripe

A gold star embroidered above the stripes on either cuff or shoulder mark means "an officer of the Line." All other devices (oak leaves predominating) indicate other branches of the Service.

RANK IN THE MARINE CORPS

The highest ranking officer in the Marine Corps is the Lieutenant General Commandant. He wears the same three silver stars that are worn by a Lieutenant General in the Army. Otherwise the insignia are the same as in the Army.

THE GOLD SHIELD OF THE COAST GUARD

The uniform of an officer of the Coast Guard is distinguished from that of an officer in the Navy by a gold shield above the stripes on his sleeve, and also by his cap devices and buttons. The highest ranking officer of the Coast Guard is the Vice-Admiral. He wears braid two inches wide with two half-inch stripes above and a shield above all on his sleeve. Otherwise insignia are the same as in the Navy.

COMPARATIVE RANKS OF THE FOUR SERVICES

Because it is almost impossible for any hostess to remember the comparative ranks of the officers in the four Services, and because it is of utmost importance that she seat each of these officers correctly—whether there be many or few at her table—the following lists are given. The officers of the same number are of the same rank but take

*Note: There are no insignia on collars of white or blue naval uniforms.

precedence according to the branch of service: Army I, Navy II, Marines III, Coast Guards IV; and also according to the dates of their commissions.

I. ARMY*
General of the Armies
1. Chief of Staff of Army
2. General (5 stars) ⎫
3. General ⎬ General Officers
4. Lieutenant General ⎪
5. Major General ⎪
6. Brigadier General ⎭
7. Colonel ⎫
8. Lieutenant Colonel ⎬ Field Officers
9. Major ⎭
10. Captain ⎫
11. First Lieutenant ⎬ Company Officers
12. Second Lieutenant ⎭
(12.) Chief Warrant Officer
13. Warrant Officer (junior grade)
(13.) Flight Officer (Office functional may be either grade W. O.)

II. NAVY*
Admiral of the Navy
1. Chief of Naval Operations
2. Admiral
3. Vice-Admiral
4. Rear Admiral
5. Commodore (Reinstated 1943)
6. Captain
7. Commander
8. Lieutenant Commander ⎫
9. Lieutenant ⎬ Junior** Officers
10. Lieutenant (junior grade) ⎭
11. Ensign
11. Commissioned Chief Warrant Officer ranks "with but below" Ensign
12. Midshipman
Warrant Officer

III. MARINE CORPS
†Commandant of Marine Corps ⎫
Major General ⎬ General Officers
Brigadier General ⎭
Colonel ⎫
Lieutenant Colonel ⎬ Field Officers
Major ⎭
Captain ⎫
First Lieutenant ⎬ Company Officers
Second Lieutenant ⎭
Commissioned Chief Warrant Officer
Warrant Officer

IV. COAST GUARD‡#
‡Vice-Admiral
Rear Admiral
Commodore (Reinstated 1943)
Captain
Commander
Lieutenant Commander ⎫
Lieutenant ⎬ Junior Officers
Lieutenant (Junior grade) ⎭
Ensign
Commissioned Chief Warrant Officer
Warrant Officer

Non-commissioned Officers—Army
Master ("Top") Sergeant
Technical Sergeant ⎱
First Sergeant ⎰
Staff Sergeant
Sergeant
Corporal
Private 1st Class
Private

Petty Officers—Navy
Chief Petty Officer
Petty Officer 1st Class
Petty Officer 2nd Class
Petty Officer 3rd Class
Seaman 1st Class ⎱
Fireman 1st Class ⎰
Seaman 2nd Class ⎱
Fireman 2nd Class ⎰
Apprentice Seaman

* Aviators are part of the Army or part of the Navy.
** The term "junior officer" is not susceptible of accurate definition because its meaning varies under different circumstances. However, officers in the Navy below the rank of Lieutenant Commander are commonly understood to be "junior officers."
† Officer serving as such holds rank of Lt. Gen'l.
‡ Highest rank in this branch of service.   # The oldest branch of service.

MILITARY AND POST-WAR ETIQUETTE

THE WOMEN'S SERVICES

Highest in rank—since *all* are commissioned officers—and certainly highest in the hearts of their countrymen, are the Army and Navy nurses.

After them come the Army's WACS, the WAVES, MARINES, the SPARS, the WAFS, etc.

In all the women's services (except the WAFS at the time of this writing) the women are governed by exactly the same regulations as are the men. Their officers are entitled to and receive the same courtesies. Their rank is identical with that of men officers of comparable grade. Rank, not sex, determines all questions of precedence on all official occasions. In only one particular are they catered to as women: they may secure permission from their C.O. to wear brides' or bridesmaids' dresses.

ADDRESSING LETTERS

An envelope addressed to a man or woman in the Service gives the full rank as the title, or the rating after the name.

Letters to officers with the rank of Commander or higher in the Navy and Captain or higher in the Army begin "Dear Captain Smith" or "Dear Commander Jones." ("Sir:" is formal.)

Warrant Officers, Cadets, and Midshipmen may be written to as either "Dear Mr. —" or "Dear Radio Electrician Smith," "Dear Cadet Brown," "Dear Midshipman Jones."

To all others in the Army: "Dear Pvt. Doe," "Dear Corporal Doe," "Dear Sgt. Doe."

In the Navy: "Dear Mr. Doe" (or "Miss" or "Nurse").

SOCIAL DIVISIONS ACCORDING TO MILITARY RANK

The most definite rule of military etiquette says that it is improper to invite enlisted men and commissioned officers together. Ordinarily no host or hostess may *thoughtlessly* overlook this regulation.

But, like almost all rules, it has exceptions. In the Air Service, for example, the social distinction between pilots with or without commissioned rank is disregarded. In the privacy of a family, of course, when some of the members are officers and some are soldiers or sailors without rank, or in a group restricted to intimate friends, the etiquette of rank is necessarily waived. At most present-day weddings, the bridegroom and ushers are of different services, ranks and grades.

INTRODUCING PEOPLE IN THE SERVICES

An officer below the rank of Commander is properly introduced by his title but thereafter spoken to as "Mister."

"Mrs. Smith, may I present Lieutenant Commander Jones. *Mr. Jones has just come from Tampa and knows your son.*" (If Lieutenant Commander Jones belonged to the WAVES, she would be spoken to as "Miss" or "Mrs. Jones.")

In peace-time, when an officer may be wearing civilian clothes, he is introduced by his title and the branch of Service to which he belongs. "Lieutenant Brown of the Marine Corps."

Introducing Senior Officers presents no difficulty, for all are spoken to and introduced by their titles. "Miss Smith, may I introduce Captain Strong?"

Junior Officers of the Medical Corps are introduced by their military titles and then called "Doctor." A doctor or surgeon who is a senior officer is addressed by his military title.

Chaplains are called "Chaplain," regardless of rank; a Catholic chaplain is called "Father."

Warrant Officers are all introduced as and called "Mister."

Non-commissioned officers in the Army are introduced as and called "Corporal" or "Sergeant."

A private or private first class is introduced as such, but no official source of information seems to know whether a civilian should then call him "Private" or "Mister." It seems to be optional.

Petty officers and enlisted men in the Navy are introduced as and called "Mister" (or "Miss" or "Mrs.").

(A Naval authority has suggested that, when a civilian is uncertain, he should ask, "How shall I introduce you?")

MEANING OF "ADDRESS"

Because of the misinterpretation of civilians who seek information in the official manuals and think the word "address" means the subscription on the envelope of a letter, it is well to remember that in military parlance "address" means "speak to."

MILITARY CUSTOMS THAT CIVILIANS ARE EXPECTED TO KNOW

Hats. A small detail, but one which is disturbing to Regional Officers, is the Reserve Officers' habit of taking off their hats. Every well brought up boy having been taught to take off his civilian hat when greeting a lady—military manual notwithstanding—instinctively reaches for his uniform hat the moment he greets a woman friend or when a lady enters the public elevator he is in. A Regular Officer keeps his on and is therefore made to seem rude. According to military etiquette, the cap is a part of the uniform and it is not proper to remove any part of the uniform outdoors.

MILITARY AND POST-WAR ETIQUETTE

Civilian etiquette is simple, and explicit. Elevators in hotels and apartment houses or any building used for domestic or social purposes are indoors, and a gentleman takes his hat off when a woman is present. Elevators in office buildings or stores, railroad terminals, and so on are outdoors and hats are kept on.

Military opinion declares: All "public" elevators are outdoors.

Salute. The remark is occasionally made that the Army men never fail to salute their friends either indoors or out, whereas Naval men don't take this trouble. This difference is again one of military regulations. The Naval personnel NEVER salute when uncovered. Those of the Army do. On the other hand, Naval custom permits saluting with left hand when right can not readily be used. Army custom holds to the right hand only. The use of the word of greeting, such as "Good morning" or "Good evening," when saluting is a Naval custom.

Precedence of rank is not enforced when an officer and an enlisted man both, stand in any one of the same lines waiting in post-offices, banks, restaurants, railroad stations, grocery stores, theatres, hotels, etc.

Miniature Insignia. Wives, Mothers, Sisters, and best girls should be advised that wearing the full-sized Army or Naval insignia is not permitted under Army or Naval regulations. There are miniature copies (similar to the sister pins of fraternities) which service men may properly give to "HER" and whomever else they please.

Decorations. When a man overseas receives a decoration and sends it home for his mother or wife to "wear," he is asking that she do what is NOT permitted. A decoration is worn only by the one upon whom it is bestowed. When it is presented posthumously, it is merely handed to his mother or wife or for the moment pinned on the breast of his child. But after the presentation it is worn by no one, ever.

DON'T ever call the Navy's men-of-war's men "gobs"!

DON'T use the word "NAVY" as an adjective. It is a Naval uniform with its Naval insignia, and it is Naval tradition, and there are Naval officers.

MAN AND GIRL PAYMENTS

Frankness about payments is illustrated by the girl who pays the taxi fare if she chooses to. While he was a civilian and they were caught in the rain, and he said nothing about getting a taxi, rather than embarrass him she let her clothes get spoiled. Now, because of uncertain rationing, she is expected to feel free to insist on a taxi and on her right to pay for it. He is expected to see her point of view. She, too, is expected to understand that he doesn't at all like to put her on the bus instead of seeing her home ... or to be vague about a future date ... or to be rude when he fails to answer some of the military questions she unthinkingly asks him. But with all this, it is hoped that the gallantry that has always characterized the well-bred man will not disappear permanently because many pleasant ways of life were given up for the duration.

TO GIRLS WHO WANT TO VISIT MEN AT CAMP

Among the propriety problems of these war days none is more difficult to solve wisely than that of the girl who wants to visit a man at training camp. There are, however, a number of rules that are generally accepted, rules which no "nice" girl flaunts—war or no war! They are guides to safe conduct.

At the top of the approved list is, of course, the situation of the fiancée who is going to camp to marry, with the consent of her family and of his. It may be that she has to make a transcontinental trip to do so. If a member of her family, or his—or best, of both—can go with her, so much the better. But if not, this is one of the "ways of war" that has to be accepted.

An approved visit to a camp is that of Mary whose engagement to John is announced, but whose marriage is not taking place until after the war. In many instances, perhaps in most of them, distance is too great and time too short for John to come home. Therefore, if they are to see each other at all, it is she who has to go to him. If it is possible, a member of her family—or of his—should go with her. If this is not possible and she has to go alone or he must sail without seeing her, the reputation he and she have built up at home must serve as her chaperon.

Even so, a young woman who is engaged to a man at camp should not stay in a near-by hotel alone. It will be best that he get her a room in the house of a well-known family. If he has made friends with people near-by and they invite his fiancée to stay with them, this will, of course, be proper.

In addition to these two, there is one other young woman who may properly go to a military camp. This is the girl from home who is invited by the man's family to go with them. In this case, since she is their guest, it is their obligation to pay her expenses.

All other young women should stay at home. The war does not give them the right to let down all the bars and do whatever unconventional things come into their heads. Moreover, they are only adding both to already strained transportation facilities and to the problems of military training.

On the word of many of the trainees themselves, a man in training camp is embarrassed and disgusted with a girl in whom he has never

MILITARY AND POST-WAR ETIQUETTE

shown serious interest who suddenly develops war-time sentiment for him.

CERTAINLY WRITE TO HIM!—WRITE TO THEM ALL

Among the peace-time rules of etiquette which have definitely "about-faced" in war-time, none is more conspicuous than the reversal of the advice to young girls not to write impulsive letters to their boy friends. Now that many of her friends are in the Services, Mary Hometown not only writes to her best boy friend in training camp, but also sends letters and packages to as many other friends in uniform as she can find time for—especially to those, whose P.O. numbers indicate the A.E.F.

In short, nothing is more welcome to the normal, home-loving man (or girl) than to hear his name called when the mail is handed out; nothing is more dispiriting than seeing others go forward for their letters or packages and never a call for himself.

DON'T FOR LETTERS OVERSEAS

Of course there are certain don'ts as well as do's of what to write or send. The don'ts at the end of Chapter 43 are the same in war- as in peace-time. Don't write anything—ever—that could embarrass you were it left lying around for everyone to read. And it might be well to remember that war-time mail may easily fall into strange hands.

And whether you are writing to a man or to a girl, don't write any home news that will cause needless distress or worry. If bad news must be told, it should come from one who can give it accurately and in detail. Nothing is more cruel than referring to illness or misfortune without giving details as to *what* is wrong with mother's health or with father's business.

Although the letter written to the one who is dearest to you is quite outside the province of this chapter, it can do no harm to remind you *not* to sob over him, or to emphasize the anxiety with which you are praying that he "will come through safely." Send him your prayer-thoughts by all means but keep fear-thoughts to yourself.

THE LONG-AWAITED FURLOUGH

The first don't which the family of every man or girl in the Service should keep in mind is: DON'T make any definite engagements for them that they have *not asked you* to make! Remember to leave them free to do what they please, and do your best to seem pleased with whatever this may be. The most practical help you can give is to see that they are not interfered with by time-wasting persons or circumstances.

WEDDING HELD FAR FROM BRIDE'S HOME

As fully explained in the wedding chapters of this book, there are very few occasions when any of the wedding preparations or expenses may be borne by the family of the bridegroom.

But a not unusual war situation is that of a bridegroom stationed near his own home, whose bride must come a long distance from hers to be married. In such a case, should his mother want to give the wedding reception, because, as one of them explained, all the guests will of necessity be the friends and relatives of the bridegroom's family, there is really no sensible reason why she may not do so. If the bride's family lived near-by, it would, of course, be different.

MARRIAGE AT CAMP

In the many cases where neither her family nor his can be present at the marriage, the bridegroom will make the arrangements for the ceremony to take place upon her arrival at camp.

The most troublesome question brought about by this reversal of custom is whether the bridegroom should pay the traveling expenses of the bride, which may be considerable. Since the whole procedure is turned around, the practical rather than the conventional point of view has to be considered. If her family can pay all her expenses, they do so, of course. If not, the bridegroom may be obliged to. In many cases their families share her expenses.

TODAY'S TYPICAL WEDDING

Preparations for the typical wedding of a man in the Service are extremely simple, and invitations are often likely as not given to relatives and friends by word of mouth. That the business of war takes second place to none is a lesson learned from the earlier experiences of many brides' families who found themselves with elaborate preparations on their hands and hundreds of invitations to cancel at the last minute.

THE UNCERTAIN DATE

When the bridegroom's arrival can not be definitely stated the bride's family order invitations with the date line left blank. The empty envelopes should be addressed and stamped. When the date is set, it is quickly written in the invitations, which are then slipped into their envelopes and mailed.

BRIDGEGROOM'S NAME ON WEDDING INVITATIONS AND ANNOUNCEMENTS

On wedding invitations, the name of a bridegroom whose rank is below Commander in the Navy or Captain in the Army is at present given this way:

John Strong
2nd Lieut., Army of the United States
(or United States Army if commissioned in regular Army)

David Deepsea
Ensign, United States Naval Reserve
(or United States Navy, if commissioned in the regular Navy)

One change (probably permanent) is that Mr. before the name of a bridegroom of lower than senior rank whose rating is indicated on the line below is fast going out of favor. It is still correct, much as Esquire is; but it is used by the few, rather than by the many.

The name of a non-com or C.P.O. or enlisted sailor or soldier is engraved John Strong, and Signal Corps, U.S.N.R. or Coast Artillery, A. of U.S. or whatever designation is his, is in smaller type directly beneath the name on the wedding invitations. Or, if the bride chooses to include Pvt. 1st Class, A. of U.S. or Apprentice Seaman, U.S.N.R. social usage is now permitting this.

The name of the bride who is in the service is engraved

marriage of their daughter
Alice Mary
Lieutenant, Women's Army Corps
or
Ensign, WAVES, United States Naval Reserve
or
Nurse Corps, United States Naval Reserve

When the bride's father is also in the Service, and absent, his name appears as follows:

Major (overseas) and Mrs. John Jones
request the honour of your presence, etc.

(On the announcements, father's address is omitted.)

If the father is in the Service and has rank below that of Captain in the Army or Commander in the Navy, the first line of the invitations and announcements is engraved

Mr. and Mrs. John Henry Jones

This is also being used by leading engravers when the bride's mother is in the Service.

NAMES ON VISITING CARDS

On their visiting cards, junior officers and all men in the service ranking below junior officers engrave their rank and branch of service either directly beneath their name or in the lower right-hand corner.

John Henry Bones
Lieut., Medical Corps
Army of the United States

John Henry Saintly
Lieut., Chaplain Corps
United States Naval Reserve

Correctly there are no double cards possible for these men and their wives. The latter continue to use their own Mrs. John Henry Jones cards, which serve adequately.

CONCERNING THE ARCH OF SWORDS

The arch of crossed swords under which the bride and bridegroom descend the outside steps of the church after the ceremony—the conspicuous feature of a military wedding—is unhappily quite out of the question when the bridegroom and his ushers are not commissioned officers and therefore have no swords.

The occasional suggestion that the ushers be supplied with swagger sticks and hold these in the semblance of an arch as the bride and groom descend the steps of the chancel has no official approval. The only approved substitute for the sword arch is to have fellow members of the bridegroom's Company or Corps or a group of his shipmates stand at attention on either side of the outside steps as the bride and bridegroom leave the church. Even at the wedding of a commissioned officer the sword arch should never be made inside the church. The church is a sanctuary, and arms—unless borne by defense guards—are out of place.

Although there is supposedly no substitute for the bridegroom's sword, which is used by the bride to cut the cake, so few service men of today have swords, social usage not only approves the use of the sword of any of the bridegroom's forebears, but finds nothing to criticise should Private Jones borrow one from a friend.

WAR TIME SIMPLIFICATIONS PERHAPS PERMANENT

ONLY ONE ENVELOPE

To the current question of whether the inner envelopes of wedding invitations and announcements may be omitted because of the paper shortage, the answer is, of course, "yes." It might, in fact, be suggested that the small double sheet with the flap cut at the top of the second page, so that when folded this second sheet becomes the envelope, be admitted. In other words, since the object is to save paper, let's discard both envelopes instead of only one until we can again choose what we prefer instead of what will help our country's need.

HALF-POSTAGE

Half-postage is another peace-time tabu that should perhaps not be banned now. Remember, however, that not a single word of writing is permitted on anything enclosed in an unsealed envelope and that third-class mail is much slower than first-class.

RETURN ADDRESSES

Since the post office requires return addresses on the *face* of all envelopes which we wish to have returned in case the addressee is not found, this usual tabu on wedding invitations is now lifted.

"... AND FAMILY"

It is still better to write as many as three lines of names above the address on the envelope of an invitation. However, when "... and Family" can be considered definite enough for the family to know how many of them are meant, it is permitted because of the paper shortage. It would, of course, be sufficient on the envelope of an announcement.

INVITATIONS TO WAR WIVES

Invitations addressed to wives properly include the name of the husband even though he is known to be absent: "Captain and Mrs. Harrison Heaume," "Pvt. and Mrs. John Jones," "Apprentice Seaman and Mrs. George Green," and mailed to wherever the wife is living.

ANNOUNCING THE NEW BABIES

Although upholders of etiquette as applied to conventional forms do not take kindly to double visiting cards reading "2nd Lieut. and Mrs. ----," still less "Ensign and Mrs. ----," and very certainly not "Apprentice Seaman and Mrs. ----," the lack of such cards has been a very real handicap for a young wife who wants to announce the birth of a baby and her husband's promotion.

Since a double card for "Ensign and Mrs. ----" is incorrect, and tying both the father's card and the baby's card to the mother's card is very awkward, the following was devised:

Henry Martin Highwaves
Ensign, U.S.N.R.
and
Mrs. Highwaves
announce the birth of their son
Henry Martin, Jr.
on July 30, 1942

Whether this card

> Apprentice Seaman and Mrs. Elmer Brown
> joyfully announce the birth of Alice
> August 3, 1942

could properly serve as a pattern cannot be stated; however, it *was* sent out by the son-in-law and daughter of an Admiral. It is said that the head of the family (who wears four stars on his shoulders) did not give his approval. But his wife (the baby's grandmother) gave it as her opinion that "under the special circumstances of the stork's visit," her husband, while not officially approving, gave no orders for its cancellation.

A birth announcement to a new father in the Armed Forces, *and sent to his military address*, is the sole exception to the general ban on sending telegrams and cables. For messages to family and friends, greeting card announcements which you can buy at your stationer's are more popular than ever. Even though varieties have been reduced, there are still plenty with beguiling pictures of babies, and their messages lack merely the date of birth and the name. The envelopes for these can be addressed ahead of time and stamped ready to mail. Don't forget that any writing whatsoever, even the word "boy" or "girl" or "August 19" in *unsealed envelopes requires first-class postage*.

On a formally worded announcement, the name of the absent father should always be included. When a new baby's father is reported missing, it is better that the mother send informal announcements.

RULES OF BEHAVIOR FOR WAR WIVES

The following is a brief list of the conventional proprieties that every wife of an absent service man would be wise to observe. You may see your friends—men and women both; go out when invited by people you like; invite them in return if and when you can. There is no objection to going to a movie now and then with a man—especially one who is an old friend of your husband's as well as your own; but it is best not to make a constant practice of going out with one man alone or of being seen sitting next the same man often enough to let anyone couple your names.

You make no exceptions to the rule against taking a man into the house, or up into your apartment, late in the evening. The fact that you share an apartment or a house with another woman is not a reliable safe-guard against gossip.

HOW TO KNOW YOU ARE RIGHT

To determine for yourself the right or the wrong of what you may do is quite simple. No matter how young or how lacking in worldly experience you may be, unless life has done something to dull the sensitiveness which all youth possesses, the right impulse will stand clearly apart from the wrong one the moment you ask yourself, "Would Jim want me to go? Or would he rather I didn't?" If the answer is "Yes" you go and find the evening gay and amusing; but if you are not quite sure that you were wise to have gone, you can find the answer in your mood when you write to Jim.

If you eagerly tell him where you went and who was there and what they said; if, time and again while you were there you kept wishing that Jim could have been there too, you'll know you need give the question of rightness no further thought. On the other hand, if you find yourself thinking it best not to tell him this or that because you may not be able to put it so he won't misunderstand, it is likely that you have been venturing toward dangerous ground.

These are, of course, just the conventional rules of behavior for every young and attractive woman who is in love with her husband, and does not want to give anyone a chance to think otherwise.

WHEN OUR VETERANS COME HOME

The blundering tactlessness of many unthinking people has made it necessary to emphasize the need for thoughtful courtesy on the part of every one of us whenever we come into personal contact with a newly returned veteran. The first rule for us to follow, therefore, is to

STOP A MOMENT AND THINK—PLEASE!

When you meet a veteran who has been in combat, do try to keep your wits about you and *think* before you begin talking about anything so unconsidered as the hardships of war-time living here at home. The girl at the soda counter who told a battle scarred hero "I guess you're glad to be home to get a real job," has many counterparts!

If he is an old friend, tell him how glad you are to see him back; and show that you are, not only by looking glad but by paying enough thoughtful attention to adjust your mood to his.

Should he seem absent-minded, untalkative or tense try to realize what he has been through and be patient. If he has been home a long time and if he has found the niche into which he fits, you need not perhaps worry about treading softly. But if he may not yet have "found himself"—meaning the job he wants or whatever it is he most wants to do—the rule of safety is to be very quiet. Try to follow his lead with friendly but uninquisitive interest in anything he has to tell you. But whatever you do *don't* ask him questions about what the war was like, or what he thinks or feels about getting home—unless he himself brings up these subjects.

OUR ATTITUDE TOWARD DISABLED VETERANS

Our behavior to strangers is quite simple. The first rules of good manners which we have learned from earliest childhood are: Don't stare; don't point; don't make personal remarks. These are the first exactions of decent behavior—whether someone has on an unusual hat or carries his arm in a sling.

The greatest kindness we can show to our badly injured is not to let our own thoughts dwell on any handicap that may be theirs. We have only to follow the attitude of the entire Nation toward President Roosevelt. Why, then, should we think of Sam Soldier's handicap? (Unless it, in some way, becomes an obligation to do so.)

If, for example, you were seated at table next a soldier whose arm is in a sling, and a piece of steak (impossible to cut with one hand) were on his plate, you would simply say, "Let me cut that for you." In the same way you would hold his coat for him, as a matter of course. If you see one who is plainly in difficulty and you don't know what to do, you may say quietly, "Tell me how to help you" and then do what you are told. In this way you can be of genuine service.

But whatever you do, try not to ask personal questions. Any questioning or attempted commiseration on the part of a complete stranger is, of course, in worst possible taste.

When you meet a friend for the first time, you might perhaps without going into personal detail, tell him briefly how sorry you were to hear of the bad time he had. Or if you know that he has shown extraordinary grit, you can tell him when you say good-bye, "Everyone says you were wonderful!" or "I want you to know how swell I think you are!" The point to keep in mind is that he wants to forget his handicap—if he possibly can—and the only way he can is for others to show they are not remembering.

WHEN THE DISABLED MAN IS HER SON OR HUSBAND OR BETROTHED

The supreme requirement of tact is that which will be exacted of the "one" whom a badly disfigured or disabled man in hospital most longs, yet most fears, to see. Whether she be wife or mother or sweetheart she will do well to be prepared for that first meeting when, with long accumulated fear he searches her face to measure the degree of his handicap by its effects on her.

One thing therefore which every woman so tested must do is school herself to meet the difficulty of keeping tears under control when she first sees the one she loves who is still bearing the evidences of suffering. In this, or in any other case, she must above everything remember that abandonment to tears is not the way to help him. The one thing that does help is to make him realize that to her he is not any different from the man he was—and to assure him that in the years to come he is *not* to be set apart.

FLAG ETIQUETTE

The flag is displayed from sunrise to sunset. The flag may be displayed at night only on special occasions when the object is to produce a patriotic effect.

The flag displayed with the Union (stars) down is the signal of dire distress.

When a flag is hung either horizontally or perpendicularly, the blue field should be at the flag's upper right corner and at the observer's left.

The flag should never be draped, but always hung in straight lines. Strips of red, white, and blue bunting instead of the flag should be used for decorating. When this bunting is used horizontally, the blue band must be at the top.

The flag should never have placed upon it or attached to it any mark, insignia, letter, figure design, picture or drawing.

The flag should never touch anything beneath it: ground, floor, water, or merchandise.

The flag should never be carried flat or horizontally, always aloft and free.

When to indicate mourning the flag is at half-staff, the flag should be hoisted to the peak for an instant and then lowered to half-staff. Before lowering for the day, it should be raised to the top and then lowered.

To indicate mourning when the flag is fastened to a small staff (as when carried in a parade), two streamers of black crêpe are attached to the spearhead and allowed to fall.

When covering a casket, absolutely nothing may be put on it—neither flowers nor leaves. The blue field of the flag is at the head of the casket and over the left shoulder of the deceased. The casket is carried foot-end-foremost. The flag must not be lowered into the grave nor allowed to touch the ground.

Nothing but the Bible should ever be placed on the flag. It should never be placed so that it could be struck by a gavel.

When the flags of several countries are displayed together, international etiquette requires that the flags be of equal size and that the flag of the home country be placed at the left (as seen by the observer) or else that it be placed in the center of many flags.

Whenever the colors are passing, every person must halt if walking or rise if sitting, and every man uncover.

When a man (or woman) is in uniform, he gives the military salute to the flag. In civilian dress, a man removes his hat and holds it over his heart; a woman simply stands quietly.

The national flag is always carried on the right or in front of other flags in a parade (as color bearers are facing) with the exception of the Church flag. When the national flag is flown from the same staff as another flag, the other flag is beneath the national flag, again excepting the Church flag.

When used on a rostrum, it should be displayed above and behind the speaker's chair.

The flag may never be worn as the whole or part of a costume. When worn as a badge, it should be worn over the left breast, or on the left lapel of a collar.

Do not display the flag on a float in a parade except from a staff. Do not embroider it upon cushions or handkerchiefs, nor print it on paper napkins.

When unfit for further use, a flag should be destroyed by respectfully committing it to the flames.

NATIONAL ANTHEM

The same exactions apply to the national anthem. We must stand whenever it is played or sung to us; this means in our presence. We do not rise, however, when it accompanies the action seen on the stage or the screen—because we have no part in the scene.

When the anthem is played to us and the flag is not displayed, all present should stand and face the music. When the flag is displayed, all stand and face the flag. Those in uniform salute at the first note and retain this position until the last note. We all show the same respect to the anthems of our allies.

When the anthem closes a performance, we must not begin to collect our belongings or to put on our hats or gloves or to even button our coats, during the playing of the "Star-Spangled Banner"

Index

Absent-mindedness, an unintended rudeness, 22
Acceptance or regret notes, 116–124; informal, 121; in official Washington, 619
Accuracy of maids' duties and schedules, 313
Acknowledgment of sympathy, 278–279
Addressing, business letters, 509; cards for newlyweds, 105; children, 506; envelopes, 92, 498, 507; important personages, 527–535, 614–616; letters to Military personnel, 627; Military marriage announcements, 100; Royalty, 3, 527; visiting cards, 98
Adoption, announcement of, 270; marriage of child of, 254
Advice, to the beginner who engages a general maid, 313–315; to the novice driver, 583; to novice travelers, 599
Afternoon meal at card party, 405
Afternoon tea parties, 114, 125; etiquette at, 130; menu for, 126, 129; proper clothes for, 458; table equipment for, 128; with dancing, 125; without dancing, 127
Air travel, special aspects of, 601
Aisle of theater, going down the, 64, 69
À la carte menu, 57
Ambassador, American, 500, 615; French, 619
"American Plan," meals, 57; hotel and tips, 606
Americans, hospitality of, 413, 431; in a foreign country, 615; in London clubs, 568; neighborhood customs, 401–406; respect to Orientals, 612; service, 363; rudeness at table, 361; tradition of, 362; traveling abroad, 609
Anniversaries, birthday, 182; engagement announced on own, 255; wedding, 253
Announcements, of adoption, 270; of birth of war babies, 635–636; of dinner, 353; of engagements, 182–184; of guests, 311, 350; of long engagement, 185; of names on telephone, 552; of new address, 105; of persons of rank, 350–351; of simplified wedding, 259; of son's engagement, 255; of wedding, 103–104; of wedding of adopted child, 254
Announcing guests, 350; persons of high rank, 350–351
Answering formal telephoned invitations, 123–124; informal invitations, 120–123; invitations on visiting cards, 89, 119; wedding invitations, 106
At the beach, 53; opera, theater, and other public gatherings, 61–70
Anxious hostess, persistence of, 424
Apology of late guest, 354; when and how to apologize, 19, 65, 69
Archbishop, addressing an, 614

Army and Navy post, etiquette, 624–628; girls visiting at, 630
Art of being a house guest, 426, 428–430
Artichokes, how eaten, 488
Artists and entertainers, courtesy toward, 433
Asking for a dance, 142
Asparagus, how eaten, 488
"At Home," cards, 115; in garden, 134; in Washington, 622; lady of the house is, 84; "Not at Home," 79, 83
Attracting attention, avoidance of, 49, 455
Automobile, etiquette of motorists, 581–586

Babies, at table, 482; thanks for present, 512
Bachelor, dance, 167; dinner, 212, 359, 360; entertaining, 165; house party, 167; invitations, 120
Back yard hospitality, 398
Bacon, eaten with fork, 489
Baggage, amount for travel, 610
Ball, 135–143; ball beautiful, 136–137; decorations, 136; distinction vanished, 139–140; dress for, 465–466; etiquette, 139; for débutante, 109–112; 146–147; host, 139; hostess receives, 138; in private house, 138; invitations, 107, 135–136; invitation asked for stranger, 136; list is borrowed, 136; not a dancing school, 143; preparation for, 135; public ball, 143; supper, 137; to be patron, 107; ushers at, 140
Banquet guests, 436
Beach, behavior at public, 53; clambake on, 398
Beauty of living, contribution to, 591–598
Behavior, as house guest, 427; at beach, 53; at circus, 69; at clubs, 565; at dancing, 141; at games, 69; at meals, 488; at opera, 62; at park, 54; at parties, 395–406; at playgrounds, 54; at restaurant, 56; at theater, 65; attracting attention, 49; cheapness of, 174; of children, 283; of confidential secretary, 554; of a lady, 589; of a gentleman; 18, 50, 587; while driving, 584
Beginning a conversation, 40–41; 43–44; a letter, 502, 507, 508, 510
Bellboy, at hotel, 603, 606; tipping, 606
Bell, draping mourning, 273
Belles of yesterday, 147
Bereavement, in time of, 271–285
Be tranquil! Don't be afraid! 40–41
Best forms of speech, 28–38
Best man, after ceremony, 232–233; at church, 230; at rehearsal, 215; at simplified wedding, 259; at small wedding, 240; choice of, 207; clothes of, 209; du-

641

ties before wedding, 222, 223; gift for, 251; position in ceremony, 215, 217, 231
Best people, xi–xiii
Beverages served, at afternoon parties, 127, 386; at bridge, 386; at formal dinner, 335; burgundy, 335; champagne, 335; cocktails, 131; coffee ceremony, 409; luncheon, 376; whiskey, 336; wines, 335, 344
Bible, simple language of, 29
Birds, not eaten with fingers, 489
Birthday cards, 89
Birthstones, 182
Blunders in table service, 369; serving dinner, 324–328
Bones removed from mouth at table, 489
Boring conversation, 42, 45; of doting mother, 41
Boutonnières for ushers, 140, 210, 230
Bow, informal, 21; "cut," 22; of ceremony, 20; of woman, 21; when to, 22
Boy, being introduced, 7, 20; clothes for college, 480; "Mr." on cards of, 74; removes hat, 20
Box visiting at theater, 62
Bread and butter, eating, 490; letter, 513–517; letter for blind date, 157; plate, 374
Breakfast, hunt, 377; in hotel room, 377, 605; invitation to, 99; setting for, 321; tray service, 421; wedding, 99, 193, 237, 241
Bride, after ceremony, 232; at double wedding, 218–219; at rehearsal, 213; bridal table, 238–239; cake, 239, 241–242; essential linen list, 200–201; flippancy or radiance, 246; goes to church, 227, 230; in ceremony, 231–232; in everyday clothes, 257–259; in her thirties, 255–256; parents provide wedding, 250; protesting, 257; receives at church, 191; receives at reception, 235, 236; record of presents, 193–194; thanks for gifts, 194; travel clothes, 243; trousseau, 197–198; unthinking, 255; wedding dress, 201–202; who goes to live in husband's town, 263
Bridegroom, at ceremony, 230; at home, 235; breach of etiquette to give wedding, 193; bridesmaid of, 207; entrance of, 216; expenses of, 251; parents of, 233, 243, 248; present of bride to, 220; toast to, 242; trousseau of, 208, 259; wedding clothes of, 209
Bridesmaids, and ushers' dinner, 212; at ceremony, 232; at double wedding, 218; at house wedding, 245–246; at morning wedding, 192; at reception, 233, 242; at small wedding, 240; carry in hand, 204–205; clothes, 203–204; cost of being a, 205; dressed alike, 257–258; gifts for, 211–212; groom's, 207–208; in mourning, 204; in the procession, 214–216; number of, 205
Bridge, after-meal ice water, 377; dessert, 404–405; giving a, 385–386; good loser, 575; guest prize, 405; lunch, 376–377;

mannerisms at table, 575; overbidding, 574; players, pleasant and unpleasant, 573–574; playing for money, 575–576; poor player, 576; refreshments, 386–387, 405, 406
Budgeting clothes of, a young man, 475; college boy, 480; college girl, 461; gentleman, 468–481; lady, 454–467; travel, 463, 609
Buffet parties, 387; begins, 390–391; guests at, 387; invitations, 388; menu, 389–390; setting table, 388
Bundles, gentlemen and, 50
Bungling a dinner, 324
Burgundy, how to serve, 335
Burial, only intimates attend, 277
Business letters, 507–508
Business, etiquette in, 544–559; announcing names on telephone, 552; a poor saleswoman, 558; business gifts, 551; business women, 547; character and tact with customers, 551–552; from the customer's point of view, 557; general stenographer, 549; good manners, 545; secretary's behavior outside business hours, 556; ideal business woman, 549; importance of suitable appearance, 556; inconsiderate customer, 559; lunching with employer, 551; office discipline, 550; perfect secretary, 548; protecting employer's interest, 553–554; reason for lost positions, 549–550; rules of poker good in, 545; saleswoman versus customers, 557; secretary prepares for journey, 555–556; self-made man, 545–546; sex banned, 547–548; should stenographer rise, 552; son of self-made man, 546–547; sportsmanship in giving and taking, 552–553; store etiquette, 556–557; successful saleswoman, 557–558; tact essential, 558–559; telephone in an office, 551; unconventional situations, 554–555; well-run office, 544–545; "x" markers, 546
Business woman, clothes of a, 462–463, 556; conduct of, 547; general stenographer, 549–552; ideal, 549; perfect secretary, 548, 552–556; sex banned in business, 547–548; saleswoman, 556–559
Butler, duties of a, 293–295; in the dining room, 337
Butter, knife for, 490; plate for, 374; spreading of, 490

Cabaret, 143
Café brûlot, how to make, 366
Cake, christening, 270; wedding, 238, 241
Camps, visits of girls to training, 630
Candles, for formal dinner, 334, 370; no place on lunch or breakfast table, 373
Candlesticks, 370
Cane, right and wrong kinds, 469
Card parties, 404, 574–576
Cards, birthday, 89; children's, 76–77; Christmas, 86–89; fold-over, 77; for reserved pews at wedding, 98; half-en-

INDEX

graved utility, 114; menu, 347; of general invitation, 113; of new or temporary address, 77; of thanks, 184, 517; on wedding gifts, 196, 252; place, 347, 571; p.p.c., 77; playing of, 385, 575; special, 77; train card, 101-102; visiting, 71-84, 89-90
Cardinals, highest ecclesiastical rank, 616; introductions to, 3
Catholic dignitaries, addressing, 614, 616; introducing, 3
Chairman at public dinner, 360
Champagne, serving of, 335
Chaperone, at Big dance, 157; at bachelor's, 167; definition, 160; duties, 161; for protection, 162-163; girl on own, 162; girls who are not particular, 163; mother hen of yesterday, 161-162; parents as, 163; proprieties repealed, 163; resident, 160; today's reversal, 161
Charm, attributes of, 39; greatest asset, 1, 174
Chauffeur, position of, 297
Cheapness, all thoroughbreds hate, 174-175; today's outstanding, 361-362
Check, when paid by a woman, 59, 171
Cheese, how eaten, 491
Chic, a woman who is, 456
Child or puppy, a friend maker, 263-264.
Children, addressing, 506; at funerals, 283; at table, 482; at telephone, 442; behavior exacted of, 283; dressed like their friends, 467; flower girls and pages, 204; in wedding procession, 206; never wear black, 283; teen-age fads, 467; their cards, 76; train bearers, 206-207; nurse for, 305; of Peers, 534; on trains, 600; use of names, 25
Christening, 266-270; arrangements of house for, 269; asking godparents, 266-267; clothes, 269; fee, 269; godparents by proxy, 267; house christening, 268-269; in church, 268; invitations, 266; obligation of being godparent, 267; time, 267-268
Christmas cards, 86-89; colored inks, 89; for whole family, 88; husband's or wife's name first, 87-88; names on, 86-88; to business acquaintances, 88; to one in mourning, 88-89
Church, christening at, 268; decorations, 191, 258; ethics, 1; funeral, 276; greetings in, 16; wedding, 187, 191, 258
Cigarette smoking ethics, 51, 395, 444
Cinderella, wedding of a, 190-191
Circus, conduct at, 69
City life, 54, 265; driving manners, 584
Clergy, at a funeral, 276; clothes of a Protestant, 480
Clothes hangers ready for guests, 413
Clothes, of a gentleman, 468-481; accessories at a glance, 478-480; boys' clothes, 480; college clothes, 480; dinner coat, 469-470, 477, 479; flannel suit, 472; formal afternoon, 470-471, 477; formal evening, 468-469, 477, 478;

jewelry, 472-473; house suit, 470; in the country, 473-474, 478, 479; of Protestant clergy, 480-481; of young man, 475; sack suit, 471-472, 478, 479; sloppy husbands, 474-475; value of valeting, 474; what to wear on various occasions, 477-478; young man budgets his, 475-477
Clothes, of a lady, 454-467; afternoon, 458; children dressed like friends, 467; country, 460; cruise, 467-468; on a boat, 463; do you know how to wear, 454-455; don't exchange a face for a mask, 457; don't get too many, 458-459; following fashion, 455; for business woman, 462-463; for dinners, balls, operas, and concerts, 465-466; hair dressing, 457; how many jewels, 456-457; in a restaurant, 458; gloves, 459-460; guests at wedding, 460-461; hostess less dressed than guests, 466-467; on a motor or train trip, 463; hat, 459; sheep, 455-456; riding, 464-465; teen-age fads, 467; to wear at home, 466; when income is limited, 457; when in doubt, 459; woman who is chic, 456; well-dressed girl at college, 461-462; vulgar clothes, 455
Clubs and club etiquette, 560-572; election to, 561-563; country, 564; good manners in, 565-566; grill and saucepan, 407-409; informal, 566; etiquette in London, Paris, and New York, 568; delegate to convention, 570-571; arrangements for guest speakers, 571; meeting, 569-570; unbreakable rules, 569; visitors in a, 566-568; perfect clubman, 566; women's, 564-565; supper, 143
Coat of arms, when used, 94, 197, 498
Cocktails, 131; serve with, 131; saying "no" to, 131-133; olives and cherries in, 492
Coffee, café brûlot, 366; ceremony, 409; informal service of, 365; in the living room, 382; ways to serve, 357n
Colds, spreading germs of, 452
College, blind date, 157-158; fraternity house party, 150-155; fraternity pin, 158; graduation, 155-156; dining room etiquette, 158; pick-ups, 158; popularity and hospitality at, 149-159; prom, 157; titles of faculty, 158; well-dressed girl at, 461-462
Colonial house of perfection, 419
Commencement invitations, 159
Community, position in, 263
Companion, position of, 290
Complimentary close for letters, 502, 514
Condiments, use for and eating of, 484, 491
Condolence letters, 524
Conduct, at a public beach, 53; at games and circus, 69; how far may girl run after man, 177; of friends of bereaved, 275-276; on street, 49-52; opera and theater, 63-69; parks and playgrounds,

54; public places, 53–54, 69; picnic, 53; restaurant, 55–60; tea, 130
Congratulatory letters, 521–524
Consideration of servants, 60, 288–289, 306–310
Conspicuous in attracting attention, 49
Contribution to beauty of living, 591–598; divorce, 592; friendly flower giving, 596; he gives her flowers, 596; in-law situations, 594, 595; old house coat habit, 591; parents who live with children, 593; respecting private lives of neighbors, 593; tact, 593–594; we must send flowers, 597–598; woman sends flowers to man, 597; young war wife, 595; whether you are hostess or guest, 426–437; art of being house guest, 426; courtesy towards artists and performers, 433–434; courtesy to celebrity, 434; don't—when you are hostess, 436; do—when you are guest, 436; favors taken for granted, 435; first aid to successful hostess, 431–432; details of interest to hostess, 431; guest no one invites again, 437–438; guest on yacht, 430; guests at banquet, 436; give and take of hospitality, 432–443; hostess enters last, 436; how expert visitors look after own comfort, 429–430; ideal house guest, 428; inexcusable behavior to friends who are professionals, 434–435; take own sports clothes, 427; receiving guests in club or restaurant, 436; to be always in demand, 429; when you leave before party is over, 430; when you stay in little house, 430; when you are hostess, 430–431; you can send yourself a telegram, 428;
Convention meeting problems, 570–572
Conversation, 40–48; beginning a, 40, 43–44; dangers, 46–47; fishing for topics, 43; if you are a doting mother, 41; cramming for, 44; the bore, 45; humor, 43; once is effective, 42; personal remarks, 47; maxims, 40–41, 42, 48; "omniscience" of the very rich, 47–48; tact, 44–46, 47; tabus, 46; think before you speak, 41; those who speak too easily, 42; time-takers, 45; topics, 41–42, 43; without introduction, 12, 13; to bridegroom, 236–237; telephone, 440–441
Cook, dress of, 299; gentleman, 408; position of, 298; submitting menu, 299
Corn on cob, to be eaten neatly, 491
Correspondence, formal, 495–526; choice of paper, 495–500; country house stationery, 499–500; complimentary close, 502–504; address plainly, 507; business letters, 507–509; bread and butter letter, 513; dating, 501; daughters, sons, and children, 506; examples, 514–517; formal notes, 511; for present sent after wedding, 512; for present to baby, 512–513; folding letter, 501–502; how to improve letter's appearance, 495; intimate notes, 511–512; letters of thanks, 510–512; mourning paper, 501; name of divorcée, 506; never "Mrs.," 514–515; note of apology, 509–510; official paper, 500–510; printing, 499; return address, 498–499; sequence of pages, 501; salutation, 502; sealing wax, 502; signature, 504; social note, 508–509; stamping, 498; woman never uses crest, 498; when "Mr." is correct, 505; use of "esquire," 506; widow uses husband's name, 506
Corsage bouquets, 596
Country, house and its hospitality, 413–425; anxious hostess, 424; breakfast tray advantages, 421; at the dinner hour, 418; bedtime, 418; clothes for, 460, 473, 478; club membership, 564; don'ts for hostesses, 424; dressing table and desk, 416; energetic hostess, 423–424; greeting of host, 413; greeting of the hostess, 414; guest card, 417–418; guest room, 414–415; guest-room service, 420–421; houses we like to stay in, 423; how tips are given, 422; hostess in her own spare room, 415–416; little house of perfection, 418–420; house party of many guests, 413; no shutters that bang, 417; plenty of hangers, 417; perfect hostess, 425; room for every guest, 414; stationery for, 499–500; tips, 421–422; tray service, 421
Courtesy, consideration of telephone operator's angle, 441–442; for those with antipathy to cats, 437; favors taken for granted, 435; inexcusable behavior to friends who are professionals, 434–435; in Far East, 612; keep your germs to yourself, 452–453; party-line, 442; radio, 447; to a celebrity, 434; to elderly domestic employees, 24; to one's household, 306, 410; toward artists and entertainers, 433–434
Courtship, 180–186
Crepe for mourning is no more, 281
Crest, 197, 498; on wedding invitations, 94–95
Cruelty of New York, 265
Cruise, clothes for, 463–464
Culture (see *Etiquette*)
Customer, manner to, 556–559
"Cut direct," 22
Cutting in, 141; on strangers, 158

Dance, after theatre, 68; asking for, 142–143; can be simple, 393; college, 157, 158; cutting in, 141–142; at wedding, 242–243; definition, 137–138; flock system, 141; formal in private house, 138; hostesses, 395; in backyard, 399; invitations, 113, 137, 393–394; music and partners, 394; program, 140–141; refusal, 142; supper, 395; teas with, 125; ushers, 140, 394
Dangerous letters to avoid, 540–542
Dates, 157–158
Daughter, conventions for, 160–170; introduction of, 6; living with, 595;

INDEX

mourning worn by, 282; only one, 90; questions and answers for, 90, 168; "running wild," 169, sorority house party for, 158, 159
Death, in time of, 271–285
Débutante, 144–148; ball for, 109, 144–145; belles of yesterday, 147–148; "don'ts" for, 147; dress, 145; friends receive, 145; in confidence to a, 145–147; invitation to ball for, 109–110; popular, 148; successful, 148
Decorations, big church made small, 191; for elaborate wedding, 189; for house wedding, 244; of bride's house, 223–225; of church, 189–190; of church for wedding, 258; of table at wedding reception, 259
Dessert, clearing table for, 346; serving of, 346, 404
Diagrams of table setting, 340–343, 348
Dinner giving, modern, 363–371; by Mrs. Three-in-One, 379–384; detailed directions for formal, 328
Dinners, at little tables, 392; at the dinner hour, 418; before theater, 63–64; clothes for, 465, 469; engagements, 329; everyday, 363–370; by Mrs. Three-in-One, 379–384; formal, 323–362; formal invitations to, 115–116, 619; giving a successful, 370; official, in Washington, 619–621; or supper, 371; out-of-doors, 410–412; public, 360–361; regrets and acceptances, 116–117
Diplomatic reception, 618
Dishes of food, how served and eaten, 129, 345, 369, 484–493; served at left, removed from right, 338
Dishing, proper way of, 369
Divorce, 592–593
Divorced parents of bride, 110–111, 247, 248; of bridegroom, 248
Divorcée, takes name of husband before last, 75, 506; remarriage of, 105
Domestic servants, 60, 288–306, 309–313; management of, 306
Don't, ask "What are you doing Saturday?" 441; be afraid, be tranquil, 40; for débutante, 147; for all house-party visitors, 152–155; for hostesses, 424; for letters overseas, 631; exchange face for mask, 457; get too many clothes, 458–459; let small child answer telephone, 442–443; make false signals, 583–584; manners that please no man, 174; smoking, 446; wear mirror-lined divers' helmets, 150
Door opened to visitor, 83
Doting mothers, 41
Drawing room, how to enter, 85
Dress, at home, 466; christening, 269; children's nurse, 305; business woman, 462–463, 556; bride, 201, 255; bridesmaids, 203; bridegroom, 209; business secretary, 292, 462–463, 556; children, 467; college girls, 461; companion, 390–391; dinner, balls, opera, and concerts, 465–466; cocktail parties, 458; gentleman, 468–481; going-away, 243; governess, 304; for a cruise, 463–464; in the country, 460; lady, 454–467; lady's maid, 302; mourning, 280–285; on motor or train trip, 463; on a boat, 463; restaurant, 55, 458; riding, 464–465; teas, 458; travel, 609–610; train bearers, 206; servants, 289–305; registered nurse, 304–305; ushers, 209–211; waitress, parlor maid and housemaid, 301; wedding guest, 460–461; well-dressed girl in college, 461–462; teen-age fads, 467; fraternity house party, 150–152; gloves, 17, 230, 231, 459–460; débutante, 145; garden party, 133; man's formal, 61; man's hat, 18–20, 61; in restaurant, 55, 458; opera, 62–63, 465; theater, 67, 465; wrong, 152
Dressing-rooms, 310, 349–350, 414; in well-appointed houses, 306
Drink and driving do not mix, 582–586
Drinks served at meals (see *Beverages*)
"Dunking," in coffee, 487; in gravy, 488

Eating etiquette, 485; bread and butter, 490; corn on cob, 491; do's and don'ts, 487; fish, 489; fowl, 489; sopping bread in gravy, 488; soup, 491; vegetables, 488; with fingers, 488, 493; zigzag, 484
Ecclesiastical precedence at functions, 616
Ecclesiastics, rank of, 616; vestments of, 480
Eggs, ways of eating, 486
Elbows on table, not attractive, 486
Election into a club, 561–563
Embarrassing food difficulties, 484
Employer-employee relationship, 438, 544–556
Endings for letters, 503, 514, 538
Enemies bury hatchets at dinner, 356
Engaging, a general maid, 313; help for a well-appointed house, 290–305
Engagements, 180–186; approved, 180; announcement, 182–183, 255, 401–403; acceptable gifts, 186; broken, 116, 186; couple and chaperone, 185–186; couple in public, 184; duties of accepted suitor, 180; before announcement, 182; etiquette of engaged, 185; fraternity pin, 158; his parents call, 180; long engagement, 185; meeting of kinfolk, 185; present, 181, 184; ring, 181; showers, 184, 401–403; importance of dinner, 329–330
Engraved card forms, 91–124
Entertaining, by bachelor, 165–168; by young girl, 164; on modest means, 173; "pay party," 174; service in formal, 310. (See *teas, formal dinner,* etc.)
Envelopes, addressing business, 507; for gentlemen, 348; formal, 91, 507; for invitations, 92; printed, 498
Etiquette, ballroom, 139; cultured speech, 27, 69; débutante, 145–147; drinking health, 183; club, 560–572; dance, 395; engaged couples, 185; funeral, 275;

guest, 426–430, 436; hostess, 430–437; house party, 152–155; paying, 171–173; radio, 447–449; public gatherings, 61–70; punctuality, 450–452; illness, 452–453; sorority house, 158–159; smoking, 444–447; table, 482–494; telephone, 438–444; store, 556–559; street, 49–52; tea, 130; theatre, 65; true meaning of, 1–2; wedding reception, 260–262; breach of, 193; gloves and napkin, 354–355; business, 544–559; in clubs of London, Paris, and New York, 568; flag, 639–640; service, 308; travel, 599–612; White House, 620

Europe, Americans in, 611–615; clothes for traveling in, 609; clubs of, 568

Evening clothes, gentleman's, 468, 469, 477, 478; lady's, 465, 466

"Excuse me, please," 69

Excuse my glove, 17

Expenses, funeral, 272; wedding, 220, 245, 250, 251

Face exchanged for mask, 457
Faculty, titles of, 158
Fashion, following of, 455–466
Fat and fashion, 466
First names, cheapness of, 23–24; of domestic employees, 24; worst taste, 25
Fish, removing bones while eating, 490
Flannels, etiquette of wearing, 472, 478
Flat silverware, choice and usage, 316–322, 370
Flowers, for guests, 571; friendly giving, 596; when he gives flowers to her, 596–597; when a woman sends to a man, 597; we must send, 597–598
Food, at little tables, 392; attacking complicated dish, 356; how served, 337, 345; out of doors, 410
Footman, position of, 295
Foreign languages, knowledge of, 611; pronunciation, 37
Fork, at table setting, 321, 331, 333, 370; or fingers, 485; proper use of, 486; uses, 318–322
Formal dinner, 323–361; announcing guests, 350; announcing persons of rank, 350–351; asking someone to fill a place, 329; attacking complicated dish, 356; bread, 345; butler in dining room, 337; can be bungled, 324–328; correct service, 337–338; courteous hostess, 343; clearing table, 346; detailed directions, 328; dishes presented, 338; dessert service, 346–347; duty of host, 352; enemies must bury hatchet, 355; envelopes for gentlemen, 348; ever-present plate, 338; exchange plate, 338; filling glasses, 343–344; gentlemen return, 358; great American rudeness, 361–362; guest of honor, 347; how a hostess receives, 351–352; in house of widow, 341–342; in a great house, 323–324; importance of dinner engagements, 329–330; late guest, 354; leaving the table, 357–358; menu, 330–331, 371; more than one service, 339; menu card, 347; manners of hostess, 353–354; manners at table, 355; napkins on plate, 333–335; place cards, 347; plate removed, 337; presenting dishes, 345; public dinner, 360–361; selection of people, 328–329; setting places, 332–333; setting table, 331–332; putting on glasses, 333; silver that shines, 335; order of precedence, 339–341; of eight — no host, 343; serving table, 345–346; seating, 347; sidewalk, hall, and dressing rooms, 349–350; "stag" dinner, 359–360; taking leave, 358–359; toasts, 360–361; turning of table, 354; table diagram, 348–349; two plates at a time, 338–339; when dinner is announced, 353; when there is no host, 353; wines, 335–337

Formal luncheon, 372–373
"Formal" and "informal," 33
Frankness of today, 578
Fraternity, dress of guests, 150–152; house-party week, 150
Friend introducing friend, 7
Friendly, at games and sports, 578; flower giving, 596; house guest, 426; notes, 121
Frock coat, of Protestant clergy, 480; when worn, 471, 478
Fruits, how to eat, 484, 490
Full dress for gentleman, accessories for, 478–480; at opera, 477; formal, 468, 477
Fundamentals of good behavior, as house guest, 427; at beach, 53; at games, 69; of a gentleman, 18, 50, 587; of a lady, 589; of a motorist, 581–584; of a secretary, 554
Funerals, 271–285; acknowledgment of sympathy, 278–279; another may write notes, 379; behavior of children, 283; clergyman, 273; crêpe veil is no more, 280; director, 272–273; "funeral home," 278; good taste in mourning, 283; hanging the bell, 273; honorary pallbearers, 273; house arrangement, 278; keep accurate list of flowers, 274; length of mourning for men, 284; little children never wear black, 283; member of family in charge, 274; memorial service, 278; arranging flowers, 274–275; conduct of friends, 275; church funeral, 276; funeral at house, 277; few attend burial, 277; mourning, 274, 279–285; music, 277; newspaper notice, 271–272; notify people, 271; poor taste in mourning, 283; processional, 276; "sitting up" no longer necessary, 275; widow's mourning, 281–282; young widow, 282
Furniture, becoming, 287; outdoor, 410–412

Games, outdoor and circus, 69; and sports, 573–580; bridge players, 573–576; don'ts for those who would be sought after, 594; if you want to go to bed, don't begin, 400; golf, 576–577; sportsmanship, 577–580

INDEX

Garden parties, 133
Gentlemen, as hosts, 167, 352, 407–414; at formal dinner, 339–343; bows, 21; and bundles, 50; cook; ladies look on, 408–409; code of a, 587–590; dress of, 468–481; envelopes for, 348; foreign, kisses hand, 17; invitations, 120; lifts hat, 19; must take initiative, 175–177; name on cards, 72, 73–74; offers his arm, 50–51; precedes lady, 51, 64, 66–67, 69; perfect clubman, 566; removes hat, 18; rises, 20; return to drawing room, 358; seats lady on right, 52; shakes hands when introduced, 16; smoke on street, 51; who substitutes for host, 342–343
Gifts, engagement, 181, 184, 186; exchanging, 211; for bride's attendants, 211; exchanging, 197; for bridegroom, 220; for ushers, 213; of bride, 220; to ushers, 213; "thank you," 152, 510–517; business, 551; wedding, 191–196, 251–252
Girl, accepts fraternity pin, 158; chaperoned, 162; college, 149, 461; débutante, 144–147; don'ts for, 152–154; engaged, 180–186; entertained by, 164; first name on correspondence, 496; graduation, 155; house party for, 150; of fifteen, 164; on overnight journey, 164; popularity of college, 149; with modern man, 171
Glasses, on dinner table, 333, 371; filling, 343
Gloom letters, 539
Gloves, gentleman removes, 17; lady never removes, 17; when to wear, 459–460
Godparents at christening, 266; by proxy, 267
Golf, etiquette of, 564, 576
Good breeding, 2, 27; business etiquette, 544–559; driving manners, 581; loser at cards, 575; manners at club, 565; manners while eating, 486; mixers, 545; speech, 27–39; taste, 2
"Good mixers," 545
Graduation of college girl, 155
Greetings, 15–22; acknowledging introductions, 15; bride and groom in church, 191; at house wedding, 244–245; at simplified wedding, 259; at wedding reception, 233–237; by stranger at wedding, 261–262; by young people, 17; of host, 413; of hostess, 414; on campus, 158; in church, 16
Grill and Sauce Pan Club, host at, 407–409
Guest, announcing a, 311, 350; art of being, 426; do—when you are, 436; guest room, 414; ideal house guest, 428; looks after own comfort, 429–430; on yacht, 430; guests at a banquet, 436, 460–461; flowers for, 511; no one invites again, 427–428; speakers, arrangements for, 576; room for every, 414; when you stay in little house, 430; when you leave before party is over, 430; who is guest of honor, 347–348, 436–437; when you are late, 354; when guests smoke, 445–446; who is guest of honor, 347–348, 436–437

Hair dressing, importance of, 457
Hand, held in lap while eating, 493
Handshake, personality of a, 17; when proper to, 9
Hat, gentleman removes, 18; lifts, 19; boy removes, 20; shall I wear a, 459
"Home" and "house" meaning of, 32
Hospitality, country house and its, 413–425; give and take of, 432; in college, 149–159; neighborhood customs, 401–406; newcomer's return of, 168; not dependent on wealth, 384; of hosts, 407–412; "pot-luck," 431; to newcomer, 168
Host, bachelor, 167–168; dons chef's cap, 407; duty of, 352; greeting of, 413–414; Grill and Sauce Pan Club, 407–409; hospitable, 407–412; the perfect, 139; substitute for, 342, 343; when there is no, 353
Hostess, alone, 392–393; anxious, 424; at the side, 348–349; after dinner, 358; courteous never served first, 343; don't when you are, 436; details of interest to, 431; dance, 395; don'ts for, 424; energetic, 423–424; first aid to successful, 431–432; greeting of, 414; in own spare room, 415–416; in restaurant, 59; enters last, 436; less dressed than guests, 466–467; manners of, 353–354; perfect, 425; receives at formal dinner, 351–352; receives at ball, 138; prepares to give ball, 135; receiving guests in club or restaurant, 436; rules of escape for helpless, 382–383; or guest, 426–437; turning of the table, 355; when you are, 430–431; whether you are hostess or guest, 426–437
Hotels, American plan, 59; arrival at, 602–603; breakfast in your room, 605; calling on people in, 608; in restaurant alone, 607–608; leaving, 608; other items of service, 605; registering, 603–604; rules of propriety, 605–606; stationery, 605; tips, 606, 610; to assure accommodations, 602
House, country, 412–425; ideal guest, 428–430; little house of perfection, 418–420; we like to stay in, 423; well-appointed, 286–315
House party, bachelor's, 167–168; don't for all visitors, 153–155; fraternity, 150–155; of many guests, 413; "thank you" present, 152
House wedding, 244–245; at least expense, 245; differs from church wedding, 245–246
Household linen, bride's, 200; marking of, 202
Housemaid, position of, 300; dress, 301
Humor, gift of, 43

"I beg your pardon," when and how to say, 19, 65, 69
Ideal, business woman, 549; hostess, 353, 431; house guest, 428–430
Ill-bred, bridge player, 576; cheapness evident, 23, 174, 361; conversational bore, 45; inconsiderate customer, 559; in letter writing, 543; hostess' "don'ts," 361, 424; motorists, 581; please no man, 174; serving dinner, 324; speech, 40–47
Important personages, how to address, 527–535
Informal, clothes, 150, 464, 477, 556; clubs, 566; dinners, 363, 410; introductions, 10; parties, 150, 387, 398; speech, 33
In-laws, difficult situations of, 594; introducing, 6; letter from bride to, 514; living with, 595; mourning worn by, 284; names for, 25; perfect relationship of, 595
Intentional slighting, 22
Interviewing household help, 313–315
Intimate correspondence, 511
Introductions, correct forms, 3–6; conversational, 5–6; conversation without, 13; another man to wife, 5; by letter, 14, 507–520; acknowledging, 15; ecclesiastical, 616; forms to avoid, 6–7; for youth, 7; husband to friends, 5; labels serve as, 571; letters of, 517; military personnel, 624–628; most ceremonious, 3; of domestic employee, 13–14; of relatives-in-law, 6; of people in services, 627–628; persons of high rank, 527–535, 613; oneself, 14; order of presentation, 3; "present," 3; response to, 8–9; roof of friend, 8; "This is," 5; typical, 4–5; when to, 11–12; when not to, 12; shake hands, 9, 16; one person to group, 11; young woman to man at dinner, 8; Washington officials, 3, 613–623
Invitations, 96–124; answer to, wedding, 106; acceptance or regret, 116–117; anniversary, 105; ball, 107, 108–112, 135–136; by organization, 118; by telephone, 123–124, 440–441; by bachelor, 120; christening, 266; dance, 113, 137; engraved forms, 91–124; expensive, 172; formal written, 115–116; for stranger, 112–113; general card of, 113–114; informal, 120–123; in place of visit, 79; luncheon, 372; on visiting card, 89, 118–119; other formal, 106–107; more than one hostess, 117; parties in garden, 134; recalled, 116; receptions and teas, 114–115; reminders, 124; showers, 401; telegraphed, 119–120; to be patron, 107; to war wives, 635; wedding, 91–103, 104–105, 187–189, 220, 251–252

Jewels, how to be worn, 456; suitable for a gentleman, 472
Jewish weddings, 248
Joining a club, 560–567
Junior etiquette (see *Boys, Girls*)

Kissing the hand of a lady, custom of, 17
Kitchen finds itself in society, 409–410; maid's position, 300
Knife, as a pusher, 488; for salads, 493; types of, for all occasions, 316–322

Lady, instincts of a, 589; on the right, 52; precedes, 69
Lady's maid, position of, 301
Language, knowledge of foreign, essential for travel, 611; thorough command of English important, 27–39; 69, 70
Lateness in keeping appointments, 69, 354, 450
Leave-taking, proper forms of, 16
Legal change of names, 26
Letters, an answer to, xi; business, 507–509; bread and butter, 157; condolence, 524–526; congratulations, 521–524; dangerous, 540–542; formal, 495–526; introduction, 517–520; formal introduction, 518; informal introduction, 519; introduction by, 519–520; indirect letter of introduction, 520; longer, 536–543; recommendation, 521–522; resignation, 521; paper, 495–497; to men in services, 627
Life in crowded cities, 54
Little Jack Horner Shelf of Welcome, 383, 384
Linen, in trousseau, 197–201; marking, 199–201; mourning, 285; table, 198–199
Liveries, for caterer's men, 138; mourning, 285; of butler, 295; of footman, 296–297
Lobster, how to eat, 492
London clubs, etiquette in, 568
Long letters, 536–543
Luggage, amount of needed, 610, condition of, 599
"Lunch," 372, 494
Lunching with employer, 551
Luncheons, breakfasts, and suppers, 372–378; bread and butter plate, 374; beverages, 376; bridge, 376–377; formal, 372–373; invitation, 372; menu, 374–375; service of, 374; table, 373

Maid of honor, as attendant, 205, 231, 234, 240, 242; dress of, 203; gift to, 212; in wedding procession, 214, 218
Maids, in well-regulated houses, 289–293, 300–303, 311; courtesy to, 410
Make-up of face, at wedding, 204; exchanged for mask, 456
Making one's position in new community, 263–265; appearing to be snob, 264; bride who goes to husband's town, 263; child—or puppy, 263–264; cruelty of New York, 265; your first visitors, 264; you who are strangers, 263
Man, and modern girl, 165–168; at formal dinner, 339–343, 358; bachelor, 165, 212, 359–360; best man at wedding, 232, 233; business etiquette of, 544–559; clothes of, 468–481; club etiquette for, 560–572; cook, 408; girl running after, 177; man-

INDEX

ners, 16–21, manners unpleasing to, 174; seats lady at right, 52; stationery, 348, 505; ushers, 140, 207, 394
Management of servants, 306–308
Manners, at a dance, 395; at opera, theater and public gatherings, 61–70; at table 356, 482–494; and "good mixers," 545; in clubs, 565–566; of hostess, 353–354; of enemies, 356; of motorists, 581–586; that please no man, 174; train, 599
Marking, engagement and wedding rings, 219; linen, 199–201; silver, 196
Marriage (see *Wedding*)
Matron of Honor, 203–205; 212
Maxims for those who talk too easily, 481
Meals (see *Dinners, Formal Dinners, Modern Dinners*)
Menus, afternoon tea, 126–127, 129–131; at house wedding, 245; at simplest reception, 259; for formal dinner, 330–331; not a formal, 371; special, 367; wedding, 237–239, 241; wedding breakfast, 240–241; submitting the, 299; lunch, 374–375; dinner by Mrs. Three-in-One, 380–382
Messages on visiting cards, 82, 90
Military and post-war supplement, 624–640, addressing letters, 627; bridegroom's name on invitations, 632–633; announcing new babies, 635–636; comparative ranks, 625–626; certainly write to him, 631; concerning arch of swords, 634; don'ts for letters overseas, 631; flag etiquette, 639–640; how to know you are right, 636–637; knowledge of military rank, 624–627; introducing people in the services, 627–628; letters to, 627; long-awaited furlough, 631; man and girl payments, 629–630; meaning of "address," 628; military customs, 628–629; marriage at camp, 632; names on visiting cards, 633–634; national anthem, 640; our attitude toward disabled veterans, 638; rules of behavior for war wives, 636; social divisions according to military rank, 627; stop a moment and think—please, 637–638; to girls who visit men at camps, 630–631; today's typical wedding, 632; uncertain date, 632; wedding held far from bride's home, 632; wartime simplifications, 634–635; when our veterans come home, 637; when the disabled man is her son or husband or betrothed, 638–639; women's services, 627
Mister, when used, 24–26; "Mr. & Mrs.," use of, 504–506; 603–604
Modern dinner giving, 363–371; American service table setting, 365; café brûlot, 366; blunders in service, 369; dishes that have condiments, 366–367; do not experiment, 368–369; do whatever you can do well, 370; encouragement of praise, 369–370; everyday dinner, 363; giving a successful, 370; informal service of coffee, 365; possibilities of plain cooking, 368; proper dishing, 369; service known as American, 363; special menus, 367–368; three classifications of table service, 363
Modern man and girl, 171–179
Morning wedding, 192; breakfast after, 99, 193, 237, 241
Mother-in-law, getting along with, 594, 595; letter from bride to, 514; introducing one's, 6; name of, 25
Motorists, manners for, 581–586; as to the manners of pedestrians, 586; autocrat of the driver's seat, 582; advice to novice driver, 583; bad manners lead to accidents, 581–582; certain bad manners and women drivers, 585; city driving manners, 584; discourteous horn blowers, 584; don't make false signals, 583–584; drink and driving, 582; drivers we like—and dislike, 584–585; driving sportsmanship, 586; good and bad drivers, 581; headlight menace, 582–583; signals, 583; snail, 582; social rating, 581; stop light, 584
Mourning, behavior of little children, 283–284; by mother, 282; by sister or daughter, 282; crêpe veil is no more, 280; for country wear, 282; for business woman, 282–283; for family-in-law, 284; for funeral, 274, 279; for men, 283; good taste in, 284; little children, 283; length of for men, 284; livery, 285; mourning materials, 280–281; poor taste in, 284; proprieties liberalized, 281; widow's, 281–282; word of economy, 281; young widow, 282
Mrs. Three-in-One gives a dinner party, 379–384; beginning with roast, 381; coffee, 382; floor-standing susans, 380; little Jack Horner shelf of welcome, 383–384; hospitality not dependent on wealth, 384; menu, 380; other details, 382; if you begin with soup, 380; salad, 381; to you who are, 379–380; rules of escape for helpless hostess, 382–383; unanswerable front door, 382
Music, for house funeral, 277; for house wedding, 245; for wedding, 217; for wedding reception, 189

Name, child's use of, 25; divorcée, 506; for parents-in-law, 25–26; first names, 23–24, 25; formality in use of title, 23; esquire, 506; giving one's on telephone, 440; legally changed, 26; on Christmas cards, 87–88; on boy's card, 74; on letters, 504–505, 509; on visiting cards, 72–77, 90; of domestic employees, 24; of safety, 23; over telephone, 26; rules for, 24–25; widow's, 72, 73, 506
Napkin, in lap, 354; on dinner plate, 333; unfolding, 493
Navy and Army Post etiquette, 624–628; girls visiting, 630
Neighbor, behavior toward, 444

Neighborhood customs, American, 401–406
New address cards, 77
Newcomer in town, 168, 263, 264, 613
"Not at home," meaning of, 79, 83
Notes, another may write, 279; bread and butter, 513–517; bride's, 194, 510–512; congratulation, 522–524; acknowledging sympathy, 278–279; informal, 120–123; of apology, 509; of sympathy, 524–526; social, 508–509; thank you, 510–513
Notice of death, 271–285
Novice, advice to, engaging maid, 313–315; motorist, 583; traveler, 599
Nurse, position of, 304
Nursery children, at table, 482; manners of, 483

Odors, bodily, reasons for lost positions, 549, 550
Office etiquette, 544–559
Official Washington, 613–623; American in foreign country, 615–616; dinners, 620–621; ecclesiastical precedence, 616; new arrival, 613; official dinners and forms, 618–619; official visits and days at home, 622; order of precedence in United States, 614–615; paying visits, 622–623; precedence, 614; university and college titles, 616; uses of titles, 616–618; White House etiquette, 620
Olives and celery, serving of, 334
One maid in the home, 311
Once is effective, twice is boring, 42–43
On the street and in public, 49–54; at a public beach, 53–54; don't attract attention, 49–50; enjoyment of public places, 53; gentlemen and bundles, 50; lady not on the left, 52; life in crowded cities, 54; gentleman offers his arm, 50–51; parks and playgrounds, 54; picnic in public, 53; on country by-paths, 51; question of paying, 52
Opera, brilliant night, 62–63; boxes, 62; dress, 63; general conduct, 61–62
Oranges, how to eat, 494
Overnight journey, 164, 599–608

Pallbearers at funeral, 273
Paper, choice of, for letter writing, 496–500
Pardon, to beg one's, 19, 65, 69
Parents, bridegroom's are divorced, 248; at table for small wedding, 240; friendly meeting of divorced, 248; are divorced, 247; groom's mother, 254; helpless mother, 169–170; of bride provide, 250–251; of groom call on bride, 180; seating at double wedding, 219; table of bride's, 239; thought for bridegroom's, 243–244; who must live with children, 595
Paris clubs, etiquette at, 568
Park and playgrounds, behavior at, 54
Parlor maid, position of, 300; dress, 301
Parties, buffet, 387–392; bridge, 172, 385, 404–405; balls and dances, 135–148; clambake, 398; cocktail, 131–133; backyard, 398–399; fraternity house, 150–155; garden, 133–134; hours for, 405–406; identical patterns for, 406; picnics, 395–399; simple, 385–400, 399; tea, 125–131; surprise, 403; warning against surprise, 403
Paying, for calls on neighbor's telephone, 444; expensive invitations, 172; man and girl payments, 629–630; poor man and nice girl, 173; "pay party," 174; question of, 52, 171; woman pays dinner check, 59, 171
Personages, cards of, 75–76; how to address, 527–536
Personality, a business asset, 549; charm of, 1, 39, 174; chief ingredient of hospitality, 414; of a handshake, 17; of a home, 413–425
Personal letters, 536–543; details of importance, 543; difficulty is beginning, 577; dangerous, 540; ending, 538; how to end, 538; how not to begin, 537; how to begin, 537–538; letter no one cares to read, 539; letters of gloomy apprehension, 539; letters of two wives, 540–541; letter everyone loves to receive, 541; letter no woman should write, 541–542; letter no gentleman writes, 542; proper letters of love, 542; the blank, 539; typewritten, 537
Persons of rank, addressing, 527–535; announcing, 350; cards of, 75, 76
Pews at church, 98, 228, 229
Picnics, building fire, 396; clambake, 398; don't try strange place, 397–398; in backyard, 398–399; in public, 53; popularity of, 395–396
Picture of girl to boy, 156–157
Pick-ups on the campus, 158
Place cards, 77, 347, 571
Plain cook, possibilities of, 368
Plates, at dinner, 331–346, 338, 339; ever-present, 338; exchange, 338; leaving food on, 486; napkins on, 333–335; removal of, 337; two plates at a time, 338
Playing for money, 575–576
Poker rules, good in business application, 545
Polish, business asset, 542–549
Popularity, 149–159; in new community, 263–265; lasting or transient, 149–150; secret of, 148, 149, 150; saying "no," 131–133
Port wine, how served, 336
Porter, tipping of, 606, 610
Potato, how to eat baked, 489
P. P. C. cards (*pour prendre congé*—Good-by), sending, 77
Position in community, 263–265; from over the tracks, 178–179
Precedence, American in foreign country, 614–615; diagrams, 340–343; ecclesiastical, 616; in Washington, 614–615; **order of** table, 339–343, 347

INDEX

Praise, encouragement of, 369
Precedence, order of seating at formal dinner, 339–341
Presenting, ecclesiasticals, 3; Royalty, 4; Washington officials, 3
"Present," use of in introduction, 3
Presents—(see Gifts)
President, introducing, 3; in seating at table, 620; Washington society, 613–623
Prinking, 67, 174
Procession and rehearsal of wedding, 206, 213–218, 227, 231
Professionals, imposing on, 433
Pronunciation, 34–36; English accent, 37; French word, 37
Propriety, how a dinner can be bungled, 324–328; a hostess receives at a formal dinner, 351; a name is "put up," 561–562; how far may girl run after man, 177; tips are given, 422–423; many jewels, 456–457; visitor takes leave, 10; a first visit is made, 82–83; to address important personages, 527–535; to begin a letter, 537; to end a letter, 538; to make a speech, 572; not to begin a letter, 537; to enter drawing room, 85; to interview an applicant, 313–315; to propose a toast, 183–184; to sit gracefully, 85–86; as hostess, 353, 430–437; as house guest, 413–428; at clubs, 560–572; at funerals, 271–285; at military camps, 626–637; at public places, 49–69; at table, 482–494; at weddings, 232–251; in business, 544–559; in hotels, 603–616; in sportsmanship, 579–580; while traveling, 599–612; with servants, 306–308
Public gatherings, 61–70
Public places, 53; beaches, 53–54; crowded cities, 54; games and circus, 69; opera and theatre, 61–70; parks and playgrounds, 54; picnics, 53
Pullman, going to bed in a, 599–600
Punctuality, importance of, 450–451; when she keeps him waiting, 451–452
Puppy, good friend maker, 263, 264

Radiance, beautiful quality of bride, 246
Radio, courtesy, 447–448; one fan's solution, 449; why can't engagement be valid, 449–450
Railroad train, children in a, 600; girl alone, 164, 602; manners in a, 599–612; sleeping in a, 599–600
Rank, addressing persons of, 527–535; ecclesiastical, 616; military personnel, 624–628; royalty, 527; Washington officials, 3, 613, 620–623
Receptions, invitations, 114; out-of-door, 125; stranger at wedding, 260–262; wedding, 233–243
Recommendation, letter of, 521
Reference given in application without permission, 157
Registering at a hotel, 603
Regret or acceptance notes, 116–124; informal, 121; to officials in Washington, 619
Rehearsal, wedding, 213–218, 227, 231
Relatives-in-law (see In-laws)
Resignation, letter of, 521
Restaurant etiquette, 55–60; at dinner given in, 56; consideration of those who serve us, 60; entering, 55; in a hotel, 607–608; manners, 60; ordering, 56, 57–58; payment, 59–60; prepayment, 59, 171; sitting, 55, 56; table d'hôte or à la carte, 57; tips, 58–59; what to wear, 458
Retort courteous, 14
Riding clothes, 464, 465
Ring, engagement, 181; wedding, 219; worn at all times, 456
Rise, 10; gentleman, 20, 60
Road manners for motorists, 581–586
Room, for every guest, 414; guest room, 414–415; spare room, 415–417
Royalty, addressing, 3, 4, 527; presenting, 527; seating, 362
R. S. V. P., correct usage of, 110, 111, 119
Rudeness, often due to absentmindedness 22; the great American, 361–362
Rules, definite, of use of names, 24–25; for sports, 577; of behavior of war wives, 626–637; of propriety in hotel, 605–616; of sportsmanship, 579–580; unbreakable, 569

Sack suit, man's, 471–472, 478
Salad eaten without knife, 493
Salesmen and saleswomen, 556–559
Sandwiches, eaten with fingers, 493
Schedule for one-maid house, 312–313
Seating, opera, 61; restaurant, 55, 56, 57; theater, 64, 65, 70
Second, helping at table, 485; marriage, 104
Secretary, perfect business, 548, 552–566; private, 291; social, 291, 292
Self-made men, 546–547
Self-respect, defined, 2
Sentiment, blindness of, 287–288
Servants, number of, 289–290, 311–312; for large house, 290–305; obligations of courtesy to, 410
Servantless house, 379–383
Service, 388–389; correct, 337–339, 345, 347; dessert, 346; American, 363–365; blunders in, 369; house with limited, 311; informal coffee, 365; informal entertaining, 310; three classifications of table, 363; bread and butter plate, 374; guest-room, 420–421
Serving, table near pantry, 345; ways of, 129, 338, 345, 369; yourself, 484
Setting table (see *Table Setting*)
Sewing and singing circles, 404
Sex appeal, banned in business, 547, **548**
Shaking hands, gloves, 17; personality of, 17; proper, 17; when to, 9–10, 16–17
Sherry, how to serve, 335
Ship, clothes for cruise, 463, **464**

Shirts, evening, of faultless linen, 468, 472, 478–480
Shoes, ladies', 458, 462, 463; men's, 474, 476, 478–480; riding, 465
Shorts, when tolerated, 456
Showers, engagement, 184, 401–403; neighborhood gatherings, 401–403; wedding, 256
Signatures, how used, 504–506, 603–604
Silver, 316–322; complete list, 316; details of table setting, 321–322; each piece in detail, 317–319; marking, 196; mixed patterns, 316–322; miscellaneous implements, 320; quantity necessary, 317; rules for choosing, 316–317; serving implements, 319–320; which fork, 320–321; who is head of the table, 322; that shines or none, 335
Simple party giving, 385–400; big dinners at little tables, 392; bridge, 385–387; buffet, 387–392; dance can be simple, 393–395; hospitality in backyard, 398–399; hostess alone, 392; if you want to go to bed, don't start games, 400; friendliest of simple parties, 399; manners, 395; picnics, 395–398
Simplified wedding details, 257–259; at the church, 259; first asset, 257–258; reception, 259
Singing and sewing circles, 404
Sit-down breakfast, 237, 240, 242, 262
"Sitting up," at funeral, no longer necessary, 275
Slang, 33–34
Small, scale entertaining, 379, 392; house of perfection, 418–420; wedding, 191, 240–242
Smokers, at dance, 395; on street, 51; etiquette of, 444–447
Snob, appearing to be, 264–265
Social importance of speech, 27–28; notes, 508–509
Socks, appropriate, to be worn, 472, 475, 478–480
Sorority house party, 158, 159
Soup, how served at lunch, 375
Speaker, introduced at public dinner, 360
Speech, 27–39; accents from London, 37; best forms, 69–70; attributes of charm of, 39; French words in English speech, 37; forms to avoid, 32–33; "formal" and "informal," 33; "home" and "house," 32; how to cultivate, 28–29; in spite of illiteracy, 28–32; pronunciation, 34–38; social importance of, 27–28; slang, 33–34; x-ray of quality, 27
Sportsmanship, 577–579; driving, 586; frankness of today, 579; rules of, 579–580
Staff of large house, 290–305; business or social secretary, 291–292; butler, 293–295; chauffeur, 297–298; children's nurse, 305; companion, 290–291; cook, 298–299; governess, 304; housemaid, 300; house footman, 295–297; housekeeper, 293; lady's maid, 301–302; parlor maid, 300; private secretary, 291; registered nurse, 304–305; tutor, 303; valet, 302–303
Stand-up breakfast or supper, 240–241; 245, 262
State dinners at Washington, 619–621
Steamer travel, 608–610
Stenographer, 549, 552
Store etiquette, 556–559
Stranger at wedding, 260–262; at reception, 261–262; at sit-down breakfast, 262; you who are, 263
Street etiquette, rules of, 49–50; gentleman carries, 50; gentleman offers arm, 50; lady on right, 52; smoking, 51
Success specialists, 148
Suits, men's, for all occasions, 469–474, 478–481; young man's, 475
Supper clubs, 143
Suppers, 377, 378; table, 378
Surprise parties, 403; warning against, 403
Sympathy acknowledgments, 278, 279

Table, bare, 373; bridge, 376–377; cigarettes at, 446–447; clearing of, 346; d'hôte, 57; leaving the, 357; luncheon, 373–374; manners at, 356, 482; seating the, 340–343, 347, 348; setting, 321–322; supper, 378; turning the, 355; who is head of, 322
Table manners, 482–494; bread in gravy, 488; eating chops, 488; elbows on, 485–486; embarrassing difficulties, 484; foods difficult to eat, 488–493; forks or fingers, 485; good manners, 485–486; graduating tests, 485; finical absurdities, 494; hand idle in lap, 493–494; how to eat an orange, 494; knife as pusher, 488; "lunch" or "luncheon," 494; leaving food on plate, 486; other don'ts, 487–488; removing bones, 489–490; general behavior, 482; second helping, 485; salad without knife, 493; salt, 493; sandwiches, 493; table tricks corrected, 482–484; unfolding napkin, 493; when helping yourself, 484–485; wipe silverware, 487
Table setting, 321–322; breakfast, 321; diagrams for, 340–343, 348; dinner, 322, for formal dinner, 331–335; luncheon or supper, 321–322; order of, 370
Table d'Hôte, 56–57
Tabus, of conversation, 46; "Mrs. Mary," 72–73
Tact, cruelty of tactless blundering, 44–45; character and, 551–552; essential to customer and clerks alike, 558–559; observations on, 593–594
Taking leave, 10, 16; forms of farewell, 16; shake hands, 16; when visitor takes leave, 83–84, 358–359
Taste, good in mourning, 284; poor in mourning, 284
Teas and other afternoon parties, 125–

INDEX

134; cocktails at, 131–133; etiquette of, 130; hostesses pour, 127; invitations, 114; menu, 126–127, 129; table, 127–129; with dancing, 125; without dancing, 127

Telegram, as invitation, 119–120; examples of, 525; sending oneself a, 428; to hotel for a room, 602

Telephone, manners and other exactions of courtesy, 438–453; announcing names on, 552; consideration for operator's angle, 441–442; business office "good morning," 438–439; don't let small child answer telephone, 442–443; giving one's name, 440; "hello" correct, 439; in an office, 551; long invitations by, 440–441; important last word, 444; long distance, 442; payment by visitors, 443–444; paying for calls on neighbor's, 444; party-line courtesy, 442; our poor, weak younger generation, 443; someone puts in call for you, 438; use of names, 26; "who is calling, please," 439–440

Thank you notes; bread and butter, 513–517; for present for baby, 512–513; of bride, 194, 510–512; formal, 511; intimate, 511–512; to intimate friends of bridegroom, 511

That which is good remains good, 173

Theater, dinner and go to the play, 63–64; entering, 64, 69; dress, 67; between acts, 70; hats, 65–66; leaving, 66–67; manners, 65; pests, 66; party, 68–69; tickets, 64; to avoid being climbed over, 65

Think before you speak, 41

Thoroughbreds hate cheapness, 174, 175

Three is a crowd, 177

Ties worn for different occasions, 469, 472, 475, 478–480

Tips, average first-class restaurant, 57; de luxe restaurant, 58; in country house, 421–423; in hotel, 606; traveling, 610

Titles, formality in use of, 23; name of safety, 23; of the faculty, 158, 616; on cards, 74; use of, 616–618

Toasts, announcement of engagement, 183–184; at public dinners, 360–361; at wedding reception, 242

Today's outstanding cheapness, 23

Topics for conversation, 41–43, dangers to be avoided, 46–47; fishing for, 43; of the very rich, 47–48; personal remarks, 47

Travel, amount of baggage, 610; bride and groom, 243–244, 255; children on train, 600; courtesy in Far East, 612; by air, 600–601; etiquette, 599–612; even when we speak English, 612; girl alone, 164; going to bed in pullman, 599–600; in hotels, 602–608; in restaurant alone, 607–608; knowledge of languages, 611; preparations for sailing, 609; selecting travel clothes, 609–610; special directions for novices, 599; tips, 606, 610; train manners, 599–602; travel bureau, 608–609; traveling for pleasure, 611; young girl alone, 602

Trousseau, bridegroom's, 208–209; definition, 197; displaying, 203; essential linen list, 200–201; marking linen, 199–200; other clothes for, 202–203; table linen, 198–199

True meaning of etiquette, 1–2

Tutor, position of, 303

Tuxedo or dinner coat, 469

Unconventional situations, 554; business woman in, 554–556; nurse's immunity to convention, 304–305

Uniforms for servants, 289–305

University and college titles, 158, 616

Untidiness, inexcusable, 447

Use of "Mrs." and "Mr.," 504–506; 603–604

Ushers, at ball or dance, 140, 394; at double wedding, 218; at wedding, 207; bride's, 207–208; gift to, 213; head usher, 211; in procession, 213–217; clothes, 209–210; dinner, 212; during ceremony, 228–229; after ceremony, 232–233; at the house, 235; at small wedding, 240; at wedding dance, 242; at house wedding, 244; at simplified wedding, 257–259

Valet, position of, 302

Valeting, value of, 474

Visiting cards, boy's, 74; children's, 76–77; correct names, 71–77; correct number, 83; fold-over, 77; invitations on, 89, 118–119; meaning of "Jr." and "2nd," 73–74; man's, 73–74; messages on, 82, 90; "Miss Onlydaughter," 90; modern card-leaving, 81–82; new address, 77; "not at home," 79–80; names of military on, 633–634; of divorcée, 75; of personages, 75–76; on tray, 83; p. p. c., 77; size and engraving, 71; special, 77; titles, 74–75; use, 71; visit of empty form, 78; widow's, 72–73; woman in business, 72–73; young girl, 73

Visitors, in a club, 566–568; girls who want to visit men in military camp, 630–631; leaves, 83–84; your first, 264

Visits, in Washington, 622–623; invitation in place of returned, 79; how a first is made, 82–83; other details, 86; postscripts on, 86; on opening the door, 83; vanishing . . . of empty form, 78; to a lady without a maid, 81; when visitor leaves, 83–84; when hostess is at home, 84–85; which everyone must make, 81–82

Voice, index of culture, 27, 39, 69, 70

Vulgarity in clothes, 152, 455, 474

Waitress, dress for, 301; hotel, 606; tips for, in country house, 421–423

War-time Supplement, 624–640
War wives, rules for, 626–637
Washington society, 347n, 350n, 351n, 613–623
Wedding invitations, addressing envelopes, 92; church, 93; double wedding, 97; enclosed in two envelopes, 91–92; engraved, 91; envelope and invitation in one, 92–93; of bride without parents, 100; to breakfast, 94; to ceremony and reception, 99; to house, 98; to wedding at house of friend, 96; when parents are divorced, 100, 101; with lozenge, 94–95; to house wedding, 101; to reception only, 102–103; to second marriage, 104–105; military wedding, 632–633; most flattering, 102; war simplifications, 634–635
Wedding expenses, at least expense, 220–221; clergyman's fee, 220; cost of being bridesmaid, 205; complete summary, 250–251; house wedding at least expense, 245; of bridegroom, 251; parents of bride provide, 250–251
Wedding presents, arranging, 195; cards left on, 196; cards with, 252; delayed, 252; from bridegroom's friends, 196; exchanging, 197; recording, 193–194; suggestions for, 251–252; when shown, 196
Weddings, announcements, 103–104; at parsonage, 192, 193; attendants, 205–208; anniversaries, 253–254; bridegroom's gift, 220; bride's gift, 220; best man, 222, 223; bride's dress, 201, 255; best man and ushers, 207; bride's usher and groom's bridesmaid, 207–208; bachelor dinner, 212; bridesmaids' and ushers' luncheon, 211; bridesmaids, 203, 204–205; addressing invitations, 92; children, 206, 304; church, 187; ceremony, 231–232; after ceremony, 232–233; collation, 241; congratulations, 236; dancing, 242; double wedding, 218–219; day of, 222–256; dress of ushers, 209; early morning, 192; evening, 191–192; expenses, 250–251; flippancy or radiance, 246; fees, 220–221, 245, 250–251; gifts for attendants, 211, 213; dress of bridegroom, 209; given by bride's family, 193, 247, 254; going away, 243, 244; guests at, 460–461; house wedding, 244–246; in front of ribbons, 228; invitations, 91–103, 187–189; in everyday clothes, 257–259; most elaborate, 189; of a Cinderella, 190; of children of divorced, 247, 248; of adopted daughter, 254; presents, 193–196, 251–252; preparation of house, 223–226; pictures, 226; reception, 99, 102, 233–243; rehearsal and procession, 213–218, 227, 231; reserved pews, 98; simplified, 257–259; shower wedding, 256; stranger at, 260–262; second marriage, 104, 249–250; small in large church, 191; silver, 196–197; preparation for church, 187–221; seating guests, 228–229, 230; ring, 219; two envelopes, 91; train card, 101–102; trousseau, 197–201, 203, 208; thanks for presents, 510–512; sit-down breakfast, 237; small wedding, 240–242; stand-up breakfast or supper, 240–241; toast, 242; usual fashionable, 189; Jewish, 248–249; war, 632–635; wedding cake, 238–239, 241–242
Week-end guests, 429, 430
Well-appointed house, 286–315; announcement of guests, 311; advice to beginning employing a general maid, 313–315; "becoming" furniture, 287; blindness of sentiment, 287–288; courtesy to one's household, 306; dressing rooms, 310; etiquette of service, 308; house with limited service, 311; how can house need many servants, 290; how many servants, 289–290; management of servants, 306–307; maids receive friends, 309–310; run by one maid, 311–312; service, 288–289; service in formal entertaining, 310; those who have persistent trouble, 307, 308; time "in" and "out," 309; work schedule, 312
Well-dressed lady, 454–467; man, 468–481
Whiskey, served at dinner, 336
White House, etiquette at, 613–623
Widow, formal dinner in house of, 341–343; keeps husband's name, 72, 506; mourning of, 281, 282
Widow's name on visiting card, 72; keeps husband's, 72; son has same, 73
Wines, 335–337, 343, 344
Wiping tableware, extremely rude, 487
Women in business, proper manners of, 544–559
Words preferred, 15n; proper use of, 27–39, 69, 70
Writing letters and note (see *Correspondence*)
Writing paper, 498, 521; mourning, 501; official, 500–510

X-ray of quality, 27

Young girl, at college, 149–159, 461; attitude toward parents, 169–170; entertains, 164; goes alone to man's apartment, 165–167; follow the crowd, 168–169; her visiting card, 73; her own chaperone, 162; not particular, 163; on over-night journey, 164; travels alone, 164, 602; typical notes of, 123
Young man, proper clothes for, 475–477
Young people afraid to say "No," 132
Young widow, 282

Zigzag eating manners, 484